Organizational
Influence
Processes

Organizational Influence Processes

Robert W. Allen
EECO Incorporated

Lyman W. Porter
University of California, Irvine

Scott, Foresman and Company
Glenview, Illinois
Dallas, Tex.   Oakland, N.J.   Palo Alto, Cal.
Tucker, Ga.   London, England

HD
58.7
.O737
1983

Library of Congress Cataloging in Publication Data
Main entry under title:

Organizational influence processes.

Includes bibliographies and index.
1. Organizational behavior—Addresses, essays, lectures. 2. Power (Social sciences)—
Addresses, essays, lectures. I. Allen, Robert W., 1931-   . II. Porter, Lyman W.
HD58.7.O737 1983   658.4   82-23148
ISBN 0-673-15318-5

1 2 3 4 5 6 - KPF - 86 85 84 83

Preface

This book grew out of a project that was both intellectually stimulating and a lot of fun—a study of organizational politics. Several years ago, two faculty members and several Ph.D. students at the University of California, Irvine, became interested in this topic and proceeded to design an empirical study. (See the articles by Madison et al. and Allen et al. that report the findings of the study in Section IV of this book.) Subsequently, the two authors of the present book decided to take a comprehensive look at not only organizational politics in particular, but organizational influence processes in general. This book is the culmination of our research.

In organizing this book, we were guided by a conviction that a useful way to view organizational influence processes was to take a *directional* approach: that is, to consider them from the perspective of downward, lateral, and upward influence. Consequently, the readings in this volume are arranged under these headings, preceded by an introductory set of articles dealing more generally with the nature of influence processes and power. The reader will find, especially in the section on lateral influence, that it is not always easy to assign every article neatly into one of these directional categories. Yet, we believe that most influence attempts in organizations are in some sense directional, and therefore, that it makes sense to group studies in these particular clusters.

In selecting the specific articles, we were guided by several key criteria: relevance to the topic of organizational influence processes; substance (i.e., "does the article make a relatively significant contribution?"); interest and appeal (i.e., "do we ourselves enjoy reading it and find it stimulating?"); and recency, a criterion we occasionally deliberately violated by choosing several articles that were over one or two decades old. In those instances, we felt the selections had a certain "timelessness" that made them appropriate for inclusion. We also hasten to point out that we found more good and appropriate articles than could be included in a book of this size. As is frequently the case in attempting to exercise influence, we were forced to make choices.

Our thanks go to several individuals. First, to our former colleagues with whom we had a number of insightful and stimulating discussions of organizational influence processes: Patty Renwick Lawler, Dan Madison, Tom Mayes, and Hal Angle. They were especially influential with us (certainly an example of lateral influence). Also, our great thanks go to Eva C. Mount and Cindy Lindsay for their cordial and competent assistance in preparation of the manuscript. Finally, our vote of grateful appreciation to a first-rate copy editor, Elizabeth Fresen.

In conclusion, we want to dedicate this book to several very influential people of the past, present, and certainly, the future: A grandson, Jeremiah Daniel; his grandmother, Luckie Cherie; a son, Bill; a daughter, Anne; and a son-in-law, Marr.

RWA
LWP

Contents

Alphabetical List of Contributors

Organizational Influence Processes

Introduction

Whenever individuals come together to accomplish some desired end result, influence processes play a part. In their attempts to achieve, men and women continuously make use of influence processes. Although social and behavioral scientists have examined influence itself, the broad range of influence processes in *organizational settings* has not always received the intensive attention that it deserves. Downward influence, especially leadership, has been the subject of numerous studies, but the explicit processes of lateral and upward influence in organizations have been relatively ignored. Recently, though, this imbalance in attention to organizational influence processes appears to be decreasing, and there is renewed interest in the influence processes that take place in organizational contexts.

Organizations: Structure and Processes

We view an organization as an entity comprised of individuals and groups pursuing a common goal, at least at some superordinate level, with a designed structure and with continuity through time. The *structure* of an organization provides a framework of vertical and horizontal differentiation—demarcation of levels of hierarchial authority and responsibility and functional areas of expertise required for goal achievement. A second function of organizational structure is to provide some sort of rational basis for coordinating or integrating the differentiated parts of the organization. Policies, procedures, operating practices, information systems, and established working relationships are examples of typical integrative devices. In addition to structural characteristics, there are the important processes inherent in the pursuit of goals in an

1

organization—communicating, decision making, problem solving, and influencing individuals and groups to behave in certain ways. This text focuses on the array of influence processes that are in operation when individuals and groups come together in an organizational setting.

Influence and Power: Relationship and Key Issues

Before we can discuss influence processes in a meaningful way we must consider the closely related concept of power. In reviewing previous literature on influence and power, it is clear that there frequently are differences among various social scientists concerning what is meant by these terms. The distinction between the terms power and influence is often unclear. Power itself has a multitude of definitions—almost as numerous as the number of individuals writing on the subject. Bierstedt (1950), in a seminal article on social power, lamented this state of affairs when he observed:

> In the entire lexicon of sociological concepts none is more troublesome than the concept of power. We may say about it in general only what St. Augustine said about time, that we all know perfectly well what it is—until someone asks us (p. 730).

The evaluative overtones that often accompany the consideration of power present a further problem. Power has been viewed in pejorative terms by some writers. For example, Archbishop Fenelon felt that "power is poison," and a well-known statement made by Lord Acton when writing to Bishop Mandell Creighton was that "power tends to corrupt; absolute power corrupts absolutely" (Catlin, 1962, p. 71). Lord Acton would undoubtedly still find considerable following among some writers and in some organizational settings. On the other hand, other writers emphasize the importance of the "positive face" of power in facilitating organization goal accomplishment.

The relative lack of research, as compared with the proliferation of theoretical/conceptual formulations, has undoubtedly also contributed to the difficulty encountered with the interpretation of the terms *influence* and *power.* In an earlier work by one of the authors of this text, a comprehensive comparison of the concepts of influence and power was conducted. It was found that many writers did not differentiate between them. Others who did distinguish between these terms tended to view power as an ability, capacity, or potential for influence, and influence as a process of producing behavioral and psychological (i.e., values, beliefs, attitudes) effects. All of the writers reviewed believed that the use of influence or power produced certain effects in the target individual(s).

The causation of certain effects has consistently been treated as a characteristic of the *use* of influence or power. However, the issue of whether specific effects are intentional has been dealt with differently by authors of power and influence literature. Most of the writers either explicitly or implicitly include intended effects as a distinguishing characteristic of the use of power or influence. But several writers explicitly exclude intentionality as a requirement. And there are authors who suggest that, although the influencing act must be intentional, the resulting effect may not be as intended. At least two aspects of intent are important to consider: first, the question of the motivations and intentions of the power or influence source (i.e., his or her state of mind); and second, the aspect of whether or not the exercise of power or influence resulted in consequences that were intended, or consequences that were unanticipated.

In reviewing the power and influence literature, at least two other important issues emerge. One issue concerns the way in which influence or power is regarded—either as a personal attribute, or as a relational concept between individuals. Although there are several examples in the literature where influence or power is considered to be an attribute of an individual, most of the literature treats power as a force between individuals or groups. Similarly, influence is seen more typically as a process between individuals or groups, rather than as a singular attribute.

A second issue concerns differing intended outcomes: the use of influence or power solely to obtain desired outcomes, or the use of influence processes as not only a way to obtain desired outcomes, but also to prevent undesired outcomes. A majority of the writing focused on using influence or power to obtain certain outcomes, giving little attention to the use of power or influence in preventing other individuals from modifying the source's own conduct in a way that he or she does not desire (i.e., the reciprocal of an influence attempt, where the source becomes the target). We believe that it is appropriate to consider both the defensive or reciprocal use of power and influence and the offensive use.

It is apparent that power is closely related to the concept of influence. The various issues highlighted earlier are important in examining either power or influence. Our view of power, consistent with many previous writers, is as a capacity or potential for influence. We regard influence as a process in organizations for producing certain intended effects in individuals or groups. We also recognize that the influence attempt may not always or even frequently be successful, and may result in unanticipated consequences.

Influence Processes in Organizations

The purpose of this text is to focus on influence processes in *organizational* settings. A carefully selected set of readings is presented in the four sections that follow. Section I concentrates on the concepts of power and influence, providing a general framework for considering the process of influencing subordinates, peers, and superiors to engage in behaviors that will provide outcomes desired by the influencing source. Sections II, III, and IV present readings discussing downward, lateral, and upward influence considerations and processes respectively.

This pattern for examining the flow of influence processes in an organization is particularly useful, because various functions and aspects of these processes often are altered significantly by organizational constraints, and by the relative positioning of individuals or groups involved. Influence processes are different for superiors influencing subordinates than they are for subordinates attempting to influence superiors, or for a person or group influencing a peer. In any categorization framework there are always exceptions, however. Indeed, the target of downward influence attempts might respond with lateral or reciprocal actions as a defensive or offensive means of coping. Despite such inevitable exceptions, we feel that to differentiate the utilization and effects of influence processes according to levels in the organizational hierarchy is constructive, and can be integrated into a broad framework that is helpful in understanding this complex and dynamic subject.

The dynamics of power and influence in organizational settings are the subject of Section I. This section serves as a framework for studying the process of influencing subordinates, peers, and superiors to engage in behaviors that will provide outcomes intended by the influencing source.

There are various aspects inherent in the process of influence. For example, each individual in an organization is expected to attain certain prescribed results. These are the outcomes required if the organization, or some subunit of the organization, is to achieve its overall goals and objectives. In addition, each organizational member desires specific outcomes that will satisfy his or her personal needs and goals. The goals and objectives of the organization, often expressed in plans or policies, are usually more explicit than are the needs and desires of individual members. We do not wish to imply that organizational objectives are more important. The point is that, whether the desired outcome is an organizational goal or a personal objective, the individual is usually dependent upon the actions of other individuals. This creates an intricate set of interdependencies, and their relationship to the achievement of outcomes desired by the organization and its members is integral to the influence process within organizations.

The reality that the desired outcome is beyond the capability of the individual invokes the necessity of getting someone else to provide assistance if the goal is to be attained. The stage is set for an influence attempt. The target must be selected, which requires that the source have an understanding of the capacity and potential willingness of other people to do what is desired. Whether a potential target can and will do what is desired depends upon the degree of interdependency that exists within the organization. The risks of attempting to get the person to comply, along with the potential costs associated with the person choosing to comply or not to comply, must be considered. The method or tactic of influence that is selected will depend upon an evaluation of the willingness of the target to comply with the influence attempt. Influence methods that are very successful with a subordinate may be unsuccessful with a peer, and totally inappropriate for a superior.

In Section II we concentrate on downward influence processes in organizations. The unique characteristic of downward influence is that the influence source is in a higher level in the organizational hierarchy and thereby possesses more organizational power than the influence target. In other words, the influence source has formal authority. In addition, the influence source may have the ability to formally reward or punish subordinates for complying or not complying with the influence attempt. Vertical differentiation within an organization typically results in lower-level individuals being more dependent upon higher-level individuals than vice versa. But interdependencies are still important in superior-subordinate relationships because the superior is dependent upon subordinates doing what he or she desires. While the possession of formal authority can be helpful in organizational settings, formal authority alone may be insufficient to influence subordinates to perform in the desired manner. There are many examples of dysfunctional behavior resulting from the abuse of formal authority in organizational settings. In some instances, authority of a superior may be resisted by lower-level individuals, rendering it relatively ineffective as a means for influencing subordinate personnel. That is why the superior must give careful attention to choosing methods of influence that are appropriate to the situation and to the degree of interdependency in the relationship between the superior and the subordinate.

In Section III our topic is lateral influence in organizations. The focus here is on influence processes that are exclusively outside the direct superior-subordinate "chain of command." The target of influence may be within the same department, or in another department or division of the organization. The influence source's and the target's positions may be at varying levels of importance within the organization, as evidenced by their pay differential. However, the influence source will not possess any formal authority over the target. The influence source and the influence target may generally be regarded as peers, regardless of whether there is a difference in the value or level of the specialty that they perform. For example, a senior engineer may attempt to influence a quality control analyst. There may be a significant difference between these two positions from a compensation level perspective; however, no formal authority exists in the relationship. Although the senior person may be more influential because of his or her expertise status, this difference can also occur between two senior engineers within the same department.

A frequent form of lateral influence is found in the socialization process. All organizations and organizational subunits have norms, or expected behaviors, that apply to their members. Both the formal and the informal organization are involved in influencing members to behave in the manner that the organization has decided is appropriate. The range of tactics used to attain the desired behavior is quite broad. In addition, the more a given individual resists the influence attempts of other organizational members, the more the recalcitrant member will become aware of the penalty of this resistance. The power of the group to influence (socialize) its members or expel them cannot be denied.

The fourth and final section of the text deals with the upward influence process in organizations. The distinguishing characteristic of upward influence is that the *target* of influence possesses more formal authority than the influence source. From a formal authority perspective, along with the inability to reward and possibly coerce, the influence source is at a disadvantage. While the overall interdependency between superior and subordinate typically favors the superior, there are many situations that will shift the dependency relationship to the advantage of the subordinate. In Section IV, David Mechanic makes this point very clear in his discussion of the power of lower participants in organizations.

Nonetheless, the lack of formal authority does restrict the influence methods available to subordinate personnel attempting to get their superiors to provide outcomes that they desire. The usual reward that a subordinate can generally provide a superior is good performance. Yet it can be reasonably argued that the superior has the right to expect good performance as a part of the employment relationship. It can be further argued that withholding this expected behavior will in the long run be more detrimental to the subordinate than to the superior. Therefore, the feasibility of providing rewards as a means of influencing a superior seems doubtful. Likewise, using threats or coercion to influence superiors would appear to be generally unsuccessful.

Perhaps the most frequent method used by subordinates to influence their superiors is persuasion. Persuasion can be effective when the influence attempt is concerned with attaining organizational outcomes of mutual interest. However, when the outcome intended involves satisfying personal desires or needs of the subordinate, persuasion may be inappropriate. A raise in pay, a promotion, a transfer to a more desirable assignment or location are examples of outcomes desired by subordinate personnel that may not be considered particularly important to a superior. Superiors may be very vehement about such matters as they apply to their personal situations, but not feel a strong conviction to provide similar outcomes to their subordinates. This may introduce the need for the subordinate to engage in a particularly interesting aspect of the upward influence process—organizational politics.

One of the distinguishing characteristics of political behavior in organizations is that it is self-serving, and may or may not be at the expense of other organizationally-oriented goals and objectives. For instance, consider the subordinate who is hoping to influence a superior to provide an outcome that is primarily self-serving. Persuasion may be neither appropriate nor effective. In such a situation the political actor may choose to conceal altogether the fact that he or she is attempting to influence the target; that is, the subordinate may attempt to manipulate the superior. While manipulation can be used as a method of influence in downward and lateral influence processes, it seems to be used most frequently in political situations. Therefore, persuasion and manipulation appear to be two methods of influence that are as readily available to subordinates as to superiors.

In focusing our attention in Section IV on organizational politics, it should not be construed that we are condoning or condemning this form of upward influence. We find it to be a particularly interesting aspect of reality in organizational settings, and believe that the systematic study of politics deserves the same emphasis that other organizational influence processes receive. It is an influence process that can be learned, understood, and managed. Therefore, it should be included as an integral part of the education of individuals interested in management and organizational behavior.

REFERENCES

Bierstedt, R. "An analysis of social power." *American Sociological Review* 15 (1950): 703-738.

Catlin, G. E. G. *Systematic politics.* Toronto: University of Toronto Press, 1962.

PART **1**

Influence and Power in Organizational Settings

In all likelihood, what you are doing now is the result of a successful influence attempt. For whatever reason, you have decided to pursue knowledge of behavior in organizations by reading this book. Your professor or instructor required you to read certain materials, your behavior was influenced, and you are doing what someone intended for you to do.

Influencing and being influenced are inherent in organizational behavior. Almost all organizational members engage in influencing others, and are in turn influenced by others. Engineers, social workers, salespeople, union members, parents, and children all share the goal of getting other individuals and groups to engage in behaviors that they desire. Indeed, the pursuit of individual and organizational objectives requires a continual process of influencing and being influenced. The success of an influence attempt depends upon the power base and/or the tactics of the influence source. However, it is important to recognize that individuals can be influenced without the source's intent, and that, with a disguised tactic, they can also be influenced without being aware of it.

The opening article by Nord sets forth the characteristics and importance of a humanized organization. After introducing the concept of power, he examines the resultant effects when the attempts by individuals or groups to attain or retain power clash with the goal of creating organizations that are humanized. Although Nord does not conclude that the realization of humanized organizations is irreconcilable with power coalitions within organizations, it is clear that he is not overly optimistic about reconciliation. Nord suggests that, at best, considerable struggle will be involved.

The second reading, in contrast with Nord's concern with the impact of power relationships on achieving more humanized organizations, focuses on considerations involved in a powerholder's selection of influence tactics. Kipnis' discussion does not concern itself with the favorable or unfavorable consequences of a chosen influence tactic. Instead, he focuses on the selection process itself, divorced from any unforeseen outcomes of the tactic selected. In keeping with the famous Lewinian formulation that behavior is a function of the person interacting with the environment, Kipnis argues that availability and selection of influence tactics are affected by the setting in which the tactics are to be exercised. While the tactic of "acting cold and saying very little" to the target may be quite effective in influencing a marriage partner, it may be ineffective or even damaging to the influence source if used on a superior in a work situation.

When rewards or punishments are used as influence tactics, it is likely that the influence source occupies a higher level position in the organization. This is because the power bases of reward and punishment are more available to people in upper-level organizational positions. On the other hand, the influencer's choice of influence tactics that are based on knowledge or expertise will most likely be independent of his or her position or level in the organization. It seems obvious that perceptive people will confine influence attempts to power bases they know or feel that they possess. But how does a powerholder with the ability to choose among broad bases of power to obtain behavioral compliance determine which influence tactics to use?

In his reading, *The Use of Power,* Kipnis discusses the importance of rational or cognitive processes as well as affective or emotional considerations in choosing influence tactics to employ. He introduces a two-stage process for making the influence choice: the process involves diagnosing the reasons why the target may refuse to comply, followed by choosing the influence tactic to be used. The effectiveness of the tactic, according to Kipnis, depends upon the accuracy of the diagnosis. For example, performance is generally considered to be a function of abilities interacting with motivation. If the influence source desires to influence the performance behavior of a subordinate, the diagnosis that a person does not possess the ability to do what is desired will dictate a different influence tactic (i.e., training, development, etc.) than if the diagnosis is that the person has the ability, but is not motivated. Kipnis also contends that assertiveness on the part of a powerholder will increase as the number of ways in which the powerholder can influence others increases. In addition, he maintains that as power increases, the powerholder will respond by making many more demands on his or her environment.

The next two articles present an interesting perspective concerning intraorganizational power. Hickson, Hinings, Lee, Schneck, and Pennings develop a theory of power within organizations by focusing on power as the dependent variable. The division of labor or subunit tasks, the functioning of these subunits, and the links between subunit activities are the independent variables that determine the power of various subunits within the organization. For example, organizational subunits that are dependent upon other subunits have less power and influence than subunits that are independent or depended upon by others. The three variables identified by Hickson, et al. as being most closely associated with intraorganizational dependency are: (1) the degree to which a subunit copes with uncertainty in the organization; (2) the extent to which a subunit's activities are substitutable; and (3) centrality—the degree to which the activities of a subunit are "pervasive" (linked with other subunits) and "immediate" (essential to the timely continuation of work flow). The article examines the definition and possible operationalization of each variable, and develops a strategic contingencies theory of power within organizations based upon the interrelationships of these variables. To conclude, the authors of the article evaluate the utility of the theory according to its ability to withstand testing against earlier published work on the concept of power.

The Salancik and Pfeffer article is an explanation and elaboration of the strategic contingency theory of power. A number of research studies are discussed, including the authors' 18-month investigation of 29 university departments. Their findings that uncertainty, scarcity and criticality of resources are likely to affect the use of power in organizations are also presented. The authors imply that changes in organizational subunits will be accompanied by power shifts to the dominant coalition (Dominant coalitions are usually those coalitions whose capabilities are appropriate to the organization's environment). Salancik and Pfeffer also maintain that, by setting forth constitutions, policies, procedures, rules, and information systems, the dominant coalition can institutionalize power to its advantage. It can limit the potential power of other organizational subunits.

The next article, a unique approach to interpreting power and its use from a behavioral perspective, was written by Thompson and Luthans specifically for this edition. They focus on behaviors "exhibited in order to *acquire* power or to exercise its *use*," discussing several previous models or frameworks of the power concept and developing an operant definition of power based on reinforcement theory. Their model provides for the environmental context that acts as the *Antecedent* to evoke certain *Behaviors* that will in turn lead to certain *Consequences*. After examining the three sets of variables, the stage is set for a discussion of the acquisition, the exercise, and the use of power.

The article by Kanter identifies important variables that are linked to power in organizations—lines of supply, lines of information, and lines of support. Kanter argues that when these lines are broken or curtailed, power is lost or reduced. She specifically singles out supervisors, staff professionals, and, surprisingly, chief executive officers as being particularly vulnerable to powerlessness due to a degradation of these all-important lines of power. Willingness to share power, the article concludes, is the most effective way to keep open supply, information, and support lines, and to thereby expand power. A special feature of Kanter's article is the examination of particular power failures that women managers experience. Note that in the article by Nord, the sharing of power was considered to be an essential, albeit elusive, ingredient of humanized organizations.

In the final reading in Section One, Kipnis and Schmidt report the results of two studies that investigate tactics used by people in work situations to influence their supervisors, co-workers, and subordinates. Using factor analysis on the content of essays written by a group of lower-level managers and on other lower-level managers' questionnaire responses, the authors identify eight dimensions of influence. These are: assertiveness; ingratiation; rationality; sanctions; exchange; upward appeals; blocking; and coalitions. Kipnis and Schmidt found that organizational size, unionization, resistance of the target person, reasons for exercising influence, relative power of the respondents and their targets of influence, and organizational status of the respondents all were related to the frequency of use of each of the eight dimensions. As we alluded to early in this overview of *Influence and Power in Organizational Settings,* we agree with the conclusion of Kipnis and Schmidt—"that everyone is influencing everyone else in organizations, regardless of job title."

Dreams of Humanization and the Realities of Power

WALTER R. NORD

For several decades American organizational psychologists have dreamed of and sought to create humanized organizations. While it is not clear exactly what a humanized organization is, various writers seem to agree that in humanized organizations members are: (a) treated as ends rather than as means; (b) engaged in meaningful, challenging work; (c) encouraged to develop their uniquely human abilities fully; (d) treated justly and with a dignity which places them well above the non-human aspects of organization; and (e) able to exercise substantial control in organizational decisions—particularly those decisions which affect them directly.

As writers have dreamed of organizations which would be characterized by at least some of these features, often they have appeared to assume that such organizations would be easy to develop. Optimists have come to see them as inevitable, whereas many of the pessimists see humanized organization as requiring only the enlightenment of managers. Recently these dreams seemed sound because organizations appeared to need these very characteristics if they were to be effective and to survive.

"Dreams of Humanization and the Realities of Power" by Walter R. Nord, *The Academy of Management Review,* July 1978, Volume 3, Number 3, pp. 674-679. Copyright © 1978 by the Academy of Management. Reprinted by permission.

A number of things pointed towards the necessity for more humanized organizations. Bennis (4) noted some of these including: (a) the exponential growth of science; (b) turbulent environments; (c) a younger, more mobile, better educated work force; (d) a growth in the confluence between persons of knowledge and persons of power; (e) a change in managerial philosophy towards the emphasis on a new concept of humanity based on complex and shifting needs; (f) a new concept of power based on collaboration and reason; and (g) new organizational values based on humanistic-democratic ideals. As Bennis and Nord (16, 17) have observed, humanized organizations have been slow to develop.

Why have organizations been so resistant to humanization? There is no simple answer, but some valuable insights can be gained by exploring the role that power and political processes play in the dynamics of organizations.

The working definition of *power* used here is derived from the work of Adams (2) and Bachrach and Baratz (3). Power is the ability to influence flows of the available energy and resources towards certain goals as opposed to other goals. Power is assumed to be exercised only when these goals are at least partially in conflict with each other. Given this conceptualization, humanizing organizations can be accomplished by altering the flow of resources and energy so that at least some of the five aspects of humanization listed above are given increased emphasis.

The quest for humanized organizations can be broken in two parts. First, consider the design of systems in which the achievement of humanized goals and organizational success on traditional criteria of effectiveness are mutually supportive. Secondly, consider those cases where the two sets of outcomes are in conflict. It is this second set of cases where consideration of power provides insights into why organizations have remained so resistant to power sharing, to just and dignified treatment of individuals, and to the provision of challenging and growth producing work. Examination of four postulates about power and organizations will help to focus on some of these constraints.

P1: *Organizations are composed of coalitions which compete with one another for resources, energy, and influence.*

Organizations are a mixture of common goals, individual goals, and sub-group goals. Conflict among competing parties for resources and energies is seldom completely resolved, and the conflicting parties are often arrayed in a number of coalitions.

As Zaleznik (23) argued, competition to become a dominant coalition (or part of one) is an intense and an important feature of life in organizations. Moreover, competing coalitions are often engaged in what approach zero-sum games. If one coalition exercises dominant control over resources and the allocation process, other coalitions cannot. Sometimes these struggles are reflected in what appear to be the palace revolts which result in the ouster of top-level corporate officials, but, as Zaleznik showed, the struggles are often more subtle and less spectacular.

While more information about the magnitude and frequency of these conflicts is needed, the climates created by such struggles are not likely to be conducive to the achievement of humanized ends of justice, dignity, etc.

The focus on organizations as coalitions highlights some other constraints upon humanization. In particular, we discover why turbulent environments have not had the straightforward effects of humanizing organizations which have often been assumed. Following the strategic contingencies theory of organizational power developed by Hickson et al. (10) and Hinnings et al. (11), it is clear that changes in the environment affect the balance of power among the various coalitions within the organization, because skills and/or resources which were highly valued become less important. Other skills and resources which were once unimportant become highly valued. Participants whose power is threatened are apt to respond defensively and/or aggressively; those who have gained power are apt to seek to consolidate their position. Consequently, the response of the total organization is not the rational adaptation of a harmonious system, but is the resultant vector of conflicting interests, distorted information, and struggle.

Contrary to the beliefs of some organizational behaviorists, because rapidly changing environments introduce power struggles within organizations, turbulent environments may be in conflict with humanizing organizations. The more turbulent the environment, the more pervasive and strong the resulting internal strife may be. There is little reason to expect that the warring parties will treat each other in humanized ways, and the scars, particularly when the resources and rights of one or more parties have been reduced or eliminated, are apt to be slow to heal.

P2: *Various coalitions will seek to protect their interests and positions of influence by moderating environmental pressures and their effects.*

It is typically assumed that rapidly changing environments humanize organizations because they induce deroutinization and consequently create the need for a large number of organizational participants to exercise greater discretion and to use a wide variety of their skills and talents. Thompson's (22) analysis suggests that, while increased discretion may occur, such increases will not be pervasive because members of the dominant coalition are often effective in routinizing the organization's core technology and protecting it from fluctuations in the environment. While there may be *an increase in size of the dominant coalition,* if the core technology is adequately buffered, the change in the environment may affect very few people.

For example, consider an automobile firm facing changes in materials, governmental regulations, and consumer preferences. The effects of these changes are frequently absorbed by engineering and other technical adjustments. There is at best a small chance that operatives on the assembly line will experience significantly more variety in their work or exercise more discretion. Members of dominant coalitions, operating under the norms of rationality, are motivated to limit the discretion of lower level participants in order to avoid disruptions in the operation of core technologies. Thus, while turbulent environments may force the dominant coalition to dilute its power slightly, there is no assurance that this dilution will humanize the work of all or even most people.

P3: *The unequal distribution of power itself has non-humanizing effects.*

The unequal distribution of power itself stimulates outcomes which are contrary to many of the characteristics of humanized organizations. Some of these outcomes stem from the influence of power inequalities on the powerful; others are due to the influence of power inequalities on the less powerful.

The powerful. Thompson (22) noted that the dominant coalition frequently attempts to design structures which reduce the discretion of lower level participants. Often, the discretion of lower level participants is limited by the explicit decisions made by those in authority. As political scientists such as Bachrach and Baratz (3) suggested, one of the most significant advantages the powerful have is the power of non-decision— the ability to suppress and/or thwart challenges by preventing an issue from being considered subject to a decision. Movement towards humanized organizations frequently will require that issues handled by non-decision in the past are negotiated in the future. As the history of trade unionism documents, such a process is often bitter, and the humanized outcomes are by no means inevitable.

In addition to the effect of reducing the ability of individuals to control their own outcomes, various processes used to increase predictability often result in perceived injustice, threats to individual esteem and dignity, and other dehumanizing consequences. O'Day's (18) description of intimidation rituals and Swingle's (21) discussion of mechanisms of bureaucratic strangulation provide some interesting examples. A number of studies (12, 13) have shown how possession of power itself leads to non-humanized treatment of lower level participants by the powerful. Kipnis concluded:

> . . . the control of power triggers a chain of events, which, in theory, at least, goes like this: (a) with the control of power goes increased temptations (sic) to influence others' behavior, (b) as actual influence attempts increase, there arises the belief that the behavior of others is not self-controlled, that it is caused by the powerholder, (c) hence, a devaluation of their performance. In addition, with increased influence attempts, forces are generated with the more powerful to (d) increase psychological distance from the less powerful and view them as objects of manipulation (12, p. 40).

Similarly, Zimbardo's (1) discussion of his mock prison and Rosenhan's (20) observations of how hospital personnel related to mental patients provide convincing evidence that the possession of power itself leads the powerful to treat the less powerful in a non-humanized fashion.

Overall, it appears that the possession of the power has important dehumanizing effects. Not only are many individuals deprived of the ability to control their own outcomes but, in McGregor's terms, there seems to be a tendency for powerful people to adopt Theory X assumptions about their subordinates.

Effects on the less powerful.   The unequal distribution of power has complementary, non-humanizing effects on the less powerful. Examples are: Harrington's (9) description of "twisted spirit" of the American poor and the "culture of poverty"; Lefcourt's (14) work on the psychology of powerlessness; Gouldner's (8) observation of feelings of dependence that result in servile attitudes toward superiors; and Nemeth's (15) report that inequalities in power inhibit cooperative behavior; these studies reveal the dehumanizing consequences of "powerlessness". Similarly, Culbert's (5) work reveals how relatively powerless individuals become trapped by shared assumptions which make them vulnerable to excess influence and induce them to accept the status quo. Thus, it seems reasonable to hypothesize that humanized relationships will be more probable when there is relative equality in power among individuals than when gross discrepancies exist.

P4:   *The exercise of power within organizations is one very crucial aspect of the exercise of power within the larger social system.*

One of the most productive outcomes of assessing the relationship between power and humanized organizations may well be that such discussions direct us to the work of political scientists. Their ideas point to some important omissions in thinking about power and control of work organizations.

Dahl (6) provides a basis for exploring some of these considerations. He observed that in America we have made a strange ideological distinction about the exercise of power. Power exercised in political organizations ought to be public and democratic, but power *within* economic organizations need not be democratic and ought to be left in the hands of the owners or managers of the firm. In his words:

. . . the prevailing ideology prescribes "private" enterprise, that is, firms managed by officials who are legally, if not de facto responsible to private shareholders . . . It is widely taken for granted that the only appropriate form for managing economic enterprise is a privately owned firm . . . Ordinarily technical arguments in favor of an alternative must be of enormous weight to overcome the purely ideological bias in favor of the private firm (6, pp. 117-118).

Dahl was more concerned with macro level analysis (e.g., the fact that the given magnitude of many decisions made by General Motors, they cannot reasonably be considered private matters) than he was with democracy *in* the work place.

Pateman (19) extended Dahl's ideas into the work place. She suggested that since organizations are so important in the lives of people, a fully democratic society is possible only if democratic voting is extended to organizations. She maintained that unless such an extension is made, voting and representation are doomed to be largely formal matters. Pateman wrote:

> The aim of organizational democracy is democracy. It is not primarily increased productivity, efficiency, or better industrial relations (even though these things may even result from organizational democracy); rather it is to further justice, equality, freedom, the rights of citizens, and the protection of interests of citizens, all familiar democratic aims. (19, pp. 18-19).
>
> It is only a radical, participatory approach to organizational democracy that is likely to foster the expertise, skills, and confidence, both in the daily work process and in the exercise of democratic citizenship within the enterprise, that are vital if members of the organization as a whole are to be equipped to meet the challenge of control that will come from the technostructure (19, p. 21).

This argument leads to a direct consideration of the right to exercise power within an organization in a democratic society. Inquiry into this question has potentially radical implications. When we start to discuss power in this way, we are beginning to ask as Ellerman (7) did, "Who is the firm?" We may come to inquire about the rights by which certain individuals or groups now exercise control and come to consider alternative bases of power as means of humanized organizations and to a more fully democratic society. We may discover that equal access to power (political democracy) is a necessary (but certainly not sufficient) condition for humanized social organization.

CONCLUSION

The feelings which underlie this article can be summarized by a comparison of the *two* Golden Rules. First, many of us who seek to humanize organizations dream of organizations where the powerful people either out of self interest or out of moral commitment, follow the first (or the normative) Golden Rule—"Do unto others as you would have them do unto you." By contrast, the second or the descriptive golden rule, which I first saw on the wall in a men's room at Washington University, states, "Them that has the gold makes the rules."

The distribution of power and resources in existing organizations supports humanized relationships only to a limited degree. Humanization of such systems is by no means inevitable, but instead may require considerable struggle. Analysis and facilitation of the process will be aided by greater emphasis on the role of power and the realization that organizations are political systems embedded in larger political systems.

REFERENCES

1. "A Pirandellian Prison," *New York Times Magazine,* April 8 (1973), pp. 38-40, 49.
2. Adams, R. N., *Energy and Structure: A Theory of Social Power* (Austin, Texas: University of Texas Press, 1975).
3. Bachrach, P., and M. S. Baratz. *Power and Poverty: Theory and Practice* (New York: Oxford University Press, 1970).

4. Bennis, W. G. "A Funny Thing Happened on the Way to the Future," *American Psychologist,* Vol. 25 (1970), 595-608.
5. Culbert, S. A. *The Organization Trap* (New York: Basic Books, 1974).
6. Dahl, R. A. *After the Revolution? Authority in a Good Society* (New Haven: Yale University Press, 1970).
7. Ellerman, D. "The 'Ownership of Firm' Is a Myth," *Administration and Society,* Vol. 7 (1975), 27-42.
8. Gouldner, A. W. *The Coming Crisis of Western Sociology* (New York: Basic Books, 1970).
9. Harrington, M. *The Other America* (Baltimore: Penguin Books, 1962).
10. Hickson, D. J., C. R. Hinings, C. A. Lee, R. E. Schneck, and J. M. Pennings. "A Strategic Contingencies' Theory of Intraorganizational Power," *Administrative Science Quarterly,* Vol. 19 (1971), 216-229.
11. Hinings, C. R., D. J. Hickson, J. M. Pennings, and R. E. Schneck. "Structural Conditions of Intraorganizational Power," *Administrative Science Quarterly,* Vol. 19 (1974), 22-44.
12. Kipnis, D. "Does Power Corrupt?" *Journal of Personality and Social Psychology,* Vol, 24 (1972), 33-41.
13. Kipnis, D., P. J. Castell, M. Gergen, and D. Mauch. "Metamorphic Effects of Power," *Journal of Applied Psychology,* Vol. 61 (1976), 127-135.
14. Lefcourt, H. M. "The Function of the Illusions of Control and Freedom," *American Psychologist,* Vol. 28 (1973), 417-425.
15. Nemeth, C. "Bargaining and Reciprocity," *Psychological Bulletin,* Vol. 74 (1970), 297-308.
16. Nord, W. R. "The Failure of Current Applied Behavioral Science: A Marxian Perspective," *Journal of Applied Behavioral Science,* Vol. 10 (1974), 557-578.
17. Nord, W. R. "Economic and Socio-Cultural Barriers to Humanizing Organizations," in H. Meltzer and F. R. Wickert (Eds.), *Humanizing Organizational Behavior* (Springfield, Illinois: Charles C. Thomas, 1976), 175-193.
18. O'Day, R. "Intimidation Rituals: Reactions to Reform," *Journal of Applied Behavioral Science,* Vol. 10 (1974), 373-386.
19. Pateman, C. "A Contribution to the Political Theory of Organizational Democracy," *Administration and Society,* Vol. 7 (1975), 5-26.
20. Rosenhan, D. L. "On Being Sane in Insane Places," *Science,* Vol. 179 (1973), 250-258.
21. Swingle, P. G. *The Management of Power* (Hillside, N.J.: Lawrence Erlbaum Associates, 1976).
22. Thompson, J. D. *Organizations in Action* (New York: McGraw-Hill, 1967).
23. Zaleznik, A. "Power and Politics in Organizational Life," *Harvard Business Review,* Vol. 48 (1970), 47-60.

The Use of Power

DAVID KIPNIS

Once a person has gained control of resources that are given weight by others he must consider how best to use these resources. Statesmen must decide when to offer to negotiate, and when threats will produce the advantageous outcome. Parents must similarly decide how to convince their children to eat their food, to dress properly, and to study.

And so it goes—for all levels of society the perplexing problem is how to gain compliance without losing the long-term affection of the target person, and yet use one's resources economically. In the face of these uncertainties, it is not surprising that there is a continual demand for books that promise to give advice on these matters. Niccolò Machiavelli in *The Prince* provides extensive advice to rulers on how to extend and consolidate their power. Similarly, books on leadership provide advice to managers on the best way to influence subordinates, and books on child psychology are continual best-sellers among parents groping their way from one "identity crisis" of their children to the next.

In the present chapter, rather than offering advice on how best to exert influence, I shall more prudently limit myself to the question of what influences a powerholder's selection of influence tactics, regardless of whether the consequences of this choice lead to favorable or unfavorable outcomes.

The reader should be aware that I have adopted the perspective of the powerholder in discussing the particular means of influence that are used. That is, if the powerholder believes he is offering to reward the target for compliance, I will accept this belief as valid, even though the target may view the offer as an insult and an outside observer may see the same promise of reward as a threat. This kind of relativity exists in defining power relationships, since they represent social acts rather than processes that are invariant with respect to who is doing the observing (Tedeschi, Smith and Brown, 1972; Bachrach and Baratz 1963). Hence different observers may disagree sharply on the benefit and meaning of any social exchange.

INSTINCTS AND POWER USAGE

One possible answer to the question of what determines the choice of means of influence comes from social philosophers who stress man's inherent enjoyment in exercising power in order to inflict harm on others. Freud, writing in *Civilization and Its Discontent,* described man's destructive impulses this way:

> Men are not gentle, friendly creatures wishing for love, who simply defend themselves if they are attacked . . . a powerful measure of desire for aggression has to be reckoned as part of their intrinsic, instinctual endowment. The result is that their neighbor is to them not only a possible helper or sexual outlet, but also someone who tempts them to satisfy their aggressiveness on him, to exploit his capacity for work without compensation, to use him sexually without his consent, to seize his possessions, to humiliate him, to cause him pain, to torture, and to kill him. Homo homini lupus. Who in the face of all his experience of life and history will have the courage to dispute this assertion?
>
> As a rule this cruel aggressiveness waits for some provocation or puts itself at the service of some other purpose, whose goal might also have been reached by milder methods. In circumstances that are favorable to it, when the mental counterforces which ordinarily inhibit it are out of action, it also manifests itself spontaneously and reveals man as a savage beast to whom consideration to its own kind is something alien . . . . The existence of this inclination to aggression, which we can detect in ourselves and justly presume to be in others, is the factor which disturbs our relations with our neighbors and which makes it necessary for culture to institute its highest demands.

Here we have Freud enumerating various coercive means by which man may harass his neighbor, and for no other reason than to satisfy primitive aggressive instincts that make up his natural endowment. If we are to take Freud seriously on this matter, the decision as to what particular means of influence to use will depend primarily on the presence or absence of societal restraining forces. In their absence, the powerholder will choose the cruellest means available. In this way he may satisfy both the manifest reason for exerting influence and the instinctual reason relating to the gratifications achieved by inflicting harm on others.

Freud's assumptions, however, are not easily verified when we examine the day-to-day behaviors of powerholders in the process of exerting influence. Except under special circumstances of intense anger we find that most powerholders tend to reject the immediate use of coercive means of influence. There is a preference for using less harsh means that will preserve a friendly relationship if possible. And if friendship is impossible, means of influence are sought that will at least allow civil intercourse between the powerholder and the target.

A study by Michener and Schwertfeger (1972) illustrates how the choice of destructive modes of influence are reserved for those persons we dislike to begin with, rather than being used indiscriminately. These investigators reported that, in conflict with a landlord over a rent increase, tenants who liked the landlord either attempted to change his decision through persuasion or by offering to move into a cheaper apartment in the same building complex. Tenants who disliked the landlord, however, appeared to follow the destructive pattern described by Freud, in that their choice of influence tactics were more likely to cause pain to the landlord. That is, tenants who initially disliked the landlord favored either forming a tenant's union to militantly resist the landlord's demands for higher rent or threatened to move elsewhere, thus depriving the landlord of any rent at all. It is mainly when strong antipathy is felt toward a target person that we appear to deliberately make our first choice of influence coercive rather than gentle.

INSTITUTIONAL SETTINGS GUIDE THE CHOICE OF INFLUENCE TACTICS

Any discussion of decisions concerning how power is used, whether benignly or with malevolent application, properly begins with the setting in which the influence is to be exercised. Each formal grouping in our society possesses some unique repertoire of influence means that are considered proper to use in that setting. This repertoire exists to provide persons directly responsible for goal achievement with the means to coordinate and guide the behavior of other participants, and so to achieve the setting's goals. In business organizations, Pelz (1951) and Godfrey, Fiedler, and Hall (1959) have found that when appointed leaders were deprived of power usually associated with their positions (by superiors not supporting their decisions), the appointed leaders were less able to influence their employees. Few of the employees listened when they realized that their supervisor's opinions about their work no longer counted. Clearly, personal charm may have only limited value for inducing behavior in settings that traditionally rely on institutionally based means of influence.

Table 1 shows the kinds of coercive means of influence that were found to be available to powerholders in three different settings—marriage, work, and custodial mental hospitals. These means of influence were gathered by the writer and his colleagues while interviewing marriage partners, first-line supervisors, and psychiatric aides. The

Table 1	Coercive Means of Influence Available in Three Settings

Marriage
1. I act cold and say very little to him/her.
2. I make the other person miserable by doing things he or she does not like.
3. I get angry and demand that he/she give in.
4. I threaten to use physical force.
5. I threaten to separate or seek a divorce.

Work
1. I chewed him out.
2. I gave him a verbal warning.
3. I threatened to give him a written warning.
4. I ignored him while being friendly with everyone else.
5. I kept riding him.
6. I scheduled him to work hours he didn't like.
7. I gave him work he didn't like.
8. I put him in a work area he didn't like.
9. I put him in an area of lower premium pay.
10. I gave him a written warning.
11. I took steps to suspend him.
12. I recommended that he be brought before the disciplinary committee.
13. He was suspended from work.
14. He was fired.

Custodial Mental Hospital
1. Warn the patient of loss of privileges (passes, cigarettes).
2. Put the patient in isolation.
3. Scold the patient.
4. Physically control the patient (restraints, etc.).
5. Give medicine to the patient (to sedate).
6. Discipline the patient by removing things or privileges that the patient wants.

targets of influence were the respondent's spouse, the employee, and the mental patient.

One of the first impressions gained from examining these listings is that the coercive power in each of these settings directs itself toward different values and needs within the target person. In marriage the coercive means of influence are based upon the ability of one spouse to withdraw emotional support and services from the other. The threat is to "move away" from the other partner. Further in the marriage setting, one has an impression that the threats used are vague and do not precisely specify exact consequences for noncompliance. In the mental hospitals, however, the threats appear to be quite precise. Also, the coercive means tend to be directed at the physical well-being of the patient. Rather than withdrawing emotional support and "moving away" from the target, psychiatric aides may threaten to "move against" the patient if compliance is not forthcoming. Among first-line supervisors the threats are directed toward withholding economic support or toward reducing the employee's self-esteem.

Another impression that is gained from examining Table 1 is that the first-line supervisors appear to control a wider range of coercive influence means than do marital partners or psychiatric aides. That is, supervisors appear to control "low keyed" threats for minor forms of resistance and massive threats (firings or suspensions) for strong forms of resistance. Having access to this range of influence means should make the first-line supervisors far more flexible in their attempts to influence employees than either marital partners or psychiatric aides, who may have to choose threats that are inappropriate for the kinds of opposition being encountered from their spouses or patients.

A good deal can be learned about the attempts of powerholders to influence others from simply tabulating the means of influence available to them in each setting. Can rewards be given out freely? What types of punishments may be threatened for noncompliance? Can the target person's environment be altered? If the answer to most of these questions is "no," one can suspect that the influence potential of the individual will be low, regardless of his personality, loquacity, or personal charm.

Suppose we observe two persons attempting to influence target persons. The first adopts a pleasant, democratic style in which mild *requests* for compliance predominate. The second person adopts a brusque, demanding tone with little concern for the feelings of the target person. If asked to explain these differences, we might guess that the first person is rather timid, while the second has an authoritarian personality. However, we would probably alter our interpretation if we were told that the first person was the president of the local Parent-Teacher Association interacting with one of the members, while the second person was a business manager talking with a subordinate. Rather than resulting from personality differences, the two styles of influence can at least in part be attributed to the fact that the PTA president has no formal sanctions available to induce compliance, while the business manager has such sanctions available.

As a general rule, one should look for increased assertiveness in powerholders as the number of ways in which they can influence others increases. Support for this general rule can be found in several studies by psychologists of the relationship between the availability of means of influence and the assertiveness of the powerholder. In one study by Columbia University psychologists Morton Deutsch and Robert Krauss (1960) it was found that persons running a simulated business game who were given the power to threaten their rivals became far more demanding and less willing to compromise with their business rivals. Seemingly, the added power encouraged the development of a belief system: "We're stronger—we deserve more."

Somewhat similar findings were also obtained by the present writer (1972) in an experimental study in which managers ran a simulated business. The job of manager required the supervision of the work of four employees. There were two conditions in the study. In the first, managers were provided with a number of different ways of influencing the employees; that is, the managers were allowed, if they chose to do so, to give pay raises, pay deductions, to shift their employees from one job to another, to train their employees, or to fire them. In a second condition, the managers were not provided with any of these means of influence. Instead they had to rely on their personal ability to persuade their employees, or on their legitimate rights as managers to issue orders.

The results of this study were that managers who controlled a broad range of ways of influencing were far more assertive and demanding in their relations with their employees than were managers who were not provided with this range of influence. Managers with many institutional powers made twice as many demands upon their employees to work harder as did managers with no institutional powers.

It seems clear, then, that as we move individuals into settings that provide additional ways of influencing others, these individuals will respond by making far more demands upon the world.

There is also a hint in the experimental literature that the kinds of demands made upon others will vary with the kinds of means of influence that are available. In a study of how two people make concessions when bargaining with each other, Schlenker, and Tedeschi (1972) provided some participants with the power to reward their opponents if the opponents complied, other participants with the power to punish noncompliance, and still other participants with both the power to reward compliance and to punish noncompliance. The finding of considerable interest was that the type of power available had important effects on the behavior of the powerholders.

Powerholders sent more threats, and actually invoked coercive power more frequently when they possessed *only* coercive power than when they possessed both coercive and reward power. Thus persons acted more aggressively when they could only punish to gain compliance than when they could choose to either punish or reward. Further, powerholders promised fewer rewards when they possessed *only* reward power than when they possessed both reward and coercive power. These findings suggest that users of power will be less benevolent and more coercive in situations where they can only reward, or only punish, as compared to situations where they control the power to both reward and punish. Perhaps the power of prison guards to threaten and coerce should be augmented with the power to provide genuine rewards to prisoners in exchange for compliance. One wonders if by this means we could reduce the number of prison-abuse incidents that occur. For if the only way we have to get our way is to threaten and bully, it seems clear from everyday observation that most of us, sooner or later, will get used to the idea of threatening and bullying.

THE INFLUENCE OF STATUS ON THE CHOICE OF MEANS

So far we have stated that simply tabulating the number and kinds of means of influence available to a powerholder in a given setting will tell us a good deal about how the powerholder is likely to behave. Here we wish to consider the implication of this statement as it relates to a person's status within the setting. To state an obvious fact, persons with high status tend to have available a wide variety of means to influence. There are also few restraints on their use of these means as compared to the restraints on persons of lower status. Children can only beg, ask, plead, or whine in order to influence their parents. Parents can legitimately punish, reward, and train their children—that is, bring strong means of influence to bear on their children.

Within institutional settings individuals with high status and great office may have unlimited access to resources, while those with less status, such as supervisors or teachers, will have only limited access to the institution's resources. A study of role conflict among business managers by Robert Kahn and his associates at the University of Michigan (1964) nicely illustrates how access to influence varies with the person's work status in the organization. In this study managers were asked the extent to which they could use a variety of means to influence various target persons with whom they worked. The respondent was either a superior, peer, or subordinate of the target person.

Table 2 shows these responses in terms of average rating by each respondent of his ability to use four means of influence: legitimate power, reward power, coercive power, and expert power. Quite clearly, top supervisors reported that they had greater latitude to use legitimate, reward and coercive powers than did subordinates. It may also be seen that all persons in the organization, regardless of level, felt that they could use their expert power to influence a target person.

This indicates that powers derived purely from participation in the organization, such as the power to reward and punish, are closely linked with level in the organization. High-status persons have a wider range of influence to choose from than low-status persons. On the other hand, when the means of influence depend upon the individual's own abilities, such as his expert knowledge, we are more likely to find persons at all levels using such means. Thus first-line supervisors can change their superior's behavior by using professional knowledge. However, first-line supervisors will hardly ever attempt to change this behavior by promising to raise their bosses' pay, that is, by using reward power. This latter power tactic is reserved for those with higher status.

Table 2	**Ability to Use Various Means of Influence at Differing Organizational Levels**			
	Top Supervisor	Immediate Supervisor	Peer	Subordinate
Legitimate power	4.6	4.3	2.3	1.6
Reward power	4.0	3.7	2.2	1.5
Coercive power	4.1	3.6	1.3	1.3
Expert power	4.1	4.1	4.1	4.1

NOTE: The higher the score the greater the ability to use the given power.
*Estimated from text's statement that all respondents averaged above 4.0 on a scale of 1 to 5 (Kahn et al. [1964], p. 200).

CALCULATION AND THE CHOICE OF INFLUENCE

The previous two sections pointed out that powerholders' willingness to assert themselves is closely tied to the kinds and amount of power bases that are available to them. Assume now that a powerholder does possess a suitable position and an array of means of influence that can be freely used. That is, assume the powerholder can choose to do whatever he wants to make the target person comply. In these circumstances, what determines the powerholder's particular choice of influence from this array? Why does he use one particular means of influence in one situation but not in another? Why in one instance does a teacher use flattery to encourage a student to study but flatly order a second student to engage in similar behavior? Why does a supervisor in one instance spend long hours training an incompetent worker to reach acceptable levels of performance but in another instance threaten to fire an equally incompetent worker? Is the answer, as Freud suggests, simply that powerholders select the means liable to do the most harm, so long as they are not punished themselves? Or are more rational processes involved?

All evidence indicates that more rational processes are almost always involved in decisions concerning tactics of influence. As Raven (1974) points out: "On the assumption that man is rational we would expect him to use the base of power which would most likely lead to successful influence" (p. 192). Raven goes on to point out that if the goal of the powerholder was to produce long-lasting changes in the behavior of the target person, then the powerholder would probably avoid coercive means of influence and perhaps attempt to influence through providing the target person with new information. If long-lasting compliance was not an issue, however, then the powerholder might decide to obtain immediate satisfaction by invoking strong sanctions.

Planning and rationality can almost always be found when powerholders are deciding which of several means of influence should be used in a given situation. This does not mean of course that emotions and feelings do not affect the powerholder's decisions. Such emotional feelings, however, appear to act by narrowing or expanding the range of influence means that the powerholder is likely to believe effective in that situation.

Gamson (1968) illustrates how emotions serve to guide the powerholder's choice of influence means. When the powerholder trusts the target person, persuasion is most likely to be used to convince the target person. Because of this trusting relationship, the powerholder is willing to allow the target person the freedom to make up his own mind, confident that the target person will freely do what the powerholder has requested. If the powerholder does not trust the target person, then it is quite likely that he will decide to invoke threats and punishments. The assumption here is that one cannot rely on influence means that allow the target person freedom of choice (such as persuasion), because with freedom the distrusted target person will probably do exactly the opposite of what the powerholder wants him to do. As Gamson notes:

"Since the probability of favorable outcomes is already very low . . . , it is hardly necessary to worry about [the target's feelings]. The attitude then that 'the only thing they understand is force' is a perfect manifestation of this trust orientation" (p. 169).

CHOICE OF INFLUENCE—A TWO-STAGE PROCESS

If we assume that powerholders act rationally when choosing how best to influence a target person, then it follows that there must be at least two stages involved in the choice of a particular means of influence. First the powerholder must diagnose the reasons for the target's refusal to comply with his request. Is the reason for the target's refusal due to the target's dislike of the powerholder, or is it because the target person does not possess the ability to do what the powerholder wants? Perhaps it is because a lack of trust exists between the two parties so that the target person will refuse any suggestion made by the powerholder, no matter how beneficial the suggestion is to both parties. Clearly, there is no end to the number of possible reasons why the target person has offered resistance.

Yet if the powerholder does not understand the reason for this resistance, he will be forced to flail about until by chance he discovers the one influence means that will produce compliance. Given this time-consuming alternative, the rational powerholder, before taking further action, prefers to spend some time analyzing why the target person has refused his request.

Frequently this stage in the decision-making process is complicated by the lack of open communication between the powerholder and the target person. The target person may lie about his reasons or sullenly refuse to talk, since once the causes of resistance have been discovered the powerholder may attempt to overcome the resistance.

Further, the powerholder can make mistakes in his diagnosis. He is in the position of the sixteenth-century physician who possessed only the crudest of diagnostic tools with which to decide what was bothering his patient. As mistakes were common then among physicians, so too are they today among powerholders. The history of modern international negotiations contains many examples where signals of one nation were misperceived by another nation, which saw hostility where in fact peace overtures were intended. We have no X-ray devices available to peer into the mind of the target person and discern there the reasons for his refusal to comply with our request. Our closest approach to such a device is perhaps the consumer surveys that seek to discover the cause of citizen antipathy toward consumer products, or toward politicians, so that precise campaigns can be planned to overcome these resistances. For most powerholders, however, diagnosing the causes of the target persons' resistance remains a subtle art based upon past encounters with the target person, hunches, and the powerholder's own perceptiveness.

Once the diagnosis is reached, regardless of whether it is correct, we reach the second stage of the decision-making process, which involves the actual choice of means of influence. Assuming that the powerholder is acting rationally, this stage is almost completely dependent upon the powerholder's initial diagnosis of the cause of the target's resistance. As the powerholder's diagnosis of the reasons for the target's lack of cooperation varies, so too will his choice of tactics vary.

This two-stage process has an analogy in the practice of medical diagnosis and treatment. When a patient appears at a physician's office and complains of feeling sick, the physician must first decide what is causing these complaints. It is only after the diagnosis has been made that the physician can select a paricular mode of treatment. Furthermore, the treatment that is selected must be the one that holds the highest promise of cure. If the physician ignores this treatment in favor of another, his action tends to be viewed as a breach of medical ethics. The concept of "treatment of choice" in medicine refers to this general rule that the treatment with the highest probability of cure must be used before any other is tried. Once the diagnosis has been made, one can predict with almost complete certainty the kinds of treatments the physician will use.

There is also a "treatment of choice" rule associated with the selection of means of influence. We have found that if powerholders agree on the reason for a target person's resistance to their influence, they will also agree on the proper means of influence to use. This two-stage process can be illustrated by studies done by myself and my colleagues William Lane and Joseph Cosentino (1962; 1969) among Navy and industrial supervisors.

The purpose of these studies was to determine how appointed leaders used their delegated powers to influence the performance of their subordinates. At the beginning of the studies we had no particular preconceived ideas as to how power would be used. Rather it was hoped to catalogue the range of means of influence that were relied upon, and to get some idea of when each means was used.

Our procedure consisted of asking supervisors in both the Navy and in various business organizations to describe a recent incident in which they had to correct the behavior of one of their subordinates. We asked the supervisors to describe the problem they faced and what they or someone else did about it. In telling us what they did, the supervisors were in effect tellng us about the kinds of influence they had the authority to use.

The reason for these influence attempts did not arise from any particularly sinister motives. Rather they arose from the supervisors' involvement in their work. As part of this work there were obligations to make sure that employees performed at acceptable levels and to force changes if this level was not reached.

The nature of the employee problems that disturbed the supervisors in the first place was also tabulated. Basically the problems could be diagnosed as those caused by an inability of the employee to do his work or by a lack of motivation to do the work or by problems of discipline, in which company rules were violated (such as the problem of habitual lateness). Sometimes a supervisor would describe a subordinate whose poor performance was due to a combination of these problems. These employees were described as manifesting "complex" problems.

Next we looked at the ways in which the supervisors said they attempted to correct their employees' performance. Their attempts involved the use of a variety of institutional means of influence, which we classified as follows: (a) coercive power—threatening or actually demoting the subordinate or assigning him to less pleasant or lower-paying work, or reducing his responsibilities, or sending him an official letter of warning, or suspending or firing him; (b) ecological control, in which the subordinate was shifted to a new job, work shift, or a new job location but not for the purpose of punishment; (c) expert power, in which new information or new skills were shown the worker; (d) legitimate power expressed in terms of direct requests or orders for change.

In addition to these institutional means of influence, supervisors also relied upon their personal powers of persuasion convincing subordinates to change by praising, reprimanding, and encouraging them to expend additional efforts. Readers who adopt a historic or cultural perspective on these kinds of findings will be quick to see how bound by time and space such attempts at influence are. That is, no supervisors mentioned physically striking their employees, as would have been done prior to the twentieth century, and no supervisors mentioned using appeals based upon family and company loyalty, as is still done in some Japanese industries.

One of the strongest findings that emerged from these studies was the discovery that there was a "treatment of choice" rule associated with the selection of means of influence. That is, the kinds of influence invoked by

Table 3   **Diagnosis of Subordinate Resistance and the Means of Influence Used to Overcome It**

	Diagnosed Cause of Poor Work			
	Simple Problems			Complex Problems
Means of Influence	Employee Lacks Motivation	Employee Lacks Ability	Employee Lacks Discipline	Combinations of Poor Attitudes, Discipline and/or Lack of Ability
Discussion	Yes	No	Yes	Yes
Extra training (expert power)	No	Yes	No	Yes
Ecological control	No	No	No	Yes
Legitimate power	Yes	Yes	Yes	Yes
Coercion	Yes	No	Yes	Yes

the supervisors were found to vary systematically with the nature of the subordinate's problem as diagnosed by the supervisor. Without any particular instruction in the use of power, most of the supervisors converged on the selection of a given means of influence for a given type of problem. These findings are summarized in Table 3.

It can be seen that, as the supervisor's diagnosis of what was causing the subordinate's poor performance changed, so too did the means of influence that were used. For instance, when the supervisor believed that the employee's problem was due to poor attitudes, the supervisor used persuasion and informational modes of influence. The supervisor's concern was to find out the reasons for the subordinate's poor attitudes and, if possible, to persuade him to change. If, however, the supervisor attributed the subordinate's poor performance to a lack of ability, then persuasion was rarely mentioned. Rather, the supervisor invoked his expert powers and devoted time to retraining his subordinate.

If the problem shown by a subordinate was complex, with elements of lack of ability and discipline, and poor attitudes, then supervisors increased the number of different means of influence directed toward the subordinate. Apparently, when the supervisors believed that several factors were causing the employee's poor performance ("He could never learn to do the simplest jobs, and on top of that he was always shooting off his mouth"), then the problem was considered more difficult to deal with. Accordingly, more powers were invoked to overcome this added resistance. For instance, 76 percent of a sample of Navy supervisors invoked two or more means of influence. (e.g., increased training and change of jobs) when their subordinates manifested complex problems. When the subordinate evidenced a simple problem, however, only 41 percent of the Navy supervisors invoked two or more means of influence. This difference was statistically reliable beyond the .01 level.

A further finding was that, when faced with complex problems, supervisors exercised power by ecological control. That is, significantly more workers were moved to a new job or work shift when their problems were complex rather than simple. The supervisors apparently reasoned: "If he's causing so much fuss on this job, let's try him somewhere else." A moment's reflection will convince the reader that this means of exercising power is not limited to harassed supervisors facing strong resistance. In schools, pupils who are considered intractable by teachers are transferred out of class, while ecological control is exerted over criminals by sending them to prison. In all instances the diagnosis of being hard to influence leads to the temptation to shift the person to a new environment considered more likely to overcome these resistances.

Here we have evidence that powerholders adjusted the kinds of influence they brought to bear to fit what they believed to be the reason for the target's resistance. If the target's resistance was seen as caused by poor attitudes, then persuasion was one of the favored means (coercion was also favored in such cases). If the resistance was seen as caused by a lack of ability, then expert power was used and little time was wasted trying to persuade the target to improve his performance. If the target was seen as manifesting a variety of problems simultaneously, then the powerholder increased the pressure for change by invoking several different kinds of influence. Simply put, as resistance increased, additional means of influence were brought to bear on the target person. And among these was an attempt to move the target person from his present environment.

These findings are consistent with the notion that the use of power involves an active cognitive search which consists of two stages. First, we see that the powerholder diagnoses the causes of the resistance. He says to himself, "The reason X is acting so badly is that . . . ." Second, the powerholder searches for the best means of influence available to him for dealing with this resistance. That is, he says, "Well, if that's why he is doing so poorly, then I'd better do this."

While this process has been illustrated in terms of work settings, it is not difficult to see how a similar search pattern might operate elsewhere. Thus, a parent whose child gets into continual mischief during the summer vacation must decide whether to promise him some benefit for good behavior, sit down and reason with him, send him to summer camp, appeal to his love for his parents, or threaten some kind of punishment. The process of choice will be actively guided by what the parent decides is causing the mischief in the first place.

LIMITATIONS TO RATIONAL CALCULATIONS

There are several reasons why powerholders may not be able to select the best means of influencing a target person. Most obviously, the powerholder may not have available the proper means of influence. For example, a supervisor may not have the authority to promise a pay raise, despite his recognition that he will be able to influence his employees to produce more if such means are used. Related to this reason is the problem that arises when the use of one means of influence may prevent the powerholder from using a second means, despite the powerholder's recognition that the use of the second means would be more appropriate. Thus for example, if one uses coercion on occasion, it becomes difficult then to switch to the use of persuasion. Researchers who have studied the use of power in penal systems point out that therapy programs in prison tend to be unsuccessful because the prisoners tend to be coerced into entering such programs.

The inhibiting effect that the use of one means of influence has upon the use of a second means is also illustrated in the complaints of social caseworkers that their control of the power to grant or withhold welfare money tends to weaken their ability to provide counseling and guidance to their poverty clients. In effect the poor are unwilling to communicate socioemotional problems to a caseworker because of the possibility that some careless revelation about themselves may cause the caseworker to withdraw funds. While many caseworkers would prefer to influence their clients through counseling, they are unable to do so because they also influence the same clients through the use of money. Similar problems have been noted by supervisors in industry who are expected to influence both task attitudes and socioemotional attitudes of their employees. It has been reported (Reed 1962) that subordinates are not willing to openly communicate problems to the supervisors because of the employees' fears that revealing negative information about themselves will reduce their chances for promotion. In both of these instances, the possession of strong economic means prevents the powerholder from using other means despite his recognition of their usefulness for exercising influence.

A second limitation to choosing the appropriate means of influence occurs when a powerholder simply misdiagnoses the causes of the target's resistance and applies the wrong means of influence. Thus, a teacher might threaten to discipline an inattentive student unless the student's behavior improved. The same teacher would rapidly change tactics if it were discovered that the cause of the student's inattention was a hearing loss. Then, perhaps, the student would be moved to the front of the class as a means of improving his attention.

Still another limitation occurs when the powerholder does not consider a particular means of influence as appropriate. For example, open expressions of love as a means of influencing a wife or child are rejected by some men who believe that such expressions are not consistent with their conceived role of manhood. In a different context, Dartmouth College political scientist David Baldwin (1974) has discussed this limitation in terms of the reluctance of government foreign-policy planners to seriously consider other nations in any terms but coercive military power. He points out that:

> students of international politics are so preoccupied with negative sanctions, threat systems, and military force that they have painted themselves into a conceptual corner which has little room for non-military factors, positive sanctions and promise systems. It is not surprising, therefore, that the recent *International Encyclopedia of the Social Sciences* included an article on military power potential but none on economic power potential. At a time when military power is losing utility in international politics and economic power is gaining utility, this omission is especially unfortunate. [p. 395]

LACK OF ABILITY OR LACK OF MOTIVATION?

Powerholders usually diagnose the causes of a target person's resistance into one of two groupings. Either the resistance is attributed to the fact that the target person is inept and lacks ability, or to the fact that the target person has deliberately chosen to refuse to comply. In this second instance, the label of "poor attitude" or "lack of motivation" is used. Thus resistance is attributed by powerholders to either the fact that external forces are controlling the target person ("He wants to help but simply doesn't know how") or to internal forces within the target person ("That s.o.b. could do it if he wanted to help out"). The distinction between internal or external forces tends to be critical for understanding the powerholder's choice of influence tactics.

Here I wish to consider briefly the question of what kinds of information powerholders use when deciding that the target's resistance is due to either internal or external forces.

University of Wisconsin social psychologist H. Andrew Michener and his colleagues (John Fleishman, Gregory Elliot, and Joel Skolnick [in press, 1975]) have used concepts derived from attribution theory to help explain this decision. Michener et al. have proposed that the powerholder's judgment is based upon four bits of information: (a) the difficulty of the demands placed upon the target person; (b) the known ability of the target person; (c) the extent to which the target person seems to be trying; and (d) whether the target person's performance improves or not. In a test of this proposal, Michener found that powerholders attributed a target person's poor performance on an experimental task (solving anagrams) to external forces or, lack of ability, when the task was known to be difficult for most people, when the target person had a prior history of ineptness in solving anagrams, when the target person signaled that he was trying as hard as he could, and when the target person's performance improved over time, even though it never quite reached the level expected by the powerholder. Powerholders attributed the target person's poor performance to a lack of motivation when the opposite of the above four bits of information were communicated to the powerholder.

In short, the process by which powerholders diagnose the causes of a target person's resistance to influence has its own logic. Basically the powerholder attempts to reach a diagnosis by comparing the target person's current behavior with past behavior. Inconsistencies between current and past behavior are considered due to deliberate resistance when the powerholder knows that what has been requested is within the capabilities of the target person. Under these circumstances it is not unusual to hear powerholders justifying their selection of influence tactics in terms of the target person's poor attitude, hostility, or lack of motivation.

SUMMARY

This chapter has examined how powerholders convert inert resources into actual influence. The basic proposal is that the decision to convert resources into influence is guided by an active cognitive search for the best means of making this conversion. This search involves two distinct stages. In the first the reasons for the target person's refusal to comply are diagnosed. The second stage involves selecting that means of influence considered by the powerholder as most likely to overcome the diagnosed causes of resistance.

It has also been suggested that there are stable linkages between the diagnosed causes of a target person's resistance and the particular means of influence that are chosen. If powerholders attribute the target person's resistance to external forces over which the target person has no control ("I'm trying, but I just can't seem to do it"), then the influence techniques chosen involve training and expert knowledge. In essence these techniques serve to restore self-control to the target person so that he can comply in future interactions.

When powerholders attribute the target person's resistance to internal forces under the control of the target person ("I refuse"), then the influence techniques chosen involve discussion and persuasion, at least initially. If, however, discussion fails, then powerholders are tempted to invoke stronger means of influence to overcome what they believe to be deliberate resistance. These stronger means of influence involve the use of both rewards and punishments.

Finally the chapter has briefly surveyed sources that restrict the powerholder's selection of the appropriate means of influence. These sources include the fact that often influence tactics are not available to a given powerholder because of his position in an organization, because he does not recognize that it is legitimate to use some influence tactic, or because he has misdiagnosed the reasons for the target person's refusal and simply has chosen the wrong means of influence.

A Strategic Contingencies'
Theory of Intraorganizational Power

D. J. HICKSON,
C. R. HININGS,
C. A. LEE,
R. E. SCHNECK,
AND J. M. PENNINGS

Typically, research designs have treated power as the independent variable. Power has been used in community studies to explain decisions on community programs, on resource allocation, and on voting behavior: in small groups it has been used to explain decision making; and it has been used in studies of work organizations to explain morale and alienation. But within work organizations, power itself has not been explained. This paper sets forth a theoretical explanation of power as the dependent variable with the aim of developing empirically testable hypotheses that will explain differential power among subunits in complex work organizations.

The problems of studying power are well known from the cogent reviews by March (1955, 1966) and Wrong (1968). These problems led March (1966: 70) to ask if power was just a term used to mask our ignorance, and to conclude pessimistically that the power of the concept of power "depends on the kind of system we are confronting."

Part of March's (1966) pessimism can be attributed to the problems inherent in community studies. When the unit of analysis is the

Reprinted from "A Strategic Contingencies' Theory of Intraorganizational Power" by D. J. Hickson, C. R. Hinings, C. A. Lee, R. E. Schneck, and J. M. Pennings published in *Administrative Science Quarterly,* Volume 16, Number 2, June 1971 by permission of The Administrative Science Quarterly.

community, the governmental, political, economic, recreational, and other units which make up the community do not necessarily interact and may even be oriented outside the supposed boundaries of the community. However, the subunits of a work organization are mutually related in the interdependent activities of a single identifiable social system. The perspective of the present paper is due in particular to the encouraging studies of subunits by Lawrence and Lorsch (1967a, 1967b), and begins with their (1967a: 3) definition of an organization as "a system of interrelated behaviors of people who are performing a task that has been differentiated into several distinct subsystems."

Previous studies of power in work organizations have tended to focus on the individual and to neglect subunit or departmental power. This neglect led Perrow (1970: 84) to state: "Part of the problem, I suspect, stems from the persistent attempt to define power in terms of individuals and as a social-psychological phenomenon. . . . Even sociological studies tend to measure power by asking about an individual. . . . I am not at all clear about the matter, but I think the term takes on different meanings when the unit, or power-holder, is a *formal group* in an *open system* with *multiple goals,* and the system is assumed to reflect a political-domination model of organization, rather than only a cooperative model. . . . The fact that after a cursory search I can find only a single study that asks survey questions regarding the power of functional *groups* strikes me as odd. Have we conceptualized power in such a way as to exclude this well-known phenomenon?"

The concept of power used here follows Emerson (1962) and takes power as a property of the social relationship, not of the actor. Since the context of the relationship is a formal organization, this approach moves away from an overpersonalized conceptualization and operationalization of power toward structural sources. Such an approach has been taken only briefly by Dubin (1963) in his discussion of power, and incidentally by Lawrence and Lorsch (1967b) when reporting power data. Most research has focused on the vertical superior-subordinate relationship, as in a multitude of leadership studies. This approach is exemplified by the extensive work of Tannenbaum (1968) and his colleagues, in which the distribution of perceived power was displayed on control graphs. The focus was on the vertical differentiation of perceived power, that is the exercise of power by managers who by changing their behavior could vary the distribution and the total amount of perceived power.

By contrast, when organizations are conceived as interdepartmental systems, the division of labor becomes the ultimate source of intraorganizational power, and power is explained by variables that are elements of each subunit's task, its functioning, and its links with the activities of other subunits. Insofar as this approach differs from previous studies by treating power as the dependent variable, by taking subunits of work organizations as the subjects of analysis, and by attempting a multivariate explanation, it may avoid some of the previous pitfalls.

ELEMENTS OF A THEORY

Thompson (1967: 13) took from Cyert and March (1963) a viewpoint which he hailed as a newer tradition: "A newer tradition enables us to conceive of the organization as an open system, indeterminate and faced with uncertainty, but subject to criteria of rationality and hence needing certainty . . . we suggest that organizations cope with uncertainty by creating certain parts specifically to deal with it, specializing other parts in operating under conditions of certainty, or near certainty."

Thus organizations are conceived of as interdepartmental systems in which a major task element is coping with uncertainty. The task is divided and allotted to the subsystems, the division of labor creating an interdependency among them. Imbalance of this reciprocal interdependence (Thompson, 1967) among the parts gives rise to power relations. The essence of an organization is limitation to the autonomy of all its members or parts, since all are subject to power from the others; for subunits, unlike individuals, are not free to make a decision to participate, as March and Simon (1958) put it, nor to decide whether or not to come together in political relationships. They must. They exist to do so. Crozier (1964: 47) stressed in his discussion of power "the necessity for the members of the different groups to live together; the fact that each group's privileges depend to quite a large extent on the existence of other group's privileges." The groups use differential power to function within the system rather than to destroy it.

If dependency in a social relation is the reverse of power (Emerson, 1962), then the crucial unanswered question in organizations is: what factors function to vary dependency, and so to vary power? Emerson (1962: 32) proposed that "the dependence of actor A upon actor B is (1) directly proportional to A's motivational investment in goals mediated by B, and (2) inversely proportional to the availability of those goals to A outside of the A-B relation." In organizations, subunit B will have more power than other subunits to the extent that (1) B has the capacity to fulfill the requirements of the other subunits and (2) B monopolizes this ability. If a central problem facing modern organizations is uncertainty, then B's power in the organization will be partially determined by the extent to which B copes with uncertainties for other subunits, and by the extent to which B's coping activities are available elsewhere.

Thus, intraorganizational dependency can be associated with two contributing variables: (1) the degree to which a subunit copes with uncertainty for other subunits, and (2) the extent to which a subunit's coping activities are substitutable. But if coping with uncertainty, and substitutability, are to be in some way related to power, there is a necessary assumption of some degree of task interconnection among subunits. By definition, organization requires a minimum link. Therefore, a third variable, centrality, refers to the varying degree above such a minimum with which the activities of a subunit are linked with those of other subunits.

Before these three variables can be combined in a theory of power, it is necessary to examine their definition and possible operationalization, and to define power in this context.

Power

Hinings *et al.* (1967: 62) compared power to concepts such as bureaucracy or alienation or social class, which are difficult to understand because they tend to be treated as "large-scale unitary concepts." Their many meanings need disentangling. With the concept of power, this has not yet been accomplished (Cartwright, 1965), but two conceptualizations are commonly employed: (1) power as coercion, and (2) power as determination of behavior.

Power as coercive force was a comparatively early conceptualization among sociologists (Weber, 1947; Bierstedt, 1950). Later, Blau (1964) emphasized the imposition of will despite resistance.

However, coercion is only one among the several bases of power listed by French and Raven (1959) and applied across organizations by Etzioni (1961); that is, coercion is a means of power, but is not an adequate definition of power. If the direction of dependence in a relationship is determined by an imbalance of power bases, power itself has to be defined separately from these bases. Adopting Dahl's (1957) concept of power, as many others have done (March, 1955; Bennis *et al.*, 1958; Emerson, 1962; Harsanyi, 1962; Van Doorn, 1962; Dahlstrom, 1966; Wrong, 1968; Tannenbaum, 1968; Luhmann, 1969), power is defined as the determination of the behavior of one social unit by another.

If power is the determination of A's behavior by B, irrespective of whether one, any, or all the types of bases are involved, then authority will here be regarded as that part of power which is legitimate or normatively expected by some selection of role definers. Authority may be either more or less than power. For subunits it might be represented by the formally specified range of activities they are officially required to undertake and, therefore, to decide upon.

Discrepancies between authority and power may reflect time lag. Perrow (1970) explored the discrepancy between respondent's perceptions of power and of what power should be. Perhaps views on a preferred power distribution precede changes in the exercise of power, which in turn precede changes in expectations of power, that is in its legitimate authority content. Perhaps today's authority hierarchy is partly a fossilized impression of yesterday's power ranking. However this may be, it is certainly desirable to include in any research not only data on perceived power and on preferred power, but also on positional power, or authority, and on participation, or exercised power (Clark [ed.], 1968).

Kaplan (1964) succinctly described three dimensions of power. The weight of power is defined in terms of the degree to which B affects the probability of A behaving in a certain way, that is, determination of behavior in the sense adopted here. The other dimensions are domain and scope. Domain is the number of A's, persons or collectivities, whose behavior is determined; scope is the range of behaviors of each A that are determined. For subunit power within an organization, domain might be the number of other subunits affected by the issues, scope the range of decision issues affected, and weight the degree to which a given subunit affects the decision process on the issues. In published research such distinctions are rarely made. Power consists of the sweeping undifferentiated perceptions of respondents when asked to rank individuals or classes of persons, such as supervisors, on influence. Yet at the same time the complexity of power in organizations is recognized. If it is taken for granted that, say, marketing has most to do with sales matters, that accounting has most to do with finance matters, supervisors with supervisory matters, and so on, then the validity of forcing respondents to generalize single opinions across an unstated range of possibilities is questionable.

To avoid these generalized opinions, data collected over a range of decision topics or issues are desirable. Such issues should in principle include all recognized problem areas in the organization, in each of which more than one subunit is involved. Examples might be marketing strategies, obtaining equipment, personnel training, and capital budgeting.

Some suggested subvariables and indicators of power and of the independent variables are summarized in Table 1. These are intended to

Table 1	Variables and Operationalizable Subvariables

Power (weight, domain, scope)
Positional power (authority)
Participation power
Perceived power
Preferred power

Uncertainty
Variability of organizational inputs
Feedback on subunit performance;
  Speed
  Specificity
Structuring of subunit activities

Coping with uncertainty, classified as:
By prevention (forestalling uncertainty)
By information (forecasting)
By absorption (action after the event)

Substitutability
Availability of alternatives
Replaceability of personnel

Centrality
Pervasiveness of workflows
Immediacy of workflows

include both individual perceptions of power in the form of questionnaire responses and data of a somewhat less subjective kind on participation in decision processes and on formal position in the organization.

It is now possible to examine coping with uncertainty, substitutability and centrality.

Uncertainty and Coping with Uncertainty

Uncertainty may be defined as a lack of information about future events, so that alternatives and their outcomes are unpredictable. Organizations deal with environmentally derived uncertainties in the sources and composition of inputs, with uncertainties in the processing of through-puts, and again with environmental uncertainties in the disposal of outputs. They must have means to deal with these uncertainties for adequate task performance. Such ability is here called coping.

In his study of the French tobacco manufacturing industry, Crozier (1964: 164) suggested that power is related to "the kind of uncertainty upon which depends the life of the organization." March and Simon (1958) had earlier made the same point, and Perrow (1961) had discussed the shifting domination of different groups in organizations following the shifting uncertainties of resources and the routinization of skills. From studies of industrial firms, Perrow (1970) tentatively thought that power might be due to uncertainty absorption, as March and Simon (1958) call it. Lawrence and Lorsch (1967b) found that marketing had more influence than production in both container-manufacturing and food-processing firms, apparently because of its involvement in (uncertain) innovation and with customers.

Crozier (1964) proposed a strategic model of organizations as systems in which groups strive for power, but his discussion did not clarify how uncertainty could relate positively to power. Uncertainty itself does not give power: coping gives power. If organizations allocate to their various subunits task areas that vary in uncertainty, then those subunits that cope most effectively with the most uncertainty should have most power within the organization, since coping by a subunit reduces the impact of uncertainty on other activities in the organization, a shock absorber function. Coping may be by prevention, for example, a subunit prevents sales fluctuations by securing firm orders; or by information, for example, a subunit forecasts sales fluctuations; or by absorption, for example, a drop in sales is swiftly countered by novel selling methods (Table 1). By coping, the subunit provides pseudo certainty for the other subunits by controlling what are otherwise contingencies for other activities. This coping confers power through the dependencies created.

Thus organizations do not necessarily aim to avoid uncertainty nor to reduce its absolute level, as Cyert and March (1963) appear to have assumed, but to cope with it. If a subunit can cope, the level of uncertainty encountered can be increased by moving into fresh sectors of the environment, attempting fresh outputs, or utilizing fresh technologies.

Operationally, raw uncertainty and coping will be difficult to disentangle, though theoretically the distinctions are clear. For all units, uncertainty is in the raw situation which would exist without the activities of the other relevant subunits, for example, the uncertainty that would face production units if the sales subunit were not there to forecast and/or to obtain a smooth flow of orders. Uncertainty might be indicated by the variability of those inputs to the organization which are taken by the subunit. For instance, a production subunit may face variability in raw materials and engineering may face variability in equipment performance. Lawrence and Lorsch (1967a) attempted categorizations of this kind. In addition, they (1967a: 14) gave a lead with "the time span of definitive feedback from the environment." This time span might be treated as a secondary indicator of uncertainty, making the assumption that the less the feedback to a subunit on the results of what it is doing, and the less specific the feedback, the more likely the subunit is to be working in a vague, unknown, unpredictable task area. Both speed and specificity of feedback are suggested variables in Table 1.

Furthermore, the copious literature on bureaucratic or mechanistic structures versus more organic and less defined structures could be taken to imply that routinized or highly structured subunits, for example, as conceptualized and measured by Pugh et al. (1968), will have stable homogeneous activities and be less likely to face uncertainty. This assumption would require empirical testing before structuring of activities could be used as an indicator of uncertainty, but it is tentatively included in Table 1.

In principle, coping with uncertainty might be directly measured by the difference between the uncertainty of those inputs taken by a subunit and the certainty with which it performs its activities nonetheless. This would indicate the degree of shock absorption.

The relation of coping with uncertainty to power can be expressed by the following hypothesis:

Hypothesis 1. The more a subunit copes with uncertainty, the greater its power within the organization.

The hypothesis is in a form which ignores any effects of centrality and substitutability.

Substitutability

Concepts relating to the availability of alternatives pervade the literature on power. In economics theory the degree of competition is taken as a measure of the extent to which alternatives are available from other organizations, it being implied that the power of an organization over other organizations and customers is a function of the amount of competition present. The same point was the second part of Emerson's (1962) power-dependency scheme in social relations, and the second requirement or determinant in Blau's (1964) model of a power relationship.

Yet only Mechanic (1962) and Dubin (1957, 1963) have discussed such concepts as explanations of organizational power. Mechanic's (1962: 358) hypothesis 4 stated: "Other factors remaining constant, a person difficult to replace will have greater power than a person easily replaceable." Dubin (1957) stressed the very similar notion of exclusiveness, which as developed later (Dubin, 1963: 21), means that: "For any given level of functional importance in an organization, the power residing in a functionary is inversely proportional to the number of other functionaries in the organization capable of performing the function." Supporting this empirically, Lipset *et al.* (1956) suggested that oligarchy may occur in trade unions because of the official's monopoly of political and negotiating skills.

The concept being used is represented here by the term substitutability, which can, for subunits, be defined as the ability of the organization to obtain alternative performance for the activities of a subunit, and can be stated as a hypothesis for predicting the power of a subunit as follows:

Hypothesis 2. The lower the substitutability of the activities of a subunit, the greater its power within the organization.

Thus a purchasing department would have its power reduced if all of its activities could be done by hired materials agents, as would a personnel department if it were partially substituted by selection consultants or by line managers finding their staff themselves. Similarly, a department may hold on to power by retaining information the release of which would enable others to do what it does.

The obvious problem in operationalization is establishing that alternative means of performing activities exist, and if they do, whether they could feasibly be used. Even if agents or consultants exist locally, or if corporation headquarters could provide services, would it really be practicable for the organization to dispense with its own subunit? Much easier to obtain are data on replaceability of subunit personnel such as length of training required for new recruits and ease of hiring, which can be regarded as secondary indicators of the substitutability of a subunit, as indicated in Table 1.

Centrality

Given a view of organizations as systems of interdependent roles and activities, then the centrality of a subunit is the degree to which its activities are interlinked into the system. By definition, no subunit of an organization can score zero centrality. Without a minimum of centrality, coping with uncertainty and substitutability cannot affect power; above the minimum, additional increments of centrality further differentiate subunit power. It is the degree to which the subunit is an interdependent component, as Thompson (1967: 54) put it, distinguishing between pooled, sequential, and reciprocal interdependence patterns. Blau and

Scott (1962) made an analogous distinction between parallel and interdependent specialization. Woodward (1965: 126) also introduced a concept of this kind into her discussion of the critical function in each of unit, large batch and mass, and process production: "there seemed to be one function that was central and critical in that it had the greatest effect on success and survival."

Within the overall concept of centrality, there are inconsistencies which indicate that more than one constitutive concept is being used. At the present stage of conceptualization their identification must be very tentative. First, there is the idea that the activities of a subunit are central if they are connected with many other activities in the organization. This workflow pervasiveness may be defined as the degree to which the workflows of a subunit connect with the workflows of other subunits. It describes the extent of task interactions between subunits, and for all subunits in an organization it would be operationalized as the flowchart of a complete systems analysis. For example, the integrative subsystems studied by Lawrence and Lorsch (1967a: 30), "whose members had the function of integrating the sales-research and the production-research subsystems" and which had structural and cultural characteristics intermediate between them, were presumably high on workflow pervasiveness because everything they did connected with the workflows of these several other subsystems. Research subsystems, however, may have been low on this variable if they fed work only to a single integrative, or production, subsystem.

Secondly, the activities of a subunit are central if they are essential in the sense that their cessation would quickly and substantially impede the primary workflow of the organization. This workflow immediacy is defined as the speed and severity with which the workflows of a subunit affect the final outputs of the organization. Zald (1962) and Clark (1956) used a similar idea when they explained differential power among institution staff and education faculty by the close relation of their activities to organization goals.

The pervasiveness and immediacy of the workflows of a subunit are not necessarily closely related, and may empirically show a low correlation. A finance department may well have pervasive connections with all other subunits through the budgeting system, but if its activities ceased it would be some time before the effects were felt in, say, the production output of a factory; a production department controlling a stage midway in the sequence of an automated process, however, could have high workflow immediacy though not high pervasiveness.

The two main centrality hypotheses can therefore be stated as follows:

Hypothesis 3a.   The higher the pervasiveness of the workflows of a subunit, the greater its power within the organization.

Hypothesis 3b.   The higher the immediacy of the workflows of a subunit, the greater its power within the organization.

Figure 1   The Strategic Contingencies Theory And Routinization

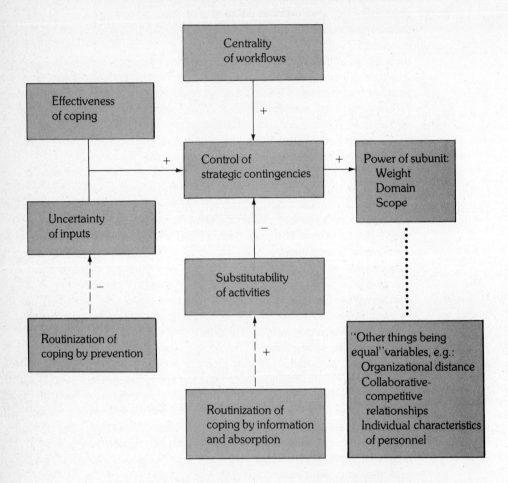

Direct relationship with power;-------indirect relationship with power;........
relationship with power other than by control of contingencies.

CONTROL OF CONTINGENCIES

Hypotheses relating power to coping with uncertainty, substitutability, and the subvariables of centrality have been stated in a simple single-variable form. Yet it follows from the view of subunits as interdependent parts of organizational systems that the hypotheses in this form are misleading. While each hypothesis may be empirically upheld, it is also hypothesized that this cannot be so without some values of both the other main independent variables. For example, when a marketing department copes with a volatile market by forecasting and by switching sales staff around to ensure stable orders, it acquires power only because the forecast and the orders are linked to the workflow of production, which depends on them. But even then power would be limited by the availability of a successful local marketing agency which could be hired by the organization, and the fact that salesmen were low skilled and easily replaceable.

To explain this interrelationship, the concept of control of contingencies is introduced. It represents organizational interdependence; subunits control contingencies for one another's activities and draw power from the dependencies thereby created. As a hypothesis:

Hypothesis 4.   The more contingencies are controlled by a subunit, the greater its power within the organization.

A contingency is a requirement of the activities of one subunit which is affected by the activities of another subunit. What makes such a contingency strategic, in the sense that it is related to power, can be deduced from the preceding hypotheses. The independent variables are each necessary but not sufficient conditions for control of strategic contingencies, but together they determine the variation in interdependence between subunits. Thus contingencies controlled by a subunit as a consequence of its coping with uncertainty do not become strategic, that is, affect power, in the organization without some (unknown) values of substitutability and centrality. A strategic contingencies theory of power is therefore proposed and is illustrated by the diagram in Figure 1.

In terms of exchange theory, as developed by Blau (1964), subunits can be seen to be exchanging control of strategic contingencies one for the other under the normative regulation of an encompassing social system, and acquiring power in the system through the exchange. The research task is to elucidate what combinations of values of the independent variables summarized in hypotheses 1-3 allow hypothesis 4 to hold. Ultimately and ideally the aim would be to discover not merely the weightings of each in the total effect upon power, but how these variables should be operationally interrelated to obtain the best predictions. More of one and less of another may leave the resulting power unchanged. Suppose an engineering subunit has power because it quickly absorbs uncertainty by repairing breakdowns which interfere with the different workflows for each of several organization outputs. It is moderately central and nonsubstitutable. A change in organization policy bringing in a new technology with a single workflow leading to a single output would raise engineering's centrality, since a single breakdown would immediately stop everything, but simultaneously the uncertainty might be reduced by a maintenance program which all but eliminates the possibility of such an occurrence.

Though three main factors are hypothesized, which must change if power is to change, it is not assumed that all subunits will act in accord with the theory to increase their power. This has to be demonstrated. There is the obvious possibility of a cumulative reaction in which a subunit's power is used to preserve or increase the uncertainty it can cope with, or its centrality, or to prevent substitution, thereby increasing its power, and so on. Nor is it argued that power or authority are intentionally allocated in terms of the theory, although the theory is open to such an inference.

Routinization

Most studies that refer to uncertainty contrast it with routinization, the prior prescription of recurrent task activities. Crozier (1964) held that the power of the maintenance personnel in the tobacco plants was due to all other tasks being routinized. A relative decline in the power of general medical personnel in hospitals during this century is thought to be due to the routinization of some tasks, which previously presented uncertainties which could be coped with only by a physician, and the transfer of these tasks to relatively routinized subunits, such as inoculation programs, mass X-ray facilities, and so on (Perrow, 1965; Gordon and Becker, 1964). Crozier (1964: 165) crystallized the presumed effects of routinization; "But the expert's success is constantly self-defeating. The rationalization process gives him power, but the end results of rationalization curtail his power. As soon as a field is well covered, as soon as the first intuitions and innovations can be translated into rules and programs, the expert's power disappears."

The strategic contingencies' theory as developed in Figure 1 clarifies this. It suggests that research has been hampered by a confusion of two kinds of routinization, both of which are negatively related to power but in different ways. Routinization may be (a) of coping by prevention, which prevents the occurrence of uncertainty; and (b) of coping by information or absorption which define how the uncertainty which does occur shall be coped with.

Preventive routinization reduces or removes the uncertainty itself, for example, planned maintenance, which maintenance in Crozier's (1964) tobacco factories would have resisted; inoculation or X-ray programs; and long-term supply contracts, so that the sales staff no longer have to contend with unstable demand. Such routinization removes the opportunity for power, and it is this which is self-defeating (Crozier, 1964: 165) if the expert takes his techniques to a point when they begin not only to cope but to routinely diminish the uncertainty coped with. Thus reducing the uncertainty is not the same as reducing the impact of uncertainty. According to the hypothesis, a sales department which transmits steady orders despite a volatile market has high power; a sales department which reduces the uncertainty itself by long-term tied contracts has low power.

Routinization of coping by information and absorption is embodied in job descriptions and task instructions prescribing how to obtain information and to respond to uncertainty. For maintenance personnel, it lays down how to repair the machine; for physicians, it lays down a standard procedure for examining patients and sequences of remedies for each diagnosis. How does this affect power, since it does not eliminate the uncertainty itself, as preventive routinization does? What it does is increase substitutability. The means of coping become more visible and possible substitutes more obvious, even if those substitutes are unskilled personnel from another subunit who can follow a standard procedure but could not have acquired the previously unexpressed skills.

There is probably some link between the two kinds of routinization. Once preventive routinization is accomplished, other coping routinization more easily follows, as indeed it follows any reduction of uncertainty.

STUDIES OF SUBUNIT POWER

Testing of Hypotheses on Earlier Work

The utility of the strategic contingencies theory should be tested on published work, but it is difficult to do this adequately, since most studies stress only one possibility. For example, Crozier (1964) and Thompson (1967) stressed uncertainty, Dubin (1963) stressed exclusiveness of function, and Woodward (1965) spoke of the critical function.

The difficulty is also due to the lack of data. For example, among several studies in which inferences about environmental uncertainty are drawn, only Lawrence and Lorsch (1967b) presented data. They combine executive's questionnaire responses on departmental clarity of job requirements, time span of definitive feedback on departmental success in performance, and uncertainty of cause and effect in the department's functional area.

Lawrence and Lorsch (1967b: 127) found that in two food-processing organizations, research was most influential, then marketing, excluding the field selling unit, and then production. However, influence, or perceived power as it is called here, was rated on the single issue of product innovation and not across a range of issues as suggested earlier in this paper; validity therefore rests on the assumption of equal potential involvement of each function in this one issue. Would research still be most influential if the issues included equipment purchase, or capital budgeting, or personnel training? Even so, on influence over product innovation, an uncertainty hypothesis could be said to fit neatly, since the subunits were ordered on perceived uncertainty of subenvironment exactly as they were on influence.

But uncertainty alone would not explain power in the other firms studied. Although in six plastics firms, coordinating sections or integrating units were perceived as having more influence than functional subunits because "integration itself was the most problematic job" (Lawrence and Lorsch 1967b: 62), it was also a central job in terms of workflow pervasiveness.

Furthermore, in two container manufacturing organizations, although the market subenvironment was seen as the least uncertain, the sales subunit was perceived as the most influential (Lawrence and Lorsch 1967b: 111). An explanation must be sought in the contingencies that the sales subunit controls for production and for research. In this industry, outputs must fit varying customer requirements for containers.

Scheduling for production departments and design problems for research departments are therefore completely subject to the contingencies of orders brought in by the sales department. Sales has not only the opportunity to cope with such uncertainty as may exist over customer requirements, it is highly central; for its activities connect it directly to both the other departments—workflow pervasiveness—and if it ceased work production of containers would stop—workflow immediacy. The effects of centrality are probably bolstered by nonsubstitutability, since the sales subunit develops a necessary particularized knowledge of customer requirements.Production and research are, therefore, comparatively powerless in face of the strategic contingencies controlled by the sales subunit.

In short, only a sensitive balancing of all three factors can explain the patterns of contingencies from which power strategically flows.

This is plain also in Crozier's (1964) insightful study of small French tobacco-manufacturing plants. Crozier (1964: 109) had the impression that the maintenance engineers were powerful because "machine stoppages are the only major happenings that cannot be predicted"; therefore, the engineers had (Crozier, 1964: 154) "control over the last source of uncertainty remaining in a completely routinized organizational system." But this is not enough for power. Had it been possible to contract maintenance work to consulting engineers, for example, then programs of preventive maintenance might have been introduced, and preventive routinization would have removed much of the uncertainty. However, it is likely that union agreements ensured that the plant engineers were nonsubstitutable. In addition, in these small organizations without specialist control and service departments, the maintenance section's work linked it to all production subunits, that is, to almost every other subunit in the plant. So workflow pervasiveness was high, as was workflow immediacy, since cessation of maintenance activities would quickly have stopped tobacco outputs. The control of strategic contingencies which gave power to the engineers has to be explained on all counts and not by uncertainty alone.

Crozier's (1964) study is a warning against the facile inference that a power distribution fitting the strategic contingencies theory is necessarily efficient, or rational, or functional for an organization; for the power of the engineers to thwart the introduction of programmed maintenance was presumably neither efficient, rational, nor functional.

A challenge to the analysis made is presented by Goldner's (1970) description of a case where there was programmed maintenance and yet the maintenance section held power over production. Goldner (1970) attributed the power of the maintenance subunit to knowing how to install and operate such programs, to coping with breakdowns as in the Crozier (1964) cases, and to knowing how to cope with a critical problem of parts supplies. The strategic contingencies theory accords with his interpretation so long as knowing how to install a program takes effect as coping with uncertainty and not yet as preventive routinization which stops breakdowns. This is where an unknown time element enters to allow for changes in the variables specified and in any associated variables not yet defined. For a time, knowing the answer to an uncertainty does confer power, but the analyses of routinization derived from the theory, as shown in Figure 1, suggests that if this becomes successful preventive routinization, it takes a negative effect upon power. The net result for power in Goldner's (1970) case would then be from the interplay of the opposed effects of activities some of which are preventively routinized, thus decreasing power, and some of which continue to be nonroutine, thus increasing power.

On the other hand, Goldner's (1970) description of the powerful industrial relations subunit in the same plant clearly supports the strategic contingencies theory by showing that coping with uncertainty, centrality, and substitutability had the effect predicted here. The industrial relations subunit exploited uncertainty over the supply and cost of personnel, which arose from possible strikes and pay increases, by (Goldner, 1970: 104) "use of the union as an outside threat." It coped effectively by its nonroutinized knowledge of union officials and of contract interpretation; and its activities were centrally linked to those of other subunits by the necessity for uniform practice on wages and employment. Industrial relations staff developed nonsubstitutable interpersonal and bargaining skills.

There are no means of assessing whether the univariate stress on uncertainty in the handful of other relevant studies is justified. Perrow (1970) explained the greater perceived power of sales as against production, finance, and research, in most of 12 industrial firms, by the concept of uncertainty absorption (March and Simon, 1958). Sales was strategic with respect to the environment. Is the one case where it came second to production the only case where it was also substitutable? Or not central?

White (1961) and Landsberger (1961) both suggested that power shifts over periods of time to follow the locus of uncertainty. Both studied engineering factories. From the histories of three firms, Landsberger (1961) deduced that when money was scarce and uncertain, accounting was powerful; when raw materials were short, purchasing was powerful; and, conversely, when demand was insatiable sales were weakened. In the Tennessee Valley Authority, a nonmanufacturing organization, Selznick (1949) attributed the eventual power of the agricultural relations department to its ability to cope with the uncertain environmental threat represented by the Farm Bureau.

Yet while these earlier studies emphasized uncertainty in one way or another, others called attention to substitutability and probably also to centrality. Again the implication is that contingencies are not strategically controlled without some combination of all three basic variables. For example, the engineers described by Strauss (1962, 1964) appeared to have more power than purchasing agents because the latter were substitutable, that is, the engineers can set specifications for what was to be bought even though the purchasing agents considered this their own responsibility. Thompson (1956: 300) attributed variations in perceived power within and between two U.S. Air Force wings to the changing "technical requirements of operations," which may have indicated changing centralities and substitutabilities.

In the absence of data, consideration of further different kinds of organization must remain pure speculation, for example, the power of surgical units in hospitals, the power of buyers in stores, the power of science faculties in universities.

Other Variables Affecting Power

In order that it can be testable, the strategic contingencies theory errs on the side of simplicity. Any theory must start with a finite number of variables and presume continual development by their alteration or deletion, or by the addition of new variables. As stated, the theory uses only those variables hypothesized to affect power by their contribution to the control of contingencies exercised by a subunit. Other possible explanations of power are not considered. This in itself is an assumption of the greater explanatory force of the theory. Blalock (1961: 8) put the problem clearly: "The dilemma of the scientist is to select models that are at the same time simple enough to permit him to think with the aid of the model but also sufficiently realistic that the simplifications required do not lead to predictions that are highly inaccurate."

In recognition of this, Figure 1 includes several "other things being equal" variables as they are called, that may affect power, but are assumed to do so in other ways than by control of contingencies. One such range of possible relevant variables is qualities of interdepartmental relationships, such as competitiveness versus collaborativeness (Dutton and Walton, 1966). Does the power exercised relate to the style of the relationship through which the power runs? Another possibility is pinpointed by Stymne (1968: 88): "A unit's influence has its roots partly in its strategical importance to the company and partly in nonfunctional circumstances such as tradition, or control over someone in top management through, for example, family relationship." The tradition is the status which may accrue to a particular function because chief executives have typically reached the top through it. Many case studies highlight the personal links of subunits with top personnel (Dalton, 1959; Gouldner, 1955). The notion might be entitled the organizational distance of the subunit, a variant of social distance.

Finally, but perhaps most important, individual differences must be accepted, that is, differences in the intelligence, skills, ages, sexes, or personality factors such as dominance, assertiveness, and risk-taking propensity, of personnel in the various subunits.

CONCLUSION

The concept of work organizations as interdepartmental systems leads to a strategic contingencies theory explaining differential subunit power by dependence on contingencies ensuing from varying combinations of coping with uncertainty, substitutability, and centrality. It should be stressed that the theory is not in any sense static. As the goals, outputs, technologies, and markets of organizations change so, for each subunit, the values of the independent variables change, and patterns of power change.

Many problems are unresolved. For example, does the theory implicitly assume perfect knowledge by each subunit of the contingencies inherent for it in the activities of the others? Does a workflow of information affect power differently to a workflow of things? But with the encouragement of the improved analysis given of the few existing studies, data can be collected and analyzed, hopefully in ways which will afford a direct test.

REFERENCES

Bennis, Warren G., N. Berkowitz, M. Affinito, and M. Malone
    1958 "Authority, power and the ability to influence." Human Relations, 11: 143–156.
Bierstedt, Robert
    1950 "An analysis of social power." American Sociological Review, 15: 730–736.
Blalock, Hubert M.
    1961 Causal Inferences in Nonexperimental Research. Chapel Hill: University of North Carolina Press.
Blau, Peter
    1964 Exchange and Power in Social Life. New York: Wiley.
Blau, Peter, and W. Richard Scott
    1962 Formal Organizations: A Comparative Approach. London: Routledge and Kegan Paul.
Cartwright, Dorwin
    1965 "Influence, leadership, control." In James G. March (ed.), Handbook of Organizations: 1–47. Chicago: Rand McNally.
Clark, Burton R.
    1956 "Organizational adaptation and precarious values: a case study." American Sociological Review, 21: 327–336.
Clark, Terry N. (ed.)
    1968 Community Structure and Decision-Making: Comparative Analyses. San Francisco: Chandler.
Crozier, Michel
    1964 The Bureaucratic Phenomenon. London: Tavistock.
Cyert, Richard M., and James G. March
    1963 A Behavioral Theory of the Firm. Englewood Cliffs, N.J.: Prentice-Hall.
Dahl, Robert A.
    1957 "The concept of power." Behavioral Science, 2: 201–215.
Dahlstrom, E.
    1966 "Exchange, influence, and power." Acta Sociologica, 9: 237–284.
Dalton, Melville
    1959 Men Who Manage. New York: Wiley.

Dubin, Robert
1957 "Power and union-management relations." Administrative Science Quarterly, 2: 60–81.
1963 "Power, function, and organization." Pacific Sociological Review, 6: 16–24.

Dutton, John M., and Richard E. Walton
1966 "Interdepartmental conflict and cooperation: two contrasting studies." Human Organization, 25: 207–220.

Emerson, R. E.
1962 "Power-dependence relations." American Sociological Review, 27: 31–41.

Etzioni, Amitai
1961 A Comparative Analysis of Complex Organizations. New York: Free Press.

French, John R. P., and Bertram Raven
1959 "The bases of social power." In D. Cartwright (ed.), Studies in Social Power: 150–167. Ann Arbor: University of Michigan.

Goldner, Fred H.
1970 "The division of labor: process and power." In Mayer N. Zald (ed.), Power in Organizations: 97–143. Nashville: Vanderbilt University Press.

Gordon, Gerald, and Selwyn Becker
1964 "Changes in medical practice bring shifts in the patterns of power." The Modern Hospital (February): 89–91, 154–156.

Gouldner, Alvin W.
1955 Wildcat Strike. London: Routledge.

Harsanyi, John C.
1962 "Measurement of social power, opportunity costs, and the theory of two-person bargaining games." Behavioral Science, 7: 67–80.

Hinings, Christopher R., Derek S. Pugh, David J. Hickson, and Christopher Turner
1967 "An approach to the study of bureaucracy." Sociology, 1: 61–72.

Kaplan, Abraham
1964 "Power in perspective." In Robert L. Kahn and Elise Boulding (eds.), Power and Conflict in Organizations: 11–32. London: Tavistock.

Landsberger, Henry A.
1961 "The horizontal dimension in bureaucracy." Administrative Science Quarterly, 6: 299–332.

Lawrence, Paul R., and Jay W. Lorsch
1967a "Differentiation and integration in complex organizations." Administrative Science Quarterly, 12: 1–47.
1967b Organization and Environment. Cambridge: Division of Research, Graduate School of Business Administration, Harvard University.

Lipset, Seymour M., Martin A. Trow, and James A. Coleman
1956 Union Democracy. Glencoe, Ill.: Free Press.

Luhmann, Niklaus
1969 "Klassische theorie der macht," Zeitschrift fur Politik, 16: 149–170.

March, James G.
1955 "An introduction to the theory and measurement of influence." American Political Science Review, 49: 431–450.
1966 "The power of power." In David Easton (ed.), Varieties of Political Theory: 39–70. Englewood Cliffs, N.J.: Prentice-Hall.

March, James G., and Herbert A. Simon
  1958 Organizations. New York: Wiley.
Mechanic, David
  1962 "Sources of power of lower participants in complex organizations."
    Administrative Science Quarterly, 7: 349–364.
Perrow, Charles
  1961 "The analysis of goals in complex organizations." American
    Sociological Review, 26: 854–866.
  1965 "Hospitals: technology, structure, and goals." In James G. March
    (ed.), Handbook of Organizations: 910–971. Chicago: Rand McNally.
  1970 "Departmental power and perspectives in industrial firms." In
    Mayer N. Zald (ed.), Power in Organizations: 59–89. Nashville:
    Vanderbilt University Press.
Pugh, Derek S., David J. Hickson, Christopher R. Hinings, and Christopher
    Turner
  1968 "Dimensions of organization structure." Administrative Science
    Quarterly, 13: 65–105.
Selznick, Philip
  1949 T.V.A. and the Grass Roots. Berkeley: University of California
    Press.
Strauss, George
  1962 "Tactics of lateral relationship: the purchasing agent."
    Administrative Science Quarterly, 7: 161–186.
  1964 "Work-flow frictions, interfunctional rivalry, and professionalism."
    Human Organization, 23: 137–150.
Stymne, Bengt
  1968 "Interdepartmental communication and intraorganizational strain."
    Acta Sociologica, 11: 82–100.
Tannenbaum, Arnold S.
  1968 Control in Organizations. New York: McGraw-Hill.
Thompson, James D.
  1956 "Authority and power in 'identical' organizations." American
    Journal of Sociology, 62: 290–301.
  1967 Organizations in Action. New York: McGraw-Hill.
Van Doorn, Jaques A. A.
  1962 "Sociology and the problem of power." Sociologica Neerlandica, 1:
    3–47.
Weber, Max
  1947 The Theory of Social and Economic Organization. Glencoe, Ill.:
    Free Press.
White, Harrison
  1961 "Management conflict and sociometric structure." American Journal
    of Sociology, 67: 185–199.
Woodward, Joan
  1965 Industrial Organization: Theory and Practice. London: Oxford
    University Press.
Wrong, Dennis H.
  1968 "Some problems in defining social power." American Journal of
    Sociology, 73, 673–681.
Zald, Mayer N.
  1962 "Organizational control structures in five correctional institutions."
    American Journal of Sociology, 68: 335–345.

Who Gets Power—And How They Hold on to It: A Strategic-Contingency Model of Power

GERALD R. SALANCIK
JEFFREY PFEFFER

Power is held by many people to be a dirty word or, as Warren Bennis has said, "It is the organization's last dirty secret."

This article will argue that traditional "political" power, far from being a dirty business, is, in its most naked form, one of the few mechanisms available for aligning an organization with its own reality. However, institutionalized forms of power—what we prefer to call the cleaner forms of power: authority, legitimization, centralized control, regulations, and the more modern "management information systems"—tend to buffer the organization from reality and obscure the demands of its environment. Most great states and institutions declined, not because they played politics, but because they failed to accommodate to the political realities they faced. Political processes, rather than being mechanisms for unfair and unjust allocations and appointments, tend toward the realistic resolution of conflicts among interests. And power, while it eludes definition, is easy enough to recognize by its consequences—the ability of those who possess power to bring about the outcomes they desire.

The model of power we advance is an elaboration of what has been called strategic-contingency theory, a view that sees power as something that accrues to organizational subunits (individuals, departments) that cope with critical organizational problems. Power is used by subunits, indeed, used by all who have it, to enhance their own survival through control of scarce critical resources, through the placement of allies in key positions, and through the definition of organizational problems and policies. Because of the processes by which power develops and is used, organizations become both more aligned and more misaligned with their environments. This contradiction is the most interesting aspect of organizational power, and one that makes administration one of the most precarious of occupations.

WHAT IS ORGANIZATIONAL POWER?

You can walk into most organizations and ask without fear of being misunderstood, "Which are the powerful groups or people in this organization?" Although many organizational informants may be *unwilling* to tell you, it is unlikely they will be *unable* to tell you. Most people do not require explicit definitions to know what power is.

Power is simply the ability to get things done the way one wants them to be done. For a manager who wants an increased budget to launch a project that he thinks is important, his power is measured by his ability to get that budget. For an executive vice-president who wants to be chairman, his power is evidenced by his advancement toward his goal.

People in organizations not only know what you are talking about when you ask who is influential but they are likely to agree with one another to an amazing extent. Recently, we had a chance to observe this in a regional office of an insurance company. The office had 21 department managers; we asked ten of these managers to rank all 21 according to the influence each one had in the organization. Despite the fact that ranking 21 things is a difficult task, the managers sat down and began arranging the names of their colleagues and themselves in a column. Only one person bothered to ask, "What do you mean by influence?" When told "power," he responded, "Oh," and went on. We compared the rankings of all ten managers and found virtually no disagreement among them in the managers ranked among the top five or the bottom five. Differences in the rankings came from department heads claiming more influence for themselves than their colleagues attributed to them.

Such agreement on those who have influence, and those who do not, was not unique to this insurance company. So far we have studied over 20 very different organizations—universities, research firms, factories, banks, retailers, to name a few. In each one we found individuals able to rate themselves and their peers on a scale of influence or power. We have done this both for specific decisions and for general impact on organizational policies. Their agreement was unusually high, which suggests that distributions of influence exist well enough in everyone's mind to be referred to with ease—and we assume with accuracy.

WHERE DOES ORGANIZATIONAL POWER COME FROM?

Earlier we stated that power helps organizations become aligned with their realities. This hopeful prospect follows from what we have dubbed the strategic-contingencies theory of organizational power. Briefly, those subunits most able to cope with the organization's critical problems and uncertainties acquire power. In its simplest form, the strategic-contingencies theory implies that when an organization faces a number of lawsuits that threaten its existence, the legal department will gain power and influence over organizational decisions. Somehow other organizational interest groups will recognize its critical importance and confer upon it a status and power never before enjoyed. This influence may extend beyond handling legal matters and into decisions about product design, advertising production, and so on. Such extensions undoubtedly would be accompanied by appropriate, or acceptable, verbal justifications. In time, the head of the legal department may become the head of the corporation, just as in times past the vice-president for marketing had become the president when market shares were a worrisome problem and, before him, the chief engineer, who had made the production line run as smooth as silk.

Stated in this way, the strategic-contingencies theory of power paints an appealing picture of power. To the extent that power is determined by the critical uncertainties and problems facing the organization and, in turn, influences decisions in the organization, the organization is aligned with the realities it faces. In short, power facilitates the organization's adaptation to its environment—or its problems.

We can cite many illustrations of how influence derives from a subunit's ability to deal with critical contingencies. Michael Crozier described a French cigarette factory in which the maintenance engineers had a considerable say in the plantwide operation. After some probing he discovered that the group possessed the solution to one of the major problems faced by the company, that of troubleshooting the elaborate, expensive, and irrascible automated machines that kept breaking down and dumbfounding everyone else. It was the one problem that the plant manager could in no way control.

The production workers, while troublesome from time to time, created no insurmountable problems; the manager could reasonably predict their absenteeism or replace them when necessary. Production scheduling was something he could deal with since, by watching inventories and sales, the demand for cigarettes was known long in advance. Changes in demand could be accommodated by slowing down or speeding up the line. Supplies of tobacco and paper were also easily dealt with through stockpiles and advance orders.

The one thing that management could neither control nor accommodate to, however, was the seemingly happenstance breakdowns. And the foremen couldn't instruct the workers what to do when emergencies developed since the maintenance department kept its records of problems and solutions locked up in a cabinet or in its members' heads. The breakdowns were, in truth, a critical source of uncertainty for the organization, and the maintenance engineers were the only ones who could cope with the problem.

The engineers' strategic role in coping with breakdowns afforded them a considerable say on plant decisions. Schedules and production quotas were set in consultation with them. And the plant manager, while formally their boss, accepted their decisions about personnel in their operation. His submission was to his credit, for without their cooperation he would have had an even more difficult time in running the plant.

Ignoring Critical Consequences

In this cigarette factory, sharing influence with the maintenance workers reflected the plant manager's awareness of the critical contingencies. However, when organizational members are not aware of the critical contingencies they face, and do not share influence accordingly, the failure to do so can create havoc. In one case, an insurance company's regional office was having problems with the performance of one of its departments, the coding department. From the outside, the department looked like a disaster area. The clerks who worked in it were somewhat dissatisfied; their supervisor paid little attention to them, and they resented the hard work. Several other departments were critical of this manager, claiming that she was inconsistent in meeting deadlines. The person most critical was the claims manager. He resented having to wait for work that was handled by her department, claiming that it held up his claims adjusters. Having heard the rumors about dissatisfaction among her subordinates, he attributed the situation to poor supervision. He was second in command in the office and therefore took up the issue with her immediate boss, the head of administrative services. They consulted with the personnel manager and the three of them concluded that the manager needed leadership training to improve her relations with her subordinates. The coding manager objected, saying it was a waste of time, but agreed to go along with the training and also agreed to give more priority to the claims department's work. Within a week after the training, the results showed that her workers were happier but that the performance of her department had decreased, save for the people serving the claims department.

About this time, we began, quite independently, a study of influence in this organization. We asked the administrative services director to draw up flow charts of how the work of one department moved onto the next department. In the course of the interview, we noticed that the coding department began or interceded in the work flow of most of the other departments and casually mentioned to him, "The coding manager must be very influential." He said "No, not really. Why would you think so?" Before we could reply he recounted the story of her leadership training and the fact that things were worse. We then told him that it seemed obvious that the coding department would be influential from the fact that all the other departments depended on it. It was also clear why productivity had fallen. The coding manager took the training seriously and began spending more time raising her workers' spirits than she did worrying about the problems of all the departments that depended on her. Giving priority to the claims area only exaggerated the problem, for their work was getting done at the expense of the work of the other departments. Eventually the company hired a few more clerks to relieve the pressure in the coding department and performance returned to a more satisfactory level.

Originally we got involved with this insurance company to examine how the influence of each manager evolved from his or her department's handling of critical organizational contingencies. We reasoned that one of the most important contingencies faced by all profit-making organizations was that of generating income. Thus we expected managers would be influential to the extent to which they contributed to this function. Such was the case. The underwriting managers, who wrote the policies that committed the premiums, were the most influential; the claims managers, who kept a lid on the funds flowing out, were a close second. Least influential were the managers of functions unrelated to revenue, such as mailroom and payroll managers. And contrary to what the administrative services manager believed, the third most powerful department head (out of 21) was the woman in charge of the coding function, which consisted of rating, recording, and keeping track of the codes of all policy applications and contracts. Her peers attributed more influence to her than could have been inferred from her place on the organization chart. And it was not surprising, since they all depended on her department. The coding department's records, their accuracy and the speed with which they could be retrieved, affected virtually every other operating department in the insurance office. The underwriters depended on them in getting the contracts straight; the typing department depended on them in preparing the formal contract document; the claims department depended on them in adjusting claims; and accounting depended on them for billing. Unfortunately, the "bosses" were not aware of these dependencies, for unlike the cigarette factory, there were no massive breakdowns that made them obvious, while the coding manager, who was a hard-working but quiet person, did little to announce her importance.

The cases of this plant and office illustrate nicely a basic point about the source of power in organizations. The basis for power in an organization derives from the ability of a person or subunit to take or not take actions that are desired by others. The coding manager was seen as influential by those who depended on her department, but not by the people at the top. The engineers were influential because of their role in keeping the plant operating. The two cases differ in these respects: The coding supervisor's source of power was not as widely recognized as that of the maintenance engineers, and she did not use her source of power to influence decisions; the maintenance engineers did. Whether power is used to influence anything is a separate issue. We should not confuse this issue with the fact that power derives from a social situation in which one person has a capacity to do something and another person does not, but wants it done.

POWER SHARING IN ORGANIZATIONS

Power is shared in organizations; and it is shared out of necessity more than out of concern for principles of organizational development or participatory democracy. Power is shared because no one person controls all the desired activities in the organization. While the factory owner may hire people to operate his noisy machines, once hired they have some control over the use of the machinery. And thus they have power over him in the same way he has power over them. Who has more power over whom is a mooter point than that of recognizing the inherent nature of organizing as a sharing of power.

Let's expand on the concept that power derives from the activities desired in an organization. A major way of managing influence in organizations is through the designation of activities. In a bank we studied, we saw this principle in action. This bank was planning to install a computer system for routine credit evaluation. The bank, rather progressive-minded, was concerned that the change would have adverse effects on employees and therefore surveyed their attitudes.

The principal opposition to the new system came, interestingly, not from the employees who performed the routine credit checks, some of whom would be relocated because of the change, but from the manager of the credit department. His reason was quite simple. The manager's primary function was to give official approval to the applications, catch any employee mistakes before giving approval, and arbitrate any difficulties the clerks had in deciding what to do. As a consequence of his role, others in the organization, including his superiors, subordinates, and colleagues, attributed considerable importance to him. He, in turn, for example, could point to the low proportion of credit approvals, compared with other financial institutions, that resulted in bad debts. Now, to his mind, a wretched machine threatened to transfer his role to a computer programmer, a man who knew nothing of finance and who, in addition, had ten years less seniority. The credit manager eventually quit for a position at a smaller firm with lower pay, but one in which he would have more influence than his redefined job would have left him with.

Because power derives from activities rather than individuals, an individual's or subgroup's power is never absolute and derives ultimately from the context of the situation. The amount of power an individual has at any one time depends, not only on the activities he or she controls, but also on the existence of other persons or means by which the activities can be achieved and on those who determine what ends are desired and, hence, on what activities are desired and critical for the organization.

One's own power always depends on other people for these two reasons. Other people, or groups or organizations, can determine the definition of what is a critical contingency for the organization and can also undercut the uniqueness of the individual's personal contribution to the critical contingencies of the organization.

Perhaps one can best appreciate how situationally dependent power is by examining how it is distributed. In most societies, power organizes around scarce and critical resources. Rarely does power organize around abundant resources. In the United States, a person doesn't become powerful because he or she can drive a car. There are simply too many others who can drive with equal facility. In certain villages in Mexico, on the other hand, a person with a car is accredited with enormous social status and plays a key role in the community. In addition to scarcity, power is also limited by the need for one's capacities in a social system. While a racer's ability to drive a car around a 90° turn at 80 mph may be sparsely distributed in a society, it is not likely to lend the driver much power in the society. The ability simply does not play a central role in the activities of the society.

The fact that power revolves around scarce and critical activities, of course, makes the control and organization of those activities a major battleground in struggles for power. Even relatively abundant or trivial resources can become the bases for power if one can organize and control their allocation and the definition of what is critical. Many occupational and professional groups attempt to do just this in modern economies. Lawyers organize themselves into associations, regulate the entrance requirements for novitiates, and then get laws passed specifying situations that require the services of an attorney. Workers had little power in the conduct of industrial affairs until they organized themselves into closed and controlled systems. In recent years, women and blacks have tried to define themselves as important and critical to the social system, using law to reify their status.

In organizations there are obviously opportunities for defining certain activities as more critical than others. Indeed, the growth of managerial thinking to include defining organizational objectives and goals has done much to foster these opportunities. One sure way to liquidate the power of groups in the organization is to define the need for their services out of existence. David Halberstam presents a description of how just such a thing happened to the group of correspondents that evolved around Edward R. Murrow, the brilliant journalist, interviewer, and war correspondent of CBS News. A close friend of CBS chairman and controlling stockholder William S. Paley, Murrow, and the news department he directed, were endowed with freedom to do what they felt was right. He used it to create some of the best documentaries and commentaries ever seen on television. Unfortunately, television became too large, too powerful, and too suspect in the eyes of the federal government that licensed it. It thus became, or at least the top executives believed it had become, too dangerous to have in-depth, probing commentary on the news. Crisp, dry, uneditorializing headliners were considered safer. Murrow was out and Walter Cronkite was in.

The power to define what is critical in an organization is no small power. Moreover, it is the key to understanding why organizations are either aligned with their environments or misaligned. If an organization defines certain activities as critical when in fact they are not critical, given the flow of resources coming into the organization, it is not likely to survive, at least in its present form.

Most organizations manage to evolve a distribution of power and influence that is aligned with the critical realities they face in the environment. The environment, in turn, includes both the internal environment, the shifting situational contexts in which particular decisions get made, and the external environment that it can hope to influence but is unlikely to control.

THE CRITICAL CONTINGENCIES

The critical contingencies facing most organizations derive from the environmental context within which they operate. This determines the available needed resources and thus determines the problems to be dealt with. That power organizes around handling these problems suggests an important mechanism by which organizations keep in tune with their external environments. The strategic-contingencies model implies that subunits that contribute to the critical resources of the organization will gain influence in the organization. Their influence presumably is then used to bend the organization's activities to the contingencies that determine its resources. This idea may strike one as obvious. But its obviousness in no way diminishes its importance. Indeed, despite its obviousness, it escapes the notice of many organizational analysts and managers, who all too frequently think of the organization in terms of a descending pyramid, in which all the departments in one tier hold equal power and status. This presumption denies the reality that departments differ in the contributions they are believed to make to the overall organization's resources, as well as to the fact that some are more equal than others.

Because of the importance of this idea to organizational effectiveness, we decided to examine it carefully in a large midwestern university. A university offers an excellent site for studying power. It is composed of departments with nominally equal power and is administered by a central executive structure much like other bureaucracies. However, at the same time it is a situation in which the departments have clearly defined identities and face diverse external environments. Each department has its own bodies of knowledge, its own institutions, its own sources of prestige and resources. Because the departments operate in different external environments, they are likely to contribute differentially to the resources of the overall organization. Thus a physics department with close ties to NASA may contribute substantially to the funds of the university; and a history department with a renowned historian in residence may contribute to the intellectual credibility or prestige of the whole university. Such variations permit one to examine how these various contributions lead to obtaining power within the university.

We analyzed the influence of 29 university departments throughout an 18-month period in their history. Our chief interest was to determine whether departments that brought more critical resources to the university would be more powerful than departments that contributed fewer or less critical resources.

To identify the critical resources each department contributed, the heads of all departments were interviewed about the importance of seven different resources to the university's success. The seven included undergraduate students (the factor determining size of the state allocations by the university), national prestige, administrative expertise, and so on. The most critical resource was found to be contract and grant monies received by a department's faculty for research or consulting services. At this university, contract and grants contributed somewhat less than 50 percent of the overall budget, with the remainder primarily coming from state appropriations. The importance attributed to contract and grant monies, and the rather minor importance of undergraduate students, was not surprising for this particular university. The university was a major center for graduate education; many of its departments ranked in the top ten of their respective fields. Grant and contract monies were the primary source of discretionary funding available for maintaining these programs of graduate education, and hence for maintaining the university's prestige. The prestige of the university itself was critical both in recruiting able students and attracting top-notch faculty.

From university records it was determined what relative contributions each of the 29 departments made to the various needs of the university (national prestige, outside grants, teaching). Thus, for instance, one department may have contributed to the university by teaching 7 percent of the instructional units, bringing in 2 percent of the outside contracts and grants, and having a national ranking of 20. Another department, on the other hand, may have taught one percent of the instructional units, contributed 12 percent to the grants, and be ranked the third best department in its field within the country.

The question was: Do these different contributions determine the relative power of the departments within the university? Power was measured in several ways; but regardless of how measured, the answer was "Yes." Those three resources together accounted for about 70 percent of the variance in subunit power in the university.

But the most important predictor of departmental power was the department's contribution to the contracts and grants of the university. Sixty percent of the variance in power was due to this one factor, suggesting that the power of departments derived primarily from the dollars they provided for graduate education, the activity believed to be the most important for the organization.

THE IMPACT OF ORGANIZATIONAL POWER ON DECISION MAKING

The measure of power we used in studying this university was an analysis of the responses of the department heads we interviewed. While such perceptions of power might be of interest in their own right, they contribute little to our understanding of how the distribution of power might serve to align an organization with its critical realities. For this we must look to how power actually influences the decisions and policies of organizations.

While it is perhaps not absolutely valid, we can generally gauge the relative importance of a department of an organization by the size of the budget allocated to it relative to other departments. Clearly it is of importance to the administrators of those departments whether they get squeezed in a budget crunch or are given more funds to strike out after new opportunities. And it should also be clear that when those decisions are made and one department can go ahead and try new approaches while another must cut back on the old, then the deployment of the resources of the organization in meeting its problems is most directly affected.

Thus our study of the university led us to ask the following question: Does power lead to influence in the organization? To answer this question, we found it useful first to ask another one, namely: Why should department heads try to influence organizational decisions to favor their own departments to the exclusion of other departments? While this second question may seem a bit naive to anyone who has witnessed the political realities of organizations, we posed it in a context of research on organizations that sees power as an illegitimate threat to the neater rational authority of modern bureaucracies. In this context, decisions are not believed to be made because of the dirty business of politics but because of the overall goals and purposes of the organization. In a university, one reasonable basis for decision making is the teaching workload of departments and the demands that follow from that workload. We would expect, therefore, that departments with heavy student demands for courses would be able to obtain funds for teaching. Another reasonable basis for decision making is quality. We would expect, for that reason, that departments with esteemed reputations would be able to obtain funds both because their quality suggests they might use such funds effectively and because such funds would allow them to maintain their quality. A rational model of bureaucracy intimates, then, that the organizational decisions taken would favor those who perform the stated purposes of the organization—teaching undergraduates and training professional and scientific talent—well.

The problem with rational models of decision making, however, is that what is rational to one person may strike another as irrational. For most departments, resources are a question of survival. While teaching undergraduates may seem to be a major goal for some members of the university, developing knowledge may seem so to others; and to still others, advising governments and other institutions about policies may seem to be the crucial business. Everyone has his own idea of the proper priorities in a just world. Thus goals rather than being clearly defined and universally agreed upon are blurred and contested throughout the organization. If such is the case, then the decisions taken on behalf of the organization as a whole are likely to reflect the goals of those who prevail in political contests, namely, those with power in the organization.

Will organizational decisions always reflect the distribution of power in the organization? Probably not. Using power for influence requires a certain expenditure of effort, time, and resources. Prudent and judicious persons are not likely to use their power needlessly or wastefully. And it is likely that power will be used to influence organizational decisions primarily under circumstances that both require and favor its use. We have examined three conditions that are likely to affect the use of power in organizations: scarcity, criticality, and uncertainty. The first suggests that subunits will try to exert influence when the resources of the organization are scarce. If there is an abundance of resources then a particular department or a particular individual has little need to attempt influence. With little effort, he can get all he wants anyway.

The second condition, criticality, suggests that a subunit will attempt to influence decisions to obtain resources that are critical to its own survival and activities. Criticality implies that one would not waste effort, or risk being labeled obstinate, by fighting over trivial decisions affecting one's operations.

An office manager would probably balk less about a threatened cutback in copying machine usage than about a reduction in typing staff. An advertising department head would probably worry less about losing his lettering artist than his illustrator. Criticality is difficult to define because what is critical depends on people's beliefs about what is critical. Such beliefs may or may not be based on experience and knowledge and may or may not be agreed upon by all. Scarcity, for instance, may itself affect conceptions of criticality. When slack resources drop off, cutbacks have to be made—those "hard decisions," as congressmen and resplendent administrators like to call them. Managers then find themselves scrapping projects they once held dear.

The third condition that we believe affects the use of power is uncertainty: When individuals do not agree about what the organization should do or how to do it, power and other social processes will affect decisions. The reason for this is simply that, if there are no clear-cut criteria available for resolving conflicts of interest, then the only means for resolution is some form of social process, including power, status, social ties, or some arbitrary process like flipping a coin or drawing straws. Under conditions of uncertainty, the powerful manager can argue his case on any grounds and usually win it. Since there is no real consensus, other contestants are not likely to develop counter arguments or amass sufficient opposition. Moreover, because of his power and their need for access to the resources he controls, they are more likely to defer to his arguments.

Although the evidence is slight, we have found that power will influence the allocations of scarce and critical resources. In the analysis of power in the university, for instance, one of the most critical resources needed by departments is the general budget. First granted by the state legislature, the general budget is later allocated to individual departments by the university administration in response to requests from the department heads. Our analysis of the factors that contribute to a department getting more or less of this budget indicated that subunit power was the major predictor, overriding such factors as student demand for courses, national reputations of departments, or even the size of a department's faculty. Moreover, other research has shown that when the general budget has been cut back or held below previous uninflated levels, leading to monies becoming more scarce, budget allocations mirror departmental powers even more closely.

Student enrollment and faculty size, of course, do themselves relate to budget allocations, as we would expect since they determine a department's need for resources, or at least offer visible testimony of needs. But departments are not always able to get what they need by the mere fact of needing them. In one analysis it was found that high-power departments were able to obtain budget without regard to their teaching loads and, in some cases, actually in inverse relation to their teaching loads. In contrast, low-power departments could get increases in budget only when they could justify the increases by a recent growth in teaching load, and then only when it was far in excess of norms for other departments.

General budget is only one form of resource that is allocated to departments. There are others such as special grants for student fellowships or faculty research. These are critical to departments because they affect the ability to attract other resources, such as outstanding faculty or students. We examined how power influenced the allocations of four resources department heads had described as critical and scarce.

When the four resources were arrayed from the most to the least critical and scarce, we found that departmental power best predicted the allocations of the most critical and scarce resources. In other words, the analysis of how power influences organizational allocations leads to this conclusion: Those subunits most likely to survive in times of strife are those that are more critical to the organization. Their importance to the organization gives them power to influence resource allocations that enhance their own survival.

HOW EXTERNAL ENVIRONMENT IMPACTS EXECUTIVE SELECTION

Power not only influences the survival of key groups in an organization, it also influences the selection of individuals to key leadership positions, and by such a process further aligns the organization with its environmental context.

We can illustrate this with a recent study of the selection and tenure of chief administrators in 57 hospitals in Illinois. We assumed that since the critical problems facing the organization would enhance the power of certain groups at the expense of others, then the leaders to emerge should be those most relevant to the context of the hospitals. To assess this we asked each chief administrator about his professional background and how long he had been in office. The replies were then related to the hospitals' funding, ownership, and competitive conditions for patients and staff.

One aspect of a hospital's context is the source of its budget. Some hospitals, for instance, are run much like other businesses. They sell bed space, patient care, and treatment services. They charge fees sufficient both to cover their costs and to provide capital for expansion. The main source of both their operating and capital funds is patient billings. Increasingly, patient billings are paid for, not by patients, but by private insurance companies. Insurers like Blue Cross dominate and represent a potent interest group outside a hospital's control but critical to its income. The insurance companies, in order to limit their own costs, attempt to hold down the fees allowable to hospitals, which they do effectively from their positions on state rate boards. The squeeze on hospitals that results from fees increasing slowly while costs climb rapidly more and more demands the talents of cost accountants or people trained in the technical expertise of hospital administration.

By contrast, other hospitals operate more like social service institutions, either as government healthcare units (Bellevue Hospital in New York City and Cook County Hospital in Chicago, for example) or as charitable institutions. These hospitals obtain a large proportion of their operating and capital funds, not from privately insured patients, but from government subsidies or private donations. Such institutions rather than requiring the talents of a technically efficient administrator are likely to require the savvy of someone who is well integrated into the social and political power structure of the community.

Not surprisingly, the characteristics of administrators predictably reflect the funding context of the hospitals with which they are associated. Those hospitals with larger proportions of their budget obtained from private insurance companies were most likely to have administrators with backgrounds in accounting and least likely to have administrators whose professions were business or medicine. In contrast, those hospitals with larger proportions of their budget derived from private donations and local governments were most likely to have administrators with business or professional backgrounds and least likely to have accountants. The same held for formal training in hospital management. Professional hospital administrators could easily be found in hospitals drawing their incomes from private insurance and rarely in hospitals dependent on donations or legislative appropriations.

As with the selection of administrators, the context of the organizations has also been found to affect the removal of executives. The environment, as a source of organizational problems, can make it more or less difficult for executives to demonstrate their value to the organization. In the hospitals we studied, long-term administrators came from hospitals with few problems. They enjoyed amicable and stable relations with their local business and social communities and suffered little competition for funding and staff. The small city hospital director who attended civic and Elks meetings while running the only hospital within a 100-mile radius, for example, had little difficulty holding on to his job. Turnover was highest in hospitals with the most problems, a phenomenon similar to that observed in a study of industrial organizations in which turnover was highest among executives in industries with competitive environments and unstable market conditions. The interesting thing is that instability characterized the industries rather than the individual firms in them. The troublesome conditions in the individual firms were attributed, or rather misattributed, to the executives themselves.

It takes more than problems, however, to terminate a manager's leadership. The problems themselves must be relevant and critical. This is clear from the way in which an administrator's tenure is affected by the status of the hospital's operating budget. Naively we might assume that all administrators would need to show a surplus. Not necessarily so. Again, we must distinguish between those hospitals that depend on private donations for funds and those that do not. Whether an endowed budget shows a surplus or deficit is less important than the hospital's relations with benefactors. On the other hand, with a budget dependent on patient billing, a surplus is almost essential; monies for new equipment or expansion must be drawn from it, and without them quality care becomes more difficult and patients scarcer. An administrator's tenure reflected just these considerations. For those hospitals dependent upon private donations, the length of an administrator's term depended not at all on the status of the operating budget but was fairly predictable from the hospital's relations with the business community. On the other hand, in hospitals dependent on the operating budget for capital financing, the greater the deficit the shorter was the tenure of the hospital's principal administrators.

CHANGING CONTINGENCIES AND ERODING POWER BASES

The critical contingencies facing the organization may change. When they do, it is reasonable to expect that the power of individuals and subgroups will change in turn. At times the shift can be swift and shattering, as it was recently for powerholders in New York City. A few years ago it was believed that David Rockefeller was one of the ten most powerful people in the city, as tallied by *New York* magazine, which annually sniffs out power for the delectation of its readers. But that was before it was revealed that the city was in financial trouble, before Rockefeller's Chase Manhattan Bank lost some of its own financial luster, and before brother Nelson lost some of his political influence in

Washington. Obviously David Rockefeller was no longer as well positioned to help bail the city out. Another loser was an attorney with considerable personal connections to the political and religious leaders of the city. His talents were no longer in much demand. The persons with more influence were the bankers and union pension fund executors who fed money to the city; community leaders who represent blacks and Spanish-Americans, in contrast, witnessed the erosion of their power bases.

One implication of the idea that power shifts with changes in organizational environments is that the dominant coalition will tend to be that group that is most appropriate for the organization's environment, as also will the leaders of an organization. One can observe this historically in the top executives of industrial firms in the United States. Up until the early 1950s, many top corporations were headed by former production line managers or engineers who gained prominence because of their abilities to cope with the problems of production. Their success, however, only spelled their demise. As production became routinized and mechanized, the problem of most firms became one of selling all those goods they so efficiently produced. Marketing executives were more frequently found in corporate boardrooms. Success outdid itself again, for keeping markets and production steady and stable requires the kind of control that can only come from acquiring competitors and suppliers or the invention of more and more appealing products—ventures that typically require enormous amounts of capital. During the 1960s, financial executives assumed the seats of power. And they, too, will give way to others. Edging over the horizon are legal experts, as regulation and antitrust suits are becoming more and more frequent in the 1970s, suits that had their beginnings in the success of the expansion generated by prior executives. The more distant future, which is likely to be dominated by multinational corporations, may see former secretaries of state and their minions increasingly serving as corporate figureheads.

THE NONADAPTIVE CONSEQUENCES OF ADAPTATION

From what we have said thus far about power aligning the organization with its own realities, an intelligent person might react with a resounding ho-hum, for it all seems too obvious: Those with the ability to get the job done are given the job to do.

However, there are two aspects of power that make it more useful for understanding organizations and their effectiveness. First, the "job" to be done has a way of expanding itself until it becomes less and less clear what the job is. Napoleon began by doing a job for France in the war with Austria and ended up Emperor, convincing many that only he could keep the peace. Hitler began by promising an end to Germany's troubling postwar depression and ended up convincing more people than is comfortable to remember that he was destined to be the savior of the world. In short, power is a capacity for influence that extends far beyond the original bases that created it. Second, power tends to take on institutionalized forms that enable it to endure well beyond its usefulness to an organization.

There is an important contradiction in what we have observed about organizational power. On the one hand we have said that power derives from the contingencies facing an organization and that when those contingencies change so do the bases for power. On the other hand we have asserted that subunits will tend to use their power to influence organizational decisions in their own favor, particularly when their own survival is threatened by the scarcity of critical resources. The first statement implies that an organization will tend to be aligned with its environment since power will tend to bring to key positions those with capabilities relevant to the context. The second implies that those in power will not give up their positions so easily; they will pursue policies that guarantee their continued domination. In short, change and stability operate through the same mechanism, and, as a result, the organization will never be completely in phase with its environment or its needs.

The study of hospital administrators illustrates how leadership can be out of phase with reality. We argued that privately funded hospitals needed trained technical administrators more so than did hospitals funded by donations. The need as we perceived it was matched in most hospitals, but by no means in all. Some organizations did not conform with our predictions. These deviations imply that some administrators were able to maintain their positions independent of their suitability for those positions. By dividing administrators into those with long and short terms of office, one finds that the characteristics of longer-termed administrators were virtually unrelated to the hospital's context. The shorter-termed chiefs on the other hand had characteristics more appropriate for the hospital's problems. For a hospital to have a recently appointed head implies that the previous administrator had been unable to endure by institutionalizing himself.

One obvious feature of hospitals that allowed some administrators to enjoy a long tenure was a hospital's ownership. Administrators were less entrenched when their hospitals were affiliated with and dependent upon larger organizations, such as governments or churches. Private hospitals offered more secure positions for administrators. Like private corporations, they tend to have more diffused ownership, leaving the administrator unopposed as he institutionalizes his reign. Thus he endures, sometimes at the expense of the performance of the organization. Other research has demonstrated that corporations with diffuse ownership have poorer earnings than those in which the control of the manager is checked by a dominant shareholder. Firms that overload their boardrooms with more insiders than are appropriate for their context have also been found to be less profitable.

A word of caution is required about our judgment of "appropriateness." When we argue some capabilities are more appropriate for one context than another, we do so from the perspective of an outsider and on the basis of reasonable assumptions as to the problems the organization will face and the capabilities they will need. The fact that we have been able to predict the distribution of influence and the characteristics of leaders suggests that our reasoning is not incorrect. However, we do not think that all organizations follow the same pattern. The fact that we have not been able to predict outcomes with 100 percent accuracy indicates they do not.

MISTAKING CRITICAL CONTINGENCIES

One thing that allows subunits to retain their power is their ability to name their functions as critical to the organization when they may not be. Consider again our discussion of power in the university. One might wonder why the most critical tasks were defined as graduate education and scholarly research, the effect of which was to lend power to those who brought in grants and contracts. Why not something else? The reason is that the more powerful departments argued for those criteria and won their case, partly beause they were more powerful.

In another analysis of this university, we found that all departments advocate self-serving criteria for budget allocation. Thus a department with large undergraduate enrollments argued that enrollments should determine budget allocations, a department with a strong national reputation saw prestige as the most reasonable basis for distributing funds, and so on. We further found that advocating such self-serving criteria actually benefited a department's budget allotments but, also, it paid off more for departments that were already powerful.

Organizational needs are consistent with a current distribution of power also because of a human tendency to categorize problems in familiar ways. An accountant sees problems with organizational performance as cost accountancy problems or inventory flow problems. A sales manager sees them as problems with markets, promotional strategies, or just unaggressive salespeople. But what is the truth? Since it does not automatically announce itself, it is likely that those with prior credibility, or those with power, will be favored as the enlightened. This bias, while not intentionally self-serving, further concentrates power among those who already possess it, independent of changes in the organization's context.

INSTITUTIONALIZING POWER

A third reason for expecting organizational contingencies to be defined in familiar ways is that the current holders of power can structure the organization in ways that institutionalize themselves. By institutionalization we mean the establishment of relatively permanent structures and policies that favor the influence of a particular subunit. While in power, a dominant coalition has the ability to institute constitutions, rules, procedures, and information systems that limit the potential power of others while continuing their own.

The key to institutionalizing power always is to create a device that legitimates one's own authority and diminishes the legitimacy of others. When the "Divine Right of Kings" was envisioned centuries ago it was to provide an unquestionable foundation for the supremacy of royal authority. There is generally a need to root the exercise of authority in some higher power. Modern leaders are no less affected by this need. Richard Nixon, with the aid of John Dean, reified the concept of executive privilege, which meant in effect that what the President wished not to be discussed need not be discussed.

In its simpler form, institutionalization is achieved by designating positions or roles for organizational activities. The creation of a new post legitimizes a function and forces organization members to orient to it. By designating how this new post relates to older, more established posts, moreover, one can structure an organization to enhance the importance of the function in the organization. Equally, one can diminish the importance of traditional functions. This is what happened in the end with the insurance company we mentioned that was having trouble with its coding department. As the situation unfolded, the claims director continued to feel dissatisfied about the dependency of his functions on the coding manager. Thus he instituted a reorganization that resulted in two coding departments. In so doing, of course, he placed activities that affected his department under his direct control, presumably to make the operation more effective. Similarly, consumer-product firms enhance the power of marketing by setting up a coordinating role to interface production and marketing functions and then appoint a marketing manager to fill the role.

The structures created by dominant powers sooner or later become fixed and unquestioned features of the organization. Eventually, this can be devastating. It is said that the battle of Jena in 1806 was lost by Frederick the Great, who died in 1786. Though the great Prussian leader had no direct hand in the disaster, his imprint on the army was so thorough, so embedded in its skeletal underpinnings, that the organization was inappropriate for others to lead in different times.

Another important source of institutionalized power lies in the ability to structure information systems. Setting up committees to investigate particular organizational issues and having them report only to particular individuals or groups, facilitates their awareness of problems by members of those groups while limiting the awareness of problems by the members of other groups. Obviously, those who have information are in a better position to interpret the problems of an organization, regardless of how realistically they may, in fact, do so.

Still another way to institutionalize power is to distribute rewards and resources. The dominant group may quiet competing interest groups with small favors and rewards. The credit for this artful form of cooptation belongs to Louis XIV. To avoid usurpation of his power by the nobles of France and the Fronde that had so troubled his father's reign, he built the palace at Versailles to occupy them with hunting and gossip. Awed, the courtiers basked in the reflected glories of the "Sun King" and the overwhelming setting he had created for his court.

At this point, we have not systematically studied the institutionalization of power. But we suspect it is an important condition that mediates between the environment of the organization and the capabilities of the organization for dealing with that environment. The more institutionalized power is within an organization, the more likely an organization will be out of phase with the realities it faces. President Richard Nixon's structuring of his White House is one of the better documented illustrations. If we go back to newspaper and magazine descriptions of how he organized his office from the beginning in 1968, most of what occurred subsequently follows almost as an afterthought. Decisions flowed through virtually only the small White House staff; rewards, small presidential favors of recognition, and perquisites were distributed by this staff to the loyal; and information from the outside world—the press, Congress, the people on the streets—was filtered by the staff and passed along only if initialed "bh." Thus it was not surprising that when Nixon met war protestors in the early dawn, the only thing he could think to talk about was the latest football game, so insulated had he become from their grief and anger.

One of the more interesting implications of institutionalized power is that executive turnover among the executives who have structured the organization is likely to be a rare event that occurs only under the most pressing crisis. If a dominant coalition is able to structure the organization and interpret the meaning of ambiguous events like declining sales and profits or lawsuits, then the "real" problems to emerge will easily be incorporated into traditional molds of thinking and acting. If opposition is designed out of the organization, the interpretations will go unquestioned. Conditions will remain stable until a crisis develops, so overwhelming and visible that even the most adroit rhetorician would be silenced.

IMPLICATIONS FOR THE MANAGEMENT OF POWER IN ORGANIZATIONS

While we could derive numerous implications from this discussion of power, our selection would have to depend largely on whether one wanted to increase one's power, decrease the power of others, or merely maintain one's position. More important, the real implications depend on the particulars of an organizational situation. To understand power in an organization one must begin by looking outside it—into the environment—for those groups that mediate the organization's outcomes but are not themselves within its control.

Instead of ending with homilies, we will end with a reversal of where we began. Power, rather than being the dirty business it is often made out to be, is probably one of the few mechanisms for reality testing in organizations. And the cleaner forms of power, the institutional forms, rather than having the virtues they are often credited with, can lead the organization to become out of touch. The real trick to managing power in organizations is to ensure somehow that leaders cannot be unaware of the realities of their environments and cannot avoid changing to deal with those realities. That, however, would be like designing the "self-liquidating organization," an unlikely event since anyone capable of designing such an instrument would be obviously in control of the liquidations.

Management would do well to devote more attention to determining the critical contingencies of their environments. For if you conclude, as we do, that the environment sets most of the structure influencing organizational outcomes and problems, and that power derives from the organization's activities that deal with those contingencies, then it is the environment that needs managing, not power. The first step is to construct an accurate model of the environment, a process that is quite difficult for most organizations. We have recently started a project to aid administrators in systematically understanding their environments. From this experience, we have learned that the most critical blockage to perceiving an organization's reality accurately is a failure to incorporate those with the relevant expertise into the process. Most organizations have the requisite experts on hand but they are positioned so that they can be comfortably ignored.

One conclusion you can, and probably should, derive from our discussion is that power—because of the way it develops and the way it is used—will always result in the organization suboptimizing its performance. However, to this grim absolute, we add a comforting caveat: If any criteria other than power were the basis for determining an organization's decisions, the results would be even worse.

A Behavioral Interpretation of Power

KENNETH R. THOMPSON
FRED LUTHANS

The study of power as an individual or an organizational phenomenon is rapidly developing to a level of importance that reflects the underlying centrality that power has in an organizational setting. While the popular notion of power has roots in the negative connotations from books such as *Clout* and *Boss,* the academic and research community has realized the importance of understanding power and power relationships in organizations. The power component is a necessary part or antecedent condition to understanding other behavioral dynamics in an organizational setting. Unfortunately, the concept of power is not conceptually well defined. Currently a host of definitions and constructs are directed toward the analysis of power, often in conflicting and confusing ways. The understanding of power is further complicated by the research difficulties inherent in measuring power in an organizational setting. For example, because of power's negative connotation, an individual often will not report accurately on actions that are taken that might be classified as related to power. Due to these limitations, much of the discussion of power is based on logical, albeit untested, frameworks or categorizations of various power types. These existing categorizations used to describe power often do not provide meaningful directions in the understanding and testing of the acquisition and use of power in organizations.

The purpose of this paper is to trace current constructs of power

Kenneth R. Thompson and Fred Luthans, "A Behavioral Interpretation of Power." Unpublished material printed with permission.

viewed from an individual level of analysis. After reviewing previous perspectives of power, an operant or behavioral approach to power acquisition and use is developed. This framework for the analysis of power in an organizational setting will aid in demonstrating the focal role of power acquisition and use in governing behavior between individuals and groups in organizations.

TRADITIONAL VIEWPOINTS OF POWER

There has been little agreement over the years on exactly what is meant by power, the most popular approach being to classify power by types. The three most widely recognized classification frameworks for power are those of French and Raven, Etzioni, and McClelland.

French and Raven (1959) recognize five distinct power types:

1. *Reward power*—based on the ability of the influencer to provide benefits to the influence target;
2. *Coercive power*—based on the ability of the influence agent to provide punishing consequences to the target for non-compliance;
3. *Expert power*—based on the special ability and/or knowledge that the influence agent has for the influence target over particular objectives that the target would like to reach;
4. *Referent power*—based on the ability of the influence target's desire to favorably identify with the influence agent, or with what the agent symbolizes to the target.
5. *Legitimate power*—based on the feeling within the influence target that the influence agent has the right and/or authority to exert influence over particular activities of the target because of the granting of power by the formal organization or through historical precedence.

A major difficulty in the French and Raven typology relates to the inconsistent identification of power types in their framework. As Patchen [1974] indicates:

It appears, then, that the five "bases of power" distinguished by French and Raven are not described in a conceptually parallel way. Instead, for different types of power, different aspects of the process underlying successful influence are highlighted. Reward and coercive are in terms of resources; referent is in terms of motivation of target (influence subject); expert in terms of characteristics of influencer; legitimate in terms of target. [p. 196]

Patchen concludes that French and Raven are not discussing types of power but instead different aspects of power. These non-parallel aspects make it difficult to make comparisons between power types and to treat power in a systematic fashion.

Etzioni [1961; 1965] expanded the power concept to include transactional properties of the influence target (the individual or group that the influence attempt is directed toward) and the influence agent (the person or group attempting to influence the target). This dyadic transactional relationship has been advocated elsewhere [Blau, 1955; 1964]. Etzioni applied the concept of power to an organizational setting, identifying three types of power that can be applied: coercive, remunerative, and normative. Coercive power can be used when the influence agent can apply sanctions upon the individual for noncompliance. Remunerative power is based on control over resources that can be used as rewards for compliance. Normative power consists of control over resources that have high symbolic value to the influence target, in that the target wishes to identify with the goals of the organization or to seek acceptance by members of the organization.

The success of the influence agent in controlling the target depends, to a great degree, upon the correct match of power type to the degree of involvement by the influence target. According to Etzioni (1961; 1965), there is a continuum of personal involvement in organizations that ranges from a high degree of individual commitment to a high degree of alienation. Midway between these two endpoints, the individual is involved in the organization only due to the amount of personal gain (calculative involvement) that is possible through being associated with the organization. According to Etzioni, the coercive influence approach is more effective with an alienative participant; the utilitarian approach with the calculative target; and use of normative power with a target that is highly committed to the values of the organization.

The Etzioni framework stresses the interactive properties of power in an organizational setting and particularly the need for the influence agent to adequately match the degree of involvement by the influence target with the appropriate influence strategy in order to increase the probability of a successful influence attempt. The Etzioni framework fails, however, to direct attention to the power acquisition stages of power development—particularly toward the specific actions taken by the power seeker and holder in order to build a more effective and enduring power base. Therefore, while Etzioni describes an important aspect of power, the approach is not comprehensive enough to provide a systematic understanding of power formation and maintenance in an organization.

McClelland [1970] defines power as an internalized state within the influence agent. McClelland's "two faces" of power consists of socialized power (power directed toward group goal acquisition) and personalized power (power directed toward an enhancement of the position of the influence agent). McClelland describes personalized power as a more coercive type of power based on the personal gain of the influence agent. On the other hand, social power is a more positive aspect of power. Social power is characterized by a "concern for group goals, for finding those goals that will move man, for helping the group to formulate them, for taking some initiative in providing members of the group with the

Figure 1

ANTECEDENT───────▶ BEHAVIOR ───────▶ CONSEQUENCE
(Environmental Context)

means of achieving such goals, and for giving members the feeling of strength and competence they need to work hard for such goals" [p. 41].

McClelland aids in building a personal behavior power perspective: behavior can be directed toward individual gain (personal power), toward building a group's power, or toward broader group or organizational goals (socialized power). As with Etzioni's model, though, the process of power acquisition and use is subordinated to a description of a dichotomy of power types.

More recent studies of power have attempted to define power more in a behavioral [for example, Hickson, Hinings, Lee, Schneck & Pennings, 1971] and process mode [for example, Tedeschi, 1972 & 1974; Blau, 1964] as opposed to the traditional perspective. Studying power as a process aids in highlighting the interactive and transactional properties of the concept. This more dynamic perspective provides a more realistic and pragmatic sense of power, as well as providing a framework in which a more empirically-based construct of power can be formulated. In this sense, some of the difficulties in studying power that led March [1966] to feel that "power is just a term used to mask our ignorance of understanding organizational relationships and behavior" will be abated.

To summarize, in previous interpretations of power, insufficient attention was given to the behavioral aspects of power acquisition and use. Power acquisition and use are natural processes in any organization. To study power empirically and to understand power more realistically, a behavioral approach is necessary as power is manifested through behavioral actions. Even perceptions of power strength and organizational support for an individual's power position are demonstrated through behavioral actions. It is with this behavioral perspective in mind that a behavioral approach to power will be discussed.

AN OPERANT APPROACH TO UNDERSTANDING BEHAVIOR

The operant paradigm appears in Figure 1. The model consists of three components; the antecedent condition, the behavior, and the consequence of the behavior.

The antecedent conditions comprise the environmental context that serves as a cue or discriminator stimulus for the individual. Given previous associations with the environment and environment-behavior-consequence relationship, the individual learns to associate or discriminate between environments and appropriate behaviors given a particular environment. An appropriate behavior is one which will lead to the desired outcome or consequence by the individual. For example, the occasion that an individual's supervisor is present may lead to a different set of behaviors being exhibited than when the supervisor is not present. An individual wishing to receive a promotion may act more responsibly on an assignment or become more assertive with subordinates (behaviors) when management is present, or when it is known that management will closely review the subordinate's actions. Through previous experiences, the individual has learned to associate these behaviors with pleasing management. The individual believes that management will then reward him/her favorably in terms of a promotion. If the behaviors lead to receiving a promotion, in essence the individual's strategy of exhibiting the behavioral patterns has been reinforced and will be repeated in subsequent situations. If the behaviors are not reinforced, the individual may either reduce the frequency of the exhibition of the behavior and try different types of behaviors or continue the same behaviors hoping that the reinforcement for these behaviors will still occur when finally acknowledged by management. Unreinforced behaviors, over time, will lead to an extinction (reduction in the frequency of occurrence) of the exhibited behaviors. Reinforcement will tend to increase the probability of future occurrence of the behaviors, given a similar environmental context.

While a full discussion of the operant approach is outside the scope of this paper [for a complete discussion see Luthans, 1981; Luthans & Kreitner, 1975], there are three considerations that are particularly germane to an understanding of a behavioral approach to power. First, the operant approach is predicated on learning associations between antecedent conditions and appropriate behaviors to match the antecedent conditions. Through a successful match of correct behaviors to an environmental setting, the probability of successful behavioral outcomes (reaching a desired consequence) will be enhanced. An individual "learns" the correct matches from direct and vicarious (learning through observing others) experiences of what has or has not worked in the past.

Second, there are many reinforcing agents in an organizational setting. Other work groups, groups in other departments, peer groups, friendships, management, and administrative groups can all be reinforcing to an individual. In many situations, an individual can be a self-reinforcing agent, reinforcing his/her own behaviors. For example, good job performance can be reinforcing to an individual because of an internally held value system that there is pride in good work. Attribution theory considers this aspect of self-reinforcement when considering internal locus of control [for example, Weiner, 1972, pp. 270-354]. These multiple reinforcers complicate an analysis and understanding of behavior in an organizational setting because determining causality of behavior actions is predicated on understanding what consequence the individual desires and from what source (s) or reinforcers the individual is attempting to receive the desired consequence.

This variability among reinforcers is the third consideration. Defining the dominant reinforcing sources in an organization cannot readily be standardized over an organization or even a subunit of the organization. The more powerful reinforcing sources are the ones which the individual perceives as having greater potential for aiding or harming his/her goal reaching ability. The goals that the individual is attempting to reach are the personal objectives of the individual which may or may not be similar to the organizational or task objectives. These personal goals include career and quality of life objectives valued by the individual. What one individual values may differ from the values of another, and what one individual perceives as a logical path to goal fulfillment may not necessarily reflect the path of another individual. These degrees of variability complicate the empirical analysis of behavioral causality in organizational settings and hinder the understanding of the motivation phenomenon.

In understanding power, there are two dimensions that need to be highlighted; power acquisition and power use. Power acquisition refers to the patterns of antecedent conditions, behaviors, and consequences that lead to the development of the ability to influence. The actual behavioral patterns, antecedent conditions, and consequences that lead to influencing a target constitute the use or exercise of power. It should be noted that power is defined as the capacity to influence; influence is the actual process of exercising power [Katz & Kahn, 1966; Allen, 1978]. Both power acquisition and use will be included in a comprehensive framework of power; however, each will first be discussed separately in order to foster an understanding of each of these main components of power.

POWER ACQUISITION

An aspiring power holder attempts to develop a power base by accumulating favorable power enhancement consequences from other power sources. These power enhancement consequences can include actual control over resources or visible symbolic designations of support from power sources. Power is not necessarily granted through a conscious action by other power holders, nor does it necessarily emanate only from one official source (such as Weber's [1947] rational-legal type of power). Instead, it is more of an evolutionary series of power granting consequences that are provided by diffused sources (individuals and groups) within an organization that, once combined, aid in the development of a power base of the power aspirant (individual or group). Figure 2 depicts this process. In the example provided in Figure 2 three different power sources are identified (the work group, upper-level management, and work-group members in another area). Note the important transactional relationship demonstrated in the example provided in Figure 2. A power aspirant does not receive power unless

Figure 2   The Acquisition Dimension Of Power

ANTECEDENT ⟶ BEHAVIOR ⟶ CONSEQUENCE

ANTECEDENT	BEHAVIOR	CONSEQUENCE

Upper level management present	works hard
	assertive with subordinates
	advocates constructive
	   changes
	initiates actions
	develops an expertise in
	   a valued area
		Upper level management rewards by:
		  more recognition
		  gives attention to suggestions
		  grants greater responsibility
		  promotes
		  gives additional status symbols
		  gives greater autonomy
		  includes in special work
		    and social activities
		  grants privileged information to
		  gives greater control over resources

Work group present	engages conversation
	initiates suggestions
	solicits suggestions for task
	advocates pro-group
	   position to management
		Group rewards through:
		  following suggestions
		  inclusion in social events
		  showing respect
		  directing questions to individual
		  asking individual's opinion
		    on group issues

Another department's work group present (B)	advocates cooperation
	makes concessions
	takes opposing
	   department's viewpoint
	friendly greetings
		Another department's work group
		rewards through:
		  cooperation with department (A)
		  working with individual
		  respecting individual's viewpoint

other sources grant it. In most likelihood, a power source will not grant power to the aspirant unless the behavior of the aspirant is such that additional power granting is warranted. If an individual desires greater power, the power aspirant must attempt to garner acceptance from power sources within the organization. For example, in Figure 2, an individual who wishes power may behave in a fashion (working hard, being assertive, initiating actions, etc.) that will indicate to upper management that the power aspirant can assume greater authority and responsibility (power). The strategy that the power aspirant can employ may include both direct (behaviors committed in the presence of management) or indirect (behaviors that will evoke positive comments to management) methods. If management is impressed and develops confidence in the individual, the power aspirant will be reinforced with power building consequences that will aid to directly reinforce the power aspirant's position.

While management may grant power, other sources in the organization are also power grantors. As noted by Barnard [1938], power is received from below as well as from above. Having management support or legitimate power only aids in providing some measure of power. A broader acceptance of a power aspirant's power is necessary for the effectiveness of an influence attempt. Garnering power from other sources (peers, work groups, friendship groups, informal management groups, subordinates) involves different types of behaviors as Figure 2 indicates. Developing a broader power base is difficult, though, in that the differing behaviors necessary to build a power base may not be compatible across power groups. Power granted from informal sources is more fragile, too, than legitimate (formally granted) power. When there is a granting of power from a legitimate power source, there usually is some public declaration (granting a change in title or duties) or symbolic designation (large private office with carpeting, special parking space, etc.). In contrast, power granting from informal sources is less public, thus easier to revoke without losing face as more formal power sources would counter.

While there are difficulties in the development of support across organizational formal and informal groups, there are definite advantages to a broader base of power. As with most cognitive decision making, the decision maker experiences some level of dissonance with a chosen course of action. Dissonance can be reduced if there is a broad base consensus that the power aspirant is worthy of receiving power. Broader support will aid to legitimize the power builder position. This only holds true, however, if there is a margin of mutual respect between power grantors. If one power group is strongly mistrusted by another power source, the second power source may have increased dissonance resulting from the first group's power-granting behavior to the same power seeker as the second group has already granted power.

There are additional risks involved. The power aspirant, through increased visibility and activity, could exhibit behaviors that may not reinforce the power granting that has taken place by other power granting sources. The individual even risks a power loss, as a power granting group loses confidence in the power aspirant because of behaviors made to garner support of other power groups. It is obvious that the entire power acquisition phase is heavily laden with potential pitfalls that can negate the development of a power base for an aspirant in an organization. The power aspirant must be sensitive to the balance of power between groups and to the political relationships between each group and the power aspirant. In essence, the power aspirant treads a fine line in meeting the demands of various organizational power sources (grantors) in the development of a power coalition. This is not only true of power acquisition, but also of power use, the second phase of a behavioral framework of power.

THE EXERCISE AND USE OF POWER

In considering the use of power, the transactional properties and behavioral dimensions must again be considered. In the exercise of power, there is an influence agent (the individual or group attempting to exercise influence) and a target of influence (an individual or a group). Figure 3 presents a model of the power-use phase of a behavioral interpretation of power. In behavioral terms there are nine distinct steps that comprise the exercise of power process. Step one involves an existing environment or antecedent condition that is present before the influence attempt (see step 1, Figure 3). The influence agent and target of influence both have some realization of the amount of power possessed by the influence agent. In a similar manner, through previous actual experiences or vicarious learning, the influence target and agent may also have some perceptions of the resources that the influence agent may have in order to extract compliance from the influence target. This combination of direct and vicarious experiences aids in the development of the antecedent environmental conditions of the relationship between the influence agent and target. During the influence attempt, the influence agent behaves (step 2) in a manner that changes the environment for the influence target. In effect, the influence agent solicits a behavioral response of compliance from the influence target. The environment of the influence target changes, given the behavior of the influence agent (step 3), eliciting a behavioral action by the influence target (step 4). The influence target's behavior indicates compliance or noncompliance. This overt behavior by the influence target acts as a consequence (step 5) of the influence agent's behavior—the consequence either reinforces or does not reinforce the action of the influence agent. If the influence attempt was successful, the behavior of the influence agent is reinforced, leading to an increase or maintenance of power. An unsuccessful influence attempt, in which the individual does not comply with the influencing action poses a threat to the influence agent. First, by noncompliance, the influence target is directly rejecting the influence agent's power. Second, the rejection of the influence agent's power (if known to the power grantors) may result in a questioning of the support of the influence agent by the power grantors. The noncompliance act by the target leads to dissonance within the power grantors. If the credibility of the demurring target is high, the dissonance will be higher. Repeated failures to influence may result in a loss of confidence by the power grantors, which would lead directly to a loss of power to the influence agent. Only through the successful use of power will the agent maintain and gain support for the granting of additional power, and retention of existing power. However, with the potential for unsuccessful influence attempts, it is obvious that the power user must consider the use of power judiciously so that power will be maintained and enhanced in the process.

Failure to exercise power, however, can also lead to a reduction of power. By not acting to preserve a power base, power may be eroded

Figure 3   The Power-Use Model

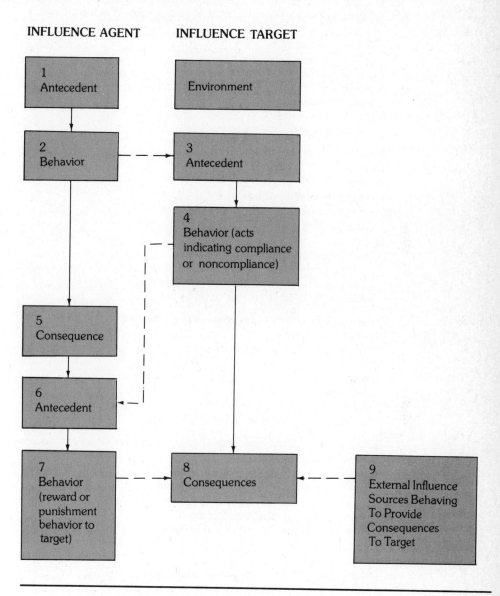

INFLUENCE AGENT   INFLUENCE TARGET

either through direct defiance of the power holder's influence, or through a deterioration of support by power grantors. As with the use of power, the decision not to use power must be made judiciously in order to maintain a power base. Failure to act or to act with imprudence can erode the support for the power holder's position.

Returning to Figure 3, the influence target's action of compliance/noncompliance becomes a consequence (step 5) to the influence agent. This consequence to the influence agent changes the environment

Table 1	Examples of Consequences of Compliance/Noncompliance Behaviors

1. Behavior to indicate acceptance: other groups support influence agent
    Benefits:
    gain of acceptance by agent
    gain of power source of autonomy
    gain of acceptance of other groups
    recognition, special favors from power sources
    status symbols granted by sources
    Costs:
    loss of autonomy, individual freedom

2. Behavior to indicate acceptance; environment does not support influence agent
    Benefits:
    gain of acceptance of agent
    recognition, special favors by agent
    status symbols granted by agent
    Costs:
    loss of individual autonomy, freedom
    alienation from other power sources
    loss of acceptance from other power sources
    exclusion from other groups' social activities

3. Behaviors to indicate noncompliance; environment supports influence agent
    Benefits:
    gain in personal freedom, autonomy
    Costs:
    loss of acceptance by agent and other power sources
    loss of inclusion in social functions by both sources
    loss of recognition, special favors
    loss of status symbols by both power sources

4. Behaviors to indicate noncompliance; environment does not support influence agent
    Benefits:
    gain of acceptance from other power sources
    recognition, special favors granted by other sources
    status symbols granted by other power sources
    individual freedom, autonomy enhanced
    Costs:
    loss of acceptance from agent
    loss of recognition, special favors from agent
    loss of status, exclusion from social ties by agent

of the influence agent providing a changed antecedent environmental condition for the agent (step 6). This change in the environment creates the condition that may cue a reactive behavior by the influence agent. The influence agent will either indicate compliance by providing some reinforcement for a behavior, or provide a nonreinforcing, or even a punishing environment for noncompliance. This reactive behavior by the influence agent acts as a consequence (step 8) for the influence target. Some possible consequences that the influence agent might provide in reinforcing or nonreinforcing the influence target are indicated in Table 1.

Table 1 provides for both behaviors of compliance and noncompliance by the influence target, given environmental conditions where other groups in the organization support or do not support the influence agent. Both positive and negative consequences to the influence target are indicated, regardless of the reinforcement or nonreinforcement provided by the influence agent. For example, under condition one, a compliance behavior will be reinforced by the influence agent and, in this case, the other organizational groups will support the compliance behavior. Given the potential reinforcement by various groups in the organization, there is a strong inducement to comply. However, compliance will also lead to a negative outcome—that of losing some of the target's own power, autonomy, and individual freedom.

Table 1 provides a sample list of possible consequences to the target; these consequences are not unknown to the target. In formulating the decision to comply, the influence target calculates the potential consequences of the particular actions of compliance/noncompliance.

It is difficult to present a complete list of positive and negative outcomes that may occur to the influence target. There is a wide variety of means to reinforce or non-reinforce individuals or groups in an organizational setting. Each target is attempting to pursue a somewhat unique set of objectives in the organization, some personally-based. One target may readily comply with an influence attempt by management, while another may feel less compelled to be influenced by management. One target may value acceptance by one particular group in the organization, and acceptance by that group may mean aversive actions taken by an opposing power faction. For example, an employee that follows work group norms of low productivity may win acceptance and support by the informal work group. Management may then punish poor work performance. Management actions, however, may not lead to improved performance as the work group is a more important source of power to the employee than management. In fact, management's sanctions against the employee may aid that employee's acceptance into the informal work group.

The example above raises an important issue seldom considered in the power literature. Power relationships (acquisition, use, compliance/noncompliance actions) in an organization are not simple, dyadic relationships as some power theorists advocate [Katz & Kahn, 1966; French, 1956; Blau, 1964]. Considerations of compliance/noncompliance often require multi-faceted decisions involving many power relationships within the organization. For example, the employee in the previous example must decide whether to comply with the influence agent. By complying, the target may lose acceptance by one or more power groups but curry acceptance with other groups, creating a complex decision in compliance/noncompliance for the influence target.

THE COMPREHENSIVE MODEL

A comprehensive behavioral model of power appears in Figure 4. It is a combination of the power acquisition and use phases, and also indicates the interrelationship between the two phases. As power is acquired or lost by a power holder or aspirant, there is a change in the environment that affects both the user of power and the potential target of the influence attempt. These changes cause a reassessment of the power relationships among agents, targets, and power grantors, leading to changes in attitudes and behaviors among the groups. A complex and constant chain of behaviors, consequences, and changing environmental conditions creates a multifaceted process of power building and use. Through direct and indirect participation and observation, a participant "learns" where the power is in the organization, what the acceptable behavioral limits are to the power holder, and the degrees of latitude the influence target may exercise without violating the norms established by the power sources in the organization.

IMPLICATIONS

Three implications result from viewing power from a behavioral perspective. First, power should be viewed as a two-phase process: power acquisition and power use. Power is derived from individuals, granted to individuals, and exercised by individuals. Power sources, users, and targets cross organizational levels and permeate all functional areas. Power is an all-encompassing process involving all participants in the organization.

A second implication relates to the compliance/noncompliance act. Actions of compliance and noncompliance tend to reinforce or dissipate the power of the influence agent. Power is a dynamic process: the use of power acts as both a threat and an opportunity to its existence. Power is an unstable entity—it must be used to be preserved. However, insufficient compliance to an influence attempt can also lead to a reduction of power.

Third, power relationships cannot be viewed as simple, isolated dyadic processes. Multiple transactions are made between groups and individual influence agents, targets, and power sources. Because power resides within individuals, power sources are also influence targets, and influence agents can readily become influence targets.

Power is obviously a complex process that involves behaviors, consequences, and a multi-faceted interaction between individuals and groups. Many of the organizational activities and constructs that are studied under the rubric of organizational behavior are directly linked to power-related behaviors. The behavioral model proposed in this paper provides a way of analyzing power in organizations, both in terms of understanding and in providing a framework for empirical analysis. Power consists of observable, measurable behaviors that can be

Figure 4   A Comprehensive Behavioral Model Of Power

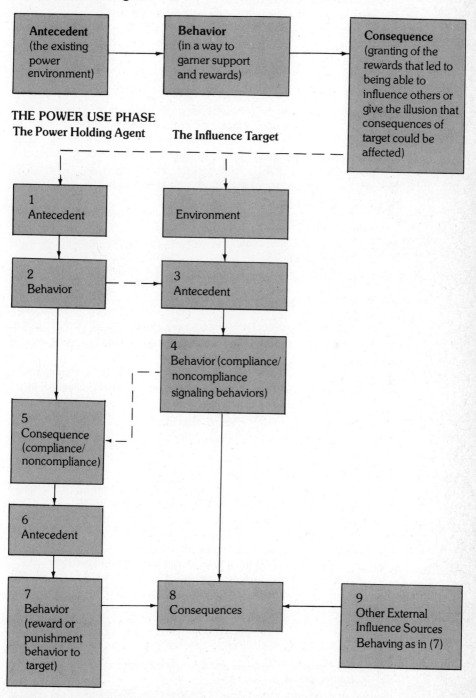

THE ACQUISITION PHASE
The Aspiring Power Agent

Antecedent (the existing power environment)

Behavior (in a way to garner support and rewards)

Consequence (granting of the rewards that led to being able to influence others or give the illusion that consequences of target could be affected)

THE POWER USE PHASE
The Power Holding Agent   The Influence Target

1 Antecedent

Environment

2 Behavior

3 Antecedent

4 Behavior (compliance/ noncompliance signaling behaviors)

5 Consequence (compliance/ noncompliance)

6 Antecedent

7 Behavior (reward or punishment behavior to target)

8 Consequences

9 Other External Influence Sources Behaving as in (7)

empirically assessed in an organizational setting. Also, power consists of cognitive perceptions of the environment of which an individual is a part. Both behavioral measures and cognitive self-reports can aid in the delineation of the power construct. More research in the future is needed to further refine the notion of power, and to understand power as it affects behavior in organizations.

REFERENCES

Allen, R. W. "Study on the choice of targets to influence in organizational settings." Unpublished doctoral dissertation, University of California, Irvine, 1978.

Barnard, C. I. *The functions of the executive.* Cambridge, Mass.: Harvard University Press, 1938.

Blau, P. M. *The dynamics of bureaucracy.* Chicago: University of Chicago Press, 1955.

Blau, P. M. *Exchange and power is social life.* New York: John Wiley & Sons, 1964.

Etzioni, A. *A comparative analysis of complex organizations.* New York: Free Press, 1961.

Etzioni, A. Organizational control structure. In J. C. March (Ed.), *Handbook of organizations.* Chicago: Rand McNally, 1965.

French, J. R. P. A formal theory of social power. *Psychological Review,* 1956, *63,* 181-194.

French, J. R. P.; & Raven, B. The bases of social power. In D. Cartwright (Ed.), *Studies in social power.* Ann Arbor: Institute for Social Research, 1959.

Hickson, D. J.; Hinings, C. R.; Lee, C. A.; Schneck, R. E.; & Pennings, J. M. A strategic contingency theory of intraorganizational power. *Administrative Science Quarterly,* 1971, *16,* 216-230.

Katz, D.; & Kahn, R. L. *The social psychology of organizations.* New York: John Wiley & Sons, 1966.

Luthans, F. *Organizational behavior.* New York: McGraw Hill, 1981.

Luthans, F.; & Kreitner, R. *Organizational behavior modification.* Glenview, Illinois: Scott, Foresman, & Co., 1975.

March, J. C. The power of power. In D. Easton (Ed.), *Varieties of political theory.* Englewood Cliffs, N.J.; Prentice-Hall, 1966, 39-70.

McClelland, D. E. The two faces of power. *Journal of International Affairs,* 1970, *24,* 29-47.

O'Connor, L. *Clout.* New York: Avon, 1976.

Patchen, M. The locus and basis of influence on organizational decision. *Organizational Behavior and Human Performance,* 1974, *11,* 195-221.

Royko, M. *Boss.* New York: New American Library, 1971.

Tedeschi, J. T. (Ed.). *The social influence process.* New York: Aldine-Atherton Press, 1972.

Tedeschi, J. T. (Ed.). *Perspectives on social power.* Chicago: Aldine Publishing Co., 1974.

Weber, M. *The theory of social and economic organizations.* New York: Oxford University Press, 1947.

Weiner, B. *Theories of motivation.* Chicago: Rand McNally & Co., 1972.

Power Failure in Management Circuits

ROSABETH MOSS KANTER

Power is America's last dirty word. It is easier to talk about money—and much easier to talk about sex—than it is to talk about power. People who have it deny it; people who want it do not want to appear to hunger for it; and people who engage in its machinations do so secretly.

Yet, because it turns out to be a critical element in effective managerial behavior, power should come out from undercover. Having searched for years for those styles or skills that would identify capable organization leaders, many analysts, like myself, are rejecting individual traits or situational appropriateness as key and finding the sources of a leader's real power.

Access to resources and information and the ability to act quickly make it possible to accomplish more and to pass on more resources and information to subordinates. For this reason, people tend to prefer bosses with "clout." When employees perceive their manager as influential upward and outward, their status is enhanced by association and they generally have high morale and feel less critical or resistant to their boss.[1] More powerful leaders are also more likely to delegate (they are too busy to do it all themselves), to reward talent, and to build a team that places subordinates in significant positions.

Powerlessness, in contrast, tends to breed bossiness rather than true leadership. In large organizations, at least, it is powerlessness that often creates ineffective, desultory management and petty, dictatorial, rules-minded managerial styles. Accountability without power—responsibility for results without the resources to get them—creates frustration and failure. People who see themselves as weak and powerless and find their subordinates resisting or discounting them tend to use more punishing forms of influence. If organizational power can "ennoble," then, recent research shows, organizational powerlessness can (with apologies to Lord Acton) "corrupt."[2]

So perhaps power, in the organization at least, does not deserve such a bad reputation. Rather than connoting only dominance, control, and oppression, *power* can mean efficacy and capacity—something managers and executives need to move the organization toward its goals. Power in organizations is analogous in simple terms to physical power: it is the ability to mobilize resources (human and material) to get things done. The true sign of power, then, is accomplishment—not fear, terror, or tyranny. Where the power is "on," the system can be productive; where the power is "off," the system bogs down.

But saying that people need power to be effective in organizations does not tell us where it comes from or why some people, in some jobs, systematically seem to have more of it than others. In this article I want to show that to discover the sources of productive power, we have to look not at the *person*—as conventional classifications of effective managers and employees do—but at the *position* the person occupies in the organization.

WHERE DOES POWER COME FROM?

The effectiveness that power brings evolves from two kinds of capacities: first, access to the resources, information, and support necessary to carry out a task; and, second, ability to get cooperation in doing what is necessary. (*Exhibit I* identifies some symbols of an individual manager's power.)

Both capacities derive not so much from a leader's style and skill as from his or her location in the formal and informal systems of the organization—in both job definition and connection to other important people in the company. Even the ability to get cooperation from subordinates is strongly defined by the manager's clout outward. People are more responsive to bosses who look as if they can get more for them from the organization.

We can regard the uniquely organizational sources of power as consisting of three "lines":

1. *Lines of supply.* Influence outward, over the environment, means that managers have the capacity to bring in the things that their own organizational domain needs—materials, money, resources to distribute as rewards, and perhaps even prestige.

Exhibit I	**Some Common Symbols of a Manager's Organizational Power (Influence Upward and Outward)**

To what extent a manager can—

Intercede favorably on behalf of someone in trouble with the organization

Get a desirable placement for a talented subordinate

Get approval for expenditures beyond the budget

Get above-average salary increases for subordinates

Get items on the agenda at policy meetings

Get fast access to top decision makers

Get regular, frequent access to top decision makers

Get early information about decisions and policy shifts

2. *Lines of information.* To be effective, managers need to be "in the know" in both the formal and the informal sense.
3. *Lines of support.* In a formal framework, a manager's job parameters need to allow for nonordinary action, for a show of discretion or exercise of judgment. Thus managers need to know that they can assume innovative, risk-taking activities without having to go through the stifling multilayered approval process. And, informally, managers need the backing of other important figures in the organization whose tacit approval becomes another resource they bring to their own work unit as well as a sign of the manager's being "in."

Note that productive power has to do with *connections* with other parts of a system. Such systemic aspects of power derive from two sources—job activities and political alliances:

1. Power is most easily accumulated when one has a job that is designed and located to allow *discretion* (nonroutinized action permitting flexible, adaptive, and creative contributions), *recognition* (visibility and notice), and *relevance* (being central to pressing organizational problems).
2. Power also comes when one has relatively close contact with *sponsors* (higher-level people who confer approval, prestige, or backing), *peer networks* (circles of acquaintanceship that provide reputation and information, the grapevine often being faster than formal communication channels), and *subordinates* (who can be developed to relieve managers of some of their burdens and to represent the manager's point of view).

When managers are in powerful situations, it is easier for them to accomplish more. Because the tools are there, they are likely to be highly motivated and, in turn, to be able to motivate subordinates. Their

Exhibit II	Ways Organizational Factors Contribute to Power or Powerlessness		
Factors	Generates power when factor is	Generates powerlessness when factor is
Rules inherent in the job	few	many
Predecessors in the job	few	many
Established routines	few	many
Task variety	high	low
Rewards for reliability/ predictability	few	many
Rewards for unusual performance/ innovation	many	few
Flexibility around use of people	high	low
Approvals needed for nonroutine decisions	few	many
Physical location	central	distant
Publicity about job activities	high	low
Relation of tasks to current problem areas	central	peripheral
Focus of tasks	outside work unit	inside work unit
Interpersonal contact in the job	high	low
Contact with senior officials	high	low
Participation in programs, conferences, meetings	high	low
Participation in problem-solving task forces	high	low
Advancement prospects of subordinates	high	low

activities are more likely to be on target and to net them successes. They can flexibly interpret or shape policy to meet the needs of particular areas, emergent situations, or sudden environmental shifts. They gain the respect and cooperation that attributed power brings. Subordinates' talents are resources rather than threats. And, because powerful managers have so many lines of connection and thus are oriented outward, they tend to let go of control downward, developing more independently functioning lieutenants.

The powerless live in a different world. Lacking the supplies, information, or support to make things happen easily, they may turn instead to the ultimate weapon of those who lack productive power—oppressive power: holding others back and punishing with whatever threats they can muster.

Exhibit II summarizes some of the major ways in which variables in the organization and in job design contribute to either power or powerlessness.

POSITIONS OF POWERLESSNESS

Understanding what it takes to have power and recognizing the classic behavior of the powerless can immediately help managers make sense out of a number of familiar organizational problems that are usually attributed to inadequate people:

· The ineffectiveness of first-line supervisors.
· The petty interest protection and conservatism of staff professionals.
· The crises of leadership at the top.

Instead of blaming the individuals involved in organizational problems, let us look at the positions people occupy. Of course, power or powerlessness in a position may not be all of the problem. Sometimes incapable people *are* at fault and need to be retrained or replaced. But where patterns emerge, where the troubles associated with some units persist, organizational power failures could be the reason. Then, as Volvo President Pehr Gyllenhammar concludes, we should treat the powerless not as "villains" causing headaches for everyone else but as "victims."[3]

First-line Supervisors

Because an employee's most important work relationship is with his or her supervisor, when many of them talk about "the company," they mean their immediate boss. Thus a supervisor's behavior is an important determinant of the average employee's relationship to work and is in itself a critical link in the production chain.

Yet I know of no U.S. corporate management entirely satisfied with the performance of its supervisors. Most see them as supervising too closely and not training their people. In one manufacturing company where direct laborers were asked on a survey how they learned their job, on a list of seven possibilities "from my supervisor" ranked next to last. (Only company training programs ranked worse.) Also, it is said that supervisors do not translate company policies into practice—for instance, that they do not carry out the right of every employee to frequent performance reviews or to career counseling.

In court cases charging race or sex discrimination, first-line supervisors are frequently cited as the "discriminating official."[4] And, in studies of innovative work redesign and quality of work life projects, they often appear as the implied villains; they are the ones who are said to undermine the program or interfere with its effectiveness. In short, they are often seen as "not sufficiently managerial."

The problem affects white-collar as well as blue-collar supervisors. In one large government agency, supervisors in field offices were seen as the source of problems concerning morale and the flow of information to and from headquarters. "Their attitudes are negative," said a senior official. "They turn people against the agency; they put down senior management. They build themselves up by always complaining about headquarters, but prevent their staff from getting any information directly. We can't afford to have such attitudes communicated to field staff."

Is the problem that supervisors need more management training programs or that incompetent people are invariably attracted to the job? Neither explanation suffices. A large part of the problem lies in the position itself—one that almost universally creates powerlessness.

First-line supervisors are "people in the middle," and that has been seen as the source of many of their problems.[5] But by recognizing that first-line supervisors are caught between higher management and workers, we only begin to skim the surface of the problem. There is practically no other organizational category as subject to powerlessness.

First, these supervisors may be at a virtual dead end in their careers. Even in companies where the job used to be a stepping stone to higher-level management jobs, it is now common practice to bring in MBAs from the outside for those positions. Thus moving from the ranks of direct labor into supervision may mean, essentially, getting "stuck" rather than moving upward. Because employees do not perceive supervisors as eventually joining the leadership circles of the organization, they may see them as lacking the high-level contacts needed to have clout. Indeed, sometimes turnover among supervisors is so high that workers feel they can outwait—and outwit—any boss.

Second, although they lack clout, with little in the way of support from above, supervisors are forced to administer programs or explain policies that they have no hand in shaping. In one company, as part of a new personnel program supervisors were required to conduct counseling interviews with employees. But supervisors were not trained to do this and were given no incentives to get involved. Counseling was just another obligation. Then managers suddenly encouraged the workers to bypass their supervisors or to put pressure on them. The personnel staff brought them together and told them to demand such interviews as a basic right. If supervisors had not felt powerless before, they did after that squeeze from below, engineered from above.

The people they supervise can also make life hard for them in numerous ways. This often happens when a supervisor has himself or herself risen up from the ranks. Peers that have not made it are resentful or derisive of their former colleague, whom they now see as trying to lord it over them. Often it is easy for workers to break rules and let a lot of things slip.

Yet first-line supervisors are frequently judged according to rules and regulations while being limited by other regulations in what disciplinary actions they can take. They often lack the resources to influence or reward people; after all, workers are guaranteed their pay and benefits by someone other than their supervisors. Supervisors cannot easily control events; rather, they must react to them.

In one factory, for instance, supervisors complained that performance of their job was out of their control: they could fill production quotas only if they had the supplies, but they had no way to influence the people controlling supplies.

The lack of support for many first-line managers, particularly in large organizations, was made dramatically clear in another company. When asked if contact with executives higher in the organization who had the potential for offering support, information, and alliances diminished their own feelings of career vulnerability and the number of headaches they experienced on the job, supervisors in five out of seven work units responded positively. For them *contact* was indeed related to a greater feeling of acceptance at work and membership in the organization.

But in the two other work units where there was greater contact, people perceived more, not less, career vulnerability. Further investigation showed that supervisors in these business units got attention only when they were in trouble. Otherwise, no one bothered to talk to them. To these particular supervisors, hearing from a higher-level manager was a sign not of recognition or potential support but of danger.

It is not surprising, then, that supervisors frequently manifest symptoms of powerlessness: overly close supervision, rules-mindedness, and a tendency to do the job themselves rather than to train their people (since job skills may be one of the few remaining things they feel good about). Perhaps this is why they sometimes stand as roadblocks between their subordinates and the higher reaches of the company.

Staff Professionals

Also working under conditions that can lead to organizational powerlessness are the staff specialists. As advisers behind the scenes, staff people must sell their programs and bargain for resources, but unless they get themselves entrenched in organizational power networks, they have little in the way of favors to exchange. They are seen as useful adjuncts to the primary tasks of the organization but inessential in a day-to-day operating sense. This disenfranchisement occurs particularly when staff jobs consist of easily routinized administrative functions which are out of the mainstream of the currently relevant areas and involve little innovative decision making.

Furthermore, in some organizations, unless they have had previous line experience, staff people tend to be limited in the number of jobs into which they can move. Specialists' ladders are often very short, and professionals are just as likely to get "stuck" in such jobs as people are in less prestigious clerical or factory positions.

Staff people, unlike those who are being groomed for important line positions, may be hired because of a special expertise or particular background. But management rarely pays any attention to developing them into more general organizational resources. Lacking growth prospects themselves and working alone or in very small teams, they are not in a position to develop others or pass on power to them. They miss out on an important way that power can by accumulated.

Sometimes staff specialists, such as house counsel or organization development people, find their work being farmed out to consultants. Management considers them fine for the routine work, but the minute the activities involve risk or something problematic, they bring in outside experts. This treatment says something not only about their expertise but also about the status of their function. Since the company can always hire talent on a temporary basis, it is unclear that the management really needs to have or considers important its own staff for these functions.

And, because staff professionals are often seen as adjuncts to primary tasks, their effectiveness and therefore their contribution to the organization are often hard to measure. Thus visibility and recognition, as well as risk taking and relevance, may be denied to people in staff jobs.

Staff people tend to act out their powerlessness by becoming turf-minded. They create islands within the organization. They set themselves up as the only ones who can control professional standards and judge their own work. They create sometimes false distinctions between themselves as experts (no one else could possibly do what they do) and lay people, and this continues to keep them out of the mainstream.

One form such distinctions take is a combination of disdain when line managers attempt to act in areas the professionals think are their preserve and of subtle refusal to support the managers' efforts. Or staff groups battle with each other for control of new "problem areas," with the result that no one really handles the issue at all. To cope with their essential powerlessness, staff groups may try to elevate their own status and draw boundaries between themselves and others.

When staff jobs are treated as final resting places for people who have reached their level of competence in the organization—a good shelf on which to dump managers who are too old to go anywhere but too young to retire—then staff groups can also become pockets of conservatism, resistant to change. Their own exclusion from the risk-taking action may make them resist *anyone's* innovative proposals. In the past, personnel departments, for example, have sometimes been the last in their organization to know about innovations in human resource development or to be interested in applying them.

Top Executives

Despite the great resources and responsibilities concentrated at the top of an organization, leaders can be powerless for reasons that are not very different from those that affect staff and supervisors: lack of supplies, information, and support.

We have faith in leaders because of their ability to make things happen in the larger world, to create possibilities for everyone else, and to attract resources to the organization. These are their supplies. But influence outward—the source of much credibility downward—can diminish as environments change, setting terms and conditions out of the control of the leaders. Regardless of top management's grand plans for the organization, the environment presses. At the very least, things going on outside the organization can deflect a leader's attention and drain energy. And, more detrimental, decisions made elsewhere can have severe consequences for the organization and affect top management's sense of power and thus its operating style inside.

In the go-go years of the mid-1960s, for example, nearly every corporation officer or university president could look—and therefore feel—successful. Visible success gave leaders a great deal of credibility inside the organization, which in turn gave them the power to put new things in motion.

In the past few years, the environment has been strikingly different and the capacity of many organization leaders to do anything about it has been severely limited. New "players" have flexed their power muscles: the Arab oil bloc, government regulators, and congressional investigating committees. And managing economic decline is quite different from managing growth. It is no accident that when top leaders personally feel out of control, the control function in corporations grows.

As powerlessness in lower levels of organizations can manifest itself in overly routinized jobs where performance measures are oriented to rules and absence of change, so it can at upper levels as well. Routine work often drives out nonroutine work. Accomplishment becomes a question of nailing down details. Short-term results provide immediate gratifications and satisfy stockholders or other constituencies with limited interests.

It takes a powerful leader to be willing to risk short-term deprivations in order to bring about desired long-term outcomes. Much as first-line supervisors are tempted to focus on daily adherence to rules, leaders are tempted to focus on short-term fluctuations and lose sight of long-term objectives. The dynamics of such a situation are self-reinforcing. The more the long-term goals go unattended, the more a leader feels powerless and the greater the scramble to prove that he or she is in control of daily events at least. The more he is involved in the organization as a short-term Mr. Fix-it, the more out of control of long-term objectives he is, and the more ultimately powerless he is likely to be.

Credibility for top executives often comes from doing the extraordinary: exercising discretion, creating, inventing, planning, and acting in nonroutine ways. But since routine problems look easier and more manageable, require less change and consent on the part of anyone else, and lend themselves to instant solutions that can make any leader look good temporarily, leaders may avoid the risky by taking over what their subordinates should be doing. Ultimately, a leader may succeed in getting all the trivial problems dumped on his or her desk. This can establish expectations even for leaders attempting more challenging tasks. When Warren Bennis was president of the University of Cincinnati, a professor called him when the heat was down in a classroom. In writing about this incident, Bennis commented, "I suppose he expected me to grab a wrench and fix it."[6]

People at the top need to insulate themselves from the routine operations of the organization in order to develop and exercise power. But this very insulation can lead to another source of powerlessness— lack of information. In one multinational corporation, top executives who are sealed off in a large, distant office, flattered and virtually babied by aides, are frustrated by their distance from the real action.[7]

At the top, the concern for secrecy and privacy is mixed with real loneliness. In one bank, organization members were so accustomed to never seeing the top leaders that when a new senior vice president went to the branch offices to look around, they had suspicion, even fear, about his intentions.

Thus leaders who are cut out of an organization's information networks understand neither what is really going on at lower levels nor that their own isolation may be having negative effects. All too often top executives design "beneficial" new employee programs or declare a new humanitarian policy (e.g., "Participatory management is now our style") only to find the policy ignored or mistrusted because it is perceived as coming from uncaring bosses.

The information gap has more serious consequences when executives are so insulated from the rest of the organization or from other decision makers, that, as Nixon so dramatically did, they fail to see their own impending downfall. Such insulation is partly a matter of organizational position and, in some cases, of executive style.

For example, leaders may create closed inner circles consisting of "doppelgängers," people just like themselves, who are their principal sources of organizational information and tell them only what they want to know. The reasons for the distortions are varied: key aides want to relieve the leader of burdens, they think just like the leader, they want to protect their own positions of power, or the familiar "kill the messenger" syndrome makes people close to top executives reluctant to be the bearers of bad news.

Finally, just as supervisors and lower-level managers need their supporters in order to be and feel powerful, so do top executives. But for them sponsorship may not be so much a matter of individual endorsement as an issue of support by larger sources of legitimacy in the society. For top executives the problem is not to fit in among peers; rather, the question is whether the public at large and other organization members perceive a common interest which they see the executives as promoting.

If, however, public sources of support are withdrawn and leaders are open to public attack or if inside constituencies fragment and employees see their interests better aligned with pressure groups than with organizational leadership; then powerlessness begins to set in.

When common purpose is lost, the system's own politics may reduce the capacity of those at the top to act. Just as managing decline seems to create a much more passive and reactive stance than managing growth, so does mediating among conflicting interests. When what is happening outside and inside their organizations is out of their control, many people at the top turn into decline managers and dispute mediators. Neither is a particularly empowering role.

Thus when top executives lose their own lines of supply, lines of information, and lines of support, they too suffer from a kind of powerlessness. The temptation for them then is to pull in every shred of power they can and to decrease the power available to other people to act. Innovation loses out in favor of control. Limits rather than targets are set. Financial goals are met by reducing "overhead" (people) rather than by giving people the tools and discretion to increase their own productive capacity. Dictatorial statements come down from the top, spreading the mentality of powerlessness farther until the whole organization becomes sluggish and people concentrate on protecting what they have rather than on producing what they can.

When everyone is playing "king of the mountain," guarding his or her turf jealously, then king of the mountain becomes the only game in town.

TO EXPAND POWER, SHARE IT

In no case am I saying that people in the three hierarchical levels described are always powerless, but they are susceptible to common conditions that can contribute to powerlessness. *Exhibit III* summarizes the most common symptoms of powerlessness for each level and some typical sources of that behavior.

I am also distinguishing the tremendous concentration of economic and political power in large corporations themselves from the powerlessness that can beset individuals even in the highest positions in such organizations. What grows with organizational position in hierarchical levels is not necessarily the power to accomplish—productive power—but the power to punish, to prevent, to sell off, to reduce, to fire, all without appropriate concern for consequences. It is that kind of power—oppressive power—that we often say corrupts.

The absence of ways to prevent individual and social harm causes the polity to feel it must surround people in power with constraints, regulations, and laws that limit the arbitrary use of their authority. But if oppressive power corrupts, then so does the absence of productive power. In large organizations, powerlessness can be a bigger problem than power.

David C. McClelland makes a similar distinction between oppressive and productive power:

The negative . . . face of power is characterized by the dominance-submission mode: if I win, you lose . . . . it leads to simple and direct means of feeling

Exhibit III	Common Symptoms and Sources of Powerlessness for Three Key Organizational Positions		
Position	**Symptoms**	**Sources**	
First-line supervisors	Close, rules-minded supervision Tendency to do things oneself, blocking of subordinates' development and information Resistant, underproducing subordinates	Routine, rules-minded jobs with little control over lines of supply Limited lines of information Limited advancement or involvement prospects for oneself/subordinates	
Staff professionals	Turf protection, information control Retreat into professionalism Conservative resistance to change	Routine tasks seen as peripheral to "real tasks" of line organization Blocked careers Easy replacement by outside experts	
Top executives	Focus on internal cutting, short-term results, "punishing" Dictatorial top-down communications Retreat to comfort of like-minded lieutenants	Uncontrollable lines of supply because of environmental changes Limited or blocked lines of information about lower levels of organization Diminished lines of support because of challenges to legitimacy (e.g., from the public or special interest groups)	

powerful [such as being aggressive]. It does not often lead to effective social leadership for the reason that such a person tends to treat other people as pawns. People who feel they are pawns tend to be passive and useless to the leader who gets his satisfaction from dominating them. Slaves are the most inefficient form of labor ever devised by man. If a leader wants to have far-reaching influence, he must make his followers feel powerful and able to accomplish things on their own . . . . Even the most dictatorial leader does not succeed if he has not instilled in at least some of his followers a sense of power and the strength to pursue the goals he has set.[8]

Organizational power can grow, in part, by being shared. We do not yet know enough about new organizational forms to say whether productive power is infinitely expandable or where we reach the point of diminishing returns. But we do know that sharing power is different from giving or throwing it away. Delegation does not mean abdication.

Some basic lessons could be translated from the field of economics to the realm of organizations and management. Capital investment in plants and equipment is not the only key to productivity. The productive capacity of nations, like organizations, grows if the skill base is upgraded. People with the tools, information, and support to make more informed decisions and act more quickly can often accomplish more. By empowering others, a leader does not decrease his power; instead he may increase it—especially if the whole organization performs better.

This analysis leads to some counterintuitive conclusions. In a certain tautological sense, the principal problem of the powerless is that they lack power. Powerless people are usually the last ones to whom anyone wants to entrust more power, for fear of its dissipation or abuse. But those people are precisely the ones who might benefit most from an injection of power and whose behavior is likely to change as new options open up to them.

Also, if the powerless bosses could be encouraged to share some of the power they do have, their power would grow. Yet, of course, only those leaders who feel secure about their own power outward—their lines of supply, information, and support—can see empowering subordinates as a gain rather than a loss. The two sides of power (getting it and giving it) are closely connected.

There are important lessons here for both subordinates and those who want to change organizations, whether executives or change agents. Instead of resisting or criticizing a powerless boss, which only increases the boss's feeling of powerlessness and need to control, subordinates instead might concentrate on helping the boss become more powerful. Managers might make pockets of ineffectiveness in the organization more productive not by training or replacing individuals but by structural solutions such as opening supply and support lines.

Similarly, organizational change agents who want a new program or policy to succeed should make sure that the change itself does not render any other level of the organization powerless. In making changes, it is wise to make sure that the key people in the level or two directly above and in neighboring functions are sufficiently involved, informed, and taken into account, so that the program can be used to build their own sense of power also. If such involvement is impossible, then it is better to move these people out of the territory altogether than to leave behind a group from whom some power has been removed and who might resist and undercut the program.

In part, of course, spreading power means educating people to this new definition of it. But words alone will not make the difference; managers will need the real experience of a new way of managing.

Here is how the associate director of a large corporate professional department phrased the lessons that he learned in the transition to a team-oriented, participatory, power-sharing management process:

> Get in the habit of involving your own managers in decision making and approvals. But don't abdicate! Tell them what you want and where you're coming from. Don't go for a one-boss grass roots 'democracy.' Make the management hierarchy work for you in participation . . . .

Women Managers Experience Special Power Failures

The traditional problems of women in management are illustrative of how formal and informal practices can combine to engender powerlessness. Historically, women in management have found their opportunities in more routine, low-profile jobs. In staff positions, where they serve in support capacities to line managers but have no line responsibilities of their own, or in supervisory jobs managing "stuck" subordinates, they are not in a position either to take the kinds of risks that build credibility or to develop their own team by pushing bright subordinates.

Such jobs, which have few favors to trade, tend to keep women out of the mainstream of the organization. This lack of clout, coupled with the greater difficulty anyone who is "different" has in getting into the information and support networks, has meant that merely by organizational situation women in management have been more likely than men to be rendered structurally powerless. This is one reason those women who have achieved power have often had family connections that put them in the mainstream of the organization's social circles.

A disproportionate number of women managers are found among first-line supervisors or staff professionals; and they, like men in those circumstances, are likely to be organizationally powerless. But the behavior of other managers can contribute to the powerlessness of women in management in a number of less obvious ways.

One way other managers can make a woman powerless is by patronizingly overprotecting her: putting her in "a safe job," not giving her enough to do to prove herself, and not suggesting her for high-risk, visible assignments. This protectiveness is sometimes born of "good" intentions to

Hang in there, baby, and don't give up. Try not to 'revert' just because everything seems to go sour on a particular day. Open up—talk to people and tell them how you feel. They'll want to get you back on track and will do things to make that happen—because they don't really want to go back to the way it was . . . . Subordinates will push you to 'act more like a boss,' but their interest is usually more in seeing someone else brought to heel than getting bossed themselves.

Naturally, people need to have power before they can learn to share it. Exhorting managers to change their leadership styles is rarely useful by itself. In one large plant of a major electronics company, first-line production supervisors were the source of numerous complaints from managers who saw them as major roadblocks to overall plant productivity and as insufficiently skilled supervisors. So the plant personnel staff undertook two pilot programs to increase the supervisors' effectiveness. The first program was based on a traditional competency and training model aimed at teaching the specific skills of successful supervisors. The second program, in contrast, was designed to empower the supervisors by directly affecting their flexibility, access to resources, connections with higher-level officials, and control over working conditions.

give her every chance to succeed (why stack the deck against her?). Out of managerial concerns, out of awareness that a woman may be up against situations that men simply do not have to face, some very well-meaning managers protect their female managers ("It's a jungle, so why send her into it?").

Overprotectiveness can also mask a manager's fear of association with a woman should she fail. One senior bank official at a level below vice president told me about his concerns with respect to a high-performing financially experienced woman reporting to him. Despite his overwhelmingly positive work experiences with her, he was still afraid to recommend her for other assignments because he felt it was a personal risk. "What if other managers are not as accepting of women as I am?" he asked. "I know I'd be sticking my neck out: they would take her more because of my endorsement than her qualifications. And what if she doesn't make it? My judgment will be on the line."

Overprotection is relatively benign compared with rendering a person powerless by providing obvious signs of lack of managerial support. For example, allowing someone supposedly in authority to be bypassed easily means that no one else has to take him or her seriously. If a woman's immediate supervisor or other managers listen willingly to criticism of her and show they are concerned every time a negative comment comes up and that they assume she must be at fault, then they are helping to undercut her. If managers let other people know that they have concerns about this person or that they are testing her to see how she does, then they are inviting other people to look for signs of inadequacy or failure.

continued

After an initial gathering of data from supervisors and their subordinates, the personnel staff held meetings where all the supervisors were given tools for developing action plans for sharing the data with their people and collaborating on solutions to perceived problems. But then, in a departure from common practice in this organization, task forces of supervisors were formed to develop new systems for handling job and career issues common to them and their people. These task forces were given budgets, consultants, representation on a plantwide project steering committee alongside managers at much higher levels, and wide latitude in defining the nature and scope of the changes they wished to make. In short, lines of supply, information, and support were opened to them.

As the task forces progressed in their activities, it became clear to the plant management that the hoped-for changes in supervisory effectiveness were taking place much more rapidly through these structural changes in power than through conventional management training; so the conventional training was dropped. Not only did the pilot groups design useful new procedures for the plant, astonishing senior management in several cases with their knowledge and capabilities, but also, significantly, they learned to manage their own people better.

Women Managers Experience Special Power Failures *continued*

Furthermore, people assume they can afford to bypass women because they "must be uninformed" or "don't know the ropes." Even though women may be respected for their competence or expertise, they are not necessarily seen as being informed beyond the technical requirements of the job. There may be a grain of historical truth in this. Many women come to senior management positions as "outsiders" rather than up through the usual channels.

Also, because until very recently men have not felt comfortable seeing women as businesspeople (business clubs have traditionally excluded women), they have tended to seek each other out for informal socializing. Anyone, male or female, seen as organizationally naive and lacking sources of "inside dope" will find his or her own lines of information limited.

Finally, even when women are able to achieve some power on their own, they have not necessarily been able to translate such personal credibility into an organizational power base. To create a network of supporters out of individual clout requires that a person pass on and share power, that subordinates and peers be empowered by virtue of their connection with that person. Traditionally, neither men nor women have seen women as capable of sponsoring others, even though they may be capable of achieving and succeeding on their own. Women have been viewed as the *recipients* of sponsorship rather than as the sponsors themselves.

(As more women prove themselves in organizations and think more self-consciously about bringing along young people, this situation may change. However, I still hear many more questions from women managers

---

Several groups decided to involve shop-floor workers in their task forces; they could now see from their own experience the benefits of involving subordinates in solving job-related problems. Other supervisors began to experiment with ways to implement "participatory management" by giving subordinates more control and influence without relinquishing their own authority.

Soon the "problem supervisors" in the "most troubled plant in the company" were getting the highest possible performance ratings and were considered models for direct production management. The sharing of organizational power from the top made possible the productive use of power below.

One might wonder why more organizations do not adopt such empowering strategies. There are standard answers: that giving up control is threatening people who have fought for every shred of it; that people do not want to share power with those they look down on; that managers fear losing their own place and special privileges in the system; that "predictability" often rates higher than "flexibility" as an organizational value; and so forth.

But I would also put skepticism about employee abilities high on the list. Many modern bureaucratic systems are designed to minimize

about how they can benefit from mentors, sponsors, or peer networks than about how they themselves can start to pass on favors and make use of their own resources to benefit others.)

Viewing managers in terms of power and powerlessness helps explain two familiar stereotypes about women and leadership in organizations: that no one wants a woman boss (although studies show that anyone who has ever had a woman boss is likely to have had a positive experience), and that the reason no one wants a woman boss is that women are "too controlling, rules-minded, and petty."

The first stereotype simply makes clear that power is important to leadership. Underneath the preference for men is the assumption that, given the current distribution of people in organizational leadership positions, men are more likely than women to be in positions to achieve power and, therefore, to share their power with others. Similarly, the "bossy woman boss" stereotype is a perfect picture of powerlessness. All of those traits are just as characteristic of men who are powerless, but women are slightly more likely, because of circumstances I have mentioned, to find themselves powerless than are men. Women with power in the organization are just as effective—and preferred—as men.

Recent interviews conducted with about 600 bank managers show that, when a woman exhibits the petty traits of powerlessness, people assume that she does so "because she is a woman." A striking difference is that, when a man engages in the same behavior, people assume the behavior is a matter of his own individual style and characteristics and do not conclude that it reflects on the suitability of men for management.

---

dependence on individual intelligence by making routine as many decisions as possible. So it often comes as a genuine surprise to top executives that people doing the more routine jobs could indeed, make sophisticated decisions or use resources entrusted to them in intelligent ways.

In the same electronics company just mentioned, at the end of a quarter the pilot supervisory task forces were asked to report results and plans to senior management in order to have their new budget requests approved. The task forces made sure they were well prepared, and the high-level executives were duly impressed. In fact, they were so impressed that they kept interrupting the presentations with compliments, remarking that the supervisors could easily be doing sophisticated personnel work.

At first the supervisors were flattered. Such praise from upper management could only be taken well. But when the first glow wore off, several of them became very angry. They saw the excessive praise as patronizing and insulting. "Didn't they think we could think? Didn't they imagine we were capable of doing this kind of work?" one asked. "They must have seen us as just a bunch of animals. No wonder they gave us such limited jobs."

As far as these supervisors were concerned, their abilities had always been there, in latent form perhaps, but still there. They as individuals had not changed—just their organizational power.

NOTES

[1]Donald C. Pelz, "Influence: A Key to Effective Leadership in the First-Line Supervisor," *Personnel,* November 1952, p. 209.

[2]See my book, *Men and Women of the Corporation* (New York: Basic Books, 1977), pp. 164-205; and David Kipnis, *The Powerholders* (Chicago: University of Chicago Press, 1976).

[3]Pehr G. Gyllenhammar, *People at Work* (Reading, Mass.: Addison-Wesley, 1977), p. 133.

[4]William E. Fulmer, "Supervisory Selection: The Acid Test of Affirmative Action," *Personnel,* November-December 1976, p. 40.

[5]See my chapter (coauthor, Barry A. Stein), "Life in the Middle: Getting In, Getting Up, and Getting Along," in *Life in Organizations,* eds. Rosabeth M. Kanter and Barry A. Stein (New York: Basic Books, 1979).

[6]Warren Bennis, *The Unconscious Conspiracy: Why Leaders Can't Lead* (New York: AMACOM, 1976).

[7]See my chapter, "How the Top is Different," in *Life in Organizations.*

[8]David C. McClelland, *Power: The Inner Experience* (New York: Irvington Publishers, 1975), p. 263. Quoted by permission.

Intraorganizational Influence Tactics: Explorations in Getting One's Way

DAVID KIPNIS
STUART M. SCHMIDT
IAN WILKINSON

Organizational psychologists have not been particularly interested in studying the ways in which people at work influence their colleagues and superiors to obtain personal benefits or to satisfy organizational goals. For the most part, interest has centered on the ways subordinates can be influenced to improve subordinate productivity and morale. This latter use of influence is customarily called the study of leadership, whereas the former can be called the study of organizational politics.

A consequence of this focus on leadership is that there is little systematic information available about how people use power to influence their colleagues or superiors. With but few exceptions (e.g., Izraeli, 1975; Schein, 1977), our thinking about this topic is guided by anecdotal evidence or armchair speculations that have been organized into rational classifications of power tactics (e.g., Etzioni, 1968, pp. 94-109; French & Raven, 1959). One problem with these classifications of power tactics, as Raven (1974) has pointed out, is that they overlap with each other, though each varies in the number of influence dimensions that are described. A further problem with existing classifications of power tactics is that when influence acts are actually

"Intraorganizational Influence Tactics: Explorations in Getting One's Way" by David Kipnis, Stuart M. Schmidt and Ian Wilkinson, *Journal of Applied Psychology*, 1980. Vol. 65, No. 4, 440-452. Copyright © 1980 by the American Psychological Association, Inc. Reprinted by permission of the American Psychological Association, Inc.

studied, it is found that people do not exercise influence in ways predicted by rational classification schemes. This point was first explicitly made in a study by Goodchild, Quadrado, and Raven (Note 1) in which college students wrote brief essays on the topic "How I got my way." It was found that many of the influence tactics described by these students could not be classified into preexisting categories. Several tactics thought to be basic when classifying influence, such as the use of expert power, were not even mentioned by the students.

There is a need, therefore, for empirical studies of the use of influence within organizations. The purpose of this article is to report two studies that sought to examine the tactics of influence used by people at work when attempting to change the behavior of their superiors, co-workers, and subordinates. In the first study, the range of tactics that people use at work was identified by applying content analysis to written descriptions by managers of their attempts to influence their bosses, co-workers, or subordinates. The second study sought to identify through factor analysis the dimensions of influence underlying the specific tactics that were uncovered in the first study.

STUDY 1: DETERMINING INTRAORGANIZATIONAL INFLUENCE TACTICS

Method

The data for this study were collected from 165 respondents, 25% women and 75% men. All respondents were taking graduate business courses part-time, in the evening. They were told to refer to their current employment experience when supplying the requested information.

The respondents were employed mainly in managerial roles as engineers, technicians, and professionals. Since most respondents came from different organizations, there were almost as many organizations as respondents represented.

Respondents were asked to describe an incident in which they actually succeeded in getting either their boss, a co-worker, or a subordinate to do something they wanted: 62 described how they got their way with their boss, 49 with a co-worker, and 54 with a subordinate. The reason for the unequal distribution of respondents over status levels was that fewer respondents had subordinates or co-workers than had bosses.

In their description of an incident, each respondent wrote in essay form what they wanted from a target person, what they did, whether there was resistance from the target, and what further influence tactics were used in response to resistance from the target. Each respondent also completed a structured questionnaire containing demographic and specific organizational job-situation questions.

The incidents were sorted first in terms of the goal sought from the target person. This sorting yielded five general categories of goals: *assistance with own job*—obtaining the assistance of the target in helping the respondent do his or her job, when it was not part of the target's

Table 1   Reasons for Exercising Influence, by Target Status (Study 1) in Percentages

Reasons	Target status			
	Boss (62)	Co-worker (49)	Subordinate (54)	Total (165)
Obtain assistance on own job	3	48	9	18
Get others to do their jobs	13	23	46	27
Obtain personal benefits	58	10	0	25
Initiate change in work	26	15	28	23
Improve target's job performance	0	4	17	7

Note. Numbers in parentheses are Ns.

legitimate job duties; *get others to do their job*—getting the target to do his or her own work; *obtain benefits*—goals that personally benefited the respondent, such as salary increase, promotion, and improved work schedule; *initiate change*—initiating new organizational programs and systems or improving the coordination of organizational activities (e.g., changing a scheduling procedure); and *improve performance*—improving the target's on-the-job performance.

These goals varied as a function of the target's job status, as shown in Table 1. Respondents sought mostly self-interest goals from their superiors. The primary goal sought from co-workers was to get assistance with the respondent's own job. The most prevalent reason for influencing subordinates was to get them to do their jobs. Finally, the goal of initiating change was sought both from bosses and from subordinates in almost equal proportion. However, the changes sought from superiors focused on job-related organizational changes, such as launching a new accounting procedure or starting a special project. But with subordinates, the changes sought dealt with job performance, such as changes in the way a job should be done or the manner of working in the organization.

Next, the influence tactics reported by the respondents in attempting to achieve these goals were identified. A total of 370 influence tactics were reported by the 165 respondents. The authors sorted these tactics into 14 categories (see Table 2). Consensus among the coders was used as the criterion for assigning a given tactic to a category. The 14 categories ranged from the use of administrative sanctions and personal threats through the use of logic and rational discussions to clandestine, dependency appeal, and ingratiating tactics. The individual tactics illustrating these 14 categories are also shown in Table 2. To determine the reliability of the assignment of items to these 14 categories, three coders who were not associated with the research independently sorted the 370 influence tactics into the 14 categories. Raters 1 and 2 agreed on the placement of items 61% of the time; Raters 1 and 3 agreed 64% of the time; and Raters 2 and 3 agreed 65% of the time. Since there were 14 categories into which any item could be placed, the degree of agreement between the three raters suggests modestly high reliability for the classification scheme. The areas of disagreement between the raters involved primarily the three categories "weak ask," "explain," and "request."

Table 2	Classification of Influence Tactics by Category (Study 1)		
Category/tactic	%[a]	Category/tactic	%[a]
Clandestine 8		**Persistence** 7	
Challenged the ability of the target		Repeated reminders	
Lied to the target		Argued	
Acted in a pseudo-democratic manner		Repeated previous actions	
Puffed up the importance of the job		Surveillance	
		Training 6	
Manipulated information		Explained how it was to be done	
Made the target feel important		Showed how to do it	
Cajoled the target		**Reward** 2	
Showed understanding (pretended) of the target's problem		Verbal reinforcement	
		Salary raise	
		Gave benefits	
Personal negative actions 8		**Self presentation** 5	
Fait accompli/went ahead on own		Demonstrated competence	
Chastised the target		Performed well, then asked	
Became a nuisance		Waited until target was in the right mood	
Slowed down on the job		Was humble	
Held personal confrontation with target		Was friendly	
		Direct request 10	
Threatened withdrawal of help		**Weak ask** 6	
Expressed anger		Showed dependency	
Threatened to leave job		Weak request	
Blocked target's actions		**Demand** 7	
Ignored target		Invoked rules	
Administrative negative actions 3		Ordered	
Filed a report with supervisor		Convened formal conference	
Sent target to superior for conference		Set time deadline	
		Told target that it must be done as I said or better proposed	
Gave unsatisfactory performance evaluations			
		Explained rationale for request 17	
Gave no salary increase		**Gathered supporting data** 6	
Threatened with unsatisfactory performance ratings		**Coalitions** 7	
		Obtained support from co-workers	
Threatened job security		Obtained support informally from superiors	
Threatened loss of promotion			
Exchange 8		Obtained support from subordinates	
Contributed in exchange for compliance		Threatened to notify an outside agency	
Compromised			
Offered to make sacrifice		Made formal appeals to higher levels	
Offered help to get the job done			
Invoked past favors			

[a]Percentage of the 370 tabulated influence tactics reported by respondents.

In addition to identifying influence tactics, the analyses of Study 1 focused on the correlates of the 14 categories of influence. To this end, a unit weight of 1 was assigned if the respondent reported using any of the items comprising a given influence tactic category; a score of 0 was assigned if none of the items comprising a category were mentioned. Thus, each respondent had 14 scores of 1 or 0. Next, multivariate analyses of variance, which if significant were followed by univariate analyses, were carried out to examine the relationship among the 14 categories of influence, the status of the target person, and the goals sought by respondents in exercising influence.

The influence tactics used by the respondents varied with the goal sought from the target person. When the goal was self-interest, the most frequently reported tactics were self-presentation and personal negative actions; when the goal was to initiate change, the most frequently reported tactics were the use of logic and rational discussions; when the goal was to improve a target's performance, respondents reported using administrative sanctions, training, and simply demanding compliance. Finally, when the goal was to get others to do the respondent's own work, the most frequently reported tactic was the use of requests. All of the above findings were statistically reliable beyond the .05 level.

The kinds of influence tactics used by the respondents varied with the power of the target person. Respondents significantly more often used the tactics of self-presentation, supporting data, and coalitions when attempting to influence their bosses. Different tactics, however, were used to influence subordinates; then respondents significantly more often used clandestine tactics, administrative sanctions, training, demanding, and explaining. Finally, the data showed that only one tactic was significantly associated with influencing co-workers—the tactic of requesting help. At the .10 level, however, the tactics of exchange, requests, and rewards were also associated with influencing co-workers.

The use of influence tactics also varied with the amount of resistance shown by target persons. When the respondents stated that the target at first refused to comply, the subsequent actions of respondents included an increase in persistence and the use of personal negative actions. Additionally, when confronting resisting bosses and co-workers, the respondents reported an increase in the use of coalitions with fellow employees. If the person resisting was a subordinate, however, the respondents reported using more administrative sanctions such as giving unsatisfactory performance evaluations.

Results

The findings of the study suggest that in organizational settings the choice of influence tactics is associated with what the respondents are trying to get from the target person, the amount of resistance shown, and the power of the target person. Combining these findings suggests that administrative sanctions and personal negative actions are more likely to be used when the target is a subordinate who is actively resisting the request of the manager and when the reasons for exercising influence are based on the respondent's role in the organization (e.g., improve target's performance).

It is also important to note that many of the tactics reported by the respondents have received little mention in the organizational literature (e.g., the use of deceit, self-presentation, and clandestine tactics). In fact, the tactics shown in Table 2 represent a bewildering combination of several classification schemes from the exchange theories of Michener and Schwertfeger (1972) to the schemes described by French and Raven (1959) and by Cartwright (1965, pp.1-47). It is clear that the many influence tactics described here do not fit easily into any single classification scheme currently found in the literature on power usage. Based on these findings, we believe that new ways of classifying such tactics are needed that use the actual influence behaviors of organizational members as the starting point. An effort in this direction is reported in the next study.

STUDY 2

Method

Many of the 14 categories of influence tactics in the first study overlapped either conceptually or empirically or both (e.g., "weak ask" vs. "request"). The purpose of Study 2 was to determine the factor structure of the tactics found in the previous study. To this end, 58 items were developed from Study 1's tactics. These items were included in a questionnaire administered to 754 employed respondents. Respondents were asked to describe on a 5-point scale how frequently during the past 6 months they had used each item to influence a target person at work. The 5-point scale had verbal anchors as follows: usually use this tactic to influence him/her (5), frequently use this tactic to influence him/her (4), occasionally use this tactic to influence him/her (3), seldom use this tactic to influence him/her (2), and never use this tactic to influence him/her (1).

There were three forms of the questionnaire: One asked respondents to describe how they influenced their bosses, another asked how they influenced their co-workers, and the third asked how they influenced their subordinates. The instructions read:

This questionnaire is a way of obtaining information about how you go about changing your boss's (or co-worker's or subordinate's) mind so that he or she agrees with you. Below are described various ways of doing this. Please do not answer in terms of what you would like to do.

Respondents were also told that if the tactics did not apply in their work to leave the space blank: blank responses were coded as "never used this tactic."

Sample. The respondents were drawn from the same managerial population as in Study 1 and were taking graduate business courses part-time: 690 were enrolled in evening courses at Temple University and 64 were enrolled at the Bernard Baruch Graduate Center in New York City. Of the 754 respondents, 225 described how they influenced their bosses, 285 described how they influenced co-workers, and 244 described how they influenced subordinates.

Reasons for exercising influence. In addition to describing how frequently each influence tactic was used, a separate scale presented respondents with five possible reasons for influencing the target person. These reasons were based on those found in Study 1 and read as follows: (a) have my boss (co-worker or subordinate) assist me on my job or do some of my work; (b) assign work to my boss (co-worker or subordinate) or tell him or her what to do; (c) have my boss (co-worker or subordinate) give me benefits, such as raises, better hours of work, time off, better job assignments, and so on; (d) have my boss (co-worker or subordinate) do his or her own work better or do what they are supposed to do; (e) have my boss (co-worker or subordinate) accept my ideas for changes, for example, to accept a new way of doing the work more efficiently or a new program or project.

For each of the five reasons, the respondents were asked to rate on a 5-point scale ranging from "very often" (5) to "never" (1) how frequently each reason had been the cause of their trying to influence the target person to do something.

Paralleling the findings of Study 1, the reasons for exercising influence varied with whether the target person was a superior, co-worker, or subordinate. Table 3 shows that the major reasons for influencing subordinates were that respondents more frequently attempted to assign them work, to improve their task performance, and to have them assist the respondents in their own work ($p < .01$ compared to co-workers or superiors). Superiors were influenced most frequently to receive

Table 3	Mean Frequency of Reasons for Respondents Exercising Influence (Study 2)			
		Target status		
Reason for exercising influence	Subordinate (244)	Co-worker (285)	Superior (225)	F
Assistance on own job	3.15$_a$	2.75$_b$	2.09$_c$	64.36**
Assign work	4.08$_a$	2.47$_b$	1.86$_c$	329.69**
Obtain benefits	1.33$_a$	1.65$_b$	2.42$_c$	90.41**
Improve performance	3.93$_a$	2.88$_b$	2.39$_c$	135.19**
Initiate change	3.54$_a$	3.27$_b$	3.47$_a$	6.66*

Note. Numbers in parentheses are Ns. Groups with different subscripts differ beyond the .05 level. High scores indicate that the goal was rated as a frequent reason for the respondent to influence the target person. *$p < .05$ ** $p < .01$.

personal benefits ($p < .01$). Finally, respondents reported that they attempted to influence both their subordinates and their superiors with almost equal frequency to convince them to initiate change. This last result was also found in Study 1.

Additional background data. The questionnaire also obtained information about the sex of the respondent, the sex of the respondent's boss, whether the organization was unionized, the number of persons employed in the respondent's work unit, and the job level of the respondent. Job level information was based on the respondent's description of his or her own work. This information was coded into four groups: clerical/sales, professional (e.g., engineer, computer technician), first-line and middle managers (e.g., supervisor, manager of clerical unit, etc.), and top-level managers (e.g., vice president of marketing).

Results

The 58 influence tactic items were factor analyzed using a principal component factor solution, with iterations for communality and varimax rotation. Forced two-factor through eight-factor solutions were carried out to aid in interpreting the findings.

Factor analyses were carried out for the entire sample and separately for each of the three target status levels (superior, co-worker, subordinate). This was done to examine the possibility that dimensions of influence would emerge at each target status level that did not emerge in the overall analysis. A second reason for carrying out separate factor analyses at each target status level was to ensure that any factors that emerged in the combined analysis also appeared in at least one of the separate factor analyses. It was assumed that a factor that did not appear in any of the separate analyses, yet appeared in the overall analysis, only reflected differences between target status levels in the exercise of influence.

The factor analysis of the entire sample yielded six interpretable factors. These six factors accounted for 38% of the total item variance. Table 4 lists the 58 tactics presented in the questionnaire and their loadings on each of the six factors. The data in Table 4 are based on the overall factor analysis utilizing all 754 respondents.

Factor 1 is identified by highest loadings on the influence tactics, including demanding, ordering, and setting deadlines. This factor is labeled *Assertiveness*. The factor emerged as a dimension of influence at all target status levels (superior, co-worker, and subordinate).

Factor 2 is described by the highest loadings on weak and nonobtrusive influence tactics. Included here were such tactics as "acting humble" and "making the other person feel important." This factor is labeled *Ingratiation*. The factor emerged as a dimension of influence at all levels of target status.

Table 4   Rotated Factors and Item Loadings

Dimension of influence/tactic	1	2	3	4	5	6	7[a]	8[b]
Assertiveness								
51. Kept checking up on him or her.	64	21	11	09	05	18	12	-15
45. Simply ordered him or her to do what was asked.	58	12	-10	27	-05	15	13	-14
18. Demanded that he or she do what I requested.	58	10	-03	29	-03	12	08	-06
39. Bawled him or her out.	54	06	07	30	04	01	03	10
11. Set a time deadline for him or her to do what I asked.	54	22	18	23	00	23	-09	35
19. Told him or her that the work must be done as ordered or he or she should propose a better way.	49	11	09	26	01	14	03	17
53. Became a nuisance (kept bugging him/her until he/she did what I wanted).	47	14	08	-11	16	08	33	-10
43. Repeatedly reminded him or her about what I wanted.	47	14	28	-04	09	14	28	-04
54. Expressed my anger verbally.	42	-13	18	17	07	01	36	08
41. Had a showdown in which I confronted him or her face to face.	34	-07	31	18	12	05	24	25
30. Pointed out that the rules required that he or she comply.	33	11	15	20	10	30	27	04
Ingratiation								
46. Made him or her feel important ("only you have the brains, talent to do this").	25	59	13	15	04	09	17	09
9. Acted very humbly to him or her while making my request.	-01	52	-02	-05	14	07	07	-02
17. Acted in a friendly manner prior to asking for what I wanted.	-02	51	11	-01	16	04	-03	-07
28. Made him or her feel good about me before making my request.	-02	51	19	10	17	03	-05	-04
37. Inflated the importance of what I wanted him or her to do.	27	51	14	20	07	06	-04	05
36. Praised him or her.	32	50	09	22	06	12	-09	19
3. Sympathized with him/her about the added problems that my request has caused.	25	47	17	05	16	15	05	12
44. Waited until he or she appeared in a receptive mood before asking.	-13	45	21	-05	16	-06	04	21
10. Showed my need for their help.	22	43	12	06	11	07	-21	11
29. Asked in a polite way.	18	38	15	01	14	07	17	02
22. Pretended I was letting him or her decide to do what I wanted (act in a pseudo-democratic fashion).	15	38	15	13	-04	07	00	23

Table 4   Rotated Factors and Item Loadings—Continued

Dimension of influence/tactic	1	2	3	4	5	6	7[a]	8[b]
Rationality								
40. Wrote a detailed plan that justified my ideas.	−06	−04	65	06	−02	21	−17	61
38. Presented him or her with information in support of my point of view.	06	17	64	04	05	−07	−15	37
31. Explained the reasons for my request.	17	20	57	−03	08	01	07	49
13. Used logic to convince him or her.	10	13	55	02	03	−02	−03	32
24. Wrote a memo that described what I wanted.	15	03	42	04	00	26	00	31
42. Offered to compromise over the issue (I gave in a little).	14	23	40	00	23	00	04	47
16. Demonstrated my competence to him or her before making my request.	−10	23	35	10	04	02	−11	17
Sanctions								
49. Gave no salary increase or prevented the person from getting a pay raise.	17	03	06	63	01	01	02	08
26. Threatened his or her job security (e.g., hint of firing or getting him or her fired).	26	05	03	59	02	08	04	11
15. Promised (or gave) a salary increase.	06	11	07	52	11	01	−05	15
6. Threatened to give him or her an unsatisfactory performance evaluation.	24	09	01	52	−04	13	02	15
34. Threatened him or her with loss of promotion.	11	00	02	46	07	11	04	−03
Exchange								
35. Offered an exchange (e.g., if you do this for me, I will do something for you).	03	21	02	03	70	08	22	06
27. Reminded him or her of past favors that I did for them.	07	19	01	04	53	03	17	−15
50. Offered to make a personal sacrifice if he or she would do what I wanted (e.g., work late, work harder, do his/her share of the work, etc).	−07	28	10	10	52	05	10	15
55. Did personal favors for him or her.	04	37	03	07	48	03	15	09
7. Offered to help if he/she would do what I wanted.	23	33	07	10	40	20	−12	14
Upward appeal								
58. Made a formal appeal to higher levels to back up my request.	10	12	09	−01	11	59	29	14
20. Obtained the informal support of higher-ups.	20	26	08	06	05	47	−05	23
25. Filed a report about the other person with higher-ups (e.g., my superior).	17	03	06	31	04	42	−02	16
33. Sent him or her to my superior.	28	09	07	13	05	40	−03	05

Table 4   Rotated Factors and Item Loadings—Continued

Dimension of influence/tactic	Factors							
	1	2	3	4	5	6	7[a]	8[b]
Blocking								
47. Threatened to notify an outside agency if he or she did not give in to my request.	17	−12	04	19	12	19	80	10
48. Threatened to stop working with him or her until he or she gave in.	10	−11	02	16	20	07	63	−03
4. Engaged in a work slowdown until he or she did what I wanted.	02	03	−08	03	07	16	59	07
5. Ignored him or her and/or stopped being friendly.	05	03	−14	08	06	01	37	−08
14. Distorted or lied about reasons he or she should do what I wanted.	06	19	04	06	13	10	33	−02
Coalitions								
12. Obtained the support of co-workers to back up my request.	06	17	35	−13	02	29	28	50
56. Had him or her come to a formal conference at which I made my request.	25	04	34	15	02	35	13	47
32. Obtained the support of my subordinates to back up my request.	06	16	35	11	−06	18	20	46
Unclassified items								
52. Kept kidding him or her until they did what I wanted.	33	34	13	−10	25	−02	−01	−09
23. Ignored him or her and went ahead and did what I wanted.	10	11	00	−08	11	01	16	05
8. Provided him or her with various benefits that they wanted.	07	22	17	25	28	07	08	19
1. Challenged his or her ability ("I bet you can't do that").	17	13	−01	13	07	09	03	07
21. Pretended not to understand what needed to be done so that he or she would volunteer to do it for me.	02	24	−04	05	10	05	18	16
2. Concealed some of my reasons for trying to influence him/her.	03	22	13	07	−01	10	24	12
% of total variance	18.2	6.5	5.2	4.2	3.2	2.9	5.7	5.0

Note. N = 754. Decimals omitted. Item numbers denote the items' original position in the questionnaire.
[a]Data based on factor analysis of tactics used to influence superiors.
[b]Data based on factor analysis of tactics used to influence subordinates.

Factor 3 is characterized by loadings on the use of rationality influence tactics and is labeled *Rationality*. It includes such tactics as "writing a detailed plan" and "explaining the reasons for my request." This factor emerged at each target status level. In the analysis of tactics directed toward subordinates, however, additional items that involved group pressure also loaded highly on this factor. These latter items will be discussed subsequently.

Factor 4 involved the use of administrative sanctions to induce compliance. Tactics with high loadings included "prevented salary increases" and "threatened job security." This factor is labeled *Sanctions.* It emerged as a dimension of influence at all levels of target status.

Factor 5 loaded on tactics involving the exchange of positive benefits. Included here were such tactics as "offering an exchange" and "offering to make personal sacrifices." This factor is labeled *Exchange of Benefits.* This factor only emerged in the factor analysis of influence tactics directed toward superiors.

Factor 6 is described by loadings on tactics that bring additional pressure for conformity on the target by invoking the influence of higher levels in the organization. Included here were such tactics as "making a formal appeal to higher levels" and "obtaining the informal support of higher-ups." This factor only emerged in the factor analysis of influence tactics directed toward superiors: it is labeled *Upward Appeal.*

Two additional factors (Factors 7 and 8) did not emerge in the overall factor analysis but were found in the subanalyses. It was decided to retain these factors for heuristic purposes.

Factor 7 emerged in the factor analysis of influence directed toward superiors. Items that loaded on this factor included "engaging in a work slowdown" and "threatening to stop working with the target person." Essentially, these tactics are attempts to stop the target person from carrying out some action by various kinds of blocking tactics. This factor is labeled *Blocking.*

Factor 8 emerged from the factor analysis of tactics directed toward subordinates. Items in this factor were part of the previously described factor Rationality. However, this subset of items described the use of steady pressure for compliance by "obtaining the support of co-workers" and by "obtaining the support of subordinates." This is labeled *Coalitions.*

Scale construction. To aid further analysis, scales were constructed whose items were selected to represent each of the eight dimensions of influence. Selection was made on the basis of two criteria. First, items were selected that loaded over .40 on a given dimension and did not load above .25 on any of the remaining dimensions. Second, from the pool of items that were selected to represent each dimension, items were selected based on an examination of each item's correlation with other items representing the factor and their correlations with items in the remaining factors. High item intercorrelation within a factor and low item intercorrelation with the remaining items were used as the final criteria for selecting items.

To determine the intercorrelation between the eight scales, correlation matrices were first computed at each of the three status levels. Next, all intercorrelations were converted to their z' equivalents, averaged, and then reconverted to product-moment correlations. This procedure provides an estimate of the correlation between the eight scales, with the variance attributable to target status partialed out. As shown in Table 5,

Table 5   **Intercorrelation of Scale Scores**

Dimension of influence	2	3	4	5	6	7	8
1. Assertiveness	.22	.32	.24	.26	.35	.21	.28
2. Ingratiation		.14	.24	.49	.28	.10	.31
3. Sanctions			.13	.24	.32	.21	.17
4. Rationality				.20	.22	−.03	.32
5. Exchange					.27	.22	.29
6. Upward appeal						.20	.36
7. Blocking							.16
8. Coalitions							

Note. N = 754.

Table 6   **Reliability of Tactic Scores (Alpha Coefficient)**

Dimension of influence	Number of items	Target status			Total
		Subordinate	Co-worker	Superior	
Ingratiation	6	.65	.73	.71	.70
Rationality	4	.61	.77	.70	.71
Assertiveness	5	.61	.68	.65	.78
Sanction	5	.69	.71	.54	.73
Exchange	5	.70	.74	.76	.73
Upward appeal	4	.65	.65	.68	.67
Blocking	3	.47	.42	.74	.53
Coalitions	2	.71	.64	.81	.75

there was a fair degree of independence among the factors, with the exception of the relationship between Ingratiation and Exchange tactics (r = .49). The remaining factors show reasonably low levels of intercorrelation, with *r*s ranging from .03 to .36. It should be noted that the individual correlation matrices at each status level closely paralleled the averaged findings reported in Table 5.

Table 6 presents the reliability of the eight scale scores (coefficient alpha) for each target status level. With the exception of low reliability for the use of Blocking tactics with subordinates and co-workers, the remaining factor scores have satisfactory reliabilities.

Correlates of Influence Tactics

Target status.   Table 7 shows the means and standard deviations of each influence dimension as a function of the status of the target. Seven of the eight dimensions were significantly associated with the relative status of the target. Basically, the findings suggest that as the status of the target person increased, respondents placed more reliance on rationality tactics. An analysis using Duncan's multiple-range test found that Assertive tactics and Sanctions were used more often to influence

Table 7   **Target Status and Average Frequency of Tactic Use**

Dimension of influence	Target status			F
	Subordinate	Co-worker	Superior	
Ingratiation				
M	15.92$_b$	16.08$_b$	14.52$_a$	16.69**
SD	3.97	4.73	4.48	
Rationality				
M	14.04$_b$	13.74$_b$	14.72$_a$	7.17**
SD	2.47	3.20	3.01	
Assertiveness				
M	12.04$_a$	8.06$_b$	6.94$_c$	243.91**
SD	3.00	2.67	2.25	
Sanctions				
M	6.39$_a$	5.27$_b$	5.16$_b$	68.18**
SD	1.95	0.91	0.62	
Exchange				
M	9.83$_b$	10.08$_b$	8.56$_a$	13.52**
SD	3.10	3.65	3.53	
Upward appeal				
M	7.05$_b$	6.83$_b$	5.43$_a$	37.16**
SD	2.31	2.29	1.99	
Blocking				
M	3.31$_a$	3.50$_b$	3.29$_a$	4.05*
SD	0.82	1.04	0.91	
Coalitions				
M	4.37	4.30	4.53	.079
SD	2.04	2.05	2.14	

Note. Groups with different subscripts differ beyond the .05 level.
*$p < .05$. **$p < .01$.

subordinates than co-workers or superiors ($ps < .01$). The tactics of Ingratiation, Exchange of Benefits, and Upward Appeal were used with equal frequency among subordinates and co-workers but significantly less often when attempting to influence superiors ($p < .01$). Finally, respondents reported that they used Rationality tactics more frequently to convince superiors than co-workers or subordinates ($p < .01$). As will be shown later, these differences in choice of tactics in part reflect the fact that respondents have different reasons for influencing target persons at different status levels.

Goals. It will be recalled that respondents in the present study rated the importance of five possible reasons for exercising influence. To determine whether different combinations of tactics were used as the reasons for influencing varied, a set of stepwise regression analyses was performed. These stepwise regression analyses examined the relation between the eight tactic scores and the rated importance of each reason for exercising influence. A restriction put on the analysis was that only tactics that correlated significantly ($p < .05$) with a given reason were entered into the regression analysis. Since we have already found that the type of tactic used and the reasons for exercising influence both varied with the status of the target person, separate regression analyses were carried out at each target status level. Table 8 shows these findings in

Table 8	Multiple Correlations Between Tactics and Rated Importance of Reasons for Exercising Influence	
Reason for exercising influence/target	Tactic category used	*R*
Receive assistance on own job		
boss	Ingratiation	.20
co-worker	Ingratiation	.16
subordinate	Assertiveness	
	Ingratiation	.29
Assign work to target		
boss	Assertiveness	.51
co-worker	Assertiveness	.28
subordinate	Assertiveness	.31
Obtain benefits from target		
boss	Exchange	
	Ingratiation	.38
co-worker	Exchange	
	Blocking	
	Ingratiation	.32
subordinate	Assertiveness	
	Coalitions	.21
Improve target's performance		
boss	Assertiveness	
	Blocking	
	Rationality	.43
co-worker	Assertiveness	
	Exchange	
	Coalitions	
	Rationality	.46
subordinate	Assertiveness	
	Rationality	.34
Initiate change		
boss	Rationality	
	Coalition	
	Ingratiation	
	Exchange	.57
co-worker	Rationality	
	Coalitions	
	Exchange	.45
subordinate	Assertiveness	
	Rationality	.42

Note. Tactics are listed in order of their entry into the stepwise multiple regression equations. All correlations are significant beyond the .05 level.

terms of the particular combination of influence tactics that best predicted each reason for exercising influence. In addition, Table 8 presents the multiple correlations of these influence tactics with each reason for exercising influence.

Table 8 shows that at all target status levels, the respondent's choice of influence tactics varied with the respondents' reasons for exercising influence. That is, respondents who frequently sought personal assistance from target persons used Ingratiation tactics; respondents who frequently assigned work to target persons used Assertiveness; and respondents who frequently tried to improve a target person's performance used Assertiveness and Rationality tactics. Finally, respondents who frequently tried to convince target persons to accept new ideas used Rationality tactics.

Another finding of interest in Table 8 is that respondents showed the least variation in choice of tactics when attempting to influence their subordinates. No matter what the reason for influencing subordinates, the use of Assertiveness was associated with each of the five reasons and accounted for the most variance for each reason. In contrast, when influencing co-workers and superiors, the use of Assertiveness was associated only with two of the five reasons.

Other situational factors.   So far it has been shown that use of the eight dimensions of influence was associated with the relative power of the target person and the reasons why the respondents wanted to influence the target person. In this section we examine the relationship between the use of tactics and five personal or situational characteristics of the respondent: sex, level in the organization, whether the respondent's unit was unionized, number of people in respondent's work unit, and sex of respondent's boss.

The findings showed that the respondent's own level in the organization was closely associated with use of influence tactics. Compared to those with low job status, respondents with higher job status reported greater use of Rationality and Assertiveness tactics when influencing both their subordinates and their superiors ($ps < .01$). In addition, respondents with higher job status used Sanctions more frequently and sought aid from their superiors less frequently when influencing their subordinates ($ps < .01$). Thus, as the respondents' own job status rose, they were more likely to use more direct tactics of influence and be less dependent upon superiors.

Size of work unit also related to the use of tactics on subordinates. In large work units, respondents more frequently used Assertiveness ($p < .01$), Sanctions ($p < .01$), and Upward Appeal ($p < .05$) when influencing subordinates. These findings are consistent with the general idea that as the number of persons in a work unit increases, a greater reliance is placed on strong and impersonal means of control.

Finally, the presence of unions was associated with the use of certain tactics. If the organization was unionized, respondents were more likely to use Ingratiating tactics to influence subordinates ($p < .01$), to avoid the use of Assertiveness when influencing co-workers ($p < .05$), and to use Rationality tactics less frequently ($p < .01$) and Blocking tactics more frequently ($p < .01$) when influencing bosses.

There were no significant relations associated with the sex of the respondent and the sex of the respondent's boss in terms of the frequency of use of the eight dimensions of influence. Thus, in the present study men and women chose similar tactics when attempting to get their way.

Discussion

In Study 1, influence tactics were sorted into 14 categories, but we suspected that a more parsimonious classification system was likely to exist. The results of Study 2 yielded eight dimensions of influence.

Four of these dimensions emerged at all status levels. These dimensions were Assertiveness, Sanctions, Ingratiation, and Rationality. The remaining dimensions were uniquely associated with influencing either superiors or subordinates. The tactics of Exchange of Benefits, Blocking, and Upward Appeal emerged when respondents described how they influenced their bosses. These dimensions did not appear in the analysis of influence tactics used among subordinates. Finally, the use of Coalitions tactics appeared only when respondents described how they influenced their subordinates.

Unfortunately, there are few studies available with which to compare the present findings. Within organizational settings, the major empirical studies of influence tactics have been based on the Ohio State-Navy leadership studies (Fleishman, 1973). These studies could identify only two dimensions of influence—consideration and initiating structure. However, this early program of research was only concerned with how leaders exercised influence over subordinates and was not concerned with the use of influence tactics among peers and bosses. Hence, the range of influence tactics used in that early research covered fewer areas than those included here.

Other factorial studies of influence tactics have focused on dimensions of influence in interpersonal settings (Falbo, 1977; Kipnis, Cohen, & Catalano, Note 2). These studies have uncovered only two or three dimensions of influence. For example, Kipnis et al. reported that dating couples used three dimensions of influence—strong, weak, and rational—as ways of changing their dating partner's behavior. The items loading on these three dimensions closely resemble the dimensions we have labeled *Assertiveness, Rationality,* and *Ingratiation* tactics. Thus, instead of acting "more loving" in order to influence, organizational members act "humble" and offer to "make sacrifices." The parallel is clearly there. The additional factors found in the present study suggest that organizational resources extend the range of tactics that organizational members can use. Thus, organizational members can invoke formal sanctions or the added authority of higher management as compliance-gaining strategies.

It is recognized, of course, that findings presented here are based on self-report measures and require replication using different methodologies. Nevertheless, the picture portrayed by these data is of organizational members actively seeking to influence peers, superiors, and subordinates for a variety of reasons, some personal and some based on their management roles. This picture supports the view of those who argue that organizational leadership is more complicated than is represented in organizational behavior textbooks (Kochan, Schmidt, & DeCotiis, 1976). Such texts mainly focus on the ways in which higher levels in the organization influence lower levels. This is called the leadership process. In fact, we would suggest that everyone is influencing everyone else in organizations, regardless of job title. People seek benefits, information, satisfactory job performance, the chance to do better than others, to be left alone, cooperation, and many other outcomes too numerous to mention.

In fact, there may be very little difference in the frequency with which people try to influence their bosses, co-workers, and subordinates, given all these various reasons for trying to influence others. What shows remarkable variation, however, are the kinds of tactics that are chosen when trying to obtain these various outcomes. The present article has shown that these tactics vary with the particular wants of the influencing agent and his or her degree of control over the target of influence. The implications of these findings for the understanding of organizational politics remain to be explored.

As a final point, the scales that have been developed to measure the various dimensions of influence can be useful in further research. Even though the use of influence within organizations is a topic of considerable interest, there have been few systematic attempts to develop a means of measuring such behavior. The present dimensions provide the potential for profiling the use of influence in a variety of organizational settings and at different levels as well as between various groups.

REFERENCE NOTES

1. Goodchild, J. D., Quadrado, C., & Raven, B. H. *Getting one's way.* Paper presented at the meeting of the Western Psychological Association, Sacramento, California, April 1975.
2. Kipnis, D., Cohen, E., & Catalano, R. *Power and affection.* Paper presented at the meeting of the Eastern Psychological Association, Philadelphia, April 1979.

REFERENCES

Cartwright, D. Influence, leadership and control. In J. G. March (Ed.), *Handbook of organizations.* Chicago: Rand McNally, 1965.

Etzioni, A. Organizational dimensions and their interrelationship. In B. Indik & F. K. Berrien (Eds.), *People, groups and organizations.* New York: Teachers College Press, 1968.

Falbo, T. The multidimensional scaling of power strategies. *Journal of Personality and Social Psychology,* 1977, *35,* 537-547.

Fleishman, E. A. Twenty years of consideration and structure. In E. A. Fleishman & J. G. Hunt (Eds.), *Current developments in the study of leadership.* Carbondale: Southern Illinois University Press, 1973.

French, J. R. P., & Raven, B. H. The bases of social power. In D. Cartwright (Ed.), *Studies in social power.* Ann Arbor: University of Michigan Press, 1959.

Izraeli, D. N. The middle manager and the tactics of power expansion. *Sloan Management Review,* 1975, *16,* 57-70.

Kochan, T. A., Schmidt, S. M., & DeCotiis, T. A. Superior-subordinate relations: Leadership and headship. *Human Relations,* 1976, *28,* 279-294.

Michener, A., & Schwertfeger, M. Liking as a determinant of power tactic preference. *Sociometry,* 1972, *35,* 190-202.

Raven, B. H. The comparative analysis of power and influence. In J. T. Tedeschi (Ed.), *Perspective on social power.* Chicago: Aldine, 1974.

Schein, V. E. Individual power and political behavior. *Academy of Management Review,* 1977, *2,* 64-72.

PART 2

Downward Influence

In organizational situations involving downward influence, someone is attempting to affect the behavior of another individual or group of individuals at a lower level in the formal organization hierarchy. Thus, in downward influence, the superior is the initiator of the influence attempt; the subordinates are the recipients of the attempt. Of course, the terms "superior" and "subordinate" used here refer to *relative* positions in the organizational hierarchy, and not necessarily to two positions at immediately adjacent levels. For instance, an example of a downward influence attempt could involve a vice president of sales trying to influence a sales representative who is several levels below the vice president. The distinguishing feature of downward influence is that the influencer is at a higher organizational level than the (potential) influencee. Therefore, the only individuals who could not engage in *downward influence* attempts, as we use the term, are those who are at the lowest operative level within the organization.

The inescapable element in downward influence is the fact that the influencer has more designated formal authority than the target of the influence. The extent to which the influence agent utilizes this formal authority and the way in which it is utilized will vary with circumstances. The point to be made, however, is that the influence agent has this tool available, and typically both he or she and the intended recipients of the attempt will be quite aware of this fact. Nevertheless, it must be emphasized that the hierarchical superior in the situation also has all of the other potential bases of power (expertise, charisma, etc.) available to anyone else in the organization. The formal authority differential is simply an "extra" not available in lateral or upward influence situations. When formal authority is utilized *effectively,* the individual is usually termed a "leader," rather than simply being designated a higher-level manager or supervisor.

There is another important consideration to keep in mind when analyzing downward influence situations. Typically, though not universally, the lower-level individual will be relatively more dependent on the higher-level person for rewards than vice versa. (See the article in Section IV by Mechanic that discusses when this dependency relationship will be equalized, or even reversed.) This means that ordinarily the recipient of the influence attempt will be more motivated to please the initiator than would be the case in lateral or upward influence situations. (Indeed, that is the problem for the influence agent in those situations—how to have an impact on someone who is not dependent on the influencing agent for rewards.) However, in downward influence situations, the existence of the typical dependency relationship does not necessarily mean that it is an easy task for the higher-level manager to use rewards effectively in bringing about influence. (This is the focus of Steven Kerr's article, presented later in this section.) It does mean, though, that those who attempt to exercise downward influence start with a particular type of advantage—formal authority—that may or may not be employed skillfully.

The articles in Section II examine a number of facets of downward influence processes. We begin with an article by Kotter that places the issue of power at the front and center of the practice of management. Kotter focuses on how effective managers both acquire and use power in relating to others in the organization, particularly those below them in the hierarchy. He begins by noting that if managers are to do a good job, they must recognize that they are dependent on others in the organization—even though the degree of *relative* dependence is greater from subordinate to boss than vice versa. Managers cannot accomplish their goals by themselves. Therefore, in Kotter's analysis, managers must learn how to establish power in their relationships with others. He identifies four means of creating power: developing a sense of obligation to the manager; developing a sense of belief in the manager's expertise; enhancing subordinates' tendencies for identification with the manager; and making salient to the subordinates their dependence on the manager. Kotter concludes with a discussion of characteristics that are common to managers who are able to generate and utilize power successfully.

The article "Power to the Powerless: Locus of Control and the Use of Power," by Goodstadt and Hjelle, presents experimental findings on power. In the experiment, the researchers identify individuals as either "externals" (those who believe that events are determined by forces outside themselves such as luck or the power of others) or "internals" (those who believe that they have considerable control themselves over what happens to them in life.) The authors label the externals as relatively "powerless" because these individuals do not believe, relatively speaking, they have much personal power. The internals, on the other hand, are characterized as having less of a sense of powerlessness. The purpose of the experiment was to determine whether internals and externals used different types of power when placed in an experimental supervisory-type situation and informed of problem work behavior of fictitious subordinates. Results revealed that the externally controlled "bosses" utilized coercive power more and persuasion less than did internally controlled "bosses." Also, it was found that the type of subordinate problem (ineptness or poor motivation) affected the type of power used by the two groups to deal with the problem. The findings from this study have some interesting implications for the selection of supervisors and for their training in identifying the "causes" of subordinate performance.

Kerr's article provides numerous examples of how organizations and managers have designed reward systems to influence or bring about certain types of behavior, but that in fact actually reward (reinforce) other (non-desired) types of behavior. After citing various examples that occur in society in general and in organizations, Kerr proceeds to analyze the causes of this seemingly paradoxical situation. Among the causes he lists are the following behaviors occurring in upper organizational echelons: "fascination with an 'objective' criterion," "overemphasis on highly visible behaviors," and sometimes even a certain degree of "hypocrisy." The author suggests several possible remedies that those administering rewards might apply. These include: selecting different types of employees (subordinates); training subordinates to value the rewards that are actually provided; and altering the reward system. The last solution is one that is often very difficult for upper-level managers to convince themselves should be done. However, it is this solution that may have the most lasting influence effects in the desired direction.

"Intimidation Rituals: Reactions to Reform" discusses how some organizations and middle-level managers deal with another type of subordinate problem—"problem" from the point of view of someone higher in the organization. O'Day discusses the situation in which a subordinate attempts to initiate "reforms" or changes in the organization that are not desired by superiors. In this sociological analysis, the author uses the term "intimidation rituals" to describe the influence actions that are sometimes employed by upper-level administrators to defeat or stop the so-called reform attempts. These actions are postulated by the author to start at a relatively low level of force and move on to more extreme forms of influence. They increase from nullification of the effort ("You don't know what you are talking about, but thank you for telling us . . . ."), through isolation and defamation of the individual, to ultimate expulsion from the organization if necessary. This characterization of influence attempts by those at lower levels who are trying to bring about changes that may be threatening to those higher up in the organization may be somewhat overdrawn. However, it does illustrate the range of downward influence attempts that can sometimes occur in organizations. In effect, the downward influence methods described by O'Day are responses to prior upward influence attempts by subordinates.

An analysis of downward influence must, of necessity, include a consideration of leadership processes. In the article by Dansereau and his colleagues, the very important point is made that any group leader or supervisor needs to deal with subordinates as individuals with unique characteristics. The authors argue that seldom, if ever, does a leader have a homogeneous set of subordinates who can be treated identically. That is, since each subordinate differs from the other subordinates, each must be responded to specifically by the leader. Thus, the term "vertical dyad linkage" (VDL) is employed. This means that if a leader or supervisor has seven subordinates, there are seven VDLs (one between the leader and subordinate A, a second between the leader and subordinate B, and so forth). The article describes a nine-month longitudinal study of how new vertical dyads (i.e., where boss and subordinate had not worked together before) are established by supervisors. The interesting results showed that within the same group of subordinates reporting to a supervisor, certain of them became "In" members and others became "Out" members in terms of their relationships with the supervisor. In 85 per cent of the situations the supervisor began early to treat the subordinates differently, giving the "Ins" much more freedom in "negotiating" how they would carry out their tasks, more support, and more attention. The findings have considerable implications for the study of downward leadership influence development in a group situation, especially with regard to how leadership tasks often are shared in the group, and how certain individuals (i.e., the "Ins") are likely to develop particularly strong commitments to the success of the group.

The final article in this section provides a case study of how the downward influence tactics utilized by a very strong, charismatic leader in a business firm had an impact that persisted even after he had vacated his top-level position. Although those remaining in the company were making attempts to shift toward more typical and conventional forms of management, there were substantial carry-over consequences of the previous leadership style. This case study demonstrates the effect that a powerful administrator can have on the way in which downward influence is exercised throughout the rest of the organization. This impact is not necessarily good or bad. It is a frequent phenomenon, however, that clearly deserves attention by those concerned about the effective functioning of organizations.

Power, Dependence, and Effective Management

JOHN P. KOTTER

Americans, as a rule, are not very comfortable with power or with its dynamics. We often distrust and question the motives of people who we think actively seek power. We have a certain fear of being manipulated. Even those people who think the dynamics of power are inevitable and needed often feel somewhat guilty when they themselves mobilize and use power. Simply put, the overall attitude and feeling toward power, which can easily be traced to the nation's very birth, is negative. In his enormously popular *Greening of America*, Charles Reich reflects the views of many when he writes, "It is not the misuse of power that is evil; the very existence of power is evil."[1]

One of the many consequences of this attitude is that power as a topic for rational study and dialogue has not received much attention, even in managerial circles. If the reader doubts this, all he or she need do is flip

Author's note: This article is based on data from a clinical study of a highly diverse group of 26 organizations including large and small, public and private, manufacturing and service organizations. The study was funded by the Division of Research at the Harvard Business School. As part of the study process, the author interviewed about 250 managers.

through some textbooks, journals, or advanced management course descriptions. The word *power* rarely appears.

This lack of attention to the subject of power merely adds to the already enormous confusion and misunderstanding surrounding the topic of power and management. And this misunderstanding is becoming increasingly burdensome because in today's large and complex organizations the effective performance of most managerial jobs requires one to be skilled at the acquisition and use of power.

From my own observations, I suspect that a large number of managers—especially the young, well-educated ones—perform significantly below their potential because they do not understand the dynamics of power and because they have not nurtured and developed the instincts needed to effectively acquire and use power.

In this article I hope to clear up some of the confusion regarding power and managerial work by providing tentative answers to three questions:

1. Why are the dynamics of power necessarily an important part of managerial processes?
2. How do effective managers acquire power?
3. How and for what purposes do effective managers use power?

I will not address questions related to the misuse of power, but not because I think they are unimportant. The fact that some managers, some of the time, acquire and use power mostly for their own aggrandizement is obviously a very important issue that deserves attention and careful study. But that is a complex topic unto itself and one that has already received more attention than the subject of this article.

RECOGNIZING DEPENDENCE IN THE MANAGER'S JOB

One of the distinguishing characteristics of a typical manager is how dependent he is on the activities of a variety of other people to perform his job effectively.[2] Unlike doctors and mathematicians, whose performance is more directly dependent on their own talents and efforts, a manager can be dependent in varying degrees on superiors, subordinates, peers in other parts of the organization, the subordinates of peers, outside suppliers, customers, competitors, unions, regulating agencies, and many others.

These dependency relationships are an inherent part of managerial jobs because of two organizational facts of life: division of labor and limited resources. Because the work in organizations is divided into specialized divisions, departments, and jobs, managers are made directly or indirectly dependent on many others for information, staff services, and cooperation in general. Because of their organization's limited resources, managers are also dependent on their external environments for support. Without some minimal cooperation from suppliers, competitors, unions, regulatory agencies, and customers, managers cannot help their organizations survive and achieve their objectives.

Dealing with these dependencies and the manager's subsequent vulnerability is an important and difficult part of a manager's job because, while it is theoretically possible that all of these people and organizations would automatically act in just the manner that a manager wants and needs, such is almost never the case in reality. All the people on whom a manager is dependent have limited time, energy, and talent, for which there are competing demands.

Some people may be uncooperative because they are too busy elsewhere, and some because they are not really capable of helping. Others may well have goals, values, and beliefs that are quite different and in conflict with the manager's and may therefore have no desire whatsoever to help or cooperate. This is obviously true of a competing company and sometimes of a union, but it can also apply to a boss who is feeling threatened by a manager's career progress or to a peer whose objectives clash with the manager's.

Indeed, managers often find themselves dependent on many people [and things] whom they do not directly control and who are not "cooperating." This is the key to one of the biggest frustrations managers feel in their jobs, even in the top ones, which the following example illustrates:

After nearly a year of rumors, it was finally announced in May 1974 that the president of ABC Corporation had been elected chairman of the board and that Jim Franklin, the vice president of finance, would replace him as president. While everyone at ABC was aware that a shift would take place soon, it was not at all clear before the announcement who would be the next president. Most people had guessed it would be Phil Cook, the marketing vice president.

Nine months into his job as chief executive officer, Franklin found that Phil Cook [still the marketing vice president] seemed to be fighting him in small and subtle ways. There was never anything blatant, but Cook just did not cooperate with Franklin as the other vice presidents did. Shortly after being elected, Franklin had tried to bypass what he saw as a potential conflict with Cook by telling him that he would understand if Cook would prefer to move somewhere else where he could be a CEO also. Franklin said that it would be a big loss to the company but that he would be willing to help Cook in a number of ways if he wanted to look for a presidential opportunity elsewhere. Cook had thanked him but had said that family and community commitments would prevent him from relocating, and all CEO opportunities were bound to be in a different city.

Since the situation did not improve after the tenth and eleventh months, Franklin seriously considered forcing Cook out. When he thought about the consequences of such a move, Franklin became more and more aware of just how dependent he was on Cook. Marketing and sales were generally the keys to success in their industry, and the company's sales force was one of the best, if not the best, in the industry. Cook had been with the company for 25 years. He had built a strong personal relationship with many of the people in the sales force and was universally popular. A mass exodus just might occur if Cook were fired.

The loss of a large number of salesmen, or even a lot of turmoil in the department, could have a serious effect on the company's performance.

After one year as chief executive officer, Franklin found that the situation between Cook and himself had not improved and had become a constant source of frustration.

As a person gains more formal authority in an organization, the areas in which he or she is vulnerable increase and become more complex rather than the reverse. As the previous example suggests, it is not at all unusual for the president of an organization to be in a highly dependent position, a fact often not apparent to either the outsider or to the lower level manager who covets the president's job.

A considerable amount of the behavior of highly successful managers that seems inexplicable in light of what management texts usually tell us managers do becomes understandable when one considers a manager's need for, and efforts at, managing his or her relationships with others.[3] To be able to plan, organize, budget, staff, control, and evaluate, managers need some control over the many people on whom they are dependent. Trying to control others solely by directing them and on the basis of the power associated with one's position simply will not work—first, because managers are always dependent on some people over whom they have no formal authority, and second, because virtually no one in modern organizations will passively accept and completely obey a constant stream of orders from someone just because he or she is the "boss."

Trying to influence others by means of persuasion alone will not work either. Although it is very powerful and possibly the single most important method of influence, persuasion has some serious drawbacks too. To make it work requires time [often lots of it], skill, and information on the part of the persuader. And persuasion can fail simply because the other person chooses not to listen or does not listen carefully.

This is not to say that directing people on the basis of the formal power of one's position and persuasion are not important means by which successful managers cope. They obviously are. But, even taken together, they are not usually enough.

Successful managers cope with their dependence on others by being sensitive to it, by eliminating or avoiding unnecessary dependence, and by establishing power over those others. Good managers then use that power to help them plan, organize, staff, budget, evaluate, and so on. *In other words, it is primarily because of the dependence inherent in managerial jobs that the dynamics of power necessarily form an important part of a manager's processes.*

An argument that took place during a middle management training seminar I participated in a few years ago helps illustrate further this important relationship between a manager's need for power and the degree of his or her dependence on others:

Two participants, both managers in their thirties, got into a heated disagreement regarding the acquisition and use of power by managers. One took the position that power was absolutely central to managerial work, while the other argued that it was virtually irrelevant. In support of their positions, each described a very "successful" manager with whom he worked. In one of these examples, the manager seemed to be constantly developing and using power, while in the other, such behavior was rare. Subsequently, both seminar participants were asked to describe their successful managers' jobs in terms of the dependence *inherent* in those jobs.

The young manager who felt power was unimportant described a staff vice president in a small company who was dependent only on his immediate subordinates, his peers, and his boss. This person, Joe Phillips, had to depend on his subordinates to do their jobs appropriately, but, if necessary, he could fill in for any of them or secure replacement for them rather easily. He also had considerable formal authority over them; that is, he could give them raises and new assignments, recommend promotions, and fire them. He was moderately dependent on the other four vice presidents in the company for information and cooperation. They were likewise dependent on him. The president had considerable formal authority over Phillips but was also moderately dependent on him for help, expert advice, the service his staff performed, other information, and general cooperation.

The second young manager—the one who felt power was very important—described a service department manager, Sam Weller, in a large, complex, and growing company who was in quite a different position. Weller was dependent not only on his boss for rewards and information, but also on 30 other individuals who made up the divisional and corporate top management. And while his boss, like Phillips's was moderately dependent on him too, most of the top managers were not. Because Weller's subordinates, unlike Phillips's, had people reporting to them, Weller was dependent not only on his subordinates but also on his subordinates' subordinates. Because he could not himself easily replace or do most of their technical jobs, unlike Phillips, he was very dependent on all these people.

In addition, for critical supplies, Weller was dependent on two other department managers in the division. Without their timely help, it was impossible for his department to do its job. These departments, however, did not have similar needs for Weller's help and cooperation. Weller was also dependent on local labor union officials and on a federal agency that regulated the division's industry. Both could shut his division down if they wanted.

Finally, Weller was dependent on two outside suppliers of key materials. Because of the volume of his department's purchase relative to the size of these two companies, he had little power over them.

Under these circumstances, it is hardly surprising that Sam Weller had to spend considerable time and effort acquiring and using power to manage his many dependencies, while Joe Phillips did not.

As this example also illustrates, not all management jobs require an incumbent to be able to provide the same amount of successful power-oriented behavior. But most management jobs today are more like Weller's than Phillips's. And, perhaps more important, the trend over the past two or three decades is away from jobs like Phillips's and toward jobs like Weller's. So long as our technologies continue to become more complex, the average organization continues to grow larger, and the average industry continues to become more competitive and regulated, that trend will continue; as it does so, the effective acquisition and use of power by managers will become even more important.

ESTABLISHING POWER IN RELATIONSHIPS

To help cope with the dependency relationships inherent in their jobs, effective managers create, increase, or maintain four different types of power over others.[4] Having power based in these areas puts the manager in a position both to influence those people on whom he or she is dependent when necessary and to avoid being hurt by any of them.

Sense of Obligation

One of the ways that successful managers generate power in their relationships with others is to create a sense of obligation in those others. When the manager is successful, the others feel that they should—rightly—allow the manager to influence them within certain limits.

Successful managers often go out of their way to do favors for people who they expect will feel an obligation to return those favors. As can be seen in the following description of a manager by one of his subordinates, some people are very skilled at identifying opportunities for doing favors that cost them very little but that others appreciate very much:

> Most of the people here would walk over hot coals in their bare feet if my boss asked them to. He has an incredible capacity to do little things that mean a lot to people. Today, for example, in his junk mail he came across an advertisement for something that one of my subordinates had in passing once mentioned that he was shopping for. So my boss routed it to him. That probably took 15 seconds of his time, and yet my subordinate really appreciated it. To give you another example, two weeks ago he somehow learned that the purchasing manager's mother had died. On his way home that night, he stopped off at the funeral parlor. Our purchasing manager was, of course, there at the time. I bet he'll remember that brief visit for quite a while.

Recognizing that most people believe that friendship carries with it certain obligations ("A friend in need . . . ."), successful managers often try to develop true friendships with those on whom they are dependent. They will also make formal and informal deals in which they give something up in exchange for certain future obligations.

Belief in a Manager's Expertise

A second way successful managers gain power is by building reputations as "experts" in certain matters. Believing in the manager's expertise, others will often defer to the manager on those matters. Managers usually establish this type of power through visible achievement. The larger the achievement and the more visible it is, the more power the manager tends to develop.

One of the reasons that managers display concern about their "professional reputations" and their "track records" is that they have an impact on others' beliefs about their expertise. These factors become particularly important in large settings, where most people have only secondhand information about most other people's professional competence, as the following shows:

Herb Randley and Bert Kline were both 35-year-old vice presidents in a large research and development organization. According to their closest associates, they were equally bright and competent in their technical fields and as managers. Yet Randley had a much stronger professional reputation in most parts of the company, and his ideas generally carried much more weight. Close friends and associates claim the reason that Randley is so much more powerful is related to a number of tactics that he has used more than Kline has.

Randley has published more scientific papers and managerial articles than Kline. Randley has been more selective in the assignments he has worked on, choosing those that are visible and that require his strong suits. He has given more speeches and presentations on projects that are his own achievements. And in meetings in general, he is allegedly forceful in areas where he has expertise and silent in those where he does not.

Identification with a Manager

A third method by which managers gain power is by fostering others' unconscious identification with them or with ideas they "stand for." Sigmund Freud was the first to describe this phenomenon, which is most clearly seen in the way people look up to "charismatic" leaders. Generally, the more a person finds a manager both consciously and (more important) unconsciously an ideal person, the more he or she will defer to that manager.

Managers develop power based on others' idealized views of them in a number of ways. They try to look and behave in ways that others respect. They go out of their way to be visible to their employees and to give speeches about their organizational goals, values, and ideals. They even consider, while making hiring and promotion decisions, whether they will be able to develop this type of power over the candidates:

One vice president of sales in a moderate-size manufacturing company was reputed to be so much in control of his sales force that he could get them to respond to new and different marketing programs in a third of the time taken by the company's best competitors. His power over his employees was based primarily on their strong identification with him and what he stood for. Emigrating to the United States at age 17, this person worked his way up "from nothing." When made a sales manager in 1965, he began recruiting other young immigrants and sons of immigrants from his former country. When made vice president of sales in 1970, he continued to do so. In 1975, 85% of his sales force was made up of people whom he hired directly or who were hired by others he brought in.

Perceived Dependence on a Manager

The final way that an effective manager often gains power is by feeding others' beliefs that they are dependent on the manager either for help or for not being hurt. The more they perceive they are dependent, the more most people will be inclined to cooperate with such a manager.

There are two methods that successful managers often use to create perceived dependence.

Finding and acquiring resources.   In the first, the manager identifies and secures (if necessary) resources that another person requires to perform his job, that he does not possess, and that are not readily available elsewhere. These resources include such things as authority to make certain decisions; control of money, equipment, and office space; access to important people; information and control of information channels; and subordinates. Then the manager takes action so that the other person correctly perceives that the manager has such resources and is willing and ready to use them to help (or hinder) the other person. Consider the following extreme—but true—example.

When young Tim Babcock was put in charge of a division of a large manufacturing company and told to "turn it around," he spent the first few weeks studying it from afar. He decided that the division was in disastrous shape and that he would need to take many large steps quickly to save it. To be able to do that, he realized he needed to develop considerable power fast over most of the division's management and staff. He did the following:

· He gave the division's management two hours' notice of his arrival.
· He arrived in a limousine with six assistants.
· He immediately called a meeting of the 40 top managers.
· He outlined briefly his assessment of the situation, his commitment to turn things around, and the basic direction he wanted things to move in.
· He then fired the four top managers in the room and told them that they had to be out of the building in two hours.
· He then said he would personally dedicate himself to sabotaging the career of anyone who tried to block his efforts to save the division.
· He ended the 60-minute meeting by announcing that his assistants would set up appointments for him with each of them starting at 7:00 A.M. the next morning.

Throughout the critical six-month period that followed, those who remained at the division generally cooperated energetically with Mr. Babcock.

Affecting perceptions of resources.   A second way effective managers gain these types of power is by influencing other persons' perceptions of the manager's resources.[5] In settings where many people are involved and where the manager does not interact continuously with those he or she is dependent on, those people will seldom possess "hard facts" regarding what relevant resources the manager commands directly or indirectly (through others), what resources he will command in the future, or how prepared he is to use those resources to help or hinder them. They will be forced to make their own judgments.

Insofar as a manager can influence people's judgments, he can generate much more power than one would generally ascribe to him in light of the reality of his resources.

In trying to influence people's judgments, managers pay considerable attention to the "trappings" of power and to their own reputations and images. Among other actions, they sometimes carefully select, decorate, and arrange their offices in ways that give signs of power. They associate with people or organizations that are known to be powerful or that others perceive as powerful. Managers selectively foster rumors concerning their own power. Indeed, those who are particularly skilled at creating power in this way tend to be very sensitive to the impressions that all their actions might have on others.

Formal Authority

Before discussing how managers use their power to influence others, it is useful to see how formal authority relates to power. By *formal authority,* I mean those elements that automatically come with a managerial job—perhaps a title, an office, a budget, the right to make certain decisions, a set of subordinates, a reporting relationship, and so on.

Effective managers use the elements of formal authority as resources to help them develop any or all of the four types of power previously discussed, just as they use other resources (such as their education). Two managers with the same formal authority can have very different amounts of power entirely because of the way they have used that authority. For example:

- By sitting down with employees who are new or with people who are starting new projects and clearly specifying who has the formal authority to do what, one manager creates a strong sense of obligation in others to defer to his authority later.
- By selectively withholding or giving the high-quality service his department can provide other departments, one manager makes other managers clearly perceive that they are dependent on him.

On its own, then, formal authority does not guarantee a certain amount of power; it is only a resource that managers can use to generate power in their relationships.

EXERCISING POWER TO INFLUENCE OTHERS

Successful managers use the power they develop in their relationships, along with persuasion, to influence people on whom they are dependent to behave in ways that make it possible for the managers to get their jobs done effectively. They use their power to influence others directly, face to face, and in more indirect ways.

Exhibit	Methods of influence		
Face-to-face methods	**What they can influence**	**Advantages**	**Drawbacks**
Exercise obligation-based power.	Behavior within zone that the other perceives as legitimate in light of the obligation.	Quick. Requires no outlay of tangible resources.	If the request is outside the acceptable zone, it will fail; if it is too far outside, others might see it as illegitimate.
Exercise power based on perceived expertise.	Attitudes and behavior within the zone of perceived expertise.	Quick. Requires no outlay of tangible resources.	If the request is outside the acceptable zone, it will fail; if it is too far outside, others might see it as illegitimate.
Exercise power based on identification with a manager.	Attitudes and behavior that are not in conflict with the ideals that underlie the identification.	Quick. Requires no expenditure of limited resources.	Restricted to influence attempts that are not in conflict with the ideals that underlie the identification.
Exercise power based on perceived dependence.	Wide range of behavior that can be monitored.	Quick. Can often succeed when other methods fail.	Repeated influence attempts encourage the other to gain power over the influencer.
Coercively exercise power based on perceived dependence.	Wide range of behavior that can be easily monitored.	Quick. Can often succeed when other methods fail.	Invites retaliation. Very risky.
Use persuasion.	Very wide range of attitudes and behavior.	Can produce internalized motivation that does not require monitoring. Requires no power or outlay of scarce material resources.	Can be very time-consuming. Requires other person to listen.
Combine these methods.	Depends on the exact combination.	Can be more potent and less risky than using a single method.	More costly than using a single method.

Continued

Exhibit   Methods of influence *Continued*

Indirect methods	What they can influence	Advantages	Drawbacks
Manipulate the other's environment by using any or all of the face-to-face methods.	Wide range of behavior and attitudes.	Can succeed when face-to-face methods fail.	Can be time-consuming. Is complex to implement; Is very risky, especially if used frequently.
Change the forces that continuously act on the individual: Formal organizational arrangements. Informal social arrangements. Technology. Resources available. Statement of organizational goals.	Wide range of behavior and attitudes on a continuous basis.	Has continuous influence, not just a one-shot effect. Can have a very powerful impact.	Often requires a considerable power outlay to achieve.

Face-to-face Influence

The chief advantage of influencing others directly by exercising any of the types of power is speed. If the power exists and the manager correctly understands the nature and strength of it, he can influence the other person with nothing more than a brief request or command:

· Jones thinks Smith feels obliged to him for past favors. Furthermore, Jones thinks that his request to speed up a project by two days probably falls within a zone that Smith would consider legitimate in light of his own definition of his obligation to Jones. So Jones simply calls Smith and makes his request. Smith pauses for only a second and says yes, he'll do it.

· Manager Johnson has some power based on perceived dependence over manager Baker. When Johnson tells Baker that he wants a report done in 24 hours, Baker grudgingly considers the costs of compliance, of noncompliance, and of complaining to higher authorities. He decides that doing the report is the least costly action and tells Johnson he will do it.

· Young Porter identifies strongly with Marquette, an older manager who is not his boss. Porter thinks Marquette is the epitome of a great manager and tries to model himself after him. When Marquette asks Porter to work on a special project "that could be very valuable in improving the company's ability to meet new competitive products,"

Porter agrees without hesitation, and works 15 hours per week above and beyond his normal hours to get the project done and done well.

When used to influence others, each of the four types of power has different advantages and drawbacks. For example, power based on perceived expertise or on identification with a manager can often be used to influence attitudes as well as someone's immediate behavior and thus can have a lasting impact. It is very difficult to influence attitudes by using power based on perceived dependence, but if it can be done, it usually has the advantage of being able to influence a much broader range of behavior than the other methods do. When exercising power based on perceived expertise, for example, one can only influence attitudes and behavior within that narrow zone defined by the "expertise."

The drawbacks associated with the use of power based on perceived dependence are particularly important to recognize. A person who feels dependent on a manager for rewards (or lack of punishments) might quickly agree to a request from the manager but then not follow through—especially if the manager cannot easily find out if the person has obeyed or not. Repeated influence attempts based on perceived dependence also seem to encourage the other person to try to gain some power to balance the manager's. And perhaps most important, using power based on perceived dependence in a coercive way is very risky. Coercion invites retaliation.

For instance, in the example in which Tim Babcock took such extreme steps to save the division he was assigned to "turn around," his development and use of power based on perceived dependence could have led to mass resignation and the collapse of the division. Babcock fully recognized this risk, however, and behaved as he did because he felt there was simply *no other way* that he could gain the very large amount of quick cooperation needed to save the division.

Effective managers will often draw on more than one form of power to influence someone, or they will combine power with persuasion. In general, they do so because a combination can be more potent and less risky than any single method, as the following description shows:

> One of the best managers we have in the company has lots of power based on one thing or another over most people. But he seldom if ever just tells or asks someone to do something. He almost always takes a few minutes to try to persuade them. The power he has over people generally induces them to listen carefully and certainly disposes them to be influenced. That, of course, makes the persuasion process go quickly and easily. And he never risks getting the other person mad or upset by making what that person thinks is an unfair request or command.

It is also common for managers not to coercively exercise power based on perceived dependence by itself, but to combine it with other methods to reduce the risk of retaliation. In this way, managers are able to have a large impact without leaving the bitter aftertaste of punishment alone.

Indirect Influence Methods

Effective managers also rely on two types of less direct methods to influence those on whom they are dependent. In the first way, they use any or all of the face-to-face methods to influence other people, who in turn have some specific impact on a desired person.

Product manager Stein needed plant manager Billings to "sign off" on a new product idea (Product X) which Billings thought was terrible. Stein decided that there was no way he could logically persuade Billings because Billings just would not listen to him. With time, Stein felt, he could have broken through that barrier. But he did not have that time. Stein also realized that Billings would never, just because of some deal or favor, sign off on a product he did not believe in. Stein also felt it not worth the risk of trying to force Billings to sign off, so here is what he did:

· On Monday, Stein got Reynolds, a person Billings respected, to send Billings two market research studies that were very favorable to Product X, with a note attached saying, "Have you seen this? I found them rather surprising. I am not sure if I entirely believe them, but still . . . . "
· On Tuesday, Stein got a representative of one of the company's biggest customers to mention casually to Billings on the phone that he had heard a rumor about Product X being introduced soon and was "glad to see you guys are on your toes as usual."
· On Wednesday, Stein had two industrial engineers stand about three feet away from Billings as they waited for a meeting to begin and talk about the favorable test results on Product X.
· On Thursday, Stein set up a meeting to talk about Product X with Billings and invited only people whom Billings liked or respected and who also felt favorably about Product X.
· On Friday, Stein went to see Billings and asked him if he was willing to sign off on Product X. He was.

This type of manipulation of the environments of others can influence both behavior and attitudes and can often succeed when other influence methods fail. But it has a number of serious drawbacks. It takes considerable time and energy, and it is quite risky. Many people think it is wrong to try to influence others in this way, even people who, without consciously recognizing it, use this technique themselves. If they think someone is trying, or has tried, to manipulate them, they may retaliate. Furthermore, people who gain the reputation of being manipulators seriously undermine their own capacities for developing power and for influencing others. Almost no one, for example, will want to identify with a manipulator. And virtually no one accepts, at face value, a manipulator's sincere attempts at persuasion. In extreme cases, a reputation as a manipulator can completely ruin a manager's career.

A second way in which managers indirectly influence others is by making permanent changes in an individual's or a group's environment. They change job descriptions, the formal systems that measure performance, the extrinsic incentives available, the tools, people, and other resources that the people or groups work with, the architecture, the norms or values of work groups, and so on. If the manager is successful in making the changes, and the changes have the desired effect on the individual or group, that effect will be sustained over time.

Effective managers recognize that changes in the forces that surround a person can have great impact on that person's behavior. Unlike many of the other influence methods, this one doesn't require a large expenditure of limited resources or effort on the part of the manager on an ongoing basis. Once such a change has been successfully made, it works independently of the manager.

This method of influence is used by all managers to some degree. Many, however, use it sparingly simply because they do not have the power to change the forces acting on the person they wish to influence. In many organizations, only the top managers have the power to change the formal measurement systems, the extrinsic incentives available, the architecture, and so on.

GENERATING AND USING POWER SUCCESSFULLY

Managers who are successful at acquiring considerable power and using it to manage their dependence on others tend to share a number of common characteristics:

1. They are sensitive to what others consider to be legitimate behavior in acquiring and using power. They recognize that the four types of power carry with them certain "obligations" regarding their acquisition and use. A person who gains a considerable amount of power based on his perceived expertise is generally expected to be an expert in certain areas. If it ever becomes publicly known that the person is clearly not an expert in those areas, such a person will probably be labeled a "fraud" and will not only lose his power but will suffer other reprimands too.

   A person with whom a number of people identify is expected to act like an ideal leader. If he clearly lets people down, he will not only lose that power, he will also suffer the righteous anger of his ex-followers. Many managers who have created or used power based on perceived dependence in ways that their employees have felt unfair, such as in requesting overtime work, have ended up with unions.

2. They have good intuitive understanding of the various types of power and methods of influence. They are sensitive to what types of power are easiest to develop with different types of people. They recognize, for example, that professionals tend to be more influenced by perceived expertise than by other forms of power. They also have a grasp of all the various methods of influence and what each can accomplish, at what costs, and with what risks. (See the *Exhibit.*) They are good at recognizing the specific conditions in any situation and then at selecting an influence method that is compatible with those conditions.

3. They tend to develop all the types of power, to some degree, and they use all the influence methods mentioned in the exhibit. Unlike managers who are not very good at influencing people, effective managers usually do not think that only some of the methods are useful or that only some of the methods are moral. They recognize that any of the methods, used under the right circumstances, can help contribute to organizational effectiveness with few dysfunctional consequences. At the same time, they generally try to avoid those methods that are more risky than others and those that may have dysfunctional consequences. For example, they manipulate the environment of others only when absolutely necessary.

4. They establish career goals and seek out managerial positions that allow them to successfully develop and use power. They look for jobs, for example, that use their backgrounds and skills to control or manage some critically important problem or environmental contingency that an organization faces. They recognize that success in that type of job makes others dependent on them and increases their own perceived expertise. They also seek jobs that do not demand a type or a volume of power that is inconsistent with their own skills.

5. They use all of their resources, formal authority, and power to develop still more power. To borrow Edward Banfield's metaphor, they actually look for ways to "invest" their power where they might secure a high positive return.[6] For example, by asking a person to do him two important favors, a manager might be able to finish his construction program one day ahead of schedule. That request may cost him most of the obligation-based power he has over that person, but in return he may significantly increase his perceived expertise as a manager of construction projects in the eyes of everyone in his organization.

    Just as in investing money, there is always some risk involved in using power this way; it is possible to get a zero return for a sizable investment, even for the most powerful manager. Effective managers do not try to avoid risks. Instead, they look for prudent risks, just as they do when investing capital.

6. Effective managers engage in power-oriented behavior in ways that are tempered by maturity and self-control.[7] They seldom, if ever, develop and use power in impulsive ways or for their own aggrandizement.

7. Finally, they also recognize and accept as legitimate that, in using these methods, they clearly influence other people's behavior and lives. Unlike many less effective managers, they are reasonably comfortable in using power to influence people. They recognize, often only intuitively, what this article is all about—that their attempts to establish power and use it are an absolutely necessary part of the successful fulfillment of their difficult managerial role.

NOTES

[1]Charles A. Reich, *The Greening of America: How the Youth Revolution Is Trying to Make America Liveable* (New York: Random House, 1970).

[2]See Leonard R. Sayles, *Managerial Behavior: Administration in Complex Organization* (New York: McGraw-Hill, 1964) as well as Rosemary Stewart, *Managers and Their Jobs* (London: MacMillan, 1967) and *Contrasts in Management* (London: McGraw-Hill, 1976).

[3]I am talking about the type of inexplicable differences that Henry Mintzberg has found; see his article "The Manager's Job: Folklore and Fact," HBR July-August 1975, p. 49.

[4]These categories closely resemble the five developed by John R. P. French and Bertram Raven; see "The Base of Social Power" in *Group Dynamics: Research and Theory,* Dorwin Cartwright and Alvin Zander, eds. (New York: Harper & Row, 1968), Chapter 20. Three of the categories are similar to the types of "authority"-based power described by Max Weber in *The Theory of Social and Economic Organization* (New York: Free Press, 1947).

[5]For an excellent discussion of this method, see Richard E. Neustadt, *Presidential Power* (New York: John Wiley, 1960).

[6]See Edward C. Banfield, *Political Influence* (New York: Free Press, 1965), Chapter 11.

[7]See David C. McClelland and David H. Burnham, "Power Is the Great Motivator," HBR March-April 1976, p. 100.

Power to the Powerless: Locus of Control and the Use of Power

BARRY E. GOODSTADT
LARRY A. HJELLE

What happens when the powerless are given power? This question has captured the attention of a number of social and behavioral scholars in recent years. Fanon (1965), in the *Wretched of the Earth,* noted that "the exploited man sees that his liberation implies the use of all means, and that of force, first and foremost [p. 48]." In a subsequent commentary on Fanon's book, Raven and Kruglanski (1970) suggested that the successful use of coercive power may serve to enhance the self-esteem of the influencing agent. Thus, the use of coercive power may not only liberate the powerless, but may also elevate their sense of worth and dignity.

There is perhaps another reason why the powerless may be inclined toward the use of coercive power. Namely, the use of coercive power may be mediated by the individual's personal beliefs concerning his effectiveness and/or competency as a source of influence. Assuming that an individual has available a range of means to influence others, he may employ coercion when he perceives that less assertive forms of influence are ineffective. Consistent with this line of reasoning is recent theorizing by Staub (1971) who suggested that a high degree of confidence in one's

"Power to the Powerless: Locus of Control and the Use of Power" by Barry E. Goodstadt and Larry A. Hjelle, *Journal of Personality and Social Psychology,* 1973, Vol. 27, No. 2, 190-196. Copyright © 1973 by the American Psychological Association, Inc. Reprinted by permission of the American Psychological Association, Inc.

abilities may be associated with a low need to influence others by aggressive means.

Support for these notions can be found in several studies (Goodstadt & Kipnis, 1970; Kipnis & Consentino, 1969) where coercive forms of influence were employed by a powerholder who encountered resistance from the target of influence, particularly where such resistance was attributed to a lack of motivation. Evidently, subjects presumed that the target's resistance was not amenable to gentler forms of influence. It was also found (Goodstadt & Kipnis, 1970; Kipnis & Lane, 1962) that persons who lacked confidence in their ability to effectively influence the target were more likely to employ coercive forms of influence than individuals who expressed confidence in their ability to influence. These confident individuals were, in turn, more apt to use personal means of persuasion (e.g., giving encouragement, praise, admonishment).

Who are the so-called powerless individuals who possess feelings of incompetency concerning their ability to effectively influence others? One psychological perspective is offered by Seeman (1963) who has characterized the locus of control construct in terms of a continuum of powerlessness. Internal-external locus of control as a dimension of personality refers to one's generalized expectancies regarding behavior-reinforcement contingencies (Lefcourt, 1966; Rotter, 1966; Rotter, Seeman, & Liverant, 1962). According to social learning theory, internally controlled persons believe that they are capable of controlling the occurrence of reinforcements, while externally controlled persons believe that such reinforcements are determined by outside forces such as luck or the power of others. Thus, within Seeman's framework, externally and internally controlled persons are seen as being high and low in "powerlessness," respectively. In essence, externals are the "psychologically powerless."

The manner by which internal and external individuals attempt to exercise power in dealing with others has been all but ignored in research to date. In order to examine this question, the present study employed a recently developed experimental paradigm (Goodstadt & Kipnis, 1970; Kipnis, 1972; Kipnis & Vanderveer, 1971) in which subjects were given a range of delegated powers with which they were instructed to supervise a group of fictitious subordinates. The delegated powers reflect French and Raven's (1959) categories of reward power, coercive power, and expert power. Based on the reasoning outlined above, it was expected that externally controlled (high-powerless) subjects would use more coercive powers (e.g., threatening a worker with pay deductions, firing) and fewer personal persuasive powers (e.g., giving encouragement, admonishing a worker, setting new standards) than would internally controlled (low-powerless) subjects when placed in a supervisory role setting. It might be noted that our category of personal persuasive power is almost identical to what Raven and Kruglanski (1970) have termed informational influence or persuasion.

An additional finding reported by Goodstadt and Kipnis (1970) was that problems of discipline evoked subjects' use of coercive powers, while problems of ineptness elicited subjects' use of expert powers (e.g., giving instructions). By employing a slight variation of these problem conditions, the authors attempted to replicate these findings.

METHOD
Subjects

Forty male students enrolled in introductory psychology classes at the State University College at Brockport participated in the experiment. Participation in experiments was a course requirement. Subjects were preselected on the basis of their scores on the Rotter Locus of Control Scale (Rotter, 1966). Twenty externally controlled subjects were selected from the top quartile (scores of 16 or above) of the distribution of scores obtained from a mass-testing program, while 20 internally controlled subjects were selected from the bottom quartile (scores of 8 or less).

Procedure

Subjects were contacted by telephone and were asked to serve as supervisors of three high school students in an industrial simulation experiment. Subjects reported individually to the laboratory and the experimenter was blind as to their scores on the internal-external (I-E) scale. Upon arrival, subjects were informed that they would not meet their workers, who were situated in an adjoining room. Subjects were informed that the workers were to be given 100 extra credit points in one of their courses for participating in the experiment. In fact, the three workers were fictitious and their job performance was preprogrammed.

In order to enhance involvement in the experiment, subjects were further told that previous studies had shown that satisfactory performance as a supervisor in this situation was indicative of success in real-life supervisory settings. Satisfactory performance was defined for subjects in terms of maintaining the productive level of the workers at or above specified standards.

Tasks

The fictitious workers were ostensibly engaged in two tasks: a coding task and a crossing-out task. All workers began on the coding task which was actually a digit-symbol substitution operation. The crossing-out task served as a possible alternative duty for the workers. The latter consisted of pages of random letters from which the workers were to cross out all Cs, Os, and Xs. Subjects were informed that the crossing-out task resulted in less money for the company and was also more boring for the workers.

At the end of each 3-minute work period, preprogrammed output from the workers was brought to the subject by the experimenter. The work output was identified by the worker's number (i.e., 1, 2, or 3). The subject's task was to tally the work output and record it on a summary sheet. Standard production for the coding task was 85 coded letters per 3-minute period, while the standard for the crossing-out task was 65 crossed out letters per work period. The experimental session consisted of six work periods, although subjects were not informed of this in advance.

In order to speak with the workers, subjects were provided with a one-way communication device consisting of a light signal and a microphone. All of the subjects' communications with each worker were recorded on tape. The workers could communicate with the subject only by means of written memos which were also preprogrammed.

Corrective Powers

During tape-recorded instructions, subjects were informed that they had a number of powers at their disposal. These delegated powers were posted on a sign in front of the subject and consisted of the following:

1. *Promise of extra-credit-point increase.* Supervisors could promise a 10-extra-credit-point increase per work period.
2. *Extra-credit-point increase.* A 10-extra-credit-point increase might actually be awarded to a worker for any work period.
3. *Threat of extra-credit-point deduction.* Supervisors could threaten a worker with the loss of 10 extra credit points in any given work period.
4. *Extra-credit-point deduction.* Ten extra credit points per work period might actually be taken away from the worker.
5. *Instruction.* Supervisors were provided with hints they might use for instructing the workers.
6. *Warning of transfer.* The supervisor could warn a worker that he was considering his transfer to the more boring crossing-out task.
7. *Transfer.* The supervisor was permitted to transfer a worker to the crossing-out task. When this occurred, the preprogrammed output from the crossing-out task was substituted for the output from the coding task.
8. *Warning of firing.* The supervisor could indicate to the worker that he was considering firing him.
9. *Firing of worker.* A worker could be fired by the supervisor. Under such circumstances the preprogrammed output from the fired worker was discontinued.

A previous study by Goodstadt and Kipnis (1970) revealed that some subjects elaborated upon their delegated powers and relied upon more informal personal persuasive powers. These powers consisted of the following:

10. *Encouragement or praise.* Workers were encouraged to increase production or were praised for their good work.
11. *Admonishment.* Workers were bawled out for their inadequate performance.

12.   *Set new standards.* New standards of performance were set for the workers.

Problem Conditions

The overall design of the experiment was a 2 × 2 factorial with two levels of locus of control (internals versus externals) and two kinds of problems (ineptness versus poor attitude).

The problem manipulation was varied as a function of the reason given for the inadequate performance of one of the workers (Worker 2). The output of this problem worker was preprogrammed to be 20-30 units below company standards for each work period. In all conditions Workers 1 and 3 exceeded company standards and tended to improve over trials, while the output of Worker 2 did not increase over trials.

Half of the subjects were assigned to the inept-problem condition and received a series of notes ostensibly coming from Worker 2. These notes were sent along with the work output and attributed poor performance to the worker's inability to perform the task. There were five such notes which were sent to the subject beginning with the second work period and continuing through the sixth. The notes read as follows: "I don't get this at all," "I don't understand how it can be done any faster," "There must be something peculiar about this task because I just don't get the hang of it," "The other two fellows seem to be doing all right. Something must be keeping me from doing as well," "I should be able to do this sort of thing, but I can't seem to do any better," "What's the use of trying, I can't do any better anyway."

In the poor-attitude condition, the notes from the problem worker conveyed that the poor performance was due to a poor attitude toward the job. These notes read as follows: "You must be putting me on. How can you expect anyone with intelligence to do this ridiculous job." "This job has to be the most boring I have ever done," "This stuff is ridiculous," "Why should I keep trying, I am bored by the whole thing," "Anybody could do this if they really wanted to. I don't want to." To establish that the problem worker in this condition was capable of adequate performance, his output met company standards during the first period. The output then dropped drastically in Trial 2 to the same level as the problem worker in the inept condition. During Trials 2-6 the performance of the problem worker in the inept and poor-attitude conditions was identical.

Postexperimental Questionnaire

At the conclusion of the experimental session subjects were asked to evaluate each of the three workers on four rating scales: ability, overall worth to the company, willingness to rehire for a second experiment, and recommendation for a promotion to supervisor. Possible scores on each of these scales ranged from 1, a very negative evaluation, to 11, a very positive evaluation.

Coding of Responses

The tape recorded verbal communications made by subjects to their workers were independently coded into categories by the authors, both of whom were blind as to the experimental conditions. In a number of instances, subjects relied on more than one power in a particular communication. An illustration of such multiple coding is as follows: "I will give you a credit point increase if you increase your production. If you do not, I will be forced to terminate you." This comment was coded: "promise of reward" and "threat of firing." The resultant interjudge agreement including multiple codings was 91.2%. In those cases where disagreement occurred, discussion was held and agreement was reached.

Subject Attrition and Suspiciousness

In addition to the 40 subjects participating in the study, 6 others participated, but were eliminated for various reasons. Two subjects were highly suspicious and stated that they did not believe there were any workers in the adjoining room. Two other subjects were eliminated because they misunderstood the directions. Finally, 2 subjects were dropped because of procedural errors occurring during the experimental session (e.g., sending the wrong notes or output).

RESULTS

Each subject's use of personal powers and various types of delegated power in dealing with the problem worker served as dependent measures in a series of 2×2 analyses of variance, with locus of control and type of problem serving as the factors. Because of differences in the problem worker's output during the first work period of the poor-attitude and inept problem conditions, all analyses were carried out only on data collected during Work Periods 2-6.

The average use of personal powers, the total use of the formally delegated powers, and the separate indexes of the different varieties of delegated power are presented as a function of experimental conditions in Table 1. These latter indexes were developed following French and Raven's (1959) categories of coercive, reward, and expert power. The coercive-power index consisted of the summation of each subject's use of threat of extra-credit-point deduction, actual deduction, threat of transfer, actual transfer, threat of firing, or actual firing. The reward-power index combined each subject's use of promise or actual delivery of a reward of extra credit points. Finally, the expert-power index simply consisted of the number of times each subject gave the problem worker instructions or hints.

On the basis of previous work, it was hypothesized that internally controlled subjects would rely more on personal persuasive powers than

Table 1   **Summary of Mean Use of Corrective Powers Directed at the Problem Worker over Periods 2-6**

Power	Internally controlled subjects		Externally controlled subjects	
	Poor attitude	Ineptness	Poor attitude	Ineptness
Reward	.40	.80	.50	.40
Coercive	2.60	2.10	4.00	2.60
Instruction	.40	1.20	.20	1.10
Total delegated powers	3.30	4.10	4.70	4.10
Personal	2.30	2.00	1.60	.70
Total delegated and personal powers	5.70	6.10	6.30	4.80

Note. The term "delegated powers" refers to those powers which were listed on a sign in front of the subjects. $n = 10$ in each condition.

would externally controlled subjects. In order to test this prediction, each subject's use of personal powers (i.e., giving encouragement, praise, admonishment, setting new standards) was analyzed. As predicted, it was found that internals used significantly more personal persuasive powers than externals ($F = 4.17$, $df = 1/36$, $p < .05$).

An analysis of the total use of formalized delegated powers did not reveal any differences between internals and externals. Turning to the specific forms of delegated power, it was predicted that externally controlled persons would be more likely to rely on coercive power than would internally controlled individuals. The analysis of the coercive-power index scores indicated that, as expected, externals did make significantly more use of punishing powers than did internals ($F = 4.80$, $df = 1/36$, $p < .05$).

Further analyses of the reward-power and expert-power indexes revealed no significant differences between externals and internals. Thus, locus of control was not predictive of subjects' reliance on rewarding powers or the use of instruction.

Type of Problem

As part of an attempt to replicate previous findings pertaining to the use of power in response to workers who exhibited either problems of ineptness or poor attitudes, subjects' use of coercive and expert power was examined across problem conditions. In an earlier study (Goodstadt & Kipnis, 1970), it had been shown that problems of ineptness evoked the subject's use of expert powers, while a poor-attitude problem made it more likely that subjects would use coercive powers. In the present study, an analysis of the coercive-power index revealed that subjects in the poor-attitude condition relied significantly more on coercive powers than did subjects in the inept condition ($F = 4.80$, $df = 1/36$, $p < .05$). The

Table 2   **Mean Evaluative Ratings of the Problem Worker in the Inept and Poor-Attitude Problem Conditions**

Item	Inept condition	Poor-attitude condition
Ability	3.95	5.90
Worth to the company	3.25	2.40
Willingness to rehire	3.10	2.55
Willingness to promote to supervisor	3.40	2.00

Note. Higher scores indicate more favorable evaluation. n = 20 in each condition.

use of expert powers was also found to be a function of the type of problem subjects faced. Subjects in the inept condition were significantly more likely to give the problem worker instruction than were subjects in the poor-attitude condition ($F = 11.55$, $df = 1/36$, $p < .01$). In total, these findings replicate differences between problem conditions previously reported by Goodstadt and Kipnis.

Postexperimental Ratings of Workers

The four 11-point ratings of each worker consisted of evaluations of the worker's ability, his worth to the company, the subject's willingness to rehire him, and the subject's recommendation that the worker be promoted to a supervisor. Mean postexperimental ratings of the problem worker are shown in Table 2. It was found that subjects in the poor-attitude condition rated the problem worker as having significantly more ability than did subjects in the inept condition ($t = 3.02$, $df = 38$, $p < .005$, one-tailed test). This finding was quite consistent with our problem manipulation insofar as the poor-attitude problem worker performed adequately during the first work period, while the inept problem worker did not.

In view of the fact that the problem worker in the poor-attitude condition was met with coercive power, it was expected that the poor-attitude problem worker would be evaluated less favorably than problem workers in the inept condition. Subjects in the inept condition and poor-attitude problem conditions did not differ in their ratings of the problem worker on the items pertaining to the worker's worth to the company and their willingness to rehire the worker, although the means were in the expected direction. When subjects were asked to give their recommendation that the worker be promoted to supervisor, subjects in the poor-attitude condition reported being significantly less willing to recommend promotion for the problem worker than were subjects in the inept condition ($t = 1.78$, $df = 38$, $p < .05$, one-tailed test). In general, it seems that problem workers exhibiting a poor attitude were seen as having more ability, but subjects were less willing to give them favorable ratings in terms of recommending promotions.

DISCUSSION

The central question raised in this experiment concerned what happens when the psychologically powerless are given power. The answer appears to be that the psychologically powerless or externally controlled individual, when faced with the problem of influencing a resistant other, was less likely to rely upon personal persuasion and more likely to use coercive power than the internally controlled individual.

These findings can be examined in light of the role that the subject must play in his position as supervisor. In order to perform satisfactorily, the subject must influence a problem worker who is exhibiting substandard production. From the subject's perspective, how might he select one sort of power from the range of powers at his disposal? Raven and Kruglanski (1970) have suggested that the powerholder anticipates the possible effectiveness of each of his bases of power and avoids using those which he believes are ineffective. Thus, it is quite conceivable that the subjects in this study based their selection of powers on the likelihood that their attempts at influence would be successful. When subjects had the expectancy that they would be successful in influencing the problem worker, they relied on milder forms of influence such as personal persuasion. Conversely, when subjects believed that they would be unable to influence the worker, they used the harshest variety of power—coercive power.

As has been pointed out earlier, an individual's relative belief in the internal or external control of reinforcement is an important determinant of his expectancy of successful influence. Externally controlled persons have the expectancy that they cannot influence people or events, and therefore the externally controlled subjects in this study probably had little expectancy for successful influence in their role as supervisor. Internally controlled persons, however, do tend to believe that they have the power to influence the events and people around them. Hence, it seems likely that internal subjects had the expectation that they could successfully influence the problem worker.

Given such differential expectancies, it seems plausible that internals' positive expectations of successful influence led them to rely on personal persuasion or what Raven and Kruglanski (1970) have called "informational influence." Conversely, the use of more coercive power by externally controlled subjects is consistent with their minimal expectancies of successful influence.

The question might now be raised as to how these findings dovetail with the research literature pertaining to locus of control. By and large, research concerning locus of control and social influence has focused on the susceptibility of the recipient of influence and his locus of control (e.g., Hjelle, 1970; Ritchie & Phares, 1969). Thus, the present investigation represents a departure from previous work in the area. To our knowledge there has been only one study to date in which internally or externally controlled influencing agents delivered a persuasive communication (Phares, 1965). The findings indicated that internals were more persuasive than externals. If our expectancy notions are indeed correct, this finding by Phares might suggest that a self-fulfilling prophecy is operational in social influence settings. That is, if internals have the expectancy that they can successfully influence others, they are indeed influential. In contrast, externals may have the expectancy that they cannot influence others and are, thus, less persuasive. Moreover, since internals are more likely to employ persuasive powers as evidenced in this study, they may be more accomplished in persuasive settings.

A second major purpose of this study was to replicate previous results pertaining to the different problem conditions. It has been shown that problems of ineptness evoked expert powers from the leader, while motivational problems such as poor attitudes resulted in a leader's reliance on coercive powers. Similar results were obtained in the present study, thus confirming these earlier findings.

Our expectancy explanation seems also to apply to findings of problem differences. Insofar as the problem worker in the poor-attitude condition appears to reject the job, it might appear easier from the subject's point of view to influence an inept worker than a worker with a poor attitude. In general, most persons believe that it is easier to influence the behavior of individuals with learning deficits rather than persons whose behavior is determined by an "unwillingness to perform." Thus, when the subject has little expectancy of influencing a worker by virtue of his poor attitudes, the subject tends to employ coercive power. When the problem worker was simply unable to carry out the task, he appears somewhat more amenable to influence and thus, the response by the subject takes the form of a gentler variety of power—instruction.

Evaluative ratings of these problem workers were also collected. As expected, subjects perceived the poor-attitude problem worker as having more ability than the inept problem worker; however, they were less willing to recommend his promotion. This result is consistent with the findings of Jones and deCharms (1957) who reported that a person with little motivation is rated more negatively than a person with little ability.

Finally, some wider societal implications might be drawn from our findings that externally controlled or psychologically powerless individuals are more likely to employ coercive power. Given a society of rapidly expanding technology and bureaucracy, it has been noted (Anonymous, 1972b) that an increasing number of individuals come to believe that they have little control over their own existence. In such a climate, dire consequences for society might result should individuals come to believe that they have no expectations for influencing the social institutions and governments that affect their lives. That is, attempted influence by such individuals may take the form of coercive power. Illustrations come readily to mind, particularly that of the peace protesters of a few years ago. At the outset, peace demonstrators were quite orderly and calm. However, when met with resistance from the government, some of these same demonstrators resorted to more violent means of persuasion, such as the recent threats to place a time bomb in the new Federal Bureau of Investigation building under construction in Washington, D.C. (Anonymous, 1972a). Thus, as Fanon (1965) suggested, perhaps the powerless do come to rely on force, first and foremost.

REFERENCES

Anonymous. Bombing the banks. *Time,* January 17, 1972, 99, 18. (a)

Anonymous. Malaise and My Lai. *Time,* January 10, 1972, 99, 10. (b)

Fanon, F. *The wretched of the earth.* New York: Grove Press, 1965.

French, J. R. P., Jr., & Raven, B. H. The bases of social power. In D. Cartwright (Ed.), *Studies in social power.* Ann Arbor: University of Michigan, 1959.

Goodstadt, B., & Kipnis, D. Situational influences on the use of power. *Journal of Applied Psychology,* 1970, 54, 201-207.

Hjelle, L. A. Susceptibility to attitude change as a function of internal-external control. *Psychological Record,* 1970, 20, 305-310.

Jones, E. E., & DeCharms, R. Changes in social perception as a function of the personal relevance of behavior. *Sociometry,* 1957, 20, 75-85.

Kipnis, D. Does power corrupt? *Journal of Personality and Social Psychology,* 1972, 24, 33-41.

Kipnis, D., & Consentino, J. Use of leadership powers in industry. *Journal of Applied Psychology,* 1969, 53, 460-466.

Kipnis, D., & Lane, W. Self-confidence and leadership. *Journal of Applied Psychology,* 1962, 46, 291-295.

Kipnis, D., & Vanderveer, R. Ingratiation and the use of power. *Journal of Personality and Social Psychology,* 1971, 17, 280-286.

Lefcourt, H. M. Internal versus external control of reinforcement: A review. *Psychological Bulletin,* 1966, 65, 206-220.

Phares, E. J. Internal-external control as a determinant of amount of social influence exerted. *Journal of Personality and Social Psychology,* 1965, 2, 642-647.

Raven, B. H., & Kruglanski, A. W. Conflict and power. In P. Swingle (Ed.), *The structure of conflict.* New York: Academic Press, 1970.

Ritchie, E., & Phares, E. J. Attitude change as a function of internal control and communicator status. *Journal of Personality,* 1969, 37, 429-443.

Rotter, J. B. Generalized expectancies for internal versus external control of reinforcement. *Psychological Monographs,* 1966, 80 (1, Whole No. 609).

Rotter, J. B., Seeman, M., & Liverant, S. Internal versus external control of reinforcement: A major variable in behavior theory. In N. F. Washburne (Ed.), *Decisions, values, and groups.* Vol. 2. London: Pergamon Press, 1962.

Seeman, M. Alienation and social learning in a reformatory. *American Journal of Sociology,* 1963, 69, 270-284.

Staub, E. The learning and unlearning of aggression: The role of anxiety, empathy, efficacy, and prosocial values. In J. L. Singer (Ed.), *The control of aggression and violence.* New York: Academic Press, 1971.

On the Folly of Rewarding A, While Hoping for B

STEVEN KERR

Whether dealing with monkeys, rats, or human beings, it is hardly controversial to state that most organisms seek information concerning what activities are rewarded, and then seek to do (or at least pretend to do) those things, often to the virtual exclusion of activities not rewarded. The extent to which this occurs of course will depend on the perceived attractiveness of the rewards offered, but neither operant nor expectancy theorists would quarrel with the essence of this notion.

Nevertheless, numerous examples exist of reward systems that are fouled up in that behaviors which are rewarded are those which the rewarder is trying to *discourage*, while the behavior he desires is not being rewarded at all.

In an effort to understand and explain this phenomenon, this paper presents examples from society, from organizations in general, and from profit making firms in particular. Data from a manufacturing company and information from an insurance firm are examined to demonstrate the consequences of such reward systems for the organizations involved, and possible reasons why such reward systems continue to exist are considered.

SOCIETAL EXAMPLES
Politics

Official goals are "purposely vague and general and do not indicate . . . the host of decisions that must be made among alternative ways of achieving official goals and the priority of multiple goals . . ." (8, p. 66). They usually may be relied on to offend absolutely no one, and in this sense can be considered high acceptance, low quality goals. An example might be "build better schools." Operative goals are higher in quality but lower in acceptance, since they specify where the money will come from, what alternative goals will be ignored, etc.

The American citizenry supposedly wants its candidates for public office to set forth operative goals, making their proposed programs "perfectly clear," specifying sources and uses of funds, etc. However, since operative goals are lower in acceptance, and since aspirants to public office need acceptance (from at least 50.1 percent of the people), most politicians prefer to speak only of official goals, at least until after the election. They of course would agree to speak at the operative level if "punished" for not doing so. The electorate could do this by refusing to support candidates who do not speak at the operative level.

Instead, however, the American voter typically punishes (withholds support from) candidates who frankly discuss where the money will come from, rewards politicians who speak only of official goals, but hopes that candidates (despite the reward system) will discuss the issues operatively. It is academic whether it was moral for Nixon, for example, to refuse to discuss his 1968 "secret plan" to end the Vietnam war, his 1972 operative goals concerning the lifting of price controls, the reshuffling of his cabinet, etc. The point is that the reward system made such refusal rational.

It seems worth mentioning that no manuscript can adequately define what is "moral" and what is not. However, examination of costs and benefits, combined with knowledge of what motivates a particular individual, often will suffice to determine what for him is "rational."[1] If the reward system is so designed that it is irrational to be moral, this does not necessarily mean that immorality will result. But is this not asking for trouble?

War

If some oversimplification may be permitted, let it be assumed that the primary goal of the organization (Pentagon, Luftwaffe, or whatever) is to win. Let it be assumed further that the primary goal of most individuals on the front lines is to get home alive. Then there appears to be an important conflict in goals—personally rational behavior by those at the bottom will endanger goal attainment by those at the top.

But not necessarily! It depends on how the reward system is set up. The Vietnam war was indeed a study of disobedience and rebellion, with terms such as "fragging" (killing one's own commanding officer) and "search and evade" becoming part of the military vocabulary. The difference in subordinates' acceptance of authority between World War II and Vietnam is reported to be considerable, and veterans of the Second World War often have been quoted as being outraged at the mutinous actions of many American soldiers in Vietnam.

Consider, however, some critical differences in the reward system in use during the two conflicts. What did the GI in World War II want? To go home. And when did he get to go home? When the war was won! If he disobeyed the orders to clean out the trenches and take the hills, the war would not be won and he would not go home. Furthermore, what were his chances of attaining his goal (getting home alive) if he obeyed the orders compared to his chances if he did not? What is being suggested is that the rational soldier in World War II, *whether patriotic or not*, probably found it expedient to obey.

Consider the reward system in use in Vietnam. What did the man at the bottom want? To go home. And when did he get to go home? When his tour of duty was over! This was the case *whether or not* the war was won. Furthermore, concerning the relative chance of getting home alive by obeying orders compared to the chance if they were disobeyed, it is worth noting that a mutineer in Vietnam was far more likely to be assigned rest and rehabilitation (on the assumption that fatigue was the cause) than he was to suffer any negative consequence.

In his description of the "zone of indifference," Barnard stated that "a person can and will accept a communication as authoritative only when . . . at the time of his decision, he believes it to be compatible with his personal interests as a whole" (1, p. 165). In light of the reward system used in Vietnam, would it not have been personally irrational for some orders to have been obeyed? Was not the military implementing a system which *rewarded* disobedience, while *hoping* that soldiers (despite the reward system) would obey orders?

Medicine

Theoretically, a physician can make either of two types of error, and intuitively one seems as bad as the other. A doctor can pronounce a patient sick when he is actually well, thus causing him needless anxiety and expense, curtailment of enjoyable foods and activities, and even physical danger by subjecting him to needless medication and surgery. Alternately, a doctor can label a sick person well, and thus avoid treating what may be a serious, even fatal ailment. It might be natural to conclude that physicians seek to minimize both types of error.

Such a conclusion would be wrong.[2] It is estimated that numerous Americans are presently afflicted with iatrogenic (physician *caused*) illnesses (9). This occurs when the doctor is approached by someone complaining of a few stray symptoms. The doctor classifies and organizes these symptoms, gives them a name, and obligingly tells the patient that further symptoms may be expected. This information often acts as a self-fulfilling prophecy, with the result that from that day on the patient for all practical purposes is sick.

Why does this happen? Why are physicians so reluctant to sustain a type 2 error (pronouncing a sick person well) that they will tolerate many type 1 errors? Again, a look at the reward system is needed. The punishments for a type 2 error are real: guilt, embarrassment, and the threat of lawsuit and scandal. On the other hand, a type 1 error (labeling a well person sick) "is sometimes seen as sound clinical practice, indicating a healthy conservative approach to medicine" (9, p. 69). Type 1 errors also are likely to generate increased income and a stream of steady customers who, being well in a limited physiological sense, will not embarrass the doctor by dying abruptly.

Fellow physicians and the general public therefore are really *rewarding* type 1 errors and at the same time *hoping* fervently that doctors will try not to make them.

GENERAL ORGANIZATIONAL EXAMPLES
Rehabilitation Centers and Orphanages

In terms of the prime beneficiary classification (2, p. 42) organizations such as these are supposed to exist for the "public-in-contact," that is, clients. The orphanage therefore theoretically is interested in placing as many children as possible in good homes. However, often orphanages surround themselves with so many rules concerning adoption that it is nearly impossible to pry a child out of the place. Orphanages may deny adoption unless the applicants are a married couple, both of the same religion as the child, without history of emotional or vocational instability, with a specified minimum income and a private room for the child, etc.

If the primary goal is to place children in good homes, then the rules ought to constitute means toward that goal. Goal displacement results when these "means become ends-in-themselves that displace the original goals" (2, p. 229).

To some extent these rules are required by law. But the influence of the reward system on the orphanage's management should not be ignored. Consider, for example, that the:

1. Number of children enrolled often is the most important determinant of the size of the allocated budget.
2. Number of children under the director's care also will affect the size of his staff.
3. Total organizational size will determine largely the director's prestige at the annual conventions, in the community, etc.

Therefore, to the extent that staff size, total budget, and personal prestige are valued by the orphanage's executive personnel, it becomes rational for them to make it difficult for children to be adopted. After all, who wants to be the director of the smallest orphanage in the state?

If the reward system errs in the opposite direction, paying off only for placements, extensive goal displacement again is likely to result. A common example of vocational rehabilitation in many states, for example, consists of placing someone in a job for which he has little interest and few qualifications, for two months or so, and then "rehabilitating" him again in another position. Such behavior is quite consistent with the prevailing reward system, which pays off for the number of individuals placed in any position for 60 days or more. Rehabilitation counselors also confess to competing with one another to place relatively skilled clients, sometimes ignoring persons with few skills who would be harder to place. Extensively disabled clients find that counselors often prefer to work with those whose disabilities are less severe.[3]

Universities

Society *hopes* that teachers will not neglect their teaching responsibilities but *rewards* them almost entirely for research and publications. This is most true at the large and prestigious universities. Cliches such as "good research and good teaching go together" notwithstanding, professors often find that they must choose between teaching and research oriented activities when allocating their time. Rewards for good teaching usually are limited to outstanding teacher awards, which are given to only a small percentage of good teachers and which usually bestow little money and fleeting prestige. Punishments for poor teaching also are rare.

Rewards for research and publications, on the other hand, and punishment for failure to accomplish these, are commonly administered by universities at which teachers are employed. Furthermore, publication oriented resumés usually will be well received at other universities, whereas teaching credentials, harder to document and quantify, are much less transferable. Consequently it is rational for university teachers to concentrate on research, even if to the detriment of teaching and at the expense of their students.

By the same token, it is rational for students to act based upon the goal displacement which has occurred within universities concerning what they are rewarded for. If it is assumed that a primary goal of a university is to transfer knowledge from teacher to student, then grades become identifiable as a means toward that goal, serving as motivational, control, and feedback devices to expedite the knowledge transfer. Instead, however, the grades themselves have become much more important for entrance to graduate school, successful employment, tuition refunds, parental respect, etc., than the knowledge or lack of knowledge they are supposed to signify.

It therefore should come as no surprise that information has surfaced in recent years concerning fraternity files for examinations, term paper writing services, organized cheating at the service academies, and the like. Such activities constitute a personally rational response to a reward system which pays off for grades rather than knowledge.

BUSINESS RELATED EXAMPLES
Ecology

Assume that the president of XYZ Corporation is confronted with the following alternatives:

1. Spend $11 million for antipollution equipment to keep from poisoning fish in the river adjacent to the plant; or
2. Do nothing, in violation of the law, and assume a one in ten chance of being caught, with a resultant $1 million fine plus the necessity of buying the equipment.

Under this not unrealistic set of choices it requires no linear program to determine that XYZ Corporation can maximize its probabilities by flouting the law. Add the fact that XYZ's president is probably being rewarded (by creditors, stockholders, and other salient parts of his task environment) according to criteria totally unrelated to the number of fish poisoned, and his probable course of action becomes clear.

Evaluation of Training

It is axiomatic that those who care about a firm's well-being should insist that the organization get fair value for its expenditures. Yet it is commonly known that firms seldom bother to evaluate a new GRID, MBO, job enrichment program, or whatever, to see if the company is getting its money's worth. Why? Certainly it is not because people have not pointed out that this situation exists; numerous practitioner oriented articles are written each year to just this point.

The individuals (whether in personnel, manpower planning, or whatever) who normally would be responsible for conducting such evaluations are the same ones often charged with introducing the change effort in the first place. Having convinced top management to spend the money, they usually are quite animated afterwards in collecting rigorous vignettes and anecdotes about how successful the program was. The last thing many desire is a formal, systematic, and revealing evaluation. Although members of top management may actually *hope* for such systematic evaluation, their reward systems continue to *reward* ignorance in this area. And if the personnel department abdicates its responsibility, who is to step into the breach? The change agent himself? Hardly! He is likely to be too busy collecting anecdoctal "evidence" of his own, for use with his next client.

Miscellaneous

Many additional examples could be cited of systems which in fact are rewarding behaviors other than those supposedly desired by the rewarder. A few of these are described briefly below.

Most coaches disdain to discuss individual accomplishments, preferring to speak of teamwork, proper attitude, and a one-for-all spirit. Usually, however, rewards are distributed according to individual performance. The college basketball player who feeds his teammates instead of shooting will not compile impressive scoring statistics and is less likely to be drafted by the pros. The ballplayer who hits to right field to advance the runners will win neither the batting nor home run titles, and will be offered smaller raises. It therefore is rational for players to think of themselves first, and the team second.

In business organizations where rewards are dispensed for unit performance or for individual goals achieved, without regard for overall effectiveness, similar attitudes often are observed. Under most Management by Objectives (MBO) systems, goals in areas where quantification is difficult often go unspecified. The organization therefore often is in a position where it *hopes* for employee effort in the areas of team building, interpersonal relations, creativity, etc., but it formally *rewards* none of these. In cases where promotions and raises are formally tied to MBO, the system itself contains a paradox in that it "asks employees to set challenging, risky goals, only to face smaller paychecks and possibly damaged careers if these goals are not accomplished" (5, p. 40).

It is *hoped* that administrators will pay attention to long run costs and opportunities and will institute programs which will bear fruit later on. However, many organizational reward systems pay off for short run sales and earnings only. Under such circumstances it is personally rational for officials to sacrifice long term growth and profit (by selling off equipment and property, or by stifling research and development) for short term advantages. This probably is most pertinent in the public sector, with the result that many public officials are unwilling to implement programs which will not show benefits by election time.

As a final, clear-cut example of a fouled-up reward system, consider the cost-plus contract and its next of kin, the allocation of next year's budget as a direct function of this year's expenditures. It probably is conceivable that those who award such budgets and contracts really hope for economy and prudence in spending. It is obvious, however, that adopting the proverb "to him who spends shall more be given," rewards not economy, but spending itself.

TWO COMPANIES' EXPERIENCES
A Manufacturing Organization

A midwest manufacturer of industrial goods had been troubled for some time by aspects of its organizational climate it believed dysfunctional. For research purposes, interviews were conducted with many employees and a questionnaire was administered on a companywide basis, including plants and offices in several American and Canadian locations. The company strongly encouraged employee participation in the survey, and made available time and space during the workday for completion of the instrument. All employees in attendance during the day of the survey completed the questionnaire. All instruments were collected directly by the researcher, who personally administered each session. Since no one employed by the firm handled the questionnaires, and since respondent names were not asked for, it seems likely that the pledge of anonymity given was believed.

A modified version of the Expect Approval scale (7) was included as part of the questionnaire. The instrument asked respondents to indicate the degree of approval or disapproval they could expect if they performed each of the described actions. A seven point Likert scale was used, with one indicating that the action would probably bring strong disapproval and seven signifying likely strong approval.

Although normative data for this scale from studies of other organizations are unavailable, it is possible to examine fruitfully the data obtained from this survey in several ways. First, it may be worth noting that the questionnaire data corresponded closely to information gathered through interviews. Furthermore, as can be seen from the results summarized in Table 1, sizable differences between various work units, and between employees at different job levels within the same work unit, were obtained. This suggests that response bias effects (social desirability in particular loomed as a potential concern) are not likely to be severe.

Most importantly, comparisons between scores obtained on the Expect Approval scale and a statement of problems which were the reason for the survey revealed that the same behaviors which managers in each division thought dysfunctional were those which lower level employees claimed were rewarded. As compared to job levels 1 to 8 in Division B (see Table 1), those in Division A claimed a much higher acceptance by management of "conforming" activities. Between 31 and 37 percent of Division A employees at levels 1-8 stated that going along with the majority, agreeing with the boss, and staying on everyone's good side brought approval; only once (level 5-8 responses to one of the three items) did a majority suggest that such actions would generate disapproval.

Furthermore, responses from Division A workers at levels 1-4 indicate that behaviors geared toward risk avoidance were as likely to be rewarded as to be punished. Only at job levels 9 and above was it apparent that the reward system was positively reinforcing behaviors desired by top management. Overall, the same "tendencies" toward conservatism and apple-polishing at the lower levels" which divisional management had complained about during the interviews were those claimed by subordinates to be the most rational course of action in light of the existing reward system. Management apparently was not getting the behaviors it was *hoping* for, but it certainly was getting the behaviors it was perceived by subordinates to be *rewarding*.

An Insurance Firm

The Group Health Claims Division of a large eastern insurance company provides another rich illustration of a reward system which reinforces behaviors not desired by top management.

Table 1   Summary of Two Divisions' Data Relevant to Conforming and Risk-Avoidance Behaviors (Extent to Which Subjects Expect Approval)

Dimension	Item	Division and Samples	Total Responses	Percentage of Workers Responding		
				1, 2, or 3 Disapproval	4	5, 6, or 7 Approval
Risk Avoidance	Making a risky decision based on the best information available at the time, but which turns out wrong.	A, levels 1-4 (lowest)	127	61	25	14
		A, levels 5-8	172	46	31	23
		A, levels 9 and above	17	41	30	30
		B, levels 1-4 (lowest)	31	58	26	16
		B, levels 5-8	19	42	42	16
		B, levels 9 and above	10	50	20	30
	Setting extremely high and challenging standards and goals, and then narrowly failing to make them.	A, levels 1-4	122	47	28	25
		A, levels 5-8	168	33	26	41
		A, levels 9 +	17	24	6	70
		B, levels 1-4	31	48	23	29
		B, levels 5-8	18	17	33	50
		B, levels 9 +	10	30	0	70
	Setting goals which are extremely easy to make and then making them.	A, levels 1-4	124	35	30	35
		A, levels 5-8	171	47	27	26
		A, levels 9 +	17	70	24	6
		B, levels 1-4	31	58	26	16
		B, levels 5-8	19	63	16	21
		B, levels 9 +	10	80	0	20
Conformity	Being a "yes man" and always agreeing with the boss.	A, levels 1-4	126	46	17	37
		A, levels 5-8	180	54	14	31
		A, levels 9 +	17	88	12	0
		B, levels 1-4	32	53	28	19
		B, levels 5-8	19	68	21	11
		B, levels 9 +	10	80	10	10
	Always going along with the majority	A, levels 1-4	125	40	25	35
		A, levels 5-8	173	47	21	32
		A, levels 9 +	17	70	12	18
		B, levels 1-4	31	1	23	16
		B, levels 5-8	19	68	11	21
		B, levels 9 +	10	80	10	10
	Being careful to stay on the good side of everyone, so that everyone agrees that you are a great guy.	A, levels 1-4	124	45	18	37
		A, levels 5-8	173	45	22	33
		A, levels 9 +	17	64	6	30
		B, levels 1-4	31	54	23	23
		B, levels 5-8	19	73	11	16
		B, levels 9 +	10	80	10	10

Attempting to measure and reward accuracy in paying surgical claims, the firm systematically keeps track of the number of returned checks and letters of complaint received from policyholders. However, underpayments are likely to provoke cries of outrage from the insured, while overpayments often are accepted in courteous silence. Since it often is impossible to tell from the physician's statement which of two surgical procedures, with different allowable benefits, was performed, and since writing for clarifications will interfere with other standards used by the firm concerning "percentage of claims paid within two days of receipt," the new hire in more than one claims section is soon acquainted with the informal norm: "When in doubt, pay it out!"

The situation would be even worse were it not for the fact that other features of the firm's reward system tend to neutralize those described. For example, annual "merit" increases are given to all employees, in one of the following three amounts:

1. If the worker is "outstanding" (a select category, into which no more than two employees per section may be placed): 5 percent
2. If the worker is "above average" (normally all workers not "outstanding" are so rated): 4 percent
3. If the worker commits gross acts of negligence and irresponsibility for which he might be discharged in many other companies: 3 percent.

Now, since (a) the difference between the 5 percent theoretically attainable through hard work and the 4 percent attainable merely by living until the review date is small and (b) since insurance firms seldom dispense much of a salary increase in cash (rather, the worker's insurance benefits increase, causing him to be further overinsured), many employees are rather indifferent to the possibility of obtaining the extra one percent reward and therefore tend to ignore the norm concerning indiscriminant payments.

However, most employees are not indifferent to the rule which states that, should absences or latenesses total three or more in any six-month period, the entire 4 or 5 percent due at the next "merit" review must be forfeited. In this sense the firm may be described as *hoping* for performance, while *rewarding* attendance. What it gets, of course, is attendance. (If the absence-lateness rule appears to the reader to be stringent, it really is not. The company counts "times" rather than "days" absent, and a ten-day absence therefore counts the same as one lasting two days. A worker in danger of accumulating a third absence within six months merely has to remain ill (away from work) during his second absence until his first absence is more than six months old. The limiting factor is that at some point his salary ceases, and his sickness benefits take over. This usually is sufficient to get the younger workers to return, but for those with 20 or more years' service, the company provides sickness benefits of 90 percent of normal salary, tax-free! Therefore . . . .)

CAUSES

Extremely diverse instances of systems which reward behavior A although the rewarder apparently hopes for behavior B have been given. These are useful to illustrate the breadth and magnitude of the phenomenon, but the diversity increases the difficulty of determining commonalities and establishing causes. However, four general factors may be pertinent to an explanation of why fouled up reward systems seem to be so prevalent.

Fascination with an "Objective" Criterion

It has been mentioned elsewhere that:

> Most "objective" measures of productivity are objective only in that their subjective elements are a) determined in advance, rather than coming into play at the time of the formal evaluation, and b) well concealed on the rating instrument itself. Thus industrial firms seeking to devise objective rating systems first decide, in an arbitrary manner, what dimensions are to be rated, . . . usually including some items having little to do with organizational effectiveness while excluding others that do. Only then does Personnel Division churn out official-looking documents on which all dimensions chosen to be rated are assigned point values, categories, or whatever (6, p. 92).

Nonetheless, many individuals seek to establish simple, quantifiable standards against which to measure and reward performance. Such efforts may be successful in highly predictable areas within an organization, but are likely to cause goal displacement when applied anywhere else. Overconcern with attendance and lateness in the insurance firm and with number of people placed in the vocational rehabilitation division may have been largely responsible for the problems described in those organizations.

Overemphasis on Highly Visible Behaviors

Difficulties often stem from the fact that some parts of the task are highly visible while other parts are not. For example, publications are easier to demonstrate than teaching, and scoring baskets and hitting home runs are more readily observable than feeding teammates and advancing base runners. Similarly, the adverse consequences of pronouncing a sick person well are more visible than those sustained by labeling a well person sick. Team-building and creativity are other examples of behaviors which may not be rewarded simply because they are hard to observe.

Hypocrisy

In some of the instances described the rewarder may have been getting the desired behavior, notwithstanding claims that the behavior was not desired. This may be true, for example, of management's attitude toward apple-polishing in the manufacturing firm (a behavior which subordinates felt was rewarded, despite management's avowed dislike of the practice). This also may explain politicians' unwillingness to revise the penalties for disobedience of ecology laws, and the failure of top management to devise reward systems which would cause systematic evaluation of training and development programs.

Emphasis on Morality or Equity Rather than Efficiency

Sometimes consideration of other factors prevents the establishment of a system which rewards behaviors desired by the rewarder. The felt obligation of many Americans to vote for one candidate or another, for example, may impair their ability to withhold support from politicians who refuse to discuss the issues. Similarly, the concern for spreading the risks and costs of wartime military service may outweigh the advantage to be obtained by commiting personnel to combat until the war is over.

It should be noted that only with respect to the first two causes are reward systems really paying off for other than desired behaviors. In the case of the third and fourth causes the system *is* rewarding behaviors desired by the rewarder, and the systems are fouled up only from the standpoints of those who believe the rewarder's public statements (cause 3), or those who seek to maximize efficiency rather than other outcomes (cause 4).

CONCLUSIONS

Modern organization theory requires a recognition that the members of organizations and society possess divergent goals and motives. It therefore is unlikely that managers and their subordinates will seek the same outcomes. Three possible remedies for this potential problem are suggested.

Selection

It is theoretically possible for organizations to employ only those individuals whose goals and motives are wholly consonant with those of management. In such cases the same behaviors judged by subordinates to be rational would be perceived by management as desirable. State-of-the-art reviews of selection techniques, however, provide scant grounds for hope that such an approach would be successful.

Training

Another theoretical alternative is for the organization to admit those employees whose goals are not consonant with those of management and then, through training, socialization, or whatever, alter employee goals to make them consonant. However, research on the effectiveness of such training programs, though limited, provides further grounds for pessimism (for example, see 3).

Altering the Reward System

What would have been the result if:

1. Nixon had been assured by his advisors that he could not win reelection except by discussing the issues in detail?
2. Physicians' conduct was subjected to regular examination by review boards for type 1 errors (calling healthy people ill) and to penalties (fines, censure, etc.) for errors of either type?
3. The President of XYZ Corporation had to choose between (a) spending $11 million dollars for antipollution equipment, and (b) incurring a fifty-fifty chance of going to jail for five years?

Managers who complain that their workers are not motivated might do well to consider the possibility that they have installed reward systems which are paying off for behaviors other than those they are seeking. This, in part, is what happened in Vietnam, and this is what regularly frustrates societal efforts to bring about honest politicians, civic-minded managers, etc. This certainly is what happened in both the manufacturing and the insurance companies.

A first step for such managers might be to find out what behaviors currently are being rewarded. Perhaps an instrument similar to that used in the manufacturing firm could be useful for this purpose. Chances are excellent that these managers will be surprised by what they find—that their firms are not rewarding what they assume they are. In fact, such undesirable behavior by organizational members as they have observed may be explained largely by the reward systems in use.

This is not to say that all organizational behavior is determined by formal rewards and punishments. Certainly it is true that in the absence of formal reinforcement some soldiers will be patriotic, some presidents will be ecology minded, and some orphanage directors will care about children. The point, however, is that in such cases the rewarder is not *causing* the behaviors desired but is only a fortunate bystander. For an organization to *act* upon its members, the formal reward system should positively reinforce desired behaviors, not constitute an obstacle to be overcome.

It might be wise to underscore the obvious fact that there is nothing really new in what has been said. In both theory and practice these matters have been mentioned before. Thus in many states Good Samaritan laws have been installed to protect doctors who stop to assist a stricken motorist. In states without such laws it is commonplace for doctors to refuse to stop, for fear of involvement in a subsequent lawsuit. In college basketball additional penalties have been instituted against players who foul their opponents deliberately. It has long been argued by Milton Friedman and others that penalties should be altered so as to make it irrational to disobey the ecology laws, and so on.

By altering the reward system the organization escapes the necessity of selecting only desirable people or of trying to alter undesirable ones. In Skinnerian terms "As for responsibility and goodness—as commonly defined—no one . . . would want or need them. They refer to a man's behaving well despite the absence of positive reinforcement that is obviously sufficient to explain it. Where such reinforcement exists, 'no one needs goodness.' "

REFERENCES

1. Barnard, Chester I. *The Functions of the Executive* (Cambridge, Mass: Harvard University Press, 1964).
2. Blau, Peter, M., and W. Richard Scott. *Formal Organizations* (San Francisco: Chandler, 1962).
3. Fiedler, Fred E. "Predicting the Effects of Leadership Training and Experience from the Contingency Model," *Journal of Applied Psychology,* Vol. 56 (1972), 114-119.
4. Garland, L. H. "Studies of the Accuracy of Diagnostic Procedures," *American Journal Roentgenological, Radium Therapy Nuclear Medicine,* Vol. 82 (1959), 25-38.
5. Kerr, Steven. "Some Modifications in MBO as an OD Strategy," *Academy of Management Proceedings,* 1973, pp. 39-42.
6. Kerr, Steven. "What Price Objectivity?" *American Sociologist,* Vol. 8 (1973), 92-93.
7. Litwin, G. H., and R. A. Stringer, Jr. *Motivation and Organizational Climate* (Boston: Harvard University Press, 1968).
8. Perrow, Charles. "The Analysis of Goals in Complex Organizations." In A. Etzioni (Ed.), *Readings on Modern Organizations* (Englewood Cliffs, N.J.: Prentice-Hall, 1969).
9. Scheff, Thomas J. "Decision Rules, Types of Error, and Their Consequences in Medical Diagnosis," in F. Massarik and P. Ratoosh (Eds.), *Mathematical Explorations in Behavioral Science* (Homewood, Ill: Irwin, 1965).
10. Simon, Herbert A. *Administrative Behavior* (New York: Free Press, 1957).

NOTES

[1]In Simon's (10, pp. 76-77) terms, a decision is "subjectively rational" if it maximizes an individual's valued outcomes so far as his knowledge permits. A decision is "personally rational" if it is oriented toward the individual's goals.

[2]In one study (4) of 14,867 films for signs of tuberculosis, 1,216 positive readings turned out to be clinically negative; only 24 negative readings proved clinically active, a ratio of 50 to 1.

[3]Personal interviews conducted during 1972-1973.

Intimidation Rituals: Reactions to Reform

RORY O'DAY

This paper characterizes the reactions of superiors in social systems to a reform-minded subordinate as a series of intimidation rituals. Each successive "ritual of control" represents an escalation in the efforts of authority to discourage an individual (and those who may support him or her) from continuing to seek reform.

MIDDLE MANAGEMENT'S MECHANISM OF CONTROL

The rituals of intimidation satisfy the two primary concerns of authorities confronted by a subordinate who appears not only able to articulate the grievances of a significant number of other system members but also capable of proposing solutions to them. Their first concern is, of course, to control the reformer so that he does not succeed in recruiting support. Their other concern is to exercise this control in ways that absolve them of any wrongdoing in the matter. The individual in question must be controlled in such a way that he neither continues to be an effective spokesman nor becomes a martyr. When superiors are confronted with a reform-minded subordinate, they want his silence or his absence, whichever is easier to achieve. The "authorities" must also preserve their

Reproduced by special permission from *The Journal of Applied Behavioral Science,* "Intimidation Rituals: Reactions to Reform," by Rory O'Day, Volume 10, Number 3, pp. 373-386, copyright © 1974, NTL Institute.

carefully managed image of reasonableness, and would prefer that the reformer leave voluntarily rather than be removed officially.

For purposes of illustration, this presentation will describe intimidation rituals used by various organizations in the service of protest-suppression, for organizational authorities prefer to *intimidate* a reform-minded individual rather than commit organizational energy to the structural and personnel changes required to transform a "nonconforming enclave" into a legitimate subunit.[1] It is further suggested that an organization undergoes major changes that incorporate and accommodate a group of dissidents only when the intimidation rituals do not succeed in silencing the individuals who constitute the "leading edges" of the reform movement.

In the discussion that follows, I will be concerned primarily with the reformer who emerges from the lower hierarchy in an organization and challenges the *middle hierarchy*. A reformer threatens middle management in three distinctly different ways. The first threat is a function of the validity of his accusations about the inadequacy of specific actions of middle-level members and his suggestions for correcting them. If the reformer is correct, those in the middle will fear that those at the top will punish them when they discover the truth. The second threat comes from the moral challenge presented by such a reformer, for his demand for action will reveal the strength or weakness of middle management's commitment to the organization. And thirdly, the reformer's challenge may indicate to people at the top that middle management is unable to maintain order in its own jurisdiction. To protect their interest, middle-level bureaucrats therefore feel their only defense against reform-minded subordinates is intimidation.[2]

The rituals of intimidation involve two phases: *Indirect Intimidation*, which has two steps, *nullification* and *isolation;* and *Direct Intimidation*, which also comprises two steps, *defamation* and *expulsion*.

PHASE I: INDIRECT INTIMIDATION
Step 1: Nullification

When a reformer first approaches his immediate supervisors, they will assure him that his accusations or suggestions are invalid—the result of misunderstandings and misperceptions on his part. His superiors, in this phase, hope that the reformer will be so awed by authority that he will simply take their word that his initiative is based on error. If, however, the reformer insists, his superiors will often agree to conduct an "investigation." The results of such an investigation will convince the reformer that his accusations are groundless and that his suggestions for enhancing organizational effectiveness or revising organizational goals have been duly noted by the appropriate authorities.

Bureaucratic justification for this response usually rests on the argument that this method copes with the system's "crackpots" and "hotheads," discouraging them from disturbing the smooth, routine functioning of the organization with their crazy ideas and their personal feuds. But middle management also uses these rituals of nullification to handle a potentially explosive (for them and others in the organization) situation quickly and quietly, in order to prevent unfavorable publicity, maintain the organization's state of pluralistic ignorance, and prevent the development of a sympathetic and concerned audience for the reformer's ideas. The explicit message is: "You don't know what you're talking about, but thank you anyway for telling us. We'll certainly look into the matter for you." Members of the middle hierarchy then proceed to cover up whatever embarrassing (for them) truth exists in the reformer's arguments.

The protest-absorption power of the ritual of nullification derives from an element inherent in bureaucracies: the always-attractive opportunity to avoid personal responsibility for one's actions. Thus, if people attempt to reform at all, they generally do not proceed beyond the first ritual, which is a process designed to quash the reformer and allow his superiors to reaffirm the collective wisdom of the organization, while clearing their consciences of wrongdoing. Nullification even gets the would-be reformer off the hook—and he may remain grateful to the organization for this added convenience. This shedding of personal responsibility allows the reformer and the authorities alike to compromise in the belief that although it might not be a perfect organizational world, it is nevertheless a self-correcting one.

Repeated exposure to the nullification ritual (the "beating your head against the wall" phenomenon) is expected to convince any sane organizational member that a reformist voice or presence is unwelcome. He is expected to take the hint and stop pestering his superiors with his misguided opinions. Gestures of generosity on the part of the middle hierarchy are not unusual if he decides to leave the organization—and such concern is usually expressed by offering to help the individual find employment opportunities elsewhere.

Step 2: Isolation

If the reformer persists in his efforts, middle management will separate him from his peers, subordinates, and superiors, thereby softening his impact on the organization and making it extremely difficult for him to mobilize any support for his position.

Middle managers argue that these procedures represent the exercise of their rights of office in the service of protecting the organization. But these attempts to isolate the reformer can also be seen as a show of force, as a way of reassuring their own superiors (if they are paying attention), their subordinates, and perhaps themselves that they can maintain order in their own jurisdiction.

Attempts at isolating the reformer include closing his communication links, restricting his freedom of movement, and reducing his allocation of organization resources. If these do not neutralize the reformer, he will be transferred to a less visible position in the organization. In these rituals, the bureaucratic message is: "If you insist on talking about things which you do not understand, then we will have to prevent you from bothering other people with your nonsense."

Systematic unresponsiveness to a reformer's criticism and suggestions is a particularly interesting form of isolation. This lack of response is meant to convince the reformer of the invalidity of his position; but if he presses his right to be heard, it may be used to create a feeling of such impotence that the reformer overreacts in order to elicit a response from his superiors. This overreaction may then be used to demonstrate the reformer's psychological imperfections.

When subjected to organizational isolation, most people come to see the error of their ways or the handwriting on the wall. When an individual learns that there is still time to mend his ways, he usually steps back in line and becomes a silent participant in the organization. When he realizes his career in the organization is at a standstill, he may decide to leave as gracefully as possible while he can still leave under his own steam. Middle managers closest to him then often offer him assistance in finding a new job, with the assurance that "*we* only want what is best for *you*."

Most forms of isolation are designed to persuade the reformer of the futility of trying to initiate change until such time as he is instructed by his superiors to concern himself with change. The reformer practically guarantees his defeat if he reacts to systematic organizational unresponsiveness by confronting his superiors in ways that violate policy or law. The temptation to confront administrative unresponsiveness in dramatic and often self-defeating ways stems in large part from the intense frustration induced by the reformer's belief that systematic unresponsiveness violates his basic rights of freedom of expression and carries with it the implication that he is personally ineffectual (Turner, 1973). Administrative unresponsiveness to what the reformer believes are crucial issues both for himself and for the organization may be sufficiently frustrating to compel him to act, however rashly, in order to clarify the situation. From the administration's point of view, this can be seen as "flushing the rebels out into the open," "giving them enough rope to hang themselves," or, more formally, deviance-heresy conversion (Harshbarger, 1973).

PHASE II: DIRECT INTIMIDATION
Step 3: Defamation

Should the reformer refuse to remain silent, and instead mobilizes support for his position, middle management will begin to impugn his character and his motives. "When legitimate techniques fail—the middle hierarchy might resort to illegitimate or non-legitimate ones" (Leeds, 1964, p. 126). Middle managers will often distort events or even fabricate instances of misconduct in order to intimidate not only the reformer but also those who would listen to or believe him.

Defamation attempts to cut the reformer off from a potentially sympathetic following by attributing his attempts at reform to questionable motives, underlying psychopathology, or gross incompetence. This three-pronged attack is meant to blackmail the reformer into submission and to transform a sympathetic following into a mistrustful crowd of onlookers or an angry mob that feels resentful at having been deceived by the reformer.

From the vantage point of the reformer, the Kafkaesque or Alice-in-Wonderland quality of the rituals of intimidation becomes particularly evident at this time. The reformer finds himself faced with charges which only he and his accusers know are either false or irrelevant in relation to the value of his reform initiatives. The reformer is in a double bind. His superiors will use their offices and positions of trust and responsibility to create the impression in the minds of others in the organization that their accusations of incompetence, self-interest, or psychopathology are true. If the reformer continues in the face of these accusations, he risks being viewed as power-hungry or irrational. If he allows himself to be intimidated by the threat of lies, he allows his supervisors to win by default.

One tactic of the superior is to accuse the reformer of acting out his Oedipal conflicts. Such a personalization of a subordinate's reform efforts (especially a younger subordinate) permits his superior to present himself as a harassed "father" faced with a troubled "son," and blocks any examination of his conduct that might reveal provocation on his part. In this way the bureaucrat hopes to persuade others in the organization to respond to the reformer as a sick person in need of therapy or as a child in need of nurturing—a stance that allows him to take on the role of "good father" in relation to other subordinates and to the reformer, if and when the latter capitulates and admits his need for help and guidance.

Rituals of defamation are undertaken by superiors in order to focus attention away from themselves and onto the reformer. The superiors hope that by casting enough doubt on the motives, intentions, and personality of the reformer, enough people in the organization will think that "where there is smoke, there must be fire." The message of this ritual is: "Don't listen to him (his message) because you can't trust a person like him."

Like the rituals of nullification and isolation, the ritual of defamation is both an end in itself and a preliminary to the final ritual of expulsion. The superiors hope by threatening to destroy the reformer's reputation and his character, he will retreat into silence and passivity or leave the organization for greener pastures; if, however, the reformer continues his efforts, his superiors have laid the groundwork for his expulsion.

If the ritual of defamation is undertaken, its target is usually indeed a reformer and not simply a nonconformist or a deviant. His superiors would not need to engage in public tactics of intimidation if there were no substance to his challenge. It is precisely the validity of his reform initiative that leads his superiors to attempt to destroy his credibility. If this destruction of the reformer's credibility with his peers, subordinates, and top management is effectively conducted, others in the organization will desert his cause and he can be dismissed easily as an undesirable member of the intact organizational team.

Step 4: Expulsion

When neither nullification, isolation, nor defamation can silence the reformer or force his "voluntary withdrawal" from the organization, the middle hierarchy seeks an official decision for his dismissal.

If successful, at least three aims may be achieved thereby. Obviously, by expelling the reformer, his superiors will cut him off from any actual or potential following and weaken any opposition to their authority. An official dismissal also serves as a warning to other budding reformers that middle management has the necessary power and authority to expel troublemakers. Finally, the act of expulsion—a verdict of unfitness— supports the contention that the reformer is an immoral or irrational person.

Of course, the middle hierarchy would prefer the reformer to withdraw voluntarily. Managers want to avoid the public and formal proceedings that often accompany an official request for dismissal of an employee, for the accuser (superior) can often then be scrutinized as carefully as the accused, if the accused person wishes to avail himself of the opportunity. The expulsion ritual involves the formal submission of evidence, the keeping of records, the establishment of independent investigative bodies, and the right of cross-examination, which all function to threaten the image of managers as reasonable, honest, and hardworking servants of the organization. Formal dismissal proceedings are also avoided by middle management because in some fundamental sense they imply that the organization has failed and that they, in particular, have shown themselves unable to maintain order.

THE RITUAL CYCLE ABSORBS AND DESTROYS

Indirect Intimidation attempts to absorb the accusations and suggestions of the reformer, first by depriving him of effectiveness or validity, then by treating him as if he were an "invisible person." The object here is to define the reformer as "harmless." It also attempts to absorb protest by psychologically and physically exhausting the reformer so that he comes to doubt his own experience of reality, his abilities to accomplish the task he sets for himself, and its significance. The authorities hope that the reformer will come to believe the task he has set for himself is humanly impossible and that his fatigue and confusion are the result of his inability to accept human nature for what it is. Short of this, they hope that the reformer will come to feel so inadequate that he will be grateful for continued employment by the organization, in any capacity. ("You're welcome to stay aboard as long as you don't rock the boat.")

Direct Intimidation attempts to destroy protest through destruction of the *character* of the reformer (defamation) or, if necessary, of his *position* in the organization (expulsion). Direct Intimidation represents middle

Figure 1   Cycles of Intimidation Rituals

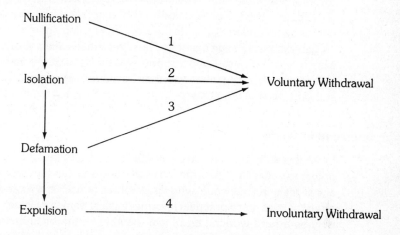

---

management's active attempt to destroy the reformer as a source of legitimate grievances and suggestions and to terrorize, if necessary, other organizational members. Successful rituals of defamation create a "bad" person, enabling the "good" organization to close ranks once again and benefit from the curative properties of solidarity when he is cast out of the system. In this sense, the ritual destruction of the person (Garfinkel, 1956) necessarily precedes the destruction of his place in the organization.

In sum, Figure 1 portrays the specific cycles of intimidation rituals. Cycle 1 is most preferred by all organizations, while Cycle 4 is the least preferred. Cycle 2 is preferred to Cycle 3.

THE REFORMER IMAGE

Throughout this discussion, the individual subjected to the rituals of intimidation has been referred to as the *reformer,* a generic term for any organizational member who resorts to voice rather than to avoidance when faced with what *he* regards as a situation of organizational deterioration or imperfection. Voice is defined as

> . . . any attempt at all to change, rather than escape from, an objectionable state of affairs, whether through individual or collective petition to the management directly in charge, through appeal to a higher authority with the intention of forcing a change in management, or through various types of actions and protests, including those that are meant to mobilize public opinion (Hirschman, 1970, p. 30).

Therefore, in the sense in which it is being used here, "reformer" includes the various meanings contained in such labels as "internal muckraker" or "pure whistle-blower" (Peters & Branch, 1972), "innovator in innovation-resisting organizations" (Shepard, 1969), "crusader for corporate responsibility" (Heilbroner, 1972), "nonconforming individual" (Etzioni, 1961; Leeds, 1964), and "heretic" (Harshbarger, 1973); but it is not intended to include the various meanings inherent in the term "organizational change agent."[3] Thus "reformer" refers to any member who acts, in any way and for any reason, to alter the structure and functioning of the organization, when he has *not* been formally delegated authority to institute change.

Why Intimidation Works

From this definition we can see that it is the organization which has the power to define the "reformer" as such, and attaches the stigma to many a well-meaning individual who does not see himself in a protest role. It is often the case that a potential reformer initially thinks of himself or herself only as a hard-working and loyal member of the organization who is simply trying to make things "better" and wishes to be "understood" by busy but well-meaning superiors. However, by the time authorities begin the rituals of defamation, the most naive individual usually realizes that, at least in the eyes of his superiors, he poses a threat to the established order (Herbert, 1972).

The inside reformer is vulnerable to all the intimidation rituals that his particular organization has at its disposal. The reformer outside an organization is usually vulnerable only to the rituals of nullification, isolation (in the form of systematic unresponsiveness), and defamation, unless the organization he is challenging is able to pressure the parent organization into doing the intimidating for it (McCarry, 1972).

Authorities in formal organizations are rarely directly challenged by subordinates. As in the Hans Christian Andersen tale, most individuals do not presume to stand in public judgment of their organizational superiors. Belief in the wisdom and power of the people at the top serves to keep most individuals silent about their grievances concerning the status quo and their ideas (if they have any) for enhancing organizational effectiveness or revising organizational goals. Subordinates do not generally demand, as part of their organizational contractual arrangements, the power to hold their superiors accountable for actions in direct and continuing ways. So intimidation rituals are held to be a last resort—reserved for organizational members who resist, for whatever reason, the usual mechanisms of social control (Millham, Bullock, & Cherrett, 1972).

In their discussion of the obstacles to whistle-blowing, Peters and Branch (1972) include the "loyal-member-of-the-team" trap, the feeling that "going public" is unseemly and embarrassing, and the fear of current and future job vulnerability. Thomson (1968) and Peters and Branch (1972) also refer to the subconscious accommodative device of the "effectiveness trap," an organizational argument that permits its members to avoid conflict on an immediate issue in order to ensure "effectiveness" on some more important issue, at some future time. The curator mentality and emotional detachment generated by the bureaucratic role; the tendency to resort to wishful thinking that organizational deterioration and the consequences of bad policy must soon stop simply because they cannot go on; and the fear that one disagrees with a particular exercise of power only because one is too weak to handle it further contribute to inaction on the part of most "loyal" organizational members (Thomson, 1968).

Reformer as Bad Guy

In point of fact, the protest-absorbing and protest-destroying power of intimidation rituals derives, in large measure, from their infrequent use by organizations. Conversely, if more members were willing to turn their various dissatisfactions into reformist activities, intimidation rituals would lose much of their power.

To understand the effectiveness of organizational intimidation one must examine the reasons why peers and subordinates usually fail to support the reformer, withdraw support, or even actively resist his efforts. Their passive or active resistance may indicate an increased desire or struggle for an organization's scarce resources (material benefits or status, power or prestige—or even dependency). It may also indicate that they perceive themselves as cast in an unfavorable light by the reformer's enthusiasm and heightened activities in pursuing present or changed organizational goals. Members of the organization may secretly believe that the reformer's efforts will be successful, and fear its implications for their position in the organization. If the reformer is successful in convincing top management to investigate the organizational "engine," many may fear that close scrutiny of the performance of the parts will find them wanting. On the other hand, on the outside chance that the reformer manages to seize the reins of power, peers and subordinates may fear that if they do not match his zeal in pursuing new as well as old organizational goals he will turn them out of their present positions.

It frequently seems that practically everyone except the reformer has a personal stake in preserving the complicated fantasy of the organization, even though conditions in the organization are in fact unsatisfying to all but a few elite members. Bion (1959) has described a similar situation in therapy groups where members engage in a variety of neurotic attempts to resist and discourage changing the structure and functioning of a group that is obviously less than fully satisfying. It seems likely, then, that subordinates in an organization actively or passively resist a peer's reform initiatives because the pain of the status quo is less intense than their fear of the unknown.

In general, the reformer finds himself initially with little or no support because there is an implicit acceptance of the bureaucratic order in our society (Wilcox, 1968) and because most people find it difficult and improper to question the actions of authority (Milgram, 1965; Peters & Branch, 1972). There is also the well-ingrained reflex of flight in the face of crisis and change, which has characterized North American society since its colonial days (Hartz, 1955; Hirschman, 1970; Slater, 1970).

Most organizational members do not support the reformer at all, or they desert him at the first opportunity because they believe he will lose in his struggle with institutional authority—and they want to be on the winning side. Moreover, as Walzer (1969) has pointed out, most people accept nondemocratic organizational conditions on the basis of the argument of tacit consent and withhold or withdraw support from the reformer, saying that he is free to go someplace else if he does not like it where he is.

Peers and subordinates may also resist a reformer because they suspect that he is committing the unforgivable sin of pride (Slater, 1963). They may come to believe that in taking it upon himself to judge the organization and its leaders he is acting in a self-righteous manner (Peters & Branch, 1972). Those who wish to desert the reformer on this ground often use as supporting data the reformer's persistent efforts in the face of the rituals of defamation.

Since the reformer's departure is usually associated with an immediate reduction or elimination of overt conflict, which in turn relieves tension in the organization, members can wrap themselves in the organizational blanket and tell themselves that he was the source of the problem all along. When the emotional ruckus dies down, most members therefore experience a heightened commitment to the organization and return to their jobs with a renewed vigor. For those organizational members who continue to harbor some doubt about the reformer's guilt, the fear of retaliation against "sympathizers" usually dampens their enthusiasm for the reformer's cause and suppresses all but ritualistic expressions of concern for his plight.

SEIZE THE DAY

It is not possible here to do more than raise the issue of whether one should attempt to change organizations from within or whether one should create alternative organizations. Large formal organizations are going to be with us for a long time to come (Heilbroner, 1972), and their members are going to have to devise ways to make them more democratic, because there really is no place to run to anymore.

The serious reformer should be prepared to take advantage of organizational crises. He must learn how to recognize, expose, and make concrete those administratively designed arrangements that do not satisfactorily resolve critical problems. For it is in a time of crisis that an organization is open to solutions to the basic problem of survival. Organizational members will be eager to adopt new structures that promise to relieve the uncertainty and anxiety generated by a crisis (Shepard, 1969). If the organization has become weak internally, if it contains corruption and indolence at various levels, if the organization is beset by energy-consuming external pressures, and if the organizational elite lack the resources or the will to initiate changes essential for organizational survival, then the organization might well be ready for successful reform from within (Leeds, 1964). Such an organization might not be capable of successfully administering the intimidation rituals.

Internal organizational reform is a difficult process. The cause of reform as well as constructive revolution cannot be served by deluding ourselves as to the ease of restructuring human society (Heilbroner, 1972; Schon, 1973). The reformer's life is not an easy one. But neither need he feel doomed from the start by the inevitability of the success of intimidation rituals mobilized against him.

REFERENCES

Bion, W. R. *Experiences in groups.* New York: Basic Books, 1959.

Etzioni, A. *A comparative analysis of complex organizations.* New York: The Free Press, 1961.

Garfinkel, H. Conditions of successful degradation ceremonies. *American Journal of Sociology,* 1956, 61, 420-424.

Harshbarger, D. The individual and the social order: Notes on the management of heresy and deviance in complex organizations. *Human Relations,* 1973, 26, 251-269.

Hartz, L. *The liberal tradition in America.* New York: Harcourt, Brace and World, 1955.

Heilbroner, R. L. *In the name of profit.* New York: Doubleday, 1972.

Herbert, A. *Soldier.* New York: Holt, Rinehart and Winston, 1972.

Hirschman, A. O. *Exit, voice, and loyalty.* Cambridge, Mass.: Harvard University Press, 1970.

Leeds, R. The absorption of protest: A working paper. In W. W. Cooper, H. J. Leavitt, and M. W. Shelly, II (Eds.), *New perspectives in organization research.* New York: Wiley, 1964.

McCarry, C. *Citizen Nader.* New York: Saturday Review Press, 1972.

Milgram, S. Some conditions of obedience and disobedience to authority. *Human Relations,* 1965, 18, 57-75.

Milham, S., Bullock, R., & Cherrett, P. Social control in organizations. *The British Journal of Sociology,* 1972, 23, 406-421.

Peters, C., & Branch, T. *Blowing the whistle: Dissent in the public interest.* New York: Praeger, 1972.

Schon, D. S. *Beyond the stable state.* New York: Norton, 1973.

Shepard, H. A. Innovation-resisting and innovation-producing organizations. In W. G. Bennis, K. D. Benne, and R. Chin (Eds.), *The planning of change,* Rev. ed. New York: Holt, Rinehart and Winston, 1969, Pp. 519-525.

Slater, P. E. On social regression. *American Sociological Review,* 1963, 29, 339-364.

Slater, P. E. *The pursuit of loneliness.* Boston: Beacon Press, 1970.

Thomson, J. C. How could Vietnam happen? An autopsy. *Atlantic Monthly,* April 1968, 221 (4), 47-53.

Turner, R. H. Unresponsiveness as a social sanction. *Sociometry,* 1973, 36, 1-19.

Walzer, M. Corporate responsibility and civil disobedience. *Dissent,* Sept.-Oct., 1969, pp. 395-406.

Wilcox, H. G. The cultural trait of hierarchy in middle class children. *Public Administration Review,* 1968, 28, 222-235.

NOTES

[1] "Nonconforming enclave" refers to the existence of a number of organizational members who, through collective effort, ". . . could potentially divert organization resources from their current commitments, undermine organizational effectiveness, or form a front capable of capturing control of the organization" (Leeds, 1964, p. 115).

[2] In a related context, Etzioni (1961, p. 241) asserts, "Once deviant charisma has manifested itself, despite . . . elaborate preventive mechanisms, counter-processes are set into motion. These are of two kinds: those which attempt to eliminate the deviant charisma; and those which seek to limit its effect."

[3] It is possible, however, that an orgnizational change agent might find himself undergoing the rituals of intimidation if he insists that effective action be taken on his proposals for change, particularly if such action would threaten certain organizational power arrangements.

A Vertical Dyad Linkage Approach to Leadership Within Formal Organizations: A Longitudinal Investigation of the Role Making Process

FRED DANSEREAU, JR.
GEORGE GRAEN
WILLIAM J. HAGA

After more than 20 years of active research, contemporary models of leadership within organizations have failed to develop beyond rather primitive levels. Recent reviews of these models testify to the underdeveloped state of these formulations (Campbell, Dunnette, Lawler & Weick, 1971; Graen, Alvares, Orris & Martella, 1970; Guion & Gottier, 1966; Korman, 1966; Nash, 1966; McMahon, 1972; Shiflett, 1972). These contemporary models typically include two assumptions about the leadership setting (see Dansereau, Cashman and Graen (1973)). The first assumption is that the members of an organizational unit who report to the same superior are sufficiently homogenous on the relevant dimensions (e.g., perceptions, interpretations and reactions) that they can be considered as a single entity: the "work group." The second assumption is that a superior behaves in essentially the same prescribed manner toward each of his members. Following these assumptions, research attention is focused upon the average or usual behavior of a superior toward his "work group." If these assumptions are inappropriate, this could help to explain the slow progress in the leadership area during the past 20 years.

One alternative approach to leadership that does not include the restrictions of these two assumptions focuses upon the vertical dyad and the relationship between a superior and a member contained in a dyad. This approach allows for the case where each of the vertical dyadic relationships contained within a unit are radically different, as well as for the traditional case where each are essentially the same. Only by focusing upon each of the dyadic relationships can the actual distribution of vertical relationships within any organizational unit be empirically discovered. Following this alternative approach, both members of the vertical dyad become the foci of investigation into the leadership process. Tersely stated, the vertical dyad is the appropriate unit of analysis for examining leadership processes because the vertical dyad reflects the processes linking member and superior.

Considering the traditional approach, one method of testing the appropriateness of measuring the behavior of the superior on the average, or toward his members in general (Average Leadership Style), is to investigate the extent of agreement between the superior and his members as a group in describing the behavior of the superior. This was done in two studies: Evans (1970) and Graham (1970) asked both superiors and their members to describe the behavior of the superior using the conventional measures of Consideration and Structure (Fleishman, 1955). In both studies, the agreement between the description obtained from the superior and that obtained by averaging his member's response was close to zero.

One method of testing the possible advantages of the vertical dyad linkage approach (VDL) is to compare the extent to which it and the traditional approach order empirical relationships. This was done in a study by Dansereau, Cashman and Graen (1973). In this study the research methods prescribed by both approaches were applied on data collected from 261 managers and their superiors. After investigating the relationship between leadership and turnover from the traditional (ALS) and Vertical Dyad Linkage perspectives the authors concluded:

> . . . this VDL approach reveals orderliness in the data that the average leadership style approach would have assumed a priori to be mainly error variance. On the other hand, the orderliness revealed by the VDL approach could not have been extracted from the data using the ALS approach (Dansereau, Cashman & Graen, 1973, p. 197).

This study suggested that the vertical dyad approach might possess a good deal of potential for uncovering the "mysteries" of leadership.

LEADERSHIP AND SUPERVISION AS TECHNIQUES

In employing the vertical dyad approach, it is necessary to focus upon each member of the dyad. Focusing first upon the behavior of the superior, Jacobs (1971) points out that much of the difficulty with the leadership literature probably stems from the failure to distinguish between the characteristics of a superior as a person and "leadership" and "supervision" as techniques which are elicited by the situation. In illustrating this point Jacobs states:

> Yet there is a continuing tendency in the literature for reference to be made to persons as leaders because some part of their role repertories consists of behaviors successful in influencing others without recourse to authority ("leadership"). This obscures the fact that almost certainly there are other parts of their repertories that are based upon . . . authority relationships ("supervision"), in order that the complicated machinery of formal organizations might operate as efficiently as possible (Jacobs, 1971, p. 288).

Briefly stated, Jacobs is suggesting that a superior may engage in role behaviors involving both leadership (influence without authority) and supervision (influence based upon only authority). Following this insightful observation to its logical consequences raises several questions concerning the conditions under which a superior can be expected to behave as a leader and when he can be expected to play the role of supervisor.

One method of seeking answers to these questions is to investigate the development of new vertical dyad linkages within an organizational context. Beginning with a superior and a member located within an organizationally new relationship, and monitoring the development of this vertical relationship over time may reveal various conditions which contribute to the emergence of leadership and supervision. Before we can proceed with a longitudinal investigation of the development of vertical dyadic linkages, we must be prepared to empirically distinguish between leadership and supervision in the dyad and during the early stages of their development in the dyad.[1]

LEADERSHIP AND SUPERVISION IN THE DYAD

A key distinction between supervision and leadership involves the nature of the "vertical exchange" that takes place between a superior and a member. Employing the supervision technique, the nature of the vertical exchange is such that a superior relies almost exclusively upon the formal employment contract in his exchanges with a member. As a condition of continued employment, the member agreed to fulfill all prescriptions and proscriptions of the formal organization regarding his position. These role prescriptions included among others that he submit to the legitimate authority of his specified superiors regarding certain specified matters. In exchange for the member's fulfillment to these conditions, the organization (not the superior) agreed to compensate the member with coin and benefits of various kinds. At the extreme, the superior can fulfill the employment contract without entering into any but the most minimal social exchange. The superior need not negotiate with the member about unit-related matters or become dependent upon him as an individual, rather he has the means to treat the member much as he would a part in a complex machine.

In contrast, employing the technique of leadership, the nature of the vertical exchange is such that the superior cannot rely exclusively upon the employment contract. Instead, he must seek a different basis for influencing the behavior of a member. This alternative basis of influence is anchored in the interpersonal exchange relationship between a superior and a member. This source of influence, theoretically untapped by formal supervision, can involve highly valued outcomes not available under supervision for both the superior and the member. The superior for his part can offer the outcomes of job latitude, influence in decision making, open and honest communications, support of the member's actions, and confidence in and consideration for the member, among others. The member can reciprocate with greater than required expenditures of time and energy, the assumption of greater responsibility, and commitment to the success of the entire unit or organization, among others. The larger the extent of this vertical exchange, the more the superior must be ready to negotiate with his member on unit-related matters. The superior is interdependent with his member and must respect his dependence upon the particular member. The use of the supervision technique by the superior to solve problems with the member can only damage and eventually destroy the leadership exchange. Although the superior employing the leadership technique possesses the formal authority to command compliance from his member by virtue of his rights of office, this authority must not be used against the member. Its use rapidly transforms the basis of influence from leadership to supervision.

LEADERSHIP AND SUPERVISION IN THE NEW DYAD

When the members of the dyad are in the initial process of organizing their roles (role making) the key outcropping of "emerging" vertical exchanges should be the extent to which the superior allows the member to negotiate job-related matters. If a member is initially given the opportunity to work through some of his job problems with his superior, the superior probably is attempting the leadership technique. However, if a member is initially allowed little or no chance to negotiate with the superior, the superior probably is employing the technique of supervision. In general, *the greater the latitude initially given to the member to negotiate job-related matters, the higher is the probability that the superior is attempting leadership and the lower the probability that he is using supervision with his member.*

Using this distinction the purpose of the present study was to examine how early attempts to employ the techniques of leadership and supervision contribute to the development of social exchanges in the dyad. Specifically this investigation focused upon the degree of negotiating latitude initially granted by the superior to his member, as a key variable in distinguishing between attempts at leadership and supervision and monitored the development of social exchange beginning at the stage of "near strangers" and following through to the stage of "established incumbents." The general hypothesis of this investigation was that negotiating latitude within the vertical dyad will produce leadership relations when given in generous amounts and will produce supervision relations when given in meager amounts.

PARTICIPANTS AND SETTING

The participants in this investigation were 60 managers whose positions formed the administrative pyramid atop a housing division within a large public university. This organization had experienced a substantial reorganization of personnel at the beginning of the academic year. One-half of the management team was brought in from outside of the organization to fill a vertical cross-section of positions. The reorganization was sufficiently extensive that it produced approximately 90% "new" vertical dyads. A vertical dyad was considered "new" if at least one member was a newcomer to his position after the reorganization. Given the personnel policies of the university, this setting produced a stable cohort of 60 managers moving together through a 9-month "shake down" period.

PROCEDURE

Data collection was divided into four interview waves: (a) The initial wave began immediately after the first month of the academic year; (b) the second wave began after the third month; (c) the third wave began after the sixth month; and (d) the final wave began after the eighth month. Each wave consisted of interviews with the 60 managers and with the superiors of these managers. Although the 60 managers in this study were superiors of other members, only the 17 managers who had members in this study were interviewed as superiors. Interviews of the 60 managers about their situation as members were conducted by one member of the research staff. Interviews with the 17 superiors about each of their members were conducted by two other staff members. For more detail on the setting, procedures, instruments and scaling methods employed, see Graen, Dansereau, Haga, and Cashman (in press) and Dansereau (1972).

INSTRUMENTS

Four sets of instruments were employed to assess (a) negotiating latitude, (b) the superior's contribution to vertical exchange in terms of his activities toward the member, (c) the member's contribution to vertical exchange in terms of his role behavior, and (d) various outcomes of the exchange process.

Table 1   Product Moment Correlations of the Negotiation Latitude Scale Across Time ($N = 60$)

Time period	Pearson product moment correlation
Second month to fourth month	.59
Second month to seventh month	.59
Second month to ninth month	.60
Fourth month to seventh month	.73
Fourth month to ninth month	.66
Seventh month to ninth month	.75

NEGOTIATING LATITUDE

Negotiating Latitude was defined as the extent to which a superior is willing to consider requests from a member concerning role development. At a conceptual level, at one end of the continuum a superior is unwilling to allow or help a member to influence his role (low negotiating latitude), while, at the other end of the continuum a superior is willing not only to allow but also to help a member to influence his role (high negotiating latitude).

Two questions were employed to assess each member's perception of two aspects of his opportunity to negotiate on various aspects of his role. The first question asked the member: "How flexible do you believe your supervisor is about evolving changes in your job activity structure?"[2] The second question asked the member: "Regardless of how much formal authority your supervisor has built into his position, what are the chances that he would be personally inclined to use his power to help you solve problems in your work?"[3] The correlations between these two component variables were .62, .71, .66, and .72 at each time period, respectively. The responses to these two measures were summed to form a measure of the member's negotiating latitude. The correlations across time for this scale are shown in Table 1.

SUPERIOR EXCHANGE

In order to measure the superior's contribution to the exchange process, some of the outcomes which could be exchanged by the superior ("Leadership Attention" and "Leadership Support") and some of the consequences of these outcomes ("Dyadic Problems" and "Superior Sensitivity") were assessed.

MEASURING LEADERSHIP ATTENTION

The first measure of leadership behavior, consisted of eight activities which included: (a) allowing a member to participate in decisions affecting him, (b) providing the member accurate information and feedback, (c) assuring the member of his confidence in him, and (d) paying attention to a member's feelings and needs, among others. The members evaluated these leadership activities in terms of (a) how much they were getting (a great deal to a little) and (b) how much they preferred to be getting (much more to much less). A superior employing the same eight activities reported how much attention each member needed to perform his role "adequately and without undue dissatisfaction" (a great deal to a little). The unit-weighted responses of the members and superiors were summed separately to form three leadership attention measures (received, preferred, and needed).

MEASURING LEADERSHIP SUPPORT

The second set of leadership activities concerned the superior's supportive behavior. The members evaluated the superior's supportive behavior in terms of 12 activities which included: (a) standing up for the member even if it made him unpopular with others, (b) backing up the member in dealing with the administration, and (c) following through on his or her promises and the like. For each activity the members indicated how often they preferred the superior to engage in the activity (more often, less often). A superior, in turn, indicated how often he supported each of his members by responding to the questions: "How often do you back up what (the member's name) suggests?" and "How often do you accept and implement changes which (the member's name) suggests?" (Never . . . Always). The unit-weighted responses of the superiors and members were summed separately to form two leadership support measures (Preference for support and Frequency of support).

MEASURING DYADIC PROBLEMS AND SUPERIOR SENSITIVITY

Two measures were employed to index the consequences of the superior's activities for the member. The first measure, labeled "Dyadic Problems," was developed from information gathered in the first interview wave. During the second wave of interviews the members and the superiors (for each of their members) indicated the severity of the following dyadic problems: Strains in the working relationship with my superior; unsure of what my superior wants me to do in this job; lack of evaluation of my job performance and back biting within the superior's unit.[4] The second set of questions designed to measure the consequences of the superior's behavior was called "superior sensitivity." This scale included the member's responses to the following five items: the extent to which the superior (a) understood his problems and needs, (b) recognized his potential, (c) helped him to know what he was supposed to be doing, (d) let him know what was expected, and (e) let him know where he stood.

MEMBER EXCHANGE

In order to measure the member's contribution to the exchange process, some of the outcomes which could be exchanged by the member (Role Behavior) *and* some of the consequences of these outcomes (Role Discrepancy and Role Congruency) were assessed.

MEASURING ROLE BEHAVIOR

Role behavior was defined as the amount of time and energy the member invested in each of the various activities included in his job. To construct a list of the activities actually performed by the members an "aided-recall" procedure (Graen, 1973) was used with the members and their superiors during the first interview wave. Using a content analytic procedure on the verbatim activities generated during this first wave, a master activity list of 22 items was constructed. During each subsequent interview wave, a member indicated how much time and energy he was spending on each of the 22 activities (member now). The superiors in turn estimated for each of their members separately (a) how much time and energy the member was expending on each of the 22 activities (superior now), and (b) how much time and energy the superior preferred that member to expend on each activity (superior ought).[5] To avoid analysis of redundant data we reduced the 22 activities by principal component factor analysis to four factor scales. The four factors were: (i) Counseling activities, (ii) Programming activities, (iii) Communicating activities, and (iv) Administrating activities. For both perspectives (superior and member) the unit-weighted time and effort scores were summed according to their factor loadings.

Within the organization three major groupings of roles which contained rather different task structures could be identified. The first group consisted of Head Residents who were responsible for the operations within a cluster of housing units. The second group consisted of Supportive Services who were responsible for the "Bricks and Mortar" throughout the organization. The third group consisted of Student Affairs who were responsible for servicing the special programs for residents throughout the organization. These three major job types showed strong relationships to the activity scales. While these relationships supported the discriminant validity of these factor scales, the purpose of the current study was to examine the effect of negotiating latitude across differing types of roles. Thus the job type variance was partialled out. By subtracting each subordinate's time and energy allocations from the average of individuals doing the same type of work, each individual's score was adjusted to reflect his time and energy allocation relative to others doing the same type of work.[6]

Employing this procedure the following two measures were used in the current analysis.

Member Now (MN). A member's estimate of the amount of time and energy he spends on a particular activity relative to others doing the same type of work. A positive value indicates that the member's time and energy allocation on a particular activity is above the average of those performing the same type of work, and a negative value indicates it is below the average.

Role Discrepancy (| SN—SO |). An estimate of the extent to which the superior perceives a particular member's activities (SN) as corresponding to his own preferences (SO) regardless of whether the member's activities are perceived as above or below the superior's expectations (the absolute value of the difference between the superior's relative perception and his relative preferences for the subordinate). A higher score indicates a larger discrepancy between what a superior reports his member doing and what he preferred that member to be doing.

A third factor analytically derived measure, Role Congruency, was employed to tap the member's perception of his ability to change his role according to his own preferences. The three questions which were summed to form this scale were the extent to which the member had (a) the opportunity to contribute as much as he wanted to his role, (b) the ability to define his role, and (c) the ability to bring about changes he wanted in his role.

ROLE OUTCOMES

The final set of instruments were designed to measure the member's attitude toward and reaction to his situation. The members' attitudes toward their situation were assessed by the Role Orientation Index (ROI). This instrument uses an adjective check list similar in format to the Job Description Index (Smith, 1967). (See Graen, Dansereau, and Minami (1972) and Dansereau (1970) for details of the development of the ROI.) Employing the ROI, members were asked to describe their situation in terms of the following outcomes: (a) the intrinsic value of their work, (b) the psychological value of their job performance rewards (pay, promotions, etc.), (c) the technical competence of their superior, and (d) the interpersonal relationship with their superior. In addition overall job satisfaction was measured by the Hoppock Job Satisfaction Blank, (Hoppock, 1935). A member's reaction to his situation also was indicated by whether he stayed with or left the organization during the 1-year period after the study.

Because the interviews with the superiors and the members were rather lengthy, all instruments were not employed at all time periods. Table 2 presents a summary of all the instruments employed. For each instrument, the respondent, method and timing is shown.

Table 2   Data Matrix

Variable	Respondent	Method	Timing months after reorganization			
			2	4	7	9
Independent variable:						
Negotiation latitude	Member	I	X	X	X	X
Dependent variables:						
Superior exchange						
Activities:						
Leadership attention						
Received	Member	Q			X	X
Preferred	Member	Q			X	X
Needed	Superior	Q			X	X
Leadership support						
Preference for support	Member	Q		X	X	X
Frequency of support	Superior	Q			X	X
Consequences:						
Dyadic problems	Member	I	D	X		
Dyadic problems	Superior	I	D	X		
Superior's sensitivity	Member	I		X	X	X
Member exchange						
Activities:						
Member's role behavior	Member	I	D	X	X	X
Consequences:						
Role discrepancy	Superior	I	D	X	X	X
Role congruency	Member	I		X	X	X
Role outcomes						
Role orientation index	Member	Q	X		X	(X)
Overall satisfaction	Member	Q	X		X	
Turnover	Records	One year period after the study				

Note: I indicates verbal interview questions; Q indicates self-administered questionnaire; X indicates data collected. D indicates if and when the measure was developed from within the sample.

ANALYSIS

Since the purpose of the current study was to focus upon attempts to employ leadership and supervision early in the dyad's development and trace the later consequences, the member's estimate of his negotiating latitude assessed one month after reorganization served as the independent variable. By holding a vertical dyad at its assessed degree of negotiating latitude early in the process, it was possible to analyze social exchanges as they developed over the remaining 7 months. One advantage of this design is that all reliable relationships with the independent variable are predictive rather than concurrent.

Examination of the distribution of scores on the negotiating latitude scale at the second month after reorganization revealed a negatively skewed distribution. This distribution suggested that the sample could be divided into two nearly equal groups with those perceiving markedly high negotiating latitude numbering 29 and those perceiving lower negotiating latitude numbering 31. Those reporting the opportunity to negotiate with the superior on their role behavior (high negotiating latitude) will be called initially "IN" with their superior; while those reporting less of a chance to negotiate with the superior will be called initially "OUT" with their superior.

In order to test the appropriateness of dividing the sample into an "IN" group and an "OUT" group, it may be assumed that this IN—OUT dichotomy capitalizes heavily on error variance. If this is the case, according to Campbell and Stanley (1963), the high scorers (or IN group) should decline on subsequent measurements of negotiation latitude, while the low scorers (or OUT group) should rise. Over time the two groups should regress to the same population mean. In order to examine the appropriateness of this dichotomy, the groups (IN and OUT) were considered as the independent variable and the measures of negotiating latitude at the fourth, seventh and ninth month were considered as the dependent variable in a repeated-measures analysis of variance design (Winer, 1972). As shown in Table 3, by employing a one-way analysis of variance with two groups at each time period (Hays, 1963), those who scored high on negotiating at 2 months after reorganization (IN group) are significantly higher in negotiation latitude at 4, 7 and 9 months. Moreover the significant repeated-measures group effect indicates that the IN group is significantly higher than the OUT group on negotiation latitude across all time periods. In addition to suggesting the appropriateness of dividing the sample into these two groups, this analysis demonstrates the statistical design to be employed through the current study.

In sum, dichotomized negotiating latitude at the second month after the reorganization served as the independent variable and the remaining measures as the dependent variables for the purpose of analysis.

Table 3	Mean Over Time of Negotiation Latitude for High and Low Negotiation Latitude Groups								
	4 months		7 months		9 months		Probability		
	Out group	In group	Out group	In group	Out group	In group	Group effect	Time effect	Group × time
Measure									
Subordinate's estimate of his Negotiation Latitude	6.2	7.4*	5.8	7.2*	5.4	7.1*	.0004	.001	.43

Note: In (High, $N = 29$) and Out (Low, $N = 31$) groups were determined by the subordinate's estimate of his own negotiation latitude at the second month after reorganization. The dependent variable is the subordinate's estimation of his negotiation latitude at 4, 7, and 9 months after reorganization.

*p < .01 t test of the difference between groups at one time period.

Figure 1   Leadership Attention Received By Member

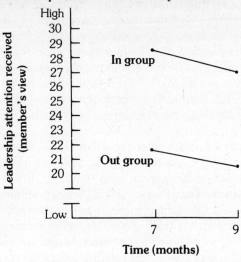

RESULTS
Unit Composition

Before considering the impact of negotiating latitude upon the development of dyadic relationships, it is helpful to examine the way in which negotiating latitude was initially perceived within each unit. One possibility corresponds to the traditional assumed case that negotiating latitude must be offered by the superior to all members equally and must be perceived in the same manner by all the members of the unit. If this view is accurate, then all of the members within a unit should be either in or out with the superior. Only 15% of the units showed all members as either "in" or "out" with the superior. The remaining 85% of the units showed a mixture of "in" and "out" members. The significant difference between these proportions (.15 vs .85, $p < .01$) suggests the units in agreement with the more traditional view (15%) were not representative of the distribution of negotiating latitude within most units (85%).[7]

Thus the labeling of the negotiation latitude groups as the "in group" and the "out group" can be said to reflect not only the level of negotiating latitude received but also the way in which negotiating latitude was initially distributed in most units. Specifically, within most units very early in their development, we find an in group (those receiving high negotiating latitude) and an out group (those receiving low negotiating latitude).

Leadership Attention

The first aspect of the nature of vertical exchange within the dyad concerned the extent to which the members reported receiving leadership attention from the superior in terms of his allowing the member to participate in decisions affecting his work, giving the member complete and accurate information and the like. As shown in Fig. 1, the in-group members reported receiving significantly higher leadership attention from the superior than that reported by the out-group members. The difference between the two groups on leadership attention at each time period and across all time periods was statistically reliable ($p < .001$). Focusing upon the member's preferences for this type of attention, as shown in Fig. 2, the out-group members reported preferring higher additional leadership attention than that reported by the in-group members. The difference between these two groups on their preferences for leadership attention was statistically reliable at each time period and across all time periods ($p < .001$). To summarize these two findings then, the out-group members reported receiving lower leadership attention but preferred higher additional attention than the in-group members. These results suggest that both groups valued leadership attention about the same; however, the in group reported receiving more of the attention than the out group.

Turning to the superior's view of leadership attention reveals the results shown in Fig. 3. In contrast to the member's reports, the superior did not report that the out-group members needed as much leadership attention as the in group members. On the contrary, the superior reported that his in-group members, in order to accomplish their jobs adequately and without undue dissatisfaction, required higher leadership attention than that reported for the out-group members. This overall difference of the superior's report of leadership attention required by the in versus out group was marginally significant across all time periods ($p < .08$). This set of results suggests that not only did the in group receive higher leadership attention but also that the superiors believed that this differential attention within the unit was required for adequate unit functioning.

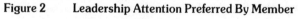

Figure 2   Leadership Attention Preferred By Member

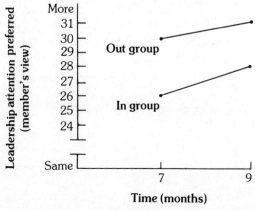

Figure 3   Leadership Attention Required By Member

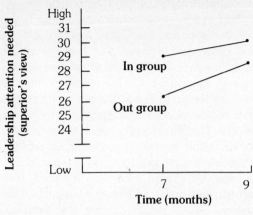

Leadership attention needed (superior's view)

High
31
30
29
28
27
26
25
24

In group

Out group

Low

7   9

Time (months)

Leadership Support

The second set of measures of the superior's activities toward the member measured the extent to which the member preferred leadership support and the extent to which the superior reported offering support to each of his members. Analysis of the member's preferences for support produce the set of results shown in Table 4. As shown in this table, the out group reported higher preferences than that reported by the in-group members. The difference between these two groups was statistically reliable at each time period and across all time periods ($p < .001$). In contrast, as shown in Table 4, the superior reported giving his in-group members somewhat higher support than that reportedly given to the out group. This difference between the two groups on the superior's report of the amount of support extended was marginally significant ($p < .06$). Taken together these results suggest that in-group subordinates were

Table 4   The Amount of Leadership Support Preferred by and Given to In Group and Out Group

	Means						Probabilities		
	4 months		7 months		9 months		Repeated measures		
Variable	Out group	In group	Out group	In group	Out group	In group	Group effect	Time effect	Group × time
Member's view:									
Preference for support	55.1	48.9*	55.2	49.6*	55.9	49.0*	.001	.870	.750
Superior's view:									
Support offered			9.0	9.4	8.9	9.7*	.060	.280	.280

*$p < .05$ t test of the difference between groups at one time period.

Table 5   **Perceived Consequences of the Superior's Behavior on the Member's Working Relationship**

	Means						Probabilities		
	2 months		7 months		9 months		Repeated measures		
Variable	Out group	In group	Out group	In group	Out group	In group	Group effect	Time effect	Group × time
Superior's view:									
Dyadic problems	7.0	5.1					.001*	NA	NA
Member's view:									
Dyadic problems	7.7	5.7					.001*	NA	NA
Superior's sensitivity	14.9	17.3*	13.9	16.8*	12.5	15.8*	.001	.001	.590

*$p < .05$ t test of the difference between groups at one time period.

receiving higher support from the superior and that the out groups' unfulfilled need for support was not reflected in the superior's supportive behavior.

Dyadic Problems and Supervisory Sensitivity

While the previous measures were concerned with a superior's behavior toward his members, the current set of measures are directed toward the consequences for the member of this behavior. A direct measure of these consequences is the extent to which the superior's behavior created problems for the members. The results of the analysis of the superior's behavior as a source of job problems for the members are shown in Table 5. As can be seen in this table, not only did the out-group members report the superior as more of a source of job problems, but also, the superior reported that the out-group members experienced more problems with him in terms of knowing what he expects and so on. Also as shown in Table 5, compared to the out-group members, the in-group members perceived the superior's behavior as higher in responsiveness to their job needs. The difference between the out group and in group on their reports of the superior's sensitivity was statistically reliable at each time period and across all time periods ($p < .001$).

Summary of Superior Exchange Results

In terms of the nature of the superior's activities within the dyad, the in group received higher leadership attention and support than the out group. Moreover, those initially receiving higher negotiating latitude (in group) reported less difficulty in dealing with the superior (for example, knowing what he expected) and perceived the superior's behavior as more responsive to their job needs (including the superior letting them

Table 6   Time and Energy Allocated Among Various Activities By In and Out Group Over Time

| | Means | | | | | | Probabilities | | |
| | 4 months | | 7 months | | 9 months | | Repeated measures | | |
Variable	Out group	In group	Out group	In group	Out group	In group	Group effect	Time effect	Time × group
Counseling	−.17	.17	.05	−.05	−.22	.22	.53	.99	.41
Planning	−.20	.20	.38	−.38	−.16	.16	.97	.99	.32
Communicating	−1.29	1.48*	−.57	.56	−.56	.61*	.01	.99	.02
Administering	−.91	.91*	−.87	.87*	−.87	.87*	.01	.99	.99

*$p < .05$ t test of the difference between groups at one time period.

know what he expected and where they stood with him, and helping them with their problems and role development, and the like). Thus those who initially received more latitude in negotiating their roles clearly were the favored members within the superior's unit.

Role Behavior

Turning to the member's behavior, Table 6 shows the average allocation of time and energy by the in group and out group. Recall that a positive value indicates greater than average expenditure relative to others doing the same type of work. A negative value indicates a lower than average expenditure of effort relative to others doing the same type of work. For counseling and planning activities (Table 6) the difference between the in group and out group is not statistically reliable. By contrast, the in-group members report expending significantly higher time and energy communicating and administering than that reported by the out-group members ($p < .01$). Moreover, the reliable group-by-time interaction ($p < .02$) on communicating indicates that the difference between the two groups on communicating becomes smaller over time. An additional analysis revealed that the in group tended to show greater variance on these four activity factors than the out group.

Analyzing the superior's evaluation of member role behavior reveals the set of results presented in Table 7. Recall that the higher the value, the larger the discrepancy between the superior's report of a member's behavior and his preferences for that member's behavior. As shown in Table 7, a superior generally tended to evaluate his in-group member's role behavior as corresponding more to his preferences than the out-group member's role behavior. A conservative estimate of overall discrepancy was calculated by summing the discrepancies for all 22 activities at each time period. The difference between the in and out groups on the overall discrepancy measure is shown in Fig. 4. This difference is statistically reliable across all time periods ($p < .04$). These results suggest that over time the superior tended to evaluate the in-group

Table 7 Role Discrepancy Between the Superiors Perceptions and Preferences

| | Means | | | | | | Probabilities | | |
| | 4 months | | 7 months | | 9 months | | Repeated measures | | |
Performance discrepancy	Out group	In group	Out group	In group	Out group	In group	Group effect	Time effect	Group × time
Counseling	.79	.61	1.07	.61	1.47	.97	.03	.01	.55
Planning	1.39	1.59	2.95	2.23	2.67	2.14	.18	.00	.11
Communicating	2.35	2.61	4.16	3.18	3.18	2.64	.07	.01	.70
Administering	2.18	2.09	1.73	1.57	1.57	1.87	.35	.03	.85

member's behavior more favorably than that of the out group (despite the apparent diversity of the in-group's role behavior).

The results for the member's perception of the extent to which he perceives his role behavior as congruent with his own preferences are presented in Fig. 5. As shown in this figure, the in-group members reported that their role was more highly congruent with their own preferences than that reported by the out-group members. This difference between these two groups on role congruency was statistically reliable across all time periods ($p < .01$).

Summary of Member Exchange Results

These results show that the in-group members spent more time and energy in communicating and administering activities than the out-group members. Moreover, the behavior of the in group was evaluated as

Figure 4 Deviation Of Member's Behavior From That Preferred By His Superior

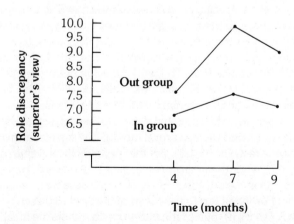

Time (months)

Figure 5   Congruence Of Role With Member's Preferences

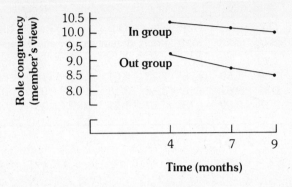

corresponding more closely to *both* the member's and the superior's preferences than was the behavior of the out group. These findings suggest that the way in which a superior initially mediated negotiating latitude had consequences for the member's opportunity to "personalize" his job. Equally important, these findings suggest that the superior may have been seeking and later evaluating a contribution from his in-group members that is far more valuable to his unit than simply a greater expenditure of effort.

Role Outcomes

The final analyses were designed to assess the member's evaluation of and reaction to his job situation. In terms of a more general satisfaction measure (Hoppock Job Satisfaction Blank), the in-group members across the second and seventh time periods expressed higher satisfaction with their jobs than that expressed by the out-group members ($p < .03$). In terms of more specific outcomes, as shown in Table 8, the in-group members expressed more positive attitudes than those expressed by the out group toward the intrinsic outcomes of their work ($p < .01$), their interpersonal relations with the supervisor ($p < .001$), their supervisor's technical competence ($p < .01$), and the value of their job performance rewards ($p < .001$). As shown in this table, the differences between the two groups on these attitudinal variables are significant at each time period except for the assessment of the psychological value of job performance rewards at the second month. The significant group × time interaction effect ($p < .03$) on the psychological value of rewards suggests that while the in group evaluated their rewards more favorably across time than the out group, this difference became more pronounced over time. For the in group the mean of the rewards received remained stable (21.7 to 21.8), but for the out-group members the mean of the job performance rewards decreased over time from 20.2 to 17.8. It may be of interest to note that one reason this role outcome was not measured at

Table 8   **Evaluation of Role Outcomes by the In Group and Out Group**

	Means						Probabilities		
	2 months		7 months		9 months		Repeated measures		
Variable	Out group	In group	Out group	In group	Out group	In group	Group effect	Time effect	Group × time
Intrinsic outcomes of work	16.5	17.3*	15.4	17.0*	15.3	16.6*	.010	.001	.370
Supervisor: Interpersonal relations	19.3	22.9*	18.8	22.4*	17.6	21.5*	.001	.001	.920
Supervisor: Technical competence	9.1	10.3*	8.5	9.3*	8.0	9.4*	.010	.001	.660
Rewards: Psychological values	20.2	21.7	17.8	21.8*			.001	.030	.030

*$p < .05$ t test of the difference between groups at one time period.

the ninth month was the strong objection by some to the relevance of these rewards in their situation. It seems plausible that these objections may have come from the out-group members. Indeed, 55% of the out-group members left the organization during the 1-year period after the study, and only 34% of the in-group members left. This set of results suggests that these two groups evaluated and reacted to the outcomes of their respective situations very differently.

DISCUSSION

The results of this longitudinal investigation of the managerial role making process, taken as a whole, produce a rather elaborate scenario of the differentiation of the organizational unit. Contrary to the views of most organizational scientists, organizational units were shown to be differentiated based upon the relationships between the superior and each of his members. Quite soon after the reorganized unit began to function, the differences in the developing vertical dyad linkages were identified in terms of the members' initial ability to negotiate with their superior. These initial differences foreshadowed the differentiation of the units into the cadre and the hired hands.

Superior Exchange

Over time, the cadre became the objects of the superior's concern and attention as compared to the hired hands. Compared to the hired hands, the cadre reported receiving higher amounts of information, influence, confidence, and concern from the superior (leadership attention). That these were valued outcomes for even the hired hands was demonstrated by the higher preferences for these outcomes reported by them compared to the cadre. The superiors for their part showed that this differential treatment was not merely a fantasy of the members by reporting that the cadre actually required higher levels of these supervisory mediated outcomes than the hired hands to perform their jobs adequately and without undue dissatisfaction. Based upon these reports from the superiors, these outcomes appear to function at least partly as inputs to adequate performance in the eyes of the superiors. This suggests that the differential treatment of members by superiors may be instrumental to adequate unit functioning. The question that these results raise is how can differential treatment aid unit functioning? The answer quickly suggested by differential psychology is based upon merit: Reward the more dependable with a more attractive package of outcomes than that given to the less dependable. But how is dependability defined by superiors?

Member Exchange

The evidence clearly indicates that the cadre members were seen by their superiors as more dependable than the hired hands. The superiors reported that the cadre were expending time and energy more closely to that preferred by them than that reported for the hired hands. On the members' part, the cadre reported higher involvement in administering and communicating activities than did the hired hands, but the cadre was also seen as doing more what the superior wanted them to do. Even though the cadre reported higher levels of latitude in performing their functions (job enrichment?) apparently this latitude was not abused but exercised dependably.

Another aspect of these differential relationships was the support the superior gave to his members. The exercise of latitude in performing one's job is closely dependent upon the support extended by the superior. Without a good deal of confidence that one's superior will support innovative approaches to problems and tasks on the job, the assumption of such risk as an exercise of latitude is not likely to occur. In this study, the superiors reported giving higher support for the actions of the cadre than that reported for the actions of the hired hands, even though the hired hands reported a higher preference for support than that reported by the cadre.

Consequences of Vertical Exchanges

Some of the costs of unit differentiation appear in the reported severity of job problems and in the reported job attitudes of the members. Both the members and the superiors reported that the hired hands experienced higher difficulty with the superior's behavior than that reported for the cadre. Judging from the sensitivity of the superior reported by the members, this set of problems, rather than being resolved somewhat over time, remained more severe for the hired hands as opposed to the cadre. Finally, the attitudes and reactions (turnover) of the members clearly reflected the reward value of the differential treatment over time.

Figure 6   Traditional Unit Becomes Differentiated During Role Making

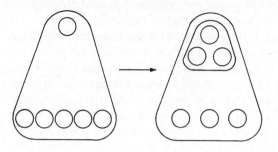

Superior-Member Exchange

Based upon these results, the fact of unit differentiation is indeed difficult to deny. However, once we have accepted the inescapable fact of unit differentiation, we must consider its implications for our understanding of how superiors react to their situation (Fig. 6).

One view of the differentiation process is that the superior of a new or reorganized unit finds himself in a problematic situation. His most valuable resource, his own time and energy, is often inadequate to perform all of the functions for which he is held primarily responsible in the eyes of his superiors. He simply cannot devote the required time and energy to each and all of his members to ensure their optimum performance. Fortunately, a subset of his members usually can perform the majority of the critical functions of the unit. Therefore, the superior invests a disproportionate amount of his time and energy in developing a select subset of his members. Once these members shoulder their share of the burden of the unit, the superior maintains his disproportionate attention to these members and their critical tasks (leadership relationship).

But what about the unselected subset of members who receive only the residual amount of time and energy of the superior? What happens to these almost forgotten members in the rush to develop and maintain a cadre of trusted assistants? How does the superior influence these impoverished ordinary members? The one concept that describes the relationship of the superiors to these hired hands is "supervision," influence by direct appeal to the formal authority of his office.

Commitment and Leadership

This view of the organizational unit as becoming differentiated based upon the superior's behavior into leadership relations with some members and supervision relations with other members is a plausible alternative to the traditional view of leadership. In addition, the findings of the present study directly contradict the traditional view that while superiors as individuals may vary in their ability to do so, they must rely solely upon their own formal authority to ensure adequate unit functioning.[8] This traditional view apparently is based upon the assumption that the member's roles are such that proper unit functioning will flow directly from a member's compliance with some legitimately prescribed role. However, our results suggest that once these roles are filled with real people, compliance with a prescribed role may not be enough to ensure the adequate fulfillment of all of the unit's functions. In addition, the adequate fulfillment of all of the unit's functions may require the personal commitment of a few key members to the success of the unit's mission. It seems likely that faced with such a situation a superior will seek to develop such commitment in some of his members.

To develop this commitment, the superior cannot employ his formal authority since commitment can only be volunteered by the members. Thus in the hope that the member will develop "ownership" feelings toward the unit and work for the success of the unit, the superior may offer the member wider latitude in his role, more leadership attention, greater support, and larger influence on the unit's operation. In sum, the superior may encourage the member to actually negotiate his duties and relationships within the unit in the hope that the member will invest some of himself in the role and assume some responsibility for the unit's success. As a result, events affecting the unit may be perceived by the member as not only having consequences for the superior but also as having consequences for the committed members. The results of this study suggest that by allowing a member to negotiate his role the superior may gain critical assistance from members committed to the unit's success. In this manner the superior can improve the survival potential of his administration.

Considering this commitment phenomenon suggests that becoming involved in this process restricts the behavior of the superior. His behavior toward his potential trusted assistants cannot, even in crisis situations, degenerate into influence based solely upon the legitimate authority of the office. This quick and effective conformity mechanism is apt to destroy the member's commitment to the unit's success. Moreover, the superior must consistently support the exercise of job latitude that results from the negotiation process as well as encouraging the selected members to take action. This is especially the case when such agreements between the superior and member are unlikely to be formally sanctioned. If the superior fails to support the member's exercise of negotiated latitude, the negotiated promise is empty and commitment would probably not occur. This suggests that the superior would be likely to offer negotiating latitude to members he believes can be trusted to accept some responsibility for the success of the unit and do the right thing or, more simply, members he can depend upon. Within most units it seems unlikely that a superior would typically perceive all of his members as "ready" for the substantial amount of latitude and support of their actions which could be involved in this negotiation process.

Supervision and Leadership as Processes

This process of allowing some members the opportunity to negotiate their roles goes beyond Jacobs' (1971) view of leadership as involving "an interaction between persons in which one presents information of a sort and in such a manner that the other becomes convinced that his outcomes (benefits/costs ratio) will be improved if he behaves in the manner suggested." The results of the current study suggest that leadership within formal organizations involves the active exchange of leadership inputs and outcomes. During the negotiation process, the trusted assistants of the leader share in both the leader's resources (superior exchange) and the leader's responsibilities (member exchange). This points to an exchange process in which the superior assists the member in developing a "vested interest" in desirable role behaviors. In a *real* sense these members' own outcomes are improved or maintained by engaging in behaviors which are desirable from the supervisor's point of view. For example in the current study the role behavior of the trusted assistants was in line not only with superior's preferences but also with the members' own role preferences.

Over time as the trusted members become trusted assistants, the superior may become more dependent upon them not only to assure adequate unit functioning but also to deal with problems that may arise within the unit. On the other side the trusted assistants may become more dependent upon the superior for the rewards of their contributions (e.g., visibility in the organization, and eventual promotions). As this interdependence (exchange) develops, a relatively tight clique may form between the superior and his trusted assistants and preclude free movement into or out of the clique over time. Additionally, the vast amounts of time invested by the superior in the trusted assistants during the negotiation process may also discourage the superior from replacing them.

In sum, these results suggest that units become differentiated into trusted assistants and ordinary members. The trusted assistants accept additional responsibilities and duties and are compensated by greater latitude in doing their job and by special treatment from the superior. In this way the superior may invest his most valued resource, his own time and energy, most efficiently to assure adequate unit functioning. As a consequence, the relationship between trusted assistants and the superior becomes characterized by leadership relations, while the relationship between the ordinary members and the superior remain characterized by supervision relations.

The Use of Leadership and Supervision

In terms of the leadership process, these results suggest that a superior may allow at least some of his members to negotiate their roles with him, in order to produce new understandings about their respective role behaviors.[9] In a functionally interdependent system, the superior is dependent upon the behavior of his members or at least some of his members, and the members are dependent upon the behavior of the superior: mutual dependence. Moreover, the superior can be expected to make demands upon his members and they upon him. One significant aspect about the organizational situation is that the superior almost always has formal authority over his members. The key distinction between leadership and supervision in the organization is the way in which a superior uses his formal authority. In supervision, a superior uses his authority to force the member to comply with some prescribed role. The cost of this to the superior probably involves the time necessary to initiate control systems and to monitor reward and punish appropriate behavior. In leadership, a superior may share his authority to gain commitment. In the current study the leader by using whatever power he had to enrich the roles of his trusted assistants, may have won the commitment of these members, thereby enhancing his control over the unit. One cost to the superior probably involves the time necessary to allow, promote and support the member in developing his role gradually over time.

Under certain conditions the use of the leadership technique can be more costly than the use of supervision. For example a number of "cost" factors may be involved in a superior's estimation of a member's dependability or "readiness" for the negotiation (leadership) process. A particular superior may be personally inclined to select members who are compatible with him in terms of technical competence and interpersonal skills. In some cases the selection may be based upon the prejudices (style) of the superior or prior experience with the member. In addition, if a superior feels sufficiently threatened by the technical or interpersonal competence or incompetence of all of his members, the superior may not use the leadership technique. Likewise, if a superior is granted little or no latitude by his superior or if the role system is a complete program, the superior's ability to negotiate with his members may be restricted and the leadership process may be unlikely to unfold. Much more research is needed to determine the boundary conditions under which a superior can be expected to use the leadership technique during the role making process.

CONCLUSION

In conclusion, the results of this investigation imply that contrary to most contemporary models of leadership a given superior can establish "leadership" relationships with some of his members and at the same time establish "supervision" relationships with other of his members.

Furthermore, this differentiation of organizational units over time based upon the apparent negotiation of the members' roles opens new and unexplored avenues for research of leadership in formal organizations. No longer need researchers examining leadership behavior be content to search only for the behavior of the leader toward his members in general on the average, but instead they might probe the exchange processes between the leader and each of his members. Rather than simply seeking the optimum balance between concern for people and concern for production, the researcher can search for the effective means of identifying and developing the appropriate mix of members required for effective unit performance on a number of dimensions, while at the same time minimizing the negative consequences of this process. Although the management of an organizational unit clearly involves dealing with the entire set of members, leadership can only occur in the vertical dyad. Long enough we have been fixated on the entire set of members. Now it is time to examine the various vertical dyads and their development over time.

REFERENCES

Bock, R. D., & Haggard, E. A. The use of multivariate analysis of variance in behavioral research. *In* D. K. Whitla (Ed.), *Handbook of measurement and assessment in behavioral sciences.* Reading, MA: Addison-Wesley, 1968.

Campbell, D., & Stanley, J. *Experimental and quasiexperimental design for research.* Chicago: Rand-McNally, 1966.

Campbell, J. P., Dunnette, M. D., Lawler, E. E., & Weick, K.E., Jr. *Managerial behavior, performance and effectiveness.* New York: McGraw-Hill, 1970.

Dansereau, F. The invisible organization. Unpublished Ph.D. dissertation, University of Illinois, 1972.

Dansereau, F., Jr. Some correlates of supervisory behavior. Unpublished M. A. Thesis, University of Illinois, 1970.

Dansereau, F., Cashman, J., & Graen, G. Instrumentality theory and equity theory as complementary approaches in predicting the relationship of leadership and turnover among managers. *Organizational behavior and human performance,* 1973, 10, 184-200.

Evans, M. G. The effects of supervisory behavior on the path-goal relationship. *Organizational behavior and human performance,* 1970, 5, 277-298.

Fleishman, E. A., Harris, E. F., & Burtt, H. E. *Leadership and supervision in industry.* Columbus: Bureau of Educational Research, Ohio State University, 1955.

Graham, W. A. Perceptions of leader behavior and evaluation of leaders across organizational levels. *Experimental publication system (APA),* 1970, 4, 144A.

Graen, G. Role making processes within complex organizations. *In* M. D. Dunnette (Ed.), *Handbook of industrial and organizational psychology,* in press.

Graen, G., Alvares, K., Orris, J. B., & Martella, J. Contingency model of leadership effectiveness: Antecedent and evidential results. *Psychology bulletin,* 1970, 74, 285-296.

Graen, G., Dansereau, F., Haga, W., & Cashman, J. *The invisible organization.* Boston, MA: Schenkman, in press.

Graen, G., Dansereau, F., Jr., & Minami, T. Dysfunctional leadership styles. *Organizational behavior and human performance,* 1972, 7, 216-236.

Graen, G., Dansereau, F., Minami, T., & Cashman, J. Leadership behaviors as cues to performance evaluation. *Academy of management journal,* 1973, 16, 611-623.

Guion, R., & Gottier, R. Validity of personality measures in personnel selection. *Personnel psychology,* 1965, 18, 135-164.

Harmon, H. H. *Modern factor analysis.* Chicago: University of Chicago Press, 1967.

Hays, W. L. *Statistics for psychologists.* New York: Holt, Rinehart & Winston, 1963.

Hoppock, R. *Job satisfaction.* New York: Harper and Brothers, 1935.

Jacobs, T. *Leadership and exchange in formal organizations.* Alexandria, VA: Human Resources Research Organization, 1971.

Katz, D., & Kahn, R. *The social psychology of organizations.* New York: Wiley, 1966.

Korman, A. K. "Consideration," "initiating structure" and "organizational criteria": A review. *Personnel psychology,* 1966, 19, 349-361.

McMahon, T. The contingency theory: Logic and method revisited. *Personnel psychology,* 1972, 25, 697-709.

Nash, A. Development of an SIVB key for selecting managers. *Journal of applied psychology,* 1966, 50, 250-254.

Shiflett, S. The contingency model: Some implications of its statistical and methodological properties. Report No. 996, US Army Medical Research Laboratory, Fort Knox, KY, 1972.

Smith, P. C. The development of a method of measuring job satisfaction: The Cornell studies. *In* E. H. Fleishman (Ed.), *Studies in personnel and industrial psychology.* Homewood, IL: Dorsey, 1967.

Stogdill, R. M., & Coons, A. E. *Leader behavior: Its description and measurement.* Columbus: Ohio State University, Bureau of Business Research, 1957.

Vroom, V., & Mann, F. Leader authoritarianism and employee attitudes. *Personnel psychology,* 1960, 13, 125-140.

Winer, B. J. *Statistical principles in experimental design.* New York: McGraw-Hill, 1972.

NOTES

[1]Jacobs (1971) does not employ the vertical dyadic approach. He does suggest that supervision and leadership are not mutually exclusive in terms of a superior's behavior. By not considering the dyads inside of the unit he fails to directly describe leadership and supervision from both the member's and superior's side of the exchange. Thus, he did not logically consider whether a member can develop both supervision and leadership relations with a superior. In order to consider this point Jacobs' (1971) view was reconceptualized in terms of role theory. The view of supervision exchange derived is similar to Katz and Kahn's (1966) role taking model. The view of leadership exchange presented is similar to that presented by Graen, Dansereau, Minami, and Cashman (1973). The difference between this view and Jacobs' view of leadership is elaborated upon in the Discussion section.

[2]The response alternatives were (1) "He sees no need for change," (2) "He sees little need for change," (3) "He is lukewarm about change," and (4) "He is enthusiastic about change."

[3]The response alternatives were (1) "No change," (2) "He might or might not," (3) "He probably would," and (4) "He certainly would."

[4]The response alternatives were "Not a problem," "A minor problem," "Somewhat of a problem," and "A major obstacle."

[5]The response alternatives for each activity were (1) "none," (2) "A little," (3) "A moderate amount," and (4) "A considerable amount."

[6]This procedure was employed for each activity factor (counseling, etc.), for each perspective (the superior and member), and for each time period separately. This last step equated time and energy allocation means between time points thereby partialling out the effect of differential calendar demands (Bock, 1968).

[7]An analysis using the average negotiation latitude in the unit as the independent variable and the same set of dependent variables as presented here, revealed results significantly weaker than presented here. This analysis suggested that the weaker results found using the traditional approach may have been due to the research strategy of averaging the member's responses and thus losing valid variance.

[8]This is basically the supervision technique. This is not to deny people may vary in their ability to use supervision. Indeed Jacobs (1971, p. 316) hypothesizes several methods or styles for reducing the cost of supervision, for example, avoiding punitive methods in supervising. Nor is this to deny that a superior may be in a position where he must use supervision and only requires compliance from the members. However, as Jacobs points out, an individual's ability to use the supervision technique is not leadership.

[9]This suggests that superiors as individuals can also vary in terms of their ability to use the leadership technique. For example Jacobs (1971) suggests that individuals may vary in their ability to effectively use and learn social exchange skills.

An Historical Discontinuity: From Charisma to Routinization

GRAEME SALAMAN

This article may be seen as a response to Peabody's (1970) argument that the study of organizations requires ". . . generalizations as to what types of authority lead to what types of consequences for different types of organizations under a variety of stable and crisis situations" (p. 328).

This is a case study of one organization at a particular time in its history—a time when senior members of the organization were self-consciously attempting to break with the past and establish new procedures and new philosophies of management. The research was part of this planned change, and the essential conclusions of the research formed the basis of a change program which is outlined below. Furthermore, the analysis presented here was openly discussed with the members of the organization on various occasions, and it formed the explicit basis of the change program.

Because this is a case study it is not possible to regard the arguments and conclusions as anything more than tentative, but it is hoped that these arguments will at least prove of sufficient interest to suggest possible areas of investigation to other researchers.

The argument, basically, is as follows. The company concerned (Browns) has for many years been dominated by a highly autocratic

"An Historical Discontinuity: From Charisma to Routinization" by Graeme Salaman, *Human Relations*, Volume 30, Number 4, 1977, pp. 373-388. Copyright © 1977 by Tavistock Institute of Human Relations. Reprinted by permission of Plenum Press.

managing director. The critical features of this man's dominance were threefold. First, he insisted on a personal involvement in all aspects of the organization and was not prepared to sacrifice his right to influence, overturn, or replace any decision or process. This undoubtedly highly competent manager was not willing to dilute his personal control and authority by vesting decision-making rights in other people or other jobs, or, if he did, such delegation was constantly liable to alteration or denial. Second, this type of centralized power was closely related to a high degree of vagueness, ambiguity, and confusion concerning job specifications. Other managers were not and could not be sure of what they were meant to do. This followed partly from the managing director's refusal to delineate his subordinates' responsibilities, and partly from his predisposition arbitrarily to change even those job responsibilities he had apparently agreed to or implied. Finally, the vast majority of the company's managers had been personally selected—often from the shop floor—by the managing director, and relations between them and their superior were extremely personal. Because most of these managers had spent all their working lives in this one company and were frequently unqualified in management, they were all the more vulnerable to their superior's arbitrary and dramatic management style.

These three interrelated features of the managing director's dominance resulted in a number of consequences for the current structure and process of the organization. It is argued that the way in which the managers of the company currently organize their work and relate to their subordinates, and their attitudes and feelings towards their colleagues and their company, are still strongly influenced by the previous managing director's behavior, even though in real organizational terms he is of greatly diminished significance. It is maintained that, ironically, the three features of his behavior described above have created a high level of role anxiety among the current directors and managers—an anxiety which is based upon ignorance of job responsibilities, uncertainty about job competence, an unwillingness to consider models of job behavior and work relationships other than very minimal ones—with the result that the current managers tend to perpetuate the forms of behavior displayed by the previous managing director. In short, the article demonstrates some of the problems inherent in a move from personal, or charismatic, authority to more routinized, more organizational forms of leadership, by suggesting that the more influential the personal authority the more likely it is that surviving members of the organization, no matter how much they may wish to initiate new methods, will be trapped in established responses, attitudes, relationships, and organizational procedures. It argues that previous forms of authority, and the organizational characteristics with which they are closely interrelated, continue to exert influence even after the actual personnel involved have left the scene, and it tries to delineate some of the mechanisms of this persisting influence.

In discussing these issues the paper touches upon a number of issues in organization theory, which can be briefly mentioned. First, it has frequently been remarked that sociological writings on organizations tend to overemphasize the collective or macro- aspects of the phenomenon and to underplay the importance of the individuals operating within it. This paper argues that it is both possible and necessary to consider organizational structure as, to some extent, the result of the behavior and decisions of the organization's leaders. This suggestion is in line with Child's recent paper (1972) in which he points out that the structure of an organization should be seen not as the result of the working out of some ineluctable logic deriving from such abstractions as "technology," "environment," or "size," but from the choices and evaluations of those who ". . . have the power to direct the organization" (p. 2). Child emphasizes that even to the extent that contextual variables are important in determining organizational structure they achieve their significance through the ways in which they are perceived, assessed, and evaluated by what he calls "the dominant coalition." Child argues for the necessity, in studying organizational structure, to consider ". . . the process of choice itself in which economic and administrative exigencies are weighed by the actors concerned against the opportunities to operate a structure of their own and/or other organizational members' preferences" (p. 16). This article, in regarding the structure of a particular organization as a consequence of patterns of behavior and superior-sub-ordinate relationships initiated by the founding father of the organization, and as a result of managers' attempts to cope with and reduce the anxieties such behaviors and relations induce, represents a further rejection of a conceptualization of organization structure in terms of inexorable contextual forces.

A second relevant theoretical issue is the question of the nature of organizational roles and their relationship to actors' experience of anxiety, strain, etc. Hickson (1966) has pointed out that organizational theory and theorists have converged on ". . . the specificity (or precision) of role prescription and its obverse, the range of legitimate discretion" (p. 225). As he points out, a number of theorists have argued that low specificity of role prescriptions results in anxiety, and others have argued that high specificity reduces confusion. However, other writers have questioned this direct relationship between specificity of role prescriptions and anxiety. This issue is discussed in the present paper with reference to the nature of the roles of members of the organization that was researched. In this way this paper may be seen as relevant to current debates about the nature and consequences of organizational roles.

Furthermore, this paper is relevant to the discussion about various alternative forms of organizational control. The traditional view, deriving from Weber, Parsons, Gouldner, Stinchcombe, Burns and Stalker, and so on, argues for two broad types, variously named, involving different methods of control. These types are seen to vary with respect to the degree of centralization and formalization, these two variables being regarded as varying together. Recently, however, it has been argued that ". . . these two expressions of bureaucratization" (Blau & Schoenherr,

1971, p. 9) need not occur together, that organizations may be relatively decentralized and yet, through the existence and employment of formalized procedures and standards, genuine autonomy and discretion may be greatly limited. Equally, Perrow (1972) has argued that even in apparently "organic" organizations, for example, those employing professionals, members' behavior can still be controlled despite the absence of ". . . conventional items of rules and commands" (p. 157) by what he calls "unobtrusive means of control" that are responsible for as much as 80% of organizational behavior. The present paper, too, maintains that formalization and centralization can vary independently, and also focuses on varieties of organizational control.

Finally, as the quotation from Peabody reveals, this article is about authority, and the relationship between forms of authority and other features of the organization. More than this, the paper investigates the difficulties of moving from a highly personal authority to a more institutionalized form, and considers the ways in which a particular type of overall leadership has consequences for all other superior-subordinate relationships.

COMPANY BACKGROUND

The company is a medium-sized manufacturing company situated in the Midlands, employing a work force of approximately 1350 on a traditional craft production system. The vast majority of the employees (1200) are engaged in the production process. Half the productive work force are women, and their work consists of applying relatively unskilled, or at most semiskilled, processes to the product. The production departments are the most important ones in the company, in terms of size, prestige, and influence. Other subsidiary and "back-up" departments are usually small and regarded as secondary to the essential and highly skilled production process. The sales department is small, since the company has traditionally relied on large and standard batch orders which are usually repeated regularly. The finished product is only manufactured to order. The company has an established reputation for the quality of its products and caters for the expensive, "quality" end of the market. It is highly successful: for the three years preceding the research (in 1971) profits had been around 12% of the annual turnover (approximately £8,000,000).

In 1962 the company was taken over by a large British multinational corporation with a wide range of interests. At this time Browns was nominally merged with two other subsidiary companies of the new parent corporation to become a three-company subgroup specializing in very similar products. The other two companies took Browns' name and, like the original Browns, came under the control of an overall divisional authority. Before the takeover Browns was a family firm.

The work force at the company is somewhat unusual in that there appears to be a high level of commitment and attachment to the company. Turnover is low, even among the unskilled women workers. Among the managers the great majority have worked at Browns all their working lives (except for service in the armed forces) and most were promoted from shop floor or office jobs. At the time of the research there had been no management trainee intake.

The company owes its current successful trading position to the early direction and leadership of a man, Mr. Brian, who is currently the chairman of the company. For many years until just before this research was conducted, Mr. Brian was managing director of the company—from before the war until the late 1960s, when he was formally installed as chairman of the company and his directorial function was taken over by a board of directors, all promoted from within the company. The formal role of chairman lacks much real influence or content.

Mr. Brian joined the company in the 1930s as a friend of the Brown family, when the company was apparently on the brink of failure. By obtaining a number of large orders he managed to set the company on the path that has led to its present successful position. Within the company he is regarded with enormous awe and deference, by managers and shop floor workers. There are three main grounds for this. First, his reputation as a businessman; second, the fact that when he was in charge of the company (as he was for 30 years) he retained complete control, often in a highly personal, arbitrary, and autocratic manner, over all sections, departments and activities; and third, because part of this control meant that he personally selected, recruited, trained, and sanctioned the present managers and directors.

Mr. Brian's personal control, when he was managing director, was retained through a highly distinctive and autocratic management style. He expected total commitment and loyalty from his hand-picked managers (who were well aware that they owed their positions entirely to him) and required them to be totally knowledgeable about every aspect of the staffing, order-processing, etc. which he thought fell within their sphere of control and responsibility. He punished any display of ignorance or any misdemeanor by administering sharp, personal, savage, and often public rebukes.

Mr. Brian's personal dominance was supported by a policy of ambiguity and vagueness concerning his subordinates' job descriptions. He refused to grant formal titles or to specify job responsibilities. He was unwilling to formalize procedures or regulations, and while he insisted that his managers did what he wanted them to do he was not prepared to specify concretely and adequately just what his expectations were. He frequently allocated the same task to more than one person, but he would not grant sufficient authority to his managers to enable them to do even those tasks that they considered to be their responsibility. (For example, he retained control over all matters of personnel selection and recruitment and giving or withholding salary increases.) Furthermore, his style of personal involvement in all aspects of the company and his lack of regard for the managers' authority meant that he would frequently contact junior managers, foremen, or skilled workers directly. This resulted in an unusual degree of personal familiarity between the managing director and the shop floor, but it also undermined the authority of the middle managers, who would discover that their orders had been countermanded, and that their subordinates were engaged in jobs which they knew nothing about. Thus their authority over their subordinates was reduced, along with their capacity to utilize efficiently and to coordinate the activities and work of their subordinates.

Under Mr. Brian the company displayed many of the features of a medieval court, rather than a modern organization. The personal and arbitrary nature of Mr. Brian's authority had direct implications not only for the culture of the organization and for the attitudes and confidence of the employees, as will be seen, but also for the structure of the company. For one thing, the structure of the company and the nature of the personnel involved reflect Mr. Brian's retention of final, and ovewhelming, authority. Hall (1972) notes that Pondy (1969) confirms this link between autocratic organizational control and organizational structure: "The data suggests that owner-managers and partnerships are less likely to add professional and administrative personnel, probably owing to their unwillingness to dilute their personal power. Although this might lead to less profitability, it maintains their existing organization and stability" (Hall, 1972, p. 127).

Another structural consequence of Mr. Brian's management style has already been noted: his highly personal, possibly charismatic authority (i.e., it was seen to inhere in him as a person rather than in his formal organizational position) was directly related to, and fed off, ambiguous and confused distribution and allocation of responsibilities and tasks. Tausky (1970) has noted this relationship: "Charismatic authority administrates by means of staff or servants devoted to the person of the leader. *The leader by whim may delegate authority to personal followers, or withdraw it. Spheres of delegated authority are rapidly changeable, as are the grounds for bestowing authority on subordinates*" (p. 124; my emphasis).

A further systematic consequence of Mr. Brian's management style, and one which is of considerable importance in any explanation of the persistence of some of the structural consequences of his domination, concerns the "followers'," in Tausky's terms, reactions to the "arbitrary delegation and withdrawal of authority" by their managing director. It was most apparent that Mr. Brian's management style and the structural ambiguities and confusions which were related to it, plus the personal part he played in the selection and promotion of the *current* management team, have severely reduced the managers' confidence in their management abilities and have directly influenced their interpretation of their job responsibilities and duties. Even though Mr. Brian is now semiretired and has more or less withdrawn from an active role in the company, the extent and style of his domination still influence the structure, culture and relationships of the company.

COMPANY STRUCTURE

The most striking characteristic of the company is its low degree of formalization, in terms of Hall's (1972) sensible definition of this concept: "Formalization is the organizational technique for prescribing how, when and by whom tasks are to be performed" (p. 196).

The structure of Browns is loosely formalized; the company lacks written or formal procedures, job descriptions, and rules. The emphasis is firmly placed on knowing through doing, on experience of the company and how it works, on personal acquaintance and personal relationships. This emphasis is obviously related to the fact that the majority of the managers have been with the company all their working lives and lack, in most cases, any formal technical or professional education or qualification. The managers' jobs are ill-defined and lines of authority are vague. It was not uncommon, during the interviews, to find that a manager might consider himself responsible for someone who, it later transpired, had no knowledge of this at all.

Frequently the managers remarked that it had taken them a long time to find out what to do, and that this had caused them uncertainty and anxiety. What they did was the result of their search for areas of responsibility and their reactions to crises which they learned to be their responsibility. If they had had a predecessor they could have imitated his behavior; but for most the gradual delineation of an area of responsibility was the result of years of trial and error. Not surprisingly, it was the errors which were most influential. Mr. Brian's responses to and treatment of his subordinates have already been described. As a result of Mr. Brian's arbitrary and undermining behavior the managers had learned to define their jobs in terms of the minimal but safest content: the supervision and control of their subordinates. Their reaction to vagueness of role specificity and to fear of rebuke was a defensive one: they devoted themselves to the inspection and monitoring of their subordinates' work activities.

But if the structure of Browns is loosely formalized, it would be a mistake to imagine that this looseness of definition is in any way similar to the sort of organizational structure which Burns and Stalker (1961) describe as "organic." This concept involves, at least, two elements. First, a looseness of definition of function: ". . . the adjustment and continual re-definition of individual tasks through interaction with others" (Burns & Stalker, 1961, p. 121) which is contrasted to the ". . . precise definition of rights and obligations and technical methods attached to each functional role" (p. 120), the latter being regarded as characteristic of the mechanistic system. A second element in the distinction concerns the distribution of authority throughout the two types. In the organic type of organization the looseness of formalization is paralleled by a high degree of decentralization of authority, with relatively autonomous members exercising discretion over a wide, unpredictable, and nonroutine number of cases whereas in the mechanistic type the operation proceeds by virtue of, and in accordance with, formalized rules and procedures and centralized authority.

The situation at Browns reveals that these two elements of degree of formalization and of centralization can vary independently. At Browns, as has been noted, formalization is loose, but centralization is high. The managers are surprisingly lacking in autonomy and authority. One aspect of this, already mentioned, is that managers have no control over subordinates' salaries, promotions, etc. Another aspect is that at every level they experience interference from the level above. Rarely are people allowed to get on with a job without some sort of high level interference from their superiors. As noted above, these superiors, like every other manager in the company, have learned to define their jobs in terms of supervision, monitoring, and interference. Furthermore, the lack of clarity about responsibilities and functions means that the managers are constantly seeking to cover and protect themselves by seeking the support, backing, and approval of their superiors, which in turn serves to confirm the latters' opinion that the subordinates require help and are unable to operate without assistance.

The culture of the organization is markedly unbureaucratic and personal. There is an atmosphere of friendliness and egalitarianism that is taken by those who work for the company not simply as a description of the ways things *are,* but also of the way things *should be.* It would seem that there is some empirical basis for these beliefs. The loosely formalized structure, the personal nature of many working relationships, and the involvement of all levels of management in their subordinates' work all serve to reduce formal hierarchical differences. But it should be clear that while these factors may lend support to a culture of egalitarianism, they do not imply anything about the actual distribution of power within the organization. In fact, despite the myths which are current within the company, power is still very tightly centralized, and this feature of the organizational structure is of paramount importance to any understanding of organizational *practice* as opposed to organizational *rhetoric.*

In short the current structure of the company reveals two essential features: first, managers' jobs and responsibilities are very loosely defined and delineated, and for various reasons the managers have reacted to this uncertainty by defining their jobs for themselves in terms of supervising and monitoring their subordinates' jobs. Second, and most important, this looseness of role specificity is not paralleled by any decentralization of decision-making. On the contrary, the managers are not even granted such authority as might be necessary for the execution of their responsibilities, and power is still very tightly controlled and retained by the board of directors. In the next section we shall see how these features of the organization—features of which the managers and directors are entirely aware, and about which they are anxious—are related to the various aspects of Mr. Brian's system of control and domination.

AUTHORITY

For obvious and sensible reasons many organizational researchers have noted the central determinant role played by patterns of control within organizations in structuring activities and relationships. Since the defining feature of organizations is the regularity and predictability they display, it is not surprising that so much interest should have been devoted to understanding the nature of, and variations in, processes of organizational control and authority. A usual and important distinction in such work is that between power and authority. Whereas power is the ". . . production of intended effects" (Russell, 1960, p. 25), authority refers to a certain sort of relationship within which the intended effects are produced by the consent of the subordinate. Under these conditions the power is regarded as legitimate. (It might of course be argued that power to establish and maintain the legitimacy of power is the most important sort of power; authority is thus not just something that can be true of any type of power, but is actually a type of power in itself. Certainly the investigation of ways in which organizations try to legitimate their patterns of hierarchy and domination is an important topic of research.)

Clearly, within organizations, which are hierarchic and inegalitarian social structures, power and authority are crucial features of organizational life. However, although a great deal of research into organizational power and authority has been carried out, most of it has focused on the bases (and correlates) of forms of legitimacy, and little has been done on the organizational and structural *consequences* of particular patterns of domination.

The situation at Browns suggests that it is unrealistic to study the nature and distribution of authority relations within an organization except in terms of the history of that enterprise and the characteristics of the early, initiating, entrepreneurs. As Moore (1959) has remarked: "The creative strategy of a business is frequently undeveloped and unbalanced in its initial form. It tends to emphasize the special interests, talents, possessions, behavior and general orientation of the founding father" (p. 221). Furthermore, particular patterns of domination tend to be related to aspects of organizational structure; indeed, to depend upon them.

But for our purposes the most striking feature of the form of managerial control exercised by the departing managing director, Mr. Brian, is not that it was related to other structural features (loose formalization, etc.) but that its effects were still apparent even after he had left the scene. It is the persistent influence of his management style which requires explanation, and the relationship between past systems of relationships and behavior and the features of the current organizational structure as outlined in the previous section that requires analysis. Why is it that the managers, although conscious of the influence of the departing managing director and keen to initiate organizational change, find themselves unable to free themselves from his influence?

The managers at Browns, as a result of their exposure to Mr. Brian's style of management and the organizational features which supported his method of domination, experience considerable role uncertainty and consequent role anxiety. Their experiences have caused them to be underconfident, to be uncertain about what they should do, and to have fears about their competence. Furthermore, the fact that these feelings and conditions are widespread within the company means that patterns of relationships actually support these feelings. Managers and directors tend to react to their subordinates.

It has been argued before that organizations, and especially those characterized by uncertainty and confusion, generate anxiety and insecurity. Theo Nichols (1969) remarks: ". . . the modern corporation is a prolific generator of anxiety and insecurity. Indeed one might expect that corporation managers would be characterized by some degree of psychological uncertainty. One might even argue that modern corporation directors are anomic, since not only do the corporation's various publics expect different things of them, but many of the objectives they claim to set themselves are often not clearly defined, or are not finite ones" (p. 125).

The managers and directors at Browns experience considerable ambiguity about what they are meant to do, and what standards of performance are expected of them. Previously, as argued above, such uncertainty was a systematic correlate of the managing director's management style. The result is anxiety: anxiety about what to do and about standards of competence. The relationship between ambiguity and anxiety has been noted before. Kahn, Wolfe, Quinn, and Snoeck (1964) remark that "The ambiguity experience is predictably associated with tension and anxiety" (p. 84). Furthermore, these authors support the point made here that ambiguity concerning role requirements (i.e., a lack or shortage of adequate information) tends to be related to certain sorts of leadership styles, and they argue that it is particularly related to autocratic forms of organizational control. "If one wants to control the behavior of others, but be master of his own organizational fate, he is tempted to arrange for complete and undistorted information flowing to himself, but to filter and control the information flowing to others" (Kahn et al., 1964, p. 78).

But this is not all. Kahn et al. also point out that one consequence of the sort of anxiety generated by role ambiguity and uncertainty is that subordinates tend to increase their communications with their superiors, presumably in some sort of attempt to establish guidelines for action, and to obtain some feedback. Exactly this sort of communication is extremely common at Browns; indeed it is so frequent that many senior managers claim it interferes with their efficiency.

But how is anxiety related to those features of the organization discussed in the previous section? Even if it were true (and it would seem, even without the evidence from the managers themselves, to be *a priori* quite likely) that exposure to Mr. Brian's management methods generated uncertainty and anxiety, how do these conditions achieve the perpetuation of loose formalization and centralization and the definition of roles and relationships apparent in the company? There are two interrelated mechanisms involved. First, the present board of directors tend to model themselves on the previous managing director. They find it difficult to avoid imitating Mr. Brian's behavior. There are many reasons for this: they are unsure of other management styles; they feel that this sort of behavior is expected of them; they admire this form of domination and they lack the confidence to initiate new patterns of relationships. A further important reason for their unwillingness to practice new and more decentralized management styles is that they not only lack confidence in their own ability, but are also far from persuaded of the competence of their subordinates. Such conceptions of their subordinates' abilities are a direct result of Mr. Brian's unwillingness to delegate authority and his confidence-reducing behavior (see section on Company Background).

The directors are therefore caught in an unfortunate dilemma: they are not prepared completely to reject Mr. Brian's methods, however much they may have suffered under them, because they are unsure of alternatives and lack confidence in their ability to initiate them. At the same time, even if they wish to instigate a process of organizational change and decentralization they feel that their subordinates are, currently at least, ill-equipped to enlarge their jobs and take on new responsibilities. Such doubts are obviously self-fulfilling and, equally obviously, sensible under the circumstances. After years of Mr. Brian's methods the managers have defined their jobs in unadventurous and defensive terms, and they *have* been deprived of opportunities to develop and practice new management skills.

But it is not only the new directors who find themselves trapped in organizational structures and relationships which are similar to those established by Mr. Brian; this is true throughout the company. The directors in perpetuating Mr. Brian's behavior not only maintain the ambiguity and confusion mentioned earlier, but actually increase it. Because the directors are doubtful of their subordinates' competence and because they are committed to a centralized conception of organizational hierarchy they involve themselves in their subordinates' work, undermine their authority, and find it hard to delegate authority. The managers at all levels react by behaving in a similar way towards their subordinates. In interviews many managers remarked that they are unwilling to delegate authority to their subordinates because they think their subordinates are undercompetent (which means that they have never seen it as part of their own job to increase their subordinates' competence) and because they are unwilling to transfer authority and autonomy to their subordinates while they are still deprived of these resources themselves.

In short, one of the mechanisms that connects the managers' anxiety to their perpetuation of particular forms of role definition and superior-subordinate relationships is that because of their uncertainty and anxiety their seniors within the organization are imposing such definitions on them. Because of their predicament the directors are unwilling to decentralize, are doubtful about their subordinates, and are uncertain about and uncommitted to new, alternative management styles, or organizational philosophies and structures. Their behavior sets off a chain reaction of similar responses throughout the organization.

But of course such responses are attractive to the managers anyway. The sort of manager-subordinate relationship evident at Browns is also the consequence of the managers' own preferences. They, and the directors *prefer* to define their roles in terms of those features of their jobs *of which they are sure:* technical quality and control of subordinates' work performances. They see management in control terms rather than any other possible conception. Control of subordinates' work performance involves close monitoring, supervision, and control over quality; in many instances the managers' supervision of their subordinates is extraordinarily fastidious and detailed. Some managers insist on checking every item or task produced or performed within their section. This means that members of the section are unlikely to develop the necessary confidence or competence to take on delegated authority, a situation which is then used as an argument in favor of the necessity of such supervision. Furthermore, this style of management is excessively concerned with the day-to-day at the expense of the long-term. Consequently the managers constantly find themselves in unforeseen crises, and in reacting to these crises they are unable to prepare for, or even to foresee, the next one, and so on.

The managers' unwillingness to depart from such conceptions of their roles and relationships is further increased by the anxiety about their own competence, as well as their subordinates'. The directors and managers were personally selected and recruited by Mr. Brian on the basis of their personal qualities, as he perceived and valued them, and their *technical competence.* But exposure to his distinctive and confidence-reducing management style, and lack of experience of other companies, has caused them to be highly uncertain about their *managerial competence,* and reluctant to initiate new methods or to escape those they are faced with.

In short, when he was managing director of the company Mr. Brian exercised a highly autocratic and personal type of authority. This management style was closely related to various organizational structural variables. Now Mr. Brian has left, but the managers, although they apparently regret it, are unable to escape from these historical forms of role definition and relationship. The reason for this strange example of an undersired historical organizational inertia lies in the high levels of anxiety that the managers experience as a result of their exposure to Mr. Brian's regime. Their lack of confidence in themselves, their colleagues, and their subordinates drives them to define their jobs in terms of supervision and control. It also makes them unwilling to try new management styles, or to delegate responsibility to their subordinates. This defensive interpretation of managerial roles and relationships is encouraged by the fact that other managers—and especially the directors—are also interpreting their jobs in terms of control and supervision; and each manager's refusal to delegate worsens the situation by limiting the resources to be distributed and increasing the atmosphere of mistrust. And so a vicious circle is sustained, with each level of the organization attributing its own behavior to the unnecessary interference and rigidity of the layer above and justifying it in terms of the incompetence of the layer below—a vicious circle whose mainspring is the anxiety generated years previously by Mr. Brian.

STABILITY AND CHANGE

In the midst of stability there is change. Despite the remarkable persistence of management styles, role definitions, and patterns of colleague relationships, it is possible to discern changes taking place in the company. It is now a truism that even the most stable social forms are actually constantly undergoing subtle but significant processes of change. Within organizations such processes are usually explicit and obvious. The striking feature of Browns—and that which constituted the problematic of this paper—is that the company demonstrates an unusual degree of inertia and continuity. But this should not be regarded as implying that no changes at all are taking place.

Not only are changes taking place, but many members of the company are very eager that they should occur. The interesting thing about the company is not only that certain organizational forms have persisted, but that many members of the company sincerely wish to alter these habits, but find themselves unable to change them. They find themselves trapped in the very cycle of anxiety, mistrust, and lack of confidence described earlier, and as a result they and their colleagues behave in ways which exacerbate the situation for each other, and, finally, for themselves. The involvement of the writer in the company and the research which forms the basis of this paper were both the direct result of the senior managers' awareness of their need to establish new forms of behavior, new expectations, and new relationships within Browns. Their difficulty was that they did not know how to effect these changes.

To a great extent their impotence was a result of their conception of the problem. Not surprisingly, in view of what has been argued above, the managers articulated the problem not in terms of their anxiety, or their inability to escape from previous habits and experiences, but in terms of the deficiencies and inadequacies of their colleagues, superiors, and subordinates. The inability to delegate, and the lack of trust and confidence of their superiors, plus the incompetence and lack of ability of subordinates, were, it was claimed, the major reasons for the managers' retention of all the authority they were granted, and were the causes for their necessary involvement in supervision and inspection, rather than management. This was how they saw it. As a result they saw the problem, initially, in terms of management development and assessment, rather than organizational change of a more basic sort.

The actual change program that has been initiated contains a number of elements. The first and most important stage was a series of research interviews with a selection of the company's management. These interviews formed the basis for the analysis outlined above. This analysis was then fed back to the directors and other members of management. The next stage was to devise a procedure whereby superiors and subordinates regularly got together to discuss the nature of the subordinate's job, his satisfaction with it, how it could be done more efficiently, what problems were involved, and so on. These interviews were intended to allow the subordinate to put pressure on his superior to gain greater autonomy and discretion. It was felt that in view of the situation in the company most of the managers would use these interviews to press for greater clarification and greater delegation. This is exactly what happened.

A third stage in the change program consisted of regular visits and interviews with samples of the managers concerned in these interviews. These visits served to ensure that the interviews were taking place and were being acted upon, and also helped to encourage the middle and junior managers to articulate, and strive for, their demands. Often these visits contained some group sessions where collections of managers would voice their difficulties, and would be supported in their suggestions.

It is too early to assess how successful this scheme has been. Certainly it has been very well received by those concerned; certainly significant and influential changes have taken place. And undoubtedly the managers themselves are sufficiently confident in the potential merit and track record of the scheme for them to be committed to it and determined to retain it. The main rationale of the program was to achieve changes in relationships, the distribution of authority, and in role definitions, *through the managers themselves*. It was felt to be arrogant and counterproductive to try to *impose* new patterns, structures, and relationships. Indeed such an imposition would feed the very passivity and dependency that constituted the nub of the problem. Consequently a program was devised which would: (a) inform the managers of the situation as described above; (b) establish procedures which would enable each manager to negotiate the changes he felt were useful, proper, and possible; and (c) assist and support them in articulating and pressing for whatever changes they considered necessary and sensible. In short, the scheme was intended to give the managers themselves both the responsibility for changing their own positions, at least, primarily, vis-á-vis their managers, *and* the necessary confidence to voice and demand such alterations.

It is interesting, finally, to consider briefly the reasons why the directors and the managers are so keen to instigate change processes within their organization. Certainly important is the fact that because of their past experiences they are uncertain of what they are meant to do, and what is expected of them. This disappearance of the charismatic authority has caused the directors to strive for new, routinized organizational forms. As Weber (1964) put it: "One of the decisive motives underlying all cases of the routinization of charisma is naturally the striving for security" (p. 370).

But outside factors are also important. The absorption of Browns into a large mulitnational organization with considerable managerial resources and the latest managerial techniques has caused the directors to worry that the possible deficiencies and weaknesses of Browns' management may be exposed. The desire for change, and finally the change itself, have followed the directors' concern about the competence and efficiency of their company in the face of internal and external changes as they perceive and define them. As we have seen, initially they defined the desired change in terms of management development and appraisal, a conception which is quite in line with Weber's comments on difficulties associated with the routinization of charisma: "The original basis of recruitment is personal charisma. With routinization, the followers or disciples may set up norms for recruitment, in particular involving tests of eligibility" (Weber, 1964, p. 367).

REFERENCES

Blau, P. M. & Schoenherr, R. A. *The structure of organizations.* New York: Basic Books, 1971.

Burns, T., & Stalker, G. M. *The management of innovation.* London: Tavistock, 1961.

Child, J. Organizational structure, environment and performance: The role of strategic choice. *Sociology,* 1972, *6*(1), 1-22.

Hall, R. H. *Organizations: Structure and process.* Englewood Cliffs, New Jersey: Prentice-Hall.

Hickson, D. J. A convergence in organization theory. *Administrative Science Quarterly.* 1966, *11,* 224-237.

Kahn, R. L. Wolfe, D. M., Quinn, R. P., & Snoeck, J. D. *Organizational stress: Studies in role conflict and ambiguity.* New York: Wiley, 1964.

Moore, D. G. Managerial strategies. In W. Warner & N. H. Martin (Eds.), *Industrial man.* New York: Harper, 1959, pp. 219-226.

Nichols. T. *Ownership, control and ideology.* London: Allen and Unwin, 1969.

Peabody, R. L. Perceptions of organizational authority. In O. Grusky & G. A. Miller (Eds.), *The sociology of organizations: Basic studies.* New York: The Free Press, 1970, pp. 319-328.

Perrow, C. *Complex organizations: A critical essay.* Glenview, Illinois: Scott, Foresman, 1972.

Pondy, L. R. Effects of size, complexity, and ownership on administrative intensity. *Administrative Science Quarterly,* 1969, *14,* 47-60.

Russell, B. *Power: A new social analysis.* London: Unwin Books, 1960.

Tausky, C. *Work organizations: Major theoretical perspectives.* Itaska, Illinois: Peacock, 1970.

Weber, M. In T. Parsons (Ed.), *The theory of social and economic organization.* New York: The Free Press, 1964.

PART 3

Lateral Influence

When considering relationships within organizations, we tend to think only of vertical interactions—boss to subordinate or vice versa. We frequently overlook the fact that a great many organizational relationships are of an essentially lateral character. For example, a manager at one level may attempt to influence another manager at roughly the same level, a group may be concerned about how one of its members is behaving in a particular type of situation, or a group may try to influence another group to meet a collective goal beneficial to both. Basically lateral relationships might also exist between a group and an organization, or between an organization and an individual. The feature that characterizes lateral influence situations is that the two parties involved do not have a *clear and unambiguous* hierarchical (vertical) differential between them. Lateral influence does not necessarily require that the amount of power possessed by the two parties be equal—only that one party does not report directly through the chain of command to the other within the organization.

In contrast to vertical influence patterns, neither party is in a position to use formal authority over the other in lateral influence situations. It is the absence of formal authority of one party over the other that distinguishes lateral influence relationships from the downward influence situations discussed in Section II.

Keep in mind that there are many variations of lateral influence situations, several of which will be discussed in the readings. One common type is represented by socialization attempts within the organization. In this example, several parties (that is, the organization, the peer group, influential fellow employees, etc.) are involved in attempting to change the behavior of a new employee, or one who is making a change to a new position or location within the organization. Of course, socialization efforts are not totally and exclusively lateral in character. Sometimes a supervisor or the organization can exert formal authority in the socialization process. However, socialization efforts do involve a great deal of lateral influence, and are therefore included in this section rather than in Section II, which deals with strictly downward influence. Other examples of purely lateral influence situations are: a peer group's influence on an individual member of the group; individuals or groups forming coalitions or alliances; and group versus group or individual versus individual competition (for example, as in some types of line-staff interactions or differing functional departments competing with each other for resources).

The readings in this section begin with two that examine organizational socialization processes. The first of these, by Schein, analyzes the process and effects of socialization. He presents the dangers of subsequent nonconformity or overconformity to both individuals and the organizations for which they work. Schein describes socialization as "the process of 'learning the ropes' . . . the process by which a new member learns the value systems, the norms and behavior patterns of the society, organization, or group which he is entering." It should be noted that socialization in organizational situations does not happen only when a person enters an organization, but also can occur when an individual takes a new position or is transferred to a new location. Particularly important in Schein's analysis is his distinction among pivotal, relevant, and peripheral norms, and how each of these relates to several types of potential responses by the individual. These responses include "rebellion," "creative individualism," and "conformity." Schein concludes with an interesting discussion of the potential for conflict between professional socialization (as carried out in schools of business or management, for example) and socialization within a specific organization.

Van Maanen's article on organizational socialization details seven major dimensions of the process. In effect, these dimensions provide the organization with strategy options for managing the socialization process. For example, organizational socialization can be highly formal or very informal, it can be focused on an individual or on a group of individuals, it can be explicitly sequential or almost totally nonsequential, and so on. The types of strategy employed by the organization in this essentially lateral influence process can have significant consequences for both the individuals (or groups of individuals) who are the target, and for the initiators (the organization).

What are the mechanisms that cause an individual's judgments to be affected by behavior of the members of a group of which he or she is a part? This is the crux of the article by Asch, in which he describes what has come to be considered a "classic" set of experimental procedures. These experiments were designed to understand the social and personal conditions that result in group influence on individual judgments. Although this article and the studies described in it are over 30 years old, the findings and their implications are as important today as they were at the time the experiments were carried out. In fact, these studies stimulated a major area of research in the realm of social psychology for at least a decade thereafter. The findings demonstrate the enormous effect that a majority opinion can have on the single individual in a group. They also show the extent of large individual differences in susceptibility to group influence. The implications of these findings carry a number of important, even crucial, messages for anyone attempting to understand this type of lateral influence situation.

The article by Janis that follows is, in many ways, a close intellectual descendent of the earlier work of Asch. Janis employs striking real-life examples from actual decision situations at the highest level of government to demonstrate how very intelligent individuals can unintentionally suppress "critical thoughts as a result of internalization of the group's norms." Janis labels this process *groupthink,* and the concept is a powerful tool for analysis of the lateral influence effects that take place within groups. The author provides a set of symptoms for recognizing groupthink, and also some suggestions or recommendations for preventing it. It is clear that where groupthink exists in organizational contexts, there is potential for damaging decisions that nobody wants, but that occur all too frequently.

In his article, *"The Abilene Paradox: The Management of Agreement,"* Harvey also deals with influence processes within groups. *The Abilene Paradox*—the derivation of this label will be clear after delving into the article—affects many decisions of groups. The paradox is that "organizations frequently take action in contradiction to the data they have for dealing with problems." As Harvey sees it, the problem is one of "mismanaged agreement." In other words, it is the difficulty that groups have when there is *apparent,* but not real, agreement. The author discusses factors that contribute to the paradox, as well as approaches for diagnosing and coping with it.

Also in the area of group influence is the article by Schein that "examines relationships between communication, group solidarity, and influenceability." This reading provides vivid examples and illustrations of the Chinese Communists' treatment of military and civilian prisoners during the Korean Conflict in the early 1950s. Although the Schein article was published a number of years ago, the analysis contained in it is regarded by those in the field as a classic. The observations that Schein, a social psychologist, made at that time are as pertinent now as they were then, even though U.S. relations with China have since changed drastically. The article focuses on how it was possible for a group (the captors) to create social alienation within a group of peers (the captives). The author analyzes the need for adequate interpersonal communication for an individual's fundamental integrity, and how the cessation of interpersonal cues and communication that confirm normal social relationships results in social alienation. This alienation, in turn, leads to heightened susceptibility to being influenced. While the prisoner of war camp context may seem far removed from typical work organizations, one should not be deterred from using Schein's analysis to gain a better understanding of the fundamental role of interpersonal communication in affecting influence processes in any type of organizational situation.

As noted earlier, individuals or groups often attempt to make alliances—usually of a temporary nature—with other persons or groups in order to obtain some common outcome or results useful to the parties involved. In organizational literature these alliances are labeled *coalitions.* The excerpt from a book by Pfeffer emphasizes the interdependence of units or positions in organizations as the necessary ingredient for the formation of coalitions. The division of labor and specialization of skills that exist in all organizations provide the impetus for building coalitions. In this manner each group or individual obtains something that is not possible by acting alone. A classic example from the realm of government is the "log rolling" that occurs in legislatures when one legislator promises to vote for the bill of another colleague if he or she in turn will reciprocate. In that case a coalition is formed to get both bills passed, each of which will greatly benefit one of the parties. Pfeffer shows that in organizations it is possible to build both external organizational constituencies (utilizing individuals or groups outside the organization to help a party within the organization) as well as internal organizational coalitions. In considering organizational coalitions, it is useful to recognize that the *formation* of coalitions in organizations is essentially a lateral influence process, but the *direction* of the coalition's efforts may be upward, lateral, or downward, depending on the goals involved.

The concluding article in this section illustrates lateral relationships among functional departments within business organizations. Based on interviews, observations, and questionnaire data, the focus in this case is on purchasing departments and how they attempt to influence other units—particularly engineering and scheduling units—within companies. Even though these other units have an "equal" status with purchasing, the article makes it clear that there exists a large repertoire of techniques available to purchasing departments for dealing with their organizational colleagues. Of course, just as the purchasing department has a range of influence methods to apply, each organizational unit has its own means for influencing the other units. The article by Strauss provides a fitting close to this section of the book because it emphasizes the ubiquitous extent of lateral influence relationships within organizations.

Organizational Socialization and the Profession of Management

EDGAR H. SCHEIN

I can define my topic of concern best by reviewing very briefly the kinds of issues upon which I have focused my research over the last several years.[1] In one way or another I have been trying to understand what happens to an individual when he enters and accepts membership in an organization. My interest was originally kindled by studies of the civilian and military prisoners of the Communists during the Korean War. I thought I could discern parallels between the kind of indoctrination to which these prisoners were subjected, and some of the indoctrination which goes on in American corporations when college and business school graduates first go to work for them. My research efforts came to be devoted to learning what sorts of attitudes and values students had when they left school, and what happened to these attitudes and values in the first few years of work. To this end I followed several panels of graduates . . . into their early career.

Organizational socialization is the process of "learning the ropes," the process of being indoctrinated and trained, the process of being taught what is important in an organization or some subunit thereof. This process occurs in school. It occurs again, and perhaps most dramatically, when the graduate enters an organization on his first job. It occurs again when he switches within the organization from one department to another, or from one rank level to another. It occurs all over again if he leaves one organization and enters another. And it occurs again when he goes back to school, and again when he returns to the organization after school.

Indeed, the process is so ubiquitous and we go through it so often during our total career, that it is all too easy to overlook it. Yet it is a process which can make or break a career, and which can make or break organizational systems of manpower planning. The speed and effectiveness of socialization determine employee loyalty, commitment, productivity, and turnover. The basic stability and effectiveness of organizations therefore depends upon their ability to socialize new members.

Let us see whether we can bring the process of socialization to life by describing how it occurs. I hope to show you the power of this process, particularly as it occurs within industrial organizations. Having done this, I would like to explore a major dilemma which I see at the interface between organizations and graduate management schools. Schools socialize their students toward a concept of a profession, organizations socialize their new members to be effective members. Do the two processes of socialization supplement each other or conflict? If they conflict, what can we do about it in organizations and in the schools?

SOME BASIC ELEMENTS OF ORGANIZATIONAL SOCIALIZATION

The term socialization has a fairly clear meaning in sociology, but it has been a difficult one to assimilate in the behavioral sciences and in management. To many of my colleagues it implies unnecessary jargon, and to many of my business acquaintances it implies the teaching of socialism—a kiss of death for the concept right there. Yet the concept is most useful because it focuses clearly on the interaction between a stable social system and the new members who enter it. The concept refers to the process by which a new member learns the value system, the norms, and the required behavior patterns of the society, organization, or group which he is entering. It does not include all learning. It includes only the learning of those values, norms, and behavior patterns which, from the organization's point of view or group's point of view, it is necessary for any new member to learn. This learning is defined as the price of membership.

What are such values, norms, and behavior patterns all about? Usually they involve:

1. The basic *goals* of the organization.
2. The preferred *means* by which these goals should be attained.
3. The basic *responsibilities* of the member in the role which is being granted to him by the organization.
4. The *behavior patterns* which are required for effective performance in the role.

5.   A set of rules or principles which pertain to the *maintenance of the identity and integrity* of the organization.

The new member must learn not to drive Chevrolets if he is working for Ford, not to criticize the organization in public, not to wear the wrong kind of clothes or be seen in the wrong kinds of places. If the organization is a school, beyond learning the content of what is taught, the student must accept the value of education, he must try to learn without cheating, he must accept the authority of the faculty and behave appropriately to the student role. He must not be rude in the classroom or openly disrespectful to the professor.

By what processes does the novice learn the required values and norms? The answer to this question depends in part upon the degree of prior socialization. If the novice has correctly anticipated the norms of the organization he is joining, the socialization process merely involves a reaffirmation of these norms through various communication channels, the personal example of key people in the organization, and direct instructions from supervisors, trainers, and informal coaches.

If, however, the novice comes to the organization with values and behavior patterns which are in varying degrees out of line with those expected by the organization, then the socialization process first involves a destructive or unfreezing phase. This phase serves the function of detaching the person from his former values, of proving to him that his present self is worthless from the point of view of the organization and that he must redefine himself in terms of the new roles which he is to be granted.

The extremes of this process can be seen in initiation rites or novitiates for religious orders. When the novice enters his training period, his old self is symbolically destroyed by loss of clothing, name, often his hair, titles and other self-defining equipment. These are replaced with uniforms, new names and titles, and other self-defining equipment consonant with the new role he is being trained for.

It may be comforting to think of activities like this as being characteristic only of primitive tribes or total institutions like military basic training camps, academies, and religious orders. But even a little examination of areas closer to home will reveal the same processes both in our graduate schools and in the business organizations to which our graduates go.

Perhaps the commonest version of the process in school is the imposition of a tight schedule, of an impossibly heavy reading program, and of the assignment of problems which are likely to be too difficult for the student to solve. Whether these techniques are deliberate or not, they serve effectively to remind the student that he is not as smart or capable as he may have thought he was, and therefore, that there are still things to be learned. . . .

Studies of medical schools and our own observations . . . suggest that the work overload on students leads to the development of a peer culture, a kind of banding together of the students as a defense against the threatening faculty and as a problem-solving device to develop norms of what and how to study. If the group solutions which are developed support the organizational norms, the peer group becomes an effective instrument of socialization. However, from the school's point of view, there is the risk that peer group norms will set up counter-socializing forces and sow the seeds of sabotage, rebellion, or revolution. The positive gains of a supportive peer group generally make it worthwhile to run the risks of rebellion, however, which usually motivates the organization to encourage or actually to facilitate peer group formation. . . .

Let me next illustrate the industrial counterpart of these processes. Many of my panel members, when interviewed about the first six months in their new jobs, told stories of what we finally labeled as "upending experiences." Upending experiences are deliberately planned or accidentally created circumstances which dramatically and unequivocally upset or disconfirm some of the major assumptions which the new man holds about himself, his company, or his job.

One class of such experiences is to receive assignments which are so easy or so trivial that they carry the clear message that the new man is not worthy of being given anything important to do. Another class of such experiences is at the other extreme—assignments which are so difficult that failure is a certainty, thus proving unequivocally to the new man that he may not be as smart as he thought he was. Giving work which is clearly for practice only, asking for reports which are then unread or not acted upon, protracted periods of training during which the person observes others work, all have the same upending effect.

The most vivid example came from an engineering company where a supervisor had a conscious and deliberate strategy for dealing with what he considered to be unwarranted arrogance on the part of engineers whom they hired. He asked each new man to examine and diagnose a particular complex circuit, which happened to violate a number of textbook principles but actually worked very well. The new man would usually announce with confidence, even after an invitation to double-check, that the circuit could not possibly work. At this point the manager would demonstrate the circuit, tell the new man that they had been selling it for several years without customer complaint, and demand that the new man figure out why it did work. None of the men so far tested were able to do it, but all of them were thoroughly chastened and came to the manager anxious to learn where their knowledge was inadequate and needed supplementing. According to this manager, it was much easier from this point on to establish a good give-and-take relationship with his new man.

It should be noted that the success of such socializing techniques depends upon two factors which are not always under the control of the organization. The first factor is the initial motivation of the entrant to join the organization. If his motivation is high, as in the case of a fraternity pledge, he will tolerate all kinds of uncomfortable socialization experiences, even to extremes of hell week. If his motivation for membership is low, he may well decide to leave the organization rather than tolerate uncomfortable initiation rites. If he leaves, the socialization process has obviously failed.

The second factor is the degree to which the organization can hold the new member captive during the period of socialization. His motivation is obviously one element here, but one finds organizations using other forces as well. In the case of basic training there are legal forces to remain. In the case of many schools one must pay one's tuition in advance, in other words, invest one's self materially so that leaving the system becomes expensive. In the case of religious orders one must make strong initial psychological commitments in the form of vows and the severing of relationships outside the religious order. The situation is defined as one in which one will lose face or be humiliated if one leaves the organization.

In the case of business organizations the pressures are more subtle but nevertheless identifiable. New members are encouraged to get financially committed by joining pension plans, stock option plans, and/or house purchasing plans which would mean material loss if the person decided to leave. Even more subtle is the reminder by the boss that it takes a year or so to learn any new business; therefore, if you leave, you will have to start all over again. Why not suffer it out with the hope that things will look more rosy once the initiation period is over.

Several of my panel members told me at the end of one year at work that they were quite dissatisfied, but were not sure they should leave because they had invested a year of learning in that company. Usually their boss encouraged them to think about staying. Whether or not such pressures will work depends, of course, on the labor market and other factors not under the control of the organization.

Let me summarize thus far. Organizations socialize their new members by creating a series of events which serve the function of undoing old values so that the person will be prepared to learn the new values. This process of undoing or unfreezing is often unpleasant and therefore requires either strong motivation to endure it or strong organizational forces to make the person endure it. The formation of a peer group of novices is often a solution to the problem of defense against the powerful organization, and, at the same time, can strongly enhance the socialization process if peer group norms support organizational norms.

Let us look next at the positive side of the socialization process. Given some readiness to learn, how does the novice acquire his new learning? The answer is that he acquires it from multiple sources—the official literature of the organization; the example set by key models in the organization; the instructions given to him directly by his trainer, coach, or boss; the example of peers who have been in the organization longer and thus serve as big brothers; the rewards and punishments which result from his own efforts at problem solving and experimenting with new values and new behavior.

The instructions and guidelines given by senior members of the organization are probably one of the most potent sources . . .

Similar kinds of lessons can be learned during the course of training programs, in orientation sessions, and through company literature. But the more subtle kinds of values which the organization holds, which indeed may not even be well understood by the senior people, are often communicated through peers operating as helpful big brothers. They can communicate the subtleties of how the boss wants things done, how higher management feels about things, the kinds of things which are considered heroic in the organization, the kinds of things which are taboo.

Of course, sometimes the values of the immediate group into which a new person is hired are partially out of line with the value system of the organization as a whole. If this is the case, the new person will learn the immediate group's values much more quickly than those of the total organization, often to the chagrin of the higher levels of management. This is best exemplified at the level of hourly workers where fellow employees will have much more socializing power than the boss.

An interesting managerial example of this conflict was provided by one recent graduate who was hired into a group whose purpose was to develop cost reduction systems for a large manufacturing operation. His colleagues on the job, however, showed him how to pad his expense account whenever they traveled together. The end result of this kind of conflict was to accept neither the cost reduction values of the company nor the cost inflation values of the peer group. The man left the company in disgust to start up some businesses of his own.

One of the important functions of organizational socialization is to build commitment and loyalty to the organization. How is this accomplished? One mechanism is to invest much effort and time in the new member and thereby build up expectations of being repaid by loyalty, hard work, and rapid learning. Another mechanism is to get the new member to make a series of small behavioral commitments which can only be justified by him through the acceptance and incorporation of company values. He then becomes his own agent of socialization. Both mechanisms involve the subtle manipulation of guilt.

To illustrate the first mechanism, one of our graduates went to a public relations firm which made it clear to him that he had sufficient knowledge and skill to advance, but that his values and attitudes would have to be evaluated for a couple of years before he would be fully accepted. During the first several months he was frequently invited to join high ranking members of the organization at their luncheon meetings in order to learn more about how they thought about things. He was so flattered by the amount of time they spent on him, that he worked extra hard to learn their values and became highly committed to the organization. He said that he would have felt guilty at the thought of not learning or of leaving the company. Sending people to expensive training programs, giving them extra perquisites, indeed the whole philosophy of paternalism, is built on the assumption that if you invest in the employee he will repay the company with loyalty and hard work. He would feel guilty if he did not.

The second mechanism, that of getting behavioral commitments, was most beautifully illustrated in Communist techniques of coercive persuasion. The Communists made tremendous efforts to elicit a public confession from a prisoner. One of the key functions of such a public confession, even if the prisoner knew he was making a false confession, was that it committed him publicly. Once he made this commitment, he found himself under strong internal and external pressure to justify why he had confessed. For many people it proved easier to justify the confession by coming to believe in their own crimes than to have to face the fact that they were too weak to withstand the captor's pressure.

In organizations, a similar effect can be achieved by promoting a rebellious person into a position of responsibility. The same values which the new member may have criticized and jeered at from his position at the bottom of the hierarchy suddenly look different when he has subordinates of his own whose commitment he must obtain.

Many of my panel members had very strong moral and ethical standards when they first went to work, and these stood up quite well during their first year at work even in the face of less ethical practices by their peers and superiors. But they reported with considerable shock that some of the practices they had condemned in their bosses were quickly adopted by them once they had themselves been promoted and faced the pressures of the new position. As one man put it very poignantly—"my ethical standards changed so gradually over the first five years of work that I hardly noticed it, but it was a great shock to suddenly realize what my feelings had been five years ago and how much they had changed."

Another version of obtaining commitment is to gain the new member's acceptance of very general ideals like "one must work for the good of the company," or "one must meet the competition." Whenever any counter-organizational behavior occurs one can then point out that the ideal is being violated. The engineer who does not come to work on time is reminded that his behavior indicates lack of concern for the good of the company. The employee who wears the wrong kind of clothes, lives in the wrong neighborhood, or associates with the wrong people can be reminded that he is hurting the company image.

One of my panel members on a product research assignment discovered that an additive which was approved by the Food and Drug Administration might in fact be harmful to consumers. He was strongly encouraged to forget about it. His boss told him that it was the F.D.A.'s problem. If the company worried about things like that it might force prices up and thus make it tough to meet the competition.

Many of the upending experiences which new members of organizations endure are justified to them by the unarguable ideal that they should learn how the company really works before expecting a position of real responsibility. Once the new man accepts this ideal it serves to justify all kinds of training and quantities of menial work which others who have been around longer are unwilling to do themselves. This practice is known as "learning the business from the ground up," or "I had to do it when I first joined the company, now it's someone else's turn." There are clear elements of hazing involved not too different from those associated with fraternity initiations and other rites of passage.

The final mechanism to be noted in a socialization process is the transition to full fledged member. The purpose of such transitional events is to help the new member incorporate his new values, attitudes, and norms into his identity so that they become part of him, not merely something to which he pays lip-service. Initiation rites which involve severe tests of the novice serve to prove to him that he is capable of fulfilling the new role—that he now is a man, no longer merely a boy.

Organizations usually signal this transition by giving the new man some important responsibility or a position of power which, if mishandled or misused, could genuinely hurt the organization. With this transition often come titles, symbols of status, extra rights or prerogatives, sharing of confidential information or other things which in one way or another indicate that the new member has earned the trust of the organization. Although such events may not always be visible to the outside observer, they are felt strongly by the new member. He knows when he has finally "been accepted," and feels it when he becomes "identified with the company."

So much for examples of the process of socialization. Let us now look at some of the dilemmas and conflicts which arise within it.

FAILURES OF SOCIALIZATION—NON-CONFORMITY AND OVER-CONFORMITY

Most organizations attach differing amounts of importance to different norms and values. Some are *pivotal*. Any member of a business organization who does not believe in the value of getting a job done will not survive long. Other pivotal values in most business organizations might be belief in a reasonable profit, belief in the free enterprise system and competition, belief in a hierarchy of authority as a good way to get things done, and so on.

Other values or norms are what may be called *relevant*. These are norms which it is not absolutely necessary to accept as the price of membership, but which are considered desirable and good to accept. Many of these norms pertain to standards of dress and decorum, not being publicly disloyal to the company, living in the right neighborhood and belonging to the right political party and clubs. In some organizations some of these norms may be pivotal. Organizations vary in this regard. You all know the stereotype of IBM as a company that requires the wearing of white shirts and hats. In some parts of IBM such values are indeed pivotal; in other parts they are only relevant, and in some parts they are quite peripheral. The point is that not all norms to which the new member is exposed are equally important for the organization.

The socialization process operates across the whole range of norms, but the amount of reward and punishment for compliance or non-compliance will vary with the importance of the norm. This variation allows the new member some degrees of freedom in terms of how far to conform and allows the organization some degrees of freedom in how much conformity to demand. The new man can accept none of the values, he can accept only the pivotal values, but carefully remain independent on all those areas not seen as pivotal, or he can accept the whole range of values and norms. He can tune in so completely on what he sees to be the way others are handling themselves that he becomes a carbon-copy and sometimes a caricature of them.

These basic responses to socialization can be labeled as follows:

Type 1   Rebellion
Rejection of all values and norms
Type 2   Creative individualism
Acceptance only of pivotal values and norms; rejection of all others
Type 3   Conformity
Acceptance of all values and norms

Most analyses of conformity deal only with the type 1 and 3 cases, failing to note that both can be viewed as socialization failures. The rebellious individual either is expelled from the organization or turns his energies toward defeating its goals. The conforming individual curbs his creativity and thereby moves the organization toward a sterile form of bureaucracy. The trick for most organizations is to create the type 2 response—acceptance of pivotal values and norms, but rejection of all others, a response which I would like to call "creative individualism."

To remain creatively individualistic in an organization is particularly difficult because of the constant resocialization pressures which come with promotion or lateral transfer. Every time the employee learns part of the value system of the particular group to which he is assigned, he may be laying the groundwork for conflict when he is transferred. The engineer has difficulty accepting the values of the sales department, the staff man has difficulty accepting the high pressure ways of the production department, and the line manager has difficulties accepting the service and helping ethic of a staff group. With each transfer, the forces are great toward either conforming or rebelling. It is difficult to keep focused on what is pivotal and retain one's basic individualism.

PROFESSIONAL SOCIALIZATION AND ORGANIZATIONAL SOCIALIZATION

The issue of how to maintain individualism in the face of organizational socialization pressures brings us to the final and most problematical area of concern. In the traditional professions like medicine, law, and teaching, individualism is supported by a set of professional attitudes which serve to immunize the person against some of the forces of the organization. The questions now to be considered are (1) Is management a profession? (2) If so, do professional attitudes develop in managers? and (3) If so, do these support or conflict with organizational norms and values?

Professionalism can be defined by a number of characteristics:

1. Professional decisions are made by means of general principles, theories, or propositions which are independent of the particular case under consideration. For management this would mean that there are certain principles of how to handle people, money, information, etc., independent of any particular company. The fact that we can and do teach general subjects in these areas would support management's claim as a profession.

2. Professional decisions imply knowledge in a specific area in which the person is expert, not a generalized body of wisdom. The professional is an expert only in his profession, not an expert at everything. He has no license to be a "wise man." Does management fit by this criterion? I will let you decide.

3. The professional's relations with his clients are objective and independent of particular sentiments about them. The doctor or lawyer makes his decisions independent of his liking or disliking of his patients or clients. On this criterion we have a real difficulty since, in the first place, it is very difficult to specify an appropriate single client for a manager, and, in the second place, it is not all clear that decisions can or should be made independent of sentiments. What is objectively best for the stockholder may conflict with what is best for the enterprise, which, in turn may conflict with what is best for the customer.

4. A professional achieves his status by accomplishment, not by inherent qualities such as birth order, his relationship to people in power, his race, religion, or color. Industry is increasingly moving toward an acceptance of this principle for managerial selection, but in practice the process of organizational socialization may undermine it by rewarding the conformist and rejecting the individualist whose professional orientation may make him look disloyal to the organization.

5. A professional's decisions are assumed to be on behalf of the client and to be independent of self-interest. Clearly this principle is at best equivocal in manager-customer relations, though again one senses that industry is moving closer to accepting the idea.

6. The professional typically relates to a voluntary association of fellow professionals, and accepts only the authority of these colleagues as a sanction of his own behavior. The manager is least like the professional in this regard, in that he is expected to accept a principle of hierarchical authority. . . .

7. A professional has sometimes been called someone who knows better what is good for his client than the client. The professional's expertness puts the client into a very vulnerable position. This vulnerability has necessitated the development of strong professional codes and ethics which serve to protect the client. Such codes are enforced through the colleague peer group. One sees relatively few attempts to develop codes of ethics for managers or systems of enforcement.

On several bases, then, management is a profession, but on several others it is clearly not yet a profession.

This long description of what is a profession was motivated by the need to make a very crucial point. I believe that management education . . . is increasingly attempting to train professionals, and in this process is socializing the students to a set of professional values which are, in fact, in severe and direct conflict with typical organizational values.

For example, I see us teaching general principles in the behavioral sciences, economics, and quantitative methods. Our applied subjects like marketing, operations management, and finance are also taught as bodies of knowledge governed by general principles which are applicable to a wide variety of situations. Our students are given very broad concepts which apply to the corporation as a whole, and are taught to see the relationship between the corporation, the community, and the society. They are taught to value the long-range health and survival of economic institutions, not the short-range profit of a particular company. They come to appreciate the necessary interrelationships between government, labor, and management rather than to define these as mutually warring camps. They are taught to look at organizations from the perspective of high ranking management, to solve the basic problems of the enterprise rather than the day-to-day practical problems of staff or line management. Finally, they are taught an ethic of pure rationality and emotional neutrality—analyze the problem and make the decisions independent of feelings about people, the product, the company, or the community. All of these are essentially professional values.

Organizations value many of the same things, in principle. But what is valued in principle by the higher ranking and senior people in the organization often is neither supported by their own behavior, nor even valued lower down in the organization. In fact, the value system which the graduates encounter on their first job is in many respects diametrically opposed to the professional values taught in school. The graduate is immediately expected to develop loyalty and concern for a particular company with all of its particular idiosyncrasies. He is expected to recognize the limitation of his general knowledge and to develop the sort of *ad hoc* wisdom which the school has taught him to avoid. He is expected to look to his boss for evaluation rather than to some group of colleagues outside the company.

Whereas the professional training tells him that knowledge is power, the graduate now must learn that knowledge by itself is nothing. It is the ability to sell knowledge to other people which is power. Only by being able to sell an application of knowledge to a highly specific, local situation, can the graduate obtain respect for what he knows. Where his education has taught the graduate principles of how to manage others and to take the corporate point of view, his organizational socialization tries to teach him how to be a good subordinate, how to be influenced, and how to sell ideas from a position of low power.

On the one hand, the organization via its recruiters and senior people tells the graduate that it is counting on him to bring fresh points of view and new techniques to bear on its problems. On the other hand, the man's first boss and peers try to socialize him into their traditional mold.

A man is hired to introduce linear programming into a production department, but once he is there he is told to lay off because if he succeeds he will make the old supervisors and engineers look bad. Another man is hired for his financial analysis skills but is not permitted access to data worth analyzing because the company does not trust him to keep them confidential. A third man is hired into a large group responsible for developing cost reduction programs in a large defense industry, and is told to ignore the fact that the group is overstaffed, inefficient, and willing to pad its expense accounts. A fourth man, hired for his energy and capability, put it this way as an explanation of why he quit to go into private consulting: "They were quite pleased with work that required only two hours per day; I wasn't." . . .

What seems to happen in the early stages of the managerial career is either a kind of postponement of professional socialization while organizational socialization takes precedence, or a rebelling by the graduate against organizational socialization. The young man who submits must first learn to be a good apprentice, a good staff man, a good junior analyst, and perhaps a good low level administrator. He must prove his loyalty to the company by accepting this career path with good graces, before he is trusted enough to be given a position of power. If he has not lost his education by then, he can begin to apply some general principles when he achieves such a position of power. . . .

CONCLUSION

The essence of management is to understand the forces acting in a situation and to gain control over them. It is high time that some of our managerial knowledge and skill be focused on those forces in the organizational environment which derive from the fact that organizations are social systems who do socialize their new members. If we do not learn to analyze and control the forces of organizational socialization, we are abdicating one of our primary managerial responsibilities. Let us not shrink away from a little bit of social engineering and management in this most important area of the human side of the enterprise.

NOTE

[1]This paper was presented as the 1967 Douglas McGregor Memorial Lecture in honor of the late Douglas McGregor, Alfred P. Sloan Professor of Management at the Massachusetts Institute of Technology.

REFERENCES

1. Blau, P. M., and Scott, R. W. *Formal Organizations*. San Francisco: Chandler, 1962.
2. Goffman, E. *Asylums*. Garden City, N.Y.: Doubleday Anchor, 1961.
3. Schein, E. H., Schneier, Inge and Barker, C. H. *Coercive Persuasion*. New York: W. W. Norton, 1961.
4. Schein, E. H. "Management Development as a Process of Influence." *Industrial Management Review,* II (1961), 59–77.
5. Schein, E. H. "Forces Which Undermine Management Development," *California Management Review,* Vol. V, Summer, 1963.
6. Schein, E. H. "How to Break in the College Graduate," *Harvard Business Review,* Vol. XLII (1964).
7. Schein, E. H. "Training in Industry: Education or Indoctrination," *Industrial Medicine and Surgery,* Vol. XXXIII (1964).
8. Schein, E. H. *Organizational Psychology*. Englewood Cliffs, N.J.: Prentice-Hall, 1965.
9. Schein, E. H. "The Problem of Moral Education for the Business Manager," *Industrial Management Review,* VIII (1966), 3-14.
10. Schein, E. H. "Attitude Change During Management Education," *Administrative Science Quarterly,* XI (1967), 601–628.
11. Schein, E. H. "The Wall of Misunderstanding on the First Job," *Journal of College Placement,* February/March, 1967.

People Processing:
Strategies of Organizational Socialization

JOHN VAN MAANEN

Socialization shapes the person—a defensible hyperbole. Organizational socialization or "people processing" refers to the manner in which the experiences of people learning the ropes of a new organizational position, status, or role are structured for them by others within the organization. In short, I will argue here that people acquire the social knowledge and skills necessary to assume a particular job in an organization differently not only because people are different, but, more critically, because the techniques or strategies of people processing differ. And, like the variations of a sculptor's mold, certain forms of organizational socialization produce remarkably different results.

Socialization strategies are perhaps most obvious when a person first joins an organization or when an individual is promoted or demoted. They are probably least obvious when an experienced member of the organization undergoes a simple change of assignment, shift, or job location. Nevertheless, certain people-processing devices can be shown to characterize every transition an individual makes across organizational boundaries. Moreover, management may choose such devices explicitly or consciously. For example, management might require all recruits or newcomers to a particular position to attend a training or orientation program of some kind. Or management may select people-processing devices implicitly or unconsciously. These strategies may simply represent taken-for-granted precedents established in the dim past of an organization's history. The precedent could perhaps be the proverbial trial-and-error method of socialization by which a person learns how to perform a new task on his own, without direct guidance.

Regardless of the method of choice, however, any given socialization device represents an identifiable set of events that will make certain behavioral and attitudinal consequences more likely than others. It is possible, therefore, to identify the various people-processing methods and evaluate them in terms of their social consequences.

BACKGROUND

Three primary assumptions underlie this analysis. First, and perhaps of most importance, is the notion that people in a state of transition are more or less in an anxiety-producing situation. They are motivated to reduce this anxiety by learning the functional and social requirements of their new role as quickly as possible.

Second, the learning that takes place does not occur in a social vacuum strictly on the basis of the official and available versions of the job requirements. Any person crossing organizational boundaries is looking for clues on how to proceed. Thus colleagues, superiors, subordinates, clients, and other work associates can and most often do support, guide, hinder, confuse, or push the individual who is learning a new role. Indeed, they can help him interpret (or misinterpret) the events he experiences so that he can take appropriate (or inappropriate) action in his altered situation. Ultimately, they will provide him with a sense of accomplishment and competence or failure and incompetence.

Third, the stability and productivity of any organization depend in large measure on the way newcomers to various organizational positions come to carry out their tasks. When positions pass from generation to generation of incumbents smoothly, the continuity of the organization's mission is maintained, the predictability of the organization's performance is left intact, and, in the short run at least, the survival of the organization is assured.

A concern for the ways in which individuals adjust to novel circumstances directs attention not only to the cognitive learning that accompanies any transition but also to the manner in which the person copes emotionally with the new situation. As sociologist Erving Goffman rightly suggests, new situations require individuals to reassess and perhaps alter both their instrumental goals (the goals they wish to achieve through their involvement in the organization) and their expressive style (the symbolic appearances they maintain before others in the organization).

In some cases, a shift into a new work situation may result in a dramatically altered organizational identity for the person. This often happens, for example, when a factory worker becomes a foreman or a staff analyst becomes a line manager. Other times, the shift may cause only minor and insignificant changes in a person's organizational identity; for instance, when an administrator is shifted to a new location or a craftsman is rotated to a new department. Yet any of these shifts is likely to result in what might be called a "reality shock" for the person being shifted. When people undergo a transition, regardless of the information they already possess about their new role, their *a priori* understandings of that role are bound to change in either a subtle or a dramatic fashion. Becoming a member of an organization will upset the everyday order of even the most well-informed newcomer. Matters concerning such aspects of life as friendships, time, purpose, demeanor, competence, and the expectations the person holds of the immediate and distant future are suddenly made problematic. The newcomer's most pressing task is to build a set of guidelines and interpretations to explain and make meaningful the myriad of activities observed as going on in the organization.

To come to know an organizational situation and act within it implies that a person has developed some beliefs, principles, and understandings, or, in shorthand notation, a *perspective* for interpreting the experiences he or she has had as a participant in a given sphere of the work world. This perspective provides the rules by which to manage the unique and recurring strains of organizational life. It provides the person with an ordered view of the organization that runs ahead and directs experience, orders and shapes personal relationships in the work setting, and provides the ground rules to manage the ordinary day-to-day affairs.

STRATEGIES OF PEOPLE PROCESSING

Certain situational variables associated with any organization transition can be made visible and shown to be tied directly to the perspective constructed by individuals in transit. The focus here is not on perspectives *per se,* however, but rather on the properties peculiar to any given people-processing situation. These properties are essentially process variables akin to, but more specific than, such generic processes as education, training, apprenticeship, and indoctrination. Furthermore, these properties can be viewed as organizational strategies that distinctly pattern the learning experiences of a newcomer to a particular organizational role.

The people-processing strategies examined below are associated to some degree with all situations that involve a person moving from one organizational position to another. Although much of the evidence comes from studies concerned with the way someone first becomes a member of an organization, the techniques used to manage this passage are at least potentially available for use during any transition a person undergoes during the course of a career. Thus the term "strategy" is used to describe each examined aspect of a transition process because the degree to which a particular people-processing technique is used by an organization is not in any sense a natural condition or prerequisite for socialization. Indeed, by definition, some socialization will always take place when a person moves into and remains with a new organizational role. However, the form that it takes is a matter of organizational choice. And, whether this choice of strategies is made by design or by accident, it is at least theoretically subject to rapid and complete change at the direction of the management.

This is an important point. It suggests that we can be far more self-conscious about employing certain people-processing techniques than we have been. In fact, a major purpose of this article is to heighten and cultivate a broader awareness of what it is we do to people under the guise of "breaking them in." Presumably, if we have a greater appreciation for the sometimes unintended consequences of a particular strategy, we can alter the strategy to benefit both the individual and the organization.

Seven dimensions on which the major strategies of people processing can be located will be discussed. Each strategy will be presented alongside its counterpart or opposing strategy. In other words, each strategy as applied can be thought of as existing somewhere between the two poles of a single dimension. Critically, across dimensions, the strategies are not mutually exclusive. In practice, they are typically combined in sundry and often inventive ways. Thus, although each tactic is discussed in relative isolation, the reader should be aware that the effects of the various socialization strategies upon individuals are cumulative—but not necessarily compatible (in terms of outcome) with one another.

I do not claim that these strategies are exhaustive or that they are presented in any order of relevance to a particular organization or occupation. These are essentially empirical questions that can only be answered by further research. I do claim and attempt to show that these strategies are recognizable, powerful, in widespread use, and of enormous consequence to the people throughout an organization. And, since organizations can accomplish little more than what the people within them accomplish, these people–processing strategies are of undeniable importance when it comes to examining such matters as organizational performance, structure, and ultimately, survival.

Formal (Informal) Socialization Strategies

The formality of a socialization process refers to the degree to which the setting in which it takes place is segregated from the ongoing work context and to the degree to which an individual's newcomer role is emphasized and made explicit. The more formal the process, the more the recruit's role is both segregated and specified. The recruit is differentiated strictly from other organizational members. In an informal atmosphere, there is no sharp differentiation and much of the recruit's learning necessarily takes place within the social and task-related networks that surround his or her position. Thus informal socialization procedures are analytically similar to the familiar trial-and-error techniques by which one learns, it is said, through experience.

Generally, the more formal the process, the more stress there is influencing the newcomer's attitudes and values. The more concerned the organization is with the recruit's absorption of the appropriate demeanor and stance, the more the recruit is likely to begin to think and feel like a U.S. Marine, an IBM executive, or a Catholic priest. In other words, formal processes work on preparing a person to occupy a particular *status* in the organization. Informal processes, on the other hand, prepare a person to perform a specific *role* in an organization. And, in general, the more the recruit is separated from the day-to-day reality of the organization, the less he or she will be able to carry over, generalize, and apply any abilities or skills learned in one socialization setting to the new position.

From this standpoint, formal socialization processes are often only the "first round" of socialization. The informal second round occurs when the newcomer is placed in his designated organizational slot and must learn informally the actual practices in his department. Whereas the first wave stresses general skills and attitudes, the second wave emphasizes specified actions, situational applications of the rules, and the idiosyncratic nuances necessary to perform the role in the work setting. However, when the gap separating the two kinds of learning is large, disillusionment with the first wave may set in, causing the individual to disregard virtually everything he has learned in the formal round of socialization.

Even when formal socialization is deliberately set up to provide what are thought to be practical and particular skills, it may be still experienced as problematic by those who pass through the process. In effect, the choice of a formal strategy forces all newcomers to endure, absorb, and perhaps become proficient with *all* the skills and materials presented to them, since they cannot know what is or is not relevant to the job for which they are being prepared. For example, in police training academies, recruits are taught fingerprinting, ballistics, and crime-scene investigation, skills that are, at best, of peripheral interest and of no use to a street patrolman. One result is that when recruits graduate and move to the mean streets of the city, a general disenchantment with the relevance of all their training typically sets in.

Even in the prestigious professional schools of medicine and law the relevance of much training comes to be doubted by practitioners and students alike. Such disenchantment is apparently so pervasive that some observers have suggested that the formal processes that typify professional schools produce graduates who have already internalized standards for their everyday work performances that are "self-validating" and are apparently lodged well beyond the influence of others both within and outside the professional and intellectual community that surrounds the occupation.

Formal strategies appear also to produce stress for people in the form of a period of personal stigmatization. This stigmatization can be brought about by identifying garb (such as the peculiar uniform worn by police recruits); a special and usually somewhat demeaning title (such as "rookie," "trainee," or "junior"); or an insular position (such as an assignment to a classroom instead of an office or job). A person undergoing formal socialization is likely to feel isolated, cut off, and prohibited from assuming everyday social relationships with his more experienced "betters."

Informal socialization processes, wherein a recruit must negotiate for himself within a far less structured situation, can also induce personal anxiety. Indeed, the person may have trouble discovering clues as to the exact dimensions of his or her assigned organizational role. Under most circumstances, laissez-faire socialization increases the influence of the immediate work group on the new employee. There is no guarantee, though, that the direction provided by the informal approach will push the recruit in the right direction so far as those in authority are concerned. Classical examples are the so-called goldbricking and quota-restriction tactics invented by employees in production situations to thwart managerial directives. Such practices are passed on informally but quite effectively to newcomers against the desires of management.

Left to his own devices, the recruit will select his socialization agents. The success of the socialization process is then determined largely on the basis of whatever mutual regard is developed between the agent and the newcomer, the relevant knowledge possessed by an agent, and, of course, the agent's ability to transfer such knowledge. In most Ph.D. programs, for example, students must pick their own advisors from among the faculty. The advisors then act as philosophers, friends, and guides for the students. And among professors—as among organization executives—it is felt that the student who pushes the hardest by demanding more time, asking more questions, and so forth, learns the most. Consequently, the recruit's freedom of choice in the more informal setting has a price. He or she must force others to teach him.

Individual (Collective) Socialization Strategies

The degree to which individuals are socialized singly or collectively is perhaps the most critical of the process variables. The difference is analogous to the batch versus unit modes of production. In the batch or mass production case, recruits are bunched together at the outset and processed through an identical set of experiences, with relatively similar outcomes.

When a group goes through a socialization program together, it almost always develops an "in-the-same-boat" collective consciousness. Individual changes in perspective are built on an understanding of the problems faced by all members of the group. Apparently as the group shares problems, various members experiment with possible solutions and report back. In the course of discussions that follow, the members arrive at a collective and more or less consensual definition of their situation.

At the same time, the consensual character of the solutions worked out by the group allows the members to deviate more from the standards set by the agents than the individual mode of socialization does. Therefore, collective processes provide a potential base for recruit resistance. In such cases, the congruence between managerial objectives and those adopted by the group is always problematic—the recruit group is more likely than the individual to redefine or ignore agent demands.

Classic illustrations of the dilemma raised by the use of the collective strategy can be found in both educational and work environments. In educational settings, the faculty may beseech a student to study hard while the student's peers exhort him to relax and have a good time. In many work settings, supervisors attempt to ensure that each employee works up to his level of competence while the worker's peers try to impress on him that he must not do too much. To the degree that the newcomer is backed into the corner and cannot satisfy both demands at the same time, he will follow the dicta of those with whom he spends most of his time and who are most important to him.

The strength of group understandings depends, of course, on the degree to which all members actually share the same fate. In highly competitive settings, group members know that their own success is increased through the failure of others. Hence, the social support networks necessary to maintain cohesion in the group may break down. Consensual understandings will develop, but they will buttress individual modes of adjustment. Junior faculty members in publication-minded universities, for instance, follow group standards, although such standards nearly always stress individual scholarship.

Critically, collective socialization processes can also promote and intensify agent demands. Army recruits socialize each other in ways the army itself could never do; nor, for that matter, would it be allowed to do. Graduate students are often said to learn more from one another than from the faculty. And, while agents may have the power to define the nature of the collective problem, recruits often have more resources available to them to define the solution—time, experience, motivation, expertise, and patience (or the lack thereof).

Individual strategies also induce personal changes. But the views adopted by people processed individually are likely to be far less homogeneous than the views of those processed collectively. Nor are the views adopted by the isolated newcomer necessarily those that are the most beneficial to him in his transitional position, since he has access only to the perspectives of his socialization agents, and they may not fully apprehend or appreciate his immediate problems.

Certainly, the newcomer may choose not to accept the advice of his agents, although to reject it explicitly may well lose him his job. Furthermore, the rich, contextual perspectives that are available when individuals interact with their peers will not develop under individual strategies. In psychoanalysis, for example, the vocabulary of motives a recruit-patient develops to interpret his situation is quite personal and specific compared with the vocabulary that develops in group therapy. Of course, individual analyses can result in deep changes but they are lonely changes and depend solely on the mutual regard and warmth that exist between agent and recruit.

Apprenticeship modes of work socialization bear some similarity to therapist-patient relationships. If the responsibility for transforming an individual to a given status within the organization is delegated to one person, an intense, value-oriented process is likely to follow. This practice is common whenever a role incumbent is viewed by others in the organization as being the only member capable of shaping the recruit. It is quite common in upper levels of both public and private organizations. Because one organizational member has the sole responsibility, he or she often becomes a role model. The recruit emulates that person's thoughts and actions.

Succession to the chief executive officer level in many firms is marked by the extensive use of the individual socialization strategy. Outcomes in these one-on-one efforts depend on the affective relationships that may or may not develop between the apprentice and his master. In cases of high affect, the process works well and the new member internalizes the values of the particular role he is eventually to play quickly and fully. However, when there are few affective bonds, the socialization process may break down and the transition may not take place.

Overall, individual socialization is expensive in terms of both time and money. Failures are not recycled or rescued easily. Nor are individual strategies particularly suitable for the demands of large organizations, which process many people every year. Hence, with growing bureaucratic structures, the use of mass socialization techniques has increased. Indeed, collective tactics, because of their ease, efficiency, and predictability, have tended to replace the traditional socialization mode of apprenticeship.

Sequential (Nonsequential) Socialization Strategies

Sequential socialization refers to transitional processes marked by a series of discrete and identifiable stages through which an individual must pass in order to achieve a defined role and status within the organization. Many banks groom a person for a particular managerial position by first rotating him or her across the various jobs that will comprise the range of managerial responsibility. Similarly, police recruits in most departments must pass successively through such stages as academy, classroom instruction, physical conditioning, firearm training, and on-the-street pupilage.

Nonsequential processes are accomplished in one transitional stage. A factory worker may become a shop supervisor without benefit of an intermediary training program. A department head in a municipal government may become a city manager without serving first as an assistant city manager. Presumably, any organizational position may be analyzed to discover whether intermediate stages of preparation may be required of people taking over that position.

When examining sequential strategies, it is crucial to note the degree to which each stage builds on the preceding stage. For example, the courses in most technical training programs are arranged in what is thought to be a progression from simple to complex material. On the other hand, some sequential processes seem to follow no internal logic. Management training is often disjointed, with the curriculum jumping from topic to topic with little or no integration across stages. In such cases, a person tends to learn the material he likes best in the sequence. If, on the other hand, the flow of topics or courses is harmonious and connected functionally in some fashion, the various minor mental alterations a person must make at each sequential stage will act cumulatively so that at the end, the person may find himself considerably different from the way he was when he started.

Relatedly, if several agents handle different portions of the socialization process, the degree to which the aims of the agents are common is very important to the eventual outcome. For example, in some officers' training schools of peacetime military organizations, the agents responsible for physical and weapons training have very different attitudes toward their jobs and toward the recruits from the agents in charge of classroom instruction. Officer trainees quickly spot such conflicts when they exist and sometimes exploit them, playing agents off against one another. Such conflicts often lead to a more relaxed atmosphere for the recruits, one in which they enjoy watching their instructors pay more attention to each other than they do to the training program. An almost identical situation can be found in many police training programs.

In the sequential arrangement, agents may not know each other, may be separated spatially, and may have thoroughly different images of their respective tasks. University-trained scientists, for example, apparently have considerable difficulty moving from an academic to an industrial setting to practice their trade. The pattern disconcerts many scientists as they discover that their scholarly training emphasized a far different set of skills and interests from those required in the corporate environment. It is often claimed that to become a "good" industrial scientist, you must learn the painful lesson that being able to sell an idea is as important as having it in the first place.

Consider, too, the range of views about a particular job an organizational newcomer may receive from the personnel department, the training division, and colleagues on the job, all of whom have a hand (and a stake) in the recruit's transition. From this standpoint, empathy must certainly be extended to the so-called juvenile delinquent who receives "guidance" from the police, probation officers, judges, social workers, psychiatrists, and correction officers. Such a sequence may actually teach a person to be whatever his immediate situation demands.

Besides the confusion that comes from the contradictory demands that are sometimes made on people, there is also likely to be misinformation passed along by each agent in a sequential process as to how simple the next stage will be. Thus, the recruit may be told that if he just buckles down and applies himself in stage A, stages B, C, D, and E will be easy. Agents usually mask, wittingly or unwittingly, the true nature of the stage to follow. Their reasoning is that if a person feels his future is bright, rewarding, and assured, he will be most cooperative at the stage he is in, not wishing to jeopardize the future he thinks awaits him.

When attempts are consistently made to make each subsequent step appear simple, the individual's best source of information on the sequential process is another person who has gone through it. If the recruit can find organizational members who have been through the process he can use them to help him obtain a more reality-oriented perspective. But some organizations go out of their way to isolate recruits from veteran members. Certain profit-making trade schools go to great lengths to be sure their paying clientele do not learn of the limited job opportunities in the "glamorous and high-paying" worlds of radio and TV broadcasting, commercial art, or heavy equipment operations. Door-to-door sales trainees are continually assured that their success is guaranteed; the handy-dandy, one-of-a-kind product they are preparing to merchandise will "sell itself." When recruits are officially allowed the privilege of interacting with more experienced organizational members, those controlling the process invariably select a veteran member who will present a sanitized or laundered image of the future.

The degree to which an individual is required to keep to a schedule as he goes through the entire sequence is another important aspect of the sequential socialization strategy. A recruit may feel that he is being pressured or pushed into certain positions or stages before he is ready. This position is similar to that of the business executive who does not want a promotion but feels that if he turns it down, he will be damaging his career. A professor may feel that he cannot turn down the chairmanship of his department without rupturing the respectful relationships with his faculty members that he now enjoys.

On the other hand, if the person does not slip, falter, fail, or seriously discredit himself in any fashion, sequential socialization over his full career may provide him with what has been called a "permanent sense of the unobtained." Thus the executive who, at thirty, aims toward being the head of his department by the time he is forty, will then be attempting to make division head by fifty, and so on. The consumer sequence that stresses accumulation of material goods has much the same character as the artistic sequence that stresses the achievement of the perfect work. Sequential socialization of this sort has a rather disquieting Sisyphus-like nature as the person seeks perpetually to reach the unreachable.

Fixed (Variable) Socialization Strategies

Organizational socialization processes differ in terms of the information and certainty an individual has regarding his transition timetable. Fixed socialization processes provide a recruit with a precise knowledge of the time it will take him to complete a given step. The time of transition is standardized. Consider the probationary systems used on most civil service jobs. The employees know in advance just how long they will be on probation. Educational systems provide another good illustration of fixed processes. Schools begin and end at the same time for all pupils. Students move through the system roughly one step at a time. Fixed processes provide rigid conceptions of "normal" progress; those who are not on schedule are considered "deviant."

Variable socialization processes do not give those being processed any advance notice of their transition timetable. What may be true for one is not true for another. The recruit has to search out clues to his future. Prisoners who serve indeterminate sentences such as the legendary and properly infamous "one to ten," must dope out timetable norms from the scarce materials available to them. Apprenticeship programs often specify only the minimum number of years a person must remain an apprentice and leave open the precise time a person can expect to be advanced to journeyman.

Since the rate of passage across any organizational boundary is a matter of concern to most participants, transition timetables may be developed on the basis of the most fragmentary and flimsiest information. Rumors and innuendos about who is going where and when characterize the variable strategy of socialization. However, if a recruit has direct access to others who are presently in or have been through a similar situation, a sort of "sentimental order" will probably emerge as to when certain passages can or should be expected to take place. And whether or not these expectations are accurate, the individual will measure his progress against them.

The vertically oriented business career is a good example of both variable socialization and the "sentimental order" that seems to characterize such processes. Take the promotional systems in most large organizations. These systems are usually designed to reward individual initiative and performance on current assignments and are therefore considered, at least by upper management, to be highly variable processes. But, for those deeply concerned with their own (and others') progress in the organization, the variable process is almost inevitably corrupted, because would-be executives push very hard to uncover the signs of a coming promotion (or demotion). These people listen closely to stories concerning the time it takes to advance in the organization, observe as closely as possible the experiences of others, and develop an age consciousness delineating the range of appropriate ages for given positions. The process is judgmental and requires a good deal of time and effort. However, in some very stable organizations, such as government agencies, the expected rate of advancement can be evaluated quite precisely and correctly. Thus, the process becomes, for all practical purposes, a fixed one.

In some cases, what is designed as a fixed socialization process more closely approximates a variable process for the individual described by the cliché, "always a bridesmaid, never a bride." The transition timetable is clear enough but, for various reasons, the person cannot or does not wish to complete the journey. Colleges and universities have their "professional students" who never seem to graduate. Training programs have trainees who continually miss the boat and remain trainees indefinitely. Fixed processes differ, therefore, with regard to both the frequency and the rate of the so-called role failure—the number of recruits who for one reason or another are not able to complete the process.

Some organizations even go so far as to provide a special membership category for certain types of role failures. Some police agencies, for example, give recruits unable to meet agent demands long-term assignments as city jailers or traffic controllers. Such assignments serve as a signal to the recruit and to others in the organization that the individual has left the normal career path.

To the extent that these organizational "Siberias" exist and can be identified by those in the fixed setting, chronic sidetracking from which there is rarely a return is a distinct possibility. On the other hand, sidetracking is quite subtle and problematic to the recruit operating in a variable socialization track. Many people who work in the upper and lower levels of management in large organizations are unable to judge where they are going and when they might get there because a further rise in the organization depends in part on such uncertain factors as the state of the economy and the turnover rates above them. Consequently, variable processes can create anxiety and frustration for people who are unable to construct reasonably valid timetables to judge the appropriateness of their movement or lack of movement in the organization.

It is clear that to those in authority within the organization time is an important resource that can be used to control others. Variable socialization processes give an administrator a powerful tool for influencing individual behavior. But the administration also risks creating an organizational situation marked by confusion and uncertainty among those concerned with their movement in the system. Fixed processes provide temporal reference points that allow people both to observe passages ceremonially and to hold together relationships forged during the socialization experiences. Variable processes, by contrast, tend to divide and drive apart people who might show much loyalty and cohesion if the process were fixed.

Tournament (Contest) Socialization Strategies

The practice of separating selected clusters of recruits into different socialization programs or tracks on the basis of presumed differences in ability, ambition, or background represents the essence of tournament socialization processes. Such tracking is often done at the earliest possible date in a person's organizational career. Furthermore, the shifting of people between tracks in a tournament process occurs mainly in one direction: downward. These people are then eliminated from further consideration within the track they have left. The rule for the tournament socialization strategy, according to Yale University sociologist James Rosenbaum, is simple: "when you win, you win only the right to go on to the next round; when you lose, you lose forever."

Contest socialization processes, on the other hand, avoid a sharp distinction between superiors and inferiors of the same rank. The channels of movement through the various socialization programs are kept open and depend on the observed abilities and stated interests of all. In perhaps 75 percent of American public high schools, school administrators and teachers have made student tracking decisions by the ninth grade (and even before). Thus only students on a college-bound track are allowed to take certain courses. But some schools practice a contest mode. They give their students great freedom to choose their classes and allow for considerable mobility in all directions within the system.

Although little empirical research has been done along these lines, there are strong reasons to believe that some version of the tournament process exists in virtually all large organizations. Often someone who is passed over for a management job once is forever disqualified from that position. And accounts from the women's movement strongly suggest that women in most organizations are on very different tracks from men and have been eliminated from the tournament even before they began. A similar situation can be said to exist for most minority-group members.

Even the so-called "high-potential employee" has something to worry about in the tournament process. Often the training for the "high potentials" is not the same as that for the other employees. The "high potential" track will differ considerably from the track afforded the average or typical recruit. But tournament strategy dictates that even among the "high potentials" once you are dropped from the fast track you can't get back on it.

As you move through higher and higher levels in the organization, the tournament strategy becomes even more pervasive. Perhaps this is inevitable. The point here is simply that the tournament socialization process (particularly if an extreme version is used across all levels in an organization) has widespread consequences.

One consequence is that when tournament processes are used, the accomplishments of an employee are more likely to be explained by the tracking system of that organization than by the particular characteristics of the person. Thus the person who fails in organization X might well have succeeded in organization Y. Also, those who fall out of the tournament at any stage can expect only custodial socialization in the future. They are expected to behave only in ways appropriate to their plateaued position, are treated coolly, and are discouraged from making further efforts. The organization, in other words, has completed its work on them. As can be seen, tournament socialization, more than the contest mode, can shape and guide ambition in a powerful way.

Consider, too, that in tournament processes, where a single failure has permanent consequences, those passing through tend to adopt the safest strategies of passage. Low risk taking, short cycles of effort, and ever-changing spheres of interest based primarily on what those above them deem most desirable at any given time are the norm. It follows that those who remain in the tournament for any length of time are socialized to be insecure, obsequious to authority, and differentiated, both socially and psychologically, from one another. On the other hand, those who do not remain in the tournament tend to move in the other direction, becoming fatalistic, homogeneous, and, to varying degrees, alienated from the organization.

The attractiveness and prevalence of tournament socialization strategies in work organizations appear to rest on two major arguments. One is that such processes promote the most efficient allocation of resources. Organizational resources, its proponents say, should be allocated only to those most likely to profit from them. The other, closely related argument, is based primarily on the faith that an accurate and reliable judgment of an individual's potential can be made early in one's career. They believe that the principles of selection and personnel psychology (which are uncertain at best) can be used to separate the deserving from the undeserving members of the organization. Various tracks are then legitimized by testing and classifying people so that each test and the resulting classification represent another level in the tournament process. The American Telephone & Telegraph Co. is perhaps the foremost proponent and user of this socialization process. Each transition from one hierarchical level to another is accompanied by the rigorous evaluation of the ever-declining cadre still in the tournament.

Contest socialization, on the other hand, implies that preset norms for transition do not exist in any other form than that of demonstrated performance. Regardless of age, sex, race, or other background factors, each person starts out equal to all other participants. As in educational systems, this appears to be the stated policy of most American corporations. However, those who have looked closely at these organizations conclude that this Horatio Alger ideal is rarely even approximated in practice.

There is some evidence (primarily from studies conducted in public schools) that contest socialization processes, where they do exist, encourage the development of such characteristics as enterprise, perseverance, initiative, and a craftlike dedication to a job well done. We also have the occasionally impressive results of the workplace experiments that are designed to create autonomous work groups, open and competitive bidding for organizational jobs, and the phasing out of the predictive types of psychological tests used to locate people in the "proper" career track (sometimes in secrecy). Instead of tests, a few organizations have moved toward simply providing people with more reliable career information and voluntary career counseling so that people can make more knowledgeable choices about where to go in the organization.

In summary, tournament socialization seems far more likely than contest socialization to drive a wedge between the people being processed. In tournament situations, each person is out for himself and rarely will a group come together to act in unison either for or against the organization. Contest strategies, as the label implies, appear to produce a more cooperative and participative spirit among people in an organization. Perhaps because one setback does not entail a permanent loss, people can afford to help one another over various hurdles and a more fraternal atmosphere can be maintained.

Serial (Disjunctive) Socialization Strategies

The serial socialization process, whereby experienced members groom newcomers about to assume similar roles in the organization, is perhaps the best guarantee that an organization will not change over long periods of time. In the police world, the serial feature of recruit socialization is virtually a taken-for-granted device and accounts in large measure for the remarkable stability of patrolman behavior patterns from generation to generation of patrolmen. Innovation in serial modes is unlikely, but continuity and a sense of history will be maintained—even in the face of a turbulent and changing environment.

If a newcomer does not have predecessors available in whose footsteps he can follow, the socialization pattern may be labeled disjunctive. Whereas the serial process risks stagnation and contamination, the disjunctive process risks complication and confusion. The recruit who is left to his own devices may rely on definitions for his task that are gleaned from inappropriate others.

But the disjunctive pattern also gives a recruit the chance to be inventive and original. Without an old guard about to hamper the development of a fresh perspective, the conformity and lockstep pressures created by the serial mode are absent. Most entrepreneurs and those people who fill newly created positions in an organization automatically fall into a disjunctive process of socialization. In both cases, few, if any, people with similar experiences are around to coach the newcomer on the basis of the lessons they have learned.

Similarly, what may be a serial process to most people may be disjunctive to others. Consider a black lawyer entering a previously all-white firm or the navy's recent attempts to train women to become jet pilots. These "deviant" newcomers do not have access to people who have shared their set of unique problems. Such situations make passage considerably more difficult, especially if the person is going it alone, as is most often the case.

Sometimes what appears to be serial is actually disjunctive. Newcomers may be prepared inadequately for spots in one department by agents from another department. This is often true when the personnel department handles all aspects of training. Only later, after the newcomers have access to others who have been through the same process, do they discover the worthlessness and banality of their training. Agent familiarity with the target position is a very crucial factor in the serial strategy.

Occasionally, what could be called "gapping" presents a serious problem in serial strategies. Gapping refers to the historical or social distance between recruit and agent. For example, a newcomer to an organization has the greatest opportunity to learn about his future from those with whom he works. But the experiences passed on to him—no doubt with the best of intentions—by those with whom he works may be quite removed from his own circumstances.

Typically, recruits in the first class will set the tone for the classes to follow. This is not to say that those following will be carbon copies, but simply that it is easier to learn from people who have been through similar experiences than it is to devise solutions from scratch. So long as there are people available in the socialization setting the recruits consider to be "like them," these people will be pressed into service as guides, passing on the consensual solutions to the typical problems faced by the newcomer. Mental patients, for example, often report that they were only able to survive and gain their release because other, more experienced, patients "set them wise" as to what the psychiatric staff deemed appropriate behavior indicating improvement.

From this perspective, serial modes of socialization provide newcomers with built-in guidelines to organize and make sense of their organizational situation. Just as children in stable societies are able to gain a pure sense of the future by seeing in their parents and grandparents an image of themselves grown older, employees in organizations can gain a sense of the future by seeing in their more experienced elders an image of themselves further along. The danger exists, of course, that the recruit won't like the image, and will leave the organization rather than face what seems to be an agonizing future. In industrial settings, where worker morale is low and turnover is high, the serial pattern of initiating newcomers into the organization maintains and perhaps amplifies an already poor situation.

The analytic distinction between serial and disjunctive socialization processes is sometimes brought into sharp focus when an organization cleans house, sweeping old members out and bringing in new members to replace them. In extreme cases, an entire organization can be thrown into a disjunctive mode of socialization, causing the organization to lose all resemblance to its former self. For example, in colleges with a large turnover of faculty, long-term students exert a lot of control. Organizations such as prisons and mental hospitals, where inmates stay longer than the staff, are often literally run by the inmates.

Investiture (Divestiture) Socialization Strategies

The last major strategy to be discussed concerns the degree to which a socialization process is set up either to confirm or to dismantle the incoming identity of a newcomer. Investiture processes ratify and establish the viability and usefulness of the characteristics the person already possesses. Presumably, recruits to most high-level managerial jobs are selected on the basis of what they bring to the job. The organization does not wish to change these recruits. Rather, it wants to take advantage of their abilities.

Divestiture processes, on the other hand, deny and strip away certain entering characteristics of a recruit. Many occupational and organizational communities almost require a recruit to sever old friendships, undergo extensive harassment from experienced members, and engage for long periods of time in what can only be called "dirty work" (that is, low-status, low-pay, low-skill, and low-interest tasks). During such periods, the recruit gradually acquires the formal and informal credentials of full and accepted membership.

Ordained ministers, professional athletes, master craftsmen, college professors, and career military personnel must often suffer considerable mortification and humiliation to pay the dues necessary before they are considered equal and respected participants in their particular professions. As a result, closeness develops among the people in that occupation and a distinct sense of solidarity and mutual concern can be found. Pervasive and somewhat closed social worlds are formed by such diverse groups as policemen, airline employees, railroad workers, nurses, symphony musicians, and funeral directors.

Investiture processes say to a newcomer, "We like you as you are; don't change." Entrance is made as smooth and troublefree as possible. Members of the organization go to great lengths to ensure that the recruit's needs are met. Demands on the person are balanced to avoid being unreasonable. There is almost an explicit "honeymoon" period. At times, even positions on the bottom rung of the organizational ladder are filled with a flurry of concern for employee desires. Orientation programs, career counseling, relocation assistance, even a visit to the president's office with the perfunctory handshake and good wishes, systematically suggest to newcomers that they are as valuable as they are.

Ordinarily, the degree to which a setting represents an ordeal to a recruit indicates the degree to which divestiture processes are operative. Rehabilitation institutions, such as mental hospitals and prisons, are commonly thought to be prototypical in this regard. But even in these institutions, initiation processes will have different meanings to different newcomers. Some "rehabilitation" settings, for example, offer a new inmate a readymade home away from home that more or less complements his entering self-image. Thus, for some people, becoming a member of, say, the thief subculture in a prison acts more as an investiture than a divestiture socialization process. In such cases, one's preinstitutional identity is sustained with apparent ease. Prison is simply an annoying interval in the person's otherwise orderly career. The analyst must examine socialization settings closely before assuming powerful divestiture processes to be acting homogeneously on all who enter.

Yet the fact remains that many organizations consciously promote initiation ordeals designed primarily to make the recruit whatever the organization deems appropriate. In the more extreme cases, recruits are isolated from former associates, must abstain from certain types of behavior, must publicly degrade themselves and others through various kinds of mutual criticism, and must follow a rigid set of sanctionable rules and regulations.

This process, when voluntarily undergone, serves, of course, to commit and bind people to the organization. In such cases, the sacrifice and surrender on the part of the newcomers is usually premised upon a sort of institutional awe the recruits bring with them into the organization. Such awe serves to sustain their motivation throughout the divestiture process. Within this society, there are many familiar illustrations: the Marine Corps, fraternal groups, religious cults, elite law schools, self-realization groups, drug rehabilitation programs, professional athletic teams, and so on. All these organizations require a recruit to pass through a series of robust tests in order to gain privileged access to the organization.

In general, the endurance of the divestiture process itself promotes a strong fellowship among those who have followed the same path to membership. For example, college teaching, professional crime, denistry, and the priesthood all require a person to travel a somewhat painful and lengthy road. The trip provides the newcomer with a set of colleagues who have been down the same path and symbolizes to others on the scene that the newcomer is committed fully to the organization. For those who complete the ordeal, the gap separating recruits from members narrows appreciably while the gap separating members from nonmembers grows.

Clearly, divestiture rather than investiture strategies are more likely to produce similar results among recruits. And, it should be kept in mind, the ordeal aspects of a divestiture process represent an identity-bestowing, as well as an identity-destroying, process. Coercion is not necessarily an assault on the person. It can also be a device for stimulating personal changes that are evaluated positively by the individual. What has always been problematic with coercion is the possibility for perversion in its use.

SUMMARY AND CONCLUSIONS

I have attempted to provide a partial framework for analyzing some of the more pervasive strategies used by organizations to control and direct the behavior of their members. For instance, the tightness or looseness of day-to-day supervision can also be depicted as a socialization strategy. So, too, could the degree of demographic and attitudinal homogeneity or heterogeneity displayed by the incoming recruits, since it could affect the probability that a single perspective will come to dominate the group of newcomers. What I have tried to do here, however, is describe those processes that are most often ignored by organizational researchers and taken for granted by organizational decision makers.

It is true that someone undergoing a transition is not *tabula rasa,* waiting patiently for the organization to do its work. Many people play very active roles in their own socialization. Each strategy discussed here contains only the possibility, and not the actuality, of effect. For example, those undergoing collective socialization may withdraw from the situation, abstaining from the group life that surrounds other recruits. Or a person may undergo a brutal divestiture process with a calculated indifference and stoic nonchalance. A few exceptions are probably the rule in even the most tyrannical of settings.

However, the preponderance of evidence suggests that the seven strategies discussed here play a very powerful role in influencing any individual's conception of his work role. By teasing out the situational processes variables that, by and large, define an organization passage, it becomes apparent that for most people a given set of experiences in an organization will lead to fairly predictable ends.

If we are interested in strategies that promote a relatively high degree of similarity in the thoughts and actions of recruits and their agents, a combination of the formal, serial, and divestiture strategies would probably be most effective. If dissimilarity is desired, informal, disjunctive, and investiture strategies would be preferable. To produce a relatively passive group of hardworking but undifferentiated recruits, the combination of formal, collective, sequential, tournament, and divestiture strategies should be used. Other combinations could be used to manufacture other sorts of recruits with, I suspect, few exceptions.

At any rate, the single point I wish to emphasize is that much of the control over individual behavior in organizations is a direct result of the manner in which people are processed. By directing focused and detailed attention to the breakpoints or transitions in a person's work career, much can be gained in terms of understanding how organizations shape the performances and ambitions of their members. And, most critically, the strategies by which these transitions are managed are clearly subject to both empirical study and practical change.

Increased awareness and interest in the strategies of people processing may be a matter of some urgency. The trend in modern organizations is apparently to decrease control through such traditional means as direct supervision and the immediate application of rewards and punishments and increase control by such indirect means as recruitment, selection, professionalization, increased training, and career path manipulation. To these more or less remote control mechanisms, we might well add the seven strategies described in this paper.

Certain features of organizations promote behavioral styles among subordinates, peers, and superiors. Since many of the strategies for breaking in employees are taken for granted (particularly for employees beyond the raw recruit level), they are rarely discussed or considered to be matters of choice in the circles in which managerial decisions are reached. Furthermore, those strategies that are discussed are often kept as they are simply because their effects are not widely understood.

People processing strategies are also frequently justified by the traditional illogic of "that's the way I had to do it, so that's the way my successors will have to do it." Yet, as I have attempted to show, socialization processes are not products of some fixed, evolutionary pattern. They are products of both decisions and nondecisions—and they can be changed. Unfortunately, many of the strategies discussed here seem to be institutionalized out of inertia rather than thoughtful action. This is hardly the most rational practice to be followed by managers with a professed concern for the effective utilization of resources—both material and human.

Effects of Group Pressure upon the Modification and Distortion of Judgments

S. E. ASCH

Our immediate object was to study the social and personal conditions that induce individuals to resist or to yield to group pressures when the latter are perceived to be *contrary to fact*. The issues which this problem raises are of obvious consequence for society; it can be of decisive importance whether or not a group will, under certain conditions, submit to existing pressures. Equally direct are the consequences for individuals and our understanding of them, since it is a decisive fact about a person whether he possesses the freedom to act independently, or whether he characteristically submits to group pressures. . . .

THE EXPERIMENT AND FIRST RESULTS

We developed an experimental technique which has served as the basis for the present series of studies. We employed the procedure of placing an individual in a relation of radical conflict with all the other members of a group, of measuring its effect upon him in quantitative terms, and of describing its psychological consequences. A group of eight individuals was instructed to judge a series of simple, clearly structured

S. E. Asch, adapted from "Effects of Group Pressure upon the Modification and Distortion of Judgments" in Harold Guetzkow, editor, *Groups, Leadership and Men: Research in Human Relations*. Copyright 1951, by Carnegie Press, copyright renewed 1979 by Harold Guetzkow. (New York: Russell & Russell, 1963). Reprinted with the permission of Russell & Russell.

perceptual relations—to match the length of a given line with one of three unequal lines. Each member of the group announced his judgments publicly. In the midst of this monotonous "test" one individual found himself suddenly contradicted by the entire group, and this contradiction was repeated again and again in the course of the experiment. The group in question had, with the exception of one member, previously met with the experimenter and received instructions to respond at certain points with wrong—and unanimous—judgments. The errors of the majority were large (ranging between ½" and 1¾") and of an order not encountered under control conditions. The outstanding person—the critical subject—whom we had placed in the position of a *minority of one* in the midst of a *unanimous majority*—was the object of investigation. He faced, possibly for the first time in his life, a situation in which a group unanimously contradicted the evidence of his senses.

This procedure was the starting point of the investigation and the point of departure for the study of further problems. Its main features were the following: (1) The critical subject was submitted to two contradictory and irreconcilable forces—the evidence of his own experience of an utterly clear perceptual fact and the unanimous evidence of a group of equals. (2) Both forces were part of the immediate situation; the majority was concretely present, surrounding the subject physically. (3) The critical subject, who was requested together with all others to state his judgments publicly, was obliged to declare himself and to take a definite stand vis-à-vis the group. (4) The situation possessed a self-contained character. The critical subject could not avoid or evade the dilemma by reference to conditions external to the experimental situation. (It may be mentioned at this point that the forces generated by the given conditions acted so quickly upon the critical subjects that instances of suspicion were rare.)

The technique employed permitted a simple quantitative measure of the "majority effect" in terms of the frequency of errors in the direction of the distorted estimates of the majority. At the same time we were concerned from the start to obtain evidence of the ways in which the subjects perceived the group, to establish whether they became doubtful, whether they were tempted to join the majority. Most important, it was our object to establish the grounds of the subject's independence or yielding—whether, for example, the yielding subject was aware of the effect of the majority upon him, whether he abandoned his judgment deliberately or compulsively. To this end we constructed a comprehensive set of questions which served as the basis of an individual interview immediately following the experimental period. Toward the conclusion of the interview each subject was informed fully of the purpose of the experiment, of his role and of that of the majority. The reactions to the disclosure of the purpose of the experiment became in fact an integral part of the procedure. We may state here that the information derived from the interview became an indispensable source of evidence and insight into the psychological structure of the experimental situation, and in particular, of the nature of the individual differences. Also, it is not justified or advisable to allow the subject to leave without giving him a full explanation of the experimental conditions. The experimenter has a responsibility to the subject to clarify his doubts and to state the reasons for placing him in the experimental situation. When this is done most subjects react with interest and many express gratification at having lived through a striking situation which has some bearing on wider human issues.

Both the members of the majority and the critical subjects were male college students. We shall report the results for a total of fifty critical subjects in this experiment. . . .

The quantitative results are clear and unambiguous.

1. There was a marked movement toward the majority. One-third of all estimates in the critical group were errors identical with or in the direction of the distorted estimates of the majority. The significance of this finding becomes clear in the light of the virtual absence of errors in control groups the members of which recorded their estimates in writing. . . .

2. At the same time the effect of the majority was far from complete. The preponderance of estimates in the critical group (68 per cent) was correct despite the pressure of the majority.

3. We found evidence of extreme individual differences. There were in the critical group subjects who remained independent without exception, and there were those who went nearly all the time with the majority. (The maximum possible number of errors was 12, while the actual range of errors was 0-11.) One-fourth of the critical subjects was completely independent; at the other extreme, one-third of the group displaced the estimates toward the majority in one-half or more of the trials.

The differences between the critical subjects in their reactions to the given conditions were equally striking. There were subjects who remained completely confident throughout. At the other extreme were those who became disoriented, doubt-ridden, and experienced a powerful impulse not to appear different from the majority.

For purposes of illustration we include a brief description of one independent and one yielding subject.

Independent. After a few trials he appeared puzzled, hesitant. He announced all disagreeing answers in the form of "Three, sir; two, sir"; not so with the unanimous answers. At trial 4 he answered immediately after the first member of the group, shook his head, blinked, and whispered to his neighbor: "Can't help it, that's one." His later answers came in a whispered voice, accompanied by a deprecating smile. At one point he grinned embarrassedly, and whispered explosively to his neighbor: "I always disagree—darn it!" During the questioning, this subject's constant refrain was: "I called them as I saw them, sir." He insisted that his estimates were right without, however, committing himself as to whether the others were wrong, remarking that "that's the way I see them and that's the way they see them." If he had to make a practical decision under similar circumstances, he declared, "I would follow my own view, though part of my reason would tell me that I might be wrong." Immediately following the experiment the majority engaged this subject in a brief discussion. When they pressed him to say whether the entire group was wrong and he alone right, he turned upon them defiantly, exclaiming: "You're *probably* right, but you may be wrong!" To the disclosure of the experiment this subject reacted with the statement that he felt "exultant and relieved," adding, "I do not deny that at times I had the feeling: 'to heck with it, I'll go along with the rest.' "

Yielding.   This subject went with the majority in 11 out of 12 trials. He appeared nervous and somewhat confused, but he did not attempt to evade discussion; on the contrary, he was helpful and tried to answer to the best of his ability. He opened the discussion with the statement: "If I'd been the first I probably would have responded differently"; this was his way of stating that he had adopted the majority estimates. The primary factor in his case was loss of confidence. He perceived the majority as a decided group, acting without hesitation: "If they had been doubtful I probably would have changed, but they answered with such confidence." Certain of his errors, he explained, were due to the doubtful nature of the comparisons; in such instances he went with the majority. When the object of the experiment was explained, the subject volunteered: "I suspected about the middle—but tried to push it out of my mind." It is of interest that his suspicion was not able to restore his confidence and diminish the power of the majority. Equally striking is his report that he assumed the experiment to involve an "illusion" to which the others, but not he, were subject. This assumption too did not help to free him; on the contrary, he acted as if his divergence from the majority was a sign of defect. The principal impression this subject produced was of one so caught up by immediate difficulties that he lost clear reasons for his actions, and could make no reasonable decisions.

A FIRST ANALYSIS OF INDIVIDUAL DIFFERENCES

On the basis of the interview data described earlier, we undertook to differentiate and describe the major forms of reaction to the experimental situation, which we shall now briefly summarize.

Among the *independent* subjects we distinguished the following main categories:

(1) Independence based on *confidence* in one's perception and experience. The most striking characteristic of these subjects is the vigor with which they withstand the group opposition. Though they are sensitive to the group, and experience the conflict, they show a resilience in coping with it, which is expressed in their continuing reliance on their perception and the effectiveness with which they shake off the oppressive group opposition.

(2) Quite different are those subjects who are independent and *withdrawn*. These do not react in a spontaneously emotional way, but rather on the basis of explicit principles concerning the necessity of being an individual.

(3) A third group of independent subjects manifest considerable tension and *doubt*, but adhere to their judgments on the basis of a felt necessity to deal adequately with the task.

The following were the main categories of reaction among the *yielding* subjects, or those who were with the majority during one-half or more of the trials.

(1) *Distortion of perception* under the stress of group pressure. In this category belong a very few subjects who yield completely, but are not aware that their estimates have been displaced or distorted by the majority. These subjects report that they came to perceive the majority estimates as correct.

(2) *Distortion of judgment.* Most submitting subjects belong to this category. The factor of greatest importance in this group is a decision the subjects reach that their perceptions are inaccurate, and that those of the majority are correct. These subjects suffer from primary doubt and lack of confidence; on this basis they feel a strong tendency to join the majority.

(3) *Distortion of action.* The subjects in this group do not suffer a modification of perception nor do they conclude that they are wrong. They yield because of an overmastering need not to appear different from or inferior to others, because of an inability to tolerate the appearance of defectiveness in the eyes of the group. These subjects suppress their observations and voice the majority position with awareness of what they are doing.

The results are sufficient to establish that independence and yielding are not psychologically homogeneous, that submission to group pressure (and freedom from pressure) can be the result of different psychological conditions. It should also be noted that the categories described above, being based exclusively on the subjects' reactions to the experimental conditions, are descriptive, not presuming to explain why a given individual responded in one way rather than another. The further exploration of the basis for the individual differences is a separate task upon which we are now at work.

EXPERIMENTAL VARIATIONS

The results described are clearly a joint function of two broadly different sets of conditions. They are determined first by the specific external conditions, by the particular character of the relation between social evidence and one's own experience. Second, the presence of pronounced individual differences points to the important role of personal factors, of factors connected with the individual's character structure. We reasoned that there are group conditions which would produce independence in all subjects, and that there probably are group conditions which would induce intensified yielding in many, though not in all. Accordingly we followed the procedure of *experimental variation*, systematically altering the quality of social evidence by means of systematic variation of group conditions. Secondly, we deemed it reasonable to assume that behavior under the experimental social pressure is significantly related to certain basic, relatively permanent characteristics of the individual. The investigation has moved in both of these directions. . . . We shall limit the present account to a sketch of the representative experimental variations.

The Effect of Nonunanimous Majorities

Evidence obtained from the basic experiment suggested that the condition of being exposed *alone* to the opposition of a "compact majority" may have played a decisive role in determining the course and strength of the effects observed. Accordingly we undertook to investigate in a series of successive variations the effects of *nonunanimous majorities*. The technical problem of altering the uniformity of a majority is, in terms of our procedure, relatively simple. In most instances we merely directed one or more members of the instructed group to deviate from the majority in prescribed ways. It is obvious that we cannot hope to compare the performance of the same individual in two situations on the assumption that they remain independent of one another. At best we can investigate the effect of an earlier upon a later experimental condition. The comparison of different experimental situations therefore requires the use of different but comparable groups of critical subjects. This is the procedure we have followed. In the variations to be described we have maintained the conditions of the basic experiment (*e.g.*, the sex of the subjects, the size of the majority, the content of the task, and so on) save for the specific factor that was varied. The following were some of the variations we studied:

1. *The presence of a "true partner."* (a) In the midst of the majority were *two* naive, critical subjects. The subjects were separated spatially, being seated in the fourth and eighth positions, respectively. Each therefore heard his judgment confirmed by one other person (provided the other person remained independent), one prior to, the other subsequently to announcing his own judgment. In addition, each experienced a break in the unanimity of the majority. There were six pairs of critical subjects. (b) In a further variation the "partner" to the critical subject was a member of the group who had been instructed to respond correctly throughout. This procedure permits the exact control of the partner's responses. The partner was always seated in the fourth position; he therefore announced his estimates in each case before the critical subject.

The results clearly demonstrate that a disturbance of the unanimity of the majority markedly increased the independence of the critical subjects. The frequency of pro-majority errors dropped to 10.4 per cent of the total number of estimates in variation (a), and to 5.5 per cent in variation (b). These results are to be compared with the frequency of yielding to the unanimous majorities in the basic experiment, which was 32 per cent of the total number of estimates. It is clear that the presence in the field of *one other* individual who responded correctly was sufficient to deplete the power of the majority, and in some cases to destroy it. This finding is all the more striking in the light of other variations which demonstrate the effect of even small minorities provided they are unanimous. Indeed, we have been able to show that a unanimous majority of three is, under the given conditions, far more effective than a majority of eight containing one dissenter. That critical subjects will under these conditions free themselves of a majority of seven and join forces with one other person in the minority is, we believe, a result significant for theory. It points to a fundamental psychological difference between the condition of being alone and having a minimum of human support. It further demonstrates that the effects obtained are not the result of a summation of influences proceeding from each member of the group; it is necessary to conceive the results as being relationally determined.

2. *Withdrawal of a "true partner."* What will be the effect of providing the critical subject with a partner who responds correctly and then withdrawing him? The critical subject started with a partner who responded correctly. The partner was a member of the majority who had been instructed to respond correctly and to "desert" to the majority in the middle of the experiment. This procedure permits the observation of the same subject in the course of transition from one condition to another. The withdrawal of the partner produced a powerful and unexpected result. We had assumed that the critical subject, having gone through the experience of opposing the majority with a minimum of support, would maintain his independence when alone. Contrary to this expectation, we found that the experience of having had and then lost a partner restored the majority effect to its full force, the proportion of errors rising to 28.5 per cent of all judgments, in contrast to the preceding level of 5.5 percent. Further experimentation is needed to establish whether the critical subjects were responding to the sheer fact of being alone, or to the fact that the partner abandoned them.

3. *Late arrival of a "true partner."* The critical subject started as a minority of one in the midst of a unanimous majority. Toward the conclusion of the experiment one member of the majority "broke" away and began announcing correct estimates. This procedure, which reverses the order of conditions of the preceding experiment, permits the observation of the transition from being alone to being a member of a pair against a majority. It is obvious that those critical subjects who were independent when alone would continue to be so when joined by another partner. The variation is therefore of significance primarily for those subjects who yielded during the first phase of the experiment. The appearance of the late partner exerts a freeing effect, reducing the level to 8.7 per cent. Those who had previously yielded also became markedly more independent, but not completely so, continuing to yield more than previously independent subjects. The reports of the subjects do not cast much light on the factors responsible for the result. It is our impression

that having once committed himself to yielding, the individual finds it difficult and painful to change his direction. To do so is tantamount to a public admission that he has not acted rightly. He therefore follows the precarious course he has already chosen in order to maintain an outward semblance of consistency and conviction.

4. *The presence of a "compromise partner."* The majority was consistently extremist, always matching the standard with the most unequal line. One instructed subject (who, as in the other variations, preceded the critical subject) also responded incorrectly, but his estimates were always intermediate between the truth and the majority position. The critical subject therefore faced an extremist majority whose unanimity was broken by one more moderately erring person. Under these conditions the frequency of errors was reduced but not significantly. However, the lack of unanimity determined in a strikingly consistent way the *direction* of the errors. The preponderance of the errors, 75.7 per cent of the total, was moderate, whereas in a parallel experiment in which the majority was unanimously extremist (*i.e.,* with the "compromise" partner excluded), the incidence of moderate errors was reduced to 42 per cent of the total. As might be expected, in a unanimously moderate majority, the errors of the critical subjects were without exception moderate.

The Role of Majority Size

To gain further understanding of the majority effect, we varied the size of the majority in several different variations. The majorities, which were in each case unanimous, consisted of 16, 8, 4, 3, and 2 persons, respectively. In addition, we studied the limiting case in which the critical subject was opposed by one instructed subject. . . .

With the opposition reduced to one, the majority effect all but disappeared. When the opposition proceeded from a group of two, it produced a measurable though small distortion, the errors being 12.8 per cent of the total number of estimates. The effect appeared in full force with a majority of three. Larger majorities of four, eight, and sixteen did not produce effects greater than a majority of three.

The effect of a majority is often silent, revealing little of its operation to the subject, and often hiding it from the experimenter. To examine the range of effects it is capable of inducing, decisive variations of conditions are necessary. An indication of one effect is furnished by the following variation in which the conditions of the basic experiment were simply reversed. Here the majority, consisting of a group of sixteen, was naive; in the midst of it we placed a single individual who responded wrongly according to instructions. Under these conditions the members of the naive majority reacted to the lone dissenter with amusement and disdain. Contagious laughter spread through the group at the droll minority of one. Of significance is the fact that the members lack awareness that they draw their strength from the majority, and that their reactions would change radically if they faced the dissenter individually. In fact, the attitude of derision in the majority turns to seriousness and increased respect as soon as the minority is increased to three. These observations demonstrate the role of social support as a source of power and stability, in contrast to the preceding investigations which stressed the effects of withdrawal of social support, or to be more exact, the effects of social opposition. Both aspects must be explicitly considered in a unified formulation of the effects of group conditions on the formation and change of judgments.

The Role of the Stimulus-Situation

It is obviously not possible to divorce the quality and course of)he group forces which act upon the individual from the specific stimulus-conditions. Of necessity the structure of the situation moulds the group forces and determines their direction as well as their strength. Indeed, this was the reason that we took pains in the investigations described above to center the issue between the individual and the group around an elementary and fundamental matter of fact. And there can be no doubt that the resulting reactions were directly a function of the contradiction between the objectively grasped relations and the majority position. . . .

One additional dimension we have examined is the magnitude of discrepancies above the threshold. . . . Within the limits of our procedure we find that different magnitudes of discrepancy produce approximately the same amount of yielding. However, the quality of yielding alters: as the majority becomes more extreme, there occurs a significant increase in the frequency of "compromise" errors.

We have also varied systematically the structural clarity of the task, including in separate variations judgments based on mental standards. In agreement with other investigators, we find that the majority effect grows stronger as the situation diminishes in clarity. Concurrently, however, the disturbance of the subjects and the conflict-quality of the situation decrease markedly. We consider it of significance that the majority achieves its most pronounced effect when it acts most painlessly.

SUMMARY

We have investigated the effects upon individuals of majority opinions when the latter were seen to be in a direction contrary to fact. By means of a simple technique we produced a radical divergence between a majority and a minority, and observed the ways in which individuals coped with the resulting difficulty. Despite the stress of the given conditions, a substantial proportion of individuals retained their independence throughout. At the same time a substantial minority yielded, modifying their judgments in accordance with the majority. Independence and yielding are a joint function of the following major factors: (1) The character of the stimulus situation. Variations in structural clarity have a decisive effect: with diminishing clarity of the stimulus-conditions the majority effect increases. (2) The character of the group forces. Individuals are highly sensitive to the structural qualities of group opposition. In particular, we demonstrated the great importance of the factor of unanimity. Also, the majority effect is a function of the size of group opposition. (3) The character of the individual. There were wide, and indeed, striking differences among individuals within the same experimental situation. . . .

BIBLIOGRAPHY

1. Asch, S. E. Studies in the principles of judgments and attitudes: II. Determination of judgments by group and by ego-standards. *J. soc. Psychol.*, 1940, *12,* 433–465.
2. Asch, S. E. The doctrine of suggestion, prestige and imitation in social psychology. *Psychol. Rev.,* 1948, *55,* 250–276.
3. Asch, S. E., Block, H., and Hertzman, M. Studies in the principles of judgments and attitudes. I. Two basic principles of judgment. *J. Psychol.* 1938, *5,* 219–251.
4. Coffin, E. E. Some conditions of suggestion and suggestibility: A study of certain attitudinal and situational factors influencing the process of suggestion. *Psychol. Monogr.,* 1941, *53,* No. 4.
5. Lewis, H. B. Studies in the principle of judgments and attitudes: IV. The operation of prestige suggestion. *J. soc. Psychol.,* 1941, *14,* 229–256.
6. Lorge, I. Prestige, suggestion, and attitudes. *J. soc. Psychol.,* 1936, *7,* 386–402.
7. Miller, N. E. and Dollard, J. *Social Learning and Imitation.* New Haven: Yale University Press, 1941.
8. Moore, H. T. The comparative influence of majority and expert opinion. *Amer. J. Psychol.,* 1921, *32,* 16–20.
9. Sherif, M. A study of some social factors in perception. *Arch. Psychol.,* N.Y., 1935, No. 187.
10. Thorndike, E. L. *The Psychology of Wants, Interests, and Attitudes.* New York: D. Appleton-Century Company, Inc., 1935.

Groupthink

IRVING L. JANIS

"How could we have been so stupid?" President John F. Kennedy asked after he and a close group of advisers had blundered into the Bay of Pigs invasion. For the last two years I have been studying that question, as it applies not only to the Bay of Pigs decision-makers but also to those who led the United States into such other major fiascos as the failure to be prepared for the attack on Pearl Harbor, the Korean War stalemate and the escalation of the Vietnam War.

Stupidity certainly is not the explanation. The men who participated in making the Bay of Pigs decision, for instance, comprised one of the greatest arrays of intellectual talent in the history of American Government—Dean Rusk, Robert McNamara, Douglas Dillon, Robert Kennedy, McGeorge Bundy, Arthur Schlesinger Jr., Allen Dulles and others.

It also seemed to me that explanations were incomplete if they concentrated only on disturbances in the behavior of each individual within a decision-making body: temporary emotional states of elation, fear, or anger that reduce a man's mental efficiency, for example, or chronic blind spots arising from a man's social prejudices or idiosyncratic biases.

I preferred to broaden the picture by looking at the fiascos from the standpoint of group dynamics as it has been explored over the past three decades, first by the great social psychologist Kurt Lewin and later in many experimental situations by myself and other behavioral scientists. My conclusion after pouring over hundreds of relevant documents—historical reports about formal group meetings and informal conversations among the members—is that the groups that committed the fiascos were victims of what I call "groupthink."

"Groupy."   In each case study, I was surprised to discover the extent to which each group displayed the typical phenomena of social conformity that are regularly encountered in studies of group dynamics among ordinary citizens. For example, some of the phenomena appear to be completely in line with findings from social-psychological experiments showing that powerful social pressures are brought to bear by the members of a cohesive group whenever a dissident begins to voice his objections to a group consensus. Other phenomena are reminiscent of the shared illusions observed in encounter groups and friendship cliques when the members simultaneously reach a peak of "groupy" feelings.

Above all, there are numerous indications pointing to the development of group norms that bolster morale at the expense of critical thinking. One of the most common norms appears to be that of remaining loyal to the group by sticking with the policies to which the group has already committed itself, even when those policies are obviously working out badly and have unintended consequences that disturb the conscience of each member. This is one of the key characteristics of groupthink.

1984.   I use the term groupthink as a quick and easy way to refer to the mode of thinking that persons engage in when *concurrence-seeking* becomes so dominant in a cohesive ingroup that it tends to override realistic appraisal of alternative courses of action. Groupthink is a term of the same order as the words in the newspeak vocabulary George Orwell used in his dismaying world of *1984*. In that context, groupthink takes on an invidious connotation. Exactly such a connotation is intended, since the term refers to a deterioration in mental efficiency, reality testing and moral judgments as a result of group pressures.

The symptoms of groupthink arise when the members of decision-making groups become motivated to avoid being too harsh in their judgments of their leaders' or their colleagues' ideas. They adopt a soft line of criticism, even in their own thinking. At their meetings, all the members are amiable and seek complete concurrence on *every* important issue, with no bickering or conflict to spoil the cozy, "we-feeling" atmosphere.

Kill.   Paradoxically, soft-headed groups are often hard-hearted when it comes to dealing with outgroups or enemies. They find it relatively easy to resort to dehumanizing solutions—they will readily authorize bombing attacks that kill large numbers of civilians in the name of the noble cause of persuading an unfriendly government to negotiate at the peace table. They are unlikely to pursue the more difficult and controversial issues that arise when alternatives to a harsh military solution come up for discussion. Nor are they inclined to raise ethical issues that carry the implication that *this fine group of ours, with its humanitarianism and its high-minded principles, might be capable of adopting a course of action that is inhumane and immoral.*

Norms.   There is evidence from a number of social-psychological studies that as the members of a group feel more accepted by the others, which is a central feature of increased group cohesiveness, they display less overt conformity to group norms. Thus we would expect that the more cohesive a group becomes, the less the members will feel constrained to censor what they say out of fear of being socially punished for antagonizing the leader or any of their fellow members.

In contrast, the groupthink type of conformity tends to increase as group cohesiveness increases. Groupthink involves nondeliberate suppression of critical thoughts as a result of internalization of the group's norms, which is quite different from deliberate suppression on the basis of external threats of social punishment. The more cohesive the group, the greater the inner compulsion on the part of each member to avoid creating disunity, which inclines him to believe in the soundness of whatever proposals are promoted by the leader or by a majority of the group's members.

In a cohesive group, the danger is not so much that each individual will fail to reveal his objections to what the others propose but that he will think the proposal is a good one, without attempting to carry out a careful, critical scrutiny of the pros and cons of the alternatives. When groupthink becomes dominant, there also is considerable suppression of deviant thoughts, but it takes the form of each person's deciding that his misgivings are not relevant and should be set aside, that the benefit of the doubt regarding any lingering uncertainties should be given to the group consensus.

Stress.   I do not mean to imply that all cohesive groups necessarily suffer from groupthink. All ingroups may have a mild tendency toward groupthink, displaying one or another of the symptoms from time to time, but it need not be so dominant as to influence the quality of the group's final decision. Neither do I mean to imply that there is anything necessarily inefficient or harmful about group decisions in general. On the contrary, a group whose members have properly defined roles, with traditions concerning the procedures to follow in pursuing a critical inquiry, probably is capable of making better decisions than any individual group member working alone.

The problem is that the advantages of having decisions made by groups are often lost because of powerful psychological pressures that arise when the members work closely together, share the same set of values and, above all, face a crisis situation that puts everyone under intense stress.

The main principle of groupthink, which I offer in the spirit of Parkinson's Law, is this: *The more amiability and esprit de corps there is*

*among the members of a policy-making ingroup, the greater the danger
that independent critical thinking will be replaced by groupthink, which is
likely to result in irrational and dehumanizing actions directed against
outgroups.*

Symptoms. In my studies of high-level governmental decision-
makers, both civilian and military, I have found eight main symptoms of
groupthink.

1. Invulnerability. Most or all of the members of the ingroup share an
    illusion of invulnerability that provides for them some degree of
    reassurance about obvious dangers and leads them to become
    over-optimistic and willing to take extraordinary risks. It also causes
    them to fail to respond to clear warnings of danger.

    The Kennedy ingroup, which uncritically accepted the Central
    Intelligence Agency's disastrous Bay of Pigs plan, operated on the
    false assumption that they could keep secret the fact that the United
    States was responsible for the invasion of Cuba. Even after news of
    the plan began to leak out, their belief remained unshaken. They
    failed even to consider the danger that awaited them: a worldwide
    revulsion against the U.S.

    A similar attitude appeared among the members of President
    Lyndon B. Johnson's ingroup, the "Tuesday Cabinet," which kept
    escalating the Vietnam War despite repeated setbacks and failures.
    "There was a belief," Bill Moyers commented after he resigned,
    "that if we indicated a willingness to use our power, they [the North
    Vietnamese] would get the message and back away from an all-out
    confrontation. . . . There was a confidence—it was never bragged
    about, it was just there—that when the chips were really down, the
    other people would fold."

    A most poignant example of an illusion of invulnerability involves
    the ingroup around Admiral H. E. Kimmel, which failed to prepare
    for the possibility of a Japanese attack on Pearl Harbor despite
    repeated warnings. Informed by his intelligence chief that radio
    contact with Japanese aircraft carriers had been lost, Kimmel joked
    about it: "What, you don't know where the carriers are? Do you
    mean to say that they could be rounding Diamond Head (at
    Honolulu) and you wouldn't know it?" The carriers were in fact
    moving full-steam toward Kimmel's command post at the time.
    Laughing together about a danger signal, which labels it as a purely
    laughing matter, is a characteristic manifestation of groupthink.

2. *Rationale.* As we see, victims of groupthink ignore warnings; they
    also collectively construct rationalizations in order to discount
    warnings and other forms of negative feedback that, taken seriously,
    might lead the group members to reconsider their assumptions each
    time they recommit themselves to past decisions. Why did the
    Johnson ingroup avoid reconsidering its escalation policy when time
    and again the expectations on which they based their decisions

turned out to be wrong? James C. Thomson, Jr., a Harvard historian who spent five years as an observing participant in both the State Department and the White House, tells us that the policymakers avoided critical discussion of their prior decisions and continually invented new rationalizations so that they could sincerely recommit themselves to defeating the North Vietnamese.

In the fall of 1964, before the bombing of North Vietnam began, some of the policymakers predicted that six weeks of air strikes would induce the North Vietnamese to seek peace talks. When someone asked, "What if they don't?" the answer was that another four weeks certainly would do the trick.

Later, after each setback, the ingroup agreed that by investing just a bit more effort (by stepping up the bomb tonnage a bit, for instance), their course of action would prove to be right. *The Pentagon Papers* bear out these observations.

In *The Limits of Intervention,* Townsend Hoopes, who was acting Secretary of the Air Force under Johnson, says that Walt W. Rostow in particular showed a remarkable capacity for what has been called "instant rationalization." According to Hoopes, Rostow buttressed the group's optimism about being on the road to victory by culling selected scraps of evidence from news reports or, if necessary, by inventing "plausible" forecasts that had no basis in evidence at all.

Admiral Kimmel's group rationalized away their warnings, too. Right up to December 7, 1941, they convinced themselves that the Japanese would never dare attempt a full-scale surprise assault against Hawaii because Japan's leaders would realize that it would precipitate an all-out war which the United States would surely win. They made no attempt to look at the situation through the eyes of the Japanese leaders—another manifestation of groupthink.

3.   *Morality.* Victims of groupthink believe unquestioningly in the inherent morality of their ingroup: this belief inclines the members to ignore the ethical or moral consequences of their decisions.

Evidence that this symptom is at work usually is of a negative kind—the things that are left unsaid in group meetings. At least two influential persons had doubts about the morality of the Bay of Pigs adventure. One of them, Arthur Schlesinger, Jr., presented his strong objections in a memorandum to President Kennedy and Secretary of State Rusk but suppressed them when he attended meetings of the Kennedy team. The other, Senator J. William Fulbright, was not a member of the group, but the President invited him to express his misgivings in a speech to the policymakers. However, when Fulbright finished speaking the President moved on to other agenda items without asking for reactions of the group.

David Kraslow and Stuart H. Loory, in *The Secret Search for Peace in Vietnam,* report that during 1966 President Johnson's ingroup was concerned primarily with selecting bomb targets in North Vietnam. They based their selections on four factors—the military advantage, the risk to American aircraft and pilots, the danger of forcing other countries into the fighting, and the danger of heavy civilian casualties. At their regular Tuesday luncheons, they weighed these factors the way school teachers grade examination papers, averaging them out. Though evidence on this point is scant, I suspect that the group's ritualistic adherence to a standardized procedure induced the members to feel morally justified in their destructive way of dealing with the Vietnamese people—after all, the danger of heavy civilian casualties from U.S. air strikes was taken into account on their checklists.

4. *Stereotypes.* Victims of groupthink hold stereotyped views of the leaders of enemy groups: they are so evil that genuine attempts at negotiating differences with them are unwarranted, or they are too weak or too stupid to deal effectively with whatever attempts the ingroup makes to defeat their purposes, no matter how risky the attempts are.

  Kennedy's groupthinkers believed that Premier Fidel Castro's air force was so ineffectual that obsolete B-26s could knock it out completely in a surprise attack before the invasion began. They also believed that Castro's army was so weak that a small Cuban-exile brigade could establish a well-protected beachhead at the Bay of Pigs. In addition, they believed that Castro was not smart enough to put down any possible internal uprisings in support of the exiles. They were wrong on all three assumptions. Though much of the blame was attributable to faulty intelligence, the point is that none of Kennedy's advisers even questioned the CIA planners about these assumptions.

  The Johnson advisers' sloganistic thinking about "the Communist apparatus" that was "working all around the world" (as Dean Rusk put it) led them to overlook the powerful nationalistic strivings of the North Vietnamese government and its efforts to ward off Chinese domination. The crudest of all stereotypes used by Johnson's inner circle to justify their policies was the domino theory ("If we don't stop the Reds in South Vietnam, tomorrow they will be in Hawaii and next week they will be in San Francisco," Johnson once said). The group so firmly accepted this stereotype that it became almost impossible for any adviser to introduce a more sophisticated viewpoint.

  In the documents on Pearl Harbor, it is clear to see that the Navy commanders stationed in Hawaii had a naive image of Japan as a midget that would not dare to strike a blow against a powerful giant.

5. *Pressure.* Victims of groupthink apply direct pressure to any individual who momentarily expresses doubts about any of the group's shared illusions or who questions the validity of the arguments supporting a policy alternative favored by the majority. This gambit reinforces the concurrence-seeking norm that loyal members are expected to maintain.

  President Kennedy probably was more active than anyone else in raising skeptical questions during the Bay of Pigs meetings, and yet he seems to have encouraged the group's docile, uncritical acceptance of defective arguments in favor of the CIA's plan. At every meeting, he allowed the CIA representatives to dominate the discussion. He permitted them to give their immediate refutations in response to each tentative doubt that one of the others expressed, instead of asking whether anyone shared the doubt or wanted to pursue the implications of the new worrisome issue that had just been raised. And at the most crucial meeting, when he was calling on each member to give his vote for or against the plan, he did not call on Arthur Schlesinger, the one man there who was known by the President to have serious misgivings.

Historian Thomson informs us that whenever a member of Johnson's ingroup began to express doubts, the group used subtle social pressures to "domesticate" him. To start with, the dissenter was made to feel at home, provided that he lived up to two restrictions. 1) that he did not voice his doubts to outsiders, which would play into the hands of the opposition; and 2) that he kept his criticisms within the bounds of acceptable deviation, which meant not challenging any of the fundamental assumptions that went into the group's prior commitments. One such "domesticated dissenter" was Bill Moyers. When Moyers arrived at a meeting, Thomson tells us, the President greeted him with, "Well, here comes Mr. Stop-the-Bombing."

6. *Self-censorship.* Victims of groupthink avoid deviating from what appears to be group consensus; they keep silent about their misgivings and even minimize to themselves the importance of their doubts.

As we have seen, Schlesinger was not at all hesitant about presenting his strong objections to the Bay of Pigs plan in a memorandum to the President and the Secretary of State. But he became keenly aware of his tendency to suppress objections at the White House meetings. "In the months after the Bay of Pigs I bitterly reproached myself for having kept so silent during those crucial discussions in the cabinet room." Schlesinger writes in *A Thousand Days.* "I can only explain my failure to do more than raise a few timid questions by reporting that one's impulse to blow the whistle on this nonsense was simply undone by the circumstances of the discussion.

7. *Unanimity.* Victims of groupthink share an *illusion* of unanimity within the group concerning almost all judgments expressed by members who speak in favor of the majority view. This symptom results partly from the preceding one, whose effects are augmented by the false assumption that any individual who remains silent during any part of the discussion is in full accord with what the others are saying.

When a group of persons who respect each other's opinions arrives at a unanimous view, each member is likely to feel that the belief must be true. This reliance on consensual validation within the group tends to replace individual critical thinking and reality testing, unless there are clear-cut disagreements among the members. In contemplating a course of action such as the invasion of Cuba, it is painful for the members to confront disagreements within their group, particularly if it becomes apparent that there are widely divergent views about whether the preferred course of action is too risky to undertake at all. Such disagreements are likely to arouse anxieties about making a serious error. Once the sense of unanimity is shattered, the members no longer can feel complacently confident about the decision they are inclined to make. Each man must then face the annoying realization that there are troublesome uncertainties and he must diligently seek out the best information he can get in order to decide for himself exactly how serious the risks might be. This is one of the unpleasant consequences of being in a group of hardheaded, critical thinkers.

To avoid such an unpleasant state, the members often become inclined, without quite realizing it, to prevent latent disagreements from surfacing when they are about to initiate a risky course of action. The group leader and the members support each other in playing up the areas of convergence in their thinking, at the expense of fully exploring divergencies that might reveal unsettled issues.

"Our meetings took place in a curious atmosphere of assumed consensus," Schlesinger writes. His additional comments clearly show that, curiously, the consensus was an illusion—an illusion that could be maintained only because the major participants did not reveal their own reasoning or discuss their idiosyncratic assumptions and vague reservations. Evidence from several sources makes it clear that even the three principals—President Kennedy, Rusk and McNamara—had widely differing asumptions about the invasion plan.

8. *Mindguards.* Victims of groupthink sometimes appoint themselves as mindguards to protect the leader and fellow members from adverse information that might break the complacency they shared about the effectiveness and morality of past decisions. At a large birthday party for his wife, Attorney General Robert F. Kennedy, who had been constantly informed about the Cuban invasion plan, took Schlesinger aside and asked him why he was opposed. Kennedy listened coldly and said, "You may be right or you may be wrong, but the President has made his mind up. Don't push it any further. Now is the time for everyone to help him all they can."

Rusk also functioned as highly effective mindguard by failing to transmit to the group the strong objections of three "outsiders" who had learned of the invasion plan—Undersecretary of State Chester Bowles, USIA Director Edward R. Murrow, and Rusk's intelligence chief, Roger Hilsman. Had Rusk done so, their warnings might have reinforced Schlesinger's memorandum and jolted some of Kennedy's ingroup, if not the President himself, into reconsidering the decision.

Products.   When a group of executives frequently displays most or all of these interrelated symptoms, a detailed study of their deliberations is likely to reveal a number of immediate consequences. These consequences are, in effect, products of poor decision-making practices because they lead to inadequate solutions to the problems under discussion.

First, the group limits its discussions to a few alternative courses of action (often only two) without an initial survey of all the alternatives that might be worthy of consideration.

Second, the group fails to reexamine the course of action initially preferred by the majority after they learn of risks and drawbacks they had not considered originally.

Third, the members spend little or no time discussing whether there are nonobvious gains they may have overlooked or ways of reducing the seemingly prohibitive costs that made rejected alternatives appear undesirable to them.

Fourth, members make little or no attempt to obtain information from experts within their own organizations who might be able to supply more precise estimates of potential losses and gains.

Fifth, members show positive interest in facts and opinions that support their preferred policy; they tend to ignore facts and opinions that do not.

Sixth, members spend little time deliberating about how the chosen policy might be hindered by bureaucratic inertia, sabotaged by political opponents, or temporarily derailed by common accidents. Consequently, they fail to work out contingency plans to cope with foreseeable setbacks that could endanger the overall success of their chosen course.

Support.   The search for an explanation of why groupthink occurs has led me through a quagmire of complicated theoretical issues in the murky area of human motivation. My belief, based on recent social psychological research, is that we can best understand the various symptoms of groupthink as a mutual effort among the group members to maintain self-esteem and emotional equanimity by providing social support to each other, especially at times when they share responsibility for making vital decisions.

Even when no important decision is pending, the typical administrator will begin to doubt the wisdom and morality of his past decisions each time he receives information about setbacks, particularly if the information is accompanied by negative feedback from prominent men who originally had been his supporters. It should not be surprising, therefore, to find that individual members strive to develop unanimity and esprit de corps that will help bolster each other's morale, to create an optimistic outlook about the success of pending decisions, and to reaffirm the positive value of past policies to which all of them are committed.

Pride.   Shared illusions of invulnerability, for example, can reduce anxiety about taking risks. Rationalizations help members believe that the risks are really not so bad after all. The assumption of inherent morality helps the members to avoid feelings of shame or guilt. Negative stereotypes function as stress-reducing devices to enhance a sense of moral righteousness as well as pride in a lofty mission.

The mutual enhancement of self-esteem and morale may have functional value in enabling the members to maintain their capacity to take action, but it has maladaptive consequences insofar as concurrence-seeking tendencies interfere with critical, rational capacities and lead to serious errors of judgment.

While I have limited my study to decision-making bodies in Government, groupthink symptoms appear in business, industry and any other field where small, cohesive groups make the decisions. It is vital, then, for all sorts of people—and especially group leaders—to know what steps they can take to prevent groupthink.

Remedies.   To counterpoint my case studies of the major fiascos, I have also investigated two highly successful group enterprises, the formulation of the Marshall Plan in the Truman Administration and the handling of the Cuban missile crisis by President Kennedy and his advisers. I have found it instructive to examine the steps Kennedy took to change his group's decision-making processes. These changes ensured that the mistakes made by his Bay of Pigs ingroup were not repeated by the missile-crisis ingroup, even though the membership of both groups was essentially the same.

The following recommendations for preventing groupthink incorporate many of the good practices I discovered to be characteristic of the Marshal Plan and missile-crisis groups:

1. The leader of a policy-forming group should assign the role of critical evaluator to each member, encouraging the group to give high priority to open airing of objections and doubts. This practice needs to be reinforced by the leader's acceptance of criticism of his own judgments in order to discourage members from soft-pedaling their disagreements and from allowing their striving for concurrence to inhibit critical thinking.
2. When the key members of a hierarchy assign a policy-planning mission to any group within their organization, they should adopt an impartial stance instead of stating preferences and expectations at the beginning. This will encourage open inquiry and impartial probing of a wide range of policy alternatives.
3. The organization routinely should set up several outside policy-planning and evaluation groups to work on the same policy question, each deliberating under a different leader. This can prevent the insulation of an ingroup.
4. At intervals before the group reaches a final consensus, the leader should require each member to discuss the group's deliberations

with associates in his own unit of the organization—assuming that those associates can be trusted to adhere to the same security regulations that govern the policymakers—and then to report back their reactions to the group.

5. The group should invite one or more outside experts to each meeting on a staggered basis and encourage the experts to challenge the views of the core members.

6. At every general meeting of the group, whenever the agenda calls for an evaluation of policy alternatives, at least one member should play devil's advocate, functioning as a good lawyer in challenging the testimony of those who advocate the majority position.

7. Whenever the policy issue involves relations with a rival nation or organization, the group should devote a sizable block of time, perhaps an entire session, to a survey of all warning signals from the rivals and should write alternative scenarios on the rivals' intentions.

8. When the group is surveying policy alternatives for feasibility and effectiveness, it should from time to time divide into two or more subgroups to meet separately, under different chairmen, and then come back together to hammer out differences.

9. After reaching a preliminary consensus about what seems to be the best policy, the group should hold a "second-chance" meeting at which every member expresses as vividly as he can all his residual doubts, and rethinks the entire issue before making a definitive choice.

How.   These recommendations have their disadvantages. To encourage the open airing of objections, for instance, might lead to prolonged and costly debates when a rapidly growing crisis requires immediate solution. It also could cause rejection, depression and anger. A leader's failure to set a norm might create cleavage between leader and members that could develop into a disruptive power struggle if the leader looks on the emerging consensus as anathema. Setting up outside evaluation groups might increase the risk of security leakage. Still, inventive executives who know their way around the organizational maze probably can figure out how to apply one or another of the prescriptions successfully, without harmful side effects.

They also could benefit from the advice of outside experts in the administrative and behavioral sciences. Though these experts have much to offer, they have had few chances to work out policy-making machinery within large organizations. As matters now stand, executives innovate only when they need new procedures to avoid repeating serious errors that have deflated their self-images.

In this era of atomic warheads, urban disorganization and ecocatastrophes, it seems to me that policymakers should collaborate with behavioral scientists and give top priority to preventing groupthink and its attendant fiascos.

The Abilene Paradox:
The Management of Agreement

JERRY B. HARVEY

The July afternoon in Coleman, Texas (population 5,607) was particularly hot—104 degrees as measured by the Walgreen's Rexall Ex-Lax temperature gauge. In addition, the wind was blowing fine-grained West Texas topsoil through the house. But the afternoon was still tolerable—even potentially enjoyable. There was a fan going on the back porch; there was cold lemonade; and finally, there was entertainment. Dominoes. Perfect for the conditions. The game required little more physical exertion than an occasional mumbled comment, "Shuffle 'em," and an unhurried movement of the arm to place the spots in the appropriate perspective on the table. All in all, it had the makings of an agreeable Sunday afternoon in Coleman—that is, it was until my father-in-law suddenly said, "Let's get in the car and go to Abilene and have dinner at the cafeteria."

I thought, "What, go to Abilene? Fifty-three miles? In this dust storm and heat? And in an unairconditioned 1958 Buick?"

But my wife chimed in with, "Sounds like a great idea. I'd like to go. How about you, Jerry?" Since my own preferences were obviously out of step with the rest I replied, "Sounds good to me," and added, "I just hope your mother wants to go."

"Of course I want to go," said my mother-in-law. "I haven't been to Abilene in a long time."

So into the car and off to Abilene we went. My predictions were fulfilled. The heat was brutal. We were coated with a fine layer of dust that was cemented with perspiration by the time we arrived. The food at the cafeteria provided first-rate testimonial material for antacid commercials.

Some four hours and 106 miles later we returned to Coleman, hot and exhausted. We sat in front of the fan for a long time in silence. Then, both to be sociable and to break the silence, I said, "It was a great trip, wasn't it?"

No one spoke.

Finally my mother-in-law said, with some irritation, "Well, to tell the truth, I really didn't enjoy it much and would rather have stayed here. I just went along because the three of you were so enthusiastic about going. I wouldn't have gone if you all hadn't pressured me into it."

I couldn't believe it. "What do you mean 'you all'?" I said. "Don't put me in the 'you all' group. I was delighted to be doing what we were doing. I didn't want to go. I only went to satisfy the rest of you. You're the culprits."

My wife looked shocked. "Don't call me a culprit. You and Daddy and Mamma were the ones who wanted to go. I just went along to be sociable and to keep you happy. I would have had to be crazy to want to go out in heat like that."

Her father entered the conversation abruptly. "Hell!" he said.

He proceeded to expand on what was already absolutely clear. "Listen, I never wanted to go to Abilene. I just thought you might be bored. You visit so seldom I wanted to be sure you enjoyed it. I would have preferred to play another game of dominoes and eat the leftovers in the icebox."

After the outburst of recrimination we all sat back in silence. Here we were, four reasonably sensible people who, of our own volition, had just taken a 106-mile trip across a godforsaken desert in a furnace-like temperature through a cloud-like dust storm to eat unpalatable food at a hole-in-the-wall cafeteria in Abilene, when none of us had really wanted to go. In fact, to be more accurate, we'd done just the opposite of what we wanted to do. The whole situation simply didn't make sense.

At least it didn't make sense at the time. But since that day in Coleman, I have observed, consulted with, and been a part of more than one organization that has been caught in the same situation. As a result, they have either taken a side-trip, or, occasionally, a terminal journey to Abilene, when Dallas or Houston or Tokyo was where they really wanted to go. And for most of those organizations, the negative consequences of such trips, measured in terms of both human misery and economic loss, have been much greater than for our little Abilene group.

This article is concerned with that paradox—the Abilene Paradox. Stated simply, it is as follows: Organizations frequently take actions in contradiction to what they really want to do and therefore defeat the very purposes they are trying to achieve. It also deals with a major corollary of the paradox, which is that *the inability to manage agreement is a major source of organization dysfunction.* Last, the article is designed to help members of organizations cope more effectively with the paradox's pernicious influence.

As a means of accomplishing the above, I shall: (1) describe the symptoms exhibited by organizations caught in the paradox; (2) describe, in summarized case-study examples, how they occur in a variety of organizations; (3) discuss the underlying causal dynamics; (4) indicate some of the implications of accepting this model for describing organizational behavior; (5) make recommendations for coping with the paradox; and, in conclusion, (6) relate the paradox to a broader existential issue.

SYMPTOMS OF THE PARADOX

The inability to manage agreement, not the inability to manage conflict, is the essential symptom that defines organizations caught in the web of the Abilene Paradox. That inability effectively to manage agreement is expressed by six specific subsymptoms, all of which were present in our family Abilene group.

1. Organization members agree privately, as individuals, as to the nature of the situation or problem facing the organization. For example, members of the Abilene group agreed that they were enjoying themselves sitting in front of the fan, sipping lemonade, and playing dominoes.
2. Organization members agree privately, as individuals, as to the steps that would be required to cope with the situation or problem they face. For members of the Abilene group "more of the same" was a solution that would have adequately satisfied their individual and collective desires.
3. Organization members fail to accurately communicate their desires and/or beliefs to one another. In fact, they do just the opposite and thereby lead one another into misperceiving the collective reality. Each member of the Abilene group, for example, communicated inaccurate data to other members of the organization. The data, in effect, said, "Yeah, it's a great idea. Let's go to Abilene," when in reality members of the organization individually and collectively preferred to stay in Coleman.
4. With such invalid and inaccurate information, organization members make collective decisions that lead them to take actions contrary to what they want to do, and thereby arrive at results that are counterproductive to the organization's intent and purposes. Thus, the Abilene group went to Abilene when it preferred to do something else.
5. As a result of taking actions that are counterproductive, organization members experience frustration, anger, irritation, and dissatisfaction

with their organization. Consequently, they form subgroups with trusted acquaintances and blame other subgroups for the organization's dilemma. Frequently, they also blame authority figures and one another. Such phenomena were illustrated in the Abilene group by the "culprit" argument that occurred when we had returned to the comfort of the fan.

6. Finally, if organization members do not deal with the generic issue—the inability to manage agreement—the cycle repeats itself with greater intensity. The Abilene group, for a variety of reasons, the most important of which was that it became conscious of the process, did not reach that point.

To repeat, the Abilene Paradox reflects a failure to manage agreement. In fact, it is my contention that the inability to cope with (manage) agreement, rather than the inability to cope with (manage) conflict is the single most pressing issue of modern organizations.

OTHER TRIPS TO ABILENE

The Abilene Paradox is no respecter of individuals, organizations, or institutions. Following are descriptions of two other trips to Abilene that illustrate both the pervasiveness of the paradox and its underlying dynamics.

Case No. 1: The Boardroom.

The Ozyx Corporation is a relatively small industrial company that has embarked on a trip to Abilene. The president of Ozyx has hired a consultant to help discover the reasons for the poor profit picture of the company in general and the low morale and productivity of the R&D division in particular. During the process of investigation, the consultant becomes interested in a research project in which the company has invested a sizable proportion of its R&D budget.

When asked about the project by the consultant in the privacy of their offices, the president, the vice-president for research, and the research manager each describes it as an idea that looked great on paper but will ultimately fail because of the unavailability of the technology required to make it work. Each of them also acknowledges that continued support of the project will create cash flow problems that will jeopardize the very existence of the total organization.

Furthermore, each individual indicates he has not told the others about his reservations. When asked why, the president says he can't reveal his "true" feelings because abandoning the project, which has been widely publicized, would make the company look bad in the press and, in addition, would probably cause his vice-president's ulcer to kick up or perhaps even cause him to quit, "because he has staked his professional reputation on the project's success."

Similarly, the vice-president for research says he can't let the president or the research manager know of his reservations because the president is so committed to it that "I would probably get fired for insubordination if I questioned the project."

Finally, the research manager says he can't let the president or vice-president know of his doubts about the project because of their extreme commitment to the project's success.

All indicate that, in meetings with one another, they try to maintain an optimistic façade so the others won't worry unduly about the project. The research director, in particular, admits to writing ambiguous progress reports so the president and the vice-president can "interpret them to suit themselves." In fact, he says he tends to slant them to the "positive" side, "given how committed the brass are."

The scent of the Abilene trail wafts from a paneled conference room where the project research budget is being considered for the following fiscal year. In the meeting itself, praises are heaped on the questionable project and a unanimous decision is made to continue it for yet another year. Symbolically, the organization has boarded a bus to Abilene.

In fact, although the real issue of agreement was confronted approximately eight months after the bus departed, it was nearly too late. The organization failed to meet a payroll and underwent a two-year period of personnel cutbacks, retrenchments, and austerity. Morale suffered, the most competent technical personnel resigned, and the organization's prestige in the industry declined.

Case No. 2: The Watergate.

Apart from the grave question of who did what, Watergate presents America with the profound puzzle of why. What is it that led such a wide assortment of men, many of them high public officials, possibly including the President himself, either to instigate or to go along with and later try to hide a pattern of behavior that by now appears not only reprehensible, but stupid? *(The Washington Star and Daily News, editorial, May 27, 1973.)*

One possible answer to the editorial writer's question can be found by probing into the dynamics of the Abilene paradox. I shall let the reader reach his own conclusions, though, on the basis of the following excerpts from testimony before the Senate investigating committee on "The Watergate Affair."

In one exchange, Senator Howard Baker asked Herbert Porter, then a member of the White House staff, why he (Porter) found himself "in charge of or deeply involved in a dirty tricks operation of the campaign." In response, Porter indicated that he had qualms about what he was doing, but that he ". . . was not one to stand up in a meeting and say that this should be stopped. . . . I kind of drifted along."

And when asked by Baker why he had "drifted along," Porter replied, "In all honesty, because of the fear of the group pressure that would ensue, of not being a team player," and ". . . I felt a deep sense of loyalty to him [the President] or was appealed to on that basis." *(The Washington Post, June 8, 1973, p. 20.)*

Jeb Magruder gave a similar response to a question posed by committee counsel Dash. Specifically, when asked about his, Mr. Dean's, and Mr. Mitchell's reactions to Mr. Liddy's proposal, which included bugging the Watergate, Mr. Magruder replied, "I think all three of us were appalled. The scope and size of the project were something that at least in my mind were not envisioned. I do not think it was in Mr. Mitchell's mind or Mr. Dean's, although I can't comment on their states of mind at that time."

Mr. Mitchell, in an understated way, which was his way of dealing with difficult problems like this, indicated that this was not an "acceptable project." *(The Washington Post,* June 15, 1973, p. A14.)

Later in his testimony Mr. Magruder said, ". . . I think I can honestly say that no one was particularly overwhelmed with the project. But I think we felt that this information could be useful, and Mr. Mitchell agreed to approve the project, and I then notified the parties of Mr. Mitchell's approval." *(The Washington Post,* June 15, 1973, p. A14.)

Although I obviously was not privy to the private conversations of the principal characters, the data seem to reflect the essential elements of the Abilene Paradox. First, they indicate agreement. Evidently, Mitchell, Porter, Dean, and Magruder agreed that the plan was inappropriate. ("I think I can honestly say that no one was particularly overwhelmed with the project.") Second, the data indicate that the principal figures then proceeded to implement the plan in contradiction to their shared agreement. Third, the data surrounding the case clearly indicate that the plan multiplied the organization's problems rather than solved them. And finally, the organization broke into subgroups with the various principals, such as the President, Mitchell, Porter, Dean, and Magruder, blaming one another for the dilemma in which they found themselves, and internecine warfare ensued.

In summary, it is possible that because of the inability of White House staff members to cope with the fact that they agreed, the organization took a trip to Abilene.

ANALYZING THE PARADOX

The Abilene Paradox can be stated succinctly as follows: Organizations frequently take actions in contradiction to the data they have for dealing with problems and, as a result, compound their problems rather than solve them. Like all paradoxes, the Abilene Paradox deals with absurdity. On the surface, it makes little sense for organizations, whether they are couples or companies, bureaucracies or governments, to take actions that are diametrically opposed to the data they possess for solving crucial organizational problems. Such actions are particularly absurd since they tend to compound the very problems they are designed to solve and thereby defeat the purposes the organization is trying to achieve. However, as Robert Rapaport and others have so cogently expressed it, paradoxes are generally paradoxes only because they are based on a logic or rationale different from what we understand or expect.

Discovering that different logic not only destroys the paradoxical quality but also offers alternative ways for coping with similar situations. Therefore, part of the dilemma facing an Abilene-bound organization may be the lack of a map—a theory or model—that provides rationality to the paradox. The purpose of the following discussion is to provide such a map.

The map will be developed by examining the underlying psychological themes of the profit-making organization and the bureaucracy and it will include the following landmarks: (1) Action Anxiety; (2) Negative Fantasies; (3) Real Risk; (4) Separation Anxiety; and (5) the Psychological Reversal of Risk and Certainty. I hope that the discussion of such landmarks will provide harried organization travelers with a new map that will assist them in arriving at where they really want to go and, in addition, will help them in assessing the risks that are an inevitable part of the journey.

ACTION ANXIETY

Action anxiety provides the first landmark for locating roadways that bypass Abilene. The concept of action anxiety says that the reason organization members take actions in contradiction to their understanding of the organization's problems lies in the intense anxiety that is created as they think about acting in accordance with what they believe needs to be done. As a result, they opt to endure the professional and economic degradation of pursuing an unworkable research project or the consequences of participating in an illegal activity rather than act in a manner congruent with their beliefs. It is not that organization members do not know what needs to be done—they do know. For example, the various principals in the research organization cited *knew* they were working on a research project that had no real possibility of succeeding. And the central figures of the Watergate episode apparently *knew* that, for a variety of reasons, the plan to bug the Watergate did not make sense.

Such action anxiety experienced by the various protagonists may not make sense, but the dilemma is not a new one. In fact, it is very similar to the anxiety experienced by Hamlet, who expressed it most eloquently in the opening lines of his famous soliloquy:

> To be or not to be; that is the question:
> Whether 'tis nobler in the mind to suffer
> The slings and arrows of outrageous fortune
> Or to take arms against a sea of troubles
> And by opposing, end them? . . . *(Hamlet,* Act
> III, Scene II)

It is easy to translate Hamlet's anxious lament into that of the research manager of our R&D organization as he contemplates his report to the meeting of the budget committee. It might go something like this:

> To maintain my sense of integrity and self-worth or compromise it, that is the question. Whether 'tis nobler in the mind to suffer the ignominy that comes from managing a nonsensical research project, or the fear and anxiety that come from making a report the president and V.P. may not like to hear.

So, the anguish, procrastination, and counterproductive behavior of the research manager or members of the White House staff are not much different from those of Hamlet; all might ask with equal justification Hamlet's subsequent searching question of what it is that

> makes us rather bear those ills we have than fly to others we know not of. *(Hamlet,* Act III, Scene II*)*

In short, like the various Abilene protagonists, we are faced with a deeper question: Why does action anxiety occur?

NEGATIVE FANTASIES

Part of the answer to that question may be found in the negative fantasies organization members have about acting in congruence with what they believe should be done.

Hamlet experienced such fantasies. Specifically, Hamlet's fantasies of the alternatives to current evils were more evils, and he didn't entertain the possibility that any action he might take could lead to an improvement in the situation. Hamlet's was not an unusual case, though. In fact, the "Hamlet syndrome" clearly occurred in both organizations previously described. All of the organization protagonists had negative fantasies about what would happen if they acted in accordance with what they believed needed to be done.

The various managers in the R&D organization foresaw loss of face, prestige, position, and even health as the outcome of confronting the issues about which they believed, incorrectly, that they disagreed. Similarly, members of the White House staff feared being made scapegoats, branded as disloyal, or ostracized as non-team players if they acted in accordance with their understanding of reality.

To sum up, action anxiety is supported by the negative fantasies that organization members have about what will happen as a consequence of their acting in accordance with their understanding of what is sensible. The negative fantasies, in turn, serve an important function for the persons who have them. Specifically, they provide the individual with an excuse that releases him psychologically, both in his own eyes and frequently in the eyes of others, from the responsibility of having to act to solve organization problems.

It is not sufficient, though, to stop with the explanation of negative fantasies as the basis for the inability of organizations to cope with agreement. We must look deeper and ask still other questions: What is the source of the negative fantasies? Why do they occur?

REAL RISK

Risk is a reality of life, a condition of existence. John Kennedy articulated it in another way when he said at a news conference, "Life is unfair." By that I believe he meant we do not know, nor can we predict or control with certainty, either the events that impinge upon us or the outcomes of actions we undertake in response to those events.

Consequently, in the business environment, the research manager might find that confronting the president and the vice-president with the fact that the project was a "turkey" might result in his being fired. And Mr. Porter's saying that an illegal plan of surveillance should not be carried out could have caused his ostracism as a non-team player. There are too many cases when confrontation of this sort has resulted in such consequences. The real question, though, is not, Are such fantasized consequences possible? but, Are such fantasized consequences likely?

Thus, real risk is an existential condition, and all actions do have consequences that, to paraphrase Hamlet, may be worse than the evils of the present. As a result of their unwillingness to accept existential risk as one of life's givens, however, people may opt to take their organizations to Abilene rather than run the risk, no matter how small, of ending up somewhere worse.

Again, though, one must ask, What is the real risk that underlies the decision to opt for Abilene? What is at the core of the paradox?

FEAR OF SEPARATION

One is tempted to say that the core of the paradox lies in the individual's fear of the unknown. Actually, we do not fear what is unknown, but we are afraid of things we do know about. What do we know about that frightens us into such apparently inexplicable organizational behavior?

Separation, alienation, and loneliness are things we do know about—and fear. Both research and experience indicate that ostracism is one of the most powerful punishments that can be devised. Solitary confinement does not draw its coercive strength from physical deprivation. The evidence is overwhelming that we have a fundamental need to be connected, engaged, and related and a reciprocal need not to be separated or alone. Everyone of us, though, has experienced aloneness. From the time the umbilical cord was cut, we have experienced the real anguish of separation—broken friendships, divorces, deaths, and exclusions. C. P. Snow vividly described the tragic interplay between loneliness and connection:

> Each of us is alone; sometimes we escape from our solitariness, through love and affection or perhaps creative moments, but these triumphs of life are pools of light we make for ourselves while the edge of the road is black. Each of us dies alone.

That fear of taking risks that may result in our separation from others is at the core of the paradox. It finds expression in ways of which we may be unaware, and it is ultimately the cause of the self-defeating, collective deception that leads to self-destructive decisions within organizations.

Concretely, such fear of separation leads research committees to fund projects that none of its members want and, perhaps, White House staff members to engage in illegal activities that they don't really support.

THE PSYCHOLOGICAL REVERSAL OF RISK AND CERTAINTY

One piece of the map is still missing. It relates to the peculiar reversal that occurs in our thought processes as we try to cope with the Abilene Paradox. For example, we frequently fail to take action in an organizational setting because we fear that the actions we take may result in our separation from others, or, in the language of Mr. Porter, we are afraid of being tabbed as "disloyal" or are afraid of being ostracized as "non-team players." But therein lies a paradox within a paradox, because our very unwillingness to take such risks virtually ensures the separation and aloneness we so fear. In effect, we reverse "real existential risk" and "fantasied risk" and by doing so transform what is a probability statement into what, for all practical purposes, becomes a certainty.

Take the R&D organization described earlier. When the project fails, some people will get fired, demoted, or sentenced to the purgatory of a make-work job in an out-of-the-way office. For those who remain, the atmosphere of blame, distrust, suspicion, and backbiting that accompanies such failure will serve only to further alienate and separate those who remain.

The Watergate situation is similar. The principals evidently feared being ostracized as disloyal non-team players. When the illegality of the act surfaced, however, it was nearly inevitable that blaming, self-protective actions, and scapegoating would result in the very emotional separation from both the President and one another that the principals feared. Thus, by reversing real and fantasied risk, they had taken effective action to ensure the outcome they least desired.

One final question remains: "Why do we make this peculiar reversal? I support the general thesis of Alvin Toffler and Philip Slater, who contend that our cultural emphasis on technology, competition, individualism, temporariness, and mobility has resulted in a population that has frequently experienced the terror of loneliness and seldom the satisfaction of engagement. Consequently, though we have learned of the reality of separation, we have not had the opportunity to learn the reciprocal skills of connection, with the result that, like the ancient dinosaurs, we are breeding organizations with self-destructive decision-making proclivities.

A POSSIBLE ABILENE BYPASS

Existential risk is inherent in living, so it is impossible to provide a map that meets the no-risk criterion, but it may be possible to describe the route in terms that make the landmarks understandable and that will clarify the risks involved. In order to do that, however, some commonly used terms such as victim, victimizer, collusion, responsibility, conflict, conformity, courage, confrontation, reality, and knowledge have to be redefined. In addition, we need to explore the relevance of the redefined concepts for bypassing or getting out of Abilene.

· *Victim and victimizer.* Blaming and fault-finding behavior is one of the basic symptoms of organizations that have found their way to Abilene, and the target of blame generally doesn't include the one who criticizes. Stated in different terms, executives begin to assign one another to roles of victims and victimizers. Ironic as it may seem, however, this assignment of roles is both irrelevant and dysfunctional, because once a business or a government fails to manage its agreement and arrives in Abilene, all its members are victims. Thus, arguments and accusations that identify victims and victimizers at best become symptoms of the paradox, and, at worst, drain energy from the problem-solving efforts required to redirect the organization along the route it really wants to take.

· *Collusion.* A basic implication of the Abilene Paradox is that human problems of organization are reciprocal in nature. As Robert Tannenbaum has pointed out, you can't have an autocratic boss unless subordinates are willing to collude with his autocracy, and you can't have obsequious subordinates unless the boss is willing to collude with their obsequiousness.

Thus, in plain terms, each person in a self-defeating, Abilene-bound organization *colludes* with others, including peers, superiors, and subordinates, sometimes consciously and sometimes subconsciously, to create the dilemma in which the organization finds itself. To adopt a cliche of modern organization, "It takes a real team effort to go to Abilene." In that sense each person, in his own collusive manner, shares responsibility for the trip, so searching for a locus of blame outside oneself serves no useful purpose for either the organization or the individual. It neither helps the organization handle its dilemma of unrecognized agreement nor does it provide psychological relief for the individual, because focusing on conflict when agreement is the issue is devoid of reality. In fact, it does just the opposite, for it causes the organization to focus on managing conflict when it should be focusing on managing agreement.

· *Responsibility for problem-solving action.* A second question is, Who is responsible for getting us out of this place? To that question is frequently appended a third one, generally rhetorical in nature, with "should" overtones, such as, Isn't it the boss (or the ranking government official) who is responsible for doing something about the situation?

The answer to that question is no.

The key to understanding the functionality of the no answer is the knowledge that, when the dynamics of the paradox are in operation, the authority figure—and others—are in unknowing agreement with one another concerning the organization's problems and the steps necessary to solve them. Consequently, the power to destroy the paradox's pernicious influence comes from confronting and speaking to the underlying reality of the situation, and not from one's hierarchical position within the organization. Therefore, any organization member who chooses to risk confronting that reality possesses the necessary leverage to release the organization from the paradox's grip.

In one situation, it may be a research director's saying, "I don't think this project can succeed." In another, it may be Jeb Magruder's response to this question of Senator Baker:

> If you were concerned because the action was known to you to be illegal, because you thought it improper or unethical, you thought the prospects for success were very meager, and you doubted the reliability of Mr. Liddy, what on earth would it have taken to decide against the plan?

Magruder's reply was brief and to the point:

> Not very much, sir. I am sure that if I had fought vigorously against it, I think any of us could have had the plan cancelled. *(Time,* June 25, 1973, p. 12.)

· *Reality, knowledge, confrontation.* Accepting the paradox as a model describing certain kinds of organizational dilemmas also requires rethinking the nature of reality and knowledge, as they are generally described in organizations. In brief, the underlying dynamics of the paradox clearly indicate that organization members generally know more about issues confronting the organization than they don't know. The various principals attending the research budget meeting, for example, knew the research project was doomed to failure. And Jeb Magruder spoke as a true Abilener when he said, "We knew it was illegal, probably, inappropriate." *(The Washington Post,* June 15, 1973, p. A16.)

Given this concept of reality and its relationship to knowledge, confrontation becomes the process of facing issues squarely, openly, and directly in an effort to discover whether the nature of the underlying collective reality is agreement or conflict. Accepting such a definition of confrontation has an important implication for change agents interested in making organizations more effective. That is, organization change and effectiveness may be facilitated as much by confronting the organization with what it knows and agrees upon as by confronting it with what it doesn't know or disagrees about.

REAL CONFLICT AND PHONY CONFLICT

Conflict is a part of any organization. Couples, R&D divisions, and White House staffs all engage in it. However, analysis of the Abilene Paradox opens up the possibility of two kinds of conflict—real and phony. On the surface, they look alike, but, like headaches, have different causes and therefore require different treatment.

Real conflict occurs when people have real differences. ("My reading of the research printouts says that we can make the project profitable." "I come to the opposite conclusion.") ("I suggest we 'bug' the Watergate." "I'm not in favor of it.")

Phony conflict, on the other hand, occurs when people agree on the actions they want to take, and then do the opposite. The resulting anger, frustration, and blaming behavior generally termed "conflict" are not based on real differences. Rather, they stem from the protective reactions that occur when a decision that no one believed in or was committed to in the first place goes sour. In fact, as a paradox within a paradox, such conflict is symptomatic of agreement!

GROUP TYRANNY AND CONFORMITY

Understanding the dynamics of the Abilene Paradox also requires a "reorientation" in thinking about concepts such as "group tyranny"— the loss of the individual's distinctiveness in a group, and the impact of conformity pressures on individual behavior in organizations.

Group tyranny and its result, individual conformity, generally refer to the coercive effect of group pressures on individual behavior. Sometimes referred to as Groupthink, it has been damned as the cause for everything from the lack of creativity in organizations ("A camel is a horse designed by a committee") to antisocial behavior in juveniles ("My Johnny is a good boy. He was just pressured into shoplifting by the kids he runs around with").

However, analysis of the dynamics underlying the Abilene Paradox opens up the possibility that individuals frequently perceive and feel as if they are experiencing the coercive organization conformity pressures when, in actuality, they are responding to the dynamics of mismanaged agreement. Conceptualizing, experiencing, and responding to such experiences as reflecting the tyrannical pressures of a group again serves an important psychological use for the individual: As was previously said, it releases him from the responsibility of taking action and thus becomes a defense against action. Thus, much behavior within an organization that heretofore has been conceptualized as reflecting the tyranny of conformity pressures is really an expression of collective anxiety and therefore must be reconceptualized as a defense against acting.

A well-known example of such faulty conceptualization comes to mind. It involves the heroic sheriff in the classic Western movies who stands alone in the jailhouse door and singlehandedly protects a suspected (and usually innocent) horsethief or murderer from the irrational, tyrannical forces of group behavior—that is, an armed lynch mob. Generally, as a part of the ritual, he threatens to blow off the head of anyone who takes a step toward the door. Few ever take the challenge, and the reason is not the sheriff's sixshooter. What good would one pistol be against an armed mob of several hundred people who *really* want to hang somebody? Thus, the gun in fact serves as a face-saving measure for people who don't wish to participate in a hanging anyway. ("We had to back off. The sheriff threatened to blow our heads off.")

The situation is one involving agreement management, for a careful investigator canvassing the crowd under conditions in which the anonymity of the interviewees' responses could be guaranteed would probably find: (1) that few of the individuals in the crowd really wanted to take part in the hanging; (2) that each person's participation came about because he perceived, falsely, that others wanted to do so; and (3) that each person was afraid that others in the crowd would ostracize or in some other way punish him if he did not go along.

DIAGNOSING THE PARADOX

Most individuals like quick solutions, "clean" solutions, "no risk" solutions to organization problems. Furthermore, they tend to prefer solutions based on mechanics and technology, rather than on attitudes of "being." Unfortunately, the underlying reality of the paradox makes it impossible to provide either no-risk solutions or action technologies divorced from existential attitudes and realities. I do, however, have two sets of suggestions for dealing with these situations. One set of suggestions relates to diagnosing the situation, the other to confronting it.

When faced with the possibility that the paradox is operating, one must first make a diagnosis of the situation, and the key to diagnosis is an answer to the question, Is the organization involved in a conflict-management or an agreement-management situation? As an organization member, I have found it relatively easy to make a preliminary diagnosis as to whether an organization is on the way to Abilene or is involved in legitimate, substantive conflict by responding to the Diagnostic Survey shown in the accompanying figure. If the answer to the first question is "not characteristic," the organization is probably not in Abilene or conflict. If the answer is "characteristic," the organization has a problem of either real or phony conflict, and the answers to the succeeding questions help to determine which it is.

In brief, for reasons that should be apparent from the theory discussed here, the more times "characteristic" is checked, the more likely the organization is on its way to Abilene. In practical terms, a process for managing agreement is called for. And finally, if the answer to the first

Organization Diagnostic Survey

Instructions: For each of the following statements please indicate whether it IS *or* IS NOT *characteristic of your organization.*

1. There is conflict in the organization.

2. Organization members feel frustrated, impotent, and unhappy when trying to deal with it. Many are looking for ways to escape. They may avoid meetings at which the conflict is discussed, they may be looking for other jobs, or they may spend as much time away from the office as possible by taking unneeded trips or vacation or sick leave.

3. Organization members place much of the blame for the dilemma on the boss or other groups. In "back room" conversations among friends the boss is termed incompetent, ineffective, "out of touch," or a candidate for early retirement. To his face, nothing is said, or at best, only oblique references are made concerning his role in the organization's problems. If the boss isn't blamed, some other group, division, or unit is seen as the cause of the trouble: "We would do fine if it were not for the damn fools in Division X."

4. Small subgroups of trusted friends and associates meet informally over coffee, lunch, and so on to discuss organizational problems. There is a lot of agreement among the members of these subgroups as to the cause of the troubles and the solutions that would be effective in solving them. Such conversations are frequently punctuated with statements beginning with, "We should do . . ."

5. In meetings where those same people meet with members from other subgroups to discuss the problem they "soften their positions," state them in ambiguous language, or even reverse them to suit the apparent positions taken by others.

6. After such meetings, members complain to trusted associates that they really didn't say what they wanted to say, but also provide a list of convincing reasons why the comments, suggestions, and reactions they wanted to make would have been impossible. Trusted associates commiserate and say the same was true for them.

7. Attempts to solve the problem do not seem to work. In fact, such attempts seem to add to the problem or make it worse.

8. Outside the organization individuals seem to get along better, be happier, and operate more effectively than they do within it.

---

question falls into the "characteristic" category and most of the other answers fall into the category "not characteristic," one may be relatively sure the organization is in a real conflict situation and some sort of conflict management intervention is in order.

COPING WITH THE PARADOX

Assuming a preliminary diagnosis leads one to believe he and/or his organization is on the way to Abilene, the individual may choose to actively confront the situation to determine directly whether the underlying reality is one of agreement or conflict. Although there are, perhaps, a number of ways to do it, I have found one way in particular to be effective—confrontation in a group setting. The basic approach involves gathering organization members who are key figures in the problem and its solution into a group setting. Working within the context of a group is important, because the dynamics of the Abilene Paradox involve collusion among group members; therefore, to try to solve the dilemma by working with individuals and small subgroups would involve further collusion with the dynamics leading up to the paradox.

The first step in the meeting is for the individual who "calls" it (that is, the confronter) to own up to his position first and be open to the feedback he gets. The owning up process lets the others know that he is concerned lest the organization may be making a decision contrary to the desires of any of its members. A statement like this demonstrates the beginning of such an approach:

> I want to talk with you about the research project. Although I have previously said things to the contrary, I frankly don't think it will work, and I am very anxious about it. I suspect others may feel the same, but I don't know. Anyway, I am concerned that I may end up misleading you and that we may end up misleading one another, and if we aren't careful, we may continue to work on a problem that none of us wants and that might even bankrupt us. That's why I need to know where the rest of you stand. I would appreciate any of your thoughts about the project. Do you think it can succeed?

What kinds of results can one expect if he decides to undertake the process of confrontation? I have found that the results can be divided into *two* categories, at the technical level and at the level of existential experience. Of the two, I have found that for the person who undertakes to initiate the process of confrontation, the existential experience takes precedence in his ultimate evaluation of the outcome of the action he takes.

· *The technical level.* If one is correct in diagnosing the presence of the paradox, I have found the solution to the technical problem may be almost absurdly quick and simple, nearly on the order of this:

"Do you mean that you and I and the rest of us have been dragging along with a research project that none of us has thought would work? It's crazy. I can't believe we would do it, but we did. Let's figure out how we can cancel it and get to doing something productive." In fact, the simplicity and quickness of the solution frequently don't seem possible to most of us, since we have been trained to believe that the solution to conflict requires a long, arduous process of debilitating problem solving.

Also, since existential risk is always present, it is possible that one's diagnosis is incorrect, and the process of confrontation lifts to the level of public examination real, substantive conflict, which may result in heated debate about technology, personalities, and/or administrative approaches. There is evidence that such debates, properly managed, can be the basis for creativity in organizational problem solving. There is also the possibility, however, that such debates cannot be managed, and, substantiating the concept of existential risk, the person who initiates the risk may get fired or ostracized. But that again leads to the necessity of evaluating the results of such confrontation at the existential level.

· *Existential results.* Evaluating the outcome of confrontation from an existential framework is quite different from evaluating it from a set of technical criteria. How do I reach this conclusion? Simply from interviewing a variety of people who have chosen to confront the paradox and listening to their responses. In short, for them, psychological success and failure apparently are divorced from what is traditionally accepted in organizations as criteria for success and failure.

For instance, some examples of success are described when people are asked, "What happened when you confronted the issue?" They may answer this way:

I was told we had enough boat rockers in the organization, and I got fired. It hurt at first, but in retrospect it was the greatest day of my life. I've got another job and I'm delighted. I'm a free man.

Another description of success might be this:

I said I don't think the research project can succeed and the others looked shocked and quickly agreed. The upshot of the whole deal is that I got a promotion and am now known as a "rising star." It was the high point of my career.

Similarly, those who fail to confront the paradox describe failure in terms divorced from technical results. For example, one may report:

I didn't say anything and we rocked along until the whole thing exploded and Joe got fired. There is still a lot of tension in the organization, and we are still in trouble, but I got a good performance review last time. I still feel lousy about the whole thing, though.

From a different viewpoint, an individual may describe his sense of failure in these words:

I knew I should have said something and I didn't. When the project failed, I was a convenient whipping boy. I got demoted; I still have a job, but my future here is definitely limited. In a way I deserve what I got, but it doesn't make it any easier to accept because of that.

Most important, the act of confrontation apparently provides intrinsic psychological satisfaction, regardless of the technological outcomes for those who attempt it. The real meaning of that existential experience, and its relevance to a wide variety of organizations, may lie, therefore, not in the scientific analysis of decision making but in the plight of Sisyphus. That is something the reader will have to decide for himself.

THE ABILENE PARADOX
AND THE MYTH OF SISYPHUS

In essence, this paper proposes that there is an underlying organizational reality that includes both agreement and disagreement, cooperation and conflict. However, the decision to confront the possibility of organization agreement is all too difficult and rare, and its opposite, the decision to accept the evils of the present, is all too common. Yet those two decisions may reflect the essence of both our human potential and our human imperfectability. Consequently, the choice to confront reality in the family, the church, the business, or the bureaucracy, though made only occasionally, may reflect those "peak experiences" that provide meaning to the valleys.

In many ways, they may reflect the experience of Sisyphus. As you may remember, Sisyphus was condemned by Pluto to a perpetuity of pushing a large stone to the top of a mountain, only to see it return to its original position when he released it. As Camus suggested in his revision of the myth, Sisyphus' task was absurd and totally devoid of meaning. For most of us, though, the lives we lead pushing papers or hubcaps are no less absurd, and in many ways we probably spend about as much time pushing rocks in our organizations as Sisyphus did in his.

Camus also points out, though, that on occasion as Sisyphus released his rock and watched it return to its resting place at the bottom of the hill, he was able to recognize the absurdity of his lot, and for brief periods of time, transcend it.

So it may be with confronting the Abilene Paradox. Confronting the absurd paradox of agreement may provide, through activity, what Sisyphus gained from his passive but conscious acceptance of his fate. Thus, through the process of active confrontation with reality, we may take respite from pushing our rocks on their endless journeys and, for brief moments, experience what C. P. Snow termed "the triumphs of life we make for ourselves" within those absurdities we call organizations.

Interpersonal Communication, Group Solidarity, and Social Influence[1]

EDGAR H. SCHEIN

The purpose of this paper is to examine some relationships between communication, group solidarity, and influenceability. Few topics in psychology have received as much attention as communication. We have looked at the nature of communication systems, at the flow of information within them, at the structural properties of languages, and at the function which communication plays in organized systems, be they groups, individuals, or neutral networks. Only more recently, however, have we begun to consider some of the more subtle semantic and communication problems which, I believe, lie at the root of social relationships. In particular, except in the study of psychotherapy, we have not given enough attention to that aspect of communication which relates to the *maintenance* of social relationships, roles, and self-images. It is this maintenance of social relationships, roles, and self-images which, I believe, accounts in large measure for the stability both of groups and of individual personalities, and which represents, therefore, one of the greatest forces against change or influenceability. When we see behavior change and social influence occurring, or when we think it should be occurring, yet it is not, we might well focus our analysis on the interpersonal communication processes which are occurring and consider their implication for the social situation and the individuals within it.

"Interpersonal Communication, Group Solidarity, and Social Influence" by Edgar H. Schein, *Sociometry,* Vol. 23, 1960, pp. 148–160. Copyright © 1960 by The American Sociological Association. Reprinted by permission of The American Sociological Association and the author.

The conceptual model which I will attempt to spell out below grew out of my studies of Chinese Communist techniques of controlling civilian and military prisoners during and after the Korean conflict (16, 17, 18). Most of my examples will be drawn, therefore, from the experiences of the prisoners. These experiences highlight the role which interpersonal communication plays in the destruction of the subject's social and personal integration and in his subsequent increase in influenceability. My aim in presenting these examples is not limited, however, to providing a socio-psychological explanation of what has popularly come to be termed as "brainwashing." An additional and perhaps more fundamental purpose is to provide some bases for a more general theory of influence which could encompass the kinds of attitude and value changes which we can witness in our own society.

A CONCEPTUAL MODEL: CREATING INFLUENCEABILITY THROUGH SOCIAL ALIENATION[2]

In any ongoing situation the things that people *say* to each other, and nonverbally *do* with respect to each other carry two kinds of information: one, information directly relevant to the task that they are engaged in, and two, information about their feelings toward each other and toward the task, reflecting in particular the value they attach to each other and to the task. In order for people to accomplish any kind of task together they must have a certain level of regard for each other, which is usually reflected in the degree of attention they give to each other, and they must have a certain level of involvement in the situation. If such regard or involvement is improperly low or high, it is a signal that the person cannot be trusted to fulfill his proper function, or worse, cannot be trusted not to take advantage of the other participants in the situation.

Such information is usually communicated through a host of gestures and non-verbal cues as well as through the content of what is said. For example, the way we dress, our social manners, the degree of deference we pay to the high status people, and the degree of energy with which we approach a task all serve to communicate to others whether we are properly involved or motivated, and therefore, whether we can be counted on to fulfill our role, be it in an office, on a combat mission, or at a party.

The importance of this type of interpersonal communication is twofold: *First,* the flow of cues which indicate that we have proper regard for each other and are properly involved in situations is critical for the maintenance of organized activity and group solidarity. *Second,* it is also critical for the maintenance of personal identity and security. Much of our personality is learned in and supported by a social context through the information which our significant others communicate to us concerning their evaluation of us. Because of this fact, we become susceptible to change when our social supports are destroyed or removed. Such potential influenceability can be hypothesized at the following levels of psychological functioning:

1.   We become more influenceable at the level of *opinions and beliefs,* particularly in regard to those beliefs which are socially shared and operate as norms or standards of conduct. If we cease to have the kinds of relationships which imply mutual trust and regard, we cease to have access to each others' opinions and beliefs which, in turn, makes it virtually impossible for us to establish, check, or enforce social norms or standards.

2.   Our *image of ourselves,* both its conscious and unconscious components, depends to a great extent on the confirmation provided to us by others through interpersonal communication. A good example is given by Goffman: In order for a girl to perceive herself as "beautiful" she must obtain from others a whole range of communication cues such as compliments, invitations to dates, "passes" made at her, etc., because beauty has no absolute standard against which it can be judged. The same sort of cues are, of course, required for us to see ourselves as intelligent, witty, manly, or what have you. In most of our daily life we operate in situations and groups which are fairly well integrated, hence we are largely unaware of the constant flow of such interpersonal communication and the confirmation of our selves which it provides. Only when such cues are absent or are manipulated in a destructive manner, as they were by the Chinese Communists, do we realize their importance.

3.   Our *fundamental values,* whether we think of them in terms of super-ego, or moral conscience, or some other concept, probably depend to a great extent on the social support of individuals or institutions which operate as surrogates for the parents or the significant others from whom they were learned. One would at least suspect this conclusion from the frequent statements by psychotherapists that change can be produced in the patient only when such surrogate relationships are exposed and re-evaluated. Again, it is difficult to see this process in ordinary social life; only when marked social disorganization occurs do we see the manner in which morals are supported by social relationships.

In summary, the ongoing integrity of the individual is at several levels of his functioning dependent on adequate social integration which, in turn, is based on adequate interpersonal communication. When interpersonal cues cease to confirm the social relationships upon which the individual depends, he becomes socially alienated and susceptible to change at the level of opinion, belief, self-image, or basic value; the degree and depth of influenceability depend on the degree of alienation, the degree of pressure to change, and the availability of new opinions, beliefs, self-images, or values.

Social relationships here are not meant to be limited to face-to-face relationships. This term applies as well to the symbolic relationships which are implied by identifications with others who are absent or identifications with groups and organizations.

Interpersonal cues which cease to confirm social relationships can be of two kinds: (a) cues which tend to be destructive—that is, cues which tell us that we are held in contempt by others, that our social value is very low; and (b) cues which tend to be neutral—that is, cues which tell us that we are not regarded highly enough to be allowed to participate in intimate relationships or share confidences, but which do not devaluate us except as potential friends or confidants. Both kinds of cues tend to destroy the kind of social integration which is required to sustain high personal integration, but there is a difference in degree, if not in kind, between the destructive effect of being held in contempt and the destructive effect of being merely mistrusted.

Thus far I have tried to argue that the reduction of confirming interpersonal cues makes a person more influenceable because it removes some of the forces which ordinarily operate to make him resist being influenced; in effect, such reduction "unfreezes" him by removing some of the "restraining forces," to use Lewin's terminology (11). If such unfreezing occurs, what is the probability that it will be followed by influence or change? The probability is high for two reasons: First, social alienation is an unsatisfying psychological state which induces strong motives toward regaining old or finding new social relationships. Such social reintegration can probably not occur without some personal change. Second, social alienation, by cutting off the individual from accustomed sources of information on which to base his judgment, heightens his susceptibility to cognitive re-definition. By cognitive re-definition I mean a process of accepting new definitions for existing concepts, placing concepts into new scales of evaluation, or shifting the anchors or neutral points on such scales. Whichever of these processes occurs, the individual's judgments and consequently his behavior will change, as a result. The adoption of new definitions, scales, or anchors occurs through the process of learning to pay attention to how others in the environment view the alienated individual and the total situation, and by identifying with them. If no alternative models are available and the situation is ambiguous, the individual probably redefines it in a direction which maximizes his immediate chances of social reintegration and also minimizes other stresses to which he is exposed.

CREATING SOCIAL ALIENATION IN POWs

In the case of the Chinese Communist treatment of United Nations prisoners of war, we have excellent examples of undermining without completely destroying the bonds which hold groups together, thus reducing the flow of confirming interpersonal cues, and thereby heightening social alienation and the individual prisoner's susceptibility to being influenced to collaborate with his captor (1, 16). This result was accomplished by manipulating the overall situation, the communication channels and the communication content.

One basic device was to destroy the authority structure of the group by systematically segregating leaders and other key personnel from the remainder of the group, or systematically undermining their own authority. As examples of the latter may be cited the rather frequent choice of low ranking enlisted men as squad leaders in prison camp, on the grounds that under Communism rank no longer had any significance and that it was the workingman who should get all the breaks. A further device was to threaten the higher ranking officers with punishment of their group if they failed to cooperate with the Chinese by providing slanted radio broadcasts or other kinds of propaganda. Attempts by the higher ranking officers to work out compromises which would satisfy the Chinese, yet which would provide increased chances of survival for their men, would often appear to the lower ranking officers like collaboration. They would then either covertly or overtly fail to obey orders, thus destroying the chain of command.

This process of social decay was aided by the fact that the first months of captivity had been marked by extreme physical privation and a high prisoner death rate which stimulated some competition for the very scarce supplies of food, medicine, and other means of survival. From the very beginning, the Chinese indicated to the prisoners that, if they were cooperative in re-educating themselves and learning the "truth" about the Korean war, they could expect better treatment. Of course, being cooperative meant being willing to give radio broadcasts and other propaganda to the effect that being a prisoner of war in Chinese hands was a pleasant affair, and so on.

In any *large* group of men such as an army, there will be a few opportunists, psychopaths, and psychotics who will take advantage of any situation for personal gain. The willingness of these men to compete and to collaborate, and the rewarding of such behavior by the Chinese began to create a general atmosphere of mutual mistrust which was heightened by several additional techniques of manipulating the POWs. For example, a sizeable group of men would be told that, if they cooperated by giving propaganda broadcasts, they would be repatriated; then the group would be split up into smaller groups some of which would be marched off in the direction of the front lines and then taken to another collection point for prisoners, leaving the impression that they had cooperated, given broadcasts, and been repatriated or rewarded in some other fashion. Also, Chinese guards would spy intensively on conversations of the most trivial and intimate nature, look for infractions of camp rules, pull in the culprit and accuse him, force him to confess, then leave him in a state of wondering how they could have known of his words or deeds unless there were more informers in camp than he had previously suspected. During interrogations a man would often be asked a question and after continued refusal to answer would be shown that the Chinese already had the answer. Then he would be asked if he would copy the answer out of the Chinese document. If he did so to get the Chinese "off his back" for a little while, his copy would be shown to another man who was being interrogated with the statement: "Why do you continue to hold out; look, your friend so-and-so has already given us the answer." These and many other devices were used to create the image that almost everyone else was collaborating, so why not you?

The Communists also prohibited any organized activity not specifically sanctioned by them. For example, religious services, social gatherings, athletic events, and so on were prohibited for most of the first two years of captivity. Thus, not even by shared rituals could prisoners reaffirm their solidarity. Any attempt at organized resistance or escape was severely punished and the group responsible split up.

The most striking examples of actual interference in the communication process were the uses of what might be called testimonials. I have already cited the example of tricking an individual into writing out material in interrogation and presenting this to another prisoner as if it had been spontaneously given. In the same category fell the utilization of a small number of men who had made germ-warfare confessions and who were then sent to various camps to give lectures and answer questions. The sincerity of their answers and the small details of their confessions were very convincing to many a prisoner. Still another device was to offer prizes like fruit or cigarettes for essays or articles in the camp newspaper. Of course, the winning essay was usually the one which most agreed with the Communist line. Once obtained by the Chinese, such an essay would be circulated widely among the other prisoners. Those few men who found themselves in a position of cooperating regularly with the Chinese would be used to try to get other prisoners to be more cooperative as well.

Identifications with groups and individuals outside of prison camp also became the targets of Chinese Communist manipulation. The best example was the selective delivery of mail. In some cases, the Chinese did not give a man any of his mail, at the same time solicitously pointing out that there had been no mail for him, which could only mean that his loved ones at home no longer cared about him. In other cases, they only delivered mail which contained bad news or was completely devoid of anything meaningful, and withheld mail which was either directly reassuring or contained news which could be reassuring. At the same time, the mass media of communication were completely saturated by Communist propaganda. Most prisoners did not see a Western non-Communist newspaper or hear a non-Communist radio broadcast during their entire captivity, unless, of course, such a medium contained news which played into Communist hands. Our manifest lack of concern about the Korean war would be a good example of the kind of news which the prisoners were surely given.

Of course the most obvious example of cutting communication channels was solitary confinement which was used for varying lengths of time up to two years or more in the case of some prisoners. However, the effects of solitary confinement were by no means clearcut. In many men it led to a tremendous need to communicate with someone, a need which interrogators have played upon for centuries; in such men it sometimes also led to real loss of assurance about their personal identity and self-image, particularly if they were deprived of the means of living in a civilized fashion, for example if they were deprived of any means of keeping clean. For other men, however, the total lack of interpersonal cues was less threatening to their integrity and sense of integration with reference groups than being systematically given cues that they were not trusted by others or were not worthy of any regard. In particular, men whose reference group identifications were very strong and whose self-images were in part organized around solitude and meditation, for example highly religious individuals, welcomed solitary confinement as a relief from pressure. This fact, by the way, highlights the superiority of actively manipulating interpersonal communication over a mere cutting of the communication channels for the production of social alienation. A man can be most alienated in the very midst of many others, as the examples below will show.

The systematic manipulation of communication and social relationships among prisoners of war produced a degree of social alienation which was characterized in most men by a systematic withdrawal of involvement from *all* social situations (18). They lived increasingly in a shell, going through certain of the motions of cooperating with the Chinese without getting overinvolved, or so they believed, at the same time giving up attempts to establish relationships with other prisoners whom they did not really trust or regard highly. However, the social alienation was not sufficient in most instances to disconfirm the prisoners' self-image or destroy his basic values. At most, the process made a man doubtful and insecure.

CREATING SOCIAL ALIENATION IN CIVILIANS IN CHINESE COMMUNIST PRISONS

To find examples of a more intensive destruction of identification with family and reference groups, and the destruction of social role and self-image we must turn to the experiences of civilian political prisoners interned within Chinese Communist prisons (e.g. 3, 4, 6, 12, 13, 14, 17, 19). In such prisons the total regimen, consisting of physical privation, prolonged interrogation, total isolation from former relationships and sources of information, detailed regimentation of all daily activities, and deliberate humiliation and degradation, was geared to producing a complete confession of alleged crimes, and the assumption of a penitent role depicting the adoption of a Communist frame of reference. The prisoner was not informed what his crimes were, nor was it permissible to evade the issue by making up a false confession. Instead, what the prisoner learned he must do was re-evaluate his past from the point of view of the Communists and recognize that most of his former attitudes and behavior were actually criminal from this point of view. For example, a priest who had dispensed food to needy peasants in his mission church had to recognize that he was actually a tool of imperialism and was using his missionary activities as a cover for exploitation of the peasants. Even worse, he may have had to recognize that he was using food as blackmail to accomplish his aims.

The key technique used by the Communists to produce social alienation to a degree sufficient to allow such re-definition and re-evaluation to occur was to put the prisoner into a cell with four or more other prisoners who were somewhat more advanced in their "thought reform" than he. Such a cell usually had one leader who was responsible to the prison authorities, and the progress of the whole cell was made contingent upon the progress of the least "reformed" member. This condition meant in practice that four or more cell members devoted all their energies to getting their least "reformed" member to recognize the truth about himself and to confess. To accomplish this they typically swore at, harangued, beat, denounced, humiliated, reviled, and brutalized their victim twenty-four hours a day, sometimes for weeks or months on end. If the authorities felt that the prisoner was basically uncooperative they manacled his hands behind his back and chained his ankles, which made him completely dependent on his cell mates for the fulfillment of his basic needs. It was this reduction to an animal-like existence in front of other humans which, I believe, constituted the ultimate humiliation and led most reliably to the destruction of the prisoner's image of himself. Even in his own eyes he became something which was not worthy of the regard of his fellow man.

If, to avoid complete physical and personal destruction, the prisoner began to confess in the manner desired of him, he was usually forced to prove his sincerity by making irrevocable behavioral commitments, such as denouncing and implicating his friends and relatives in his own newly recognized crimes. Once he had done this he became further alienated from his former self, even in his own eyes, and could seek security only in a new identity and new social relationships. Aiding this process of confessing was the fact that the crimes gave the prisoner something concrete to which to attach the free-floating guilt which the accusing environment and his own humiliation usually stimulated.[3]

INFLUENCE THROUGH IDENTIFICATION AND SOCIAL REINTEGRATION

As I indicated previously, I am assuming that adult humans are powerfully motivated to know themselves, to have some kind of positive viable self-image and a set of social roles which are confirmed in interaction with others. A state of social alienation, therefore, implies powerful motives toward personal and social integration, and initiates searching behavior on the part of the alienated individual for some meaningful relationship, role, and self-image. The usual case, both in the prisoner of war camps and in the political prisons, was that the only relationships which were permitted to grow were with the Communists or with prisoners who were cooperating with them. Such relationships were strongly encouraged and facilitated by a variety of means. A good example was the plight of the sick and wounded prisoners of war who, because of their physical confinement, were unable to escape from continual contact with their interrogator or instructor, and who therefore often ended up forming a close relationship with him. Chinese Communist instructors often encouraged prisoners to take long walks or have informal talks with them and offered as incentives cigarettes, tea, and other rewards. If the prisoner was willing to cooperate and become a "progressive," he could join with other "progressives" in an active group life.

Within the political prison, the group cell provided not only the forces toward alienation but also offered the road to a "new self." Not only were there available among the fellow prisoners individuals with whom the prisoner could identify because of their shared plight,[4] but, once he showed any tendency to seek a new identity by truly trying to re-evaluate his past, he received again a whole range of rewards of which perhaps the most important was the interpersonal information that he was again a person worthy of respect and regard. The force of the motivation to have some identity can be deduced from the fact that positive relationships typically formed in the group cell in spite of the ever present atmosphere of mutual hostility.

INFLUENCE THROUGH COGNITIVE RE-DEFINITION

When groups become disorganized through the kinds of manipulation cited above for POW groups, not only does it become impossible to communicate and enforce existing norms, but it becomes impossible to share in the formation of new norms for situational contingencies not previously encountered. Being a prisoner of war, in the first place, and being handled in the pseudo-benevolent manner which characterized the Chinese Communist approach, in the second place, were for most men highly novel and highly ambiguous situations to which our cultural norms and standards of conduct did not readily apply. The problem, then, was not that a man became unsure of his moral principles, such as the wrongness of collaborating with the enemy. Rather, the new and ambiguous situation made it difficult to determine what sort of behavior would actually be a violation of such moral principles.[5] The Chinese put considerable effort into providing the prisoner with suitable rationales for collaborative behavior, which would allow him to re-define his situation in a manner that would absolve him. Such re-definition might take the form of not recognizing that his behavior was in fact helping the enemy, or might take the form of re-evaluating relative priorities where conflicting values were involved. An officer might see less harm in giving the Chinese propaganda than in risking having his men shot; a prisoner might see greater importance in letting his loved ones at home know that he was alive by making a radio broadcast than in preventing the Chinese from getting a bit of propaganda out of him; or to put the matter more extremely, a man might see less harm in collaborating than in letting a friend die because the Chinese would not give him medicine unless he collaborated.

The important point about these examples is that they all involve some cognitive evaluations and some judgments concerning the consequences of a given course of action. The ambiguity of the situation, the Chinese saturation of the informational environment with their concept of the "truth," and the physical pressures on the men made it quite likely that some shifts in scales of judgment would occur, and that errors in assessing the consequences of collaborative behavior would also occur. However, it was also quite likely that in the whole prisoner population there were many who, because of previous experience or specialized knowledge, could have made more accurate assessments which could have become the basis for shared norms and standards of conduct. However, in a situation in which men were prevented from communicating with each other, did not trust each other, or had low regard for each other, there was no opportunity to share such knowledge. This statement is confirmed by the accounts of many men that successful resistance was usually organized around a few key individuals, often non-commissioned officers with broad experience, who were able to maintain clandestine relationships with other prisoners of war, and who would advise them how far they could cooperate with the Chinese without giving them anything of real propaganda value or getting involved with them in an irrevocable fashion. These instances of failure to produce alienation highlight the importance of effective communication channels as prerequisites to resistance.

In the political prison the pressure toward cognitive re-definition was, of course, present to an even more intense degree. Not only was there unremitting pressure on the prisoner to shift his frame of reference and to re-evaluate his own self-image and past behavior, but there were available ever present models of how to do this, combined with complete isolation from all contacts which could in any manner affirm the old self-image or social norms. Through identifying with cell mates, the prisoner came to pay attention to their point of view which led to re-defining of his own. Behavior previously seen as innocent could then be judged as criminal, and a past life based on capitalist premises could be seen as evil.[6]

RECAPITULATION AND CONCLUSIONS

Social and personal integration depend on interpersonal cues which confirm social norms and the individual's beliefs, self-image, basic values, and social role. When such cues are absent or disconfirming, the individual becomes socially alienated, which makes him susceptible to influence for three reasons: First, forces against change are reduced or removed; second, motives toward re-integration are induced; and third, cognitive redefinitions are facilitated.

My reasons for emphasizing this kind of influence model are twofold. First, we need a better understanding of the technique employed by the Communists in attempting to influence captives and their potential or actual effects. Certainly we need to go beyond some of the thinking often expressed in our mass media—that the behavior of prisoners of the Communists is either the result of mysterious occult devices or is the result of personal weakness reflecting social pathology in our society. Second: we need conceptual tools with which to explore further those institutions within our own society which are presumably geared to producing profound and lasting changes in their adult inmates, students, or patients.

When one examines institutions such as prisons, mental hospitals, basic training centers, intensive educational workshops, and so on, one is struck by the need to conceptualize what goes on in them at a level somewhat broader than is reflected in most experimental studies of social influence. In particular, one is struck by the number of similarities of such institutions with respect to the manipulation of social relationships. For example, a frequent practice in prisons, mental hospitals, educational workshops, reformatories, religious retreats, basic training centers, monasteries, nunneries, academies, and so on, is to isolate the inmates from their former social relationships, either by physically confining them or by regimenting their daily routine to such an extent that they do not have time to maintain such relationships.

In authoritarian institutions, like prisons, to which inmates are sent involuntarily, there also tend to be systematic efforts on the part of the staff to destroy the internal organization of the inmate group. This fact has been noted in the prison situation and is embodied in the admonition to prisoners to "serve their *own* time" (5). Evidences of internal organization among prisoners result in punishment for some men; removal to another cell block for others. At the same time, social alienation is fostered by the bestowing of special favors, rewards, or privileges for cooperation with the authorities. In reformatories in which there is a reasonably high rate of success of reform, one finds the key to this success in the identification of the inmates with one or more members of the staff through whom they learn new norms, self-images, and values. Such identifications can only occur when old social bonds have been undermined.

In the mental hospital we have recognized that therapy operates through the medium of forming a relationship with a psychiatrist or some other member of the staff. What we have recognized less often is that sometimes the hospital staff will, in a number of subtle ways, destroy the internal organization of the patient group, usually by moving patients from one ward to another, thus preventing stable friendships. Whether the alienation of the patient from other patients is an aid or hindrance to therapy I am not prepared to say, but it would seem to be a problem worthy of investigation. In many of these institutions, a major function of reducing inmate organization is to maintain better control over the inmate population, but perhaps such practices have other functions as well.

By focusing on social alienation, I do not wish to bypass the fact that in many change-producing institutions social organization among inmates is encouraged and is considered to heighten rather than weaken influenceability. This emphasis would certainly be true of educational workshops, religious revivals, voluntarily entered group therapy, and so on. The fact that these institutions are voluntary would appear to be one common feature which differentiates them from prisons and mental hospitals. They also differ in that the participants presumably are motivated to change or be influenced, and that the staff does not feel it necessary to impose its own authority coercively over the inmates. Instead, participants themselves are expected to assume a certain amount of responsibility and authority. An interesting middle ground is found in institutions which are entered voluntarily and with motivation to change, but which involve total submission to authority—for example, monasteries and academies. The fact that such institutions initially tend to destroy the internal organization of inmates would suggest that such destruction is more closely related to the nature of authority in the institution than to the degree of voluntariness of entry or motivation to change.

It is my hope that a model of influence such as is presented here will provide a useful approach both to the comparative study of influence within organizations and to the study of those influence processes which have major consequences for the personalities of the individuals who become its targets.

REFERENCES

1. Biderman, A. D., "Communist Attempts to Elicit False Confessions from Air Force Prisoners of War," *Bulletin of the New York Academy of Medicine,* 1957, 33, 616–625.
2. Biderman, A. D., and J. L. Monroe, "Reactions to the Korean POW Episode." Paper read before the American Psychological Association Meetings, Washington, D.C., August 30, 1958.
3. Bonnichon, A., "Cell 23—Shanghai," *The Month,* March, 1955, 1–32.
4. Bull, Geoffrey T., *When Iron Gates Yield,* Chicago: Moody Press, 1955.
5. Cressey, D. L., and W. Krossowski, "Inmate Organization and Anomie in American Prisons and Soviet Labor Camps," *Social Problems,* 1957-58, 5, 217–230.
6. Ford, R. W., *Wind between the Worlds,* New York: David McKay Company, 1957.
7. Goffman, E., "On Face-work," *Psychiatry,* 1955, 18, 213–231.
8. Goffman, E., "Alienation from Interaction," *Human Relations,* 1957, 10, 47–60.
9. Goffman, E., "On the Characteristics of Total Institutions," *Proceedings of the Symposium on Preventive and Social Psychiatry,* Washington, D.C.: Walter Reed Army Institute of Research, 1957.
10. Goffman, E., "The Structure and Function of Situational Properties." Unpublished manuscript, 1958.
11. Lewin, K., "Frontiers in Group Dynamics: Concept, Method, and Reality in Social Sciences," *Hum. Relat.,* 1947, I, 5–42.

12.   Lifton, R. J., " 'Thought Reform' of Western Civilians in Chinese Communist Prisons," *Psychiatry,* 1956, 19, 173–195.

13.   Lifton, R. J., " 'Thought Reform' of Chinese Intellectuals: A Psychiatric Evaluation," *Journal of Social Issues,* 1957, 13, 5–20.

14.   Rickett, A., and Adele Rickett, *Prisoners of Liberation,* New York: Cameron Associates, 1957.

15.   Rigney, Harold, *Four Years in a Red Hell,* Chicago: Henry Regnery, 1956.

16.   Schein, E. H., "The Chinese Indoctrination Program for Prisoners of War," *Psychiatry,* 1956, 19,149–172.

17.   Schein, E. H., Inge Schneier, and C. Barker, *Coercive Persuasion: A Socio-psychological Analysis of Chinese Communist Treatment of American Civilian Prisoners,* Cambridge: Center for International Studies, Massachusetts Institute of Technology, 1960.

18.   Strassman, H., Margaret Thaler, and E. H. Schein, "A Prisoner of War Syndrome: Apathy as a Reaction to Severe Stress," *American Journal of Psychiatry,* 1956, 112, 998–1003.

19.   Yen, Maria, *The Umbrella Garden,* New York: MacMillan, 1954.

NOTES

[1]Invited address delivered to the International Council for Women Psychologists on August 28, 1958, Washington, D.C.

[2]For many of the ideas in this formulation, I am indebted to the sociologist Erving Goffman (7, 8, 9, 10).

[3]The number of cases in which such a process occurred is extremely small. The description presented here is included to illustrate the model of influence, not as a typical account of how prisoners fared in Chinese Communist prisons. In many such prisons the thought reform program was ineffective and could be successfully resisted by the prisoner.

[4]Any degree of communication with either cell mates or interrogators heightened susceptibilities to identification, because even minimum communication requires some degree of taking the role of the other person. Some prisoners reported, by way of confirmation of this point, that they had a tougher time resisting thought reform if they knew the Chinese language.

[5]This ambiguity is actually still present after the fact, as evidenced by the difficulty in our own country of enunciating a clear policy toward POW behavior. Accounts in the press and popularized analyses have shifted markedly in the last few years from blaming collaboration on Communist mistreatment to blaming it on POW misconduct (2).

[6]The degree of permanence of the change which was produced in a few individuals by a process such as that described depended, of course, on the kinds of interpersonal cues they were exposed to following their repatriation. If their newly acquired identity and set of attitudes were not acceptable to their "significant others" back home, a new and comparable influence process was set into motion. In the few cases where such changes have persisted, there is good evidence that the individuals sought out and attached themselves emotionally to others who would support the new identity and attitude structure. These observations are based on a recent follow-up study of some of the civilian repatriates (17).

Coalitions

JEFFREY PFEFFER

Our attention will focus . . . on some processes through which additional power and support is mustered for political contests within organizations. Organizations are, above all else, systems of interdependent activity. Because of the division of labor and specialization of tasks which occur within formal organizations, interdependence is created among subunits and positions. By interdependence we mean that in order for one subunit to accomplish something, it requires the efforts and cooperation of other subunits. In order for the sales department to sell the product, it may have to rely on production for satisfactory delivery times and product reliability. In order for production to keep its costs down, it may have to rely on the purchasing department to provide high quality input supplies on an assured basis. This interdependence within organizations means that there is often a great deal of contact across subunit boundaries. And, this interdependence means that the potential for both conflict and cooperation exists. The interdependence creates conflict because the goals and values within each of the various interacting organizational units may not be consonant. The potential for cooperation and coalition formation exists because organizational participants are used to working with and through others in order to get things done.

Thus, organizational politics may involve the formation of coalitions with others either inside or outside of the formally designated organizational boundaries. In some sense, the use of the outside expert can be viewed as a coalition formation strategy with an external party. In that case, the inside subunit or groups form a coalition with an outside expert or set of experts to advocate their position on a set of decision issues. Since the expert is presumably value neutral and objective, the visibility and explicitness of the coalition formation process is lower than in the instances to be described later.

Although there is an extensive theory of coalition formation and coalition size developed in the literature on political science (cf. Riker, 1962; Leiserson, 1970), there are two difficulties in transferring that literature directly to the issue of analyzing coalition formation in formal organizations. The literature in political science has been virtually exclusively developed in one of two contexts: the study of voting blocs and coalitions in legislatures (e.g. Rosenthal, 1970) or the study of coalition formation in small, experimental groups (e.g. Gamson, 1964).

Neither context is representative of the situation confronted within formal organizations. In the legislature context, it is individuals who are bargaining, log-rolling, and forming coalitions, whereas one of the distinctive features of formal organizations is the fact that much of the activity takes place on the level of the organizational subunit. Additionally, the degree of socialization, interdependence, and consequently, solidarity is somewhat different in the two contexts. Most organizations have much more elaborate control and socialization systems, which means that there exists an ideology of an overarching organizational goal and there is probably more trust and commonly shared values than in legislatures. The small, experimental groups have suffered until quite recently from the fact that they were constructed so as to have no history and to play a very short sequence of games. In contrast, in an ongoing organization, there is a history and a future to social interaction which constrains the strategies participants will use against each other and which provides some moderation and stability to the action.

The second problem, which is in some sense even more troublesome, is that most theories of coalition formation and operation proceed from assumptions of rationality and calculation which are not completely consistent with either observed events or theories of social behavior from psychology or sociology. We could pick on many such premises, but one of the most prominent will serve to illustrate this point. One of the theoretical ideas emerging from coalition research is that participants in the political struggle seek to form coalitions that are of the minimum winning size (Riker, 1962). This is because of the assumption that although actors want to win in order to share in the rewards acquired by the winning coalition, they want to share these rewards with as few others as possible; hence, a coalition of the smallest size necessary to win is the most desirable. Importing these ideas into an organizational context, one would predict that a decision would be made whenever enough support was mustered behind one position or the other to ensure that a decision could be made.

But this is not what is observed in many instances. Many times, long after the preponderance of support in an organization has come down on one side of an issue, the discussion, debate and decision process continues in an attempt to build a broader base of support for the decision. Indeed, the goal of building consensus behind some policy or decision is one that is empirically observable in many choice situations. The desire for widely shared consensus at times means that making the decision rapidly or as soon as it is politically possible to do so is sacrificed in the interests of getting as many organizational interests as possible behind the decision. One difference from the theory of the minimal winning coalition is that the situation addressed by the traditional, political science theories of coalitions is one in which the decision making ends the action, and a policy is decided and the rewards are divided. In ongoing organizations, implementation of and commitment to the decision may be as important, if not more so, than the decision itself. Making a decision in a context in which there is enough opposition so that implementation in an interdependent set of actors is problematic, is probably an almost useless activity. Many excellent decisions have been doomed by implementation problems. Thus, in formal organizations instead of the observation of the principle of the minimum winning coalition size, what is observed more often is the maximum possible coalition size principle. In this case, the making of a decision is delayed until all the interests that can possibly be lined up in support of the decision have been approached and courted. It is only when it becomes clear that almost no additional concessions or political action can produce additional support for the decision, that the decision will be finally made. Although this principle presumes some lack of immediate time pressure, this practice of consensus building is frequently followed even when there is some pressure for fairly rapid action. As Bucher (1970: 45) has noted, "most of the opposition to an idea is worked through . . . or else the proposal dies."

Yet another difference involves the zero versus increasing sum nature of the game being played. Studies of coalition behavior in experimental groups or legislatures take a situation or construct a situation in which the total rewards to be distributed among the participants are fixed at the outset. By contrast, competition and conflict among those interacting in the situation in organizations are on occasion somewhat more like a varying sum game in which one party's gain may not be the other's loss. Even when, as in the case of budget allocations or promotion decisions, there is a relatively fixed sum to be distributed, because of the values and norms stressing the goals and success of the total organization, the losers can be given symbolic assurances that the choice maximizes their long-term welfare and increases the overall well-being of the total organization. We will consider the symbolic use of political language in detail in the next chapter. For the moment we assert that the myth of organizational goals serves to transform the decision situation into somewhat less of a zero-sum game than what typically is faced in the arena of legislative politics or experimental games.

What this means is that although the analysis of coalition formation and coalition behavior in organizations can start with ideas from political science, it will have to develop its own theory and empirical base because of the differences between organizational contexts and legislative and small-group contexts. We have already suggested one difference in the argument about the size of the coalition desired. One could refine that argument to further suggest that the attempt to maximize the size of the coalition will be observed more in situations in which commitment and motivation in the organization has a stronger normative (as contrasted with utilitarian) basis. Thus, the consensus building and coalition size maximization which is described is more likely to be observed in universities or social service agencies than in business firms; within business firms, is more likely to be observed in organizations which rely heavily on shared values, socialization and inculturation as forms of control (Ouchi and Jaeger, 1978).

We have also implicitly suggested that coalition formation activity will be more prevalent to the extent that there is more task and resource interdependence within the organization. The creation of self-contained subunits or the provision of slack resources, both of which reduce interdependence among subunits (Galbraith, 1973), will tend to reduce the coalition formation activity. An extension of this argument would maintain that coalition formation activity would increase and revolve around those decisions within the organization that involve task or resource interdependence. So, the most political activity in terms of attempting to garner support and allies for one's position can be observed in situations in which there is a higher degree of resource interdependence within the organization. The amount of coalition formation activity will be reduced to the extent that units face environments of more resources or are less interdependent.

BUILDING EXTERNAL CONSTITUENCIES

There are two foci for coalition formation activity. The first focus is outward to groups in contact with the organization, and the second focus is within the organization to other social actors whose support may be obtained. Both types of supporters are sought, and each has its own advantages and disadvantages. Allies external to the organization are less likely to be in direct competition with the subunit in question for resources, power or decision outcomes within the organization. It is, in some sense, more feasible to expect to find a symbiotic rather than competitive relationship with an external group or organization. By the same token, however, allies within the organization are closer to the actual decision process and therefore are somewhat more valuable in influencing decision outcomes. An external ally may have less conflict of interest with the internal subunit. However, because of its distance and lack of direct involvement in the decision process, the external group can apply pressure to the organization but can less easily intervene in the decision process to advocate and selectively use information. Allies more proximately connected to the decision sequence are potentially more helpful in affecting the decision outcome.

Another cost of building and using alliances with participants outside of the organization is that an activity can be viewed as being disloyal to the organization and its goals. As argued previously, the ideology of most organizations suggests the existence of a common goal or set of goals sought by those within the organization. To build alliances with external groups suggests a rejection of the organization's interests for selfish interests of the subunit, a view which is likely to be seen as going against the norms of internal cooperation and goal sharing. For this reason, it might be hypothesized that the building of external alliances and constituencies will be done somewhat more circumspectly, particularly in contexts in which the concept or belief in shared goals and values within the organization is particularly strong.

At the same time, it is clear that in many organizational contexts subunits attempt to develop relationships with external groups as a way of enhancing their power within the organization and increasing the likelihood of getting their way in organizational decisions. This process can be illustrated with several examples.

At a small electronics firm in the Southwest, the purchase of components and raw materials had been centralized and delegated to a purchasing department. This department had instituted procedures to select vendors and evaluate their quality as well as to ensure that price and quality control standards were met. The manufacturing operation within the firm, then, dealt through the purchasing department to obtain necessary supplies. Over time conflict developed between the two units. Manufacturing was most concerned about having enough materials of high enough quality on a timely basis. The manufacturing unit was much less concerned with the cost of the materials, and whether or not the suppliers had favorable or unfavorable credit terms. The unit was particularly unconcerned with the bureaucratic niceties of the procurement process, the filling out of requisitions, obtaining bids, evaluating vendors, and placing of orders. Finally, manufacturing went to the president of the company and argued that it should be allowed to purchase directly. This would fulfill its requirements more satisfactorily and also permit the corporation to save money by eliminating the purchasing department.

Having gone through the process of establishing relationships with certain vendors for various supply requirements, purchasing had, of course, developed close and at times personal relationships with these vendors. The vendors could not be sure that if the acquisition process were changed, they would still be able to generate the same volume of business. In addition, they had grown accustomed to the procedures and people in purchasing. To change and develop a new set of relationships would be time consuming and uncertain. Thus, the external constituency, those currently selling to the firm, was there to be mobilized.

The purchasing personnel informed the current vendors about what was going on within the firm and, furthermore, implied that if manufacturing took over the ordering, it was not too likely that the same business relationships would be maintained. The various vendors then wrote to the president of the firm, noting that the procedures and practices followed by the purchasing department in this firm and by similar departments in other firms enabled the vendors to plan production rates, quality standards, and specifications for the product. If the firm were to use another acquisition process, it was possible that order delivery, product reliability and willingness to work with the firm might be harmed. The firm, as previously noted, was relatively small. Input quality and delivery were important factors in controlling manufacturing costs, in ensuring product quality and, therefore, in affecting the success of the firm. Rather than risk offending these necessary and powerful suppliers for the sole reason of satisfying a subunit within the firm, the president maintained the present organizational arrangements. The future of purchasing thus was more secure than ever and the department had even more power than before.

As another example, consider the power of many accounting groups within business schools. In some instances, accounting has been able to institute its own separate master's degree program. In other instances accounting has been able to offer the largest number of doctoral courses. Typically, accounting faculty are paid somewhat more than other faculty within the school. Accounting students and faculty may receive more financial support from the school. This has tended to come about in those cases in which the accounting group has been able to build strong relationships with the professional accounting community, and this professional constituency has become active in donating money and other forms of support to the school. Once this relationship is established, every time a suggestion is made to cut down accounting enrollments, equalize resources across groups, or in some other way shift power within the schools, the accounting faculty quickly call up their external supporters who place pressure on the school to continue to favor accounting. The implied threat is that if accounting is not maintained in its favored position, the donated resources, which are of use to other groups as well, will dry up.

Finally, no setting is better for illustrating the development of external constituencies than governmental agencies. Agencies that deliver social services, money, or other benefits to various groups typically develop effective contact with those groups so that these external constituencies can be mobilized if funding is about to be reduced or the program cut back in some other way. Although this constituency building is done throughout government, it was quite evident in the various poverty, housing and training programs that were the legacy of Lyndon Johnson's War on Poverty Program. One of the things mandated by these programs was the development of community-based organizations to help with the delivery of services and with the policy formulation and management of these various activities on the local level. Ironically, these community action boards, manpower planning agencies, and housing and development boards were then politically organized and potent supporters of the various programs that were the domain of their related government bureaucracies. Any attempt to reduce funding for a given program would trigger an immediate outcry of protest from the local groups that had been established by the program itself. In this case the agency did not have to try very hard to establish an external constituency which would support it in internal struggles for resources; such organizations were decreed by the very content of the legislation which established the programs in the first place.

Building external constituencies requires contact with some organizations or groups outside the organization that are interdependent with the organization and that can be mobilized to support related internal subunits. Thus, although this strategy is certainly used, it is one that is not as readily open to every participant within the organization. However, all organizational actors can engage in building coalitions and alliances with others within the organization.

INTERNAL ALLIANCES

Just as in the case of building external constituencies, internal alliances are founded on common interests among the various participants. Internal alliances are likely to be particularly sought by the less powerful actors in the organization. Because of their limited power, the best way to ensure that these less powerful actors can achieve their interests in the organization is by finding common interests with others, particularly those with more power. Pfeffer and Salancik (1977a), for example, noted that knowledge of the internal power distribution was more highly related to resource allocations, controlling other factors, for those departments that were themselves less powerful. They argued that it was particularly necessary for the less powerful university departments to know the distribution of power because it was these departments that would find it most necessary to form alliances and find powerful sponsorship for their interests. Thus, one can predict that organizational coalitions are more likely to be sought more vigorously by the less powerful social actors within an organization.

Coalitions with other groups on issues where common positions can be identified make it possible for each group to obtain its desired outcomes. Two examples will serve to illustrate this point. In one grocery store corporation personnel did not have much power and issues of employee relations and management development had for a long period been ignored because they were excluded from the agenda of high level meetings. That same corporation illustrates the importance of allies within the organization.

None of the staff groups had much power, for the power in the firm was held by retailing, the store management function. The most powerful of the groups, however, was the legal department. Lawyers held a certain expertise and a mystique regarding that expertise that brought power. In addition, some of the members of the board of directors were themselves lawyers. With the increasing amount of litigation, not only concerning employee relations, but also dealing with advertising, product quality and product liability, legal constraints and contingencies were slowly being recognized as being more important to the firm.

The personnel staff individual had come into contact with the legal department on some fair employment litigation. The personnel staff member had performed statistical analyses and had participated in a very helpful and competent manner in designing hiring and evaluation procedures to solve the current problems and help prevent new ones. As a consequence of that contact, the personnel and the legal departments formed an alliance. This alliance was based on their common interest of increasing the corporation's concern with compliance issues and a respect for the type of technical expertise represented in both departments that was helpful in dealing with these issues. It was, if you will, these two departments allied against the retailing department. In the various meetings that occurred concerning the litigation, the personnel staff member would point out how well the legal department had handled the negotiations and managed the case and how the department should be consulted earlier and more frequently on these issues before they came to litigation. The head of the legal department came out quite strongly in favor of the kinds of training and survey and analysis activities that the personnel unit wanted to undertake. In fact, when the key personnel staff member threatened to quit, the legal department went to the president of the corporation and argued that to replace his expertise by using outsiders would be substantially more expensive and the department offered him an alternative of various consulting relationships and affiliations. It is clear that the two departments' reinforcement of each other was mutually beneficial. However, personnel, the lower power function, particularly benefited from the support of its objectives provided by the chief corporate counsel. Later, when personnel's attempts to introduce new procedures, training and evaluation were resisted by the tradition-bound retailing section, there was recourse to the legal necessity and legal support for these activities. With this outside expertise in support, personnel activity was greatly expanded in both power and scope at the corporation.

The second example has to do with the introduction of a workload measurement system at a professional school. The school was comprised of various disciplines because, as is the case for many professional schools, the school was interdisciplinary. One or two of the groups in the school were heavily burdened by the task of supervising graduate projects. These were specialists that were quite popular with the students, and many chose to do their required projects under the tutelage of persons from those disciplines. One or two of the other groups were heavily burdened by the necessity of teaching a large number of hours. Even though the formal teaching load was the same for all, some courses met only three hours a week while others met four and one-half hours, or 50% more. Because of the distribution of elective and required courses, two of the groups had much more than their share of longer courses.

A proposal was floated to provide explicit teaching credit and thus, course relief for the supervision of these graduate projects. Such a proposal, however, was favored only by the two groups that did most of this work. At the same time, the two groups that did most of the four and one-half hour course teaching were interested in adjusting the workload measurement and allocation system to recognize the fact that an n-course load teaching all classes that met three hours was not the same as an n-course load teaching classes that met for four and one-half hours. There was not a lot of support for that idea as again only a small portion of the entire school was affected. What finally happened was that the two sets of groups formed a coalition. The group burdened with project supervision supported the measurement and assignment of workload on the basis of classroom hours rather than courses, while the other group supported, in turn, the measurement and provision of teaching credit for the supervision of graduate projects. In the end, both had their workloads reduced. With the passage of the combined proposal, each group was able to benefit by its joint action with the other.

This last example illustrates an important point about coalitions, that they are unstable and shift depending on the particular issues involved. Bucher (1970: 34) has noted:

> *Most coalitions are shifting alliances, depending upon the issues. As issues come up, faculty within the department who are concerned shop around seeking out those who might be allies in relation to the particular issue.*

Politics indeed makes strange bedfellows. As long as there is enough commonality on a set of issues so a deal can be made, the other characteristics of the coalition participants may not be relevant.

Tactics of Lateral Relationship: The Purchasing Agent

GEORGE STRAUSS

This is a study of the tactics used by one functional group in an organization—purchasing—to influence the behavior of other functional departments of relatively equal status. It deals in part with "office politics" and "bureaucratic gamesmanship."

Most studies of human relations in management have dealt with *vertical* relations between superiors and subordinates or between line and staff.[1] Yet the purchasing agent's[2] internal relationships (as opposed to his external relationships with salesmen) are almost entirely *lateral;* they are with other functional departments of about the same rank in the organizational hierarchy—departments such as production scheduling, quality control, engineering, and the like. Most agents receive relatively little attention from their superiors; they must act on their own, with support being given by higher management only in exceptional cases. They are given broad freedom to define their own roles and are "controlled" chiefly by the client departments with which they deal.

Although purchasing is technically a staff department, its relations with other departments can best be analyzed in terms of work flow rather than according to the typical staff-line concept. At the beginning of the typical work flow the sales department receives an order; on the basis of this the engineering department prepares a blueprint; next the production scheduling department initiates a work order for manufacturing and a

Reprinted from "Tactics of Lateral Relationship: The Purchasing Agent" by George Strauss published in *Administrative Science Quarterly,* Volume 7, Number 2, September 1962 by permission of The Administrative Science Quarterly.

requisition for purchasing; with this requisition the purchasing department buys the needed parts.

But this process does not always work smoothly. Each department has its specialized point of view which it seeks to impose on others, and each department is struggling for greater authority and status. The purpose of this exploratory study is to illustrate the range of tactics available in the interdepartmental conflict which almost always results.

RESEARCH METHOD

The research methodology included a considerable number of informal contacts with agents, observation of them at work for periods of up to one week, twenty-five formal interviews, a written questionnaire, a review of purchasing journals, and an analysis of how agents, both individually and in groups, handled specially prepared case problems.[3] In the selection of firms to be studied there was a strong bias in favor of those with large engineering staffs, since agents in these firms face the most complex problems.

The discussion which follows will be largely impressionistic and will deal with broad aspects of tactics used by purchasing agents, since their problems vary greatly and various means are used to solve them. It should also be noted that the examples illustrate extreme cases, which, being extreme, illustrate some of the basic dilemmas which most agents face, though often in an attenuated form. This study is primarily concerned with the agent himself, the man who heads the purchasing office. It does not directly concern the buyers and expediters under him or the added complications that occur when divisions or plant agents have a staff relationship with a corporation-wide purchasing office.

CAUSES OF FRICTION

The agent originally had two primary functions: (1) to negotiate and place orders at the best possible terms—but only in accordance with specifications set by others—and (2) to expedite orders, that is, to check with suppliers to make sure that deliveries are made on time. This arrangement gave the agent broad power in dealing with salesmen but made him little more than an order clerk in terms of power or status within the company.

The ambitious agent feels that placing orders and expediting deliveries are but the bare bones of his responsibilities. He looks upon his most important function as that of keeping management posted about market developments: new materials, new sources of supply, price trends, and so forth. And to make this information more useful, he seeks to be consulted before the requisition is drawn up, while the product is still in the planning stage. He feels that his technical knowledge of the market should be accorded recognition equal to the technical knowledge of the engineer and accountant.

Specifically, the ambitious agent would like to suggest (1) alternative materials or parts to use, (2) changes in specifications or redesign of components which will save money or result in higher quality or quicker delivery, and (3) more economical lot sizes, and to influence (4) "make or buy" decisions. The agent calls these functions "value analysis."

One way of looking at the agent's desire to expand his influence is in terms of interaction. Normally orders flow in one direction only, from engineering through scheduling to purchasing. But the agent is dissatisfied with being at the end of the line and seeks to reverse the flow. Value analysis permits him to initiate for others. Such behavior may, however, result in ill feeling on the part of other departments, particularly engineering and production scheduling.

Conflicts with Engineering

Engineers write up the *specifications* for the products which the agents buy. If the specifications are too tight or, what is worse, if they call for one brand only, agents have little or no freedom to choose among suppliers, thus reducing their social status internally and their economic bargaining power externally. Yet engineers find it much easier to write down a well-known brand name than to draw up a lengthy functional specification which lists all the characteristics of the desired item. Disagreements also arise because, by training and job function, engineers look first for quality and reliability and thus, agents charge, are indifferent to low cost and quick delivery, qualities of primary interest to purchasing.

All these problems are aggravated by the "completion barrier." Usually the agent seeks to change specifications only after the engineer has already committed his plans to blueprints and feels he has completed his work—in fact, he may be starting another project; the agent's interference inevitably threatens the engineer's feeling of accomplishment and completion. In any case engineers are jealous of their professional status and often resent the efforts of the agent to suggest new techniques or materials. These are areas in which the engineer feels that he is uniquely competent. Finally, agents are particularly anxious to prevent "backdoor selling" which occurs when a salesman bypasses them and seeks to influence someone else in the organization (usually an engineer) to requisition the saleman's product by name or—more subtly—to list specifications which only this product can meet. Backdoor selling threatens the agent's status in two ways: (1) it encourages specification by brand and (2) it makes both salesmen and engineers less dependent on him.

Conflicts with Production Scheduling

The size of the order and the date on which it is to be delivered are typically determined by production scheduling. The agent's chief complaint against scheduling is that delivery is often requested on excessively short notice—that schedulers engage in sloppy planning or "cry wolf" by claiming they need orders earlier than they really do—and thus force the agent to choose from a limited number of suppliers, to pay premium prices, and to ask favors of salesmen (thus creating obligations which the agent must later repay). Schedulers, on the other hand, claim that "short lead times" are not their fault, but the fault of departments farther up the line, such as engineering (which delays its blueprints) or sales (which accepts rush orders). In addition agents claim that schedulers order in uneconomic lot sizes and fail to consider inventory costs or the savings from quantity discounts. In some instances, as we shall see, the purchasing agent seeks to solve these problems through combining production scheduling, inventory control, and purchasing into one "materials handling" department, which he hopes he will head.

TECHNIQUES FOR DEALING WITH OTHER DEPARTMENTS

Normally the agent attempts to fill requisitions as instructed. The majority of interdepartmental contacts are handled routinely and without friction in accordance with standard operating procedures. Yet many difficult problems cannot be easily programmed. Other departments are constantly placing pressures on the agent, who must take countermeasures, if only to preserve the *status quo*. And if the purchasing agent wishes to expand his power aggressively, as many do, he will inevitably run into conflict.

Understandably, then, successful agents have developed a variety of techniques for dealing with other departments, particularly when they wish to influence the terms of the requisitions received. These techniques will first be summarized briefly under five general headings and then be discussed in greater detail.

1. *Rule-oriented tactics*
   a. Appeal to some common authority to direct that the requisition be revised or withdrawn.
   b. Refer to some rule (assuming one exists) which provides for longer lead times.
   c. Require the scheduling department to state in writing why quick delivery is required.
   d. Require the requisitioning department to consent to having its budget charged with the extra cost (such as air freight) required to get quick delivery.
2. *Rule-evading tactics*
   a. Go through the motions of complying with the request, but with no expectation of getting delivery on time.
   b. Exceed formal authority and ignore the requisitions altogether.
3. *Personal-political tactics*
   a. Rely on friendships to induce the scheduling department to modify the requisition.
   b. Rely on favors, past and future, to accomplish the same result.

   c. Work through political allies in other departments.
4. *Educational tactics*
   a. Use direct persuasion, that is, try to persuade scheduling that its requisition is unreasonable.
   b. Use what might be called indirect persuasion to help scheduling see the problem from the purchasing department's point of view (in this case it might ask the scheduler to sit in and observe the agent's difficulty in trying to get the vendor to agree to quick delivery).
5. *Organizational-interactional tactics*
   a. Seek to change the interaction pattern, for example, have the scheduling department check with the purchasing department as to the possibility of getting quick delivery *before* it makes a requisition.
   b. Seek to take over other departments, for example, to subordinate scheduling to purchasing in an integrated materials department.

Note that neither the over-all categories nor the tactics listed under them are all-exclusive and that there is a great deal of overlapping. They are proposed not as comprehensive tools of analysis, but merely as fairly common examples of bureaucratic gamesmanship.

Each agent interviewed in the study was evaluated in terms of his reported success (in terms of specific accomplishments) in getting other departments to accept a wider role for purchasing. Although this measure was crude and subjective,[4] there seemed to be quite clear differences between the tactics used by those who looked upon their job description as a defensive bastion and those who sought to expand their power beyond it. (Note that success is measured here in terms of expansion of power, rather than money saved for the company.)

RULE-ORIENTED TACTICS

The tactics listed below are rule-oriented in the sense that the agent's approach is perfectly legitimate under the formal rules of the organization. Agents who emphasize these tactics seem to fit into Melville Dalton's category of "systematizers."

Appealing to the Boss

According to traditional organizational theory, whenever two executives on about the same level cannot agree, they should take the problem to their common superior for solution. Yet, most agents looked upon this as a drastic step, to be taken only when other means failed.

Only five of the agents interviewed mentioned appealing to their superior as a reasonably common means of dealing with interdepartmental problems. In three cases low status seemed to be largely responsible for their inability to handle problems on their own.

Two of these agents were new to the job. For example, one was a man in his early twenties, who had only a few months' experience and who commented that his chief problems were his age and his inability to understand what engineers were talking about. This man met daily to review his problems with his boss and commented that his boss ran interference for him, at least in big problems.

The purchasing agent of a large scientific laboratory was very successful in extending his authority. In dealing with research departments, however, he used the laboratory manager "as a buffer between me and the department heads." But in regard to equipment-maintenance departments, whose heads had much lower status than did the scientists, he commented that "if there were differences, I would discuss them with them. If we didn't agree the laboratory manager would have to arbitrate. But this has never happened here." Significantly, this agent did not have a college degree, while many of the scientists were Ph.D's.

The other two agents who frequently worked through their superiors came from branch plants of nation-wide firms, which placed strong emphasis on individual responsibility to live within rigid rules.

The more expansionist agents rarely relied on their superiors to help them in interdepartmental disputes (in part because they had little success in doing this). They often explained that they would take problems to a man's superior if necessary but that they rarely found it necessary. Many repeated versions of the following:

> We have a policy against engineers having lunch with salesmen. Since the engineer is on my level I couldn't *tell* him to stop it. But in a nice way I could talk to him. If this didn't work, I'd see the plant manager.

Q: Have you ever done this [appealed to the boss]?
A: No.

The general feeling, particularly among stronger agents, was that too frequent reference to the superior would weaken their relations both with the superior and with their fellow employees. ("After all you've got to live with them.") To bring in top management too often would, in effect, be an admission that the agent could not handle his own problems. Moreover, there is a myth in many corporations of being "one great big happy family," and, as a consequence, it is difficult to bring conflicts out in the open. Furthermore, since the agent is usually the aggressor, in the sense that he is seeking to expand his power beyond its formal limits, he is unlikely to go to the boss unless his case is unusually good.

On the other hand, the threat of going to the boss loses it effectiveness as a weapon if the threat is *never* carried out. The following quotation summarizes a common position:

> It depends on how much fuss you want to make. If it is really important, you can tell him you will discuss it with his boss. But, I don't want you to get the wrong impression. If you have to resort to this, you are probably falling down on the job. By and large, we have a good relationship with our engineers.

However, there are times when you have to take a tough position. You aren't doing your job if you always go along with them in a wishy-washy fashion.

One agent explained how he "educated" engineers to accept substitute products instead of insisting on one brand.

We prepared our evidence and we were all set to take it to the top—and then, at the last minute, we backed down and told them it was too late in the game. But we indicated that in the future we would take similar issues to the top and they knew we would. So there has been much more understanding. . . . You have to risk making a few enemies once in a while.

Use of Rules

A second traditional bureaucratic means of dealing with other departments is to cite applicable rules or to rely on a formal statement of authority (such as a job description). For instance, an agent may circumvent pressure to place an order with a given company by referring to company rules requiring competitive bidding on all purchases in excess of $10,000. Most agents agreed, in theory, that rules of this sort are useful weapons, but they varied greatly in the extent to which they relied upon them in practice.

Some agents went very much "by the book," day in and day out. In general, these were men without college training, and they worked for larger, rule-oriented companies that were not changing rapidly. In answer to questions, these men often said, "This matter is governed by corporate policy" or made references to manuals and procedures. They also had a tendency to draw the lines of responsibility quite tightly, so that there were few areas of joint decision making; for example, "Engineering has the final word as far as specs are concerned. But we decide from whom to buy, provided they meet the specs." On the other hand, many agents operated very effectively without any formal written statement of their authority; their authority was understood by everybody in the organization and there was no need to put it in writing.

The evidence suggests that the most successful expansionists preferred to operate informally until there was an open conflict with another department. When this happened, they were very glad to refer to rules to bolster their position. Thus, paradoxically, we found strong agents who worked hard to introduce purchasing manuals and then paid relatively no attention to them in daily practice. In effect these agents take the position of "speak softly and carry a big stick." Indeed, the use of rules involves an implicit threat to appeal to higher management if the rules are not obeyed. ("When everyone in the organization knows what your responsibility is—and that you are backed up—then there is no need to mention it constantly.")

If flexibly used, procedure manuals provide the agent with an added bargaining weapon in dealing with other departments. Even though he may permit rules in the manual to be ignored most of the time, he can always do this as a favor in return for which he may ask favors. And the rules put a legal stamp on his efforts whenever he decides to ensnarl another department in a mass of red tape. But the expansionist agent must be careful not to become too rule-oriented. After all, his goal is to expand his influence beyond the areas over which the rules give him definite authority—not to retreat behind them.

Requiring Written Acceptance of Responsibility

Another bureaucratic technique used by many agents is to require others to justify their decisions in writing. For example, if a production scheduler orders a part for delivery with very short lead time, the agent can ask him to explain in writing why there is such a rush. He hopes the scheduler will be embarrassed unless he has a good excuse—and in any case, the effort will make him reluctant to make such last-minute requests in the future. Certainly this helps expose the scheduler who constantly cries "wolf."

Agents may ask for written explanations to clear themselves. Just as often, however, this is done to make others hesitate or to have evidence against them later. In insisting that such reports be written, the purchasing agent can refer to company rules or to possible audits. Thus in asking for such a statement, agents often say, "I need it to document my records."

Again, it is the weaker, noncollege agent who makes the most persistent use of such tactics. Many seem to feel that an approach of this sort is cowardly and defeatist. As one put it, "If you are trying to get a man to say 'yes,' I don't see any value in forcing him to put his 'no' in writing. Then he will never move." And another said, "I suppose you do punish an engineer by forcing him to give you a long written explanation, but that's hardly the way to win friends or advance your point of view." Furthermore, "You can always ask an engineer to give you a formal test result, but if he wishes he can always make the test fail."

Financial Charges

Cost-accounting procedures may also be used as a lever. A number of agents made comments like this:

Whenever I get a request for a rush delivery, I ask the department which wants it whether they are willing to authorize overtime[5] or air freight. Since this gets charged against their budget, they usually hesitate a bit. If they go along I know they really need it. And if they have too many extra charges the auditor starts asking questions.

This tactic resembles the one previously discussed, particularly when the agent enters a statement into his records that the product would have been cheaper had the requisition been received on time. (Some companies charge inbound freight to the budget of the purchasing or traffic department; in such cases purchasing's leverage is somewhat less effective.)

Some companies have what is often called an efficiency (or profit) improvement plan. According to such a plan each department (and sometimes each executive) receives credit[6] for the cost savings which can be attributed to the department's activities. Agents in two companies reported that engineers showed little enthusiasm for value analysis because the purchasing department got all the credit, even though part of the work was done by the engineering department. The situation greatly improved in one of these companies when "primary" credit was transferred to engineering, with purchasing retaining "participating" credit.

RULE-EVADING TACTICS

Literal Compliance

In dealing with pressures from other departments the agent can always adopt a policy of passive resistance—that is, he can go through the motions in hopes of satisfying the demands. This tactic of feigned acceptance[7] is often used with production scheduling. For instance, after completing a lengthy phone call in which he half-heartedly tried to persuade a vendor to make a very quick delivery, an agent commented, "My buyer tried already and I knew that they just weren't going to be able to deliver that soon. Still production scheduling was screaming and they threatened to go to the plant manager. So I tried to handle it in such a way as not to hurt my relations with the vendor. They knew why I had to call."

This game of passive resistance can be skillfully played in such a way as to set a trap for the other department.

Example. One agent told how he dealt with an engineer who had placed a requisition for one company's products after having been lavishly entertained by its salesman. The agent wrote a long memo explaining why he felt this to be a poor choice and presented it to the engineer in a fashion which he knew the engineer would reject. The agent then placed the order. As he had predicted, the products arrived late and were totally inappropriate. The subsequent investigation led both to this engineer's transfer and demotion and to other engineers having greater respect for the agent's advice.[8]

It should be noted, however, that these tactics were reported by only a minority of agents. In almost every case the agent was "weak" (in terms of expansionism) or worked in large companies where there was considerable emphasis on following formal rule books. Instead of passively seeming to accept unreasonable requests, the stronger agents actively opposed them.

Exceeding Authority

Occasionally agents may revise the terms of requisitions on their own initiative, even though they have no formal authority to do so. For instance, an agent may extend a lead time if he knows the production scheduler has set the delivery date much earlier than is really required.

Where a requisition calls for a given brand, he may purchase a substitute which he feels sure is an equivalent. Or, he may buy a larger quantity than requested in order to take advantage of quantity discounts.

When an agent revises requisitions in this manner, he may or may not tell the requisitioning department what he is doing. In either case he is exceeding his formal authority. In effect, he is daring the requisitioning department to make an issue of it. This requires considerable courage. No sensible agent will expose himself in this way unless (1) his over-all political position is secure and (2) he feels the terms of the original requisition were clearly so unreasonable that the requisitioning department will hesitate to raise the issue and expose its mistake.

Most agents were reluctant to use this tactic. Even if they could safely change orders in a given case, continual flouting of the requisitioning department's desires would create too much antagonism in the long run.

PERSONAL-POLITICAL TACTICS

Friendships and exchange of favors are used in almost every organization to get things done and to oil the wheels of formal bureaucracy. The agent is no exception to this rule; yet the author found to his surprise that informal relations played a less important role than he had expected. Agents, on the whole, seemed oriented to doing things "through channels."

None of the tactics which follow are contemplated by the company's formal scheme; all involve the use of personal relations. It would seem that Dalton's "adapters" would make greatest use of these tactics.

Friendships

Most agents prefer to deal with friends. Friendships help reduce the kinds of tensions to which agents are commonly subject. Even where friendship is not involved, it is easier to deal with people when you know their idiosyncrasies and special interests. Not surprisingly, comments like this were common: "[In handling problems] friendships count a lot. Many of the people here started when I did twenty-five years ago. We are all at about the same level and most of them are pretty good friends of mine. A lot is a matter of trust and confidence."

Agents seem to rely on friendship contacts as a means of communication and of getting quick acceptances of proposals that could be justified on their merits in any case. Rarely do agents rely on friendship alone. As one put it, "You can accomplish some things on the basis of friendship, but you can't do too much or you will strain your friendship."

Exchange of Favors

To some extent agents operate on the principle of "reward your friends, punish your enemies," and are involved in a network of exchange of favors—and sometimes even reprisals. Favors of various sorts may be given. Most agents are under pressure to make personal purchases, for example, to help someone in management buy a set of tires at wholesale rates. Since there are usually no formal rules as to such extracurricular purchasing, the agent has a strong incentive to help those who help him most. Similarly an agent is in a position to suggest to a salesman that it might be strategic to take a "co-operative" engineer to lunch. And there are always people in management who would like him to do a favor for a friend or relative who is a salesman or who owns a small business.

Other favors are more work-related. An agent may expedite delivery for a production scheduler who normally gives plenty of lead time for his orders but who now has a real emergency on his hands. Or he may rush parts for an engineer who is building a prototype model. "If a man is reasonable with me," one agent commented, "I'll kill myself to get him what he wants." The agent is less likely to exert himself for the man who has been unco-operative in the past. Yet, in general, agents seem to play down the exchange of favors, perhaps because they have relatively few favors to offer, other than trivial ones such as personal purchases or lunches for salesmen.[9]

The use of reprisals can be seen most clearly in dealing with salesmen. As one agent put it, "I play ball with those who play ball with me. If a salesman operates behind my back, he's going to have a hell of a time getting me to give him an order." Reprisals are more risky in dealing with management.

Example.   One assistant agent, for example, told how he "delayed" getting catalogues for "uncooperative" engineers and gave "slow service" to engineers who habitually cried wolf. However, both this man's supervisor and his personnel director expressed concern over his poor human relations and his tendency to antagonize others.

The typical agent, however, seemed to feel that if he used such techniques he ran the risk of permanently impairing his relations with others. Furthermore, these techniques might always backfire; for example, if production were delayed because components were delivered late, he would be blamed.

Interdepartmental Politics

In addition to their personal relations with people, agents inevitably get involved in interdepartmental power struggles. Indeed, as the following quotation suggests, the agent is often a man in the middle, subject to conflicting pressures from all sides:

Production scheduling wants quick delivery, engineering wants quality, manufacturing wants something easy-to-make, accounting wants to save money, quality control has their own interests. And then you've got to deal with the supplier—and present the supplier's position back to your own organization (sometimes you think you are wearing two hats, you represent both the supplier and the company). Everybody has his own point of view and only the agent sees the over-all picture.

Much of the agent's time is spent seeking informal resolution of such problems[10]—and in these meetings he often acts as a mediator. The following is a common situation:

Example. Production scheduling has been pushing hard to get early delivery of a particular component (perhaps because the sales department has been pressing for increased production). In response to this pressure the vendor puts new, inexperienced men on the job. But when the components are delivered, quality control declares the work is sloppy, rejects it in *toto,* and wants to disqualify the vendor from doing further work for the company. Production scheduling and the vendor are naturally upset; the vendor insists that the defects are trivial and can be easily remedied; and purchasing is placed in the difficult position of trying to mediate the issue.

If the agent is not careful in situations like this, he may become a scapegoat; everyone may turn on him and blame him for the unhappy turn of events. On the other hand, the successful agent is able to play one pressure off against another and free himself—or he may enlist the support of a powerful department to back him. If he is shrewd, he can get both sides to appeal to him to make the final decision and thus gain prestige as well as bestow favors which he may later ask returned.

Like it or not, agents of necessity engage in power politics. In doing this, they necessarily develop allies and opponents. Each department presents a special problem.

1. *Engineering.* Unless the relationship with engineering is handled with great tact, engineering tends to become an opponent, since value analysis invades an area which engineers feel is exclusively their own. Purchasing is at a disadvantage here. Engineers have the prestige of being college-trained experts, and engineering is much more strongly represented than purchasing in the ranks of higher management.

2. *Manufacturing.* There is often a tug of war between purchasing and manufacturing over who should have the greatest influence with production scheduling. These struggles are particularly sharp where purchasing is trying to absorb either inventory control or all of production scheduling.

3. *Comptroller.* The comptroller is rarely involved in the day-to-day struggles over specifications or delivery dates. But when purchasing seeks to introduce an organizational change which will increase its power—for example, absorbing inventory control—then the comptroller can be a most effective ally. But the agent must present evidence that the proposed innovation will save money.

4. *Sales.* Sales normally has great political power, and purchasing is anxious to maintain good relations with it. Sales is interested above all in being able to make fast delivery and shows less concern with cost, quality, or manufacturing ease. In general, it supports or opposes purchasing in accordance with this criteria. But sales is also interested in reciprocity—in persuading purchasing "to buy from those firms which buy from us."

5. *Production scheduling.* Relations with production scheduling are often complex. Purchasing normally has closer relations with production scheduling than any other department, and conflicts are quite common. Yet these departments are jointly responsible for having parts available when needed and, in several companies at least, they presented a common front to the outside world. Unfortunately, however, production scheduling has little political influence, particularly when it reports relatively low down in the administrative hierarchy.

The shrewd agent knows how to use departmental interests for his own ends. Two quotations illustrate this:

> Engineering says we can't use these parts. But I've asked manufacturing to test a sample under actual operating conditions—they are easy to use. Even if engineering won't accept manufacturing's data, I can go to the boss with manufacturing backing me. On something like this, manufacturing is tremendously powerful.

> [To get acceptance of new products] I may use methods and standards. Or I might go to engineering first and then to methods and standards if engineering shows no interest. If I go to methods and standards I have to emphasize the cost-saving aspect [as contrasted to engineering's interest in quality].

EDUCATIONAL TACTICS

Next we come to a set of tactics designed to persuade others to think in purchasing terms.

Direct Persuasion

Direct persuasion—the frank attempt to sell a point of view—is, of course, the agent's typical means of influencing others. Successful persuasion means "knowing your products backwards and forwards . . . building your case so that it can't be answered . . . knowing what you are talking about."

Most agents feel it essential that they have complete command of the facts, particularly if they are to bridge the status gap and meet engineers on equal terms. As one of them said, "The engineer thinks he is the expert; the only way you can impress him is to know more than he does." Thus many agents go to considerable lengths to acquire expertise; they spend a great deal of time learning production processes or reading technical journals.

Yet some of the stronger agents pointed out that too much expertise can be dangerous in that it threatens the other man's status. "Never put a man in a corner. Never prove that he is wrong. This is a fundamental in value analysis. It doesn't pay to be a know-it-all." Thus some agents look upon themselves primarily as catalysts who try to educate others to think in purchasing terms:

> Actually it is an asset not to be an engineer. Not having the [engineering] ability myself, I've had to work backwards. I can't tell them what to do but I can ask questions. They know that I'm not trying to design their instrument. . . . You have to give the engineer recognition. The less formal you are in dealing with them the better. It doesn't get their dander up.

Indirect Persuasion

Recognizing the danger of the frontal approach, agents often try forms of indirection—manipulation, if you like—which are designed to induce the other departments to arrive at conclusions similar to those of the agent but seemingly on their own. For example:

> We are paying $45.50 a unit, but I found a vendor who was producing a unit for $30 which I felt would meet our needs just as well. There was a lot of reluctance in engineering to accept it, but I knew the engineer in charge of the test was susceptible to flattery. So I wrote a letter for general distribution telling what a good job of investigating he was doing and how much money we'd save if his investigation was successful. . . . That gave him the motivation to figure out how it *could* work rather than how it *could not* work.

Indirect persuasion often involves presenting the facts and then letting the other person draw his own conclusions. The agent may ask the engineer to run a test on a product or even simply attach a sample of the product to an interoffice buck slip, asking, "Can we use this?" Similarly, choosing which salesmen may see engineers, he can indirectly influence the specification process. (In fact, once an agent decides that a product should be introduced, he and the salesman will often co-ordinate their strategies closely in order to get it accepted by others in management.)

Most agents feel engineers should have no part in negotiating prices; they feel this would be encroaching on purchasing's jurisdiction. But one successful agent encourages engineers to help out in the bargaining because "that's the best way I know to make these engineers cost conscious." Another arranges to have foremen and production schedulers sit in while he negotiates delivery dates with salesmen. "In that way they will know what I'm up against when they give me lead times which are too short for normal delivery."

ORGANIZATIONAL-INTERACTIONAL TECHNIQUES

Organizational factors play an important part in determining (1) whether the agent's relations with other departments will be formal or informal (for example, whether most contacts will be face-to-face, by phone, or in writing), (2) whether it will be easy or hard for other departments to initiate for purchasing, and (3) whether purchasing can make its point of view felt while decisions are being considered—or can intervene only after other departments have already taken a position. All these involve interaction patterns. We shall consider here only two types of organizational changes: informal measures which make it easier for other departments to initiate change in the usual flow of orders and formal changes involving grants of additional authority.

Inducing Others to Initiate Action

In most of the examples discussed here, the agent seeks to initiate change in the behavior of other departments. He is the one who is trying to change the engineer's specifications, the production scheduler's delivery schedules, and so forth. The other departments are always at the receiving (or resisting) end of these initiations. As might be expected, hard feelings are likely to develop if the initiations move only one way.[11]

Recognizing this, many of the stronger agents seem to be trying to rearrange their relations with other departments so that others might initiate changes in the usual work flow more often for them. Specifically they hope to induce the other departments to turn instinctively to purchasing for help whenever they have a problem—and at the earliest possible stage. Thus one agent explained that his chief reason for attending production planning meetings, where new products were laid out, was to make it easier for others to ask him questions. He hoped to encourage engineers, for example, to inquire about available components before they drew up their blueprints. Another agent commented, "I try to get production scheduling to ask us what the lead times for the various products are. That's a lot easier than our telling them that their lead times are unreasonable after they have made commitments based on these."

Some purchasing departments send out what are, in effect, ambassadors to other departments. They may appoint purchase engineers, men with engineering background (perhaps from the company's own engineering group) who report administratively to purchasing but spend most of their time in the engineering department. Their job is to be instantly available to provide information to engineers whenever they need help in choosing components. They assist in writing specifications (thus making them more realistic and readable) and help expedite delivery of laboratory supplies and material for prototype models. Through making themselves useful, purchase engineers acquire influence and are able to introduce the purchasing point of view before the "completion barrier" makes this difficult. Similar approaches may be used for quality control.

Work assignments with purchasing are normally arranged so that each buyer can become an expert on one group of commodities bought. Under this arrangement the buyer deals with a relatively small number of salesmen, but with a relatively large number of "client" departments within the organization. A few agents have experimented with assigning men on the basis of the departments with which they work rather than on the basis of the products they buy. In one case work assignments in both purchasing and scheduling were so rearranged that each production scheduler had an exact counterpart in purchasing and dealt only with him. In this way closer personal relations developed than would have occurred if the scheduler had no specific individual in purchasing to contact.

Even the physical location of the agent's office makes a difference. It is much easier for the agent to have informal daily contacts with other departments if his office is conveniently located. Some companies place their agents away from the main office, to make it easier for salesmen to see them. Although this facilitates the agents' external communications, it makes their internal communications more difficult. Of course, those companies that have centralized purchasing offices and a widespread network of plants experience this problem in an exaggerated form. Centralized purchasing offers many economic advantages, but the agent must tour the plants if he is not to lose all contact with his client departments.

Value analysis techniques sharply highlight the agent's organizational philosophy. Some agents feel that value analysis should be handled as part of the buyer's everyday activities. If he comes across a new product which might be profitably substituted for one currently used, he should initiate engineering feasibility studies and promote the idea ("nag it" in one agent's words) until it is accepted. Presumably purchasing then gets the credit for the savings, but resistance from other departments may be high. Other agents, particularly those with college training, reject this approach as unnecessarily divisive; they prefer to operate through committees, usually consisting of engineers, purchasing men, and production men. Though committees are time consuming, communications are facilitated, more people are involved, more ideas are forthcoming—and, in addition, the purchasing department no longer has the sole responsibility for value analysis.

To the extent that he allows others to take the initiative, the agent himself must take a passive role. Not all agents are emotionally prepared to do this.[12] Some feel that it smacks too much of the "order clerk." A number commented, in effect, "I don't want to be everyone's door mat." Many asked questions like, "How far do you go in cost estimating, in getting quotes for hypothetical orders? . . . What do you do if a man throws a label at you and says get me some of this? After all, our time is limited."

Formal Organizational Change

The final approach is for the agent to seek to expand the formal grant of authority given his department (which might mean a larger budget too), as, for example, to place other functions such as traffic, stores, or even inventory control and production scheduling in one combined materials department. Agents who exert their energies in this direction generally reject the "human relations" or "participative" approach to management. They like to resolve problems through memoranda ("it helps keep emotions down") and are not particularly optimistic about the possibilities of converting other departments to think in purchasing terms ("after all every department has its own point of view—that's natural"). They spend considerable time developing statistical means of measuring their own efficiency and that of their subordinates, and they are more likely to be in companies that have similar philosophies. For example, one agent explained why value analysis in his organization was concentrated in the purchasing department, "[Our company] doesn't believe in joint assignments or committees. If a man isn't competent to do the job himself, then we find another man. We don't want weak sisters." And another argued, "The responsibility must be concentrated in one department or another. It can't fall between two stools."[13]

CHOICE OF TECHNIQUES

The foregoing list of tactics are presented not as a formal typology but merely to illustrate the *range* of techniques available to the agent. Most agents use all of these techniques at one time or another, depending on the problem. A different technique might well be used in introducing a major policy change than in handling routine orders. In trying to promote changes, one agent observed:

> You have to choose your weapons. I vary them on purpose. . . . I ask myself, who has the final decision? How does the Chief Engineer operate? What does he delegate? What does he keep for himself? It all involves psychological warfare. Who are the people to be sold? Who will have the final say?

And even in dealing with one problem, a mixture of tactics will generally be used. Nevertheless, the over-all strategies used by various agents seem to vary greatly in terms of which tactics receive the greatest emphasis.

1. Some agents seek formal grants of power (for example, to get inventory placed under purchasing); others merely seek influence (for example, to persuade inventory control to order in more economic lot sizes).
2. Some agents want to influence decisions *before* they are made (for example, through encouraging engineers to turn instinctively to purchasing for help whenever they are even considering the use of a new component); others *after* (for example, through having their decisions upheld often enough for engineering to hesitate to make an issue of a request whenever purchasing questions a specification).
3. Some agents think in terms of their long-run position and thus seek to improve procedures; whereas others are interested chiefly in exerting their influence in each conflict as it comes along.

We have already noted a difference between successful expansionists and those content with their roles as they are. On the whole, expansionists seemed to be more likely to choose informal tactics such as indirect persuasion, inducing others to make changes in the work flow, and interdepartmental politics. They had long-run strategies and sought to influence decisions before they were made. Those who were successful in achieving more formal power were also well aware of the value of informal influence; those who merely *talked* about formal power seemed to be relatively unsuccessful even in informal influence. In fact, one of the most noticeable characteristics of successful expansionists was their flexibility. Most were equally adept at using both formal and informal tactics and were not averse to turning the formal organization against itself.

Differences in success in expansionism seem to be due to a number of factors:

1. *Technology.* Obviously the agent cannot expand very much in a service industry or one where only raw materials are bought. He has his greatest chance for power in companies which make goods to order and in which there is a great deal of subcontracting.

2. *Management philosophy.* Where lines of authority are sharply drawn, the agent has little chance to extend his influence—except through direct seizure of another department's power, which is not easy. Note the comments of one agent in a highly rule-oriented company:

   We are a service department . . . We must see that parts are here at the proper time. . . . I usually let engineering pretty much make its own decisions. I may try to persuade an engineer to accept a new product. But if he says "no" all I can do is wait till he gets transferred and try to persuade his successor.

   Of the agents interviewed, the most successful was one in the company which had just introduced a new management and in which all relationships were in flux.

3. *Education.* Purchasing agents who were college graduates seemed to be more expansionist than those who were not. This may be due to their higher level of aspiration. Moreover, any company that appoints a college graduate may well expect to grant him greater influence. The college-trained man may feel more as an equal of the engineer and therefore more willing to come into conflict with him.

Furthermore, the more educated men (and particularly those with a business school background) seemed more prone to rely on techniques that were informal and not rule-oriented. Specifically, they were less likely to rely on formal statements of authority, to require others to take formal responsibilities for decisions, or to insist that an agent should "yell loudly whenever his rights are violated"; and they were more willing to work through committees.[14]

CONCLUSION

Traditional organization theory emphasizes authority and responsibility; it deals largely with two types of relationships: (1) those between superiors and subordinates, which it conceives as being primarily authoritarian (though perhaps modifiable by participation, general supervision, and the like) and (2) those of staff and line, which are nonauthoritarian. Though the purchasing department is traditionally classified as a staff department, my own feeling is that the staff-line dichotomy in this case (as perhaps for most other purposes) tends to obscure more problems than it illuminates. As we have seen, the purchasing department's relations with other departments cannot be explained by any one simple phrase, such as "areas of responsibility," "exchange of favors," "advice," "control," or the like. Instead the skillful agent blends all these approaches and makes use of authoritarian and persuasive tactics as the situation requires. His effectiveness is largely dependent on the political power he is able to develop.

Recent authors have suggested that the study of organization should begin first with "the work to be done and resources and techniques available to do it."[15] The emphasis is on the technology of the job ("technology" being defined broadly to include marketing problems and the like as well as external environment) and the relationships between people which this technology demands. "Organizations should be constructed from the *bottom up,* rather than from the *top down.* In establishing work-group boundaries and supervisory units, management should start with the actual work to be performed, an awareness of who must co-ordinate his job with whom, when, and where."[16]

Some of us who are interested in this area are groping toward a concept of *work flow,* meaning the communications or interactions required by the job and including the flow of raw materials and products on the assembly line, the flow of paper work when a requisition moves through engineering, scheduling, and purchasing, as well as the flow of instruction, which may move down the chain of command from president to janitor.

This has been an exploratory study of the interrelationship between power struggles and lateral work flow. Of particular interest in this study are: (1) the agent's strong desire for increased status, which upsets the stability of his relationship with other departments, (2) his attempts to raise his status through influencing the terms of the requisitions he receives and thus make interactions flow both ways, (3) the relatively limited interference on the part of higher management, which makes the lateral relationship especially important for the agent, (4) the "completion barrier," which requires the agent to contact an engineer before a blueprint is finished if the agent is to be successful in influencing the terms of the requisition, and (5) the differing vested interests or terms of reference of the various departments, which make agreement more difficult.

Finer mapping and more intensive research into interdepartmental relations is required; interactions should be precisely counted[17] and work should be done with specialties other than purchasing.

NOTES

[1]There have been many studies of lateral relations within or among primary work groups, but such studies have been concerned primarily with rank-and-file workers, not management. Three notable studies of horizontal relations within management are Melville Dalton, *Men Who Manage* (New York, 1959); Elliot R. Chapple and Leonard Sayles, *The Measure of Management* (New York, 1961); and Henry A. Landsberger, The Horizontal Dimension in a Bureaucracy, *Administrative Science Quarterly,* 6 (1961), 298–332.

[2]Henceforth, I shall refer to the purchasing agent as the "agent."

[3]I am indebted for assistance to the the Buffalo and Northern California Association of Purchasing Agents and to the chairmen of their respective Committees for Professional Development, Messrs. Roger Josslyn and M. J. McMahon. Helpful criticism was provided by Profs. Delbert Duncan, E. T. Malm, and Lyman Porter at the University of California, Berkeley; Prof. John Gullahorn of Michigan State College; Prof. Leonard Sayles at Columbia University; and Dean Arthur Butler and Prof. Perry Bliss at the University of Buffalo. Part of the research was done while the author was a research associate at the Institute of Industrial Relations, University of California, Berkeley.

[4]*Reported success* obviously involves a fair amount of wishful thinking—aspiration rather than accomplishment—but for the general character of this study this limitation was not too serious. It should be emphasized, however, that whether an agent was a successful expansionist depended not only on his personality and his choice of techniques but also on the institutional characteristics of the organization in which he worked.

[5]That is, the vendor is authorized to make an extra charge for having his men work overtime.

[6]Though there is no direct pay-off, performance under the plan is often taken into account in determining bonuses or promotions.

[7]Dalton, *op. cit.,* p. 232.

[8]A tactic like this can always backfire. The agent himself may be blamed for the failure.

[9]Reciprocity in the broader sense, as suggested by Gouldner and others, is, of course, inherent in the entire framework of relations discussed here. Cf. Alvin W. Gouldner, The Norm of Reciprocity: A Preliminary Statement, *American Sociological Review,* 25 (1960), 161–177.

[10]Dalton (*op. cit.,* pp. 227–228) points out the function of meetings in short-circuiting formal means of handling problems.

[11]Actually, of course, initiations do occur in both directions. The production schedulers initiate for the agent when they file requisitions and the engineers initiate when they determine specifications. This normal form of programmed, routine initiation is felt to be quite different from the agent's abnormal attempts to introduce innovation. This distinction is quite important.

[12]After all, a certain type of active, initiating sort of personality is required if the agent is to bargain successfully with the suppliers; it is hard for the same individual to adopt a passive role within the organization.

[13]Yet it could be argued that the committee system does not itself divide responsibility; it merely recognizes the fact that responsibility for value analysis is of necessity divided among departments.

[14]These conclusions are consistent with the findings of the questionnaire sample (N = 142). The results are in the direction indicated for both degree of education and business school background (each taken separately) although only three out of eight relationships are significant at the .05 level. The questionnaire data are somewhat suspect, however, since the values which agents report are not always consistent with their observed behavior; in answering questionnaires many agents seem to place greater emphasis on formal techniques than they do in practice.

[15]Wilfred Brown, *Explorations in Management* (London, 1960), p. 18. See Chapple and Sayles, *op. cit.*; William F. Whyte, *Men at Work* (Homewood, Ill., 1961).

[16]George Strauss and Leonard R. Sayles, *Personnel: The Human Problems of Management* (Englewood Cliffs, N.J., 1960), p. 392. The sentence is Sayles's.

[17]Albert H. Rubenstein of Northwestern University has completed an unpublished quantitative study of communications within a purchasing department.

PART 4

Upward Influence

A subordinate who is attempting to get a superior to behave in a manner desired by the subordinate is practicing an upward influence attempt. This section examines those influence attempts that are directed at a target that possesses more formal authority in the organization than the influence source. Certain bases of power that organizations provide to supervisors and managers—such as the ability to give or withhold rewards, issue orders, make decisions, and if necessary take punitive action—are less available to subordinate personnel. This necessarily reduces the repertoire of influence methods or tactics that the subordinate influence source can reasonably employ.

However, the subordinate is by no means powerless. It simply means that the subordinate must rely on personal bases of power such as expertise or charisma in persuading the superior to provide the desired outcomes. Another method of influence besides persuasion that is just as available to the subordinate as it is to the superior is manipulation. As we use it here, manipulation means influencing a person to do what is desired without the person being aware that he or she is a target of influence. Manipulation can also be used as a method of downward or lateral influence, of course, as well as in upward influence attempts.

Much of the upward influence that is attempted by subordinates takes place in the course of normal routine working relationships directed toward accomplishing organizational goals and objectives. These influence attempts range from getting the immediate superior to approve the purchase of a new typewriter to obtaining upper management approval or support for proceeding with a new product design or construction of a major new facility. Another type of upward influence occurs when the subordinate attempts to influence his or her superior to provide outcomes that will satisfy the personal needs or self interests of the subordinate—anything from getting a more desirable work space (such as an office with windows) to getting selected for a promotional opportunity. Those upward influence attempts that are primarily intended to promote or protect the self-interest of the influence source are closely associated with a concept widely known as *organizational politics.*

Only recently has the subject of organizational politics found its way into the formal education of students interested in learning about behavior in organizations. Unlike leadership and group influence processes, organizational politics has been largely ignored, yet its existence has seldom been denied! Why is it that only upon becoming an organizational member does the graduated student beginning a business or public sector career receive an education in politics? This lack of prior understanding of organizational politics can result in reality shock and a label of naiveté for the new employee. In turn, this creates a state conducive to anxiety, frustration, and conflict—inherent elements of stress. We do not contend that having an understanding of organizational politics and other upward influence processes will necessarily reduce organizational stress. We do believe, however, that understanding this pervasive process in organizations is essential to the education of students interested in organizations and their management.

There are some writers who believe that organizations are political entities and, therefore, that all behaviors are politically motivated. We prefer to consider politics as a subset of organizational behaviors. More specifically, we consider politics to be predominantly a subset of upward influence processes. The rationale for this preference has been previously set forth in the Porter, Allen, and Angle article in this section:

> "It appears reasonable to say that, while not all (or even most) upward influence involves political behavior, most political behavior (in organizations) does involve upward influence. Taking the first part of this statement, much of upward influence involves, of course, the normal routine—reporting relationships that exist in all organizations. There is a substantial segment, however, that we would contend involves what can be labeled as 'political behavior' . . . . What the ratio is of non-political to political upward influence behavior in organizations is an empirical question. The other part of the statement about the relationship between the two topics—that most political behavior in organizations involves upward influence—is based on the assumption that the typical object of influence will be someone or some group possessing more formal, legitimate power than the would-be political actor. While it is possible to cite clear exceptions to this proposition, we would, nevertheless, contend that the vast majority of *political* attempts at influence are in the upward direction."

With the exception of the opening article, then, the focus in this last section primarily will be on organizational politics as a very interesting and crucial aspect of the upward influence process in organizational settings.

Although the first reading in this section is over 20 years old, it has been widely influential. David Mechanic dispels any idea that only persons in lofty positions possess power. As with many other power writers, he argues that power is closely related to dependence. He contends that individuals within organizations can make others dependent upon them and thereby acquire power if they control information, persons, and instrumentalities (e.g., resources). He discusses how such factors as expertise, effort and interest, attractiveness, rules, coalitions, and location and position serve to increase the power of lower-level participants in an organization. In turn, this enables the lower-level participants to exert considerable influence over other higher-ranking individuals within the organization: this influence can be directed toward the attainment of organizational goals and objectives, as well as the attainment of personal goals and self-interests of the lower participant.

The article by Mayes and Allen represents an early attempt to develop a definitional framework for viewing politics in organizations. The authors consider politics to be a dynamic process of influence intended to produce organizationally relevant outcomes beyond the simple performance of job tasks. The definition focuses on influence means and influence ends, and whether or not these means and ends are organizationally sanctioned. When both the means and ends of a behavior are sanctioned by the organization, the behavior is categorized as non-political. An important feature of the Mayes and Allen definition is that not all political behavior is necessarily dysfunctional to the organization. The political actor could conceivably use influence tactics that are not necessarily sanctioned by the organization, but tactics that could nevertheless result in outcomes or goals perceived as potentially functional to the organization. One example is the political process involved in cutting through red tape to assure the satisfaction of a key customer: this is not to say that the ends will always justify the means, but to establish that political behavior in organizations need not be viewed only in a negative way. Mayes and Allen make the point that organizational politics is a process that can be learned and managed just as any other process in an organization. Greater understanding of the important influence process of organizational politics increases the likelihood that end results can fulfill organizational needs, as well as the needs of its political actors.

In the third article, Frost and Hayes make this same point. They cite Baldridge's proposition that organizational members "tend to coalesce around shared interests in order to better seek common organizational outcomes." The authors, consistent with many previous writers, view organizations as a marketplace for the exchange and distribution of resources. An important characteristic of the framework offered by Frost and Hayes is that this exchange process involves two phases—the negotiation of the exchange, and the enactment of the exchange once it has been negotiated. It is in the negotiating for resources phase where politics most likely are exercised. The enactment phase involves administration of programmed decision outcomes resulting from the negotiating phase, with a lesser likelihood of the necessity for political behaviors.

Frost and Hayes identify three sets of behaviors as relevant to the negotiating-enactment exchange process: administrative, discretionary, and political. Administrative behaviors are viewed as being organizationally prescribed or routine in nature, while discretionary behaviors are nonroutine or nonorganizationally prescribed. Discretionary behaviors nonetheless reflect a consensus within the organization or between exchanging parties concerning the appropriateness of the behavior. Frost and Hayes consider behavior to be political only when resources in an exchange are used in ways that would be resisted if recognized by other members involved in the exchange. This is called non-consensus behavior. Both administrative and discretionary behaviors are viewed as consensus behaviors, therefore, legitimate in terms of the exchange. It is important to note that, though political behavior is viewed as non-consensus behavior, Frost and Hayes intend no evaluative connotation. An evaluation or assessment of the outcomes of the behavior would be required before the behavior could be considered good, bad or indifferent.

Tushman presents a macro approach to political behavior in organizations: his emphasis is on the organization and major subunits within the organization as the primary units of study (a micro approach would focus on individuals or small groups within an organization). The author concentrates on the characteristics of organizational structure and processes inherent in a group of individuals vying for their share of limited or scarce resources. He uses a systems perspective that views the organization as a set of interactions between interconnected but differentiated parts. A key proposition of this presentation is that the greater the amount of differentiation in an organization, the greater will be the amount of uncertainty and ambiguity. Uncertainty creates significant opportunities for political coping behavior. Recall that in Section I, Hickson et al. related the power of subunits to the subunits' ability to cope with strategic contingencies. Tushman further discusses the relationship of power and political behavior, also emphasizing the close connection between the two concepts. Note the considerable similarity between Tushman's "Decision Making Typology" and the "Dimensions of Organizational Politics" discussed by Mayes and Allen in the second article in this section. In addition, Tushman introduces a provocative set of organizational political implications for the study and understanding of organization development.

In direct contrast with Tushman's macro view of political behavior in organizations, Porter, Allen, and Angle discuss the politics of upward influence in organizations from a micro, or "one-on-one political influence situation" perspective. Note that the definition of upward influence and organizational politics presented by these authors is generally consistent with those of earlier writers. However, special attention should be paid to the four defining characteristics of organizational political behavior presented in this article. It would be helpful to compare these characteristics to the other writers' definitional framework for organizational politics. Of particular interest is a comparison of Frost's and Hayes' administrative, discretionary, and political behavior perspective with the view of Porter, Allen, and Angle, who consider discretionary behaviors to be an integral part of a definitional framework of political behavior.

The readings contained in Section III and your own experiences in organizations should leave little doubt about the importance of norms in organizational settings. Indeed, many pivotal norms are translated into laws in our society and formally documented as policies and procedures in organizations. In this connection, Porter, Allen, and Angle emphasize the importance of political norms and their structure as a key consideration of political influence in organizations. Norms clearly can play an important role in what Mayes and Allen (in the second article in Section IV) refer to as the management of influence—downward and lateral, as well as upward. However, Porter, Allen, and Angle argue that it may be difficult to learn what the political norms are in any given organization. This is particularly true of norms that condone rather than condemn political behaviors.

A second important aspect of upward political influence discussed by Porter, Allen, and Angle is situational factors. Consistent with Tushman in the previous article, situational ambiguity, resource scarcity, and personal stake in the outcome are included as situational elements that are conducive to political activity. Characteristics of the political actor, selection of a target to influence in a political situation, and the methods of upward influence used are other important considerations in upward political influence. Note the "classification of methods" of upward political influence—the inclusion of manipulative persuasion as a method is an elaboration on models offered in previous writings about influence methods.

Cavanagh, Moberg, and Velasquez provide a contrast to the definite, nonevaluative tone of most of the other articles in this section that concern political behaviors. As indicated earlier, outcomes of political behaviors would require assessment before those behaviors could be considered good or bad. This assessment of ends is the direct concern of Cavanagh, Moberg, and Velasquez, who believe that current management theory tends to focus more on the value of the outcomes themselves than on the means chosen for accomplishing the ends. The authors are led to the conclusion that explicit consideration must therefore be given to the development of ethical criteria relevant to political uses of power in organizations. Those of you who are interested in professional management careers will find the discussion of the three basic kinds of moral behavior (utilitarian, theory of rights, and theory of justice) educational as well as thought provoking. Indeed, providing outcomes that are consistent with a sound ethical framework may be considered a defining characteristic of truly professional management.

The concluding three articles in this section present empirical findings regarding organizational politics. Gandz and Murray's primary concern is with organizational processes. Specifically, they ask which processes were perceived by their respondents as being most political, and how subjects felt about individuals who engage in political behavior. Note the considerable similarity in Gandz and Murray's findings to the results reported by Madison et al. in the subsequent article. This similarity is of particular interest because Gandz and Murray's sample was apparently composed of recent graduates and "part-time MBA students," while the sample in the Madison et al. study was a mixture of top, middle, and lower-level management personnel. One area of contrast between the two studies, however, was in how the two respondent groups viewed whether organizational politics is a positive or negative process. The Gandz and Murray sample tended in general to view politics and political behavior negatively—most of the sample considered workplace politics to be detrimental to organizational effectiveness. The practicing managers in the Madison et al. study, however, recognized helpful as well as harmful aspects of political behavior. The reader is left to speculate why younger, though highly educated, respondents might view organizational politics in more pejorative terms than did the practicing managers.

Additional findings of the Madison et al. research are that practicing managers: (1) viewed marketing and sales as functional areas where there is the highest amount of political activity; (2) believed that political behavior is most prevalent in upper levels of the organization; and (3) perceived reorganization changes, personnel changes, and budget allocations as situations most conducive to politicking. Also of note is their finding concerning the respondents' perceptions about the relative effectiveness of performance versus organizational politics for obtaining promotions, salary increases, and transfers. Generally, the subjects viewed organizational politics as useful instrumentalities for attaining such organizational rewards. On the other hand, respondents were unanimous in saying that organizational politics could also harm the individual in one or more ways.

In the final article, Allen, Madison, Porter, Renwick, and Mayes report and discuss findings regarding managerial observations about tactics used in organizational politics and characteristics of political actors. It would be instructive to try to fit the specific tactics set forth in this article into the more general framework of methods discussed in *The Politics of Upward Influence in Organizations*. Give particular attention to the authors' discussion of Attribution Theory and Organizational Politics. This discussion may help to explain the differences between Gandz and Murray's young managers' perceptions and those of the practicing managers studied by Madison et. al. regarding the favorableness of organizational politics.

This last set of readings concludes our examination of organizational influence processes. As we have seen, in organizational settings, power and influence processes are multidirectional. Regardless of their position or organizational level, all individuals are both potential targets and potential sources of influence. Organizational structure is achieved through vertical and horizontal differentiation, thereby creating levels of formal authority and functional areas of specialization. To successfully integrate the many differentiated parts of an organization, and to efficiently channel behaviors so that both individual and organizational goals can be achieved, a manager must make effective use of power and organizational influence. For these important reasons, we believe that the study of organizational influence processes is essential to the education of anyone who is anticipating or continuing a career in organizational behavior management.

Sources of Power of Lower Participants in Complex Organizations

DAVID MECHANIC

It is not unusual for lower participants[1] in complex organizations to assume and wield considerable power and influence not associated with their formally defined positions within these organizations. In sociological terms they have considerable personal power but no authority. Such personal power is often attained, for example, by executive secretaries and accountants in business firms, by attendants in mental hospitals, and even by inmates in prisons. The personal power achieved by these lower participants does not necessarily result from unique personal characteristics, although these may be relevant, but results rather from particular aspects of their location within their organizations.

INFORMAL VERSUS FORMAL POWER

Within organizations the distribution of authority (institutionalized power) is closely if not perfectly correlated with the prestige of positions. Those who have argued for the independence of these variables[2] have taken their examples from diverse organizations and do not deal with situations where power is clearly comparable.[3] Thus when Bierstedt argues that Einstein had prestige but no power, and the policeman power but no prestige, it is apparent that he is comparing categories that are not

Reprinted from "Sources of Power of Lower Participants in Complex Organizations" by David Mechanic published in *Administrative Science Quarterly,* Volume 7, Number 3, December 1962 by permission of The Administrative Science Quarterly.

comparable. Generally persons occupying high-ranking positions within organizations have more authority than those holding low-ranking positions.

One might ask what characterizes high-ranking positions within organizations. What is most evident, perhaps, is that lower participants recognize the right of higher-ranking participants to exercise power, and yield without difficulty to demands they regard as legitimate. Moreover, persons in high-ranking positions tend to have considerable access and control over information and persons both within and outside the organization, and to instrumentalities or resources. Although higher supervisory personnel may be isolated from the task activities of lower participants, they maintain access to them through formally established intermediary positions and exercise control through intermediary participants. There appears, therefore, to be a clear correlation between the prestige of positions within organizations and the extent to which they offer access to information, persons, and instrumentalities.

Since formal organizations tend to structure lines of access and communication, access should be a clue to institutional prestige. Yet access depends on variables other than those controlled by the formal structure of an organization, and this often makes the informal power structure that develops within organizations somewhat incongruent with the formally intended plan. It is these variables that allow work groups to limit production through norms that contravene the goals of the larger organization, that allow hospital attendants to thwart changes in the structure of a hospital, and that allow prison inmates to exercise some control over prison guards. Organizations, in a sense, are continuously at the mercy of their lower participants, and it is this fact that makes organizational power structure especially interesting to the sociologist and social psychologist.

Clarification of Definitions

The purpose of this paper is to present some hypotheses explaining why lower participants in organizations can often assume and wield considerable power which is not associated with their positions as formally defined within these organizations. For the purposes of this analysis the concepts "influence," "power," and "control" will be used synonymously. Moreover, we shall not be concerned with type of power, that is, whether the power is based on reward, punishment, identification, power to veto, or whatever.[4] Power will be defined as *any force that results in behavior that would not have occurred if the force had not been present.* We have defined power as a force rather than a relationship because it appears that much of what we mean by power is encompassed by the normative framework of an organization, and thus any analysis of power must take into consideration the power of norms as well as persons.

I shall also argue, following Thibaut and Kelley,[5] that power is closely related to dependence. To the extent that a person is dependent on another, he is potentially subject to the other person's power. Within organizations one makes others dependent upon him by controlling access to information, persons, and instrumentalities, which I shall define as follows:

a. *Information* includes knowledge of the organization, knowledge about persons, knowledge of the norms, procedures, techniques, and so forth.
b. *Persons* include anyone within the organization or anyone outside the organization upon whom the organization is in some way dependent.
c. *Instrumentalities* include any aspect of the physical plant of the organization or its resources (equipment, machines, money, and so on).

Power is a function not only of the extent to which a person controls information, persons, and instrumentalities, but also of the importance of the various attributes he controls.[6]

Finally, following Dahl,[7] we shall agree that comparisons of power among persons should, as far as possible, utilize comparable units. Thus we shall strive for clarification by attempting to oversimplify organizational processes; the goal is to set up a number of hypothetical statements of the relationship between variables taken two at a time, "all other factors being assumed to remain constant."

A Classic Example

Like many other aspects of organizational theory, one can find a classic statement of our problem in Weber's discussion of the political bureaucracy. Weber indicated the extent to which bureaucrats may have considerable power over political incumbents, as a result, in part, of their permanence within the political bureaucracy, as contrasted to public officials, who are replaced rather frequently.[8] Weber noted how the low-ranking bureaucrat becomes familiar with the organization—its rules and operations, the work flow, and so on, which gives him considerable power over the new political incumbent, who might have higher rank but is not as familiar with the organization. While Weber does not directly state the point, his analysis suggests that bureaucratic permanence has some relationship to increased access to persons, information, and instrumentalities. To state the hypothesis suggested somewhat more formally:

H1   Other factors remaining constant, organizational power is related to access to persons, information, and instrumentalities.
H2   Other factors remaining constant, as a participant's length of time in an organization increases, he has increased access to persons, information, and instrumentalities.

While these hypotheses are obvious, they do suggest that a careful scrutiny of the organizational literature, especially that dealing with the power or counterpower of lower participants, might lead to further formalized statements, some considerably less obvious than the ones stated. This kind of hypothesis formation is treated later in the paper, but at this point I would like to place the discussion of power within a larger theoretical context and discuss the relevance of role theory to the study of power processes.

IMPLICATIONS OF ROLE THEORY FOR THE STUDY OF POWER

There are many points of departure for the study of power processes within organizations. An investigator might view influence in terms of its sources and strategies; he might undertake a study of the flow of influence; he might concentrate on the structure of organizations, seeing to what extent regularities in behavior might be explained through the study of norms, roles, and traditions; and, finally, more psychologically oriented investigators might concentrate on the recipients of influence and the factors affecting susceptibility to influence attempts. Each of these points of departure leads to different theoretical emphases. For our purposes the most important emphasis is that presented by role theorists.

Role theorists approach the question of influence and power in terms of the behavioral regularities which result from established identities within specific social contexts like families, hospitals, and business firms. The underlying premise of most role theorists is that a large proportion of all behavior is brought about through socialization within specific organizations, and much behavior is routine and established through learning the traditional modes of adaptation in dealing with specific tasks. Thus the positions persons occupy in an organization account for much of their behavior. Norms and roles serve as mediating forces in influence processes.

While role theorists have argued much about vocabulary, the basic premises underlying their thought have been rather consistent. The argument is essentially that knowledge of one's identity or social position is a powerful index of the expectations such a person is likely to face in various social situations. Since behavior tends to be highly correlated with expectations, prediction of behavior is therefore possible. The approach of role theorists to the study of behavior within organizations is of particular merit in that it provides a consistent set of concepts which is useful analytically in describing recruitment, socialization, interaction, and personality, as well as the formal structure of organizations. Thus the concept of role is one of the few concepts clearly linking social structure, social process, and social character.

Many problems pertaining to role theory have been raised. At times it is not clear whether role is regarded as a real entity, a theoretical construct, or both. Moreover, Gross has raised the issue of role consensus, that is, the extent to which the expectations impinging upon a position are held in common by persons occupying reciprocal positions to the one in question.[9] Merton has attempted to deal with inevitable inconsistencies in expectations of role occupants by introducing the concept of role-set which treats differences in expectations as resulting, in part, from the fact that any position is differently related to a number of reciprocal positions.[10] Furthermore, Goffman has criticized role theory for its failure to deal adequately with commitment to roles[11]—a factor which Etzioni has found to be related intimately to the kind of power exercised in organizations.[12] Perhaps these various criticisms directed at role theory reflect its importance as well as its deficiencies, and despite the difficulties involved in role analysis, the concept of role may prove useful in various ways.

Role theory is useful in emphasizing the extent to which influence and power can be exercised without conflict. This occurs when power is integrated with a legitimate order, when sentiments are held in common, and when there are adequate mechanisms for introducing persons into the system and training them to recognize, accept, and value the legitimacy of control within the organization. By providing the conditions whereby participants within an organization may internalize the norms, these generalized rules, values, and sentiments serve as substitutes for interpersonal influence and make the workings of the organization more agreeable and pleasant for all.

It should be clear that lower participants will be more likely to circumvent higher authority, other factors remaining constant, when the mandates of those in power, if not the authority itself, are regarded as illegitimate. Thus as Etzioni points out, when lower participants become alienated from the organization, coercive power is likely to be required if its formal mandates are to be fulfilled.[13]

Moreover, all organizations must maintain control over lower participants. To the extent that lower participants fail to recognize the legitimacy of power, or believe that sanctions cannot or will not be exercised when violations occur, the organization loses, to some extent, its ability to control their behavior. Moreover, in-so-far as higher participants can create the impression that they can or will exert sanctions above their actual willingness to use such sanctions, control over lower participants will increase. It is usually to the advantage of an organization to externalize and impersonalize controls, however, and if possible to develop positive sentiments toward its rules.

In other words, an effective organization can control its participants in such a way as to make it hardly perceivable that it exercises the control that it does. It seeks commitment from lower participants, and when commitment is obtained, surveillance can be relaxed. On the other hand, when the power of lower participants in organizations is considered, it often appears to be clearly divorced from the traditions, norms, and goals and sentiments of the organization as a whole. Lower participants do not usually achieve control by using the role structure of the organization, but rather by circumventing, sabotaging, and manipulating it.

SOURCES OF POWER OF LOWER PARTICIPANTS

The most effective way for lower participants to achieve power is to obtain, maintain, and control access to persons, information, and instrumentalities. To the extent that this can be accomplished, lower participants make higher-ranking participants dependent upon them. Thus dependence together with the manipulation of the dependency relationship is the key to the power of lower participants.

A number of examples can be cited which illustrate the preceding point. Scheff, for example, reports on the failure of a state mental hospital to bring about intended reform because of the opposition of hospital attendants.[14] He noted that the power of hospital attendants was largely a result of the dependence of ward physicians on attendants. This dependence resulted from the physician's short tenure, his lack of interest in administration, and the large amount of administrative responsibility he had to assume. An implicit trading agreement developed between physicians and attendants, whereby attendants would take on some of the responsibilities and obligations of the ward physician in return for increased power in decision-making processes concerning patients. Failure of the ward physician to honor his part of the agreement resulted in information being withheld, disobedience, lack of co-operation, and unwillingness of the attendants to serve as a barrier between the physician and a ward full of patients demanding attention and recognition. When the attendant withheld co-operation, the physician had difficulty in making a graceful entrance and departure from the ward, in handling necessary paper work (officially his responsibility), and in obtaining information needed to deal adequately with daily treatment and behavior problems. When attendants opposed change, they could wield influence by refusing to assume responsibilities officially assigned to the physician.

Similarly, Sykes describes the dependence of prison guards on inmates and the power obtained by inmates over guards.[15] He suggests that although guards could report inmates for disobedience, frequent reports would give prison officials the impression that the guard was unable to command obedience. The guard, therefore, had some stake in ensuring the good behavior of prisoners without use of formal sanctions against them. The result was a trading agreement whereby the guard allowed violations of certain rules in return for co-operative behavior. A similar situation is found in respect to officers in the Armed Services or foremen in industry. To the extent that they require formal sanctions to bring about co-operation, they are usually perceived by their superiors as less valuable to the organization. For a good leader is expected to command obedience, at least, if not commitment.

FACTORS AFFECTING POWER

Expertise

Increasing specialization and organizational growth has made the expert or staff person important. The expert maintains power because high-ranking persons in the organization are dependent upon him for his special skills and access to certain kinds of information. One possible reason for lawyers obtaining many high governmental offices is that they are likely to have access to rather specialized but highly important means to organizational goals.[16]

We can state these ideas in hypotheses, as follows:

H3   Other factors remaining constant, to the extent that a low-ranking participant has important expert knowledge not available to high-ranking participants, he is likely to have power over them.

Power stemming from expertise, however, is likely to be limited unless it is difficult to replace the expert. This leads to two further hypotheses:

H4   Other factors remaining constant, a person difficult to replace will have greater power than a person easily replaceable.

H5   Other factors remaining constant, experts will be more difficult to replace than nonexperts.

While persons having expertise are likely to be fairly high-ranking participants in an organization, the same hypotheses that explain the power of lower participants are relevant in explaining the comparative power positions of intermediate- and high-ranking persons.

The application of our hypothesis about expertise is clearly relevant if we look at certain organizational issues. For example, the merits of medical versus lay hospital administrators are often debated. It should be clear, however, that all other factors remaining unchanged, the medical administrator has clear advantage over the lay administrator. Where lay administrators receive preference, there is an implicit assumption that the lay person is better at administrative duties. This may be empirically valid but is not necessarily so. The special expert knowledge of the medical administrator stems from his ability legitimately to oppose a physician who contests an administrative decision on the basis of medical necessity. Usually hospitals are viewed primarily as universalistic in orientation both by the general public and most of their participants. Thus medical necessity usually takes precedence over management policies, a factor contributing to the poor financial position of most hospitals. The lay administrator is not in a position to contest such claims independently, since he usually lacks the basis for evaluation of the medical problems involved and also lacks official recognition of his competence to make such decisions. If the lay administrator is to evaluate these claims adequately on the basis of professional necessity, he must have a group of medical consultants or a committee of medical men to serve as a buffer between medical staff and the lay administration.

As a result of growing specialization, expertise is increasingly important in organizations. As the complexity of organizational tasks increases, and as organizations grow in size, there is a limit to responsibility that can be efficiently exercised by one person. Delegation of responsibility occurs, experts and specialists are brought in to provide information and research, and the higher participants become dependent upon them. Experts have tremendous potentialities for power by withholding information, providing incorrect information, and so on, and to the extent that experts are dissatisfied, the probability of organizational sabotage increases.

Effort and Interest

The extent to which lower participants may exercise power depends in part on their willingness to exert effort in areas where higher-ranking participants are often reluctant to participate. Effort exerted is directly related to the degree of interest one has in an area.

> H6   Other factors remaining constant, there is a direct relationship between the amount of effort a person is willing to exert in an area and the power he can command.

For example, secretarial staffs in universities often have power to make decisions about the purchase and allocation of supplies, the allocation of their services, the scheduling of classes, and, at times, the disposition of student complaints. Such control may in some instances lead to sanctions against a professor by polite reluctance to furnish supplies, ignoring his preferences for the scheduling of classes, and giving others preference in the allocation of services. While the power to make such decisions may easily be removed from the jurisdiction of the lower participant, it can only be accomplished at a cost—the willingness to allocate time and effort to the decisions dealing with these matters. To the extent that responsibilities are delegated to lower participants, a certain degree of power is likely to accompany the responsibility. Also, should the lower participant see his perceived rights in jeopardy, he may sabotage the system in various ways.

Let us visualize a hypothetical situation where a department concludes that secretarial services are being allocated on a prejudicial basis as a result of complaints to the chairman of the department by several of the younger faculty. Let us also assume that, when the complaint is investigated, it is found to be substantially correct; that is, some of the younger faculty have difficulty obtaining secretarial services because of preferences among the secretarial staff. If in attempting to eliminate discretion by the secretarial staff, the chairman establishes a rule ordering the allocation of services on the basis of the order in which work appears, the rule can easily be made ineffective by complete conformity to it. Deadlines for papers, examinations, and the like will occur, and flexibility in the allocation of services is required if these deadlines are to be met.

Thus the need for flexibility can be made to conflict with the rule by a staff usually not untalented in such operations.

When an organization gives discretion to lower participants, it is usually trading the power of discretion for needed flexibility. The cost of constant surveillance is too high, and the effort required too great; it is very often much easier for all concerned to allow the secretary discretion in return for co-operation and not too great an abuse of power.

> H7   Other factors remaining constant, the less effort and interest higher-ranking participants are willing to devote to a task, the more likely are lower participants to obtain power relevant to this task.

Attractiveness

Another personal attribute associated with the power of low-ranking persons in an organization is attractiveness or what some call "personality." People who are viewed as attractive are more likely to obtain access to persons, and, once such access is gained, they may be more likely to succeed in promoting a cause. But once again dependence is the key to the power of attractiveness, for whether a person is dependent upon another for a service he provides, or for approval or affection, what is most relevant is the relational bond which is highly valued.

> H8   Other factors remaining constant, the more attractive a person, the more likely he is to obtain access to persons and control over these persons.

Location and Position

In any organization the person's location in physical space and position in social space are important factors influencing access to persons, information, and instrumentalities.[17] Propinquity affects the opportunities for interaction, as well as one's position within a communication network. Although these are somewhat separate factors, we shall refer to their combined effect as centrality[18] within the organization.

> H9   Other factors remaining constant, the more central a person is in an organization, the greater is his access to persons, information, and instrumentalities.

Some low participants may have great centrality within an organization. An executive's or university president's secretary not only has access, but often controls access in making appointments and scheduling events. Although she may have no great formal authority, she may have considerable power.

Coalitions

It should be clear that the variables we are considering are at different levels of analysis; some of them define attributes of persons, while others define attributes of communication and organization. Power processes within organizations are particularly interesting in that there are many channels of power and ways of achieving it.

In complex organizations different occupational groups attend to different functions, each group often maintaining its own power structure within the organization. Thus hospitals have administrators, medical personnel, nursing personnel, attendants, maintenance personnel, laboratory personnel, and so on. Universities, similarly, have teaching personnel, research personnel, administrative personnel, maintenance personnel and so on. Each of these functional tasks within organizations often becomes the sphere of a particular group that controls activities relating to the task. While these tasks usually are co-ordinated at the highest levels of the organization, they often are not co-ordinated at intermediate and lower levels. It is not unusual, however, for coalitions to form among lower participants in these multiple structures. A secretary may know the man who manages the supply of stores, or the person assigning parking stickers. Such acquaintances may give her the ability to handle informally certain needs that would be more time-consuming and difficult to handle formally. Her ability to provide services informally makes higher-ranking participants in some degree dependent upon her, thereby giving her power, which increases her ability to bargain on issues important to her.

Rules

In organizations with complex power structures lower participants can use their knowledge of the norms of the organization to thwart attempted change. In discussing the various functions of bureaucratic rules, Gouldner maintains that such rules serve as excellent substitutes for surveillance, since surveillance in addition to being expensive in time and effort arouses considerable hostility and antagonism.[19] Moreover, he argues, rules are a functional equivalent for direct, personally given orders, since they specify the obligations of workers to do things in specific ways. Standardized rules, in addition, allow simple screening of violations, facilitate remote control, and to some extent legitimize punishment when the rule is violated. The worker who violates a bureaucratic rule has little recourse to the excuse that he did not know what was expected, as he might claim for a direct order. Finally, Gouldner argues that rules are "the 'chips' to which the company staked the supervisors and which they could use to play the game";[20] that is, rules established a punishment which could be withheld, and this facilitated the supervisors' bargaining power with lower participants.

While Gouldner emphasizes the functional characteristics of rules within an organization, it should be clear that full compliance to all the rules at all times will probably be dysfunctional for the organization. Complete and apathetic compliance may do everything but facilitate achievement of organizational goals. Lower participants who are familiar with an organization and its rules can often find rules to support their contention that they not do what they have been asked to do, and rules are also often a rationalization for inaction on their part. The following of rules becomes especially complex when associations and unions become involved, for there are then two sets of rules to which the participant can appeal.

What is suggested is that rules may be chips for everyone concerned in the game. Rules become the "chips" through which the bargaining process is maintained. Scheff, as noted earlier, observed that attendants in mental hospitals often took on responsibilities assigned legally to the ward physician, and when attendants refused to share these responsibilities the physician's position became extremely difficult.[21]

> The ward physician is legally responsible for the care and treatment of each ward patient. This responsibility requires attention to a host of details. Medicine, seclusion, sedation and transfer orders, for example, require the doctor's signature. Tranquilizers are particularly troublesome in this regard since they require frequent adjustment of dosage in order to get the desired effects. The physician's order is required to make each change in dosage. With 150 patients under his care on tranquilizers, and several changes of dosages a week desirable, the physician could spend a major portion of his ward time in dealing with this single detail.
> Given the time-consuming formal chores of the physician, and his many other duties, he usually worked out an arrangement with the ward personnel, particularly the charge (supervisory attendant), to handle these duties. On several wards, the charge called specific problems to the doctor's attention, and the two of them, in effect, would have a consultation. The charge actually made most of the decisions concerning dosage change in the back wards. Since the doctor delegated portions of his formal responsibilities to the charge, he was dependent on her good will toward him. If she withheld her co-operation, the physician had absolutely no recourse but to do all the work himself.[22]

In a sense such delegation of responsibility involves a consideration of reward and cost, whereby the decision to be made involves a question of what is more valuable—to retain control over an area, or to delegate one's work to lower participants.

There are occasions, of course, when rules are regarded as illegitimate by lower participants, and they may disregard them. Gouldner observed that, in the mine, men felt they could resist authority in a situation involving danger to themselves.[23] They did not feel that they could legitimately be ordered to do anything that would endanger their lives. It is probably significant that in extremely dangerous situations organizations are more likely to rely on commitment to work than on authority. Even within nonvoluntary groups dangerous tasks are regarded usually as requiring task commitment, and it is likely that commitment is a much more powerful organizational force than coercive authority.

SUMMARY

The preceding remarks are general ones, and they are assumed to be in part true of all types of organizations. But power relationships in organizations are likely to be molded by the type of organization being considered, the nature of organizational goals, the ideology of organizational decision making, the kind of commitment participants have to the organization, the formal structure of the organization, and so on. In short, we have attempted to discuss power processes within organizations in a manner somewhat divorced from other major organizational processes. We have emphasized variables affecting control of access to persons, information, and facilities within organizations. Normative definitions, perception of legitimacy, exchange, and coalitions have all been viewed in relation to power processes. Moreover, we have dealt with some attributes of persons related to power: commitment, effort, interest, willingness to use power, skills, attractiveness, and so on. And we have discussed some other variables: time, centrality, complexity of power structure, and replaceability of persons. It appears that these variables help to account in part for power exercised by lower participants in organizations.

NOTES

[1]The term "lower participants" comes from Amitai Etzioni, *A Comparative Analysis of Complex Organizations* (New York, 1961) and is used by him to designate persons in positions of lower rank: employees, rank-and-file, members, clients, customers, and inmates. We shall use the term in this paper in a relative sense denoting position vis-à-vis a higher-ranking participant.

[2]Robert Bierstedt, An Analysis of Social Power, *American Sociological Review,* 15 (1950), 730-738.

[3]Robert A. Dahl, The Concept of Power, *Behavioral Science,* 2 (1957), 201-215.

[4]One might observe, for example, that the power of lower participants is based primarily on the ability to "veto" or punish. For a discussion of bases of power, see John R. P. French, Jr., and Bertram Raven, "The Bases of Social Power," in D. Cartwright and A. Zander, eds., *Group Dynamics* (Evanston, Ill., 1960), pp. 607-623.

[5]John Thibaut and Harold H. Kelley, *The Social Psychology of Groups* (New York, 1959). For a similar emphasis on dependence, see Richard M. Emerson, Power-Dependence Relationships, *American Sociological Review,* 27 (1962), 31-41.

[6]Although this paper will not attempt to explain how access may be measured, the author feels confident that the hypotheses concerned with access are clearly testable.

[7]*Op. cit.*

[8]Max Weber, "The Essentials of Bureaucratic Organization: An Ideal-Type Construction," in Robert Merton *et al., Reader in Bureaucracy* (Glencoe, Ill., 1952), pp. 18-27.

[9]Neal Gross, Ward S. Mason, and Alexander McEachern, *Explorations in Role Analysis* (New York, 1958).

[10]Robert Merton, The Role-Set: Problems in Sociological Theory, *British Journal of Sociology,* 8 (1957), 106-120.

[11]Erving Goffman, *Encounters* (Indianapolis, Ind., 1961), pp. 85-152.

[12]Etzioni, *op. cit.*

[13]*Ibid.*

[14]Thomas J. Scheff, Control over Policy by Attendants in a Mental Hospital, *Journal of Health and Human Behavior,* 2 (1961), 93-105.

[15]Gresham M. Sykes, "The Corruption of Authority and Rehabilitation," in A. Etzioni, ed., *Complex Organizations,* (New York, 1961), pp. 191-197.

[16]As an example, it appears that 6 members of the cabinet, 30 important subcabinet officials, 63 senators, and 230 congressmen are lawyers (*New Yorker,* April 14, 1962, p. 62). Although one can cite many reasons for lawyers holding political posts, an important one appears to be their legal expertise.

[17]There is considerable data showing the powerful effect of propinquity on communication. For summary, see Thibaut and Kelley, *op. cit.,* pp. 39-42.

[18]The concept of centrality is generally used in a more technical sense in the work of Bavelas, Shaw, Gilchrist, and others. For example, Bavelas defines the central region of a structure as the class of all cells with the smallest distance between one cell and any other cell in the structure, with distance measured in link units. Thus the most central position in a pattern is the position closest to all others. Cf. Harold Leavitt, "Some Effects of Certain Communication Patterns on Group Performance," in E. Maccoby, T. N. Newcomb, and E. L. Hartley, eds., *Readings in Social Psychology* (New York, 1958), p. 559.

[19]Alvin W. Gouldner, *Patterns of Industrial Bureaucracy* (Glencoe, Ill., 1954).

[20]*Ibid.,* p. 173.

[21]Scheff, *op. cit.*

[22]*Ibid.,* p. 97.

[23]Gouldner, *op. cit.*

Toward A Definition of Organizational Politics

BRONSTON T. MAYES
ROBERT W. ALLEN

Viewing organizations as political entities is not a recent phenomenon. March (7) suggested that organizations are political coalitions in which decisions are made and goals are set by bargaining processes. Other writers stressed the utility of taking a political perspective when studying organizations (1, 6, 9, 22). Anyone associated with almost any form of organization eventually becomes aware of activities that are described by employees as "political", but what is termed political by one observer may not be viewed as political by another. To understand the nature of political processes in organizations, some agreement as to what constitutes political behavior must be developed. This article attempts to shed light on the organizational political process by constructing a literature-derived definition of organizational politics (OP). Guiding this effort are the following assumptions:

1. Behavior referred to as politics takes place in varying degrees in all organizations.
2. Not all behavior in organizations can be categorized as political.
3. The organizational political process can be described in non-evaluative terms.
4. While many variables involved in describing organizational politics may be familiar to other organizational behavior concepts, a combination of these variables constitutes a unique process that

cannot be described adequately by existing paradigms. This unique process is organizational politics.

EARLIER ATTEMPTS TO DEFINE ORGANIZATIONAL POLITICS

Claims Against the Resource Sharing System

Political behavior in an organization has been viewed as actions that make a claim against the organization's resource sharing system. Harvey and Mills (4) utilized this definition in their treatment of the political aspects of adaptation to change. Their basic premise was that any adaptive change will produce conflict through its effect on the distribution of scarce resources among organizational units. This conflict was thought to be resolved by political processes including coalition formation, bargaining, side-payments, etc.

In a study of decision processes employed in purchasing computer equipment, Pettigrew (11) defined the political process as generation of demands for resources and mobilization of support for the demands generated.

Although some claims against an organization's resource sharing system may constitute political behavior, normally many of these claims would not be considered political. For example, an employee's asking for a salary raise, which constitutes a claim against the resource sharing system, would not be political behavior, but the use of threat to unionize to obtain a raise would be considered a political act. Circumstances surrounding the demand process must be considered in defining OP.

Conflict Over Policy Preferences

Wildavsky (21) suggests that the budgeting process is a political method of allocating financial resources, a notion consistent with the earlier Cyert and March (3) proposal that the budget represents the outcome of bargaining in the organization coalition. Wildavsky defines politics as conflict over whose preferences are to prevail in the determination of policy.

To define politics as a form of conflict seems too narrow an approach, especially when one limits politics to the conflict over policy decisions. The administration of policy involves political activities in its own right. Thus, a suitable definition of OP must include the politics of policy implementation as well as the politics of policy determination.

Another view of politics in the determination of policy is proposed by Wamsley and Zald (19). Their work relating to public organizations defines politics as the structure and process of the uses of authority and power to define goals, directions, and major parameters of the organizational economy. This definition may be suitable at upper levels of the organization but political processes also take place at lower levels where policy or system-wide decisions are not made.

Relationships of Control and Influence

In discussing power tactics used by executives, Martin and Sims (8) state that politics is concerned with relationships of control or influence. Although control, power, and influence are key issues in the study of OP, this approach allows inclusion of behaviors and forms of influence not normally considered political. An example of a non-political means of control in an organization is the periodic performance review when done in accordance with policy guidelines normally provided for this purpose. The review/appraisal constitutes a form of feedback to the ratee on his/her job performance and is a form of influence or control in that the employee is expected to correct performance deficiencies.

Burns (2), viewed politics as the exploitation of resources, physical and human, for achievement of more control over others, and thus of safer, more comfortable, or more satisfying terms of individual existence. Although this is a quite agreeable definition of politics, it fails to account for the fact that controlling others for personal benefit makes determination of what is political and what is not a province of the intent of the actor. A more rigorous approach would allow a definition of OP based on observable criteria exclusive of the actor's intent.

Self-Serving Behavior

Some writers have considered politics as behavior directed toward personal gain (2, 14). Although this approach is intuitively appealing, the argument can be made that all willful behavior ultimately serves some self-interest. If personal gain is the underlying motive for all calculated behavior, its inclusion in the definition of political activity adds nothing and may detract from definitional clarity. How is behavior classified if it is specified by the organization but also obtains rewards for the actor? Including self-interest in the definition of OP forces consideration of routine job performance as a political act. A suitable definition of OP must allow exclusion of routine job performance from consideration.

Field Research

A growing body of literature relates to the social influence process involving use of power and its effects on both the agent and the target of influence (17, 18). Almost no research has been conducted to explore organizational politics per se. Studies in print are concerned primarily with the effects of influence and power on decision processes.

Interviews and questionnaires were used by Strauss (16) to determine which techniques purchasing agents used to expand their power/influence in an organization. Of thirteen tactics discovered, he classified three as personal-political. Purchasing decisions were also studied by Pettigrew (11) and Patchen (10). Both field studies focused on who was influential in making purchasing decisions, what bases of power were used, and what methods of conflict resolution were apparent. Although Pettigrew addressed the issue of situational uncertainty in its effect on the power base of political actors, purchasing decisions would usually be considered rather structured and programmable in nature. Thus political activity surrounding these decisions might be restricted by rational problem solving techniques.

Although purchasing decisions are generally well structured, budget allocations are not. Recent work assessed the political nature of budgeting decisions in a university (12, 15). Researchers used unobtrusive measures to study the effects of departmental power on allocation of budgets. Departmental power was highly related to the department's ability to obtain outside grants and contracts. The greater the department's power, the less budget allocations were dependent on universalistic criteria of departmental work load and student demand for the department's courses. To assess the effects of uncertainty on criteria used to make research grant allocations, this research team in a later study (13) again employed unobtrusive measures. Their findings indicate that social influence is more likely to be used in uncertain situations. Unfortunately, none of these budgeting studies involved collecting data from individual actors in the decision processes. Influence effects were inferred from outcomes rather than measurement of processual elements.

TOWARD A DEFINITION OF ORGANIZATIONAL POLITICS

The definitions and research briefly presented above allow us to formulate a definition of OP that meets certain necessary conditions. First, a suitable definition would allow either micro or macro levels of analysis—consideration of both individual and organizational political phenomena. Second, it must allow for the use of politics in other than decision processes surrounding resource allocation. Third, any suitable definition of OP must clearly discriminate between political and non-political behaviors. For example, routine job performance is not a political activity but could be considered so if earlier constructs are employed.

What, then, is an acceptable definition of organizational politics? A thread of continuity through the existing literature is best recognized as influence. If outcomes alone are not sufficient to define political behavior, the processes whereby outcomes are influenced must be examined. Thus the notion of influence is a necessary but not sufficient condition for the inference of political action. A supervisor making routine job assignments influences the behavior of subordinates, but this form of influence is not political. Likewise, some forms of influence may not be intentional. Politics implies calculated influence maneuvering. But even restricting politics to calculated influence is not a sufficient condition, in that some forms of calculated influence should also be excluded from the OP construct. Is not the organization itself a form of influence calculated

Table 1   **Dimensions of Organizational Politics**

Influence Means	Influence Ends	
	Organizationally Sanctioned	Not Sanctioned by Organization
Organizationally Sanctioned	I. Non-Political Job Behavior	II. Organizationally Dysfunctional Political Behavior
Not Sanctioned by Organization	III. Political Behavior Potentially Functional to the Organization	IV. Organizationally Dysfunctional Political Behavior

to restrict the behavior of its members? The organization structure as it exists at some given point in time should be excluded from the OP construct, although *changes* made to the existing structure could be politically relevant.

Therefore OP is a dynamic process of influence that produces organizationally relevant outcomes beyond the simple performance of job tasks. Common organizational practice is to provide each member of the organization with a description of duties that specifies the organizationally desired job outcome and the limits of discretionary behavior acceptable in attaining those outcomes. Thus, the existing organization delineates both acceptable outcomes and appropriate means to their attainment for each job position. Activities within these sanctioned boundaries must be considered non-political. These considerations lead us to the following definition of OP:

> *Organizational politics is the management of influence to obtain ends not sanctioned by the organization or to obtain sanctioned ends through non-sanctioned influence means.*

This approach to a definition of OP is schematically represented in Table 1. Quadrant I, characterized by organizationally specified job behavior, is the only non-political quadrant in the classification system. Quadrant II contains political activities recognized by some bureaucratic theorists as abuses of formal authority/power (20). Behavior in this quadrant is dysfunctional from the standpoint of the organization, in that organizational resources are being utilized to further non-organizational objectives. The bureaucratic form of organization can be viewed as an attempt to eliminate this type of behavior.

Quadrant III defines political behavior undertaken to accomplish legitimate organizational objectives. The use of charisma or side-payments to accomplish sanctioned objectives would be included in behaviors assigned to this quadrant. Quadrant III activity could be

Figure 1   **The Influence Management Process**

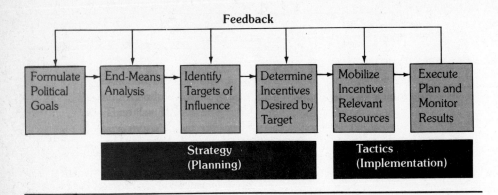

functional to the organization if undesirable side-effects did not occur. Indeed, some writers view organizationally functional Quadrant III behavior as leadership (5).

Quadrant IV behavior, like Quadrant II behavior, is dysfunctional from the organizational perspective. It deviates from organization norms with respect to both outcomes and methods. This form of OP will not be tolerated if it is discovered. Due to the possibility of being dismissed from the organization for such actions, individuals engaging in such behavior probably will be highly secretive, making Quadrant IV resistant to research attempts.

The management of influence (the process of politics) can be viewed as formulation of political objectives, ends-means analysis leading to decisions of strategy and tactics, execution of tactics, and feedback/control methods. Figure 1 is a simplified representation of the process of influence management.

In formulating political objectives, an individual within an organization shoul first take stock of whether desired outcomes are sanctioned by the organization. The political actor would determine if these outcomes are attainable through solitary action or if other persons must be involved. This ends-means analysis would lead to identification of targets of influence and the incentives required to effect the desired target behavior (see Figure 1). At this point in the process a political objective can be inferred if an individual other than the actor must be involved and if either the outcomes desired or the means of influencing the other person are not sanctioned by the organization (see Table 1). Thus the combination of outcomes and means employed to reach the outcomes defines the political nature of the influence process, while the process itself is a traditional managerial approach to problem-solving.

Although the influence management process is represented as a series of discrete actions, in reality it may be impossible to demonstrate clear distinctions among them. For example, identification of influence targets and their desired incentives would be expected to originate in the process of ends-means analysis rather than to follow it discretely. The concurrent execution of two or more stages of the influence management process is highly probable. But this should not detract from the utility of this conceptualization of the process.

This view of OP as an influence management process allows inclusion of variables already recognized by prior researchers. Even the earliest political writers were concerned with ends-means analysis as a strategic activity. The vast literature dealing with power and its effects fits into the political process model since influence targets (persons) and power bases (resources) are included in both strategic and tactical model elements. Also implied in this model is the concept that political activity can be an on-going organizational phenomenon such that one political act can trigger a chain of related political occurrences.

With an acceptable definition of organizational politics a logical step should be to formulate an integrated theory of OP. The dynamic nature of the political process seems to dictate a systems approach to political conceptualization. Within such systems, attention must be directed to individual as well as situational variables. For example, personality characteristics of political actors should be identified; politicians are hypothesized to differ from other employees in their willingness to pursue non-sanctioned objectives or in their use of non-sanctioned influence means. Non-political employees would be expected to discard objectives rather than to violate organizational sanctions. Situational or structural variables would be expected to interact with personality variables in the conduct of the political process. Some individuals might be expected to evidence political behaviors only under certain conditions, for example where goals or procedures are ill defined or in situations where the organization faces considerable uncertainty. Others may derive intrinsic benefits from engaging in politics and may do so in almost any situation. Clearly an opportunity exists in developing OP theory to provide a linkage between micro-oriented and macro-oriented organizational theoreticians.

REFERENCES

1. Allison, G. T. "Conceptual Models and the Cuban Missile Crisis," *American Political Science Review,* Vol. 63, No. 3 (1969), 689-718.
2. Burns, T. "Micropolitics: Mechanisms of Institutional Change," *Administrative Science Quarterly,* Vol. 6 (1961), 257-281.
3. Cyert, R. M., and J. G. March. *A Behavioral Theory of the Firm* (Englewood Cliffs, N.J.: Prentice-Hall, 1963).
4. Harvey, E., and R. Mills. "Patterns of Organizational Adaptation: A Political Perspective," in Mayer Zald (Ed.), *Power in Organizations* (Nashville, Tenn.: Vanderbilt University Press, 1970), pp. 181-213.
5. Katz, D., and R. L. Kahn. *The Social Psychology of Organizations* (New York: Wiley, 1966).
6. Kaufman, H. "Organization Theory and Political Theory," *The American Political Science Review,* Vol. 58, No. 1 (1964), 5-14.
7. March, J. G. "The Business Firm as a Political Coalition," *Journal of Politics,* Vol. 24 (1962), 662-678.

8. Martin, N. H., and J. H, Sims. "Power Tactics," in D. A. Kolb, I. M. Rubin, and J. M., McIntyre (Eds.), *Organizational Psychology: A Book of Readings* (Englewood Cliffs, N.J.: Prentice-Hall, 1974), pp. 177-183.

9. Pandarus. "One's Own Primer of Academic Politics," *American Scholar,* Vol. 42 (1973), 569-592.

10. Patchen, M. "The Locus and Basis of Influence on Organizational Decisions," *Organizational Behavior and Human Performance,* Vol. 11 (1974), 195-221.

11. Pettigrew, A. M. *The Politics of Organizational Decision-Making* (London: Tavistock, 1973).

12. Pfeffer, J., and G. R. Salancik. "Organizational Decision Making as a Political Process: The Case of a University Budget," *Administrative Science Quarterly,* Vol. 19, No. 2 (1974), 135-151.

13. Pfeffer, J., G. R. Salancik, and H. Leblebici. "The Effect of Uncertainty on the Use of Social Influence in Organizational Decision Making," *Administrative Science Quarterly,* Vol. 21 (1976), 227-245.

14. Robbins, S. P. *The Administrative Process: Integrating Theory and Practice* (Englewood Cliffs, N.J.: Prentice-Hall, 1976).

15. Salancik, G. R., and J. Pfeffer. "The Bases and Use of Power in Organizational Decision Making: The Case of a University," *Administrative Science Quarterly,* Vol. 19, No. 4 (1974), 453-473.

16. Strauss, G. "Tactics of Lateral Relationships: The Purchasing Agent," *Administrative Science Quarterly,* Vol. 7 (1962), 161-168.

17. Tedeschi, J. T. (Ed.), *The Social Influence Process* (Chicago: Aldine, 1972).

18. Tedeschi, J. T. (Ed.), *Perspectives on Social Power* (Chicago: Aldine, 1974).

19. Wamsley, G. L., and M. N. Zald. *The Political Economy of Public Organizations* (Lexington, Mass.: Heath Co., 1973).

20. Weber, M. *The Theory of Social and Economic Organization* (New York: Free Press, 1947).

21. Wildavsky, A. "Budgeting as a Political Process," in David L. Sills (Ed.), *The International Encyclopedia of the Social Sciences* (New York: Crowell, Collier, and Macmillan, 1968), pp. 192-199.

22. Zaleznik, A. "Power and Politics in Organizational Life," *Harvard Business Review,* Vol. 48, No. 3 (1970), 47-60.

An Exploration in Two Cultures of a Model of Political Behavior in Organizations

PETER J. FROST
DAVID C. HAYES

In the past few years, research interest in the concept of organizational politics has increased significantly. Early research by Dimock (1952) on conflict in bureaucracy, the writings of Burns (1961) on institutional change. March (1962) on political coalitions, and Wildavsky (1964) on the politics of the budgetary process, provide some of the historical antecedents to the current focus on the topic. More recently, Pettigrew (1973) has described, in a seminal book, a two-year study of politics and organizational decision-making in a retail organization. Pfeffer and Salancik (1974) studied the allocation of the university budget as a political process. Wergin (1976) outlines a political model for assessing organizational policy making. Efforts to conceptualize and define organizational politics can be found in the works of Burns (1961), Harvey and Mills (1970), MacMillan (1977), Mayes and Allen (1976), Pettigrew (1973), Porter (1976), and Robbins (1976). Pfeffer's (1977) discussion of power and resource allocation in organizations and Mechanic's (1962) views on sources of power of lower participants relate closely to the political domain of organizational behavior, without explicit development of a model of organizational politics. Despite some significant efforts to provide a theoretical understanding of organizational politics as a concept and a few pioneering ventures into its empirical examination, we feel that there is still no comprehensive definition of organizational politics and that there is ample room for extensive research into its antecedents and its consequences.[1]

A Context for Defining Politics in Organizations

As our starting point in developing a conceptualization of organizational politics, we have taken the view of organizations as market places for the exchange of incentives by both individuals and groups or coalitions of individuals who are members of the organization (Georgiou, 1973). Organizational incentives are perhaps most readily defined in terms of resources available for allocation among organizational members. Likely resources include money, information, goals, policy commitments and so forth. Organizational members, in this view of organization, tend to coalesce around shared interests in order to better seek common organizational outcomes (Baldridge, 1971; March 1962; Cyert and March, 1963). We view these coalitions of individuals as including groups of organizational members formally designated, such as the "Production Department", the "Executive Team", and the "Bargaining Unit", as well as combinations or groupings of individuals with shared interests and commonly desired outcomes who are less formally or less permanently drawn together. These latter coalitions are sometimes recognized by labels such as "concerned workers", or "young Turks", or the "inner circle". Clearly, all such coalitions in an organization are not equal. Some coalitions of organizational members tend to dominate others through their ability to control important resources, and can be viewed as dominant coalitions in the organization (Child, 1972; Thompson, 1967).

We have, at this point, a perception of organizations which includes the notion of exchange of resources between and among individual organization members, coalitions of individual organizational members, coalitions of coalitions, and individuals and coalitions, where one or more coalition may be dominant relative to others in the organization.

The Distribution of Resources

The distribution of resources in an organization can be thought of as being accomplished through agreements and trade-offs among individuals and coalitions of individuals in their bids to obtain influence over decisions perceived to be of most importance to them (Barnard, 1938; Blau, 1964; March and Simon, 1958; Pondy, 1970; White, 1974). There appear to be two phases to this process of exchange of resources in the organization; one phase has to do with the negotiation of an exchange, the other with the enactment of the terms of the exchange once negotiated. The negotiation phase would seem to be best represented as one in which values, goals, and priorities are problematic, to be worked out rather than given (Peery, 1975). Concern is with trading-off or bargaining between two or more organizational members (individuals or coalitions). This is the organizational arena which we would term political (Dimitriou, 1973), in which conflict is institutionalized (Cyert and March, 1963; Pettigrew, 1973). The enactment phase, on the other hand, is perhaps best represented as one in which values, goals and priorities are given. Concern is with the implementation of an exchange between two or more organizational members. Examples include activities such as payment of salary in return for work produced, or with a dominant coalition providing scarce research dollars to other organizational members in return for their having agreed to pursue dominant coalition objectives. We would term this the rational or administrative arena in which consensus rather than conflict is institutionalized (Peery, 1975; Dimitriou, 1973).

The Role of the Contract

An important linkage between these two phases of an exchange is the contract between the organizational members party to the exchange. Such contracts vary in degree of explicitness and formality and are established through negotiation. The contract itself specifies actions and activities to be undertaken in the enactment or implementation phase. In the ongoing process of organization, contracts are both outcomes of exchanges and important inputs to subsequent exchanges. The content of a given contract may provide the basis of precedent or serve as a memory source for subsequent exchanges. It is possible, therefore, to depict both stable and changing aspects of the organization process. Cyert and March (1963) make a similar point in their treatment of mutual control systems such as budgets and function allocation, both of which can be represented by the contract concept.

An exchange contract should represent the content of what each party to the exchange will provide in terms of resources and what each party expects of themselves and the other party so as to fulfill the contract. In addition to the programmed steps incorporated in such a contract, there are two less obvious aspects. Such a contract specifies, or at least implies, a discretionary or nonroutine zone of behavior for each party to the contract, which can be deployed to fulfill the contract terms. This is akin to the "zone of indifference" concept of Barnard (1938), or the "zone of acceptance" concept of Simon (1976). There is an additional indifference area of behavior within such contracts, however. This behavior centers on the use of organizational resources by one party to an exchange with which the other parties have no interest or concern. Such behavior would be considered by the parties as incidental to, unrelated to, or not intruding on the exchange between the parties to that exchange.

To summarize thus far, we assume that organizational members engage in an exchange process to acquire or influence the development and deployment of resources available in the organizational marketplace. We assume also that the outcome of such an exchange is a contract which specifies (in varying degrees of explicitness) expected behavior from each party to the exchange toward its enactment, areas of discretion or nonroutine behavior relevant to enactment of the exchange, and areas of indifference in which each party to the exchange uses organizational resources in ways of no interest or concern to the other parties to the exchange. We perceive the negotiating phase of the exchange process to be the likely arena of organizational politics. We perceive the enactment phase of the exchange process to be the likely arena of administrative (programmed) behavior.[2] Discretionary (acceptable, nonroutine) behavior is more difficult to locate within a single phase. It seems likely that discretionary behavior will be associated with both the negotiating and the enactment phases. It differs from political behavior in terms of acceptability and from administrative behavior in terms of routineness.

The Mechanism of Organizational Politics: The Role of Power

While the two primary phases involving a contract are concerned with negotiating or establishing a contract and its enactment, we perceive a number of subphases associated with the contract. Within the negotiation phase, attempts can be made to change the contract, unilaterally or multilaterally; efforts can also be made to resist change of the contract by one or more parties to the contract.

The resources available in the organizational marketplace derive from both the historical and current contributions which organizational members make to the marketplace. Members bring to an exchange the resources they have available to them. Such resources should provide the basis for participation in the exchange, and each such base can be conceptualized in terms of power (Dahl, 1957). Power is viewed here as the property of a social relationship (Emerson, 1962) and is defined after Dahl (1957), in the sense that A is powerful relative to B if A can get B to do something which B would not otherwise do. The probability that A will accomplish this is a function of B's dependence on A for the resources A has, as well as the degree of interest or need B has for the resources A offers (Emerson, 1962). The concept of coalitions of individuals allows a network view of power involving organizational members A and B with other members, so that dependencies among members are linked to availability and interest in the resources in the organizational marketplace. Power can be viewed as being both asymmetrical and reciprocal in a relationship between actors (Wrong, 1968). Thus, power may be balanced between or among actors to an exchange or it may be imbalanced, with power monopolized or centralized by one party. Wrong terms these intercursive and integral power respectively. Typically, exchanges involving a dominant coalition and other coalitions or individuals will be imbalanced in terms of relative power. A further important distinction introduced by Wrong is of alternating power differences. Actors in an exchange may alternate the roles of power holder and power subject (as in exchanges where a mix of professional (expert) and administrative resources are exchanged). Power differences may also be consistently reversed in given situations, one organizational member having greater power in one situation and the other member having greater power in another situation within the exchange. An example here is of union power in hiring and firing decisions and management power in long range technical planning. It is possible on this basis to view exchange and the establishment of contracts as dynamic processes in which the exercise of a power base by organizational members in an exchange relationship is characterized by degrees of symmetry, reciprocity and directionality. We have applied one further contribution from Wrong. He defines politics as "a struggle for power and a struggle to limit, resist and escape from power". (Wrong, 1968: 675-6).

DEFINING POLITICAL BEHAVIOR IN ORGANIZATIONS

Integrating the various perspectives on power, we observe that Dahl's (1957) definition of power connotes one party forcing another party to do something the latter would rather not do, whereas Emerson (1962) identifies the relational nature of power in the exchange process (as does Wrong), and Wrong (1968) conveys the sense of politics as a struggle involving power. What emerges from a consideration of these three perspectives, and of the resource exchange view of organization, is an image of organizational politics as having to do with behavior of organizational members which is imposed on another party to the exchange, is judged unacceptable by that party, and (implicitly) is resisted by that party. In terms of this definition, recognition of the behavior as an imposition and as unacceptable by one or more parties to the exchange qualifies the behavior as political in the eyes of these parties. Resistance to the behavior assessed as political is incorporated into the definition in the form of intent. Actual resistance is likely to be determined by variables such as the power difference between the parties involved, as well as the anticipated or perceived consequences of the political behavior.

We perceive political behavior to be associated with the negotiation phase and sub-phases of an exchange. Political behavior is expected to occur when one or more parties attempt to exchange resources or to limit, resist, or escape from a given resource exchange agreement in ways which are imposing to other parties to the exchange and likely to be resisted if recognized.

Operationalizing Political Behavior

We have suggested three types of behavior relevant to the two-phase exchange process. We expect political behavior to be most prevalent and most pertinent to the negotiation phase of the exchange process, and administrative behavior as most prevalent and pertinent to the enactment phase of the process. We expect to find discretionary behavior as pertinent and as occurring in both phases of the process. It becomes important to define these behaviors operationally in order to make explicit the distinctions among the three behavior types and to allow us to explore them empirically. The definitions derive from the considerations of exchange, contract and power discussed earlier and are as follows:

Administrative Behavior   The activities and actions of organizational members (individuals as well as formal and informal coalitions) when they use resources (for example, money, time, manpower) to enhance or protect their share of an exchange (involving themselves and other organizational members) in ways which are organizationally prescribed or routine.

Discretionary Behavior   The activities and actions of organizational members (individuals, as well as formal and informal coalitions) when they use resources (for example, money, time, manpower) to enhance or protect their share of an exchange (involving themselves and other organizational members) in ways which are nonorganizationally prescribed or nonroutine. Such nonprescribed or nonroutine behaviors reflect a consensus within the organization or between the parties to the exchange that the behaviors, while informal, are acceptable or are behaviors to which other parties to the exchange are indifferent.

Political Behavior   The activities and actions of organizational members (individuals, as well as formal and informal coalitions) when they use resources (for example, money, time, manpower) to enhance or protect their share of an exchange (involving themselves and other organizational members) in ways which would be resisted, or ways in which the impact would be resisted, if recognized by the other parties to the exchange.

Examination of these definitions of behavior reveals a major distinction between administrative and discretionary behavior on the one hand, and political behavior on the other hand. Administrative and discretionary actions and activities are viewed by parties to the exchange as *consensus* behavior. There is agreement that the behavior is legitimate in terms of the exchange. Political actions and activities, however, are resisted or will be resisted if their intent is recognized, by one or more parties to the exchange. There is a lack of consensus, a *non-consensus* about the legitimacy of the behavior among parties to the exchange. While political behavior represents non-consensus behavior as we have defined it, it must be emphasized that no evaluative connotations are intended for the concept of political behavior (Mowday, 1976; Porter, 1976). That is, political behavior is neither good nor bad. Evaluation of behavior, political or non-political, as good or bad requires an assessment of its outcomes as it relates to the exchange itself and to the parties to the exchange. Political behavior may result in benefits or costs (or both) to the party invoking it and to one or more of the other parties. The perceptions of each of the parties to an exchange are important if we are to establish that a behavior is political, discretionary or administrative.

Defining political behavior in the context of a resource exchange view of organization has several advantages. It allows us to deal with political behavior at several levels of organizational analysis: individual, unit/group, and multi-unit levels. It avoids the need to describe and analyze political behavior with reference to theoretical abstractions such as "*the* organization", and "*the* organization's goals and desired outcomes". It enables us to treat political behavior not as an isolated or separate phenomenon, but as an integral part of a model of organization which focuses on resource exchange between and among organizational members.

Other attempts have been made to capture the meaning of organizational politics and of political behavior in organizations. Mayes and Allen (1976) have categorized other definitions of organizational politics in the literature into those describing it as a process involving claims against the resource sharing system, as conflict over policy preferences, or as self-serving behavior. Given an assumption that organizations are marketplaces for resource exchange we would describe all behavior as primarily self-serving in the sense that exchanges are entered into first for what they have to offer and second for what must be given in return. Behavior is self-serving, but it can also be intended to serve others. Self-serving behavior is political as we define it when the intent or the perceived intent is not to serve others, or is to misserve others. In similar vein, claims against the resource system and conflict over policy preferences may or may not be political, depending on whether the behavior is viewed as consensual by the parties involved.

Mayes and Allen provide their own deductive definition of organizational politics as "the management of influence to obtain ends not sanctioned by the organization or to obtain sanctioned ends through non-sanctioned influence means" (Mayes and Allen, 1976:8). The definition makes a step toward a more analytic treatment of the concept than had earlier definitions. Introducing the notion of non-consensus *means* and non-consensus *ends* provides for the possibility of differences in tactics and focus of political behavior. However, the definition is limited in our view, by exclusive emphasis on self-serving behavior and by being tied to considerations of *the* organization, issues we have discussed earlier. Nevertheless, the links between this definition and our own become clear if we modify the Mayes and Allen approach by replacing *the* organization by "other parties to an exchange" and by interpreting the "management of influence" to mean the use of power. The use of nonsanctioned means (to sanctioned ends) and the pursuit of non-sanctioned ends (by sanctioned means) then become specific types of political behavior available to a party or parties involved in negotiating an exchange. Porter's (1976:5) definition of organizational politics as self-interested behavior outside that required or desired by the organization, or forbidden by the organization, also has ties with our approach if one relinquishes notions of *the* organization and behavior forbidden (by the organization) in favor of concepts such as coalitions, exchange processes and consensus and non-consensus behavior.

THE STUDY

The exploration of our model of organizational politics was conducted in two technological institutes, one in Australia, the other in Canada. These two educational institutions are similar along several dimensions although differing substantially in some of their structural characteristics. Focus in this study was on the departmental or unit level of analysis.

The Organizations Studied

Both organizations are institutes of technology offering courses in several disciplines and subdisciplines. The Australian institute has four faculties or schools (Business, Applied Science, Engineering and General Studies). The Canadian institute has four faculties or divisions (Business, Engineering, Health Services and a Core Division comprising departments of Physics, Chemistry, Mathematics and English). The current full time enrollment figures are 4000 (Australian) and 3100 (Canadian). Both institutes have a fundamental emphasis on teaching rather than research (with consequent heavy teaching loads), and instructors stress pragmatism and technology rather than theoretical aspects of the various subjects they teach. The Australian institute offers a three-year degree program and a two-year diploma program; the Canadian institute offers a two-year diploma program.

There are several structural differences between the two organizations. In 1973, the Australian institute was incorporated with other such institutes into a national network of Colleges of Advanced Education which are federally funded. The Canadian institute became an autonomous organization within its education system in 1974, and is funded by the province in which it is located. The faculty in the Australian institute are not formally unionized; the faculty below department head in the Canadian institute are unionized. A union of administrative staff also exists in this latter organization. The Australian institute is in the midst of an extensive appraisal of its structure and decision-making process. Currently, key decisions concerning allocation of resources as well as major policy formulation are made by the Director of the Institute (President) in informal consultation with the Deans of the four faculties. Interestingly, the Canadian institute has been through a similar process in the past two years. It has decentralized decision-making considerably through formation of an education committee comprising the Deans of faculties, heads of key service departments (e.g., library, career programs) and an executive director who links with the Principal of the Institute and his executive committee. This formally constituted committee has considerable discretion with respect to allocation of resources.

In general it would appear that the Canadian institute has a more extensively developed formal structure than its Australian counterpart, and is also in the process of implementing formal performance evaluation procedures and systems for long-range planning, which are not in evidence in the Australian institute.

METHOD

The Sample

The total sample of respondents, twenty-two at the Canadian institution and eleven in the Australian, was reduced, for purposes of the study, to twenty respondents, ten from each institute. This was done as a control device to attempt a closer match of respondents in terms of functions and responsibilities. For reasons of time and access, different strategies of data gathering were employed at each institution. In the Australian sample an in-depth study of one faculty (Dean, department heads and individual faculty members) as well as three service departments located in other faculties was performed. In the Canadian institution, a cross-sectional study of Deans and department heads in all faculties and general service areas was undertaken.

The sample of respondents from the Canadian institution included in this report represents department heads in the faculty corresponding to the Australian institution as well as those of service departments to this faculty. The major difference in terms of hierarchical level and function, therefore, is the inclusion of respondents in non-administrative positions in only one sample. It should be emphasized, however, that a departmental or group level of analysis was the emphasis in both samples, and that, in effect, both "line" and "staff" positions were studied in each institute.

Data Collection

The steps employed in the study are diagrammed in Figure 1 to enhance understanding of the procedures we followed.

A patterned interview was undertaken with each of the participants in the study. The interviews were tape recorded. The questions were of two main types. First, background information questions were asked to elicit demographic data on respondents, to set the general tone for the interview (i.e., the department/group focus) and to make the respondents feel at ease with the tape recorder. Second, questions derived from the definition of organizational politics, dealing with the establishment, maintenance and alteration of resource exchange agreements among departments were asked. (These are listed in the Appendix.) These questions deal with activities which are undertaken to set up arrangements such as joint program development, service course arrangements and joint equipment usage; activities which are undertaken to maintain satisfactory arrangements of these types; and activities which are undertaken by either party to an arrangement to unilaterally alter the arrangement or to avoid its implementation. Emphasis in the interview was placed on eliciting specific examples of behavior which each interviewee was able to relate to each of these phases of an arrangement. The analysis reported here deals with responses to this series of (eight) questions.

Figure 1

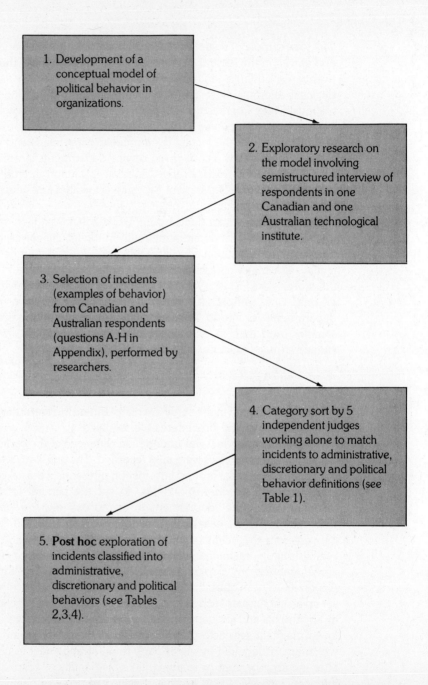

1. Development of a conceptual model of political behavior in organizations.

2. Exploratory research on the model involving semistructured interview of respondents in one Canadian and one Australian technological institute.

3. Selection of incidents (examples of behavior) from Canadian and Australian respondents (questions A-H in Appendix), performed by researchers.

4. Category sort by 5 independent judges working alone to match incidents to administrative, discretionary and political behavior definitions (see Table 1).

5. **Post hoc** exploration of incidents classified into administrative, discretionary and political behaviors (see Tables 2,3,4).

*Two additional steps were employed between (3) and (4) but are not reported in this paper. The effect of these steps was to "clean up" the incidents sorted by the judges in step 4, via the elimination of a large number of incidents.

ANALYSIS

The transcripts of the interviews from both sets of subjects were analyzed for actual examples of departmental behavior provided in response to these questions (see Appendix). One hundred fifty-nine such examples were obtained, typed on separate sheets, numbered randomly and presented to a group of judges for content analysis. This part of the analysis was performed in order to determine whether independent judges, given no information other than the examples of behavior, would be able to group them into categories resembling administrative, discretionary and political behavior, as well as being able to determine the similarities and overlaps between such categories. The content analysis and associated retranslation by a different set of judges derived six dimensions of behavior which, though of value, did not yield the categories of interest in this study and are not reported in this paper. What we report herein is the outcome of a classification exercise by a third set of judges asked to categorize a subset of examples of behavior according to the operational definitions of political, administrative and discretionary behavior which we provided. The behavioral incidents to be classified were items which had survived the initial judging and retranslation process and which we considered to be unambiguous and unidimensional as a result of the earlier two judgement stages. We assigned five judges to work independently at this final task,[3] and instructed them to attempt to place the examples in one of four categories—administrative behavior, discretionary behavior, political behavior, or "unclear"; the latter category for items which the judges could not comfortably fit into the other three categories.

The prior analyses, omitted from this paper as indicated above, had the effect of reducing the set of examples given to this group of judges down to 60 incidents (slightly more than one-third of the original sample). In order to give greater confidence in interpretation of the classifications (in terms of administrative, discretionary and political behavior), we included for analytical purposes only the items on which either all, of four out of five, judges agreed on a given categorization. This left slightly less than half of the items for purposes of discussion and analysis (29 out of 60). If a simple majority-rule for inclusion of items had been adopted, 56 out of 60 items would have survived, indicating almost unanimous agreement among judges on classification. We felt more comfortable applying the "80 per cent or greater" inclusion rule in terms of the degree of confidence it allowed us in interpreting our results. Nevertheless, the impact of this decision in reducing the sample size should be recognized.

Table 1   Behavioral Categories by Country of Institution

	Administrative	Discretionary	Political
Canada	4	2	8
Australia	5	5	5

As presented in Table 1 (on page 379), the final items were almost evenly split between the two institutions (14 Canadian and 15 Australian) reflecting the even distribution in the set of sixty items examined by the judges.[4]

DISCUSSION

As indicated in the Appendix, the questions asked of respondents focused on specific examples of behavior which occurred when departments set up, carried out, resisted or unilaterally changed arrangements between themselves and other departments. (We did not mention to our interview subjects our administrative/discretionary/political behavior distinctions. They were not aware that the study focused on political behavior.) The incidents categorized by the independent judges on the basis of the definitions we provided have several interesting characteristics which we explore in this section of the paper.

It must be borne in mind that the nature of the data and the small size of the sample make generalization inappropriate. The discussion which follows is, like the study, intended to be exploratory and illustrative of what we perceive to be a potentially rich perspective on behavior in organizations. The ideas and interpretations offered are not made in the usual sense of being generalizable to other situations, but rather as bases for further research in the area. This *caveat* is critical for the reading of the remainder of the paper.

As a first step in interpreting data, we observe from the Appendix and Tables 2–4 that, as would be predicted by our definitions of political and nonpolitical behavior, items provided in response to questions eliciting examples of activities involved in *enacting* or *implementing* arrangements (question B) only appear in the administrative and discretionary categories. The judges did not perceive these activities to be political in terms of the definition provided. Examples dealing with the *setting up* of arrangements also fall into these two categories, and not that of political behavior. Finally, although some items in response to questions involving *unilateral change* of arrangements (questions C, D, E, G, H) and some activities aimed at *increasing* the share of resources (question F) are classified as discretionary or administrative, the majority of examples provided were perceived to be political. In other words, the enactment phase behaviors analyzed were judged as either administrative or discretionary. Most negotiation phase (and subphase) behaviors were judged political, but a few behaviors generated in response to "negotiation phase" interview questions were classified by judges as discretionary or administrative. This finding highlighted the need for an examination of the examples for possible similarities in the political, discretionary and administrative behaviors linked to the negotiation phase, as well as an assessment of whether there were differences between such administrative and discretionary behaviors and those linked with the enactment phase.

Table 2	Representative Examples of Administrative Behavior (Questions which elicited the response are indicated)

(F) When there is a general requirement for more funds, we build the arguments on the size of the department—staff numbers, student numbers, number of programs offered, service courses provided to others and so on.

(A) For example, we're giving a course; we're already providing training for real estate salesmen for industry in cooperation with the university, and our students have gone out in the industry and have done exceptionally well. We have the industry actually recruit our students for jobs in various aspects of real estate where students have had no specific real estate training. So it's a question here of showing what we have done and what we can do, what our strengths at the Institute are.

(E) We've had a problem with a number of requests for servicing involving noneducational activities. People were coming to us direct to develop publicity materials and that sort of thing and it became quite embarrassing to have to refuse a Dean. In that case, I approached our Dean and the registrar, and they issued a formal statement saying that we were not to do these things unless authorized by the registrar.

(G) I would venture to say six months, it has got to be almost six months ago, two faculties came to the Education Committee with recommendations that they revert from the quarter system to semester system. These things were tabled and left hanging and all the rest of it. And they were lifted from the table and a decision was made. And the decision that was made bounced back on us in the Education Committee. Then a committee was struck to look at it again and the committee came in with recommendations, came back to the Education Committee. Finally one of the two faculties said: "Look we've got to go with it, the decision was made, it is done."

(A) We use the Educational Development Committee fairly extensively. We have extended the committee recently by appointing what we term Educational Development Unit liaison officers, who are people in each department to liaise between the Educational Development Unit and their department.

(B) We have improved the equipment circulation service and I have figures every month on cost of staff, statistics every month as to what equipment was used by what department as well as periodic reports from supervisors and complaints or comments from the various departments—we monitor the situation that way.

Examining for patterns within categories, it appears from the examples, provided in Table 2 that there are differences in focus within the category of administrative behavior. The focus varies from construction of arguments to acquire resource increments through the formal mechanisms of the organization, to public relations exercises, to use of the formal hierarchy to protect one's department against encroachment, to formal integration mechanisms, to system perfor-

Table 3   Representative Examples of Discretionary Behavior
(Questions which elicited the response are indicated)

(G) The elaborate laboratory set-up we have now and the radical revisions in our beginning course's educational methods were effectively the ideas of one person and the team of staff he got working for him. From that beginning on his own initiative, we put in a special proposal to the government funding body to fully fund the preparation of the necessary special materials for this course, which was granted for one year. At the end of that time it was so successful that we were able to convince the institute to pick up the tab for the on-going costs in future years.

(B) For instance, at the graduate diploma level, we make sure we only have people teaching who can relate to students. This is because when I came most of our department confirmed everyone else's prejudices of our being a soft area. So we've been very conscious of the fact that we've had to market ourselves.

(A) We recently developed a joint program with another faculty. That was quite an exciting thing as there seems to be some traditional feelings that the two faculties don't get on well. We were able to win support in principle for that combined degree, and then we were able to win support right down the line that it was a worth while thing.

(A) It's happened with another department this last spring; they decided they would like an elective course for their second-year students—the first-year students get math as a requirement, but an elective for their second-year students. So the department head came to me and said, "Would this be possible?" , and I went back to my department and asked were they willing to staff it in spite of their overload. The department is overloaded relative to institute. They said yes—on a one-year basis they would try it. And so I went back to the other department and said "Yes". Then I got the instructor who agreed to teach it, and we talked to them. It's a very sort of unstructured process. . . .

(A) They say what they think they would like and we say whether we think this is pedagogically possible in the time allotted. Then there is a lot of compromise and then a course outline and then it starts.

(B) The other way, from that Faculty servicing us, is most inefficiently operated at the moment, and that's a criticism of ourselves. We look for occasional *ad hoc* feedback by bumping into someone in the hall and by being reasonably friendly with the people who take classes, to every now and then just have a talk and say: "How is it going, do you have any particular problems?"

mance monitoring. In each of the examples, a different use is made of the administrative system. Some refer to internal (to the department) mechanisms; others, which are external, refer to formal interdependencies within the organization. It is interesting to note that these uses of "administrative" behavior are not judged as political, since, as described, they do not constitute actions and activities which other parties to an exchange do, or would find to be unacceptable and so a cause for resistance. That is, they are consensus behaviors.

However, the examples of administrative behavior generated in response to negotiation phase questions were not anticipated, given the conceptual framework discussed in the initial portion of the paper. While no conclusive statements can be made on this observation given the sample sizes in the study, it does emphasize the need for a careful test of the assumptions we make about behavior and the exchange phases in developing our conceptual framework. The observed external focus of such behavior also highlights the need to assess perspectives of all parties to an exchange if we are to accurately capture the nature of the three categories of behavior we have developed.

Similarly, the examples of discretionary behavior in Table 3 show differences in focus. There appear to be parallels to the situations involving administrative behavior. Internal activities, such as the establishment of new teaching programs, and external activities with varying degrees of (informal) interdependencies, e.g., joint program development and the gathering of *ad hoc* feedback on performance, all fall within the category of discretionary behavior as judged in this study. The same broad dichotomy of focus, internal *versus* external (interdependence), is not in evidence within the category of political behavior. The thrust of each instance of political behavior is clearly external to the particular department or unit; that is, it is directed toward other departments. Examples from Table 4 include attempts to increase resources available to a department, efforts to resist resource increments to others, and reactions against imposition of change by others. That is, the focus of the political behavior example is on negotiation with other units not enactment of previously negotiated contracts nor the administration or operation of a particular subunit.

Interestingly, the items in this study which have been judged as political describe behavior which is strikingly similar to that discussed by Pfeffer (1977) in his treatment of power and its use in maintaining and allocating resources. For example, Pfeffer talks about the way in which subunits can achieve power through alliances with internal and external groups (Pfeffer, 1977: 259). Both such alliances are described as political behavior in items reported in this study. The hiring of auxiliary people and $2500 subscription is an example. As a second example, Pfeffer talks about the use of committees to legitimate allocation decisions in organizations (Pfeffer, 1972: 242). A reported behavior in our study describes the use of a committee and the timing of a committee meeting to "push through" a unilateral decision to reduce the number of hours taught in a particular course.

Thus, in terms of our definition of political behavior, we see examples of actions which reflect non-consensus behaviors. However, it should be noted in this context that the nature of exchange agreements, and the negotiating and enactment of such agreements, involves at least two parties. In all of the examples in this study, given the methodology employed, we are only dealing with one perception of the particular

Table 4   Representative Examples of Political Behavior
(Questions which elicited the response are indicated)

(F) You have to cheat a little, be a little unethical perhaps. Here is an example. We need something here in the department right now we should have. However, the commercial outlet that supplies it will not supply it to an academic institution. OK, right now we are speaking to a person who is in industry downtown, who can get it. So we are saying, "You take the $2,500 subscription and we will share the cost with you, and you give us 50% of the material because they send things in multiple copies. You give us the material—they don't really want it. Alright, at the same time I mentioned this to a university director here in the city. And he said, "When you get it, I want to share the cost too." So now we have three people, so we are reducing the cost. The only thing anyone here is going to see is "Hey, we have got access to this information." The Bursar will see it, because suddenly he is going to transfer money to some industry for a service to the department. The only person that will not see is the Institute that is supplying the material. As far as they are concerned it is coming to an industry.

(F) We do need staff. Our service has grown and needs for it have grown and we've asked for staff and we were frustrated in our request for fulltime staff members last year. We've been running with auxiliaries. I made damn sure we spent every cent we had in anything related to staff. As a matter of fact, I tried to overspend. Not in a wasteful sort of way, because the need is there and the services have been valuable, but I just made damn sure that every cent was spent. So that, in fact, is going to be a bottom line. At least it will be completely absorbed iout every cent that I had and you know some of them are full time regular positions. So that's the thing—spending money, plus actually soliciting the departments we're to serve, to say "For God sakes, let your department heads and Deans know that you want this service if you actually want it. I'll work for you if you work for yourself." This sort of thing. And so this information now is pumping up to Deans. "Yes, we do need a full-time person in a permanent position instead of this auxiliary situation."

(D) The Dean of one Faculty actually put to the Senate (in other words, the top academic group), that courses which involved a statistical content should be taught, as a matter of principle, by his faculty. And he then went even further to actually nominate subjects which he felt they ought to be teaching, which included, among others, marketing research. Now, his argument was based on the fact that you could always get the applied knowhow, a veneer of that, but you can't get the real theoretical stuff, you know, you've got to have a full mathematical type degree. Where of course, we argue, our students don't have to know how to prove a formula. What we do want is people who know how to apply it. And so there is a fundamental division in philosophy. Now, when he presented that, it was thrown out, and it was just agreed not to discuss it as being not worthy of discussion by this board. That, in fact, people accepted the principle that the course leaders know what are the needs of the courses. However, it is recognized at the same time that anybody who can contribute to a course should be given that opportunity,

Table 4	Representative Examples of Political Behavior (Questions which elicited the response are indicated)

because otherwise we could end up having mathematicians in every single department. So, in the sciences, all their people became unemployed.

(C) I went to see the Graduate division at the time, on my own and told them this proposal was going to cost them $5,000 to $6,000 a year. In my view, it's a worse deal. In other words, I attempted to sabotage what they were doing by a direct approach to the President of the Institute. But it didn't work. He had been bought off or didn't understand the issues. I don't quite know what, but as far as I was concerned, we lost that fight.

(E) If a system is introduced and I don't want to carry it out, I can tie it up from the purchase order end, the shipping end, the receiving end, the supplier end. It's tight knots from that point of view as far as once the item finally arrived, if it did, you know through the technical delays, this sort of thing. I can just keep on going. The unit comes in, it's say not approved, has to go back, comes in. You know you can use that type of thing. Budget, transfer many different ways, the institute is an incredibly complex place and the bureaucracy can work against you but it can also work for you, if you want it to. Basically that's what I would do, use bureaucracy to kill it or at least slow it down until finally people got so frustrated they just say "Oh, the hell with it."

(H) Some people use the staff society (a union) to resist change.

(H) For example, if I wanted to prevent the implementation of some recent recommendations, all I would have to do would be to go around and tell people it was the greatest load of crap that had ever been written and to ignore it, seeing I was on the committee that wrote it. I wouldn't do that, of course. You could, in my view, sabotage it quite easily. There's other people trying to do that, so I don't need to.

(H) In response to a recent report suggesting changes to be made in the institution, I set out on paper my own objections. I then circulated that to as wide an audience as possible within the organization. I am looking for support so as to be able to say "This group opposes it," not just "I oppose it."

(C) But if in fact I'm servicing somebody else's thing and they say, we want it that particular way well hopefully, the conflict is somehow resolved, you know, in a mutually satisfactory way. If it really came to the crunch, where we're told things, then I guess we would threaten as we did, in fact at the Senate, that "O.K., if that's the way you want it, we'll employ our own people. We'll get a statistician in here, don't you worry about it any more, you look after your place and we'll look after ours." And so in an ultimate situation, the people who direct the programs, who are ultimately responsible for them, would argue that if they won't cooperate with us, that we'll do it our way.

(D) One of the departments cut their math hours from 5 hours to 4 hours in quarter A, and 3 hours in quarters B and C, and this was done without any

Table 4	Representative Examples of Political Behavior Continued (Questions which elicited the response are indicated)

consultation wih anybody. In fact, I didn't know anything about it, until one of my instructors said: "Hey, how come I've only got 3 on my time table." In that case it was hopeless. It was partly a case which fell through the cracks in the system. (The Senior Education committee had just started.) The Acting Dean of our faculty was told about 3 o'clock in the afternoon that the Committee had an emergency meeting to be held at 4:30, could he come? He was not told the agenda. He said, "No, I have another meeting. I can't come." At that meeting they got this through the Committee. The Executive Director of the Committee should have killed it at that stage but he didn't. It went to the Academic Sub-Committee of the Board that night and to the full Board 2 days later and it was done. I think it was an intentional strategy partly due to anxiety and pressure in the department itself. They were under pressure to reduce the physical sciences content. I think it was due in part to a personality clash between the previous Head of our department and the Head of that department. I think it was partly a convenient thing for them to do, if they could get it that way. Kind of, "We'll take what we want if we can, or we'll justify it if we have to."

exchange, that of the reporter of each example.[5] Potentially, focus on a particular exchange as the research emphasis and obtaining the perceptions of the other parties to the exchange would lead to a more complete understanding of the behavior and to the delineation of networks in which perceptions as to the intent or result of particular actions would likely vary considerably among network members.

For example, take the case of a multilateral exchange involving five parties, A–E. A's intent in the exchange may be political, but only perceived to be so by B; parties C, D and E may perceive A's behavior as discretionary. Such multiple and conflicting perceptions of behavior are to be expected in complex systems, and reflect the nuances of coalition formation and operation, and the networks of interdependencies in such systems. The description of such networks of perceptions would, in effect, provide us with interesting snapshots of significant organizational exchanges processes: we would be able to more fully explore the exercise of power, perceptions of power bases, rationales for particular courses of action, the nature of the formal administrative system and how it operates, potential "bugs" or "loopholes" in enacted contracts represented in control or budget systems, etc. Even with the one-sided perspective which our examples provide, this richness comes out in several of the examples classified as representative of political behavior. As an illustration, take the item in which the individual boasts that he can tie things up in a number of ways in order to prevent implementation (Table 4). His intent is readily discernible, yet given his knowledge of the operation of the formal administrative system of the organization, and his potential ability to shrug off complaints by others by making reference to "red-tape" and "bureaucracy", he can keep such intent well hidden. In fact, others may perceive the problem to be one of too much "bureaucracy", and not due to the exercise of power by the individual reporting the incident. Their response might be very different if the political nature of the behavior was recognized. Such covert behavior (behavior which would be resisted but is not since it is not recognized) would seem to capture the essence of what Bachrach and Baratz (1962) refer to as the "hidden face of power". The behavior by the department which ties up the bureaucracy has a non-consensus intent but it is also of a nature that it is not resisted because it is so well hidden that it is not recognized for what it is. Clearly, the methodological problems involved in exploring this notion of power are formidable. It remains, nevertheless, an intriguing area of political behavior for further investigation.

Contrasting with this "hidden power" activity is behavior which is more openly political. It is behavior which imposes, is not consensual, but is sufficiently overt that it can be recognized by other parties. Resistance by the other party to the exchange may follow, depending on circumstances and variables not captured in this study.

Instances of such behavior are given by some items in Table 4. One example deals with the recognition that some people use the union to resist changes: this is overt behavior, visible to other parties, and thus methods of resistance to it may develop. Similarly, the example of the use of the committee system to push through a change, although partially hidden in the particular example, is overt behavior capable of being resisted.

An important issue relating to the operational definitions of administrative, discretionary and political behavior concerns ability to discriminate among the three classes of behavior. This issue can be approached in two ways. Some evidence of discrimination is provided by the five independent judges completing their tasks with a relatively high degree of interjudge agreement. As indicated above, twenty-nine of the sixty items met the stringent inclusion rule of unanimous or 80% agreement among judges; another twenty-seven items were agreed to by three of the five judges. A 60 per cent agreement rule, therefore, would have included 56 out of the 60 items.

Additional evidence is provided by examination of the behaviors themselves. Administrative and discretionary behaviors have two characteristics not shared by political behavior. First, they represent consensus behaviors; behaviors which the parties to an exchange either tacitly or formally agree are appropriate or acceptable. Political behavior is non-consensus behavior; it is behavior which at least one party to the exchange does not perceive to be appropriate or acceptable. The second characteristic concerns the process aspect of the behaviors: the acts or procedures that are involved in their performance. Administrative and discretionary behaviors are, in some sense, voluntary processes: parties to an exchange act in ways they either wish to or normally do. Disagreeable or unusual actions and procedures are not involved. The very essence of political behavior, on the other hand, is that it represents an exercise of power, the imposition of the will of one party on one or more others, forcing them to do things they would not otherwise do.

Administrative behavior is distinguished from discretionary behavior on the basis of its routineness.

Further insights into the nature of what we perceive to be the process of political behavior in organizations can be garnered from items excluded from the original set by judges on the grounds that they were multidimensional. These items would seem to have a mix of administrative, discretionary and political behavior and indicate the dynamic nature of the process, as evidenced, for example, by the following illustrations:

> The senior person in part of our department is very keen to have another senior person to assist her. She didn't know that I had arrived at this same decision, privately too, and had already started the machinery in motion—because I didn't want her to be disappointed if we missed out. She came to discuss it with me, and I told her that I'd already put something in train to this effect—and that I thought I had a good chance of success if I did. It's now been stymied temporarily. So, I've said to her, 'Now, you've got to bring pressure to bear on the Dean.' He happened to wander into her office the week after he and I had had a contretemps—and he didn't know that I'd filled her in totally on the picture. So he said, 'How are things going?', and she hit him right between the eyes with 'I need another senior lecturer!'

And, from a service department head:

> One of the nuts I've been trying to crack is Department X. There is a tremendous amount of potential for visuals and for various other things in that Department. Their teaching methods in my opinion are quite archaic. I started off with the Department meeting. I threw out a few pieces of bait, in terms of what we could do and this sort of thing. I identified, from comments within the meeting, that there were some people who were fairly interested. Then I provided follow-up with one of those individuals. In fact, I went up and did some slides for them of Frank Lloyd Wright. Then I sat down with him knowing that he has a good rating with his instructors, knowing that his approach is reasonably well received by the students. I believe that if I can get that person singing the praises of the sort of thing I've done for him, then in fact I've got a good number of the department because there are some other people on the verge. So we are doing exhaustive research for him in terms of finding what packages are available, we're servicing him to death. Bring the stuff in, look at it, great, if it's not great, fine, talk with our graphic art shop designer. 'We'll make it for you.' We're servicing him to death. . . . Unless something fouls it up, which could be one of the segments of our service falling down and really annoying the person, we are going to be in that department.

As the above examples indicate, the administrative, discretionary and political behaviors do not necessarily occur on their own. Rather, we see evidence in these examples of the behaviors occurring in a sequential fashion. It is clear to us that the study of this mix, the nature of the sequencing, and interrelationships between the behaviors is an exciting and potentially fruitful area for future research.

We would also envisage within organizational contexts, different mixes of administrative, discretionary and political behavior. Potentially, these could be reflected in the form of profiles, empirically derived, which would depict this mix. (For example, Behavior emphasis: Situation A, administrative high, discretionary moderate, political low; Situation B, administrative low, discretionary moderate, political high; etc.) Our expectation is that several variables, such as managerial values, core technology and organizational structure, would be possible correlates of, influences on, or outcomes of this behavioral mix. We anticipate that such mixes would differ in appropriateness within different organizational contexts. For example, an over-emphasis on administrative programmed behavior (and by implication on contract enactment) may be dysfunctional when a task process is unpredictable. On the other hand a high incidence of political behavior may be the appropriate organizational response to rapidly changing environmental conditions.

CONCLUSION

This exploratory study has provided some interesting insights into political behavior in organizations. While the number of subjects as well as the number of organizations involved was too small to make any meaningful inferences, we can suggest, in a tentative way, that the institute members in each organization encounter similar types of problems and respond in similar kinds of ways to such problems. Much more detailed and extensive research is needed to substantiate this observation.

Some insights into the implications of organizational politics and to the distinction we have suggested between administrative, discretionary and politial behavior have been gained in the study. We are encouraged by the finding and intend to pursue several avenues of further investigation, which we hope will lead eventually to the development of a predictive model of behavior. As indicated earlier, the analysis employed in the study was extremely labor intensive, such that replication in a large number of organizations and involving a large number of respondents poses problems of cost and time. As one approach to further study of political behavior, we intend to utilize the preliminary results obtained as a means to constructing a different data gathering methodology which will attempt to capture patterns we perceive in the responses through clustering or factoring techniques. From questionnaire data, it should be possible to construct behavioral profiles which measure the relative "amounts" of the multiple categories of behavior as seem to be apparent in some of the incidents reported. We shall also attempt to explore the multidimensionality and sequencing of behaviors we have observed. Given the unobtrusive nature of political behavior and the importance of understanding its process, and the interdependence of parties whose behavior we study, it remains crucial, nevertheless, to pursue other "softer" techniques of research (such as interviews and participant observation) in our subsequent research on this concept. Further, the effect that political behavior has on other aspects of organization is a critical area of future research, the major area of interest being perhaps its impact in terms of organizational effectiveness.

The study of organizational politics is exciting. We believe that studying its occurrence, as well as its antecedents and consequences, will be an important field for organizational research in the years ahead.

REFERENCES

Bachrach, P. and M. S. Baratz. "The Two Faces of Power." *American Political Science* Review. 947–952, 1962.

Baldridge, J. F. *Power and Conflict in the University.* New York: John Wiley, 1971.

Barnard, C. I. *The Functions of the Executive.* Cambridge, Mass.: Harvard University Press, 1938.

Blau, P. M. *Exchange and Power in Social Life.* New York: John Wiley, 1964.

Burns, T. "Micro Politics: Mechanisms of Institutional Change." *Administrative Science Quarterly.* 6:257–81, 1961.

Child, J. "Organization Structure, Environment and Performance: The Role of Strategic Choice." *Sociology.* 6:1–22, 1972.

Cyert, R. and J. G. March. *A Behavioral Theory of the Firm.* Englewood Cliffs, N. J.: Prentice-Hall, 1963.

Dahl, R. A. "The Concept of Power." *Behavioral Science.* 2:201–218, 1957.

Dimitriou, B. "The Interpenetration of Politics and Planning." *Socio-Economic Planning Sciences.* 7:55–65, 1973.

Emerson, R. M. "Power-Dependence Relations." *American Sociological Review.* 27:31–41, 1962.

Freund, J. E. *Mathematical Statistics.* 2nd Edition, Englewood Cliffs, N.J.: Prentice-Hall, 1971.

Georgiou, P. "The Goal Paradigm and Notes Towards a Counter-Paradigm." *Administrative Science Quarterly.* 16:216–229, 1973.

Hall, R. H. *Organizations: Structure and Process.* 2nd Edition, Englewood Cliffs, N.J.: Prentice-Hall, 1977.

Harvey, E. and R. Mills. "Patterns of Organizational Adaptation: A Political Perspective." In M. Zald (ed.), *Power in Organizations:* 181–213. Nashville, Tenn.: Vanderbilt University Press, 1970.

MacMillan, I. C. "Organizational Politics—A Prerequisite Perspective for General Managements." In M. E. Nasser *et al.* (eds.), *Organizational Behavior: Readings for Management:* 93–110. New York: McGraw-HIll, 1977.

March, J. G. "The Business Firm as a Political Coalition." *Journal of Politics.* 24:662–678, 1962.

March, J. G. and H. A. Simon. *Organizations.* New York: John Wiley, 1958.

Mayes, B. T. and R. W. Allen. "Toward a Definition of Organizational Politics." Paper presented at the Summer, 1976 meeting of the Academy of Management. Kansas City, Missouri, 1976.

Mechanic, D. "Sources of Power of Lower Participants in Complex Organizations." *Administrative Science Quarterly,* 3:349–64, 1962.

Mowday, R. "The Exercise of Influence in Educational Organizations." Paper presented at Annual Meeting of the Academy of Management. Kansas City, Missouri, 1976.

Peery Jr., N. "Technical Rationality and Political Behavior Within Organizations." Proceedings of Academy of Management 35th Annual Meeting. Summer 1975, 179–181, 1975.

Pettigrew, A. M. *The Politics of Decision Making.* London: Tavistock, 1973.

Pfeffer, J. "Power and Resource Allocation in Organizations." In B. M. Staw and G. R. Salancik (eds.). *New Directions in Organizational Behavior.* 235–265. Chicago, Ill.: St. Clair Press, 1977.

Pfeffer, J. and G. R. Salanick "Organizational Decision Making as a Political Process: The Case of a University Budget." *Administrative Science Quarterly,* 19:135–51, 1974.

Pondy, L. R. "Toward a Theory of Internal Resource Allocation." In M. N. Zald (ed.), *Power in Organizations.* Nashville: Vanderbilt University Press, 1970.

Porter, L. W. "Organizations as Political Animals." Presidential Address, Division of Industrial-Organizational Psychology. American Psychological Association 84th Annual Meeting, Washington, D.C., 1976.

Robbins, S. P. *The Administrative Process: Integrating Theory and Practice.* Englewood Cliffs, N.J.: Prentice-Hall, 1976.

Simon, H. A. *Administrative Behavior.* 3rd Edition, New York: The Free Press, 1976.

Thompson, J. D. *Organizations in Action.* New York: McGraw-Hill, 1967.

Wergin, J. F. "Evaluation of Organizational Policy Making: A Political Model." *Review of Educational Research.* 46:75–84.

White, P. E. "Resources as Determinants of Organizational Behavior." *Administrative Science Quarterly.* 19:366–79, 1974.

Wildavsky, A. *The Politics of the Budgetary Process.* Boston: Little, Brown, 1964.

Wrong, D. H. "Some Problems in Defining Social Power." *American Journal of Sociology.* 73(6):673–81, 1968.

APPENDIX: PATTERNED INTERVIEW QUESTIONS

A. What kinds of activities or things did your Department or would your Department concentrate on to set up an arrangement with other Departments? (Tell me what it would do now if you can't recall activities involved in the past.) By activities I mean anything you would consider as important to ensure you reached an arrangement suitable to your Department, the strategies you would employ, the issues you would consider, etc.

B. Suppose your Department had established a satisfactory arrangement with another Department in the organization. If we look at what your department does to carry out the terms of the arrangement, can you think of what such an arrangement might look like for your department? What activities would your Department concentrate on to maintain the arrangement?

C. Let's look at a situation now where your Department wants to change an existing arrangement with another Department: one your Department was satisfied with but isn't now. Can you think of an example of such a situation relating to your department? What activities would your Department concentrate on in trying to change the arrangement?

D. Let's consider a different case now. Suppose that another Department has an arrangement with yours. Your Department is happy with the arrangement, but the other Department wants to change or even terminate the arrangement. What activities would your Department concentrate on to try to maintain or continue the arrangement?

E. Suppose you had an arrangement with another Department and you don't want to carry out the terms of the arrangement. You aren't trying to change the arrangement now, but to avoid carrying it out. Can you think of some examples of this? What activities would your Department concentrate on to resist implementing the arrangement?

F. Suppose it is budget time and your Department wants to change the size of the allocation of money, supplies and equipment, academic or support staff that you had been allocated. What kinds of activities would the Department concentrate on to try to accomplish this?

G. In general, in this organization, what do people do when they want changes made in the organization either within the Department, the faculty, or the institution as a whole?

H. In general, in this organization, what do people do when they want to prevent changes being made? Again, either in the Department, the faculty or the institution as a whole?

NOTES

[1] This research was generously supported in part by the Certified General Accountants' Association of British Columbia. We would like to thank the respondents to the interviews at the two institutions studied for their cooperation. We cannot name them individually due to the guarantee of anonymity provided.

[2] It is interesting to note, in this context, the recent observation on exchange and organizational interdependency by Hall (1977:238), "Once an exchange agreement had been reached, the nature of the interaction shifts. The interactions are more regularized and routine. The parties in the relationship give it less attention until a new exchange issue arises." Simon (1976) discussing "fact" and "value" in decision making and distinctions between policy and administration appears to be addressing the same issue.

[3] All judges were members of the Commerce Faculty at U.B.C., with teaching and research interests in the behavioral area.

[4] A chi-square test found no differences between institutions in terms of the behavioral categories.

[5] To this extent, we have a perspective of political behavior from one vantage point only, that of the department represented by the interviewee. More precisely, we have an interpretation of the nature of this behavior once-removed, since ascribing the behavior as political is done by a consensus of judges studying a behavior incident. To have asked the interviewee if the behavior was political would have been disruptive in this study, since it would have signalled our intent and biased the outcomes.

A Political Approach to Organizations: A Review and Rationale

MICHAEL L. TUSHMAN

Recent literature (2, 9, 43, 49, 65, 70) suggests a growing interest in viewing organizations as political systems. This kind of conceptual development is important for organizational analysis in providing a counter-point to more traditional views of organizations.

A political approach to organizations flows from the following assumptions:

1. Organizational analysts must make explicit their assumptions about organizations. Conceptual clarity at this level is important, since assumptions of organizational processes influence research and application projects at individual, group, inter-group, and inter-organizational levels of analysis. Argyris (6) made a similar point for clarifying one's assumptions of humanity.
2. Systems theory provides a useful framework for analyzing organizational behavior (OB). Conflict, bargaining, and other aspects of political behavior can be seen as a logical deduction of systems thinking
3. To understand OB, the unit of analysis must be the basic subunits which make up an organization. Following the systems framework, OB can be seen as a result of interactions among subunits within the organization. Individual behavior and individual differences, while important issues, will be tangentially considered in this discussion.

"A Political Approach to Organizations: A Review and Rationale" by Michael L. Tushman, *The Academy of Management Review*, April 1977, Volume 2, Number 2, pp. 206–216. Copyright © 1977 by the Academy of Management. Reprinted by permission.

Although the political approach to organizations is not new, it has been a neglected aspect of organizational functioning (13, 64, 65). More traditional views of organizations underemphasize the importance of power, conflict, and non-bureaucratic procedures. This article interprets theoretical and social issues which have resisted development of this political approach, as well as theoretical perspectives which have led to increased interest in it. A set of working assumptions is proposed as the basis of a political perspective, and the organizational development (OD) literature is briefly discussed from this political perspective.

DEFINITION OF TERMS

Sensitizing definitions for some terms must be introduced (the development of the area does not yet permit more formal definitions). *Politics* refers to the structure and process of the use of authority and power to effect definitions of goals, directions, and other major parameters of the organization (91, p. 18). From a political perspective, decisions are not made in a rational or formal way, but rather through compromise, accommodation, and bargaining. This perspective emphasizes differences in objectives and preferences of subunits and concentrates on processes by which these differences get resolved. Implicit in this definition is the issue of *conflict.* Conflict (where one group seeks to advance its own interests at the expense of another group) arises in organizations when interdependent subunits have inconsistent goals, have differing perceptions on how to reach a commonly held goal, or must share scarce resources (58, 78).

A subunit's relative political strength depends on its *power* over other areas for a particular issue. While this concept has not been neglected, analysts have not yet agreed upon its definition (57). Power will be defined here as the potential (or capacity) of an actor to influence the behavior of another actor in a particular issue area (26, 46). As in Emerson's (33) operationalization, power can be viewed as the obverse of dependence. Thus Unit A has power over Unit B to the extent that A controls resources important to B and/or to the extent that A monopolizes those resources.

PARADIGM DEVELOPMENT: AN APPROACH TO ORGANIZATIONS AND CONFLICT

Kuhn (51) and Allison (2) emphasize the influence of systematic approaches (paradigms) on the development of scientific disciplines. According to Kuhn, paradigms provide researchers with a set of conceptual lenses from which to view phenomena. The study of organizations has dominant paradigmatic elements (63, 72); trends developed during 1945-1960 pervade the literature. Schein's early definition reflects this more traditional view of organizations:

> An organization is the *rational coordination* of the activities of people for the achievement of some common *explicit purpose or goal,* through the division of labor and function, and through a *hierarchy of authority and responsibility* (77, p. 9, my emphases).

The emphasis here is on explicit and commonly accepted goals, rationality, and (while not stated in Schein's definition) cooperation, as basic organizational characteristics (10, 62). Conflict, disharmony, and ongoing organizational processes working against cooperation were not considered central organizational issues.

Some attention was paid to conflict, power, and political issues—for instance, conflict between the individual and the organization (3, 71). But most research on intergroup conflict did not pursue this conflict and its dynamics beyond the intragroup level without the use of superordinate goals (e.g., 32, 50, 95). There were important exceptions to this superordinate goal orientation (20, 30). Other OB studies concentrated on intergroup behavior independent of group or organizational processes (23, 37).

The literature on power in organizations has concentrated on the power of one person (the leader) over others (63, 75). This focus on vertical interpersonal power has resulted in a paucity of research dealing with differences in power between groups in organizations.

Systems Analysis: An Approach to Systems and Conflict

Before 1960, much of organizational thought and research was internally oriented (44). With the 1960's came systems theory and the notion that social systems could not be viewed in isolation. Organizational input, through-put, and output processes as they impacted and were effected by the environment became important research considerations (46, 58, 85). Uncertainty and its control became key organizational issues (85).

Besides increasing the importance of environmental issues, systems theory required that conceptual models of organization become more complex by emphasizing internal differentiation into subsystems. This differentiation has been associated with the development of local (idiosyncratic) perceptions, rationalizations, norms, and values as each subunit deals with its particular task and environmental requirements (53, 58). Cognitive, task, and hierarchical specialization, in turn, create conditions for vertical and horizontal conflict (46). Vertical conflict arises from status, hierarchy, mobility, and career differences (21, 28), while horizontal conflict arises from organizational specialization by task and environment (52, 58). If systems logic holds, these two strains of conflict are inherent in organizations; they can be moderated but not eliminated.

The advent of systems analysis was theoretically adverse to the notion of subunit goal congruence, to cooperation, and to integration at the organizational level of analysis (36). But these internally oriented implications were not pursued. Instead, the environment and its impact on the organization became a major theoretical and research area. With some important exceptions (27, 53, 98, 99), the benefits of systems thinking were not brought to bear on intra-organizational behavior.

Inter-Organizational Analysis (Organization-Environment Relations)

Empirical work on organization-environment relations is often phrased in political terms. Given a set of assumptions dealing with uncertainty and dependency as antithetical to organizations, Thompson (85) developed propositions and organizational strategies for reducing technological and environmental dependence. His design strategies involve organizational decisions regarding internal coordination costs and boundary spanning activities.

In dealing with the environment, Thompson (85, pp. 32-38) hypothesized, and Pfeffer (68, 69) and Kochan et al. (49) studied alternatives including: *competitive strategies* of maintaining environmental alternatives, seeking prestige, and seeking power; and *cooperative (collusive) strategies* of bargaining, coopting, and coalitions. The cooperative strategies are termed negotiated environments. Industrial organizations (53, 68), medical centers (39), universities (9), hospitals (69), and public agencies (88, 92) have been studied using this environment oriented inter-organization analysis.

While much is equivocal and contradictory in this research (61), systematic work has been done at the inter-organization level of analysis. But most organization analysts stop short of following through their inter-organizational and systems thinking. Thompson (85) and Child (22) recognize political behavior at the organization level of analysis, yet treat the organization as a black box controlled by dominant coalitions or what Hage and Dewar (38) call the organizational elite. The internal implications of systems and analysis have yet to be taken seriously, even with numerous case studies emphasizing the central role of power and conflict in intra-organizational decision making (19, 26, 29, 82, 96). Given the paradigmatic values of integration, superordinate goals, and cooperation at the organization level of analysis, a shift in emphasis towards treating conflict and bargaining as inherent organizational processes has made relatively little progress.

TOWARDS A POLITICAL PERSPECTIVE

Working Assumptions

Taking the systems framework and literature, a set of four working assumptions is developed, providing the basis for a political approach to OB. The utility of this approach for different decision making situations is then discussed.

The systems framework suggests that organizations can be seen as open systems which must be able to cope with environmental uncertainty (e.g., raw materials must be gathered and final product distributed) as well as task related uncertainty (e.g., technologies may be changing or tasks may require extensive coordination with other areas in the organization). To deal with sources of uncertainty, organizations tend to differentiate; they develop specialized subunits to deal with relatively homogeneous tasks and specific components of the task environment (46, 85). These subunits will be interdependent to varying degrees and will have to share scarce resources. This leads directly to the first working assumption:

A1:   *To understand the behavior of organizations, one must understand the dynamics and relationships among and between the subunits which make up the organization.*

Given resource scarcity and interdependent tasks, organization subunits must engage in joint decision making, but they are not equally powerful (43, 63, 70). In line with the systems framework and Emerson's (33) definition of power, subunits will be more powerful to the extent that they are able to control or cope with strategic contingencies or organizationally important sources of uncertainty (42, 64, 65). Since a subunit could control contingencies for one set of decisions and not others (e.g., market vs. technological decisions), the subunit power must be specified for the relevant issue areas.

A2:   *Subunits may not be equally powerful over different issue areas; subunits which are better able to deal with critical sources of uncertainty in a particular decision making area will be more powerful than other subunits in that issue area.*

The issue of power and influence is more complex. Since tasks and task environments are at least potentially unstable, the control of uncertainty and strategic contingencies must also be potentially unstable.

A2a: *The distribution of power and status within organizations will not be fixed or stable.*

This instability must be considered for a particular issue area as well as between issue areas. Given this potential flux, "the organization" may have meaning only in the short run. If so, a more appropriate concept, which captures this potential variability, is what Weick (94) calls organizing.

Assumptions 2 and 2a suggest that the distribution of power is not, in general, a stable organizational characteristic. Assumption 3 takes this source of organizational instability one step further:

A3:   *Subunits will act to decrease their internal dependence on others in order to limit the uncertainty which they must face and to increase their opportunities for growth and survival.*

This suggests that subunits will attempt to act on their environments in order to increase their power over critical issue areas.

Support for Assumption 3 can be derived from the systems ideas of subunit growth and development (46), and from Thompson's (85) speculations on organizational response to environmental dependence. Thompson has suggested, and other researchers have found, that subunits move to decrease their internal dependence through cooperative, competitive, and structural strategies (25, 30, 76). Weick's (94) idea of organizing explicitly recognizes these internal and external dynamics which continually redefine the organization.

A number of consequences result from subunit differentiation (A1) and the push of subunits towards greater autonomy and control (A3). The most important aspect of organizational differentiation may be development of particularistic norms, values, and languages to facilitate task accomplishment and to justify the subunit's growth and development (46, 58). Differentiation is also associated with development of subunit goals and interests which may or may not overlap with goals of other groups in the organization (36).

Differentiation creates organizational boundaries and internal dynamics which in turn adversely affect the ability to communicate between interdependent subunits. The greater the differentiation, the greater communication impedance and the greater the potential for conflict (53). These points lead to the final working assumption:

> A4:   *The greater the differentiation between subunits, the greater the difficulty of distortion-free communication, and the greater the potential for organizational conflict.*

These four assumptions suggest the basic outlines of a political approach to organizations. Assumptions A1 and A2 set the stage, while assumptions A3 and A4 provide the dynamics for political processes. OB can be seen as a result of decisions made by the bargaining and dealings of differentially powerful subgroups as they vie for scarce resources and cooperate on tasks which require mutual coordination. Different decisions will be of differing importance to the various subgroups and will set into motion internal haggling, eventually resulting in strategic decisions (22, 85). The dominant coalition (i.e., cliques that evolve to make the decisions) will not in general be the same over issue areas, nor is stability likely, even over similar issue areas, given environmental instability (9, 93).

Cyert and March (27) discuss sequential attention to goals and quasi-resolution of conflict, while Katz and Kahn see conflict as regulated through the dynamic of compromise and accommodation:

> . . . it is much easier for management to meet conflicts on a day to day basis, making concessions first to one part of the organization, then to another part, than it is to attempt the thorough reorganization which abstract logic might dictate. The alteration of concessions in response to the mobilization of forces means that organizations often jolt along and move by jerks and jumps (46, p. 95).

Whatever the term, quasi-resolution of conflict or the dynamic of compromise, the processes that result in "jerks and jumps" are the outputs of political processes carried out at the subsystem level of analysis. The political perspective directs attention to these processes. Although this perspective is not new, it has been of only tangential concern to organizational analysts (65, 87).

A Contingent Approach

This set of working assumptions, mapping out some components of a political approach to organizations, does not replace more traditional perspectives on organizations; it is a complementary approach, providing another viewpoint from which to look at OB. Its usefulness is contingent on the nature of the decision making situation (58).

The political perspective focuses on decision making processes between differentially powerful groups within the organization. If there is no need for joint decision making (i.e., no interdependence), and if there is no resource scarcity, then the subunits can make independent decisions (78). But if groups are interdependent and must share scarce resources, they must engage in joint decision making. Under these ubiquitous conditions, the political perspective has the most relevance.

Not all joint decisions are alike; they vary in the degree to which they are programmable. The political perspective is particularly useful for less programmable decisions. Thompson (85) distinguishes between two decision making dimensions: (a) the extent to which cause and effect relations are known (similar to a task or technology dimension); and (b) the degree to which standards of desirability (or goals) are agreed upon. These dimensions can be used in a decision making typology.

In cell A, more bureaucratic or universalistic decision making procedures can be used to reach a joint decision, since there is agreement on both means and ends. Most operational type decisions (work load, work scheduling, etc.) would fall into this category. While political issues are involved in such decisions (i.e., Dalton's factory or Crozier's industrial organization), it can be hypothesized that the political dynamics are less intense than in the other cells. This may be because it is relatively easy to measure outcomes for these types of decisions, or because the decision making structure is more likely to be centralized or governed by formal standard operating procedures (SOP's).

Cell D represents the other extreme from cell A. Decisions must be made where knowledge about cause and effects is unclear and where there is disagreement over desired outcomes. Strategic or long range decision making would fit in this cell (46). Such decisions cannot be easily evaluated or measured, and they involve resolution of conflicting preferences, beliefs, and goals. They cannot be rationalized (18).

Figure 1	**A Decision Making Typology.**		
Knowledge about Cause and Effect	Standards of Desirability		
		Clear	Ambiguous
	Complete	A	B
	Incomplete	C	D

Adapted from: J. D. Thompson, *Organizations in Action* (New York: McGraw-Hill, 1967).

Non-bureaucratic or political processes will evolve to make these decisions. There is substantial support for this hypothesis. Stagner (81), Wildavsky (96), and MacMillan (55) illustrate the political aspects of budgetary decision making; Baldridge (9) and Salancik and Pfeffer (75) use a political model to track strategic decision making in universities; while Rogers (73) and Pettigrew (64, 65) use a political model to study strategic decision making in industrial organizations.

When there is disagreement over objectives or over the relationships between action and outcomes (cells B or C), strategies of compromise or judgment are likely to be employed (86). Bowman (17) and Katz and Kahn (46) suggest that most managerial decisions fall into these categories, where decisions are made through consideration of both universalistic and particularistic issues (70).

This decision typology suggests that decisions between subunits can be broadly classified on the extent to which they are programmable, and therefore easily measured and evaluated. The less the decision can be systematically analyzed, the greater the influence of non-bureaucratic processes. The appropriate unit of analysis for studying political processes is a joint decision making situation. If all organizations must make operational, managerial, and strategic decisions, then all organizations will be moved by both universalistic and political processes. Of course various types of organizations will have different proportions of these types of decisions: organizations with a lower proportion of cell A decisions will be more political than organizations with a high proportion of cell A decisions (e.g., university vs. manufacturing organization).

Even for strategic decisions, political processes do not go unchecked. On the contrary, a number of organizational considerations constrain and stabilize non-bureaucratic processes (9, 96). Decision making precedent; organizational ideology, norms, and values; and task environment present the context and limits within which bargaining and negotiations take place. Organizational structures such as budgets, control systems, career paths, and the range of SOP's also constrain these political processes (97). Finally, the intensity of intergroup conflict is often limited since units which are competing with each other today may have to cooperate with each other in the future. Extreme conflict is rare in organizations. Baldridge (9) suggests the notion of strategic conflict, which recognizes the necessity of both conflict and cooperation in organizational decision making.

Political processes arise not because of individual or group perversity, but because of the nature of organizational processes and decision making under uncertainty. If decisions must be made without enough information or in the face of diverse goals, then non-bureaucratic methods must evolve to attend to the differences in preferences, values, and beliefs about cause and effect relations. If even the most objective issues are open to multiple interpretations (2), and if organizational participants often derive different meanings from the same information base (31), then bureaucratic decision making procedures will unambiguously decide only a limited set of organizational decisions. A political perspective is needed to better understand both internal and external organizational activities.

With this political perspective come its own conceptual lens and perceptual filters. Conflict is inherent in the system whose social structure is seen as pluralistic, fractured by subgroups with divergent interests. Decision making is characterized by bargaining and negotiation as the interest groups, with parochial priorities and perceptions, vie for organizational control. Organizations are mixed motive situations with OB as a political resultant: *political* in the sense that the activity from which decisions emerge is characterized by compromise, accommodation, and bargaining among individuals and groups with diverse interests and unequal influence; *resultant* in the sense that what happens is not necessarily chosen as a solution to a problem, but may rather result from processes of compromise and accommodation (2, 9, 18, 40).

IMPLICATIONS OF THE POLITICAL PERSPECTIVE

Assuming that the political perspective has some merit, what difference does it make? If it is different from other organizational frameworks, it should lead to different emphases, concepts, explanations, and predictions. This final section focuses on organization development (OD) literature as viewed from a political perspective. Implications for other application areas have been discussed in Tushman (90).

Given the political perspective, the usefulness of OD is more limited or more complex than is typically suggested (11, 34). While Friedlander and Brown (35) define OD in broad terms, this article takes OD as the area of concern that has grown from NTL and related developments over the past 20 years (45). Theory and results pertaining to individual approaches to change, some OD tools (e.g. team building), and the systems viewpoint can be reviewed from the political perspective.

Much OD work has been centered on individual or small group methods as primary levers for change (35). For example, Blake and Mouton (14), Argyris (4, 6, 7), and Beckhard (11) have focused on organizational change through individual and small group methods. These results have been equivocal (63, 84). Argyris (7) emphasizes interpersonal competence, usually learned in the laboratory, as the major lever for planned change. Yet the stability of what he terms World A, even after individual (and structural) interventions (5, 41, 93), may be traced to underemphasis on basic structural and political processes which the values and perspectives of laboratory training often encourage (13, pp. 77-79).

A more effective approach to changing organizations may be a sequencing of individual, structural, and strategic actions after systematic diagnosis of the client's task environments (35, 89). The diagnosis should be based on a model capable of capturing the organization's complexity. This does not say that laboratory training is irrelevant, but de-emphasizes its utility for organization level change. A more effective training program, particularly for high level individuals, could focus on economic, financial, and strategic training, with less emphasis on interpersonal competence.

Team building and a related set of techniques are the core of an OD technology. These tools are often based on assumptions of individual trust, openness, and organizational commitment (34). From the political perspective, these assumptions, while possibly useful within groups, may be inappropriate at the organization level of analysis. For instance, where team building may be effective within a subunit, these new skills and associated values may be counter-productive at the organizational level where the various sub-systems vie for scarce resources, given their frequently divergent interests.

From the political perspective, organizational equilibrium is a function of power and influence differentials with overall organizational effectiveness as one of many competing system goals. A case study by Lewicki and Alderfer (54) dealing with an abortive union-management intervention graphically described union-management posturing for their own ends, their basic goal differences, and their orientations to the change and the change agents.

What happens when a change agent cannot work from the top, as a number of OD theorists suggest (11)? What if there is no organizational summit and the organization is ruled by a committee or board of conflicting interests? The OD literature is equivocal here. A case reported by Rubin et al. (74) documents the difficulties and consequences of extending this top down approach to medical centers where deans frequently have little real power (39).

Recent work on OD has emphasized the importance of viewing the organization as a system (12, 60, 77). While this is exactly what is argued for here, a systems perspective that ignores the political implications of systems logic is severely limited. Much of the OD literature suggests that organizations are open systems which either support or react only passively to the intervention (11, 12). In these open systems, internal processes operating to resist OD interventions tend to be downplayed or discussed within a superordinate goal framework.

Perhaps because of these kinds of conceptual perspectives, the results of OD technology have been equivocal (8, 16, 63, 84). Bowers found that survey guided data feedback was more effective than all other OD techniques in his longitudinal study of organization change. King (48) demonstrated that the results of an OD program were due not to the intervention itself, but to the high expectations of the individuals involved. The widespread enthusiasm for OD techniques in the face of uncertain external evaluation speaks for the influence of OD values and beliefs and what King (48) calls expectation effects or what Kimberly and Nielsen (47) call the philosophy of OD.

With this rather pessimistic view of OD literature, what can the political approach offer to the analyst or practitioner? A clue can be taken from Mintzberg's (59) study of high level managers. He found that the development of relatively complex and comprehensive conceptual models assisted the manager in effectively *diagnosing* and *taking action* on a multitude of decisions.

These and similar results (24) suggest that the manager's conceptual model of OB is an important organizational change tool. To the extent that the political perspective provides an alternative framework for conceptualizing and diagnosing the system, it will be an important tool to systematically guide and direct managerial behavior. If the political approach provides a more accurate set of assumptions and a more illuminating picture of the organization, then it can lead to more informed and systematic interventions. Given more accurate diagnoses, strategic decisions incorporating some combination of structural and behavioral levers can be made (35, 89).

Beyond diagnosis, the political approach has direct action implications for the consultant. Pettigrew (66) cogently argues that organizational change must be viewed as a politically sensitive issue. Effective consultants must have a politically sensitive diagnostic model, and also be able to mobilize and use political processes to achieve change. The interventionist must take advantage of potential power within the client system. Although practitioners may operate with well developed political models, the change literature does not reflect this awareness.

The political perspective contributes directly to the diagnosis and action phases of an intervention. While interpersonal training is important, it should be combined with concentration on bargaining and strategic decision making skills, along with developing model of organizational functioning which recognizes political dynamics.

CONCLUSION

The political perspective presented here begins to develop an organization level framework consistent with systems thinking and the work on organization-environment relations. This view has been presented in an historical-developmental sequence which suggests that the dynamics of conflict and power have been at the periphery of organizational theory and research. Increased awareness of these issues should be brought more to the forefront of organizational thinking and research.

This viewpoint is meant to complement more traditional conceptions of organizational behavior. As organizations become more complex internally and as the change rate of technical and economic environments increases, the internal dynamics of organizations must be understood. The importance of a political perspective is then accentuated. As analysts become involved in a wider range of organizations (74), the political approach can yield additional insights. The explicit framework remains to be developed conceptually and empirically. But the shift will be worth the effort, since it will bring organization studies more in line with organizational reality—a benefit to those thinking about and those working with organizations.

REFERENCES

1. Aldrich, H. "Organizational Boundaries and Inter-Organizational Conflict," *Human Relations,* Vol. 23 (1971), 279–293.
2. Allison, G. *Essence of Decision* (Boston: Little, Brown, 1971).
3. Argyris, C. *Personality and Organization* (New York: Harper, 1957).
4. Argyris, C. *Interpersonal Competence and Organizational Effectiveness* (Homewood, Ill.: Dorsey Press, 1962).
5. Argyris, C. *Some Causes of Ineffectiveness in the Department of State* (Center for Int. Syst. Research, Department of State, 1967).
6. Argyris, C. *The Applicability of Organizational Sociology* (London: Cambridge Press, 1972).
7. Argyris, C. "Personality and Organization Theory Revisited," *Administrative Science Quarterly,* Vol. 18 (1973), 141–167.
8. Back, K. *Beyond Words* (New York: Russell Sage Foundation, 1972).
9. Baldridge, J. V. *Power and Conflict in the University* (New York: Wiley & Sons, 1971).
10. Barnard, C. *The Functions of the Executive* (Cambridge: Harvard University Press, 1938).
11. Beckhard, R. *Strategies of Organizational Development* (Reading, Mass.: Addison-Wesley, 1969).
12. Beer, M., and E. Huse. "A Systems Approach to Organizational Development," *Journal of Applied Behavioral Science,* Vol. 8 (1972), 79–101.
13. Bennis, W. *The Nature of Organization Development* (Reading, Mass.: Addison-Wesley, 1969).
14. Blake, R. R., and J. Mouton. *The Managerial Grid* (Houston: Gulf Publishing, 1964).
15. Blau, P. *Power and Exchange in Social Life* (New York: Wiley, 1964).
16. Bowers, D. "O.D. Techniques and Their Results in 23 Organizations," *Journal of Applied Behavioral Science,* Vol. 9 (1973), 21–44.
17. Bowman, N. "Epistemology, Corporate Strategy, and Academe," *Sloan Management Review* (Winter 1974), 35–51.
18. Braybrooke, D., and C. Lindbloom. *A Strategy of Decision* (Glencoe, Ill.: Free Press, 1963).
19. Bucher, R. "Social Process and Power in Medical Schools," in M. Zald (Ed.), *Power in Organizations* (Nashville, Tenn.: Vanderbilt Press, 1970), pp. 3–49.
20. Burns, T. "Micropolitics: Mechanisms of Institutional Change," *Administrative Science Quarterly,* Vol. 6 (1961), 257–289.
21. Burns, T., and G. Stalker. *Management of Innovation,* 2nd ed. (London: Tavistock., 1966).
22. Child, J. "Organization Structure, Environment, and Performance," *Sociology,* Vol. 6 (1972), 1–22.
23. Cohen, A., E. Robinson, and J. Edwards. "Experiments in Organizational Embeddedness," *Administrative Science Quarterly,* Vol. 14 (1969), 208–221.
24. Cohen, M., and J. March. *Leadership and Ambiguity* (New York: McGraw Hill, 1974).
25. Crozier, M. *The Bureaucratic Phenomenon* (Chicago: University of Chicago Press, 1964).
26. Crozier, M. "Problem of Power," *Social Research,* Vol. 40 (1973).

27. Cyert, R. and J. March. *A Behavioral Theory of the Firm* (Englewood Cliffs, N.J.: Prentice-Hall, 1963).

28. Dahrendorf, R. *Class and Class Conflict in Industrial Society* (Stanford, Calif.: Stanford Press, 1959).

29. Dalton, G., L. Barnes, and A. Zaleznick. *The Distribution of Authority in Formal Organizations* (Cambridge, Mass.: M.I.T. Press, 1968).

30. Dalton, M. *Men Who Manage* (New York: Wiley, 1959).

31. Dearborn, R., and H. Simon. "Selective Perceptions in Executives," *Sociometry,* Vol. 21 (1958), 140–144.

32. Deutsch, M. "An Experimental Study of the Effects of Cooperation and Competition upon Group Processes," *Human Relations,* Vol. 2 (1949), 199–232.

33. Emerson, R. "Power-Dependence Relations," *American Sociological Review,* Vol. 27 (1962), 31–40.

34. French, C., and C. Bell. *Organization Development* (Englewood Cliffs, N.J.: Prentice-Hall, 1973).

35. Friedlander, F., and L. Brown. "Organization Development," in J. Rosenzweig and L. Porter (Eds.), *Annual Review of Psychology* (Palo Alto, Calif.: Annual Reviews, Inc., 1974).

36. Georgiou, Petro. "Goal Paradigm and Notes Towards a Counter Paradigm," *Administrative Science Quarterly,* Vol. 18, (1973), 281–310.

37. Glanzer, M., and R. Glaser. "Techniques for the Study of Group Structure and Behavior," *Psychological Bulletin,* Vol. 58 (1961), 1–27.

38. Hage, J., and R. Dewar. "Elite Values vs. Organization Structure in Predicting Innovation," *Administrative Science Quarterly,* Vol. 18 (1973), 279–290.

39. Hagedorn, H., and J. Dunlop. *The Academic Medical Center* (Cambridge, Mass.: A. D. Little Co., 1971).

40. Hah, C., and R. Lindquist. "The 1952 Steel Seizure Revisited," *Administrative Science Quarterly,* Vol. 20 (1975), 587–605.

41. Harrison, R. In C. Argyris (Ed.), *Interpersonal Competence and Organizational Effectiveness* (Homewood, Ill.: Dorsey Press, 1962), Chapter 10.

42. Hickson, D., C. Hinings, R. Lee, R. Schneck, and J. Pennings. "A Strategic Contingencies Theory of Intra-Organizational Power," *Administrative Science Quarterly,* Vol. 16 (1971), 216–229.

43. Hinings, C., D. Hickson, J. Pennings, and R. Schneck. "Structural Conditions of Intra-Organizational Power," *Administrative Science Quarterly,* Vol. 19 (1974), 22–45.

44. Homans, G. *The Human Group* (New York: Harcourt Co., 1950).

45. Hornstein, H., B. Burke, B. Bunker, M. Gindes, and R. Lewicki. *Social Intervention: A Behavioral Science Approach* (New York: Macmillan, 1971).

46. Katz, D., and R. Kahn. *The Social Psychology of Organizations* (New York: Wiley, 1966).

47. Kimberly, J., and W. Nielsen. "Organization Development and Change in Organizational Performance," *Administrative Science Quarterly,* Vol. 20 (1975), 190–206.

48. King, A. "Expectation Effects in Organizational Change," *Administrative Science Quarterly,* Vol. 19 (1974), 221–231.

49. Kochan, T., G. Huber, and L. Cummings. "Determinants of Intraorgani-

zational Conflict in Collective Bargaining in the Public Sector," *Administrative Science Quarterly,* Vol. 20 (1975), 10–23.

50.   Kornhauser, W. *Scientists in Industry* (Berkeley: University of California Press, 1962).

51.   Kuhn, T. "Logic of Discovery of Psychology of Research," in Lakatos and Musgrave (Eds.), *Criticism and the Growth of Knowledge* (London: Cambridge Press, 1970), pp. 1–24.

52.   Landsberger, H. "The Horizontal Dimension in Bureaucracy," *Administrative Science Quarterly,* Vol. 6 (1961), 299–322.

53.   Lawrence, P., and J. Lorsch. *Organization and Environment* (Boston, Mass.: Harvard University, Graduate School of Business Administration, 1967).

54.   Lewicki, R., and C. Alderfer. "Tensions Between Research and Intervention in Inter-Group Conflict," *Journal of Applied Behavioral Science,* Vol. 9 (1973), 424–449.

55.   MacMillan, I. "Organizational Politics: A Prerequisite Perspective," *Business Management,* Vol. 6 (1975), 11–20.

56.   March, J. "Business Firm as a Political Coalition," *Journal of Politics,* Vol. 24 (1962), 662–678.

57.   March, J. "The Power of Power," in D. Easton (Ed.), *Varieties of Political Theory* (Englewood Cliffs, N.J.: Prentice-Hall, 1966).

58.   March, J., and H. Simon. *Organizations* (New York: Wiley, 1958).

59.   Mintzberg, H. *The Nature of Managerial Work* (New York: Harper and Row, 1973).

60.   Nadler, D., and P. Pecorella. "Differential Effects of Multiple Interventions in an Organization," *Journal of Applied Behavioral Science,* Vol. 11 (1975), 348–366.

61.   Osborn, R., and J. Hunt. "Environment and Organizational Effectiveness," *Administrative Science Quarterly,* Vol. 19 (1974), 231–247.

62.   Parsons, T. "Suggestions for a Sociological Approach to the Theory of Organizations," *Administrative Science Quarterly,* Vol. 1 (1956), 224–239.

63.   Perrow, C. *Complex Organizations* (Glenview, Ill.: Scott, Foresman, 1972).

64.   Pettigrew, A. "Information Control as a Power Resource," *Sociology,* Vol. 6 (1972), 187–204.

65.   Pettigrew, A. *The Politics of Organizational Decision Making* (London, Tavistock, 1972).

66.   Pettigrew, A. "Towards a Political Theory of Organizational Intervention," *Human Relations,* Vol. 28 (1975), 191–208.

67.   Pfeffer, J. *Organizational Ecology: A Systems Approach* (Ph.D. dissertation, Stanford University, 1972).

68.   Pfeffer, J. "Merger as a Response to Organizational Interdependence," *Administrative Science Quarterly,* Vol. 17 (1972), 383–395.

69.   Pfeffer, J. "Size, Composition, and Function of Hospital Boards of Directors," *Administrative Science Quarterly,* Vol. 18 (1973), 240–264.

70.   Pfeffer, J., and G. Salancik. "Organizational Decision Making as a Political Process," *Administrative Science Quarterly,* Vol. 19 (1974), 135–152.

71.   Presthus, R. *The Organizational Society* (New York: Knopf, 1962).

72.   Pugh, D. S. "Modern Organization Theory," *Psychology Bulletin,* Vol. 66 (1966), 235–251.

73.   Rogers, R. *The Political Process in Modern Organizations* (Jericho, N.Y.: Exposition Press, 1971).

74. Rubin, I., M. Plovnick, and R. Fry. "Initiating Planned Change in Health Care Systems," Sloan School Working Paper (Cambridge, Mass.: MIT, 1973).

75. Salancik, G., and J. Pfeffer. "Bases and Use of Power in Organizational Decision Making," *Administrative Science Quarterly,* Vol. 19 (1974), 453–473.

76. Sapolsky, H. *Polaris System Development* (Cambridge, Mass.: Harvard University Press, 1972).

77. Schein, E. *Organizational Psychology,* 2nd ed. (Englewood Cliffs, N.J.: Prentice-Hall, 1970).

78. Schmidt, S., and T. Kochan. "Conflict: Toward Conceptual Clarity," *Administrative Science Quarterly,* Vol. 17 (1972), 359–370.

79. Selznick, P. *T.V.A. and the Grass Roots* (Berkeley: University of California Press, 1949).

80. Selznick, P. *Leadership in Administration* (Evanston, Ill.: Harper, 1957).

81. Stagner, R. "Corporate Decision Making," *Journal of Applied Psychology,* Vol. 53 (1969), 1–13.

82. Strauss, A. "The Hospital and its Negotiated Order," in Friedson, E. (Ed.), *The Hospital in Modern Society* (New York: Free Press, 1963).

83. Strauss, G. "Tactics of Lateral Relationships," *Administrative Science Quarterly,* Vol. 7 (1962), 161–186.

84. Strauss, G. "Organizational Development: Debts and Credits," *Organizational Dynamics,* Vol. 1 (Winter 1973), 2–16.

85. Thompson, J. D. *Organizations in Action* (New York: McGraw-Hill, 1967).

86. Thompson, J., and A. Tuden. "Strategies, Structures, and Processes of Organizational Decisions," in J. Thompson and A. Tuden (Eds.), *Comparative Studies in Administration* (Pittsburgh: University of Pittsburgh Press, 1959).

87. Tichy, N. "An Analysis of Clique Formation and Structure in Organizations," *Administrative Science Quarterly,* Vol. 18 (1973), 194–208.

88. Turk, H. "Comparative Urban Structures from an Interorganizational Perspective," *Administrative Science Quarterly,* Vol. 18 (1973), 37–56.

89. Tushman, M. *Organizational Change: An Exploratory Study and Case History* (Ithaca, N.Y.: Cornell University, 1974).

90. Tushman, M. "Organizations as Political Systems," *Working Paper No. 114* (New York: Graduate School of Business, Columbia University, 1976).

91. Wamsley, G., and M. Zald. *The Political Economy of Public Organizations* (Lexington, Mass.: Heath Co., 1973).

92. Warren, R. "Inter-Organizational Field as a Focus for Investigation," *Administrative Science Quarterly,* Vol. 12 (1967), 396–419.

93. Warwick, D., and T. Reed. *A Theory of Public Bureaucracy* (Cambridge, Mass.: Harvard Press, 1975).

94. Weick, K. *The Social Psychology of Organizing* (Reading, Mass.: Addison-Wesley, 1969).

95. Whyte, W. F. *Pattern for Industrial Peace* (New York: Harper, 1951).

96. Wildavsky, A. *The Politics of the Budgetary Process* (New York: Little, Brown, 1964).

97. Wilensky, H. *Organizational Intelligence* (New York: Basic Books, 1967).

98. Zald, M. *Power in Organizations* (Nashville, Tenn.: Vanderbilt Press, 1970).

99. Zald, M. "Political Economy," in M. Zald (Ed.), *Power in Organizations* (Nashville, Tenn.: Vanderbilt Press, 1970), 221–262.

The Politics of Upward Influence in Organizations[1]

LYMAN W. PORTER
ROBERT W. ALLEN
HAROLD L. ANGLE

The existence of political processes in organizations has been well recognized in the "popular" management press, yet a mid-1970's survey of more than 70 textbooks in industrial-organizational psychology, management and organizational behavior revealed only 70 pages in which the topic of organizational politics was addressed—about 2/10 of one percent of the textbook content! A review of eight of the most appropriate academic journals revealed less than a dozen articles on the topic, out of a total of more than 1700 articles over a 16 year period (Porter, 1976). In light of this scarcity of serious attention to the topic, therefore, it is our contention that a joint examination of organizational politics and upward influence may help point the way toward some important issues in analyzing behavior processes in organizations.

It is worth noting that the two topics are not unrelated. It appears reasonable to say that while not all (or even most) upward influence involves political behavior, most political behavior (in organizations) does involve upward influence. Taking the first part of this statement, much of upward influence involves, of course, the normal routine reporting relationships that exist in all organizations. We would contend, however, that there is a substantial segment of upward influence that involves what can be labeled as "political behavior" (to be defined later). The other part of the statement about the relationship between the two topics—that most political behavior in organizations involves upward influence—is based on the assumption that the typical object of influence will be someone or some group possessing more formal, legitimate power than the would-be political actor. While it is possible to cite clear exceptions to this proposition, we would, nevertheless, contend that the vast majority of *political* attempts at influence are in the upward direction.

In this paper, we intend to maintain a focus on political influence as an individual phenomenon. This is not because we consider coalitional political processes in organizations either uninteresting or unimportant. On the contrary, the many-on-one (or many-on-several) influence event is a fairly common fact of organizational life. However, we believe that the one-on-one political influence situation is a particularly prevalent, albeit little-understood, organizational reality. In the ensuing analysis, therefore, the focus will be on gaining a better understanding of the decision logic of the individual "politician."

Before proceeding further, two definitional matters must be dealt with: (1) "upward influence"; and (2) "political behavior." The first is simple, the second complex. For our purposes, we will define upward influence as "attempts to influence someone higher in the *formal hierarchy* of authority in the organization." The fact that the person attempting to exercise influence cannot rely on formal authority results in a situation that is distinctly different from that of downward influence.

"Political behavior in organizations" or "organizational politics" is not an easy term to define. Despite this, a number of authors have recently offered definitions (e.g., Frost & Hayes, 1977; Mayes & Allen, 1977; Robbins, 1976), and our definitional framework will be consistent generally with the thrust of these definitions. However, any one of them may not include all four of the elements contained in our definition. For the purposes of the present paper, *organizational political behavior* is defined as:

(1) Social influence attempts
(2) that are discretionary (i.e., that are outside the behavioral zones prescribed or prohibited by the formal organization),
(3) that are intended (designed) to promote or protect the self interests of individuals and groups (units),
(4) and that threaten the self interests of others (individuals, units).

A few brief comments seem in order about each of the four components of the definition. First, we take it as a given that regardless of what else it is, political behavior is behavior aimed at influencing others; behavior carried out in such a way that there are no intended direct effects on others would fall into the category of non-political behavior. Second, any behavior that the organization ordinarily requires and expects is non-political; e.g., coming to work every day and carrying out the assignments and expectations of the formal role. Likewise, behavior forbidden by formal rules or commonly accepted standards of behavior (e.g., fighting, stealing, etc.) would be excluded. That leaves discretionary behavior relating to the work situation (and meeting the other definitional requirements) as that which would be labeled "political." Third, we believe that the intention of promoting or protecting self interests is a necessary (though not sufficient) element of political behavior. Of course, attributions of intention often vary widely between those who are the source of the behavior and those who are observing or labeling the behavior. It is our contention that if the behavior is *seen* by organizational participants as intended to promote or protect self interests then (meeting the other criteria) the label "political" is appropriate. Finally, we believe that unless the behavior threatens the self interests of others, it is non-political. This puts political behavior squarely in the camp of competitive as opposed to collaborative behavior, and focuses on the zero-sum aspect of organizational resource allocation. In the words of Frost and Hayes (1977), this last part of the definition emphasizes that political behavior is "non-consensus" behavior.

KEY CONSIDERATIONS

Certain considerations emerge as particularly salient when one considers the present state of knowledge (or gaps in our knowledge) of political influence in organizations. What (if any) political norms exist in organizations and how do organizational members learn about them? What situational factors influence the prevalence of political activity? Further, what kinds of individuals are prone to engage in organizational politics? Finally, what factors lead to selection of particular organizational members as political influence targets, and what methods are available, and preferred, for political influence?

Political Norms

Our definition of organizational politics has incorporated the notion that organizationally-political behaviors fall outside the range of those either prescribed or prohibited by the organization. At first blush, the implication would seem to be that "political" behaviors in organizations take place outside the normative framework. No such conclusion, however, is intended. It is very likely that strong norms do exist in organizations, relative to "political" activity. However, the basis for these norms will not be found in official prescriptions originated by the formal organization. Rather, the signals by which the organizational member pieces together a picture of "political reality" originate from the informal organization, and are apt to be sent in disguised format and against a noisy background.

The two basic issues appear salient with respect to the micro-political norms of upward influence. First, what norms exist? Do norms ever permit or prescribe upward political influence attempts, or are all such attempts acts of deviance? What are the contingent factors? Do political norms differ in different parts of the organization? How does the goal or purpose behind an influence attempt bear upon its acceptability? Do norms prescribe or proscribe particular influence tactics?

A second general issue relates to the way political norms are learned in organizations. How clear are the "norm messages" regarding upward political influence? Are they transmitted "in the clear," or are they buried in subtlety and innuendo? This raises the parallel issue of norm consensus. Is there sufficient exchange of unambiguous norm information to permit consensual validation? How accurate are individual perceptions of the extent to which upward influence is attempted and the purpose or intent of the actor when such attempts are perceived?

Political Norm Structure

There is ample reason to believe that informal "political" norms abound in organizations. Schein (1977) asserted that political processes "may be as endemic to organizational life as planning, organizing, directing and controlling" (p. 64). It is unlikely, however, that these political norms are invariant, either across all situations, or in all parts of the organization.

Political behavior that clearly would be considered "deviant" at certain times may be seen as less so at other times. For instance, it has been suggested that the process of allocating scarce organizational resources typically has two phases. In the earlier phase, conflict is clearly institutionalized. Interested parties are expected to maneuver and bargain, in order to clarify the organization's values, goals and priorities (Frost & Hayes, 1977). Later on, after values, goals and priorities have been defined, *consensus* rather than conflict—becomes institutionalized. "Political" behaviors, that may have been tolerated earlier, are now considered clearly inappropriate.

Not only will political norms vary over time, they may also differ with location in the organization. One study, for example, found that more than 90 percent of managers interviewed reported that organizational politics occurred more frequently at upper and middle levels of management that at lower managerial levels (Madison, et al, 1980). A related study (Allen et al; 1979b) found that lower-level managers describe the traits of political actors in more pejorative terms than do upper-level managers, indicating perhaps that political activity is more often considered counter-normative at lower hierarchical levels. In addition, managers in the Madison et al. study reported political activity as more prevalent in staff, as opposed to line positions. Departments in which organizational politics was seen as most prevalent were marketing and sales, while accounting/finance and production were seen as lowest in political activity.

It appears, then, that the "politically active" functional areas are those in which uncertainty is most prevalent. Organizational members in such roles may need to rely on political skill to deal with the conflicting demands of intra- and extra-organizational associates. Thus, norms that favor political influence as a means of conducting the day's business may arise, out of necessity, in such subunits.

In summary, searching for "the" organization's political norms might be far too simplistic a pursuit. We should, instead, be prepared to discover a mosaic of political-norm subsystems embedded in organizations.

Learning the Norms of Upward Political Influence

The period of organizational entry is always especially stressful. The initiate is faced with an intrinsically ambiguous, yet crucial task—that of "learning the ropes." We believe that the learning of *political* norms will pose special difficulties. Unlike many organizational norms, these are exclusively the purview of the informal organization. Since the formal organization neither prescribes nor forbids political behaviors, such norms cannot be transmitted in the form of explicit organizational policy. Moreover, there are constraints on feasible modes of communication, even by the "informal" organization. Unlike the cues provided for other types of norms, political norm cues frequently will be implicit, requiring considerable sensitivity on the part of the receiver. In this respect, messages regarding norms that *condone* political behaviors may be more vague than those that *condemn* such behaviors.

A key aspect of our definition of organizational politics is the idea that "political" behavior is self-serving while at the same time not intended to serve others (or intended, in fact, to misserve others). Such behavior, then will be resisted, *if recognized* by others (Frost & Hayes, 1977). The implication is that the actor often will take pains to conceal attempts at political influence, adding to the ambiguity encountered by observers.

In discussing the acquisition of organizational power, a pursuit closely related to political influence, Moberg (1977) asserted that societal norms require unobtrusiveness. The "politician" must take care to avoid having his/her behavior attributed, by others, to a self-serving intent. Creation of the impression that behavior is legitimate (or nonexistent) may be accomplished by acting in ways that make reliable attributions difficult. Some of the "smokescreen" tactics aimed at manipulating observers' attributions might include making certain that there is a reasonably credible organizational rationale for one's actions, by acting so enigmatically that observers lose confidence in their attributions, or by publicly advocating a "version" or interpretation of organizational goals that actually serves personal objectives.

Such tactics can seriously undermine "political" social learning. An individual's ability to behave appropriately in a social situation is determined in part by the accuracy with which she or he perceives the existing system norms. It is commonly assumed that social system members both share and are aware of each others' norms for the behavior of all members (Biddle, 1964). However, when either communication or behavior observation is restricted, a state of "pluralistic ignorance" can exist. In effect, members of a social group might come to share a wholly-mistaken view of the group's norms. Furthermore, the false consensus concerning these norms may become self-perpetuating. In view of the particular problems that surround political norm learning, it would appear that political-influence norms in organizations constitute a prime candidate for "pluralistic ignorance."

Thus, a misleading consensus may come to exist with respect to which "political" behaviors the informal organization condemns, and which such behaviors are condoned. This, in turn, may lead political actors to overestimate the extent of their own deviancy, resulting in their taking great pains to disguise their behavior. The vicious circle thus created can perpetuate a situation in which discovery of the "real" political norms in an organization may pose serious problems for researchers and organization members, alike.

As we have seen, informal political norms are a critical contextual factor in the politics of upward influence. There are also other contextual considerations surrounding any potential political act. The following section discusses several such situational factors.

Situational Factors

There is some evidence that certain organizational situations tend to be intrinsically "political." Madison et al. (1980) reported that managers saw certain situations as characterized by relatively high levels of political activity. Examples of such situations included reorganization changes, personnel changes and budget allocation. On the other hand, such organizational situations as rule and procedure changes, establishment of individual performance standards and the purchase of major items were characterized as relatively low in prevalence of political activity. These differences were discussed by Madison et al. in terms of three variables: (1) uncertainty; (2) importance of the activity to the larger organization; and (3) salience of the issue to the individual.

The situations in which political activity may be most prevalent seem to combine situational ambiguity with sufficient personal stake to activate the individual to consider actions that fall outside the boundaries of the formal organizational norm system. While lack of structure or situational ambiguity may provide recognition of *opportunity* to engage in upward political influence, it is personal stake that may provide the *incentive* to engage in political behavior, per se.

Another situational factor which appears particularly relevant to organizational politics is resource scarcity. The essence of the political process is the struggle over the allocation of scarce resources, i.e., who gets what, where and when (Lasswell, 1951). The relative abundance of resources represented by various organizational issues may have a great deal of influence regarding the extent to which "political" means become employed in their resolution.

While the preceding discussion of norms and of situational factors has described some aspects of what the potential political actor *finds* in the way of contextual factors—factors that may influence his/her "political" activity in the organization—it is also necessary to consider what the individual *brings* to the situation. These actor characteristics will now be considered.

Actor Characteristics

Each potential agency of upward political influence brings to the scene a rich array of personal characteristics. Such individual factors could easily lead two different organizational members either to perceive an identical situation differently or, even if they share identical perceptions, to behave characteristically in different ways. This now leads us to consider some particular classes of individual differences that might help predict organizational members' relative propensities to engage in upward political influence.

Beliefs about action-outcome relationships.   The truism, "organizational behavior is a function of its perceived consequences," is certainly as applicable in the arena of organizational politics as it is in other spheres of organizational life. It is a basic psychological tenet that behavior that has been rewarded in the past becomes more probable in the future.

From the perspective of expectancy theory (Vroom, 1964), organizational members are believed to behave in a manner that maximizes their net outcomes. This, in turn, suggests that organization members undertake a series of subjective cost-benefit analyses, using salient available information. Some of the more explicit information available is the political actor's knowledge of the results of past attempts at social influence. Thus, the individual's "expectancy set" regarding the efficacy of engaging in upward political influence will be at least in part determined by what has gone before.

Manifest needs.   Most substantive or content theories of human motivation are based on the premise that individuals harbor a relatively stable set of needs, and that these needs incite action directed toward need satisfaction. While the assumption base underlying the need-satisfaction paradigm has not gone unchallenged, the concept of manifest needs, stemming from Murray's (1938) pioneering work, continues to influence research.

Although Murray's taxonomy included as many as twenty needs, recent focus, particularly in organizational settings, seems to have settled on need for achievement (nAch) and need for power (nPow) (Atkinson & Feather, 1966; McClelland, 1965; McClelland & Burnham, 1976). In particular, nPow appears to be a likely candidate for investigation as a correlate of political activity in organizations.

Researchers have found nPow to be widely distributed, particularly among successful managers, in organizations (McClelland and Burnham, 1976). While power motivation, according to McClelland, can often be "socialized" (i.e., oriented toward organizational, rather than personal objectives), nPow can also center on the desire to further one's own goals. Shostrom (1967) characterized man as a manipulator, and set forth the view that, for many, control of others can become its own record apart from any extrinsic accomplishment that might be the ostensible object of the maneuver. Among the individual differences that might influence the accuracy of Shostrom's characteristics, it would seem that nPow would be rather important.

Locus of control. The theory (Rotter, 1954, 1966) that highlights this variable holds that people differ systematically in their beliefs that their personal successes and failures are the result either of uncontrollable external forces, or of their own actions. "Internals" tend to view their outcomes as the result of ability or effort, while "externals" would attribute personal consequences as the result of innate task difficulty or to luck (Weiner, 1974). Thus, when faced with a problem in which upward political influence might be within the feasible set of coping strategies, it might seem reasonable that an "internal" might arrive at a different expectancy computation than would an "external." For the average outcome, an "internal" will probably assume a higher expectancy of effort leading to attainment. This might, in turn, lead "internals" to favor political activism, while "externals" might be more prone toward political apathy.

Risk-seeking propensity. Decision makers differ in their psychological reaction to risk. While some exhibit a conservative bias, avoiding risk when possible, others appear to place a positive value on risk, per se. In the language of decision theory, the former are termed risk averters while the latter are called risk seekers (Keeney & Raiffa, 1976). (There are also many people, of course, who are essentially "risk neutral.") To the extent that an organizational member is a risk seeker, it might be reasonable to expect that he/she would be tempted to engage in a political influence attempt (which can indeed be dangerous) that might be shunned by a risk averter.

Next, we turn to consideration of the other participant in the dyadic process of upward political influence—the influence target.

Target Selection

Importance of power. Engaging in organizational politics necessitates the selection of a target(s) of influence. An essential ingredient that a chosen target must possess is the control of scarce resources, or the ability to influence scarce resource controllers. This is basically a question of who has either the *power* to allocate desired resources or the ability to *influence* other desired resource powerholders. Power is considered to be the capacity to influence, while influence is viewed as a process of producing behavioral or psychological (e.g., values, beliefs, attitudes) effects in a target person. The political actor is concerned with identifying and selecting as a target an individual(s) who possesses an appropriate base, or bases, of power that as indicated earlier is sufficiently high to do or get done what the political actor desires. This point was recognized by Tedeschi, Schlenker, and Lindskold (1972), when they indicated that individuals possessing relatively greater expertise, status or prestige than the source will be prime candidates as targets of influence.

Costs of approaching target.   It seems clear that the potential risks or costs to the political actor are also an important consideration in choosing among various powerholders in the organization, as potential targets of political influence. The target must possess sufficient power to accomplish the outcome desired by the source *and* at a minimal, or acceptable, cost to the political actor. By costs to the agent, we are referring to possible negative outcomes that may be experienced by the agent as a result of the influence attempt. These negative outcomes range from the agent's failure to promote or protect self interests in the specific situation at hand, to loss of the ability to promote or protect self interests in other future situations. Indeed, the ultimate cost could be loss of position within the organization.

Therefore, while especially powerful individuals may be able to do what the agent desires, these are the same individuals who can impose the greatest adverse effects (costs) upon the agent. The power that makes a person attractive as a target could be used, were the target so to choose, against the source. Tedeschi et al. (1972) clearly recognized this point when they proposed that the most probable influence target would be the weakest person who possesses sufficient power to enable the influencer to realize his or her goal. It was suggested that, with respect to target selection in organizations, "people have a 'natural' tendency to go through the channels of authority" (p. 314), i.e., the most likely target of influence would be the immediate superior. Allen, Angle, and Porter (1979a) found that the immediate superior is, in fact, the most frequent target of attempted influence. About two thirds of their respondents (143) selected their immediate superior as a first-choice target of influence.

Agent-target relationship.   An important consideration concerning the potential costs in selecting a target from among various powerholders in the organization may be the concept of interpersonal attraction between the agent and the potential target(s). Ideally, the selected target will possess sufficient power to provide the outcomes desired by the political actor *and* sufficiently high interpersonal attraction to be willing to do so at minimal or acceptable costs to the agent.

In upward influence, the political actor does not enjoy a given target, or even a "natural" set of targets. The appropriateness of a particular individual as an influence target is situationally determined, i.e., the target will vary according to the outcomes desired by the source. The common denominator of potential political targets is the possession of sufficient power to provide, or assist in providing, outcomes desired by the political actor. It is the political actor's task to identify, select, and induce these organizational influentials to comply, willingly or unwittingly, with the intent of the political actor.

Methods of Upward Influence

The one inescapable fact about upward influence—that the agent of influence possesses less formal authority than the target of influence— colors any examination of the selection of methods of upward political influence. The fact that the political actor cannot rely on formal authority, and most likely has considerably less power (compared to a downward situation) to wield positive and negative sanctions, means that the search for an effective method or methods of upward influence will be different from the search that takes place in downward attempts.

Before discussing a classification of possible methods of upward political influence and the factors that will affect the choice of methods, it is important to keep in mind another aspect of the situation; the methods can be utilized (as Allen et al., 1979b, have pointed out) to promote self-interests (usually in a proactive manner) or protect those interests (usually in a reactive manner). The former use refers to upward influence attempts designed to advance self interests and move the agent from a current position (in terms of access to organizational resources and rewards) to a better position. Such upward influence attempts typically require *initiation* by the agent. In the latter mode, ordinarily requiring a *response* by the agent, attempts are made to reduce or minimize potential damage to self interests that would tend to move the agent from a current position to a less desirable position. It is clear that political attempts at upward influence can be exercised in either of these modes.

Classification of methods. A categorization scheme that may be useful for the purposes of analyzing upward political influence is shown in Table 1. As can be seen, influence methods have been classified into two major categories: sanctions and informational. In turn, sanctions have been divided into the familiar sets, "positive" and "negative," while informational methods have been divided into three types: "persuasion" (both the actor's objective and the influence attempt are open); "manipulative persuasion" (the objective is concealed but the attempt is open); and "manipulation" (both the objective and the attempt are concealed).

Each of the five methods listed in Table 1 can be considered for possible use by individual political actors. As will be discussed below, and as shown in Table 1, we have indicated what we think is the relative frequency of use: namely, positive and negative sanctions are not likely,

Table 1	Classification of Methods of Upward Political Influence	
	Types of Methods	Predicted Relative Frequency of Use
I. Sanctions	A. Positive	Low
	B. Negative	Low
II. Informational	A. Persuasion	Low to Medium
	B. Manipulative Persuasion	High
	C. Manipulation	High

persuasion is low to medium in likelihood, and manipulative persuasion and manipulation are (relatively) highly likely.

Considering each of the five methods in turn:

Positive Sanctions: In upward political influence situations, it is unlikely (though certainly by no means impossible) that positive sanctions, i.e., rewards and promises of rewards, will be a very widely utilized method by individuals. The apparent reason is that the individual vis-a-vis his/her upward target is unlikely to control a wide range of rewards. To put it simply, while the upward target can do a lot for the would-be political actor in the way of providing rewards, he/she is relatively limited in the rewards that can be administered upward. The source does have his/her own performance that can serve as a reward—it can , for example, help make the boss look good—but since relatively good performance is such an expected part of normal organizational behavior, it is not likely to serve as a frequent reward in an upward direction unless it is truly exceptional performance. Other types of rewards (e.g., favors) can be promised by the lower level individual attempting upward influence, but on balance they are likely to be of limited and circumscribed impact.

Negative Sanctions: As Mechanic (1962) noted, "secretaries . . . accountants . . . attendants in mental hospitals, and even . . . inmates in prisons" (p. 350) can individually, if they wish, "gum up the works" by various tactics. Whether this is a very prevalent method, however, is a function of the possible costs or penalties for doing so. In particular, when influence is being attempted hierarchically upward, there are normative restrictions on the use of negative sanctions. While both the superior and subordinate may fully understand that the subordinate is in a threatening posture, face-saving norms (Goffman, 1955) may require that neither party openly acknowledge the subordinate's threat. Were the threat to become overt, the superior would likely be compelled to retaliate. Thus, upward threats seldom will be explicit; rather, to the extent they exist at all, upward negative sanctions will tend to take the form of what Berne (1964) termed "covert transactions." In general, it is our view that negative sanctions will not be selected often as a viable upward influence method.

Persuasion: The term "persuasion" is usually substituted as a shorthand term or open informational methods. It seems obvious that persuasion, or the open utilization of an informational base, is a frequent and common method of *non*-political upward influence on the part of the individual agent. However, when the aim of such persuasion is the promotion or protection of the self interests of the influence agent, and where the self interests of others are threatened, its uses becomes far more problematical. Since the intentions of the influence agent are open as well as the method (i.e., a direct attempt to convince), the response will be based directly on the target's evaluation of the message and the source of the message. The "costs," therefore, may be greatly increased because of the possibility of a negative reaction on the part of the target—as opposed to perhaps mere indifference in non-political situations. For this reason, we would argue that the likelihood of persuasion being utilized in upward political influence situations would be low to moderate.

It should be noted that the nature of the arguments in persuasion can take many forms, including pointing out probable consequences to the target for complying or failing to comply with the agent's wishes. Tedeschi et al. (1972) refer to this type of argument as the use of "warnings and mendations" (as contrasted with such direct sanctions as threats, punishments, and promises of rewards). "The important distinction between threat and a warning is that the source controls the punishment in the first instance but not in the second" (p. 292).

Manipulative Persuasion: The essence of this method of upward influence involves the deliberate attempt of the agent to conceal or disguise his/her true objectives, *even though* the agent is *open* about the fact that an influence attempt is taking place—it is the objective, not the influence attempt, that is concealed. This is illustrated by the well-known "hidden agenda" phenomenon.

We contend that manipulative persuasion is a frequently utilized approach to upward influence of a political sort. The reason, of course, is the influence agent's belief that if the (higher level) target knew what the source was trying to accomplish, the target would reject or ignore the message and thus avoid being influenced, or might even penalize the source. In this method, the agent is openly attempting to influence but is simultaneously attempting to disguise his/her intentions. The effectiveness of the influence method, therefore, depends on how effective is the disguise of objectives. There is probably no message so *ineffective* as one that is labeled by the target: "He/she is *only* trying to get me to do that because it will advance his/her own self interests."

Manipulation: This form of influence involves the concealment of *both* the intent of the political actor *and* the fact that an influence attempt is taking place. This obviously involves greater effort on the part of the influence agent, as both intentions and the attempt must be disguised. Despite the potential difficulties, this is a common method of upward political influence. For example, in a study of managerial perceptions of the utilization of political tactics, Allen et al. (1979b) found that "the instrumental use of information" was one of the three most commonly observed tactics mentioned by the managerial respondents from 30 small-to-medium sized industrial firms. As these authors pointed out, this category of tactics involved withholding, or distorting information (short of outright lying), or overwhelming the target with too much information. The other two tactics most frequently cited by the respondents in the Allen et al. study could also be interpreted as the utilization of pure manipulation: namely, "attacking or blaming others" and "image building/impression management." Obviously, the success of these and similar tactics, including ingratiation, would appear to depend largely on how effectively the influence agent's intentions and the attempt at influence are concealed. Attacking others, for example, is likely to be dismissed if it is regarded as being only, or primarily, in the service of the attacker's self interests and/or as an influence attempt.

Factors in the choice of method. If we assume that someone (individual or group) in an organization has made a decision to attempt upward influence for the purpose of promoting or protecting self-interests, then that person or group faces the choice of what method to use. Since we are focusing on *upward* influence, that choice will be greatly affected by the knowledge that the target has more formal authority than the agent. A choice that might be effective in downward influence might not, as noted earlier, be equally effective in the upward direction.

The choice of method is likely to be affected by the agent's instrumental motivation—the attempt to obtain particular outcomes (with satisfaction deriving from the attainment of the outcomes rather than from the process of attaining them). The agent is presumed to have some notion of what values he or she places on certain outcomes, and some idea of the probability that a given action will lead to various outcomes. It is this latter factor, the calculation of the probability that a particular method will lead to valued outcomes, that would seem to be the key ingredient in the choice of methods of influence. Alternatively, this could be thought of as a calculation of cost/benefit ratios for various possible methods. Those methods would be chosen which would bring the greatest benefits for the lowest cost.

Such calculations can be presumed to be dependent on the agent's assessment of: (1) Agent (self) characteristics; (2) Target characteristics; (3) Characteristics of the situation; and (4) The characteristics of the method. Agent characteristics would include the agent's assessment of the various resources he/she possesses vis-a-vis the target: e.g., degree of expertise, potential to provide the target with positive or negative outcomes, possession of exclusive information, ability to disguise true intentions, general persuasive ability, risk-taking propensity, and the like. Target characteristics would include such variables as: perceived susceptibility to persuasion, likelihood of attributing self-interest motivation to the agent, power to provide the desired outcome, and so forth. Finally, some assessment would be made of the characteristics (costs and benefits) of the method itself. For example, in deciding whether to use some form of manipulation such as withholding information or attempting ingratiation, the *perceived* costs involved in detection may or may not be viewed as greater than the potential gains of straightforward persuasion. It would appear, then, that the choice of methods of influence, particularly in an upward situation, is a complex process.

CONCLUDING OBSERVATIONS

Some years ago, Leavitt (1964) observed: "People perceive what they think will help satisfy needs; ignore what is disturbing; and again perceive disturbances that persist and increase" (p. 33). It is interesting to apply the selective-perception framework to the relative prominence given by the field of organizational behavior to downward and lateral influence processes, on the one hand, compared to the lack of attention given to upward influence processes and organizational politics, on the other. We believe there has been an over-focus on the former, and that the field needs to redress the imbalance by giving increased emphasis to the latter.

One can speculate as to why this imbalance has occurred. In part, at least, it has come about because those who run organizations traditionally have been interested in improving the performance of those being led or managed. Hence, they have pressed social and behavioral scientists to learn more about leadership and motivation. This has created a ready market for knowledge directed toward influencing subordinates to perform in a desired manner. Another factor shaping research, particularly with respect to both downward and lateral influence proceses, has been the small group tradition in social psychology. When only small groups, as opposed to (large) formal organizations, are the object of study, it is likely that the focus will be strongly downward, or perhaps lateral—as in the case of group dynamics. Chains of authority exist only in organizations of some size, and thus if only groups are being researched, it is difficult to investigate the intricacies of upward influence linkages—except for the limited case of the group's impact on the immediate leader (and, it should be stressed that even this circumscribed type of upward influence has only recently begun to be examined by organizational behavior researchers). Our point is not that upward influence is more important than lateral or downward influence, only that it should be studied as much as the other two types. And, when one gets into the topic of upward influence in organizations, one is *inevitably* drawn into the realm of organizational politics. This, in turn, is a subject that has long been regarded as somewhat "taboo" by both organizations and researchers because of its mildly disturbing negative connotations—clandestine, self-serving, dysfunctional, etc.

Finally, we feel that a broadened influence perspective—one that incorporates the concept of organizational politics—can contribute significantly to an understanding of many facets of organizational behavior, such as decision making, organizational design, communication, motivation and organizational development.

REFERENCES

Allen, R. W., H. L. Angle, and L. W. Porter (1979a) "A study of upward influence in political situations in organizations," unpublished manuscript, University of California, Irvine.

Allen, R. W., D. L. Madison, L. W. Porter, P. A. Renwick, and B. T. Mayes (1979b) "Organizational politics: Tactics and personal characteristics of political actors," *California Management Review*, 1979, *22* (4), 77-83.

Atkinson, J. W. and N. T. Feather (eds.) (1966) *A Theory of Achievement Motivation*, New York: Wiley.

Berne, E. (1964) *Games People Play*, New York: Grove Press.

Biddle, B. J. (1964) "Roles, goals, and value structures in organizations," in W. W. Cooper, H. J. Leavitt, and M. W. Shelly II (eds.) *New Perspectives in Organization Research*, New York: Wiley.

Frost, P. J., and D. C. Hayes (1977) "An exploration in two cultures of political behavior in organizations," paper presented at the Conference on Cross-Cultural Studies of Organizational Functioning, University of Hawaii, Honolulu, HI, September.

Goffman, E. (1955) "On facework," *Psychiatry 18,* 213-231.

Keeney, R. L., and H. Raiffa (1976) *Decisions and Multiple Objectives: Preferences and Value Tradeoffs,* New York: Wiley.

Lasswell, H. D. (1951) "Who gets what, when, how," in the *Political Writings of Harold D. Lasswell,* Glencoe, IL: Free Press.

Leavitt, H. J. (1964) *Managerial Psychology,* Revised Edition, Chicago: University of Chicago Press.

Madison, D. L., R. W. Allen, L. W. Porter, P. A. Renwick, and B. T. Mayes "Organizational politics: An exploration of managers' perceptions," *Human Relations,* 1980, *33,* 79-100.

Mayes, B. T. and R. W. Allen (1977) "Toward a definition of organizational politics," *Academy of Management Review 2,* 672-678.

McClelland, D. C. (1965) "Toward a theory of motive acquisition," *American Psychologist 20,* 321-333.

McClelland, D. C. and D. H. Burnham (1976) "Power is the great motivator," *Harvard Business Review 54 (2),* 100-110.

Mechanic, D. (1962) "Sources of power of lower participants in complex organizations," *Administrative Science Quarterly 7,* 349-364.

Moberg, D. J. (1977) "Organizational politics: Perspectives from attribution theory," paper presented to the 1977 Meeting of the American Institute for Decision Sciences, Chicago, IL.

Murray, H. A. (1938) *Explorations in Personality,* New York: Oxford University Press.

Porter, L. W. (1976) "Organizations as political animals," Presidential Address, Division of Industrial-Organizational Psychology, 84th Annual Meeting of the American Psychological Association, Washington, D. C.

Robbins, S. P. (1976) *The Administrative Process: Integrating Theory and Practice,* Englewood Cliffs, NJ: Prentice-Hall.

Rotter, J. B. (1954) *Social Learning and Clinical Psychology,* Englewood Cliffs, NJ: Prentice-Hall.

Rotter, J. B. (1966) "Generalized expectancies for internal versus external locus of control," *Psychological Monographs 80,* 1-28.

Schein, E. (1977) "Individual power and political behaviors in organizations: An inadequately explored reality," *Academy of Management Review 2,* 64-72.

Shostrom, Everett L. (1967) *Man, the Manipulator,* Nashville, TN: Abingdon Press.

Tedeschi, J. T., B. R. Schlenker, and S. Lindskold (1972) "The exercise of power and influence: The source of influence," in J. T. Tedeschi (ed.), *The Social Influence Process,* Chicago: Aldine-Atherton.

Vroom, V. H. (1964) *Work and Motivation,* New York: Wiley.

Weiner, B. (1974) "An attributional interpretation of expectancy-value theory," in B. Weiner (ed.), *Cognitive Views of Human Motivation,* New York: Academic Press.

NOTE

[1]Adapted from a chapter published in: *Research in Organizational Behavior,* Volume 3, edited by B. Staw and L. Cummings, JAI Press, 1981.

The Ethics of Organizational Politics

GERALD F. CAVANAGH
DENNIS J. MOBERG
MANUEL VELASQUEZ

Power is the cornerstone of both management theory and management practice. Few concepts are more fundamental to the study of organizations, and power is a vital and ubiquitous reality in organizational life [Dahl, 1957; Zald, 1970; Zaleznik, 1970]. Our primary purpose here is to develop a framework for evaluating the ethical quality of certain uses of power within orgnizations. We will first distinguish political from nonpolitical uses of power and then canvass the literature of normative ethics in order to construct a model of ethical analysis that can be applied to political uses of power in organizations.

ORGANIZATIONAL POLITICS

The contemporary view of power in organizations is that it is the ability to mobilize resources, energy, and information on behalf of a preferred goal or strategy [Tushman, 1977]. Thus, power is assumed to exist only when there is conflict over means or ends [Drake, 1979; Pfeffer, 1977]. More specifically, this view of power is based on two fundamental propositions:

1. Organizations are composed of individuals and coalitions that compete over resources, energy, information, and influence

"The Ethics of Organizational Politics" by Gerald F. Cavanagh, Dennis J. Moberg and Manuel Velasquez, *The Academy of Management Review*, 1981, Volume 6, Number 3, pp. 363-374. Copyright © 1981 by the Academy of Management. Reprinted by permission.

[Hickson, Hinings, Lee, Schneck, & Pennings, 1971; Thompson, 1967].

2. Individuals and coalitions seek to protect their interests through means that are unobtrusive when compared to existing controls, norms, and sanctions [Allen, Madison, Porter, Renwick, & Mayes, 1979; Pfeffer & Salancik, 1974].

This perspective has led some authors to distinguish between political and nonpolitical uses of power [Gandz & Murray, 1980]. For example, Mayes and Allen [1977] draw the distinction in terms of organizational sanctions: nonpolitical uses of power are those that involve sanctioned means for sanctioned ends, and political uses involve unsanctioned means, or sanctioned means for unsanctioned ends. That is, when individuals and coalitions choose to move outside of their formal authority, established policies and procedures, or job descriptions in their use of power, that use is political. When they use power within these sanctions for ends that are not formally sanctioned through goal statements, this too is a political use of power, according to the Mayes and Allen definition.

Unlike more encompassing conceptualizations that equate politics with *any* use of power [e.g., Martin & Sims, 1956], the Mayes and Allen definition underlines the discretionary nature of organizational politics. In spite of formal systems designed to control the use of power, organizational members can and do exercise political power to influence their subordinates, peers, superiors, and others [Schein, 1977]. And coalitions may employ politics in their reaction to policy changes that threaten their own interests [Crozier, 1964; Pettigrew, 1973].

When individuals and coalitions move outside formal sanctions, the traditional authority/responsibility linkage is broken, and important ethical issues emerge. However, current treatments of organizational politics either beg the ethical issues entirely [e.g., Kotter, 1977] or offer simplistic ethical criteria. For example, Miles asserts that "it is . . . important to recognize that politics need not be bad, though common parlance uses the term in a pejorative sense. The survival of an organization may depend on the success of a unit or coalition in overturning a traditional but outdated formal organization objective or policy" [1980, p. 155]. However, there are a host of political actions that may be justified in the name of organizational survival that many would find morally repugnant. Among these are such Machiavellian techniques as "situational manipulation," "dirty tricks," and "backstabbing."

There is, then, a clear need for a normative theory of organizational politics that addresses ethical issues directly and from the standpoint of the exercise of discretion. Unfortunately, the business and society literature, where one might expect to find such issues discussed, offers little guidance in this regard. The emphasis in this literature is on institutional interactions (e.g., government regulations) and on broad human resource policy issues (e.g., affirmative action), and not on the day-to-day political decisions made in the organization.

Discussions of political tactics in the management literature also offer little guidance. The literature is, of course, rich with political guidelines: there are leadership theories, lateral relations prescriptions, notions about how to design and implement reward and control systems, conflict resolution strategies, and the like, all of which provide fodder for the development of political behavior alternatives (hereinafter PBA). However, the form of these theoretical notions tends to reduce decisions to *calculations based on effect*—that is, they provide the manager with an understanding and prediction of what PBAs are likely to evoke in terms of an outcome or set of outcomes. Armed with contemporary leadership theories, for example, managers can presumably determine the type of face-to-face direction that will result in the desired level of performance and satisfaction. This calculative emphasis defines theoretical debate over ethics in terms of the desirability of outcomes and tends to ignore the value of the activities, processes, and behaviors involved, independent of the outcomes achieved. What a manager *should* do is thus determined by the desirability of the outcomes and not by the quality of the behaviors themselves. Such an emphasis inevitably leads to a kind of ends-justify-the-means logic that fails to provide guidance for managers beyond linking alternatives to outcomes. Consider the following case.

Lorna is the production manager of a noncohesive work group responsible for meeting a deadline that will require coordinated effort among her subordinates. Believing that the members of the work group will pull together and meet the deadline if they have a little competition, Lorna decides in favor of a PBA. She tries to create the impression among her subordinates that members of the sales department want her group to fail to meet the deadline so that sales can gain an edge over production in upcoming budgetary negotiations.

How might we evaluate this PBA? Management theory tends to focus our attention on consequences. One might argue that if it works and Lorna's group pulls together and meets the deadline, it's okay. Or, a more critical observer might argue that even if the objective is accomplished, an important side effect could be the loss of a cooperative relationship between the sales and production departments. What we tend to lose sight of, though, is that "creating an impression" is a euphemism for lying, and lying may not be ethically acceptable in this situation.

This example illustrates what may be termed the teleological or goal-oriented form of management theory [Keeley, 1979; Krupp, 1961; Pfeffer, 1978]. This leads managers and management scholars alike to restrict normative judgments about organizational behavior to outcomes (e.g., performance, satisfaction, system effectiveness) rather than consider the ethical quality of the means employed.

In contrast, the field of normative ethics provides fertile ground on which to develop a normative theory of organizational politics. We will therefore turn to the literature of this field in order to draw out a set of principles that can provide the basis for a normative analysis of organizational politics that may reduce the ethical uncertainty surrounding the political use of power.

ETHICAL CRITERIA RELEVANT TO POLITICAL BEHAVIOR DECISIONS

Work in the field of normative ethics during this century has evolved from three basic kinds of moral theories: utilitarian theories (which evaluate behavior in terms of its social consequences), theories of rights (which emphasize the entitlements of individuals), and theories of justice (which focus on the distributional effects of actions or policies). Each of these has a venerable heritage. Utilitarian theory was precisely formulated in the eighteenth century [Bentham, 1789; Mill, 1863; Sidgwick, 1874]. Formulations of rights theories appeared in the seventeenth century [Hobbes, 1651; Locke, 1690; Kant, 1785]. Aristotle and Plato first formulated theories of justice in the fifth century B.C. This past decade has seen a continuing discussion of a subtle and powerful variant of utilitarianism called "rule utilitarianism" [Brandt, 1979; Sobel, 1970], an elaboration of several rights theories [Dworkin, 1978; Nozick, 1974], and the publication of sophisticated treatments of justice [Bowie, 1971; Rawls, 1971].

Utilitarian Theory

Utilitarianism holds that actions and plans should be judged by their consequences [Sidgwick, 1874; Smart, 1973]. In its classical formulation, utilitarianism claims that behaviors that are moral produce the greatest good for the greatest number [Mill, 1863]. Decision makers are required to estimate the effect of each alternative on all the parties concerned and to select the one that optimizes the satisfactions of the greatest number.

What can be said about the ethical quality of PBAs from a utilitarian standpoint? In its present form, utilitarianism requires a decision maker to select the PBA that will result in the greatest good for the greatest number. This implies not only considering the interests of all the individuals and groups that are affected by each PBA, but also selecting the PBA that optimizes the satisfactions of these constituencies. Obviously, this can amount to a calculative nightmare.

Accordingly, there are several shortcuts that may be used to reduce the complexity of utilitarian calculations. Each of these involves a sacrifice of elegance for calculative ease. *First,* a decision maker can adopt some ideological system that reduces elaborate calculations of interests to a series of utilitarian rules. For example, some religious ideologies specify rules of behavior that, if followed, are supposed to result in an improved human condition (e.g., the Golden Rule). Certain organizational ideologies, like professionalism, allow complex utilitarian calculations to be reduced to a focus on critical constituencies [Schein, 1966]. *Second,* a decision maker can adopt a simplified frame of reference in evaluating the interests of affected parties. For example, an economic frame of reference presupposes that alternatives are best evaluated in terms of dollar costs and dollar benefits. In this way, utilitarian calculations can be quantified. And *third*, a decision maker can place boundaries on utilitarian calculations. For example, a decision maker can consider only the interests of those directly affected by a decision and thus exclude from analysis all indirect or secondary effects. Similarly, a decision maker can assume that by giving allegiance to a particular organizational coalition or set of goals (e.g., "official goals"), everyone's utilities will be optimized.

Calculative shortcuts like these do not automatically free decision makers from moral responsibility for their actions. Normative ethicians typically suggest that decision makers should periodically assess these simplifying stategies to assure themselves that certain interests are not being ignored or that decision rules do not lead to suboptimal outcomes [e.g., Bok, 1980].

Whatever form of utilitarianism is employed, two types of PBAs are typically judged unethical: (1) those that are consistent with the attainment of some goals (e.g., personal goals) at the expense of those that encompass broader constituencies (e.g., societal goals), and (2) those that constitute comparatively inefficient means to desired ends. Take the case of an employee of a company who uses personal power to persuade policy makers to grant unusually high levels of organizational resources to a project by systematically excluding important information about the progress of the project. This PBA is unethical if other resource allocation schemes would better satisfy a greater number of individuals or if persuasion of this kind is less efficient than being more open about how the project is progressing.

Theory of Rights

A theory of moral rights asserts that human beings have certain fundamental rights that should be respected in all decisions. Several fundamental rights have been incorporated into the American legal system in the form of the Constitutional Bill of Rights. In light of these Constitutional guarantees, advocates of moral rights have suggested the following:

1. *The right of free consent.* Individuals within an organization have the right to be treated only as they knowingly and freely consent to be treated [Bennis & Slater, 1968; Hart, 1955].
2. *The right to privacy.* Individuals have the right to do whatever they choose to do outside working hours and to control information about their private life, including information not intended to be made public [Miller, 1971; Mironi, 1974; Wasserstrom, 1978].
3. *The right to freedom of conscience.* Individuals have the right to refrain from carrying out any order that violates moral or religious norms to which they adhere [Ewing, 1977; Waltzer, 1967].

4. *The right of free speech.* Individuals have the right to criticize conscientiously and truthfully the ethics or legality of the actions of others so long as the criticism does not violate the rights of other individuals [Bok, 1980; Eells, 1962; Walters, 1975].
5. *The right to due process.* Individuals have the right to a fair and impartial hearing when they believe their rights are being violated [Ewing, 1977, 1981; Evan, 1975].

Making decisions based on a theory of rights is much simpler than with utilitarian theory. One need only avoid interfering with the rights of others who might be affected by the decision. This can be complicated, of course, but generally a theory of rights does not involve the decision complexities that utilitarianism requires.

Theory of Justice

A theory of justice requires decision makers to be guided by equity, fairness, and impartiality. Canons of justice may specify three types of moral prescriptions: distributive rules, principles of administering rules, and compensation norms.

Distributive rules. The basic rule of distributive justice is that differential treatment of individuals should not be based on arbitrary characteristics: individuals who are similar in the relevant respects should be treated similarly, and individuals who differ in a relevant respect should be treated differently in proportion to the differences between them [Perelman, 1963]. This rule is the basis for contentions that certain resource allocations are "fair." When applied to salary administration, for example, it would lead to a distribution of rewards such that those whose jobs are equal in terms of importance, difficulty, or some other criterion receive equal rewards.

A second distributive rule is that the attributes and positions that command differential treatment should have a clear and defensible relationship to goals and tasks [Daniels, 1978]. Clearly, it is unjust to distribute rewards according to differences unrelated to the situation at hand.

Principles of administering rules. Justice requires that rules should be administered fairly [Feinberg, 1973; Fuller, 1964]. Rules should be clearly stated and expressly promulgated. They should be consistently and impartially enforced. They should excuse individuals who act in ignorance, under duress, or involuntarily [Rawls, 1971].

Compenstion norms. A theory of justice also delineates guidelines regarding the responsibility for injuries [Brandt, 1959]. First, individuals should not be held responsible for matters over which they have no control. Second, individuals should be compensated for the cost of their injuries by the party responsible for those injuries.

Table 1   **Ethical Theories Relevant to Judging Political Behavior Decisions**

Theory	Strengths as an Ethical Guide	Weaknesses as an Ethical Guide
Utilitarianism (Bentham, Ricardo, Smith)	1. Facilitates calculative shortcuts (e.g., owing loyalty to an individual, coalition, or organization). 2. Promotes the view that the intersts accounted for should not be solely particularistic except under unusual circumstances (e.g., perfect competition). 3. Can encourage entrepreneurship, innovation, and productivity.	1. Virtually impossible to assess the effects of a PBA* on the satisfaction of all affected parties. 2. Can result in an unjust allocation of resources, particularly when some individuals or groups lack representation or "voice." 3. Can result in abridging some persons' rights to accommodate utilitarian outcomes.
Theory of Rights (Kant, Locke)	1. Specifies minimal levels of satisfaction for all individuals. 2. Establishes standards of social behavior that are independent of outcomes.	1. Can encourage individualistic, selfish behavior—which, taken to an extreme, may result in anarchy. 2. Reduces political prerogatives that may be necessary to bring about just or utilitarian outcomes.
Theory of Justice (Aristotle, Rawls)	1. Ensures that allocations of resources are determined fairly. 2. Protects the interests of those who may be underrepresented in organizations beyond according them minimal rights.	1. Can encourage a sense of entitlement that reduces entrepreneurship, innovation, and productivity. 2. Can result in abridging some persons' rights to accommodate the canons of justice.

*Political behavior alternative

While a theory of justice does not require the complicated calculations demanded by utilitarian theory, it is by no means easy to apply. There is the problem of determining the attributes on which differential treatment is to be based. There are fact-finding challenges associated with administering rules. And there is the thorny problem of establishing responsibility for mistakes and injuries.

However, as applied to political behavior decisions, these canons of justice are useful in clarifying some ethical issues. First, PBAs for the purpose of acquiring an advantageous position in the distribution of resources are ethically questionable if there is no legitimate basis for the advantage. Second, PBAs based on an exchange of rule leniency for other favors are patently unethical unless everyone qualifies for the same level of leniency. Finally, political advantage should not be based on favorable attributions of responsibility or the compensation for injury [Allen et al., 1979]. In short, a theory of justice demands that inequality or advantage be determined fairly.

AN ANALYTICAL STRUCTURE FOR EVALUATING POLITICAL BEHAVIOR DECISIONS

Each of the three kinds of ethical theories has strong and weak points, as depicted in Table 1 (on page 429). Most important for our purposes, each can be shown to be inadequate in accounting for issues accounted for by another. Utilitarian theory cannot adequately account for rights and claims of justice [Lyons, 1965]. Rights theories proved deficient in dealing with social welfare issues [Singer, 1978]. And theories of justice have been criticized for both violating rights [Nozick, 1974] and diminishing incentives to produce goods and services [Okum, 1975]. One solution to the problem of theoretical inadequacy is to combine these three theories into a coherent whole.

To that end, we have incorporated all three normative theories in a decision tree, diagrammed in Figure 1. The three categories of ethical criteria that bear on a political behavior decision are arbitrarily arranged in the diagram. In addition to incorporating all three theories, the decision tree accounts for overwhelming factors that preclude the application of any of these criteria. These overwhelming factors will be specified after two cases illustrating the use of the decision tree have been presented.

Illustrative Cases

Sam and Bob are highly motivated research scientists who work in the new-product department lab at General Rubber. Sam is by far the most technically competent scientist in the lab, and he has been responsible for several patents that have netted the company nearly six million dollars in the past decade. He is quiet, serious, and socially reserved. In contrast, Bob is outgoing and demonstrative. While Bob lacks the technical track record Sam has, his work has been solid though unimaginative. Rumor

Figure 1   A Decision Tree for Incorporating Ethics Into Political Behavior Decisions

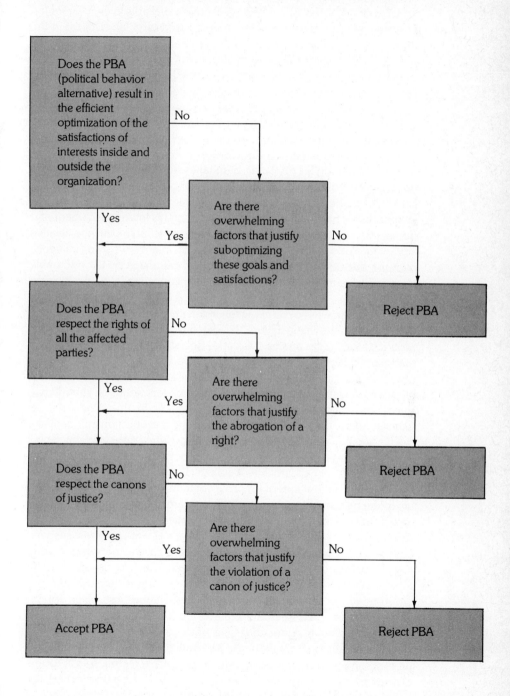

has it that Bob will be moved into an administrative position in the lab in the next few years.

According to lab policy, a $300,000 fund is available every year for the best new-product development idea proposed by a lab scientist in the form of a competitive bid. Accordingly, Sam and Bob both prepare proposals. Each proposal is carefully constructed to detail the benefits to the company and to society if the proposal is accepted, and it is the consensus of other scientists from blind reviews that both proposals are equally meritorious. Both proposals require the entire $300,000 to realize any significant results. Moreover, the proposed line of research in each requires significant mastery of the technical issues involved and minimal need to supervise the work of others.

After submitting his proposal, Sam takes no further action aside from periodically inquiring about the outcome of the bidding process. In contrast, Bob begins to wage what might be termed an open campaign in support of his proposal. After freely admitting his intentions to Sam and others, Bob seizes every opportunity he can to point out the relative advantages of his proposal to individuals who might have some influence over the decision. So effective is this open campaign that considerable informal pressure is placed on those authorized to make the decision on behalf of Bob's proposal. Bob's proposal is funded and Sam's is not.

An ethical analysis of Bob's action in this case could begin by using the decision tree shown in Figure 1. The first question in the sequence requires a utilitarian analysis. Clearly, Bob's interests are better served than Sam's. However, the nature of the two proposals seems to require one of the two to be disappointed. Moreover, the outcome in terms of broader interests (i.e., company, society) appears not to be suboptimal, since both proposals were judged equivalent in the blind reviews. Consequently, it is appropriate to answer the first question affirmatively.

The second question inquires into the rights respected by Bob's behavior. Here again, the evidence seems persuasive that no one's rights were violated. Sam did not have (did not create) the same opportunity to point out the advantages of his proposal to those at whom Bob directed his lobbying campaign, but Bob's open campaign involved no deceit, and Sam's inaction may be taken as implied consent.

It is in light of the third question that Bob's actions are most suspect. Justice would have best been served in this case if there had been a clear situation-relevant difference between the two proposals. The blind reviews found them equivalent, so some other basis for differentiating between the proposals presumably had to be found. Bob's efforts served to create irrelevant differences between them. If anything, Sam's superior technical track record would have been a more relevant factor than Bob's initiative and social skills in determining who should be favored to perform a technical task. Bob's actions in this regard were therefore unjust. Interestingly, had the proposals required supervision of others or the ability to persuade others, Bob's approach would have been justified.

Let us examine another case. Lee, 61, has been Director of

Engineering for American Semiconductor for 14 years. He is very bright and a fine supervisor but he has not kept abreast of new developments in technology.

American Semiconductor's manufacturing process creates substantial quantities of toxic materials. Lee's rather casual attitude toward the disposal of these chemicals has resulted in a number of environmental citations. The firm is now tied up in court on two cases and will probably be forced to pay a considerable amount in damages. Yet, Lee still does not perceive the disposal problem as urgent. For three years, Charlie, the executive vice president, has tried to persuade Lee to make this a priority issue but has failed. Charlie has reluctantly concluded that Lee must be taken out of his position as Director of Engineering.

Charlie recognizes that it would demoralize the other managers if he were to fire Lee outright. So, Charlie decides that he will begin to tell selected individuals that he is dissatisfied with Lee's work. When there is an open support for Lee, Charlie quietly sides with Lee's opposition. He casually lets Lee's peers know that he thinks Lee may have outlived his usefulness to the firm. He even exaggerates Lee's deficiencies and failures when speaking to Lee's coworkers. Discouraged by the waning support from his colleagues, Lee decides to take an early retirement.

In response to the first question in the decision tree, we can conclude that getting Lee out of his position may indeed bring about the "greatest good for the greatest number," presumably a suitable replacement can be found. Not only is Lee hindering the achievement of the apparent goals of the organization, but he is also causing external diseconomies in the disposal of the toxic wastes. Both of these problems, especially when taken together, bring us to the conclusion that Lee is hurting both American Semiconductor and many other people. Thus, Charlie's PBA seems to pass utilitarian criteria.

On the issue of rights, however, there are some difficulties with Charlie's PBA. Namely, Lee's right of free consent was violated. Lee has the right to be treated honestly and forthrightly and Charlie's attempt to destroy Lee's reputation behind his back failed to respect this right.

Overwhelming Factors

A still-unexplained qualification in the decision tree we have described is the concept of an "overwhelming factor"—i.e., a situational factor that may, in a given case, justify overriding one of the three ethical criteria: utilitarian outcomes, individual rights, or distributive justice. What counts as an overwhelming factor?

Conflicts between criteria.   As we have suggested, the three criteria are intended to systematically focus our attention on three kinds of decision factors: (1) the congruence between the decision and the efficient satisfaction of the greatest number of people, (2) the effect of the decision on individuals who have rights, and (3) the distributional consequences of the decision. Obviously, these three factors may come into conflict. As in the American Semiconductor case, the decision maker may be faced with a situation in which a choice must be made between, on the one hand, a course of action that achieves the greatest good for the greatest number but at the price of violating an individual's rights, and, on the other hand, a course of action that respects the individual's rights but at the price of a substantial reduction in the achievement of the greatest good.

There are no well-defined rules for solving the moral dilemmas that these conflicts pose. The dilemmas can be resolved only by making a considered judgment concerning which of the conflicting criteria should be accorded the most weight in the given situation. In some cases the judgment may be easier than in others. Suppose, for example, that violating an employee's right to privacy on the job is the only way to stopping continuing thefts that deprive thousands of customers from getting quality pharmaceutical products. Then the utilitarian criterion may be given greater weight than the rights criterion—employee's rights must be sacrificed for the "greatest good."

Although there are no hard and fast rules for resolving moral dilemmas of this sort, there is a systematic procedure for handling them—the *principle of double effect.* Stated simply, this principle holds that it is acceptable to make a decision that has two effects, one good and one bad, provided that the decision maker's dominant motivation is to achieve the good effect and provided that the good effect is important enough to permit the bad effect [Grisez, 1970].

Conflicts within criteria.   Not only may the three criteria conflict with each other, but each may conflict with itself as well. *First,* there may be conflict between the utilitarian consequences of those involved or with the means chosen to accomplish the appropriate goals. This is probably typical in organizations that have coalitions with conflicting goals or where there is conflict among coalitions about the appropriate means to consensual goals. *Second,* there may be conflict between the rights of competing individuals. The decision maker may be forced to choose between permitting one person to preserve the right to privacy and allowing another person to exercise the right of free speech. *Third,* there may be a conflict between different canons of justice. Administering a rule with literal consistency, for example, may conflict with the principle that individuals who differ in relevant ways should be treated differently. Or there may be a conflict between individuals. A situation may, for example, call for hard choices between using seniority or using merit as the basis for deciding who is to be given preference.

As with conflicts between ethical criteria, there are no well-defined rules for the dilemmas within ethical criteria. Again, the decision maker is forced to employ a weighting procedure. For example, when rights come into conflict, the decision maker must make a conscientious judgment concerning the relative importance of the interests protected by one right as compared to the interests protected by the conflicting right. Although sometimes easy and obvious, such judgments can also be exceedingly difficult to make.

Lack of capacity to employ the criteria.   Three kinds of factors might legitimately relieve the decision maker of the responsibility of adhering to the ethical criteria relevant to a certain decision. All three of these factors relate to the decision maker's personal incapacity to adhere to the relevant criteria.

First, the decision maker may legitimately lay aside a certain ethical criterion if there is no freedom to use it. For example, a manager may be so pressured by others that ethical criteria cannot be brought to bear on the decision. Or a decision maker may be only in partial control of a certain decision and thus unable to use a specific ethical criterion.

Second, the decision maker might legitimately fail to employ a certain ethical criterion owing to a lack of adequate information for using that criterion. As we have seen, this is more often the case with the utilitarian and justice criteria than with the rights criterion.

Third, the decision maker who has strong and reasonable doubts about the legitimacy of an ethical criterion can legitimately be excused from adhering to that criterion. There is nothing sacred about the specific ethical criteria proposed in this article. They represent a consensus among normative ethicians, but that does not preclude other, more or less constraining norms being employed, as long as they are arrived at conscientiously.

Faced with any of these three kinds of incapacitating factors, the decision maker may legitimately accord a lesser weight to one criterion. The underlying rationale for such systematic devaluation of ethical criteria is simple. Persons cannot be held responsible for matters they cannot control or for matters about which they are ignorant or sincerely in doubt. However, determining whether a decision maker's lack of freedom, lack of information, or lack of certitude is sufficient to abrogate ethical responsibility requires one to make some exceedingly difficult judgments.

IMPLICATIONS

An important implication of any research on ethics lies in the area of education and development. This is particularly true regarding the subject of organizational politics. Presented in an ethically bland fashion, theories of organizational politics tend to evoke an unfortunate combination of cynicism, defeatism, and paranoia. Without ethical paradigms, individuals too often infer that success is controlled by others or attained only by those who engage in unproductive behavior. In contrast, confronting the ethical issues in organizational politics leads individuals to assume responsibility for their political behavior decisions. It is unlikely that such an approach will enable individuals to solve all the ethical dilemmas they will face in their careers, but it may stimulate "moral" development [Kohlberg, 1973].

Several lines of research are also suggested by the foregoing analysis. First, there would be some value in further developing ethical paradigms for other areas of discretion faced by organizational members. For example, the areas of obedience, whistle blowing, self-promotion, and bottom-up social intervention all cry out for ethical guidance. Second, there is a need to conduct empirical research regarding what rights, canons of justice, and utilitarian rules are commonly accepted in general and in specific dilemmas. Third, the *process* of ethical judgment about politics and other issues needs empirical work. For example, what antecedent conditions are associated with ethical actions? Similarly, how do ethical codes formalized in an organization influence political behavior decisions?

CONCLUDING REMARKS

As should be clear from this discussion, reducing the ethical uncertainty surrounding political behavior decisions places significant cognitive burdens on the decision maker [Simon, 1976]. Judging the normative equality of PBAs can involve confronting complicated ethical dilemmas. Yet, there seems to be no satisfactory substitute for individual discretion that addresses these complexities directly and to the limits of one's cognitive capabilities.

As we have seen, management theory offers little guidance in this regard. Its calculative form influences us to be ethically myopic when we evaluate political behavior. Instead of determining whether human rights or standards of justice are violated, we are often content to judge political behavior according to its outcomes. This orientation invites cynicism about what are termed the political realities of organizational life [Nord, 1978]. For example, in describing a patently unethical political act, one writer asserted "many people think it is wrong to try to influence others in this way, even people who, without consciously recognizing it, use this technique themselves" [Kotter, 1977], as if to justify the action. We do not intend to replace cynicism of this kind with Polyanna assertions that ethical managers (politicians) will be more successful than unethical ones. They may or may not be, but that is really not the point. Ethics involves standards of conduct, not guidelines for personal gain. When it comes to the ethics of organizational politics, respect for justice and human rights should prevail for its own sake.

REFERENCES

Allen, R. W.; Madison, D. L.; Porter, L. W.; Renwick, P. A.; & Mayes, B. T. Organizational politics: Tactics and characteristics of its actors. *California Management Review*, 1979, 22(4), 77-83.

Aristotle. *The Nicomachean ethics* (J. A. K. Thomson, trans.). London: Allen & Unwin, 1953. (330 B.C.)

Bennis, W.; & Slater, P. *The temporary society.* New York: Harper & Row, 1968.

Bentham, J. *An introduction to the principles of morals and legislation.* New York: Hafner, 1948. (1789)

Bok, S. Whistleblowing and professional responsibilities. In D. Callahan & S. Bok (Eds.), *Ethics teaching in higher education.* New York: Plenum, 1980.

Bowie, N. E. *Toward a new theory of distributive justice.* Amherst: University of Massachusetts Press, 1971.

Brandt, R. B. *A theory of the good and the right.* New York: Oxford University Press, 1979.

Crozier, M. *The bureaucratic phenomena.* Chicago: University of Chicago Press, 1964.

Dahl, R. A. The concept of power. *Behavioral Science* 1957, *2*, 201-205.

Daniels, N. Merit and meritocracy. *Philosophy & Public Affairs,* 1978, *7*, 206-223.

Drake, B. *Normative constraints on power in organizational decision making.* Unpublished manuscript, School of Business Administration, Wayne State University, Detroit, 1979.

Dworkin, R. *Taking rights seriously.* Cambridge: Harvard University Press. 1978.

Eells, R. *The government of corporations.* New York: Free Press, 1962.

Evan, W. M. Power, conflict, and constitutionism in organizations. *Social Science Information* 1975, *14*, 53-80.

Ewing, D. W. *Freedom inside the organization.* New York: McGraw-Hill, 1977.

Ewing, D. W. Constitutionalizing the corporation. In T. Bradshaw & D. Vogel (Eds.), *Corporations and their culture.* New York: McGraw-Hill, 1981.

Feinberg, J. *Social philosophy.* Englewood Cliffs, N. J.: Prentice-Hall, 1973.

Fuller, L. *The morality of law.* New Haven: Yale University Press, 1964.

Gandz, J.; & Murray, V. V. The experience of work place politics. *Academy of Management Journal,* 1980, *23*, 237-251.

Grisez, G. *Abortion: The myths, the realities, and the arguments.* New York: Corpus Books, 1970.

Hart, H. L. A. Are there any natural rights? *Philosophical Review,* 1955, *64*, 175-191.

Hickson, D. J.; Hinings, C. R.; Lee, C. A.; Schneck, R. E.; & Pennings, J. M. A strategic contingencies theory of intraorganizational power. *Administrative Science Quarterly,* 1971, *19*, 216-229.

Hobbes, T. *The leviathan.* New York: Bobbs-Merrill, 1958. (1651)

Kant, I. *The metaphysical elements of justice* (J. Ladd, trans.) New York: Library of Liberal Arts, 1965. (1797)

Keeley, M. *Justice versus effectiveness in organizational evaluation.* Paper presented at the annual meeting of the Academy of Management, Atlanta, 1979.

Kohlberg, L. *Collected papers on moral development and moral education.* Cambridge: Center for Moral Education, Harvard University, 1973.

Kotter, J. P. Power, dependence, and effective management. *Harvard Business Review*, 1977, *53*(3), 125-136.

Krupp, S. *Patterns of organization analysis*. New York: Holt, Rinehart & Winston, 1961.

Locke, J. *The second treatise of government*. New York: Liberal Arts Press, 1952. (1690)

Lyons, D. *The forms and limits of utilitarianism*. Oxford: Clarendon Press, 1965.

Martin, N. H.; & Sims, J. H. Power tactics. *Harvard Business Review*, 1956, *34*(3), 25-36.

Mayes, B. T.; & Allen, R. W. Toward a definition of organizational politics. *Academy of Management Review*, 1977, *2*, 672-678.

Miles, R. H. *Macro organizational behavior*. Santa Monica, Calif.: Goodyear, 1980.

Mill, J. S. *Utilitarinism*. Indianapolis: Bobbs-Merrill, 1957. (1863)

Miller, A. R. *The assault on privacy*. Ann Arbor: University of Michigan Press, 1971.

Mironi, M. The confidentiality of personal records: A legal and ethical view. *Labor Law Journal*, 1974, *25*, 270-292.

Nord, W. R. Dreams of humanization and the realities of power. *Academy of Management Review*, 1978, *3*, 674-679.

Nozick, R. *Anarchy, state, and utopia*. New York: Basic Books, 1974.

Okum, A. M. *Equality and efficiency: The big-trade-off,* Washington: Brookings Institution, 1975.

Perelman, C. *The idea of justice and the problem of argument,* New York: Humanities Press, 1963.

Pettigrew, A. M. *The politics of organizational decision making*. London: Tavistock, 1973.

Pfeffer, J. Power and resource allocation in organizations. In B. Staw & G. Salancik (Eds.), *New directions in organizational behavior*. Chicago: St. Clair Press, 1977, pp. 235-266.

Pfeffer, J. The micropolitics of organizations. In M. W. Meyer and associates (Eds.), *Environments and organizations*. San Francisco: Jossey-Bass, 1978, pp. 29-50.

Pfeffer, J.; & Salancik, G. Organizational decision making as a political process. *Administrative Science Quarterly*, 1974, *18*, 135-151.

Rawls, J. *A theory of justice*. Cambridge, Mass.: Belknap Press, 1971.

Schein, E. H. The problem of moral education for the business manager. *Industrial Management Review*, 1966, *7*, 3-11.

Schein, V. E. Individual power and political behaviors in organizations: An inadequately explored reality. *Academy of Management Review*, 1977, *2*, 64-72.

Sidgwick, H. *The methods of ethics*. New York: Dover, 1966.

Simon, H. A. *Administrative Behavior* (3rd ed.). New York: Free Press, 1976.

Singer, P. Rights and the market. In J. Arthur & W. Shaw (Eds.), *Justice and economic distribution*. Englewood Cliffs, N. J.: Prentice-Hall, 1978, pp. 207-221.

Smart, J. J. C. An outline of a system of utilitarian ethics. In J. C. C. Smart & B. Williams (Eds.), *Utilitarianism for and against,* New York: Cambridge University Press, 1973, 3-74.

Sobel, J. H. Utilitarianism: Simple and general. *Inquiry*, 1970, *13*, 394-449.

Thompson, J. D. *Organizations in action.* New York: McGraw-Hill, 1967.

Tushman, M. T. A political approach to organizations: A review and rationale. *Academy of Management Review,* 1977, *2,* 206-216.

Waters, K. D. Your employee's right to blow the whistle. *Harvard Business Review,* 1975, *53*(4), 26-34.

Walzer, M. The obligation to disobey. *Ethics,* 1967, *77*(3), 163-175.

Wasserstrom, R. Privacy and the law: In R. Bronaugh (Ed.), *Philosophical law.* Westport, Conn.: Greenwood Press, 1978.

Zald, M. N. (Ed.), *Power in organizations.* Nashville: Vanderbilt University Press, 1970.

Zaleznik, A. Power and politics in organizational life. *Harvard Business Review,* 1970, *48*(2), 47-60.

The Experience of Workplace Politics

JEFFREY GANDZ
VICTOR V. MURRAY

For many years people who work in complex organizations have talked about company politics, politicians, and political decisions. It is only comparatively recently, since the early 1960s, that explicit references to politics in the workplace have begun to appear with regularity in the organizational behavior literature. A survey of the literature undertaken as preparation for this project revealed 3 references directly on workplace politics before 1962, 5 between 1963 and 1967, 7 between 1969 and 1972, and 11 between 1973 and 1977. Most of this writing was at the conceptual and theoretical level. Only a small proportion reported on empirical studies.

There is a lack of uniformity in the ways in which different writers define organizational or workplace politics. In one category are those who define it in a "neutral" fashion as the occurrence of certain forms of behavior associated with the use of power or influence. A second group tend to define it in terms of an actor's subjectively realized intention of engaging in self-serving behaviors at the expense of others in the organization.

Within the first category there are a number of groups, as Mayes and Allen (1977) have pointed out. There are those (Harvey & Mills, 1970; Wildavsky, 1964) who see any conflict over the allocation of scarce resources as a political process. A second group (Walmsley & Zald, 1973; March, 1962) broaden the definition to include conflict over any policy decision, not just those relating to the allocation of scarce resources. A third group (Butler, Hickson, Wilson, & Axelsson, 1977; Martin & Sims, 1956) sees the use of *any* power or influence as political.

Within the second category, those defining politics in terms of consciously self-serving behaviors, there are also a number of subdivisions. One of these sees political behavior as both self-serving and contrary to organizational effectiveness. Another sees it as the pursuit of self-interest which conflicts with the interest of any organizational member. In the first group, Batten and Swab (1965, p. 13), for example, say that "men engage in company politics because they believe that they can best achieve what they want in a devious, indirect and underhanded way." Pettigrew (1973) defines company politics as the by play that occurs when one man or group of men want to advance themselves or their ideas regardless of whether or not those ideas would help the company. Porter's (1976) definition is substantially the same, and Mayes and Allen (1977) are quite emphatic in defining politics as the use of influence for ends or means that are not sanctioned by the organization.

Burns (1961), Butler (1971), and Frost and Hayes (1977) avoid reifying the organization, viewing it as a constantly shifting set of groups and individuals seeking to impose their views of the organization's purpose on others. Typical is this definition of Frost and Hayes:

> Political behavior (is) the activities of organizational members . . . when they use resourcs to enhance or protect their share of an exchange . . . in ways which would be resisted, or ways in which the impact would be resisted, if recognized by the other party(ies) to the exchange (1977, p. 8).

The empirical research on workplace politics has used the "neutral" definition of politics discussed above. This research tends to be restricted almost exclusively to lateral conflicts in budget setting (Wildavsky, 1964), purchasing decisions (Strauss, 1964), or general policy setting (Pfeffer & Salancik, 1974). Those writing about workplace politics as a subjective process, involving the conscious pursuit of self-interest, have not undertaken research based on this conception.

In sharp contrast to the studies of social scientists, with their reluctance to study the subjective side of workplace politics, is the approach of the writers of organizational fiction and the journalists who analyze the workings of business and government policy makers. These writers subscribe fully to the concept of politics based on the pursuit of self-interest. Uninhibited by strictures to be "objective," they unasham-edly impute all kinds of motives, schemes, and plots to the minds of their subjects. Any group of academic organization theorists gathered for a social chit-chat blithely do the same thing . . . as long as it is not for publication!

PURPOSE OF RESEARCH

The authors were curious about what organizational processes managers subjectively experienced as being the most pervaded by politics and how they felt about those who engage in political behaviors. They also were interested in the personal, job, and organizational variables that might affect managers' perceptions and feelings, although a comprehensive examination of these was not the primary aim of the study.

From inferences derived from related research, the authors' employment experiences, and unstructured preliminary interviews with managerial and nonmanagerial employees, a number of tentative general hypotheses were developed to guide the research. These were:

1. *Talk about "politics" and "politicians" would be common in most organizations.*

The hypothesis was based solely on preliminary interviews with managers and personal experience. No previous research has been reported on the frequency of political talk in work settings.

2. *The perception of politics would occur primarily around issues and events that were not guided by explicit policy or precedent nor derived from an obvious techno-economic rationale.*

This hypothesis is inferred from the work of March (1962), Cyert and March (1963), and others who define all nonroutine decision making as political. Although none of these authors has suggested that managers in organizations will consciously perceive the decision making process in the same way as they themselves do, it is not unreasonable to assume they would. Hence those issues and processes involving change in a context that does not permit strict cost/benefit analysis with widely shared criteria would be the most likely to be perceived as political by organizational members as well as by academics writing about organizations.

3. *Organization politicians and political actions would tend to be seen as self-serving and detrimental to organizational effectiveness.*
4. *People would believe that political astuteness is a necessary condition for advancement in organizational hierarchies.*

Again, for these two hypotheses it was necessary to fall back on the preliminary interview results and personal experience because no prior research reports on attitudes toward politics or belief systems associated with the perception of workplace politics.

5. *People who see their organizations as highly political would tend to be those at lower levels in the organization who are dissatisfied with their jobs and pessimistic about future success in their organizations. Such people would be responding as "victims" of political actions.*

If one assumes that most managers feel negatively about politics, it follows that they would not be likely to admit that they personally would consciously and willingly engage in such behavior. Conversely, it is possible to infer that those who are seen as causing dissatisfaction for an actor are likely to be seen as engaging in political behavior. From the opposite point of view, those seen as engaging in a great deal of disliked political behavior will create a sense of job dissatisfaction in the perceiver. In either case one would expect to find an association between the level of job satisfaction and the amount of workplace politics perceived. Also, because previous research (Locke, 1976) indicates that dissatisfaction is greater at lower hierarchial levels, more politics will be perceived by people at these levels. This argument is derived primarily from cognitive dissonance theory (Festinger, 1957). The perceived existence of political behavior, negative affect toward it, and high job satisfaction are not consonant cognitive states.

6. *Public sector employees would be likely to see their organizations as more political than would those in the private sector.*

This hypothesis is derived directly from the same rationale as that for Hypothesis 2 coupled with the literature on public sector organizations, e.g., Downs (1967), Warwick (1975), and Rainey, Backoff, and Levine (1976). This latter writing indicates quite clearly that decision making in public sector organizations is less susceptible to the application of technoeconomic rationality. Hence the process will tend to be viewed as more political.

SAMPLE AND RESEARCH METHOD

A mailed, self-administered questionnaire was sent to North American resident graduates and current part-time MBA students of a large metropolitan Canadian business school. From a total of 590 question-naires mailed out, 428 usable responses were returned, a 72 percent response rate. This sample was not representative of managers in general as it was heavily biased toward younger, highly educated males. There was, however, a good distribution of respondents in different types of public and private sector organizations, organizational functions, and hierarchical levels.

The questionnaire consisted of three sections. In the first section respondents were asked (a) the extent to which talk about politics was common in their organizations and the extent to which political considerations influenced 11 organizational processes such as pay determination, promotion, disciplinary penalties and interdepartmental cooperation; (b) the levels in the organization in which they considered political activities to be most prevalent; and (c) how they felt about politics in terms of their impact on organizational effectiveness, the success and effectiveness of executives in organizations, and the general effect.

In the second part of the questionnaire, respondents were asked to provide data on (a) selected demographic variables; (b) previous job experience and employment history; (c) current functional and supervisory responsibilities; (d) dimensions of their job contexts including autonomy, variety, feedback on performance, social interaction, opportunity for promotion, and overall job satisfaction; (e) organizational characteristics including size, product or service markets, and economic sector (business or government).

In the third section of the questionnaire, respondents were asked to describe an actual situation, involving either themselves or others, that was to them "a good example of workplace politics in action." In this section, 123 (31 percent) of the respondents provided usable stories, which were content analyzed for major themes by one of the investigators. The content analysis of the narratives was done independently of the analysis of the questionnaire responses to minimize coder bias.

RESULTS

The Extent of Political Talk

As anticipated, politics is the subject of much of the casual conversation that goes on over coffee breaks and lunch at work. Of all respondents, 60 percent agreed with the statements that "most casual conversation appears to be about things I would consider as workplace politics" or "it is among the more popular topics of conversation," while 35 percent agreed that "it only comes up now and then." The remaining 5 percent agreed that "it rarely or never comes up at all."

Perceived Politicization of Organizational Processes

Two approaches were taken to assessing the extent to which certain organizational processes were perceived as being pervaded by political behaviors. The first involved presenting, in the self-administered questionnaire, 11 organizational processes in which politics may play a part and asking respondents the extent (never = 0; rarely = 1; frequently = 2; always = 3) to which these processes were influenced by politics in their organizations. The second approach was the content analysis of the 132 narratives of political incidents provided by the respondents.

The scores on the 11 processes presented in the questionnaire, their relative rankings, and the results of a nonparametric analysis of variance are shown in Table 1. Although objective measures of the degree to which managerial discretion is involved in each of these processes are not at hand, it appears as if the ones that are seen as most politicized, such as interdepartmental coordination, the delegation of authority, and promotion and transfers, are those in which there are usually few established rules of standards and criteria tend to be "fuzzy" or open to great subjectivity. Those seen as least political, such as the application of personnel policies, hiring, and the application of disciplinary penalties, are those in which policies, some objective criteria, or precedents exist.

Table 1 **Perceived Politicization of Organizational Processes**

Process	Mean Rank	Mean Score[a]	% Always or Frequency
Promotions and transfers	7.4	1.65	59.5
Hiring	4.7	1.03	22.5
Pay	5.4	1.21	33.1
Budget allocation	5.5	1.27	37.6
Facilities, equipment allocation	6.6	1.48	49.2
Delegation of authority	7.3	1.65	58.7
Interdepartmental coordination	7.8	1.77	68.4
Personnel policies	5.2	1.14	28.0
Disciplinary penalties	4.5	.98	21.5
Work appraisals	6.2	1.37	42.4
Grievances and complaints	5.4	1.22	31.6

Friedman 2-way ANOVA[b]
$x^2 = 462.5; D. F. = 10; p < .001$

[a]Scores: $0 = $ never, $1 = $ sometimes, $2 = $ frequently, $3 = $ always.
[b]All interprocess differences were significant ($p < .001$) in a Wilcoxon matched pairs signed rank test except: promotions and transfers/delegation of authority; promotions and transfers/interdepartmental coordination; hiring/personnel policies, disciplinary penalties; pay/personnel policies; budget allocation/personnel policies, work appraisals; facilities, equipment allocation/work appraisal.

The analysis of the narratives provided by the respondents yielded 192 "political" incidents, and the results tended to support the findings from the self-administered questionnaire. Promotions, transfers, demotions, and dismissals were mentioned in 32 percent of the political incidents. These stories dealt with perceived inequities in the decisions of superiors about their subordinates. Of these, the most common theme was that of employees bypassed for promotion by someone else with "pull" with the supervisor based on friendship, although the person overlooked allegedly had superior competence.

The assessment of work performance was the second most common theme in the narratives, featuring in 31 percent of the incidents. The stories dealt with avoiding blame for poor work performance, fear of superiors, perceptions of superiors judging performance on hidden or uncontrollable criteria, superiors who were nonsupportive, or superiors and colleagues who spent most of their time "covering their asses" (Warwick, 1975)

Of the incidents cited, 20 percent mentioned interunit competition for authority: who should have control over special projects, new functions, or the transfer of old functions to new units. Competition for authority between superiors and subordinates featured in 17 percent of the incidents. They involved head offices trying to get control of a project or function from field offices or vice versa, subordinates trying to "end-run" superiors, subordinates resisting the orders, or influence-attempts of others. Stories about who should, or should not, have been assigned to particular tasks or projects were the subject of 14 percent of the incidents.

Table 2   Locus of Political Behavior by Managerial Level and Occupational Category Means of Respondent Scores

Locus of Political Behavior[b]	Grand Mean	Managerial Level of Respondents				K-W ANOVA[b] x^2
		Senior	Middle	Lower	Non-managerial	
Top Management	1.22	.91	1.18	1.29	1.36	15.5** (n = 420)
Middle management	1.07	.75	1.08	1.18	1.16	15.7** (n = 417)
Lower management	.73	.56	.67	.84	.80	6.2** (n = 413)
Technical and professional	.54	.49	.54	.60	.50	3.3 (n = 408)
Clerical and white collar	.50	.61	.44	.41	.57	12.9** (n = 408)
Production and blue collar	.18	.35	.19	.12	.11	5.9 (n = 373)
Friedman test ANOVA x^{2c}	354.2** (n = 365)	17.3* (n = 59)	108.6** (n = 107)	137.0** (n = 98)	106.9** (n = 99)	

[a]Respondents asked the extent (always = 3; frequently = 2; rarely = 1; never = 0) to which the climate at different managerial levels and in different occupational groups is "political."
[b]Kruskal-Wallis nonparametric one-way analysis of variance.
[c]Friedman test.
*$p < .01$
**$p < .001$

Locus of Political Behaviors

Both in their questionnaire responses and in their narratives, respondents indicated that they perceived the climate to be more political at higher managerial levels in the organization and less political at lower managerial and among nonmanagerial occupational groups.

Table 2 shows the extent to which respondents in each of four managerial groups (top, middle, lower, and nonmanagerial) considered the overall climate to be political within three managerial groups (senior, middle, lower) and three other occupational categories (technical-professional, clerical and white collar, production and blue collar). The two nonparametric analyses of variance presented in this table indicate that:

a. In the respondent sample as a whole, the climate is considered to be more political at higher managerial levels and less political among lower managerial and nonmanagerial groups.

b. More senior managerial respondents viewed the climates at each managerial level to be less political than did less senior and nonmanagerial respondents. There were no significant differences between respondent groups in the extent to which they perceived the climate as political in the nonmanagerial occupational groups.

c. Within each level of respondents, the climate was seen to be more political at higher managerial levels within the organization.

Levels of management were identified in 105 of the 132 narrative cases. The most frequently mentioned level involved in the incidents was middle management (department and division managers, plant managers, etc.), featured in 42 percent of the cases. Top management (presidents, chief executive officers, vice-presidents, etc.) was mentioned in 29 percent. First-line management was identified as acting politically in 14 percent of the narratives and nonmanagerial employees in 15 percent. The difference between the narratives and the questionnaire responses, in terms of the relative politicization of upper and middle management, is believed to be attributable to the lack of knowledge of specific incidents at the top management level. The respondents were mainly at lower and middle levels in the organization.

Attitudes and Beliefs about Workplace Politics

Respondents were asked the extent to which they agreed or disagreed with 10 statements about a number of aspects of workplace politics. They included items relating to the impact of politics on organizational effectiveness, whether political organizations were "happy" ones, whether politics was played by weak or powerful executives, the locus of political activity, how common politics was in organizations, and the relationship between political astuteness and executive success.

General affect toward workplace politics was investigated with a 9-item semantic differential anchored by adjectives such as good/bad, rational/irrational, fair/unfair, and dirty/clean.

Table 3   Responses to Statements about Workplace Politics

Statement	Mean Score[a]	Standard Deviation	Strong or Moderate Agreement %
(a) The existence of workplace politics is common to most organizations	1.59	.71	93.2
(b) Successful executives must be good politicians	1.75	.88	89.0
(c) The higher you go in organizations, the more political the climate becomes	1.99	1.10	76.2
(d) Only organizationally weak people play politics[b]	2.21	1.17	68.5
(e) Organizations free of politics are happier than those where there is a lot of politics	2.34	1.09	59.1
(f) You have to be political to get ahead in organizations	2.37	1.13	69.8
(g) Politics in organizations are detrimental to efficiency	2.57	1.14	55.1
(h) Top management should try to get rid of politics within the organization	2.67	1.23	48.6
(i) Politics help organizations function effectively[b]	2.76	1.13	42.1
(j) Powerful executives don't act politically[b]	3.87	1.15	15.7

[a]Score: 1—strongly agree; 2—slightly agree; 3—neither agree or disagree; 4—slightly disagree; 5—strongly disagree.
[b]Reverse scoring.

The responses to both these item sets showed a certain amount of amibivalence in the view of workplace politics held by respondents. On the one hand, over 70 percent agreed with statements to the effect that workplace politics are common, successful and powerful executives act politically, the higher one climbs in an organization the more political the climate becomes, and that one must be a good politician to get ahead. On the other hand, 68 percent indicated strong or moderate agreement with the statement that organizationally weak people play politics; 55 percent felt that organizations free of politics are happier than those in which there is a lot of politics; 55 percent felt that politics is detrimental to organizational effectiveness, and 49 percent felt that top management should attempt to get rid of politics in the organization. In terms of general affect, respondents felt that politics are generally bad, unfair, unnecessary, unhealthy, and conflictual. In short, respondents felt that workplace politics are common and inevitable, particularly at higher levels in the organization. But, while realizing this and recognizing that to be successful they may have to be good at playing politics, they don't feel that this is the way that it *ought* to be.

The analysis of the narratives showed that 73 percent of the political incidents described depicted political activity as harmful to the organization as a whole, to some unit of it, or to the protagonists in the story. Fully 84 percent of the stories described some deviation from "businesslike practice" or techno-economic rationality.

Factors Influencing Perceived Politicization

It was suggested at the outset of this paper that workplace politics may best be conceived of as a state of mind rather than as an objective state. Conflicts may exist, power plays and negotiations may go on, and they may not be defined as political by some organizational members. Others may define the application of a routine bureaucratic procedure as intensely political.

The results presented above show substantial variance in the extent to which respondents view different organizational processes as politicized and in the feelings, attitudes, and beliefs about workplace politics and politicians. The primary objective of this study was not to explain this variance. It was expected that most of the explanation would lie in variables relating to the personality, cognitive processes, hopes and aspirations, and life experiences of the respondents. This was not investigated in this initial study. However, two specific hypotheses were tested.

1. *People who see their organization as highly political would tend to be at lower levels in the organization, dissatisfied with their jobs, and pessimistic about opportunities for promotion.*
2. *Public sector employees would be likely to see their organizations as more political than would those in the private sector.*

The dependent variable in the test of these hypotheses was a scale of perceived politicization formed by summing scores on the 11 organizational processes described in Table 1. This scale has a mean interitem Pearson product moment correlation of .36 and a coefficient of reliability (standardized item alpha) of .86. A high score on this scale indicates that the respondent considers the organization as highly political.

The independent variables were:

1. Seven-point items relating to overall job satisfaction, autonomy, variety, feedback on performance, social interaction on the job, and the opportunity for promotion (Hackman & Oldham, 1974).
2. Managerial level in the organization. Respondents were assigned to groups on the basis of their responses to a number of questions on job title, job description, number of levels of authority above and below, and number of people directly and indirectly supervised. Agreement between two coders on a random sample of 100 respondents was 93 percent. The categories were: top management—chief executive officers, presidents, vice-presidents, directors of government agencies; middle management—department or division heads, functional heads below vice-president level, assistants to directors of governmental agencies; lower management—first line supervisors and managers; and nonmanagement—technical, sales, and professional personnel.
3. A nominal variable indicating whether the respondent was employed in a private (business) or public (federal, provincial, municipal government) organization.
4. Other variables, such as age, income, years of work experience and size of organization (number of employees), that might moderate the hypothesized relationships.

In a bivariate correlation analysis, shown in Table 4, perceived politicization was significantly ($p < .01$) but weakly associated with lower managerial level, lack of variety and autonomy in the job, low amounts of feedback, and poor opportunities for promotions. However, in a test of differences between respondents in private and public sector organizations, perceived politicization was not significantly different ($t = 1.84$, $p > .05$) between the groups.

In a stepwise multiple regression analysis, perceived politicization was regressed on all 13 variables shown in Table 4 with dummy variable coding used for managerial levels and private/public sector. Job dissatisfaction, low autonomy, and poor opportunity for promotion were the only significant ($p < .05$) regression coefficients. It was possible to account for only 11 percent of the variance in the regression sample ($n = 322$) with shrinkage to 5 percent in the hold-out, validation sample ($n = 106$). In short, a substantial amount of variance is not accounted for on the basis of these variables, and the hypothesized relationships among managerial level, private/public sector, and perceived politicization, were not supported in the multivariate analysis.

Table 4   **Correlations Between Perceived Politicization and Personal,
Job, and Organizational Characteristics**

Spearman Rank Order Correlations ($372 \leq n \leq 428$)

	1	2	3	4
1. Politicization				
2. Managerial level	−.12*			
3. Age	.09	.47**		
4. Income	−.10	.58**	.61**	
5. Years of work experience	−.08	.54**	.86**	.69**
6. Years present employer	−.05	.34**	.50**	.49**
7. Job variety	−.12*	.30**	.17**	.29**
8. Job autonomy	−.19**	.28**	.20**	.33**
9. Social interaction	−.09	.08	.04	.07
10. Feedback	−.11	.13*	.03	.13*
11. Job satisfaction	−.21**	.24**	.14*	.25**
12. Promotion opportunity	−.12*	−.18**	−.28**	−.13*
13. Size of organization	.07	−.33**	−.08	−.05

*$p < .01$
**$p < .001$ one-tailed test

The bivariate relationship between perceived politicization and job satisfaction ($p = -.21, p < .001$) suggested one other hypotheses: *that viewing one's organization as political might be a source of job dissatisfaction.* Job satisfaction was regressed against the variables in Table 4, a dummy variable for private sector, and the perceived politicization scale. As expected, job variety, opportunity for promotion, and feedback on performance were the main contributors to a total explained variance of 48 percent in the validation sample. However, perceived politicization also had a significant ($p < .02$) coefficient in this regression equation, suggesting that it may be one facet of overall job satisfaction, heretofore ignored in the voluminous literature on this complex construct.

DISCUSSION

In this study, an attempt was made to develop an understanding of the meaning of workplace politics to those who work in a variety of business and government organizations. In some respects, the picture is clear. Talk about politics is common in the workplace; respondents see politics as deviations from techno-economic rationality, as pervading discretionary more than other types of organizational processes, and as more prevalent among higher and middle managerial levels than among lower and nonmanagerial levels.

The narratives focused on self-serving and self-advancing behavior of which the narrators clearly disapproved. In general, the sample viewed politics and political behavior unfavorably, most of them viewing work-place politics as detrimental to organizational effectiveness. Clearly,

5	6	7	8	9	10	11	12
.62**							
.22**	.09						
.28**	.15**	.47**					
.08	.04	.28**	.24**				
.03	.03	.21**	.26**	.21**			
.13*	.08	.47**	.39**	.29**	.36**		
−.28**	−.20**	.08	.09	.16**	.15*	.29**	
−.04	.14	−.10	−.11	.00	−.10	−.08	.16**

the preference of the sample was for the Weberian dream of the ideal decision making process, impersonal and *sine ira ac studio*. However, with this preference is the belief, perhaps realistic or perhaps cynical, that executive success is contingent on political astuteness.

As previously noted, earlier writing on this subject has tended to view it from two distinct points of view. One, striving for value neutrality, has used the term to refer to any use of power, influence, or negotiating behavior that occurs within an organization. The other is based on the subjective, conscious intent on the part of one or more organizational members to gain self-interests at the expense of others.

Clearly, it does not facilitate the further development of this subject to retain such diverse definitions of its meaning. This study indicates that, although politics is viewed by the majority in the sample as a deviation from techno-economic rationality in decision making and usually involves conflict and the use of influence, it is not always viewed this way. It appears that the orderly development of this element of organizational theory would be best served if the concept of organizational politics is not used synonymously with the well-established concepts of organizational conflict, power, and influence. It should be restricted to denote *a subjective state in which organizational members perceive themselves or others as intentionally seeking selfish ends in an organizational context when such ends are opposed to those of others.*

Given this more restricted definition, future research should seek to clarify the impact of a number of variables on perceptions, attitudes, and beliefs about workplace politics and politicians. The present study provides only a beginning in providing some directions for future research and some insight into the problems and pitfalls that may be encountered. It is suggested that future research focus on the characteristics of organizational processes, the characteristics of the organizational actors, and the interactions of the two in the following manner.

Characteristics of the Process

Certain organizational processes lend themselves to being viewed as more political than others. They are processes in which managerial discretion is high and which relate to success or failure at work, relationships with superiors, and interunit lateral relations. Insofar as an individual, or others positively regarded, may not succeed to the level expected, it is convenient to believe the decisions were not rational and hence were political. To the extent that processes such as work appraisals, promotions, or transfers rest *in fact* on ill-defined, poorly known, or ambiguous criteria, such perceptions will be exacerbated. Previous writers (Thompson, 1967; Lawrence & Lorsch, 1967; Galbraith, 1977) have indicated that interunit lateral relations are the aspects of organizational integration that are most difficult to subject to routinization and techno-economic rationality. Further research should seek to define the specific characteristics of processes that influence their perception as political.

Characteristics of Perceivers

Certain functions, because of the nature of the job and the interactions with other functions, especially tend to involve people in organizational processes that might be considered political. Mintzberg (1973) and others have shown that both ambiguity and difficulty in applying technoeconomic rationality in decision making increase as one moves higher up in the hierarchy. The sample in this study confirmed this by indicating that political behavior was greater at higher levels.

One of the paradoxes revealed in the study, however, was the denial of the pervasiveness of politics by executives in the top management group, even though others indicated that they think politics are more prevalent at higher levels in the organization. There are a number of possible reasons for this paradox. It may reflect the self-image of the senior executives as techno-economic rationalists and the dissonance reduction sufficient to balance their predominantly negative view of politics and politicians. On the other hand, managerial level correlates significantly with job satisfaction in total and with other job situation variables such as variety and autonomy. The top executives were a highly satisfied group who, presumably, have had many of their expectations satisfied within their organizations and have no reason to look for political explanations for their own failure to achieve desired goals.

Even within the specific managerial levels and in the context of particular organizational processes, there is substantial variation in perceived politicization, attitudes, and beliefs. Job satisfaction has been shown to be one variable related to both perceived politicization and attitudes and beliefs about politics. One cannot rule out, on the basis of the data, the possibility that perceived politicization is one component of that job satisfaction. Although not measured in this study, it would be expected that both personal experiences and the personality of the perceiver would influence perceptions, attitudes, and feelings. It would be expected that the more one came to believe, through experience or teaching, that decisions could and should be made in terms of techno-economic rationality, and the more this is coupled with a cynical belief that people always seek to benefit themselves without regard to organizational well-being, then the more politics would be seen as occurring in the workplace. Such probing of past experience and the detailed attitudinal and personality inventories that would be needed to test such hypotheses were not included in this study. They present an opportunity for future research.

In conclusion, it is hoped that this study has brought some order to a burgeoning literature on workplace politics and clearly positioned it as a subjectively experienced phenomenon. The methodological problems in studying such a subject empirically are profound. Only rarely will protagonists in political events reveal their innermost thoughts to unknown researchers. In part, this can be overcome, as was done in this project, by asking respondents to report not on their own involvement, but on the behaviors of others which they would term political. The main alternative to this approach is the use of unobtrusive measures in participant observation studies.

Aside from further research on the determinants of the subjectivity experienced political climate in organizations, perhaps the most important unanswered question having to do with workplace politics is its impact on organizational decision making. Once a significant proportion of those involved in decision making come to believe that the organization's politics are the result of individuals pursuing purely selfish interests, what does this do to the quality of subsequent decisions and the way they are implemented?

Questions such as these illustrate the importance of shifting future research on workplace politics from *a priori* definitions to those with a phenomenological basis.

REFERENCES

1. Batten, J. D., & Swab, J. L. How to crack down on company politics. *Personnel,* 1965, 42, 8-20.
2. Burns, T. Micropolitics: Mechanisms of institutional change. *Administrative Science Quarterly,* 1961, 6, 257-281.
3. Butler, E. A. Corporate politics—Monster or friend? *Generation,* 1971, 3, 54-58.
4. Butler, R. J., Hickson, D. J., Wilson, D. C., & Axelsson, R. Organizational power, politicking and paralysis. Working Paper, Organizational Analyses Research Unit, University of Bradford, England, 1977.
5. Cyert, R. M., & March, J. G. A behavioral theory of the firm. Englewood Cliffs, N. J.: Prentice-Hall, 1963.
6. Downs, A. *Inside bureaucracy.* Boston: Little Brown, 1967.

7. Festinger, L. *A theory of cognitive dissonance*. Evanston, Ill.: Row Peterson, 1957.

8. Frost, P. J., & Hayes, D. C. An exploration in two cultures of political behavior in organizations. Paper presented at the Conference on Cross Cultural Studies in Organizational Functioning, Hawaii, September 1977.

9. Galbraith, J. *Organizational design*. Reading, Mass.: Addison-Wesley, 1977.

10. Hackman, J. R., & Oldham, G. R. *Job diagnostic survey: An instrument for the diagnoses of jobs and the evaluation of job redesign projects*. Technical Report No. 4, Department of Administrative Sciences, Yale University, 1974.

11. Harvey, E., & Mills, R. Patterns of organizational adaptation: A political perspective. In Mayer Zald (Ed.), *Power in organizations*. Nashville, Tenn.: Vanderbilt University Press, 1970, 181-213.

12. Lawrence, P., & Lorsch, J. W. *Organizations and environment*. Boston: Division of Research, Graduate School of Business Administration, Harvard University, 1967.

13. Locke, E. A. The nature and causes of job satisfaction. In M. Dunnette (Ed.), *Handbook of industrial and organizational psychology*. Chicago: Rand-McNally, 1297-1350.

14. March, J. G. The business firm as a political coalition, *Journal of Politics*, 1962, 24, 662-678.

15. Martin, N. H., & Sims, J. H. Power tactics. *Harvard Business Review*, 1956, 34, 25-36.

16. Mayes, B. T., & Allen, R. W. Toward a definition of organizational politics. *Academy of Management Review*, 1977, 2, 672-677.

17. Mintzberg, H. *The nature of managerial work*. New York: Harper and Row, 1973.

18. Pettigrew, A. M. *The politics of organizational decision making*. London: Tavistock, 1973.

19. Pfeffer, J., & Salancik, G. R. Organizational decision making as a political process: The case study of a university budget. *Administrative Science Quarterly*, 1974, 19, 135-151.

20. Porter, L. W. Organizations as political animals. Presidential Address, Division of Industrial Organizational Psychology, American Psychological Association 84th Annual Meeting, Washington, D. C., 1976.

21. Rainey, H. G., Backoff, R. W., & Levine, C. H. Comparing public and private organizations. *Public Administration Review*, March/April, 1976, 223-244.

22. Stauss, G. Workflow frictions, interfunctional rivalry, and professionalism: A case study of purchasing agents. *Human Organizations*, 1964, 23, 137-149.

23. Thompson, J. D. *Organizations in action*. New York: McGraw-Hill, 1967.

24. Wamsley, G., & Zald, M. *The political economy of public organizations*. Lexington, Mass.: Heath Co., 1973.

25. Warwick, D. P. *A theory of public bureaucracy*. Cambridge, Mass.: Harvard University Press, 1975.

26. Wildavsky, A. *The politics of the budgeting process*. New York: Little Brown, 1964.

Organizational Politics:
An Exploration of Managers' Perceptions

DAN L. MADISON
ROBERT W. ALLEN
LYMAN W. PORTER
PATRICIA A. RENWICK
BRONSTON T. MAYES

INTRODUCTION

Casual observations and the popular press sometimes give the impression that behavior commonly referred to as "political" is rampant in most organizations today. This apparent pervasiveness is in sharp contrast to the dearth of empirical and conceptual attention given the phenomenon by scholarly researchers (Mayes & Allen, 1977; Porter, 1976; Tushman, 1977). There are indications, however, that various members of the research community have recognized both the neglect and the importance of understanding political behaviors in organizations (e.g., Baldridge, 1971; Bucher, 1970; Pettigrew, 1973; Robbins, 1976; Scott, 1974).

An examination of the available literature on organizational politics reveals a collection of views, models, and lists of tactics that do not always seem to address the same phenomenon (Burns, 1961; Harvey & Mills, 1970; Martin & Sims, 1974; Robbins, 1976; Strauss, 1962; Tushman, 1977; Walmsley & Zald, 1973; Wildavsky, 1968). It is also apparent that the behaviors and situations examined in this literature are those which the *researchers* feel are political, irrespective of whether the members of organizations perceive them as political (e.g., Pettigrew, 1973; Pfeffer &

"Organizational Politics: An Exploration of Managers' Perceptions" by Dan L. Madison, Robert W. Allen, Lyman W. Porter, Patricia A. Renwick and Bronston T. Mayes, *Human Relations*, Volume 33, Number 2, 1980, pp. 79-100. Copyright © 1980 by Tavistock Institute of Human Relations. Reprinted by permission of Plenum Press.

Salancik, 1974; Rogers, 1971; Strauss, 1962). The perceptions of members of working organizations who, in the final analysis, actually engage in organizational politics should provide useful insights into the process as well as suggest fruitful areas for further research.

One might argue that reliance on perceptual data invites attribution of self-serving biases, and self-defensive interpretations of the events by the respondents. Indeed, we would agree. However, by concentrating on the subjects' perceptions of who or what is political, a more accurate description of the "world of everyday thought and experience," which Calder (1977, p. 183) calls "first-degree constructs," may be obtained. The approach adopted by the researchers is quite consistent with Calder's view that two primary ways to develop scientific concepts and terms (which he calls "second-degree constructs") are to abstract from a world of behavior or simplify from the everyday world of thought. In the case of organizational politics, the field of inquiry has seldom, if ever, been defined from the point of view of the organizational members. In keeping with that view, one of the purposes of this study is to explore perceptions of practicing managers regarding the overall incidence and characteristics of organizational politics, conditions associated with increased occurrence of organizational politics, and the impacts that organizational politics are perceived to have on individuals and the organization.

The perceptions and attributions of organizational politics held by members of organizations may serve as a basis for the development of second-degree constructs and formal models to be used in further research. Such information may aid in the definition of specified units (constructs), laws of interaction among the units, and boundary conditions within which the laws of interaction hold true as required in the formation of a well-developed theory (Dubin, 1978). On the other hand, organizational politics may be a special case of influence processes, distinguished only by the attribution of organizational members and researchers. However, we feel that Calder's (1977) admonition to study the everyday experience of leadership for its' own sake applies equally well to organizational politics; substituting for his use of the term "leadership":

> If it does nothing more than call attention to the need for understanding the everyday, nonscientific, meaning of [organizational politics] for specific groups of actors, attribution theory represents an advance for both [organizational politics] research and training. (p. 202)

A common theme running through the literature on organizational politics is that political behavior and power are intimately related (e.g., Dahl 1968; Gross, 1968; Lasswell, 1951; Pfiffner & Sherwood, 1960; Wergin, 1976, Wrong, 1968). To say that power and political behavior are intimately related is not the same as saying that they necessarily are the same thing. Rather, we would maintain, organizational politics is a process of influence or the "management of influence" as described by Mayes and Allen (1977), while power is a reservoir of potential influence consistent with the definitions of power and influence given by Cartwright and Zander (1968) and Katz and Kahn (1966). By way of analogy, power may be thought of as similar to wealth, while influence processes (such as organizational politics) are similar to cash flows by which the wealth is accumulated or dispersed. Wealth and cash flow are clearly related, but distinguishable, concepts. It is not necessary to have one to have the other, but it is likely that most people would argue that it helps.

While we would agree with authors who have related power and politics conceptually, there appears to be little empirical evidence available in the literature either to support or refute that relationship. Part of the intent of this study is to determine whether managers perceive a direct relationship between power and politics in the organizational setting. In addition, if it can be shown empirically that variables closely related to power are also perceived as related to organizational politics, additional inferential support may be provided for linking the concepts of power and politics. Such empirically demonstrated links may not only support the existence of relationships between power and politics, but also contribute to a better understanding of these relationships.

From the literature, it is possible to identify at least three separate variables that have been related to power and that may offer potential connecting links to organizational politics. These three variables are: (1) the degree of uncertainty in the situation; (2) the importance of the activity to the larger system of the organization, defined by Hickson, Hinings, Lee, Schneck, and Pennings (1971) as "centrality of workflow" and "substitutability of activities"; and (3) the salience to the individual actor, described by Patchen (1974) as "stake in the decision". The relationships between these variables and power have extensive support in the literature and are discussed briefly below.

The relationship between uncertainty and power has been widely noted. Crozier (1964) proposed that power is related to "the kind of uncertainty upon which depends the life of the organization" (p. 164). A similar argument was advanced by Perrow (1961). Lawrence and Lorsch (1967) discussed the greater influence of marketing, compared to other functional departments, in container firms and food processing firms. This appeared to be due, at least in part, to involvement with the relatively uncertain and innovative functions of the firm. These arguments concerning the importance of uncertainty in gaining power are consistent with Hickson et al. (1971), who stressed that it is the coping with uncertainty that is the real basis of power, rather than the presence of uncertainty alone.

Other writers have argued that neither the uncertainty, nor the ability to cope with uncertainty, are sufficient in themselves for the development of power. Blau (1964) and Emerson (1962) suggest that considerations of availability of alternative actions or resources are important in discussions of power at the macro level. Dubin (1957) introduced the ideal of ease of substitution as relevant to power within the organization. Hickson et al. (1971) added to the notion of substitutability by observing that the substitution could be from outside the organization, as well as from within it. Both internal and external alternatives are combined in the term "substitutability" in their strategic contingencies theory.

The linkage between "salience of issue," or "decision," for an individual has been studied by Patchen (1974). He shows that the degree of involvement in the decision process and the amount of information gained by (or given to) the individual are related to the individual's own assessment of the salience of the issue and to the concern attributed to that individual by others. Although Patchen specifically discusses the amount of influence available to an individual based on the salience of the issue, the commonly accepted definition of power as potential influence (Katz & Kahn, 1966) serves to relate his work to the present discussion of variables related to power.

The relationships between power and the three variables mentioned above—(1) uncertainty, (2) importance to the organization, and (3) salience to the individual—are well established in the literature. Confirming the linkages of politics to any one—or all—of these variables would reinforce the inference that politics is also related to power. Indeed, Pettigrew (1973) explicitly made the connection between politics and the first of these variables, uncertainty, which was only implied in earlier writings on power. After following a somewhat different path through the literature than that described here, Pettigrew (1973) stated that political behavior is "likely to be especially pronounced in the uncertain task environment surrounding an innovative decision" (p. 30). He observed and reported behaviors that he defined as political in the uncertainty of a major purchase decision but did not measure whether the participants *perceived* the activity as political.

The present study focused on providing information on managerial *perceptions* concerning political phenomena (i.e., what managers think takes place in organizations concerning politics). No attempt was made to measure actual situations or behaviors. However, Lewin (1936) and others have argued that behavior is in response to perception of reality rather than to some objective reality. Porter (1976) has added that perceptions are important "whether or not they are misperceptions of what 'actually' happens."

Specific attention in this investigation was given to the following areas:

(1)   The perceived incidence of organizational politics, both overall and in specific hierarchial levels and functional locations within the organization.

(2)   The general organizational characteristics (e.g., size, uncertainty) considered by the respondents to be associated with the increased incidence of political behaviors.

(3)   The typical organizational situations, or events, (e.g., personnel decisions, budgetary allocations, reorganization changes) perceived to be associated with the occurrence of organizational politics.

(4)   The positive and negative instrumentalities that organizational politics may be perceived as having for the attainment of both individual and organizational outcomes.

METHOD

Organizational politics is a potentially sensitive subject. In certain types of research, such as studies of political activity to which the respondents may be a party or the amount and nature of politics within the respondents' organization, we would agree with Pettigrew (1973) when he implies, citing Burns (1961), that "politics" may be a term too sensitive for use in direct investigations. However, in cases where the research can be placed in an impersonal and nonthreatening frame of reference, it may not be necessary to cloak the term in some euphemism to avoid harsh reactions or stereotypical answers when a research question is posed to practicing managers.

In this study, the respondents were invited to discuss organizational politics based upon their total experience in all organizations for which they had worked (including, but not limited to, their present organization), with the understanding that these statements did not necessarily apply to themselves, their current subunit, or their current organization. This approach was chosen in order to allow respondents to discuss organizational politics freely without identification with themselves or their current organizational ties. However, it is likely that the reported perceptions would reflect current conditions in the respondents' organizations. As Secord and Backman (1964) have discussed, perception is influenced by response salience. That is, "certain contemporary conditions predispose the organism to make certain responses" (p. 16). Given several equally practiced responses, a particular response will occur based on the immediately preceding conditions.

When doing research on a relatively unexplored phenomenon, it is considered advisable to start with loosely controlled conditions in a field survey setting before moving on to more controlled and "objective" explorations (McGrath, 1964). Because of the exploratory nature of the present research, the structured interview was selected as an appropriate method of data collection. In addition to the usual assurances of complete confidentiality of responses and the nonidentification with current organizational ties described above, the respondents were further assured that the interviewer had no preconceived notion of the "best" definition of organizational politics, or whether it was good or bad, and that our purpose was to learn something about organizational politics from the point of view of practicing managers in business organizations. To this end, each interview was started by asking the manager to define organizational politics and to use that definition as a frame of reference for all of his/her responses. No definition was provided by the interviewer nor, it is interesting to note, did any respondent ask what was meant by organizational politics. Every effort was made to make the interview and the interviewer's questions and responses as nonthreatening as possible. The evidence of the validity of this approach lies in the fact that respondents did not deny the existence of organizational politics and spoke freely about the topic. Although no specific test for social desirability was performed, the broad range of both positive and negative impacts of politics mentioned by nearly every respondent and summarized in the results indicates no apparent bias toward social desirability.

It would have been preferable to sample a large number of respondents and organizations so as to avoid a narrow perspective that might severely limit the generalizability of the findings. However, the interview method of data collection mitigated against as large a set of both organizations and individual respondents as would have been feasible using a questionnaire technique. A total of three managers from each of 30 organizations was decided upon as a reasonable sample for the purposes of this study. It was also decided that all organizations would be from a single basic industry to provide for some comparability of results.

Each organization chosen was a small to medium size independent firm, or a relatively autonomous division or subsidiary of a large corporation, within the electronics industry in Southern California. These firms could be described as primarily engaged in special item production, research and development of products, or small batch production as defined by Woodward (1965). This industry is generally considered to be high in external environmental conditions of uncertainty and diversity described by Lawrence and Lorsch (1967), as well as "technically diffuse" as this term was used by Harvey (1968). However, no attempt was made to determine the specific operating mode or the structure of the individual respondent firms.

Three managers were selected from each organization. They included: (1) the chief executive officer (CEO) of the firm or division; (2) a high-level staff manager, preferably the personnel manager; and (3) the lowest-level manager of a task area, excluding "lead worker" or working foremen. The last group are referred to in the study as "supervisors." For the staff manager, when there was no personnel manager or that person was unavailable, the CEO was asked to provide the name and title of three high-level administrative staff managers and the interviewer selected the one whose job most closely paralleled the personnel manager position. The supervisor was chosen by asking the CEO to name at least three supervisors of task groups and the interviewer arbitrarily selected one of these individuals. A total of 87 managers were interviewed. Three of the 30 organizations were unable to arrange interviews with one of the managers within the time constraints of the study, giving a final sample of 30 CEO's, 28 high staff managers, and 29 supervisors.

Interviews were conducted confidentially and lasted approximately 1 to 2 hours. Many of the questions were open ended. In those cases where the respondent was asked to make a choice or give scaled reponses, further comment was encouraged and recorded by the researcher on the interview schedule. Examples of the types of questions posed to the respondents are shown below.

(1) How frequent is the occurrence of organizational politics in each of the following functional areas? A list of nine functional areas was provided, and interviewers recorded the responses on a scale from 1 ("very low") to 5 ("very high").

(2) How can the occurrence of organizational politics be helpful or harmful to the *individual?* To the *organization?* (Open-ended response).

In tabulating the results, a coding scheme was prepared by the research team using a randomly selected sample of interview reports. To establish coding categories, all responses were coded independently by an analyst trained in the use of the coding schemes, and by at least one member of the research team. All differences in coding were discussed and resolved prior to statistical analysis of the data.

RESULTS

The interviews indicate that managers share clearly defined perceptions of the general nature of organizational politics as well as the characteristics or conditions which are associated with its occurrence. Specifically, these perceptions may be classified into four areas: (1) the overall incidence and general characteristics of organizational politics; (2) the relative incidence of organizational politics in various types of positions delineated either vertically or horizontally within the organization; (3) the types of situations (e.g., budget allocation, reorganization changes) most associated with the occurrence of organizational politics; and (4) the instrumentalities of politics for obtaining certian individual and organizational outcomes.

Overall Incidence and General Characteristics of Organizational Politics

Managers were asked to estimate the overall incidence of organizational politics based upon their total working experience. They also were asked to describe any overall characteristics of the organization related to increased political activity and whether it was directed toward advancing or protecting the interest of individuals or groups.

Managers from all three levels in the companies surveyed indicated that organizational politics was a very frequent activity. On a 5-point scale ("very infrequent" to "very frequent"), 60% of the managers indicated that organizational politics occurred either "frequently" or "very frequently." The mean response for all managers was 3.91. An analysis of variance indicated that the perceived incidence of organizational politics was related to the respondent's level in the organization ($F(2, 78) = 3.01, p = .055$), with CEO's estimating a higher frequency of political activity than that reported by either staff managers or supervisors.

In an open-ended question, interviewees were asked to cite any general characteristics that were related to a high occurrence of political behavior. The response most frequently mentioned was organizational size. Specifically, 44% of the respondents associated large size with the increased incidence of political activity, compared to only 8% who felt that small size was associated with organizational politics. "Ambiguity of roles and goals" and "conflict among people or departments" were mentioned by 25% of the respondents as characteristics related to the increased frequency of organizational politics. These last two characteristics seem to reflect the presence or the potential presence of uncertainty within the organization.

In addition, CEO's—in contrast to the other respondents—mentioned two characteristics of high-level managers that they perceived to be associated with increased political activity. The first of these, often described as the "personality" of the manager, referred to those managers who engaged in organizational politics and, thereby, set an example or encouraged such behavior on the part of others. This characteristic was cited by 33% of the CEO's responding, compared to only 9% of the two lower levels combined. Significant differences were observed for the three groups of respondents ($x^2 = 8.4, df = 2, p < .05$).

Organizational politics was perceived as being practiced by individuals representing individual interests far more often than by individuals representing the interests of groups. When asked whether the political actor represented individuals, groups, or both, 74% of the managers responded that individual interests were represented, compared to 16% who said that group interests were primarily represented and 9% who were undecided ($x^2 = 64.29, df = 2, p < .001$). No differences were observed among the responses of CEO's, staff managers, and supervisors.

Relative Incidence of Organizational Politics in Various Parts of the Organization

The respondents clearly differentiated the involvement of managers in political activities based upon the organizational position of the actor. This difference in the perceived amount of organizational politics was related to both vertical differentiation (hierarchial level of the political actor) and to horizontal differentiation (either by line and staff functions or by the specific organizational function of the political actor).

On the vertical dimension, over 90% of all of the managers agreed that organizational politics occurred more frequently at middle and upper levels of management than at lower levels of management. It is interesting to note that in a later question, when each manager was asked to define the term "power," in nearly every case the manager said that the term was synonymous with hierarchial level. Also, over 90% of the total sample of managers expressed the belief that a positive relationship exists between power and the successful application of organizational politics. These findings provide empirical evidence of the perceived relationship of power to the successful practice of organizational politics. They also support the conceptual literature and are another indication of the perceived positive relationship between the organizational level of the actor and the practice of organizational politics.

When viewing horizontal differentiation of the organization, the respondents were able to discriminate clearly concerning which organizational members are most actively involved in organizational politics. Managers were asked whether people in "line" positions or "staff" positions more frequently engaged in political behavior, or whether they were about equal. Over 60% of the combined sample stated that political activity is related to "staff" positions more than "line" positions, compared to 13% who saw political activity as related to "line" more than "staff" positions; 25% reported that political activity occurred as frequently in line positions as in staff positions. These differences were statistically significant beyond the .001 level ($x^2 = 32.64$, $df = 2$) and were not influenced by the respondent's own level in the organizational hierarchy.

In addition, respondents were asked to rate nine functional areas (e.g., marketing, production, personnel) on the relative occurrence of organizational politics engaged in by individuals in each of those functional areas. The responses were scored on a 5-point scale of 1 ("very low") to 5 ("very high"). A 3 (level of respondent) × 9 (functional area) analysis of variance with function repeated over subjects was used to examine the effects of organizational level on the perceived location organizational politics. The dependent variable was the perceived level of political activity.

A significant main effect for functional area ($F(8, 392) = 16.16$, $p < .001$) indicated that some functions were perceived to be higher in political activity than were others. Neither the main effect for level of respondent nor the interaction term were significant. Thus, the respondent's level in the organization did not influence perceptions concerning the functional location of organizational politics.

Mean ratings of the perceived level of political activity for each of nine functional areas are shown in Table I. It can be seen that the highest level of political activity was perceived to take place among the marketing staff, followed by the Board of Directors and sales. The function perceived as involving the least political activity was production.

Situations Associated with the Occurrence of Organizational Politics

Again, as was true with perceptions of organizational politics in different functional areas (e.g., marketing, production, accounting), the respondents were able to discriminate clearly among different types of situations (e.g., organization changes, rules and procedures changes) in their perceptions of the frequency of political activities. A list of nine specific situations was presented to the respondents, and they were asked to rate each situation on the frequency of organizational politics using a scale of 1 ("very low") to 5 ("very high") A 3 (level of respondent) × 9 (situation) analysis of variance with situation repeated over subjects was used to examine the effects of organizational level on perceptions of what situations were associated with the incidence of organizational politics. Perceived level of political activity was the dependent variable.

Table 1   Means and Standard Deviations of the Perceived Level of Organizational Politics Occurring in Each Functional Area

Functional area	Combined sample	
	X	SD
Marketing staff	4.27	1.16
Sales	3.74	1.43
Manufacturing staff	3.05	1.44
Personnel	3.01	1.50
Purchasing	2.67	1.47
Research and development (includes product design)	2.62	1.61
Accouting and finance	2.40	1.49
Production	2.01	1.19
Board of directors	3.88	1.65

A significant main effect for situation ($F(8, 616) = 20.37$, $p < .001$) indicated that some situations were perceived to be associated with higher levels of political activity than were others. Although neither the main effect for level of the respondent nor the interaction term was significant, the interaction did approach significance ($p = .08$). In particular, the supervisory level saw much lower political activity in budgeting situations and higher activity in dealing with outsiders (e.g., unions).

Means and standard deviations for the perceived incidence of organizational politics in each of the nine situations examined appear in Table II. "Reorganization changes" were identified as the most political situation, followed by "personnel changes." Situations directly related to the accomplishment of tasks were rated as the lowest in perceived political activity. These included "rules and procedures changes" and "establishing individual performance standards."

Respondents were given the opportunity to suggest any situation which may have been overlooked in the structured interview schedule that they regarded as particularly high in political activity. The situations identified by the respondents in the open-ended question (Table II) are particularly noteworthy in that they were not suggested by the interviewers, but represent views suggested by the respondents. These views may offer possible variables for future research efforts. The two most frequently mentioned situations were conflicts between people or departments and situations involving status or ego.

Perceived Instrumentalities of Organizational Politics

The instrumentalities of political behavior for obtaining specific outcomes for the individual and for the organization were examined. In each of these cases, organizational politics was shown to be related both to

Table 2   **Means and Standard Deviations of the Perceived Incidence of Organizational Politics in Different Situations**

Type of situation	Combined sample	
	X	SD
Reorganization changes	4.44	1.10
Personnel changes	3.74	1.52
Budget allocation	3.56	1.38
Dealing with outsiders (government, vendor, union)	3.30	1.64
Setting goals and objectives	3.25	1.61
Policy changes	3.12	1.54
Purchase of major items	2.63	1.53
Establish individual performance standards	2.39	1.43
Rules and procedures changes	2.31	1.35

Other Situations Identified in Open-Ended Questions as Associated with the Increased Incidence of Organizational Politics

	Percent of respondents mentioning item
Conflicts (departmental or personal)	15.29
Status or ego involved	12.95
Traumatic change or pressure	9.41
New product	8.24
Unfavorable characteristics of top management	4.91

positive outcomes (helpful) and to negative outcomes (harmful).

First, a comparison was made between two major paths—(1) job performance and (2) the use of organizational politics—for obtaining three specific types of individually desired outcomes within the organization: promotions, salary increases, and transfers. Although 53% of the sample felt that job performance was more important in achieving faster-than-average promotion, 26% saw job performance and political activity as equally important, and as many as 20% of the respondents stated that organizational politics was more important ($x^2 = 14.46$, $df = 2$, $p < .001$). In achieving higher-than-average salary increases, the results were nearly the same, with 51% reporting that job performance was more important, 27% stating that politics and performance were equally important, and 22% responding that organizational politics was more important ($x^2 = 11.62$, $df = 2$, $p < .01$).

While roughly one-fifth of the respondents viewed organizational politics as more important in achieving promotions and faster-than-average salary increases, the perceptions concerning transfers presented a

Table 3   **Perceived Ways that Organizational Politics Can Be Helpful or Harmful to the Individual**

	Percent response by group			
	Combined	CEO	Staff	Supervisor
Helpful				
Advance career	60.9	56.7	53.6	72.4
Recognition, status	21.8	13.3	25.0	27.6
Enhance power, position	19.5	20.0	25.0	13.8
Accomplish personal goals	14.9	26.7	10.7	6.9
Get the job done	11.5	13.3	14.3	6.9
Self ideas, projects, programs	10.3	10.0	7.1	13.8
Feelings (achievement, ego, control, success, etc.)	8.1	6.7	10.7	6.9
Survival	4.7	3.3	0.0	10.3
Harmful				
Loss of power, strategic position, credibility	39.1	33.3	39.3	44.8
Loss of job, demotion, etc.	31.0	30.0	32.1	31.0
Negative feelings of others	21.8	33.3	14.3	17.2
Passive loss of promotion, transfers, etc.	19.5	6.7	32.1	20.7
Internal feelings, guilt	12.6	6.7	14.3	17.2
Promotion to level of incompetence	9.2	6.7	0.0	20.7
Job performance hampered	3.5	0.0	0.0	10.3

strikingly different picture. When "transfer to a more desirable unit" was considered as the outcome, 66% of the combined sample stated that organizational politics was more important, compared to 17% who responded that job performance was more important, and an additional 17% who felt that job performance and organizational politics were equally instrumental ($x^2 = 36.03$, $df = 2$, $p < .001$). None of these results was appreciably influenced by the respondents' own level in the organizational hierarchy.

In terms of impact, organizational politics was perceived as highly instrumental in achieving positive outcomes for individual members of the organization, despite any dangers it might hold for some people. Even impacts on the organization as a whole, perceived as somewhat more negative than impacts on individuals, were seen as largely offset by potentially positive effects. These results reflect a strongly held belief that an understanding of the effective application of organizational politics is beneficial in attaining individually desired outcomes and, potentially at least, positive results for the organization.

Although respondents perceived politics as a path to certain goals, they nevertheless express ambivalence concerning whether the net result of organizational politics was helpful or harmful to the individual. In response to an open-ended question, nearly 95% of the respondents named at least one way that organizational politics could *help* an individual. On the other hand, they are unanimous in saying that organizational politics could *harm* the individual in one or more ways. This is particularly true if the actor were seen as unsuccessful in the process of political behavior. A list of the ways that the respondents perceived that organizational politics could be helpful or harmful to the individual, that were mentioned by more than 10% of any one level of the respondents, is shown in Table III.

By far the greatest agreement on the ways organizational politics could help an individual was that it could advance an individual's career either in specific ways, such as promotion, salary increases, and preferred jobs, or more generally, in terms of "being successful" in a job or career. Over 60% of the respondents mentioned at least one of these types of career advancement. The most frequently mentioned harm to individuals that might result from organizational politics was loss of power, strategic position, or credibility. Examples of more concrete losses, such as loss of job or demotion, were second in frequency.

The most strongly held views concerning the impact of organizational politics on organizations revolved around goal accomplishment. Impacts on the organization cited by more than 10% of any level of managers are

Table 4   **Perceived Ways that Organizational Politics Can be Helpful or Harmful to the Organization**

	Percent response by group			
	Combined	CEO	Staff	Supervisor
Helpful				
Organization goals achieved, get job done	26.4	30.0	28.6	20.7
Organization survival, health, processes	26.4	26.7	25.0	27.6
Visibility of ideas, people, etc.	19.5	16.7	21.4	20.7
Coordination, communication	18.4	23.3	17.9	13.8
Develop teams, group functioning	11.5	16.7	7.1	10.3
Esprit de corps, channel energy	10.3	10.0	10.7	10.3
Decision making, analysis	6.9	3.3	14.3	3.5
No response (unable to mention helpful result)	14.9	10.0	10.7	24.1
Harmful				
Distract from organizational goals	44.8	43.3	35.7	55.2
Misuse of resources	32.3	36.7	32.1	27.6
Divisiveness, splits, fights	21.8	20.0	21.4	24.1
Climate, tension, frustration	19.5	16.7	21.4	20.7
Incompetents advanced	14.9	3.3	21.4	20.7
Lower coordination, communication	10.3	3.3	10.7	17.2
Damage organization image, reputation	10.3	6.7	10.7	13.8
No response (no harm mentioned)	3.5	3.3	7.1	0.0

shown in Table IV (on page 467). More managers expressed the opinion that organizational goal accomplishment was harmed in some way (45% of the respondents) than stated that goal achievement was helped (26%). About one-third of all respondents felt that misuse of some type of resources resulted from organizational politics. Time and energy were often mentioned as wasted resources, either in the effort used to engage in political behavior or through expenditure of effort on projects inappropriately (from the respondent's viewpoint) given priority through political actions. However, more managers reported that they perceived communication and coordination as improved by political activities than reported that these were hindered by political activities. On balance, organizational politics was seen as improving the internal processes of the organization (e.g., communication), while detracting from specific tasks and goals deemed important to respondents.

DISCUSSION

The results of this research indicate that most of the managers sampled view organizational politics as a "two-edge sword." The practicing managers were, for the most part, able to discriminate clearly in their perceptions which levels, functions, and situations of the organization were associated with the most frequent occurrence of organizational politics. Responses to a majority of the questions showed remarkable consistency across levels of management for all firms in the combined research sample. However, for certain questions, the responses were in agreement within a level of management across all firms, while diverging sharply among the perceptions of managers at different levels.

Taken as a whole, the findings seem to suggest three tentative conclusions. First, amount of power is strongly related to perceived political activity. Second, there appear to be three underlying conditions related to high levels of perceived political activity. These conditions are consistent with the three paths linking power and politics which were described in the introduction and include: (a) the situation of uncertainty; (b) the importance of the uncertain situation to the organization; and (c) the salience of the issue to the individual. Third, organizational politics is perceived as being instrumental in achieving both positive and negative outcomes for the individual members and for the organization as a whole. Each of these three areas (i.e., power and organizational politics, underlying conditions related to organizational politics, and instrumentalities of organizational politics) will be discussed separately.

Power and Organizational Politics

The direct relationship between power and politics proposed by the writers cited in the introduction is consistent with the managerial perceptions obtained in this study. For example, over 90% of the managers in the sample reported that the successful application of organizational politics was related to a high level of power. More specifically, over 70% of the respondents saw organizational politics as instrumental in achieving a higher level of power directly or saw a higher power level and politics as interdependent. When asked how they defined "power," the respondents consistently stated that power was synonymous with position and formal authority. From these combined responses, it seems clear not only that the relationship between power and organizational politics described in the results of this study are consistent with the literature, but, in addition, that the particular form of power implied in these responses is consistent with "legitimate" power or authority as defined by French and Raven (1968). In summary, the successful practice of organizational politics is perceived to lead to a higher level of power, and once a high level of power is attained, there is more opportunity to engage in political behavior.

Conditions Related to Organizational Politics

Differences in the perceived level of political activity suggest that organizational politics is related to: (1) uncertainty; (2) the importance of the activity to the larger organization; and (3) the salience of the issue to the individual. Our discussion of (1) and (2) draws freely from the strategic contingencies theory of Hickson et al. (1971), and (3) is consistent with the work of Patchen (1974). Specific results from the present research will be used to illustrate how these three underlying conditions may be viable sources of explanation for the perceived level of political activity in a variety of instances.

The history of electronics manufacturing in Southern California since the 1960's is one of intensive competition among many firms, based on rapid increases in technology and involvement in the aerospace industry. The business is characterized by special orders, relatively short-term contracts, and an established practice of "importing" technology by hiring from the large pool of technically trained people in the area, or subcontracting work to specialty firms when internal costs or difficulties are seen as too high. With the competition for orders, it is not surprising that marketing and sales divisions are perceived as areas high in political activity, as these two functional groups deal with the uncertainties introduced by customers. They are central to the "life blood" of this type of organization; that is, they must provide a constant stream of new contracts or customers. Following the same logic, the production function and the accounting and finance functions are certainly important to the organization, but are typically engaged in more clearly defined tasks and are perceived as less political. Katz and Kahn (1966) have discussed how specialized subsystems such as marketing try to shield the production function from uncertainty. It is, therefore, consistent that production is perceived to be low in political activity while marketing is high. This line of reasoning is further supported by joining Catlin's view (cited by Lasswell & Kaplan, 1950) that the "political process is the shaping, distribution and exercise of power" to March and Simon's (1958) discussion of "uncertainty absorption." March and Simon describe the amount and locus of uncertainty absorption as affecting the influence structure of the organization, and add that "uncertainty absorption is frequently used, consciously and unconsciously, as a technique for acquiring and exercising power" (p. 166). A review of the results obtained in this study shows clearly that the groups or departments engaged in absorbing uncertainty are seen as relatively more political, while the groups engaged in functions shielded from uncertainty are seen as less political.

A similar argument may be employed to explain *situations* seen as high in political activity. Reorganization changes (by far the most political situation in this study) introduce great uncertainty relating to amount of power, resources, and assignment of tasks and responsibilities for every person or department. The outcomes are not only likely to be highly uncertain; they are also likely to have very high salience for a wide set of members in the organization. To a lesser degree, these same conditions apply to the development of a budget, ranked third in situations related to organizational politics. Budgets determine the available resources assigned to individuals or departments for a comparatively long period and, through these resources, reflect a distribution of power (Pfeffer & Salancik, 1974; Wildavsky, 1968).

The situations perceived as low in political activity also involve dealing with or "absorbing" uncertainty in one sense. However, rules and procedural changes and the establishment of individual performance standards (the two situations judged lowest in political activity) are situations which introduce certainty and fall well within the usual definition of the legitimate function of management. Barnard (1938) would include these task definition activities as within the probable "zone of indifference" for most members of the organization. As long as these rules and standards fall within the constraints of being a normal activity of management (not creating new uncertainties), and are not seen as threatening (therefore, low salience), it is reasonable to expect that they would be perceived as relatively nonpolitical.

Salience, defined as degree of concern of the individual for the outcome, was shown by Patchen (1974) to be related to involvement in the influence process and to amount of influence over a decision. This same issue of salience can be shown to be related to perceptions of organizational politics. As discussed earlier, the function of marketing and the situation of reorganization change impact on many members of the organization, and therefore, the concern is widespread. In these areas, perceptions of political activity are consistently high. In other functions and situations, however, the difference in level of involvement and concern appear to be more pronounced among particular levels or positions of management and significant differences appear in the perceptions of political activity. For example, supervisors were often less involved in the actual preparation of major budgets and frequently described them as "given" or determined by task load. Indeed, level of political activity perceived by supervisors regarding budgets was distinctly lower than the other two groups.

Perceived Instrumentalities and Effects of Organizational Politics

In previous organizational behavior and management literature, job performance has almost always been the exclusive focus of studies dealing with behavioral "paths" to desirable outcomes. A striking finding of the present investigation was that organizational politics may be a comparably crucial path, particularly in the management sectors of organizations. As a path to "faster-than-average salary increases" and "faster-than-average promotions," it was seen as more important than performance by one-fifth of the respondents; when the goal was "transfer to a more desirable unit," it ovewhelmed performance as a perceived path (65% to 17%). Our evidence thus indicates that political behavior is seen by many managers as a potentially viable instrumentality for attaining certain kinds of personal outcomes.

It is clear that the respondents were quite ambivalent concerning the effects of organizational politics on the organization. As was the case with the perceived impact of organizational politics on individuals, the area of impact on the organization perceived as benefiting the most from political activity was also the one perceived as the most likely to suffer as a result of politics. This area concerned goal accomplishment: 45% of the respondents reported that organizational politics facilitated their achievement of company objectives, and about the same percentage felt that politics detracted from organizational accomplishment. Most of the potential advantages perceived as accruing to the organization as a result of political behavior can be described as improving internal organizational processes. For example, gaining visibility for ideas, improving coordination and communication, developing teams and groups, and increasing *espirit de corps* were often cited by the respondents.

CONCLUSION

It is apparent from both the literature and this study that a close relationship exists between power and politics, and that politics is viewed as a pervasive process in organizational settings. Power may be considered as either positive or negative in *affect* (Bertle, 1967; McClelland, 1974; Thompson, 1967) and, again, the same has been found to be true of managerial perceptions of the process of organizational politics. In addition, the respondents perceived politics as both positive and negative in *effect*. The results obtained in this research have shown perceived organizational politics to be related to the conditions of uncertainty, the importance of the activity to the larger organization, and the salience of the issue to the individual in much the same manner as these conditions have been related to power in the literature. While it is true that the specific results pertaining to individuals in the positions and functions perceived to engage most actively in organizational politics may not generalize to other individuals in other organizations, it is reasonable to expect that these three conditions may be useful in explaining the occurrence of political activity in other organizational settings.

An important distinction emerges from the results of this investigation; that is, political activity is often attributed to those in positions of high legitimate power (i.e., "authority") and successful political activity is perceived to lead to higher positions of legitimate power. However, it is not the direct exercise of authority *per se* that is perceived as political. To the contrary, the responses in this study indicate that the more legitimated and routine the influence activity, the less likely were the respondents to make political attributions. The pattern of the results suggests that perceived political activity is an influence attempt outside the traditional use of authority to direct the activity of others. Therefore, even though the bases of power for these influence attempts may accrue most often to those in positions of legitimate authority, and successful political activity may result in higher positions of authority, political activity is perceived as proceeding from a base outside the traditionally defined limits of legitimate power.

With the results of this research, we might suggest that many of the ideas contained in the strategic contingencies theory of Hickson et al. (1971) could serve as a useful framework for understanding the reciprocal interdependence of power and organizational politics. For our purposes, expressing the activities in political terms and adding a feedback path from the results of the political act to the base of power will serve to extend the basic theory into a political model. This extended theory would suggest that conditions of uncertainty would provide greater opportunity for coping activities, insofar as these uncertainties are perceived by members of the organization. These attempts to cope with uncertainty are often perceived as politics. The individuals for whom the outcome of the situation has the greatest salience will be more inclined to engage in influence attempts and may be perceived as acting politically. The more important the issue to the organization and the less substitutable the resources of the political actor, the more probable that the action will be accepted (i.e., the political act will be successful). Successful applications of organizational politics lead to greater acquisition of power. A higher level power places one in a position to better discern areas of uncertainty relevant to the organization and provides access to the resources necessary to cope with these uncertainties, thus increasing the opportunities for—and the effectiveness of—future political activity. Engaging in political activities in areas seen as irrelevant by other members of the organization, or engaging unsuccessfully in politics, may lead to reductions both in power and in opportunities for future successful applications of organizational politics. Thus, organizational politics can be related to power in an interdependent manner; therefore, in a general sense, it might be said that "the rich get richer and the poor get poorer."

REFERENCES

Baldridge, J. V. *Power and conflict in the university.* New York: Wiley, 1971.

Barnard, C. I. *The functions of the executive.* Cambridge, Mass.: Harvard University Press, 1938.

Berle, A. A. *Power.* New York: Harcourt, Brace and World, 1967.

Blau, P. *Exchange and power in social life.* New York: Wiley, 1964.

Bucher, R. Social process and power in a medical school. In M. N. Zald (Ed.), *Power in organizations.* Nashville, Tenn.: Vanderbilt Press, 1970.

Burns, T. Micropolitics: Mechanisms of organizational change. *Administrative Science Quarterly,* 1961, *6,* 257-281.

Calder, B. J. An attribution theory of leadership. In B. M. Staw & C. R. Salancik (Eds.), *New directions in organizational behavior.* Chicago: St. Clair Press, 1977.

Cartwright, D., & Zander, A. Power and influence in groups: An introduction. In D. Cartwright & A. Zander (Eds.), *Group dynamics.* New York: Harper & Row, 1968.

Crozier, *The bureaucratic phenomenon.* Chicago: University of Chicago Press, 1964.

Dahl, R. A. Power. In D. L. Sills (Ed.), *International encyclopedia of social sciences* (Vol. 12). New York: Macmillan and the Free Press, 1968.

Dubin, R. Power and union-management relations. *Administrative Science Quarterly,* 1957, *2,* 60-81.

Dubin, R. *Theory building* (Rev. ed.). New York: The Free Press, 1978.

Emerson, R. E. Power-dependent relations. *American Sociological Review,* 1962, *27,* 31-41.

French, J. R. P., & Raven, B. The bases of social power. In D. Cartwright & A. Zander (Eds.), *Group Dynamics.* New York: Harper & Row, 1968.

Gross, B. M. Political process. In D. L. Sills (Ed.), *International encyclopedia of the social sciences* (Vol. 12). New York: Macmillan and the Free Press, 1968.

Harvey, E. Technology and structure of organizations. *American Sociological Review,* 1968, *33,* 249.

Harvey, E., & Mills, R. Patterns of organizational adaptation. In M. Zald (Ed.), *Power in organizations.* Nashville, Tenn.: Vanderbilt Univeristy Press, 1970.

Hickson, D. J., Hinings, C. R., Lee, C. A., Schneck, R. E., & Pennings, J. M. A strategic contingencies theory of intraorganizational power. *Administrative Science Quarterly,* 1971, *11,* 216-217.

Katz, D., & Kahn, R. L. *The social psychology of organizations.* New York: Wiley, 1966.

Lasswell, H. D. Politics—Who gets what, when, how. In *The Political Writings of Harold D. Lasswell.* Glencoe, Ill.: The Free Press, 1951.

Lasswell, H. D., & Kaplan, A. *Power and society.* New Haven: Yale University Press, 1950.

Lawrence, P., & Lorsch, J. W. *Organization and environment.* Boston: Division of Research, Graduate School of Business Administration, Harvard University, 1967.

Lewin, K. *Principles of topological psychology.* New York: McGraw-Hill, 1936.

March, J. G., & Simon, H. A. *Organizations.* New York: Wiley, 1958.

Martin, N. H., & Sims, J. H. Power tactics. In D. A. Kolb, I. M. Rubin, & J. M. McIntyre (Eds.), *Organizational psychology: A book of readings* (2nd ed.). Englewood Cliffs, New Jersey: Prentice-Hall, 1974.

Mayes, B. T., & Allen, R. W. Toward a definition of organizational politics. *Academy of Management Review,* 1977, *2*(4), 672-678.

McClelland, D. C. The two faces of power. In D. Kolb, I. Rubin, & J. McIntyre (Eds.), *Organizational psychology: A book of readings* (2nd ed.). Englewood Cliffs, New Jersey: Prentice-Hall, 1974.

McGrath, J. E. Toward a "theory of method" for research in organizations. In W. W. Cooper, H. J. Leavitt, & M. W. Shelly (Eds.), *New perspectives in organizational research.* New York: Wiley, 1964.

Patchen, M. The locus and basis of influence on organizational decisions. *Organizational Behavior and Human Performance,* 1974, *11,* 195-221.

Perrow, C. The analysis of goals in complex organizations. *American Sociological Review,* 1961, *26,* 854-866.

Perrow, C. Departmental power and perspectives in industrial firms. In M. N. Zald (Ed.), *Power in organizations.* Nashville, Tenn.: University Press, 1970.

Pettigrew, A. M. *The politics of organizational decision-making.* London: Tavistock, 1973.

Pfeffer, J., & Salancik, G. Organizational decision making as a political process: The case of the university budget. *Administrative Science Quarterly,* 1974 *19*(2), 135-151.

Pfiffner, J. M., & Sherwood, J. P. *Administrative organization.* Englewood Cliffs, New Jersey: Prentice-Hall, 1960.

Porter, L. W. *Organizations as political animals.* Presidential Address, Division of Industrial-Organizational Psychology, 84th Annual Meeting of American Psychological Association, Washington, D. C., September 4, 1976.

Robbins, S. P. *The administrative process: Integrating theory and practice.* Englewood Cliffs, New Jersey: Prentice-Hall, 1976.

Rogers, R. E. *The political process in modern organizations.* New York: Exposition Press, 1971.

Scott, A. Management: A political process: Overt vs. covert. *American Council on Education,* 57th annual meeting, October 10, 1974.

Secord, P. F., & Backman, C. W. *Social psychology.* New York: McGraw-Hill, 1964.

Strauss, G. Tactics of lateral relationships: The purchasing agent. *Administrative Science Quarterly,* 1962, *7,* 161-186.

Thompson, J. D. *Organizations in action,* New York: McGraw-Hill, 1967.

Tushman, M. T. A political approach to organizations: A review and rationale. *Academy of Management Review,* 1977, *2*(2), 206-216.

Walmsley, G. L., & Zald, M. N. *The political economy of public organizations.* Lexington, Mass.: Heath, 1973.

Wergin, J. F. The evaluation of organizational policy making: A political model. *Review of Educational Research,* 1976, *46*(1), 75-116.

Wildavsky, A. Budgeting as a political process. In D. L. Sills (Ed.), *The international encyclopedia of the social sciences.* New York: Crowell, Collier, and Macmillan, 1968.

Woodward, J. *Industrial organization: Theory and practice.* London: Oxford University Press, 1965.

Wrong, D. H. Some problems in defining social power. *American Journal of Sociology,* 1968, *73,* 673-681.

Organizational Politics:
Tactics and Characteristics of Its Actors

ROBERT W. ALLEN
DAN L. MADISON
LYMAN W. PORTER
PATRICIA A. RENWICK
BRONSTON T. MAYES

Organizational politics is conspicuous by its relative absence in the management and organizational theory and research literature. The reason for this absence is somewhat unclear. It is not because politics occurs infrequently in organizational settings or because behavior commonly referred to as political goes unnoticed. Practicing managers are familiar with politics in organizational settings from experience, as targets or observers, rather than from systematic inquiry.

Organizational politics involve intentional acts of influence to enhance or protect the self-interest of individuals or groups. "The study of politics is the study of influence and the influential . . . the influential are those who get most of what there is to get."[1] How do the influential get what there is to get? What tactics are used by political actors "in working the system to get what [they] need?"[2] What are the personal characteristics of politically effective individuals? This article reports the results of an exploratory study of managerial perceptions concerning these aspects of politics in organizations.

The Study

Eighty-seven managerial personnel (thirty chief executive officers, twenty-eight high-level staff managers, twenty-nine supervisors) were interviewed using questions developed by the authors. The managers represented thirty different organizations in the electronics industry in Southern California. Each interview was conducted confidentially and lasted one to two hours. Two of the questions asked the managers were:

- Organizational politics takes many forms. What are the tactics of organizational politics of which you are aware?
- What are the personal characteristics of those people you feel are most effective in the use of organizational politics?

A coding system was developed and the open-ended responses were categorized independently by an analyst and at least one of the authors. The few differences between the coders in assigning the responses to the various categories were discussed and reconciled.

Respondents were asked to describe organizational political tactics and personal characteristics of effective political actors based upon their accumulated experience in *all* organizations in which they had worked. They were told their statements need not apply to their own behavior, their current subunit, or their current organization. No definition of organizational politics was given to the respondents, nor did any of them ask what was meant by the term. They were asked to provide a definition and use it in their responses. The definitions they provided convinced the authors that they and the respondents were talking about the same thing.

Organizational Politics—Tactics

Many writers concerned with behavior in organizations focus on an individual's reaction to others or to events, with less attention to proactive or initiating behavior. Typically, reactive behavior is intended to protect self-interest while proactive promotes self-interest. Organizational politics involve both.

Table 1 shows the eight categories of political tactics mentioned most frequently by each of the three groups of respondents (chief executive officers, high-level staff managers, supervisors). The first four categories are examined individually below.

Blaming or attacking others.   This tactic, identified by over half of each of the three groups of respondents, is reactive and proactive in nature. The reactive behavior centers around "scapegoating," used when a situation is negatively evaluated or when the individual feels he may be associated with an outcome that is failing or has failed. Respondents indicated that the political actor minimizes or avoids his association with the undesirable situation or result. Scapegoating tends to be impersonal, the emphasis on "getting off the hook" as in the old cliche, "When something goes wrong the first thing to be fixed is the blame."

Table 1   Managerial Perception of Organizational Politics Tactics

Tactic	Percent of Respondents that Mentioned Tactic			
	Combined Groups	Chief Executive Officers	Staff Managers	Supervisors
Attacking or blaming others	54.0	60.0	50.0	51.7
Use of information	54.0	56.7	57.1	48.3
Image building/ impression management	52.9	43.3	46.4	69.0
Support building for ideas	36.8	46.7	39.3	24.1
Praising others, ingratiation	25.3	16.7	25.0	34.5
Power coalitions, strong allies	25.3	26.7	17.9	31.0
Associating with the influential	24.1	16.7	35.7	20.7
Creating obligations/ reciprocity	12.6	3.3	14.3	30.7

Proactive blaming or attacking tactics are far more personal and appear to be geared toward reducing the competition for scarce resources, with other individuals or subunits viewed as rivals for promotions, salary increases, status, budgets. Proactive behavior includes making the rival look bad in the eyes of influential organizational members—blaming competitors for failures or denigrating their accomplishments as unimportant, poorly timed, self-serving, or lucky. The organizational politician finds a negative situation that might be blamed on a rival.

Use of information.   Almost half the supervisors and over half the chief executive officers and staff managers identified information as a political tool. The tactics of information use can be proactive, reactive, or both depending upon the situation. Information is withheld, distorted, or used to overwhelm another.

Few managers believed outright lying or falsification is a widely used technique due, at least in part, to the dire consequences of such acts if discovered. A variety of information uses were described, including withholding information when it might be detrimental to self-interest, avoidance of individuals and situations that might require explanation reflecting unfavorably on an individual, and distortion of information to create an impression by selective disclosure, innuendo, or "objective" speculation about individuals or events. Overkill, the opposite of withholding information, overwhelms the target with data, not all of it pertinent. The purpose of this tactic may be to bury or obscure an important detail the political actor believes could harm him, when the risk of withholding information is too great. The more data, the less likely the detail will be noticed. That the target was notified can be claimed if it later comes to light. Inundating a target with "evidence" is effective in exploiting any feeling that volume of information is a measure of the importance of an issue or the validity of an argument. The political actor assumes competition between the parties whose arguments are of equal merit will be decided in favor of whoever can muster the greatest volume of alleged supporting information. The impression of rationality and logic is given by the use of quantitative data in the form of graphs, formulas, tables, summations. One manager indicated that one of his most effective techniques is to arrive at a wholly subjective decision and then have his staff collect "objective" data to support it.

Creating and maintaining a favorable image.   This tactic was the third kind of political behavior most mentioned by respondents. It is predominantly, if not exclusively, proactive—designed to promote self-interests. Image building includes general appearance, dress and hair style, sensitivity to organizational norms, drawing attention to successes, even those the individual is not responsible for, and creating the appearance of being on the inside of important activities. Other types of image building center on enhancement of personal characteristics, developing a reputation of being liked, enthusiastic (not too aggressive or ambitious), thoughtful, honest, and such attributes as the individual considers to be thought desirable by influential members of the organization.

A particularly heinous image-building tactic, in the view of supervisors, is the taking of credit for the accomplishments or good ideas of someone else. This may be done with misleading statements, but is more likely to involve passing on an idea without reference to the source (unless the idea is ridiculed or leads to failure). Accepting recognition without explanation or making reference to the help of others in such a way as to appear humble and eager to share the recognition with "the team" rather than in honest admission that one was not responsible for the achievement are forms of this tactic.

Developing a base of support.   Higher-level managers are more sensitive than lower-level managers to the importance of the proactive behavior of idea support building as a political tactic. Does occupying a higher-level position make a manager more sensitive to this tactic or does the successful use of this tactic lead to promotion to higher levels? The latter would cause one to expect that of the 24 percent of the supervisors describing this tactic, those who successfully practice it might be the future members of higher-levels groups.

Idea support building as seen by respondents includes getting others to understand one's ideas before a decision is made, setting up the decision before the meeting is called, and getting others to contribute to the idea (possibly making them feel it is theirs) to assure their commitment.

Other tactics. The fifth most frequently mentioned tactic was ingratiation. Lower-level managers mentioned the use of this technique much more frequently than the higher-level managers, twice as often as chief executive officers. The tone and context of the descriptions seemed to change with the level of the respondent. Higher-level managers tended to speak in terms of praising others and establishing good rapport. Supervisors used expressions such as "buttering up the boss," "apple polishing," and other more colorful, but less printable, remarks.

The sixth and seventh most frequently mentioned tactics were developing strong allies and forming power coalitions, and associating with influential persons in business and social situations. An interesting tactic mentioned most often by supervisors, least by chief executive officers—indicating a trend toward greater use of it at lower levels—concerned performing services or favors to create obligations. The norm of reciprocity is invoked when assistance is required,[3] "You scratch my back, I'll scratch yours."

Use of rewards, coercion and threats in influencing others, mentioned by less than 10 percent of the respondents, is not shown on Table 1. The wide variation between the mention of it by the chief executive officers (20 percent) and other managerial respondents (staff managers, 7 percent; supervisors, 3 percent) is worth noting. It appears that promises and threats may be more instrumental to individuals at higher levels than to those at lower levels. The latter may have little to promise and be quite sensitive to the personal dangers involved in making threats.

Personal Characteristics of Effective Political Actors

Table 2 shows those personal characteristics perceived as conducive to successful organizational politics mentioned by 10 percent or more of the respondents, and the percentage of each group that mentioned them. Three distinct profiles of effective political actors come from the responses from these three groups. Not all members of a group will match the stereotype, nor can the profiles be generalized to individuals in similar levels in other organizational groupings, but the following picture seems to reflect the stereotype held by each group.

Chief executive officers' perspective. In the chief executive officers' view, a successful politician must, first, be sensitive to other individuals, situations, and opportunities. He is highly articulate, usually highly intelligent, ambitious, and success-oriented, but does not forget the well-being of the organization.

Staff managers' perspective. Staff managers agree with the chief executive officers that the successful political actor must be articulate: they see this as his most important attribute. The politician must be socially adept, must understand the social norms of the organization and

Table 2   Personal Characteristics of Effective Political Actors

Personal Characteristics	Percent of Respondents that Mentioned Characteristic			
	Combined Groups	Chief Executive Officers	Staff Managers	Supervisors
Articulate	29.9	36.7	39.3	12.8
Sensitive	29.9	50.0	21.4	17.2
Socially adept	19.5	10.0	32.1	17.2
Competent	17.2	10.0	21.4	20.7
Popular	17.2	16.7	10.7	24.1
Extroverted	16.1	16.7	14.3	17.2
Self-confident	16.1	10.0	21.4	17.2
Aggressive	16.1	10.0	14.3	24.1
Ambitious	16.1	20.0	25.0	3.4
Devious	16.1	13.3	14.3	20.7
"Organization man"	12.6	20.0	3.6	13.8
Highly intelligent	11.5	20.0	10.7	3.4
Logical	10.3	3.3	21.4	6.9

behave so as to be perceived by influential others as "fitting in well," not as a "rebel" or "trouble maker." Staff managers, as contrasted to the other two groups, said it is important for the politician to be logical and inoffensively clever. Successful politics, they said, requires competence and, agreeing with the chief executive officers, sensitivity to others and varying situations.

Supervisors' perspective. A somewhat different picture of the successful politician emerges from the supervisory group. They see him as being aggressive, popular, and competent, also devious. There was less agreement among the supervisors than at higher levels on what personal characteristics are important to successful politicking: sensitivity and articulateness were mentioned by 50 percent and 36.7 percent of the chief executive officers; articulateness and socially adeptness by 39.3 and 32.1 percent of staff managers. The two characteristics, named most often by supervisors, being aggressive and being popular, were identified by only 24.1 percent of the supervisory respondents.

The eyes of the beholder. Chief executive officers see the effective political actor as sensitive to varying situations. He is articulate, commendably ambitious, and of sufficiently high intellect. The major difference between the characteristics named by staff managers and chief executive officers is the staff managers' emphasis on social adeptness and playing down of the importance of sensitivity. This is understandable when viewed from each perspective. Chief executive officers perceive the effective political actor as behaving in a way that will increase the chance of accomplishing what is desired, regardless of whether he is socially adept. Being perceived as socially adept might be more instrumental for a staff manager, particularly in interactions with influential individuals, than for the relatively more powerful chief executive officer.

The viewing lens of supervisors tended to focus on a political actor striving for popularity. They agreed with the higher levels on his aggressiveness but not on the commendability of this behavior. The supervisors also said that political actors are competent, but saw them as more devious than did the higher levels. The responses of chief executive and staff officers referred to and favored politically effective individuals at their levels in the organization, while the supervisors referred to these same individuals, but less favorably.

Attribution Theory and Organizational Politics

Managers in this study identified readily the tactics and personal characteristics of political actors. Observing behavior and naming attributes is the concern of the social psychological theory of attribution. This theory can be used to further understand political actors.

Attribution theory focuses on explaining how individuals account for the behavior of people. Attributions refer to the dispositional nature of the individual being observed or the situational forces confronting the person. "That's just the way he is" would be a dispositional attribution, "That's not like her but she had little choice," a situational attribution. A dispositional attribution refers to something within the person causing the observed behavior (as honesty), while a situational attribution uses external factors to explain behavior. According to attribution theory, most people tend to use dispositional explanations to understand the behavior of others.[4]

The tactics of organizational politics can be examined with attribution theory. Dennis Moberg points out:

> The legitimacy norm requires that observers do not attribute such behavior to legitimate (self-serving) motives. . . . In attribution terms, politicians must avoid having their behavior attributed by others to a particular intent (illegitimate or self-serving motives). They may do so first by "creating the impression" that they have legitimate motives.[5]

To the extent that individuals perceive behavior as self-serving rather than legitimate (as was often the case in the present study), it appears that many actors are unsuccessful in their attempts to "create the impression." It also raises the question of how often the attributions of legitimate motives are the result of successful manipulative tactics.

Attribution theory can explain why the chief executive officers and staff managers view personal characteristics of political actors in more favorable terms than do supervisors. Politicking is thought to occur more frequently at higher levels of an organization, so higher-level participants may be attributing favorable characteristics to themselves. Supervisors, who have less power in the organization, may be less able as a group to practice politics successfully and less generous in attributing favorable characteristics to the most high-level politicians.

Conclusions and Implications

The managers in this study were able and willing to identify organizational political tactics. Politics is an important behavioral process in organizational settings. It was not the purpose of the article to praise political behavior as "good" for organizations or individuals nor to condemn it as "bad." Politics is an important social influence process with the potential of being functional or dysfunctional to organizations and individuals.

In a recent study, managerial respondents indicated a high degree of ambivalence when asked to consider the harmful or helpful effects of politics on individuals and the organization.[6] Advancement of career and increased power were cited as self-interests that could be furthered through politics. Loss of an individual's credibility was perceived as a risk. The managers mentioned that politics could improve communications and coordination in the organization, but pointed out that political behavior could threaten task accomplishment. These findings and those in this article imply practicing managers should learn more about political processes to enable them to play a larger role in its management.[7]

There was considerable consistency among the three levels of respondents concerning tactics most used in organizations. More proactive than reactive behavior was identified, indicating greater use of politics for promotion than for protection of self-interests—the best defense, a good defense.

From an organization's perspective, tactics of withholding and distorting information are probably most potentially dysfunctional. Information and control systems can be designed to minimize this. Each tactic named above could be studied by management and channelled by them so as not to jeopardize organizational goals—again, the best defense.

There were differences in the perceptions of the groups of respondents as to what makes a good politician, but the nine most cited personal characteristics could also be considered attributes of an effective leader. The similarities between the influence processes of leadership and politics may be greater than their differences, particularly when viewed by higher level members of management. Lower-level supervisors may discriminate between personal objectives and the organizational interests that concern their leaders. Higher-level managers may feel what is good for them is good for the organization and vice versa, blurring the distinction between politician and leader.

REFERENCES

1. Harold D. Lasswell, "Politics—Who Gets What, When, How," *The Political Writings of Harold D. Lasswell* (Glencoe, Illinois: The Free Press, 1951).
2. Ann Scott, "Management: A Political Process: Overt vs. Covert," *American Council on Education* (Fifty-Seventh Annual Meeting, 10 Oct. 1974).

3. Alvin W. Gouldner, "The Norm of Reciprocity: A Preliminary Statement," *American Sociological Review* (1960), pp. 161-178.

4. Philip G. Zimbardo, Ebbe B. Ebbesen, and Christina Maslach, *Influencing Attitudes and Changing Behavior* (Reading, Mass.: Addison-Wesley, 1977).

5. Dennis J. Moberg, "Organizational Politics: Perspective from Attribution Theory," Paper presented to meeting of American Institute for Decision Sciences, Chicago (1977), p. 1.

6. Unpublished study recently completed at the Graduate School of Administration, University of California, Irvine. Manuscript in preparation.

7. Bronston T. Mayes and Robert W. Allen, "Toward a Definition of Organizational Politics," *Academy of Management Review* (1977), pp. 672-678.

INDEX